THE
LAST
COACH

A Life of
Paul "Bear" Bryant

ALLEN BARRA

W. W. NORTON & COMPANY

NEW YORK   LONDON

To my daughter Maggie,

my nieces, Jennifer and Jamie Rogers,
Heather Lokey, and Lauren Blake,

my nephews, Josh White and Zac and Kris Bonta,

and my grandnephew Tyler Blake.

So they'll know what it was like.

Frontispiece: Courtesy of The Paul W. Bryant Museum, University of Alabama

For information about permission to reproduce selections from
this book, write to Permissions, W. W. Norton & Company, Inc.,
500 Fifth Avenue, New York, NY 10110

Manufacturing by R. R. Donnelley, Harrisonburg
Book design by Lovedog Studio
Production manager: Amanda Morrison

Library of Congress Cataloging-in-Publication Data

Barra, Allen.
The last coach : a life of Paul "Bear" Bryant / Allen Barra.— 1st ed.
p. cm.
Includes bibliographical references.
ISBN 0-393-05982-0 (hardcover)
1. Bryant, Paul W. 2. Football coaches—United States—Biography.
3. University of Alabama—Football—History. I. Title.
GV939.B79B37 2005
796.332'092—dc22
2005014609

ISBN-13: 978-0-393-32897-4 pbk.
ISBN-10: 0-393-32897-X pbk.

W. W. Norton & Company, Inc.
500 Fifth Avenue, New York, N.Y. 10110
www.wwnorton.com

W. W. Norton & Company Ltd.
Castle House, 75/76 Wells Street, London W1T 3QT

1 2 3 4 5 6 7 8 9 0

". . . the long legend . . . the shaggy tremendous shape . . . an anachronism indomitable and invincible out of an old dead time . . . the old bear."

—William Faulkner, "The Bear"

Contents

Introduction

If you're from Alabama and lived through the Bear Bryant era, you know where you were the day he died. On January 26, 1983, I was finishing up a newspaper assignment in California and heading back to my apartment in Park Slope, Brooklyn. I didn't know he was gone until I got off the red-eye and saw the tabloids. The *New York Post*'s back page read, "Crimson Tears: Nation Weeps Over Death of Legendary Bear Bryant, 69." The *Daily News*, God bless them, ran the story on the front page with a picture of Bryant in his familiar houndstooth hat: "'Bear' Bryant of Alabama is dead at 69."

I was stunned but not surprised. I had interviewed Bryant about a year earlier at a press conference for a film version of his life and left with the impression that he was a very sick man. There were times in that final season when he didn't appear to have the strength to make it across the field to shake hands with the opposing coach after a game. He always walked a little slower, though, when Alabama lost, and they lost too often in that last season.

Upon my return home, there were twelve Bear-related messages from all parts of the country on my answering machine. There was one from my mom: "Honey, I guess you heard about Coach Bryant. I'll save you the papers. Talk to you later." Another, from a friend in Birmingham: "It's a little strange down here. Everything seems a little different." I tried to return some of the calls but couldn't get through; I later found out that the entire area code for the state of Alabama, then 205, had been shut down from overload.

Several of the calls came from former high school and college classmates, most of them reflecting the same ambivalence we had always felt about the man. No one ever doubted that Bear Bryant was the greatest college football coach who ever lived; his all-time record of 323 victories obliterated any argument to the contrary. And though other coaches have come along since to surpass him in number of wins, none has approached his overall achievement. (Bryant won more national championships than the other top four coaches combined.) No, we never had any reservations about Bear Bryant as a winner. What we could never quite decide was whether all those victories and championships and awards translated into anything tangible off the football field. What did Bear Bryant *mean* to us?

Many of us had never been able to decide if we actually *liked* Bear Bryant, or rather, we had never been able to come to terms with the public man we were exposed to on a daily basis in Birmingham during the 1960s and 1970s. I suppose it had something to do, at least for many of us, with all those photographs of George Wallace, his arm around the only man in the Deep South more famous than himself. At that time there was no way for us to know of the contempt in which Bryant held Wallace or of Bryant's genuine though ineffectual efforts to integrate the Alabama football team. For that matter, we were never told anything at all about Bear Bryant's politics. I asked dozens of his friends who his favorite president was, and no one was ever able to give me a definitive answer. A recording of Bryant's surprise sixty-fifth birthday party given to me by Jake Reiss, former president of the Birmingham Touchdown Club, provided the answer; in the course of his speech, the Bear revealed that his favorite president was Harry Truman. Of course. "The buck stops here." We should have guessed that one.

Then there was the embarrassment of living in a state where there was so little to boast about to the rest of the country *except* Bear Bryant. Alabamians liked to joke, "Thank God for Mississippi," meaning that whatever Alabama ranked forty-ninth in, such as public spending on education, Mississippi was bound to be fiftieth. Last or not, Mississippi could claim William Faulkner and Eudora Welty, Jimmie Rogers, the father of country music, and Robert Johnson, the king of the delta blues singers. All Alabama had was a football coach.★

What so many college students like ourselves couldn't see was not only how much football meant to so many people in Alabama—white and black, male and female, old and young—but how much it mattered to us. We had felt superior to football, seeing it through the Vietnam-era mist of skepticism and alienation that permeated even Alabama's football-crazy colleges; it had served only to distract us from the important issues. Football was, we liked to say, Alabama's version of grits and circuses. Years later, gathering with friends to watch Alabama on cable television at Manhattan bars or seeing some TV documentary on Bryant, we realized how important the game and all of its cultural baggage had been to us. And always, when we came to talk of such things, Bear Bryant dominated our conversations.

IT WASN'T easy explaining to my father's relatives in New Jersey what it was like to be in Birmingham on the weekend of a big game like when Alabama played Louisiana State or Tennessee. Or, especially, Auburn, where, as Geoffrey Norman wrote in *Alabama Showdown,* "one or two people every year die of a heart attack right there in Legion Field. The better the game, the more who die."[1] People from Texas understood; it was like when the University of Texas played Texas A&M, or Oklahoma. Oklahomans understood; it was like Oklahoma against Texas, or Nebraska. People from Michigan and Ohio understood—it was like Michigan playing Ohio State. Once you got a few minutes outside Philadelphia, Pennsylvanians understood. It was like Penn State against the University of Pittsburgh. But in New Jersey, there were no easy comparisons. "You mean like the Eagles and Giants?" my aunts and uncles and cousins would ask when I described Alabama-Auburn games. Not quite, I'd reply. Nobody died at Eagles-Giants games; the year didn't hinge around Eagles-Giants games. People in Philadelphia and New York got married on the day of Eagles-

---

★ If Mississippi can claim Jimmie Rogers and Robert Johnson, then Alabama should feel free to claim the great Hank Williams, the greatest of all country musicians. But Williams's hellacious life and early death have always discouraged respectable Alabamians from promoting him as an icon.

Giants games. *Nobody* gets married in Alabama on the weekend of the Alabama-Auburn game.

It was also difficult to convey to them Bear Bryant's stature in college football and the reverence with which he was held in the South. I think I came close—and this definitely made an impression on an Italian family—when I compared Bryant to Vince Lombardi. In the South, pro football was what you watched on Sunday afternoon—if it didn't conflict with a college coach's TV show or the replay of Saturday's big game. For Alabamians, Sunday was built around watching *The Bear Bryant Show*, even if it meant missing part of the Green Bay–Dallas game.

In Alabama, the answer to who was the greater coach came as easy as skipping flat rocks over lake water. (Benny Marshall, a long-time columnist for the *Birmingham News*, actually once referred to Vince Lombardi as "a poor man's Bear Bryant.") Outside of Alabama, the question of whose stature was greater was a toss-up, depending on where you lived and whether you were more attached to pro or college football.

The most famous football coach in the first half of the twentieth century was, of course, Notre Dame's Knute Rockne. Pro football scarcely existed for most sports fans until the mid-1950s. After that, the two best-known figures in pro and college football were Lombardi and Bryant. Anyone who called himself a football fan in the 1960s and 1970s could not fail to recognize either the squat, sturdy figure of Lombardi on the Green Bay Packer sidelines, usually wearing a tan topcoat and brown fedora, or the tall, broad-shouldered Bryant, standing near the Alabama bench, clad in a sport coat and his famous houndstooth hat.

Bryant's domain, I argue, was larger than Vince Lombardi's or any other pro football coach's. Lombardi was head coach for the Green Bay Packers and pro football's dominant figure for nine seasons. Bryant, for nearly three decades, was the king of what Dan Jenkins called "Saturday's America"—the world of small towns and college communities that, from Labor Day through New Year's, gives their unqualified devotion to college football, displaying the kind of unbridled enthusiasm that can only be faked or imitated in pro football stadiums. (Those who would take issue with that statement have not experienced both pro and college football.) Both men shared an abiding passion for the game of football and a fierce, unwavering conviction that it was the pathway to the American dream. Their backgrounds are radically different, but there are some extraordinary parallels and similarities in their lives too.

Born in Brooklyn into an Italian family, Vince Lombardi was one of five children raised by a tyrannical father. His worldview was molded by a strict Catholic school education. Born of Celtic blood, Paul Bryant grew up dirt poor in an Arkansas farming community so small that it didn't qualify as a town, and he never finished high school. His family was even larger than Lombardi's—Paul was the eleventh of twelve children (three died in infancy). His mother, Ida Mae, was the single most important influence on his life.

Both men were born in 1913, during the presidency of Woodrow Wilson and one year before the outbreak of World War I. Both played for legendary college teams, starring as offensive linemen—Lombardi as one of Fordham's famed "Seven Blocks of Granite" and Bryant as a member of Alabama's great Rose Bowl championship teams of the 1930s, which established the Crimson Tide as a national power. Though no previous account of their lives mentions it, they narrowly missed playing against each other when Alabama met Fordham at the Polo Grounds in New York in 1933. (Lombardi had been to prep school the year before and was thus ineligible for the varsity squad, but he was almost certainly in the stands that day, as was his custom, rooting for the Rams.)

The football philosophy of both men was shaped by a strong connection to Knute Rockne. Lombardi learned football at Fordham from Jim Crowley, one of Rockne's Four Horsemen at Notre Dame; Bryant learned football from the great Frank Thomas, who had played quarterback for Rockne.

In the 1950s, both coached at schools with strong military traditions—Lombardi as an assistant at West Point and Bryant as head coach at Texas A&M. In the early 1950s, both men's careers were greatly affected by scandals at their universities, though neither was implicated in any way. In 1953, Lombardi left West Point in the wake of the cadets' cheating scandal, which occurred during the reign of Red Blaik, the nation's most celebrated college football coach at the time; in the same year, Bryant would leave Kentucky in the aftermath of the point shaving scandal that occurred while Adolph Rupp, the country's most celebrated college basketball coach, was in power. In the late 1950s both found the team that would link them with destiny—Bryant returning to coach at the University of Alabama in 1958 and Lombardi leaving his job as offensive coordinator with the New York Giants to assume the head coaching job at Green Bay a year later. Both turned their teams sharply around in their first seasons. Both earned their first national titles in the same season, 1961—Lombardi winning the first of five National Football League (NFL) titles, Bryant claiming the first of six national college championships.

Both men developed close and lasting relationships with rebellious prodigies whom they publicly disciplined—Lombardi with Paul Hornung (whom Bryant very nearly recruited for the University of Kentucky), Bryant with Joe Namath. Both were uncompromising taskmasters who were often accused of brutalizing their players. (In fact, they were singled out on this charge in a much-discussed *Sports Illustrated* story.) Both coaches were enthusiastic advocates of what William Walter "Pudge" Heffelfinger (Walter Camp's first All-America selection and the first pro football player) liked to call "red meat football," meaning an emphasis on blocking and tackling rather than strategy. Of both coaches it was regularly said that they were not innovators but pragmatists who borrowed and honed other coaches' ideas; both laid out their principles in ghostwritten books that became bibles for their disciples. Both were accused by their detractors of being martinets (an unfair accusation according to nearly all of those who played for them). Both preferred overachieving players with "team" skills to superathletes who were more difficult to coach. They tended toward smallish offensive and defensive lines that whipped their opponents through better conditioning.

Bryant and Lombardi stressed defense as the backbone of a championship football team and were constantly regarded as conservative on offense, emphasizing the running game. Yet both were brilliant students of the passing game who regularly ambushed bigger, more talented teams in important games with dazzling air attacks. (And both had their favorite "trick" plays—Lombardi his halfback option pass, Bryant his tackle-eligible pass.) Both emphasized the importance of the kicking game and won important games with substitute kickers.

The parallels, though, go well beyond the football field. Both men married young and stayed married to the same woman their entire lives, though Bryant's wife, Mary Harmon—it was, in the southern tradition of calling females by both their first and middle names, always "Mary Harmon," never just plain "Mary"—was much more the prototype of the "football wife" than Lombardi's wife, Marie, who was always in the background of Lombardi's life. Mary Harmon sometimes seemed to be enjoying the celebrity life more than her husband; it was joked that she would make a better First Lady than Bryant would a governor. Both Bryant and Lombardi had two children, a son and a daughter, with the son given the same first name as his father.

"Intense" was a word often used to describe both men's personalities by those who were close to them (though Joe Drach, who played for Bryant at Maryland and who knew Lombardi when he coached Green Bay, made the distinction that Lombardi was "violently intense," while Bryant was "violently laid back"). Both inspired devout loyalty and affection in their players, assistants, and colleagues. Both had bedrock family values and formed lifelong attachments to their schools and communities. (And both were the subject of biographies titled *Coach*, which is how even their former players addressed them.)

Surprisingly, the two most famous football coaches of the last three-quarters of the century met only once: in 1961, at the MacArthur Bowl ceremony in which Alabama was presented a trophy as the best college team in the nation. Shaking hands with Alabama quarterback Pat Trammell, Lombardi told him, "I'd like to have you in Green Bay." "Vince," Bryant responded, "you let him go finish medical school." (Trammell took Bryant's advice.) No photographer, as far as is known, recorded the only meeting of perhaps the two greatest coaches in the history of the game.

No player, coach, or sportswriter ever recalls Bryant having mentioned Lombardi, and, as near as I've been able to determine, there is only one known instance of Lombardi having mentioned Bryant. Former Alabama coach and current ESPN college football analyst Bill Curry played against Bryant's Alabama teams while at Georgia Tech and later played center for Lombardi at Green Bay. In 1966 Curry relates, "Just before we played the Cleveland Browns, Coach Lombardi was trying to get me fired up for practice, and while I was doing pushups he walked up with a big grin on his face and said, loud enough for others to hear, 'Curry, did ja hear what Bear Bryant says in his book about guys from Georgia Tech? He says they're pantywaists!' Coach Bryant didn't actually say that, but he did imply that practices at Georgia Tech weren't as intense as at other southeastern schools. Anyway, it struck me later that that was practically the only time I'd ever heard Vince Lombardi mention another football coach."★

Lombardi did vote for Bryant as the greatest college football coach ever in a poll taken by *The Sporting News* in 1969 on the one-hundredth anniversary of the Princeton-Rutgers game. J. David Briley, a Tennessean working on a book on racial integration in Alabama football, discovered the ballots among the papers of Tom Siler, former editor of the *Knoxville News-Sentinel.* Or, rather, Lombardi voted Bryant second after his former boss at West Point, Red Blaik, which is certainly understandable as Bryant put his former boss at Alabama, Frank Thomas, number one. (General Robert Neyland, the man who established Tennessee as a national power and whom Bryant never defeated, was the Bear's second choice.)

Bryant and Lombardi transcended football to become figures in American folklore. Both contributed catch phrases to the American lexicon. "Winning isn't everything, it's the only thing" is attributed to Lombardi, though Lombardi's greatest biographer, David Maraniss, traced the phrase to a John Wayne movie. (Lombardi apparently did say something on the order of, "Winning isn't everything, but wanting to win is."†) Bryant is credited with "A tie is like kissing your sister." Bryant claimed that he actually heard that first from Maryland coach Jim Tatum, and Tatum said he first remembers hearing it from Bryant, as well as "Winning isn't everything, but it sure beats anything that comes in second."

Both men have become American cultural icons. In the punk rock classic *Rock and Roll High School*, the students burn down Vince Lombardi Memorial High, and in Richard Ford's novel *The Sportswriter*, the central character stops on the New Jersey Turnpike to muse over the significance

---

★ Curry's memory might be a bit fuzzy. Bryant's autobiography was published in 1975, seven years after Curry left Green Bay. However, Bryant did take a swipe at Georgia Tech in one of his 1966 articles for *Sports Illustrated.* The articles were cowritten with *SI*'s John Underwood, who later worked with Bryant on *Bear: The Hard Life and Good Times of Alabama's Coach Bryant.*

† Actually, it appears that "Winning isn't everything, it's the only thing" predates the John Wayne movie, *Trouble along the Way.* The screenwriter for the film, Melville Schavelson, said that he heard it from his Hollywood agent, who also represented UCLA football coach Henry "Red" Sanders. Bryant would have laughed had he known this; Sanders was his boss at Vanderbilt during the 1940 and 1941 seasons.

of the Vince Lombardi rest stop. In the movie *Forrest Gump*, the Alabama football coach who recruits Tom Hanks goes unnamed, though he is easily recognized by his houndstooth hat. In the thriller *Crimson Tide*, Gene Hackman, commander of the submarine USS *Alabama*, has a dog named "Bear Bryant."

In 2003, ESPN aired a fictionalized account of Jim Dent's best-selling book about Bryant's first season at Texas A&M, *The Junction Boys*, with Tom Berenger as Bryant. The coach in *Remember the Titans*, starring Denzel Washington, buses his team far from the prying eyes of parents to a training camp where he subjects them to grueling, boot camp–type workouts with no water—it's a high school version of *The Junction Boys*. (To emphasize the point, the school's uniforms are Alabama crimson.) In the recent movie *Radio*, the camera scans around the office of the high school football coach, played by Ed Harris. Amidst the trophies and certificates, there is a single photo of a football coach, unnamed but quickly identified by, of course, his houndstooth hat.★ And on a night in the winter of 2005, when I took a break from completing this book, I turned on *Law and Order* and heard Fred Thompson, actor and former senator from Tennessee, tell someone that "If not for Osama Bin Laden, September 11 would only be remembered as Bear Bryant's birthday."

Bryant's influence has been both more profound and more enduring than Lombardi's. This is partly because his career was much longer, but also because Bryant, more than Lombardi and in fact more than any other football coach, had that rare ability to nurture protégés. Many men quoted Lombardi's axioms and tried to follow his pattern for success, but none of them were big winners. More than fifty of Bryant's assistants and players became coaches; several of them, including Paul Dietzel, Howard Schnellenberger, and Gene Stallings, won national college championships, and several more, including Jack Pardee, Bum Phillips, and Ray Perkins, had winning records with the pros. When Bill Parcells, an ardent Bryant admirer, returned to pro football in 2003 with the Dallas Cowboys, Texas writers openly speculated that he wanted to be "Pro Football's Bear

---

★ My twelve-year-old daughter, God bless her, did spot an error. On Harris's desk, there is a Coca-Cola bottle commemorating Bryant's 315th coaching victory, which made him the first man to pass the record of Amos Alonzo Stagg. I have the same bottle on my office desk. "Daddy," she whispered to me in the theater, "that's wrong. That bottle didn't come out until 1982, and this movie is set in 1976."

Bryant." (Bryant turned four college programs around; if Parcells succeeds with Dallas, it will be his fourth NFL turnaround.)

Bryant's influence still pervades every level of the game, from small colleges to the pros. One of the recent success stories in college football is Howard Schnellenberger's Florida Atlantic University Owls, who were 20-6 for the 2003–2004 seasons. Ozzie Newsome, one of his first great black All-America players, is currently general manager of the Baltimore Ravens and the highest-ranking black executive in the NFL. John Mitchell, the first black player to start for the University of Alabama and Bryant's first black assistant coach, is currently defensive line coach with the Pittsburgh Steelers. The college football story of 2004 was the hiring of Sylvester Croom, an All-America center and Bryant's second black assistant coach, as the first black head coach at a Southeastern Conference (SEC) school, Mississippi State, not, alas, Alabama.

Nearly every time there is a controversy or some issue that involves college football, Bryant's name is invoked, and when it is, his legacy looks better and better. Every time a coach runs up the score on a beaten opponent just to improve his position in the polls, every time a receiver or ball carrier dances in the end zone after a touchdown, every time a hotshot quarterback pads his Heisman Trophy credentials by throwing his fifth touchdown pass in a shutout victory, every time a defensive player taunts a prostrate foe after a vicious hit, many longtime college football fans think wistfully of Bear Bryant and the dignity and respect for sportsmanship he imparted to his players and, through them, to the fans of Alabama football.

There are disturbing aspects, though, to Bryant's legacy as well, questions that not only linger but seem to grow more important with every passing season. For instance, the question of college football and its continued viability as an amateur sport is more pertinent than ever. Even in New Jersey, there is an ongoing debate as to whether or not Rutgers University should continue to compete in Division I-A football. (Luckily for me no one was debating this question 135 years ago in 1869, when Rutgers won the first intercollegiate football game against Princeton, thus starting football down the path that would lead to Bear Bryant and this book.) In a letter to the *Newark Star-Ledger*, one of Rutgers's football critics, a professor at the university, phrased it thusly: "We can't afford a great library *and* great linebackers."[2] (One might counter with something like, "Rutgers must have a damn good library, because they sure don't seem to have spent any money at all on linebackers," but that would be unfair and also beside the point.) A serious study of Bryant's career and his impact on the game must come to terms sooner or later with what might well be the most important question in American sports in the twenty-first century, namely, how did America's colleges become, and why do they continue to be, cost-free minor leagues for professional sports?

And a large part of the answer relates to the enormous personal magnetism of Bear Bryant and a handful of others who transformed college football from a game with a large cult following into the most lucrative spectator sport in the world. Not that Bear Bryant had an inkling that he was bringing about this sports revolution. No man tried harder to stress the importance of a football team as a representative of its university (I honestly think he'd have conceded the point that the university needs a great library before great linebackers), and yet no man did more to accelerate the trend toward isolating football players from mainstream university life. Bryant was one of the first coaches to insist that his players sleep and eat entirely apart from the student body, and he was absolutely adamant in rejecting the label of "student-athletes," created and approved by the National Collegiate Athletic Association (NCAA). "My players," he insisted on numerous occasions, "are athletes first and students second." Even his severest critics must concede that his lack of hypocrisy on this matter was refreshing if for no other reason than that even a casual observer of the modern college football scene could hardly fail to recognize what Bear affirmed decades ago and what the NCAA continues to deny.

Bryant, I'm convinced, would not have approved of the turn college football has taken in the two decades since his death. Among the developments he would have soundly rejected are the hypocrisy of conference playoffs, in which, in order to generate more TV revenue, a team is often given a shot at winning a title in a postseason game that its regular season performance didn't merit; the overtime tie-breaking system, in which the ball is placed on the opponent's twenty-five yard line; the lack of emphasis on punting, field position, and most of the other things Bryant loved about football in favor of artificially induced offensive pyrotechnics; and even the increasing sentiment, at least among sportswriters and television executives, if not among college football fans themselves, toward a major college football playoff system. He once told me, "We've already got a perfectly good system in college football. It's called a regular season. Anything that ain't settled by the end of it plus one bowl game should stay unsettled."

Paul Bryant would have been disgusted by the ever-increasing power of the NCAA. Billy Neighbors, one of Bryant's greatest players, said his coach was constantly damning the NCAA as "useless." "You could always hear him saying," said Neighbors, "that the NCAA never did anything for anybody but themselves." Most of all, he would not have liked what the college game on the field has evolved into, that is, a junior version of the pro game with the rules and tactics so absurdly favoring passing that everything that was once unique to college football—the different formations, the varying styles and strategies that once made football at Alabama or Texas or Southern Cal or Notre Dame or Michigan so special—has now all but vanished, its place taken by 150 or more little NFL clones in college colors.

When Bear Bryant began his career, the NFL wasn't even a tail to the dog; college football was the whole dog. Bryant's only intention was to field winning college football teams, not train players for the professionals. How, though, could the greatest coach in football *not* send great players to the pros? It's arguable that no college coach produced as many players that had so much impact on the pros. If one tallies up the names from his first year at Kentucky in 1946 through his final season at Alabama in 1982, the list includes Bob Gain, George Blanda, Babe Parilli, Jack Pardee, John David Crow, Lee Roy Jordan, Joe Namath, Ray Perkins, Ken Stabler, John Hannah, Richard Todd, Ozzie Newsome, Tony Nathan, Dwight Stephenson, Don McNeal, Woodrow Lowe, and Bob Baumhower, to name just a few of the most prominent. Yet, even in the late 1970s, when Alabama's players dominated NFL rosters, the vast majority of Bear's boys went to college with no serious intentions of becoming professional football players.

Instead of grooming his players to become pros, for thirty-eight years Bryant coached as if he had a sacred obligation to make their lives better for having played football for him. And today, almost to a man, the men who played for him look you in the eye and tell you that that is indeed the case, that they are better men, that they lived richer, more responsible lives, because they played football for Bear Bryant. Only a cynic would argue that they are wrong about the therapeutic value of football.

What no one could foresee during Bryant's lifetime was the degree to which his own greatness as a football coach and the singularity and force of his personality would accelerate change in the game of college football. There is little doubt that, had he so desired, Paul Bryant could have been the highest-paid coach in either college or the pros. Instead, he wasn't even among the highest-paid coaches of his era, choosing for himself, at peak, a salary one dollar lower than that of the university president. At a time when coaches no sooner win a championship than they commence the bidding for their services, such humility seems almost storybookish, the type of thing that we read about in children's biographies of great men (and in fact the kind of humility that was emphasized time and again in the children's books that have been written about Bryant).

But Bear, more than any other great football coach, was responsible for leading us into this era of spandex and steroids, of mercenary coaches who jump from colleges to the pros and back again, of football players who owe little or no allegiance to the fans or schools whose colors they wear and whose closest relationship is with the agent who will represent them in the NFL draft. This despite the fact that Bear Bryant epitomized everything that was great about college football and that he still stands as a beacon for what the game could become once again. Did Bear Bryant contradict himself? All right, then, he contradicted himself. To accept him, we must accept him in his contradictions.

Time has not yet resolved any of those contradictions or softened any of his rough edges. On the contrary, the Bear seems more interesting and more appealing—more *authentic*—with every passing year. Like a craggy-faced Janus, Bryant looks to both the past and the future of football. He was the last coach of the Heroic Age, of what he liked to call "eleven man and sic 'em" football, with, in the words of his good friend Mickey Herskowitz, a bloodline that can be traced to Amos Alonzo Stagg, whose victory record he broke and who practically invented the college game, and to Knute Rockne, the first of the great psychologists of whom Bryant may have been the last.

His greatest failure as a leader was his lack of moral force, his hesitancy to do the right thing—to do what he very clearly understood was the right thing—when it was time to racially integrate the most storied football program in the South. Perhaps his greatest achievement as a leader was the thoroughness with which he integrated the team and the coaching staff once the commitment was made.

Bryant created the blueprint for the modern, superstar coach—or, rather, he created it with assists from Roone Arledge, who had much to do with creating Bryant's public image through ABC's college football broadcasts, and Bill Battle, one of Bryant's former players and later coaching rivals whose marketing acumen was little short of genius. There is some argument as to whether or not Paul Bryant was the first coach to have his own local television show, but there is no question that he was the first to turn that show and his own image into a gold mine. (Keith Jackson, who did play-by-play on ABC for many of Bryant's most famous games, thought him "a marketing genius. He was the only southern football coach who regularly came to New York, where the media centers were.")[3] Battle put Bryant's face and name on everything from stuffed bears wearing houndstooth hats to Coca-Cola bottles to "Bear Bryant Commemorative Vans" that sold for up to twenty-five thousand dollars. By the time Bryant approached Amos Alonzo Stagg's record for career victories, he had hawked for everyone, from Ford trucks to South Central Bell, establishing a pattern that many coaches who didn't share Bryant's old-fashioned values about not showing up the college president were still happy to emulate.

Some of those coaches, including a couple from Alabama, drunk with their endorsement deals and dazzled by their press clippings, deluded themselves into thinking they were the second coming of Bear Bryant, and nearly wrecked their lives. They didn't get the message that Bryant spent his entire coaching career repeating, that no one, not even the greatest coach in football history, is bigger than the game. They also couldn't understand what we have only just now begun to see, that there was never going to be another Bear Bryant—that he was indeed the last coach.

Prologue

ON THE MORNING OF Wednesday, December 15, 1982, Lynda Cardwell, an undergraduate at the University of Alabama and stringer for her hometown paper, left her English class early to cover the biggest story of her life. About halfway to Memorial Coliseum, she broke into a jog, fearing the consequences if she dared to enter the room after the press conference began. Cardwell had attended other press conferences presided over by Paul "Bear" Bryant, and she knew only too well how a glare from the Coach could wither a young journalist. Small chance for a teenage coed writing her first feature story to screw up at a Bryant press conference and emerge unscathed.

Cardwell barged through the back entrance to the conference room, hoping to slip in without drawing attention. No such luck. As she ran down the hall, without warning, Bryant's office door swung open and the most famous man in Alabama, the most famous football coach in America, led his entourage into the hallway. Cardwell's forward motion couldn't be slowed, and she collided with the Bear. "It was like running into a Coke machine," she later recalled.

"I'm so sorry, Coach," she stammered, desperately trying to apologize for being late, inexperienced, and female—three things writers who covered Alabama in Bryant's era weren't supposed to be. Bryant didn't speak to her, but he gently took her arm. Softly singing, "I was sinking deep in sin,

Far from the peaceful shore . . . ," he escorted her to his final press conference. Cardwell recognized the hymn as one she had heard and sung maybe a thousand times at Glencoe Church of Christ.

Opening the door to the conference room, Bryant sang the refrain: "Love lifted me . . ." Moments before, Cardwell had been in a state of near panic. Now, being led to her seat "like a prom queen on the arm of her king," she was calmed. She would not have been had she known how many others had quaked over the years upon hearing the Coach croon the old hymn, which had been a favorite of his mother's back in Moro Bottom, Arkansas.

"Whenever we heard him singing that song," said Jerry Duncan, an offensive lineman on the great Alabama national championship teams of the mid-1960s, "we knew somebody's ass was going to wind up in a sling."

But not on this day. The room was packed, not only with the Alabama media but also with writers assigned by the *Washington Post, New York Times, USA Today,* Associated Press, and others, some of whom had taken red-eyes to Birmingham on the strength of speculation that had begun filtering out the previous afternoon. The New York media scooped the locals on this one; Herschel Nissenson, the college football writer for Associated Press, caught wind of the news in New York when Giants coach Ray Perkins, a two-time All-America for Bryant at Alabama, told his players Bryant would be leaving the team. Nissenson not only broke the story of Bryant's retirement, but was able to name his successor. It was, he would say later, his most satisfying accomplishment as a sportswriter.

Bryant patted Cardwell on the arm; she slipped into the back row, mercifully unnoticed, as all eyes followed Bryant to the podium. Reading from a prepared statement, he proceeded to tell everyone that he'd "done a poor job of coaching" that season and that "the players deserve better," and announced his retirement.

Most of those present and hundreds of thousands listening on radio were numbed. Rumors had been rampant for nearly a month, since Alabama had been upset by Southern Mississippi at Bryant-Denny Stadium in Tuscaloosa—the first time the Crimson Tide had lost there in nineteen years, a streak that extended through fifty-seven games and the terms of six U.S. presidents.

But now that the time had come, scarcely anyone in Alabama could believe it. All over the state, grocery store lines halted and Muzak ceased as the conference was relayed over PA systems. A man at Baptist Medical Center Montclair in Birmingham demanded that his impending operation be delayed for a few minutes until Bryant had made his announcement. (The Bear would have been greatly amused to find out that the patient was an Auburn fan.) People pulling out of their driveways on the way to work stopped their cars to listen; those already at work sipped coffee and huddled around radios.

"There comes a time when you need to hang it up," said Bryant, looking perhaps ten years older than his actual sixty-nine, "and that time has come for me as head football coach at the University of Alabama. I'm a tired old man, but I'll never get tired of football." There was just one more game to be played, on December 29, against the University of Illinois at the Liberty Bowl in Memphis.

"If I quit coaching," he was fond of telling friends, "I'd croak in a week."

PART ONE

Paul Bryant as a Fordyce High School Redbug, circa 1928–1930.
"All I had was football," he would say in his autobiography,
"and I hung on as though it was life or death."

Chapter 1

Up from
the Bottom

One night after the 1979 Sugar Bowl, the goal line stand
game, we were having a victory party in his suite at the
Hyatt. Paul had on a T-shirt, a new one, but it had a hole
in it. One of the guests said "Coach your shirt has a hole in
it." He said, "Yeah, I know. I always tear a small hole in my
T-shirts so I'll never forget where I came from."

—*Related by former Alabama broadcaster*
John Forney[1]

THE STATE OF ALABAMA owes much to Graham MacNamee. A failed
crooner from St. Paul, Minnesota, MacNamee was the nation's first celebrity
sports announcer. Starting out in the early 1920s on WEAF in New York, he
was for nearly a decade the voice, indeed the only voice, of the World Series,
the Rose Bowl, and heavyweight championship fights. Red Barber, who
succeeded MacNamee in the World Series booth, called his rich baritone
"the most exciting voice, the one that electrified everyone." One of those
he electrified was twelve-year-old Paul William Bryant.★

★ In his 1970 book, *The Broadcasters*, Barber quotes Ring Lardner as saying, "I don't
know which game to write about—the one I saw today or the one I heard Graham
MacNamee announce." (p. 25)

In 1927 MacNamee broadcast the most anticipated match in sports history, the Gene

On January 1, 1926, MacNamee called the play-by-play for the Rose Bowl match between the Crimson Tide from the University of Alabama and the Huskies from the University of Washington. Although Bryant never said where he listened to the game, it was probably at his uncle's hotel in Fordyce, a rural town in south-central Arkansas, as his own family was much too poor to afford a luxury like a radio. The Rose Bowl at that time wasn't merely the biggest football game of the year, it was the only postseason bowl game, and the Tide's trip to Pasadena captured the imagination not just of Alabama but of the entire South in an age where many could still personally recall the end of the Civil War. "Our team," said Alabama president Dr. George Hutcheson "Mike" Denny, "will strive to represent worthily our great commonwealth and our great section. Win or lose . . . this trip means more widespread and sustained publicity for Alabama than any recent event in the history of the state."[2]

MacNamee and the Crimson Tide won Paul over, as Alabama came back from a 12–0 halftime deficit to win a thrilling 20–19 victory, after which the *Los Angeles Evening Herald* announced, "Tuscaloosa, Alabama, which Western fans didn't know was on the map, is the abiding place of the Pacific Coast Football Championship today."[3]

"I never imagined anything could be that exciting," Bryant would recall many years later. "I still didn't have much of an idea what football was, but after listening to that game, I had it in my mind that what I wanted to do with my life was go to Alabama and play in the Rose Bowl like Johnny Mack Brown." Brown, the first great idol of Alabama football, was the kind of player that Pudge Heffelfinger had in mind when he wrote in his 1954 classic *This Was Football*, "Southern ball-carriers run with reckless abandon, a wild fanaticism that's rarely found in backs

---

Tunney–Jack Dempsey rematch for the heavyweight title, from Soldier Field in Chicago. In the seventh round, Dempsey floored Tunney, bringing on the famous "long count" controversy when Dempsey refused to go to a neutral corner and the referee gave Tunney an extra few seconds to recover. MacNamee whipped the radio audience (over forty million, the radio network would later claim) into a frenzy, screaming, "Tunney is down! Tunney is down!" when the champion hit the canvas. According to Frederick Lewis Allen in his informal history of the 1920s, *Only Yesterday*, "Five Americans dropped dead of heart failure at their radios." Another five died later from heart strain caused by overexcitement.

from other parts of the nation."[4] Tall, good looking, and topped with dark, wavy hair, Johnny Mack parlayed two spectacular touchdowns in the Rose Bowl into a Hollywood career. He was so much in demand in the late 1920s and early 1930s that he even took some coveted roles (such as Billy the Kid in King Vidor's 1931 production) from a former Southern Cal lineman named Marion Morrison. Morrison, renamed John Wayne, would one day be everyone's favorite choice to play Paul Bryant on the big screen.

So young Paul heard a football game before he ever saw one—in fact, before he had ever seen a football—or at least that's what the legend says. According to his 1975 autobiography, *Bear*, he was in the eighth grade—which would make him about thirteen years old, or about a year after he listened to the Rose Bowl broadcast—when he walked past the field where the Fordyce High School football team was practicing. According to Bryant, the coach "naturally noticed a great big boy like me, and asked if I wanted to play." By some accounts, that would have been head coach Bob Cowan, later to be named by Bryant as one of the biggest influences on his life; others say it was assistant coach Dan Walton. Bryant himself never identified the man, but continued:

> I said, "Yessir, I guess I do. How do you play?"
>
> He said, "Well, you see that fellow catching the ball down there?"
>
> "Yeah."
>
> "Well, whenever he catches it, you go down there and try to kill him."

This would be the version related in numerous newspaper and magazine stories over the years. In a children's biography of Bryant's life, *Paul Bryant, Football Legend* by Sylvia B. Williams, the coach's instructions to Paul would be softened to, "When he catches it, you go down there and smash him," but more than likely the coach told Paul to "kill," just as Bryant remembered it.[5] Football in Fordyce, Arkansas, as Paul Bryant had just discovered, was taken very seriously.

Fordyce seemed like an ideal town to grow up in. Nestled in Dallas County, the handsome little town lies almost seventy miles south of Little Rock at the intersection of two major railroads, the Georgia Pacific from the east and the Union Pacific from the west—hence the town's unofficial title of "South Arkansas' Best Located City." It began as a railroad town, named after Samuel Fordyce, a Confederate officer who immediately saw the value in rebuilding and developing the railroads that the Union Army had taken such pains to destroy. (Samuel Fordyce was also famous for building the Fordyce Bath House in Hot Springs, which would later be visited by such underworld luminaries as Owney "The Killer" Madden, Charles "Lucky" Luciano, and "Pretty Boy" Floyd.)

The population in 2000 was 4,799, perhaps twelve hundred more than when Bryant was growing up. A trade center for a fertile five-county area, Fordyce was closer to being self-sufficient than many towns in the Deep South, and thus a better place than most in which to weather the Depression. Among the town's traditional attractions is the "Fordyce on the Cotton Belt Festival," which features the Rex Raney Top Gun Bull Challenge and the Redbug Reunion Rally—Fordyce boasts the only high school in America to claim the name "Redbug" for its football team (and, as one lifelong resident adds, "The only high school that would want to"). The Reunion Rally is open not merely to graduates of Fordyce High School but to anyone who ever attended, which was fortunate for Paul Bryant, as he never graduated. The town's biggest attraction, as far as any living resident can recall, is football. "When I was growing up," says Larry Lacewell, director of scouting for the Dallas Cowboys and son of one of Bryant's high school teammates, "nobody asked a boy if he *wanted* to play football—they asked you what position you were *going* to play."

Fordyce proved perfect for Paul Bryant, except for two things. First, his parents didn't approve of football, and, second, Paul Bryant wasn't from Fordyce. In fact, he was born in a place called Moro Bottom in 1913. Fordyce, however far behind the rest of the country, was at least aware of changes in the outside world; folks would meet in places like the general store owned by the Kilgore brothers, Paul's uncles, and would discuss the policies of the new president, Woodrow Wilson—a white southern democrat who had been president of Princeton—and the trouble that was brewing over in Europe. They would shake their heads over the outlandish new fashion trend toward looser and more revealing clothes for women as reflected in newspaper photographs, or marvel at the descriptions of the newly completed Panama Canal. Many were suspicious about the news that the Ford Motor Company was using a moving assembly line to build automobiles faster; none of them could suspect that, within the next ten years, many of their children would be heading north to find jobs in such plants. But in 1913, Moro Bottom was scarcely influenced by Fordyce, much less the rest of the world.

You would have to call Moro Bottom a place, because it wasn't a town. It wasn't marked on any map when Paul Bryant was born, and is marked on some maps today only because he was born there.* Moro Bottom—the name is sometimes given as Moro's Bottom and pronounced by the locals as "Moe'-Row"—was a few miles north of Fordyce. No one knows precisely where Moro Bottom got its name, which is to say no one knew where Moro Creek, which ran through it, got its name. "I hated that name," Louise Bryant Goolsby, the tenth of the twelve Bryant children, told an interviewer. "It made us seem like a bunch of morons."

Moro Bottom was the reality of which Al Capp's Dogpatch, the home of L'il Abner, was the hideous caricature. It simply wasn't possible to be more backwoods than Moro Bottom. There were no stores, just a handful of families living along a creek that would cut off the inhabitants from Fordyce or nearby Kingsland when the water level rose, usually in the spring. (Bryant would later recollect the number of families as six; other sources suggest perhaps a dozen.) During a driving rain, Paul's enterprising older brother Jack would keep a team of mules hitched, ready, for a reasonable fee, to pull a stalled car or flooded wagon out of the creek. Though reporters and profilers over the years would invariably identify his hometown as Fordyce, Bryant never denied Moro Bottom. Not that he was particularly proud of it. When Bryant began coaching at Texas A&M, Mickey Herskowitz, a Texas sportswriter who became one of Bryant's closest friends, asked him if he was from Fordyce. Herskowitz didn't quite understand the mumbled reply.

"Moro what?" he asked.

"Bottom," Bryant replied. "Like your ass. Moro Bottom."

PAUL'S FATHER, Wilson Monroe Bryant—called by his middle name, which was pronounced "Mahn'-row," by those who knew him—was,

---

* Nearly half a century later, Paul's great-nephew, Ray Bryant, erected a large wooden sign near the site where the house had stood that proclaimed Moro Bottom as "The Birthplace of Paul Bear Bryant." Every now and then a tourist comes by just to see the

according to family tradition, descended from Georgia farmers who had made their way through the wilderness to Arkansas. The family of his mother, Ida Mae Kilgore, had traveled east from Texas to settle in Arkansas. "His father's people were from Georgia, his mother's from Texas," says Colonel Jimmy Phillips of the Dallas County Museum in Fordyce. "You can't get more southern than that." None of the Bryants seem to have had any interest in tracing their ancestral roots. ("I don't know what kind of name Bryant is," Paul would tell *Sports Illustrated*'s John Underwood, "or where the family got started.") W. J. Cash, in his 1941 classic *The Mind of the South*, defined the class and the Celtic stock from which families like the Bryants sprang, as well as the social and economic circumstances which spawned them:

> The poor whites in the strict sense were merely the weakest elements of the old backcountry population, in whom these effects of the plantation had worked themselves out to the ultimate term; those who had been driven back farthest—back to the red hills and the sandlands and the pine barrens and the swamps—to all the marginal lands of the South; those who, because of the poorness of the soil on which they dwelt or the great inaccessibility of markets, were, as a group, most completely barred off from escape or economic and social advance. They were the people to whom the term "cracker" properly applied—the "white-trash and 'po' buckra" of the house-niggers, within the narrowest meaning of those epithets, which, however, were very far from being always used with nice discrimination.[6]

No Bryant, of course, would have referred to himself as "white-trash" nor suffered the insolence of any man who dared refer to them as such. Cash drew a bead on the temperament of Bryant men in the most oft-quoted passage from *The Mind of the South*, in explanation of why the Confederate infantry soldier, despite his unruly nature, was "one of the world's very finest fighting men": "the thing that sent him swinging up the slope at Gettysburg on that celebrated, gallant afternoon was before all else nothing more or less than the thing which elsewhere accounted for his violence—

---

sign and the site and to be regaled by a story or two from Ray Bryant, who built a new house on the family land.

was nothing more or less than his conviction, the conviction of every farmer among what was essentially only a band of farmers, that nothing living could cross him and get away with it." The Bryants, like "thousands and ten thousands—possibly the majority—of non-slaveholders," wrote Cash, "were really yeoman farmers."[7]

Paul would later describe the family homestead as "a truck farm"; the term wasn't derisive. The Bryants had 260 acres of land, much of it excellent for growing vegetables and a little cotton. Franklin Roosevelt's Tennessee Valley Authority, which brought electricity to much of the rural South, was more than a decade away; Paul was raised in a four-room wood-plank house with no electricity or running water. There was a kitchen, a "big room" in which checkers was played and the family Bible read aloud, and two bedrooms—the parents' and the children's. The children slept in beds—one for the girls and one for the boys—and on pallets on the floor, sometimes huddling together for warmth. (One of Bryant's sisters remembered, "There were cracks in the walls.") But the Bryant kids ate well, and so did their guests. Dean Kilgore, Ida's nephew, slept over one night "on a pallet" and, nearly seventy-five years later, in an interview for the Dallas County Historical Society, recalled waking "to the smell of that good country ham and biscuits and red eye gravy. Man oh man, that was some good eatin'."[8] The Bryants grew enough vegetables and watermelons and raised enough chickens and hogs to feed the large family and still have some left over to sell. Some of their customers were black families who lived within a few miles of the creek. Not knowing that he wasn't supposed to get along with them, Paul developed an easy rapport with blacks that stayed with him all his life. It was white folks he would have his first trouble with.

Paul got his size from his father and his personality from his mother. Monroe Bryant was a large, big-boned man, but by the time Paul began school, his father was a semi-invalid. The precise nature of Monroe's illness was never determined; Paul thought his father suffered from high blood pressure, while others who knew him from a distance seemed to think it was some combination of physical and mental problems. Visitors to the Bryant home, including a few family members, often speculated that Monroe was simply lazy. One cousin told of going to the Bryant farm to look at a cow he was thinking of buying. Monroe, seated in a chair on the porch, didn't walk to the barn with him but simply pointed and told him to "go over and look at it."[9] Louise Goolsby recalled several occasions when her father was found wandering aimlessly in the woods. One night Ida awoke to find him missing from their bed, and after searching outdoors, found him sitting in a mud puddle in the middle of the road that ran by the house. Monroe had no explanation for how or why he got there.

Though Monroe wasn't much of a factor in his son's life, Paul loved his father and was much distressed by his death, at age forty-six, in 1933 of an apparent bout with pneumonia (one source suggested food poisoning). The cause of death was never determined, as the Bryants never went to doctors. Devout members of the Church of God, the family didn't believe in seeking secular help when dealing with illness. "Mother and Daddy believed that if you had enough faith, you didn't need doctors," said Louise. Paul had just begun to attend classes at the University of Alabama when he received a letter from his cousin, Collins Kilgore, telling of his father's death. The combination of grief and homesickness caused him to consider dropping out of school. Collins straightened him out with a telegram that read, "GO AHEAD AND QUIT JUST LIKE EVERYBODY PREDICTED YOU WOULD." Collins intended no malice with his message. Paul was the first Bryant to make it to college, and no one in the family wanted to see him fail. Paul got over his homesickness, but he would harbor an ambivalence toward organized religion until the last few years of his life. He wasn't shy about letting his brothers and sisters know that he was angry about their father's death and that he felt the man had suffered and perhaps died needlessly because of misguided religious beliefs. His parents' religion, though, would influence Paul in ways he never acknowledged: among other things, he developed a lifelong skepticism toward doctors.

Paul would never, of course, have dreamt of making negative statements about religion to his mother. Ida Mae Kilgore Bryant was, literally, the stuff from which legends were made. There are no passages from W. J. Cash on the toughness and resilience of the common southern woman, but it isn't hard to hear accounts of Ida's life and not believe that had she been one of those swinging up the slopes at Gettysburg in 1863, the war might have turned out differently. It was Ida who gave order and purpose to Paul's life, and it was from her that he derived his steel resolve. She was his earliest and, until he entered grade school, practically his only influence, and it would last throughout a lifetime. On the last day of 1975, Alabama was preparing to play Penn State in the Sugar Bowl, the first game ever to be played in the New Orleans Superdome. Nittany Lions coach Joe Paterno, the man who would eventually surpass Bryant's record for victories among

Division I-A coaches, saw Bryant leaning against a goal post and noticed he wasn't wearing his trademark houndstooth hat. Paterno asked him why. "My mama always told me to take my hat off when I was indoors," he replied. The toughest man ever to come out of Fordyce, Arkansas, never hesitated to say it: "I was a mama's boy."

"I don't know how to describe her," he wrote in *Bear*, "except that she was my favorite person in the world, and that she looked great to me. . . . I suppose you would call her a handsome woman. She was a little taller than average, and her hair was already gray"—one assumes Bryant meant by the time of his first memories of her—"and there was something about her eyes that got your attention. You could look at her and tell she had class, despite all she had been through. She had it tough from the day she was born."

She had it even tougher after Monroe was unable to work. By the time Paul was seven, the three older brothers were out trying to make their own way in the world. For the next few years, until he was nearly twelve, Paul had a life of unending toil involving grueling physical labor. The nearest elementary school was in Kingsland, about nine miles from their home, and the only way to get there was by a mule-powered wagon. Ida, her three youngest daughters, and Paul rose about two hours before daybreak; the girls milked the cows and Paul hitched up the mules, Pete and Joe, for the ride to school. His school clothes consisted of a pair of overalls; when the weather got colder, he was given one of his father's old long-sleeved shirts. In order to make it to school on time, the family had to be on the road before sunup. On cold days, they heated bricks to warm their feet and posteriors. Crossing Moro Creek wasn't always a simple matter. If the creek was high, the mules actually had to swim the wagon across, with the sideboards up and the tarp over the edges to keep the water from spilling in and ruining the hard-grown produce being brought to market.* While the

---

* In a 1978 young adult biography, *Young Bear: The Legend of Bear Bryant's Boyhood* by S. C. Lee, a story is told of the time when the creek appeared too high to cross. Young Paul, after chewing on a watermelon and giving the matter some though, says,

"Say, what about this, Mama? Maybe we could build a raft." He thought for a moment, took another bite of melon, then spoke again. "But of course we don't have time, and it probably wouldn't work, either." One of his favorite stories happened to be Tom Sawyer, though of course poling a raft on the Mississippi River differed from poling a heavy load across a swollen, rapidly flowing stream.

"Nine things out of ten that we worry about never come true," says Mrs. Bryant.

children were in school, Ida would be off selling eggs and vegetables and picking up loads of laundry to do at home. At recess, Paul left the other kids to play and went to feed the mules.

While attending the Stonewall School in Kingsland, Paul encountered one of his first examples of class snobbery. The strenuous job of preparing the mules and then the long ride into town caused him to sweat considerably. "We had a lady teacher in the fifth or sixth grade," he recalled, "who was always preaching hygiene. I didn't know what she was talking about until one day after a long lecture on cleanliness she made me trade seats with one of the boys in the back. I can still hear those giggly girls, enjoying my embarrassment."

DESPITE SUCH harsh conditions, it would be wrong to characterize Bryant's adolescence as miserable. The work was relentless, but Paul and his siblings had no other life to compare theirs to. His mother doted on him, and there were plenty of opportunities for Mark Twain–like adventures. Once, while his mother attended a Church of God revival meeting at Mt. Lebanon, Paul, craving attention, took what he called "a little old cat" and tossed it through an open window and onto a little girl's lap. Ida, who was a lay preacher for the church, couldn't afford to let the incident go unpunished, but according to Paul, she waited almost two months before whipping him for it. Mrs. Bryant was a busy woman.

Another tale about young Paul that has taken on an air of legend is the

---

"And not even that often with Christians. The Lord must mean it when He says, 'Everything works for good to them who love the Lord.'"

Mr. Bryant then chips in with, "And the Scriptures also say, 'Come unto Me all ye that labor and are heavy laden and I will give you rest.' Now that must have something to do with a heavy-loaded wagon crossing a creek, wouldn't it?" he added with a faint smile.

Needless to say, Paul eventually finds a way to turn the family wagon into a raft, saving their precious load of eggs, butter, and vegetables.

There would seem to be no conceivable way that Paul could have heard of Tom Sawyer at that age, though the book was included in his curriculum later at Fordyce High. Also, there is no record from anyone in the family of Monroe Bryant ever having smiled.

"hant" story. Like so many country boys, Paul was terrified of ghosts or, in this particular instance, "hants."* Behind the smokehouse on the Bryants' farm was an old grave with a tombstone. One night, Paul's brother Jack promised him thirty-five cents if he would walk up to the headstone and look for hants. Dazzled by the prospect of making thirty-five cents, Paul swallowed his fear and approached the grave. Suddenly, a ghostly figure arose from behind the tombstone—a hired hand known by the family as Mr. Dukes, under a white sheet. Paul shrieked, ran, and finally stumbled into the house. The night was also memorable as the only time Paul ever saw his father show anger, threatening to run the two conspirators off the farm.

Despite the incident, or perhaps because of it, Paul would recall Mr. Dukes with fondness. Mr. Dukes was a part-time worker whose employment was made possible by Ida's butter-and-egg money. He helped Paul with odd errands and took him possum, squirrel, and rabbit hunting. (The dead rabbits would be hung on the fireplace in the house's "big room," waiting to be skinned and cooked.) "Mr. Dukes," Paul would recall, "was proud to work for us, and I was glad to have him . . . though I have to say he might not have been the best influence."

Mr. Dukes introduced Paul to the great southern art of creative cursing and gave him his first glimpse into the mysterious world of girls. The hired hand was infatuated with a Moro Bottom farm girl named Zora Jarrett, who was less than half his age. Donning a cowboy hat, he would ride his horse up and down the path in front of her family's house to get her attention. His persistence would eventually pay off when he and Zora were finally married. Paul was impressed; it was possible, after all, to overcome class differences and to win the woman of your dreams. It was a lesson he would remember in just a few short years. (Years later, while serving in the navy, Bryant was happy to see his old friend again in a chance encounter at the Veterans Hospital in Little Rock.)

The extra manpower provided by Mr. Dukes gave Ida Bryant the opportunity for a capitalistic venture in Fordyce, a much larger town than Kingsland. Early one Saturday morning, most likely in 1923, Paul, who was about ten, helped load the family wagon with butter, buttermilk, eggs, and

---

* Southerners also used the term *haint*. Both terms were derived from *haunt* and referred to a wide variety of ghosts, spirits, and even animated corpses.

vegetables and rode with his mother into Fordyce. Fordyce was the closest thing to a city in the area, and this trip may have been Paul's first glimpse of it. He was in for a shock, one that would have a profound effect on him.

Schools in Fordyce at that time held Saturday sessions. Paul thought that the purpose was to "keep the children off the streets"; another possible reason was to make up for lost classroom time when kids were let out of school to help with the fall harvest.* In any event, Ida and Paul usually "wound up at old Arch Weathers's at ten to twelve and in front of the school at twelve." Paul, barefoot and in old overalls, was stunned by the sight of so many well-dressed city kids, howling with gleeful derision at the country folk from the Bottom. They laughed at the creaking wagon, the old mules, at Paul, and, most unbearable of all, his mother. Paul burned with humiliation. One of the kids who laughed at them was Kelsey Kaplinger, who, nearly eighty years later, recalled for the Dallas County Historical Society, "Paul got so mad he started throwing turnips at us and fell off the wagon." In just a few short years, Kaplinger would line up opposite Paul for football practice and pay dearly for his taunts. "He whupped me all over the field," Kelsey told the historical society in an earlier interview. "I couldn't hardly walk after that practice."[10] Kaplinger wasn't the only school kid whose taunts Paul Bryant didn't forget. More than half a century later, in his autobiography, he said that "I can pass that school now and hear those voices. . . . I still remember the ones that did it."

Ida's brother, Ransom Dean Kilgore, was one of the most propertied men in Fordyce, owning both a hotel and a general store. Ida and Paul finished their day with a stop at Kilgore Brothers, where they could always count on selling the rest of their produce. According to Ida's nephew, Dean Kilgore, Ida was usually treated to an early-afternoon dinner in the hotel dining room, but Paul, intimidated at the prospect of eating in a restaurant, invariably declined. "He'd say, 'No, I'm going to go through the store and get some cheese and crackers and go down to the Cotton Belt [the main line of what would become the Union Pacific railroad] and watch that

---

* My wife remembers spending summers with her grandparents in Blount County, Alabama, as late as the mid-1960s and noticing the kids started school in early August instead of September. Her grandfather, Ben Hammond, explained that even though there was scarcely any cotton grown by individual farmers, the area school systems still followed a schedule that closed school for two weeks in September so the kids could pick cotton.

train go through.' He liked to go down and watch them freight trains go through."[11] ("I had such an inferiority complex," Bryant said in *Bear*, "I was too ashamed to go with her. I didn't know whether to use the knife or the spoon or what.")

SO SIGNIFICANT is the episode in which Paul Bryant actually wrestled a live bear that almost all the events in his life that transpired between 1924 and 1931 are measured by their proximity and distance from this one stunt. The problem is that hardly anyone can agree on exactly when that was. The timeline for this entire period is fuzzy.

A previous Bryant biographer, Keith Dunnavant, believed that Ida moved the family to a small house in Fordyce when Paul was eleven, taking in boarders to make ends meet while maintaining the family farm on weekends. The reason for the move, Dunnavant says, was primarily educational. Fordyce promised better schools and the opportunity to get ahead. If Paul had not had the chance to play football for Fordyce High School, he might have lived his entire life in Moro Bottom.[12]

According to everyone's story, including Dunnavant's and Bryant's, he was already playing football by the time he started at Fordyce High. Dunnavant, taking his information from Bryant, has him playing in his first organized football game the Friday after he saw his first football practice. But at what level of football was Bryant playing? Surely he could not have been playing on a high school team while still in the eighth grade—or perhaps he could. Agnes Phillips, director of the Dallas County Museum, remembers hearing that "they were pretty slack about those things then, and remember, the town was less than 4,000 people and this was before integration, so there wasn't much of a talent pool to draw from. I've always heard they let younger kids play with the high school if they were big and aggressive enough." The problem is that Bryant, in *Bear*, was quite clear on the length of time he played high school ball: "For a little school like Fordyce, we had terrific football teams *my three years there*" (emphasis added). So where could he have been playing football at ages thirteen and fourteen? There were no Pop Warner–type leagues for him to play in in Fordyce in the early 1920s. It's difficult to find anyone who can remember back that far, but Buster Garlington, who was ninety-eight when I interviewed him, swears that Fordyce elementary school didn't have the resources for a football team back then. And if it did, how could the team have been playing on a Friday night, a time reserved for the high school games?

There are a couple of possibilities, the most likely being that Bryant's memory simply jumped ahead by a year, or even two, to put himself in that first Friday-night game. The second is that Bryant was engaging in a bit of myth-mongering about his own past. First of all, to go back to the original story about seeing his first football practice, is it likely that Bryant lived in a football-crazy town like Fordyce for even a few months without even knowing what a football was?

It is possible that the high school coach, confronted with such a strapping boy (Paul was approaching six feet by the time he was in the eighth grade), jumped at a chance to take advantage of his size and aggressiveness by hustling him onto the team a year early. But no matter how you spin the story, it is highly improbable that a thirteen-year-old with no previous experience could have played in his first organized game just one week after seeing a football for the first time, especially—and this is the big hurdle to accepting Bryant's story—on a team with the reputation of the Fordyce Redbugs.

The time sequence for Bryant's first couple of years in Fordyce is hopelessly skewed, and there seems almost no way, nearly eighty years later, to set it straight. Bryant told *Sports Illustrated*, "About that time, Mama took a couple of rooms up in Kingsland—a little apartment—because it was so cold riding in. I'll tell you when it was: it was when Floyd Collins was in the cave in Kentucky, because we walked down to the railroad station every afternoon and the train came by and brought the papers. We didn't buy the paper, we just looked at the headlines. Anyway, instead of having to drive those mules around and unharness them and turn them out at noon when everybody else was playing basketball and stuff, I got my first chance to play."[13] (By *play*, Bryant apparently meant not only to play basketball but any sport; he makes no mention of any game or sport before this.)

Floyd Collins was a spelunker who found himself trapped while looking for an opening to Mammoth Cave on January 30, 1925. He died on February 16 when rescue attempts failed. Paul was eleven years old during Collin's ordeal and, by his own account, not yet living in Fordyce but in Kingsland.

Neither Dunnavant nor Mickey Herskowitz in his *Legend of Bear Bryant* mention anything about Paul or Ida living in Kingsland. Dunnavant places them in Fordyce at the time Bryant says his mother got the apartment in Kingsland. One thing is certain: Paul wasn't living in Fordyce long before he became enamored with football. "All I had was football," he would say. "I hung on as though it was life or death." "My daddy didn't want me to play football. He said he'd whip me if I did. He wanted me to farm. But I got Mama on my side. She never said I could play, but she wasn't saying I couldn't, and finally Papa quit saying anything about it."[14]

From the time he began playing football for the Redbugs to the end of his mother's life in 1954, Paul didn't recall a single thing his mother said about the game, good or bad. Whether she approved of the game or not, she apparently perceived right away that it provided her son with one thing that she could not—social status. Years later as a coach at the University of Kentucky and Texas A&M, Paul would talk her into going along on the bowl game trips, but "she never went to see the games. She just stayed in the hotel with the kids."

"I think," he would say after her death, "she would have loved for me to have been a preacher. I was the only one in the family who got to go to college, and I'm sure she thought it a waste of time for me to wind up coaching football. I used to tell her that coaching and preaching were a lot alike, but she didn't believe it."

What he never knew was that his mother prayed on his behalf. Fifteen years after Bryant's death, in a videotape made by the Dallas County Museum, Dean Kilgore revealed how Ida would call his mother Dru and say, "Dru, we've got to get together and pray for Paul to win this game."★

It's possible that Ida realized even before Paul that football was his ticket out of a life in a textile mill or truck farm. According to Bryant, it was his mother who took his high-top black shoes down to Mr. Clark, the shoemaker, and told him to put football cleats on them. Years later, some friends and family members would doubt the story as told by Bryant. "His mama didn't approve of his playing football," a teammate named Jack Benham said. "I don't think she would have taken his first pair of shoes and had football cleats put on them."[15] The notion that the black high tops were

---

★ The game that his mother and his aunt prayed for Paul to win is not specified in the tape, though Dean Kilgore does say, "It was that team that he never could beat." That would indicate General Neyland's Tennessee Volunteers, who even Ida's prayers could not vanquish.

Bryant's first pair of shoes came from Paul himself in numerous interviews over the years, but it isn't likely that he meant "first" as in first pair of shoes he ever wore. In many large families at the time, one's "first" pair of shoes meant first *new* pair of shoes as opposed to hand-me-downs. Benham might have been suggesting that Paul had done it without his mother's knowledge. Mr. and Mrs. Bryant disapproved of football as well as most other forms of entertainment, so it doesn't seem, on the face of it, that Ida would have taken the step of having the cleats put on. But it seems just as unlikely that Paul would have taken *any* shoes to Mr. Clark without Ida's approval, so she may just well have had the shoes made over.

Whatever the truth about the shoes, they had a magical effect on Paul: "Boy, talk about proud! I wore those cleats to football, to class, to Sunday school. I wore them in the house, everywhere. . . . I'll never forget how much those high-top black shoes with the cleats meant to me." For the first time in his life, Paul Bryant had an identity. He was a football player.

Twenty years later, at the University of Kentucky, Bryant would notice that his young quarterback, George Blanda, a tough kid from a Pennsylvania steel town, was always hanging back, refusing to take the lead. Bryant tried to motivate him, but nothing worked. One day after a loss to Mississippi, Bryant saw Blanda walking across campus, went up to put his arm around him, and noticed that Blanda had stuffed cardboard in the bottom of his shoes.

About two days later, says Blanda, "Coach called me into his office. . . . 'Say, George. You know, you're only going to get better as a quarterback, and when you do, the newspaper people are going to be coming around and snapping a lot of pictures. Why don't you go down to Graves-Cox [a local clothing store] and buy yourself some new clothes, and maybe some new shoes, too. In fact, get a couple pair.'" Blanda was taken aback. "'Coach, I just don't know when I'll be able to pay you back.' 'George,' he said, 'this is for the University, not for you. You're going to be in the public eye, and it will look good for Kentucky for you to look good in the papers. Don't worry about the money. The way you're going, you'll be playing professional football some day. You can pay me back then.'"

Blanda got the new clothes and shoes, earned his newspaper photos, and went on to play a record twenty-six seasons in the National Football League. "I paid him back every possible way I could over the years," says Blanda, "but I never really felt like I made up the debt for those shoes."

DAVEY CROCKETT claimed to have grinned a bear into surrender, but he never said he wrestled one. There is disagreement about when Paul Bryant wrestled a bear, but most place it in 1927 and a few, later. But nobody remembers it happening as early 1925, and it seems beyond belief that a twelve-year-old—*any* twelve-year-old, even young Paul Bryant—could have wrestled a bear at age twelve. Paul could never quite get the year straight—but he was always clear on who his companions were: Ike Murray, a future attorney general for the state of Arkansas, and the Jordan twins, Clark and George, better known around town as "Click" and "Jud." They were all teammates on the Fordyce High football team, so that probably places the event in 1927 when Paul was fourteen.

There are two main versions of the story, and both confirm that the conclusion was pretty scary. In the first, related by Bryant in *Bear*, Bryant and his pals, hungry for entertainment, drifted over to the Lyric Theater. According to Buster Garlington, who later owned the hardware store in the building where the Lyric once was, "It wasn't much of a theater. There were about 200 seats, and it was narrow and had a high stage that kept people in the first row or two from seeing much of what was going on. But it was the only theater we had." Traveling musicians, mostly stars of what was then called hillbilly and would later be called country music, performed there. The most popular of all country artists, the legendary Jimmie Rodgers, "The Singing Brakeman" from Meridian, Mississippi, played there, as did the equally legendary Carter family, from which June Carter Cash would one day emerge as a solo singer and the wife of Johnny Cash, from nearby Kingsland. The movies were mostly comedies (starring, among others, Charlie Chaplin, Buster Keaton, and Mack Sennett), Douglas Fairbanks–type adventures, and westerns (Tom Mix was the favorite).

One night, the Lyric featured a bonus act: bear wrestling with a dollar-a-minute prize. The Lyric's owner was agitated; the man who was scheduled to wrestle the bear hadn't shown up. Somebody asked Paul why he didn't take the man's place. Bryant had spent the summer chopping cotton for fifty cents a day for his brother Jack on the family farm at Moro Bottom, and a dollar a minute seemed like a great deal of money. As he would tell *People* magazine nearly fifty years later, "I felt I would wrestle King Kong for a dollar a minute." Paul, in his own words, was "big-dogging it" to impress a pretty red-headed older girl named Drucilla Smith, who worked at the theater. Besides, "there wasn't anything else to do anyway, and the picture cost a dime." The owner, Mr. Smith, agreed to let Paul and all his friends in for free.

An earlier, more plausible story of how the incident came about has been rejected by many because it appeared twelve years after *Bear* was published, in Mickey Herskowitz's memoir, The *Legend of Bear Bryant*, and thus, some believe, gave Bryant more time to embellish it. But Herskowitz insists that the story in his book was told to him in the 1950s when Bryant was at Texas A&M, and so it predates Bryant's own in *Bear*. In this version, a carnival was passing through Fordyce and, as Bryant told Herskowitz, "They had this little ole scraggly bear. A man was offering anybody a dollar a minute to wrestle it. Somebody dared me to do it. I said I would." So, for most of the day, the carnival folk paraded through the streets of Fordyce with a sign that read, PAUL BRYANT WILL WRESTLE A BEAR TONIGHT AT 8 AT THE LYRIC THEATER. Hence, Paul Bryant did not wrestle a bear on a whim but had all day to think about it.

In this telling also, Bryant was lured by the money and out to impress a girl, who goes unnamed. And he wasn't about to suffer the embarrassment of backing out of a deal that everyone in town knew about. This goes much further than the story Bryant related in *Bear* in explaining why a fourteen-year-old boy would go up in front of an audience and wrestle a wild animal; it's hard to believe that anything less would have gotten even so bold a youth as Paul Bryant to do something so foolhardy. That the town's folk had all day to buzz about the incident also explains why, according to those who were present, there was standing room only in the theater.★

In none of Bryant's various accounts does he come off as heroic. His friend Ike Murray said the bear was the scrawniest thing he had ever seen, but then, as Bryant pointed out, Murray didn't volunteer to wrestle it. "To me, it looked 30 feet tall. I must have wanted that money real bad."

★ Paul had already acquired something of a reputation as a daredevil. A friend, Douglas Phillips, relates that on one Sunday "Willard Clary and a group of boys were hanging around the local watering hole. They bet 'Bear' that he couldn't run the eight-mile distance from Kingsland to Fordyce in one hour or less. Bear readily accepted. It was a warm, summer afternoon. Bear ran the eight miles, fully clothed, in fifty-nine minutes and fell flat on his face as he stepped on the pavement entering Fordyce." Although the incident was supposed to have happened before Paul wrestled the bear, his friends, in their recollections, invariably predate the nickname.

At the moment of conflict, it suddenly occurred to Paul that he didn't know how to wrestle at all, let alone a bear. Keeping his wits, though, he quickly realized that the bear didn't know how to wrestle either. He quickly concocted a game plan that would appall him years later when other football coaches used it: he would run out the clock and settle for a tie. All that he knew about wrestling was that "if you got hold of somebody and kept your body away from him, he'd have a hard time breaking your hold." His game plan was to wrestle the bear as he would wrestle a man.

The bear reared up and Paul opted for the offensive, charging the animal, pulling him down, and holding him on the floor. This plan was working fine for Paul—"For a dollar a minute I wanted to hold him till he died"—but the bear's owner wanted action. He kept screaming, "Let him up! Let him up!" in Paul's ear. The bear worked itself free, Paul tried the same plan again, and they rolled and thrashed around on stage for another few seconds.

Then, somehow, the animal's muzzle came off. One account has the owner loosening it, but that doesn't seem likely, as he could have been arrested for attempted murder. More than likely, it had simply come off during the tussle. However it came off, it was off. Paul's sister Louise, who was in the second row, recalled, "A few women screamed. The men first thought it was part of the show and laughed." It was not. The bear's teeth were real. A few seconds after the muzzle came off, Paul felt a burning sensation on his ear and realized that blood was pouring down his neck. "I was being eaten alive! I jumped off that stage and nearly killed myself hitting the empty front seats with my shins"—the front row had been cleared for the bear-wrestling portion of the show. The people sitting closest to the stage jumped out of their chairs. Years later he would get a kick out of pulling up his trouser cuffs and showing off the marks on his legs from his crash with the seats.

Louise said, "You should have seen him jump off that stage when he realized that thing had bit him! He was brave enough to get up there and wrestle that bear, but he wasn't about to let it eat him alive!"

Bryant learned an important lesson that night: get your money up front. By all accounts, the show had lasted in excess of two and possibly as long as three minutes, so Paul had a handsome purse coming to him. But the bear and its owner skipped town.*

---

*Years later, while an assistant coach at Alabama, Bryant was bird hunting with former teammate Don Hutson near the town of Fayette when he saw both the man and the

Feeling that he "had achieved a certain amount of dignity," he refrained from beating the money out of the man. "He probably needed it more than I did anyway." All he ever got out of wrestling that bear, he would say, was a nickname.

The bear-wrestling tale became more embellished with time. In an account written for the Dallas County Museum, Mr. Douglas Phillips wrote, "It took place at the old Smith Theater (the Lyric was owned by Mr. Smith) back around '27-'28-'29 . . . the 'Bear Wrassling event' was bally-hooed for a week before the actual date . . . after much discussion among his crowd, 'Bear' was cajoled into fighting the bear for a five dollar fee." And, according to Buster Garlington, a Miss Irene Ramsay "saw the whole thing and claimed that Paul not only wrestled that bear inside the theater, but went outside and took him on again in the alley."

Roy Blount Jr. found a story to top Miss Ramsay's. In a September 1975 article for *Esquire*, "Bear Bryant's Stompin' School," he wrote, "I have spent only ten or twelve days in Arkansas in my life, but I've already met two different people who claimed they witnessed that event. One of them said that he, in a suit, was the bear; but he was drinking and I believe he would have said anything. In Arkansas. I don't think he would have said that around many folks in Alabama."

Choose the story that you like best; to paraphrase the newspaperman in *The Man Who Shot Liberty Valance:* this is the South; when the fact becomes legend, print the legend. Whatever really happened, says Buster Garlington, "The stage where he wrassled that bear still exists inside Benton Hardware and probably should have a historic marker in front of it." There is, at least, a stuffed bear in the Dallas County Museum—"A fine-looking specimen," says the museum's curator, Mrs. Agnes Phillips, "but one that undoubtedly pales beside the bear that Paul Bryant wrestled." The museum's bear is black; the one Bryant wrestled was brown. "Accounts of Paul Bryant wrestling a small, scraggly, toothless bear are," says Mrs. Phillips, "both unacceptable and inaccurate."

---

bear at a carnival. According to some folktales, Paul demanded a rematch (as Bryant was already famous for the confrontation, the rematch could have been billed as "Bear versus The Bear.")

———

AMID THE jokes and exaggerations that grew around Bryant's bear-wrestling adventure, a dark truth is sometimes missed: young Paul Bryant had a genuine predilection for violence. He was the first to admit it. "I'm embarrassed to say it," he told Underwood, "but I lived with a chip on my shoulder in those days. I enjoyed fighting. I suppose it was a way of expressing myself, and I never missed a chance." He was also quick to add, "I didn't go undefeated or anything."

The first altercation to work its way into the Bryant legend occurred when Paul was thirteen and involved a grown man whom, Paul claimed, was trying to get out of paying him for some groceries he had delivered while working for his uncles. The man tried to push him out of his store; Paul "hit him a few times and got him to appreciate my position." After that, he said, they were pals.

The story as Bryant told it, and as has often been repeated, doesn't quite come together. It's doubtful that any respectable citizen in Fordyce would have refused to pay for the groceries, particularly if he risked offending influential merchants like the Kilgores. Some seventy years later, Dean Kilgore offered a more plausible story when he told the historical society that Paul "came back one day from delivering some groceries to Mr. Cunningham's company store and said, 'You know, that man's a real smart ass.'" Dean's older brother Collins asked Paul what he meant. "He said to me, 'You're one of those Bryants from Moro Bottom, aren't ya?'" Apparently Mr. Cunningham was making fun of Paul's country accent.

According to Dean, Collins, needling Paul a bit, said, "Why, you don't have to take that from him. Why don't you go back there and pop him one?" Paul left, and Collins went about his business. A while later, Paul came in with a grin on his face, "Well, I done what you told me to do." "Whaddya you mean, what I told you to do?" said Collins. "I went out there and popped that smart feller one," said Paul.

Collins was horrified. "Man, I never told you to do no such thing. Boy, you gonna get yourself in trouble doing things like that."[16] (Nothing came of the incident, and apparently on future deliveries the man showed country boys more respect.)

The ninety-six-year-old Dean Kilgore recollected that Paul might have been guilty of a far more serious offense than hitting Mr. Cunningham.

Dean spoke of an incident in which Paul was suspended for knocking Dan Clary, the school superintendent, down some stairs; perhaps this occurred sometime between the ages of twelve and fourteen, but neither Bryant nor any member of his family ever offered any details. Dean claimed that Paul was ready to quit school, but Collins talked him into going back. Curiously, no one else has ever mentioned the incident, including Paul himself, who was pretty frank about his own mistakes.

Paul did admit that Clary suspended him once for missing a couple of weeks of school—but mentioned no more. At the halftime of an October game, Clary interrupted Coach Cowan's pep talk by pointing at Paul and saying, "Boy, you haven't been to school!" Paul pleaded extenuating circumstances: "I told him I had been picking cotton." "Well," Clary told him, "you are ineligible." Paul didn't know what *ineligible* meant, but he got an inkling when Cowan held him out of the second half of the game. By the following week, Paul was back in the lineup.

Whether Paul pushed Mr. Clary or not, Ike Murray may not have been joking about his old classmate when he told a visiting journalist, "If I had been writing the class prophecy for our senior class, I'd have written this about Paul: 'He'll be lucky to stay out of the penitentiary.' "[17]

Murray probably never knew about one of Paul's worst scrapes. In the summer of 1926, Paul and his pal "Chink" (so-named for his slanted eyes) Lacewell hitchhiked to Ohio to visit Paul's sister Ouida, who lived in Parma, an industrial town about seven miles from Cleveland, where white southerners migrated in search of factory jobs. Paul got a job with a company that made headlights for automobiles and rode the trolley to work every day, then switched to a job closer to Ouida's house, working for a company that made spokes for automobile wheels. He wiled away part of the summer at Dunn Field in Cleveland watching the Indians play.★

Paul was contemplating relocating to Parma and playing football for West Tech High, but his plans took a serious reverse one Friday morning when he got into a fight with another boy at the factory whose girlfriend Paul had been paying too much attention to. Actually, it wasn't much of a fight. The boy threatened Paul, but Paul got in the first punch, tearing up the kid's mouth so badly that Paul fled back to his sister's house to grab his

---

★ Wes Farrell, he remembered, pitched for the Indians at the first game he went to. The game stirred in Bryant a lifelong passion for baseball.

clothes and hop a freight train back to Arkansas. He now considered him-self reformed. Not quite, as it turned out.

At the Pine Bluff station he was grabbed by a railroad bull and taken to the dispatcher's office. There, he got lucky: the chief dispatcher's son played football for Pine Bluff High and recognized Paul from the Fordyce–Pine Bluff game. The dispatcher put him on a train back to Fordyce; Paul arrived in time for Redbug football practice.

There were other railroad adventures. Larry Lacewell relates a story from his father about Chink and Paul hopping a late-afternoon freight train headed for Texas. "Their intention was to become cowboys," says Lacewell. "They hid in a coal car until they got outside of Texarkana at way past midnight. They hadn't eaten anything, and they didn't have any money, so they gave up the cowboy plan and hitchhiked back to Fordyce. Dad said they got in just before sunup, and no one even knew they had been gone."

In between freight train jaunts Paul worked at several jobs at the Kilgore's Hotel, where he was night clerk for a while, and at the family general store, where it was quickly evident that he wasn't cut out for shop keeping. "He was so clumsy," said Dean," I didn't think he would amount to anything."

On one occasion, Paul spilled so much sugar on the floor that he was reassigned to butcher duty. That didn't work either. A young black girl came in to purchase three pounds of sausage at a nickel a pound. Paul flung the sausage onto the scales so carelessly that some of it hit the girl in the face. Dean was perturbed. "Paul, what's the matter with you? You're gonna drive all my customers away!" He sent Paul back to the sugar detail.

On another occasion, on a hot summer day, Dean heard popping noises in the store's balcony and went to investigate. "Paul," he asked, "have you got something to do with that?" Paul said nothing, but his sheepish grin gave the game away: he and a friend had made some home brew and hid-den it in the balcony, and the crude bottle tops couldn't contain the heat-accelerated fermenting process. Luckily for Paul, his mother, a strict teetotaler, never heard about it.[18]

BY THE age of fourteen Paul had tried his hand at factory work and shop keeping without much success and had given up on the notion of becom-ing a cowboy. He had long since realized that he wasn't cut out to be a farmer. In Fordyce, that didn't leave many other career opportunities, unless one displayed an aptitude for academics. But the years at Moro Bottom had left him woefully inadequate in academic skills, and there was no way to catch up now.

That left football. Paul quickly came to understand that football addressed virtually every one of his needs. First and foremost, it gave him an opportunity to channel his natural aggressiveness. It also provided him with the first real father figure he had ever known, Coach Cowan, and Paul, though naturally rebellious, was smart enough to understand that Cowan could teach him something. Despite his mother's best efforts, Paul's life up to that point had been aimless, wavering between harmless boyhood mischief and genuine delinquency; now a strong, purposeful man, someone who had achieved an authentic level of respect in his community, was insisting, against all apparent evidence, that Paul might develop into something worthwhile. No one would prove more influential in Paul's life than Cowan.

Just like Bryant in later life, Cowan was a fierce disciplinarian but, more than that, an excellent teacher. He broke down each phase of the game into a series of problems that could be addressed through proper mechanics and preparation. He yelled at his players to hit harder, but showed them the proper positioning and leverage needed to deliver the hit. Most of all, he took a rowdy bunch of farm hands and mill workers and showed them the value of respecting each other and working together. There wasn't a great deal of technique to his teaching, just an understanding of basics and the importance of repeating them until they became second nature. But, as Bryant would recall, "he had our allegiance, no doubt about that. He was the kind of guy you could tie to."

His football coach didn't speak much to Paul. "I look back," he would write years after Cowan's death, "realizing how much he tried to help me, and if I could do it over, I would appreciate it more and take advantage of his guidance. I know I respected him." Player and coach would become close only after Paul left high school. Paul and his teammates would visit Cowan at home, where Mrs. Cowan would serve them quail and homemade biscuits and gravy. When Bryant coached at the University of Kentucky, Cowan often drove up to visit him, but Cowan kept a personal distance from his players while he was their coach. This made a particularly strong impression on Paul: a coach and a player could never be friends.

Perhaps as much as anything else, Cowan instilled in his players a sense of pride, the idea that they were "special"—that if they showed enough discipline to endure his practices and made the team, they were no longer ordinary, that through their individual and team efforts they had achieved something more important. Fifty-five years later Bryant would tell me, "Coach Cowan's words couldn't have made more of an impression on me if he chiseled them into stone right there in practice."

Throughout his coaching years, he would repeat Cowan's words, as best as he could remember them, to his own players: "You're something special, and don't you ever forget that. If you're willing to work hard and sacrifice, you can achieve anything. The costs of victory are high, but so are the rewards."[19] In Bryant's 1960 book *Building a Championship Football Team*, the first man he mentioned in the dedication was Robert A. Cowan.

THERE IS no better cure for rootlessness than being planted into a tradition. By the time Paul Bryant arrived, Fordyce already had the proudest high school football tradition in the state, if not the entire South. In fact, the first high school football team in Arkansas was organized there in 1904. The program was built by a former New Yorker named Tom Meddick, who brought with him to Fordyce, in the words of J. Willard Clary, "a queer-shaped ball filled with air that had a crazy way of bouncing."[20] (J. Willard Clary was the Fordyce correspondent for the *Arkansas Gazette* and the grandson of the founder of the Clary Training School.)

In 1908, Fordyce football went big time when the local team from the Clary Training School traveled to the state capital for a game against Little Rock High School. In the *Arkansas Gazette*, Clary reported that the game "was filled with plays bordering on the sensational, but none were in the manner of foul tactics and even had the home team lost, the spectators would have been forced to admit it was the best game ever seen in Little Rock." The visitors lost 13–0, but they gave a fine display of courage against a team that had what Clary called "twenty times the manpower to draw upon."[21] The crowd was estimated to be four hundred, which many thought was the largest number to see a football game in Arkansas up to that time.

In 1909 Clary got its first crosstown rival when Fordyce High School fielded its first team. The two-year rivalry culminated in a match between the two unbeaten teams on Thanksgiving Day in 1911. Going out in a blaze of glory, the last team fielded by Clary whipped Fordyce, 39–0.

Shortly afterward, Clary closed its doors, and the faculty and students moved to Fordyce High.

What was the secret of the teams from sparsely populated south Arkansas? In 1956, Clary wrote,

> South Arkansas is covered with pine thickets and the main sport of the boys is rabbit hunting.
>
> When they go out rabbit hunting, the fast boys sidestep and dodge through the pine saplings. They make good backfield men. The slower boys run over the pines. They make good linemen.[22]

Paul could sidestep, dodge, *and* run over those pine trees. In later years, Bryant would perpetuate the myth that he was a poor athlete who got by on desire and cunning. No one doubted his desire. "He was the most aggressive player I ever saw," said Jack Benham, who played with him on perhaps the two greatest high school teams Fordyce ever produced. Coach Cowan liked to use him as a model: " 'Here, watch Bryant show you how to block' and Bryant would knock the guy five yards off the line."[23]

Bryant was huge by the high school norm of his time. By his junior year he had reached his full adult height of six feet three inches and weighed close to 190 pounds. On defense, he was a superb tackle, not merely stronger but quicker than most of the boys he was up against. On offense though, Coach Cowan quickly saw that his talents would be wasted in the interior line, so he put him at offensive end. As a sophomore he made the All-State team. As a senior he caught a seventy-yard touchdown pass that helped Fordyce beat Little Rock, 34–0.

Forty-nine years later he would recall the play with a thrill. "Click Jordan called the play, and I ran right under it, closed my eyes, and kept running. Ran right through the end zone fence." That he didn't catch more passes in those years was simply due to the lack of sophistication on offense. Passing techniques in those days were rather crude, and the softer footballs were much more conducive to kicking than throwing. But when the ball was thrown Paul's way, he generally caught it and ran with it.

His best play was an open-field, downfield block to help spring one of his teammates open for a big game. These were the hits he most relished, as they were the most visible to fans on the sidelines, not to mention his coaches. "You go down there and try to kill him."

With Paul in the lineup, the Redbugs fielded outstanding teams for three consecutive years beginning in 1928. In 1930 they were state champions. The whole town, the whole state, the whole South took notice. Scouts from numerous college football powers came sniffing around.

In 1929 the Redbugs traveled to play Little Rock. The train ride was the first time Paul had ridden on the *inside* of a passenger car as a paying customer. Modern passengers who know only Amtrak can't imagine how luxurious this must have seemed to the teenage boy; the seats were covered in leather and the armrests were mahogany, polished by an attentive, uniformed staff. Speed was not a premium; the leisurely steady roll of the heavy-gauge train allowed the boys to exchange pleasantries and wisecracks with onlookers as they rode through different stations. The excitement didn't abate when they reached Little Rock, which was one of the metropolises of the South. With almost eighty thousand people, Little Rock boasted a seven-story building, a public library with more than six thousand books, and modern marvels of technology such as elevators, in which Paul, acting as if he were in an amusement park, quickly availed himself of an opportunity to ride. For the first time ever, the Redbugs beat Little Rock, 7–0. The 1930 game, also at Little Rock, was the first time Paul had ever played under lights. (Dave Cash of nearby Rison, a cousin of singer Johnny Cash, rode in the Redbugs car and won several bales of cotton on the game.)

Bryant was by no means the only or even the most potent force on the Redbugs. Most would have awarded that honor to the Jordan twins, Click and Jud, Paul's best friends. They were both faster and better skilled at ball handling than Bryant. Later, at the University of Arkansas, they would make it into *Ripley's Believe It Or Not* by scoring four touchdowns between them in the space of two minutes, thirty-nine seconds.

One of Paul's friends in high school was Ike Murray, the team's offensive center, though they were not as close then as they would become later; at the time, they were romantic rivals. In Paul's junior year, the dream season of 1929, they were playing a team from Warren in nearby Bradley County and winning 58–0 late in the fourth quarter, with the ball on Warren's two-yard line. Paul wanted to impress a girl in the stands whom Ike was also sweet on. Click Jordan, the quarterback, announced in the huddle that they were going to "let old Bear score a touchdown"—he was going to let Bryant play quarterback for one play so he could carry the ball. Murray was having none of it: "That sonofabitch is not scoring any touchdowns while I'm centering." Jordan overruled him, but he couldn't control how Murray snapped the ball; it soared several feet over Paul's head, practically to midfield.

Murray's ploy worked; he ended up marrying the girl in the stands. A gracious winner, Ike showed up to deliver the introductory speech when Bryant was inducted into the Arkansas Hall of Fame thirty-six years later.

There were other romantic mishaps. In an interview recorded by the Dallas County Historical Society, Dean Kilgore related a story that came from his older brother, Collins: Paul and his two cousins were living in the unfinished wing of the Kilgore's Hotel when Paul returned one night with his face badly scratched. "Man, what happened to you?" Collins inquired. "She wouldn't cooperate," was Paul's only reply. "Man," said Collins, "you gonna get yourself in trouble acting like that." Nearly seventy years after the incident, when asked who the girl was, Dean would only say, "I'm not telling."[24]

Larry Lacewell's mother, Eloise, called Paul "the most handsome boy ever out of Fordyce High," but told her son that "he had a reputation around school as a boy you shouldn't get caught alone in a room with." He had to sneak around with a girl named Julia Sparks; though he was a football star, her parents didn't want her to associate with a boy from "the wrong side of the tracks."

"None of my true loves ran smooth," Bryant admitted.

One girlfriend was Mildred Byrd. Her father drove a Cadillac, and she came to watch the Redbugs games. She lived in Camden, which was about a thirty-minute ride from Fordyce if the freight trains were running fast. When Paul rode the train to visit her, Mildred and her mom would meet him at the station, then they would go to Mildred's house, sip lemonade, and talk. Paul would return to the station and grab the next freight to Fordyce, a little after midnight. One night he rode for twenty-seven miles on the outside of a train, clinging to the door; crossing the Ouichita River, he felt the trestle beams rush by his head. He would usually slip into his room at the Kilgore's Hotel before 1:00 a.m. With Collins covering for him, Ida never found out.

Paul was to lose Mildred to a basketball player from her own school, Camden High. Smarting from the dual humiliation of his romantic setback and a football loss to Camden—back then most of the same boys played on the football and basketball teams—Paul instigated what was very nearly a major riot at a basketball game in his senior year. He was spoiling for a fight the entire game, and just as the whistle for the final play blew, he got it.

The Mendoza brothers, Camden's only Jewish students, were known as tough court enforcers, and they weren't intimidated by Paul's reputation as a bear wrestler. One of the brothers gave him some lip as they were walking off the court, and Paul reached over and punched him in the face. Fans spilled out of the stands while coaches pinned the arms of the battling players. When one Camden player cursed him, Paul broke free and belted the kid, and the fighting started all over again. It wasn't pretty. Police were called in to escort the Redbugs to their team bus while Camden fans threw rocks. The Camden-Fordyce rivalry was suspended for three years.

There were other sports-related brawls. In Paul's junior year, the Redbugs took a bus to Hope, close to the Texas border, and beat the locals 20–0. There was some controversy about the integrity of the officials—three touchdowns by Click and Jud Jordan were called back—and the game ended in a donnybrook. After the game, Paul sat in the dressing room holding a shoe in case he needed a weapon.

The day stood out for Bryant as the one on which the Philadelphia Athletics rallied for eight runs in the ninth inning to beat the Chicago Cubs in the World Series. That would have made it October 12, 1929, about two and a half weeks before the stock market crash. Significantly, the trip to play Hope was not connected in his memory with the stock market crash. In fact, the crash is not mentioned at all in his autobiography nor in any other period memoirs from Fordyce residents. Southerners in the Bryant family's social and economic class at that time did not have any stock market investments and scarcely noticed a change after the crash. Paul was barely aware of the Depression at all; as far as he could see, it didn't alter his life in any substantial way.

Paul was far from the only high school athlete at Fordyce to get into fights. Game-interrupting scraps in both football and basketball were as common in southern high schools then as professional hockey fights are now, and in many, the coaches were slow to break them up. "It was a way to get out the bad blood," says Jimmy Parker, current coach of the Redbugs and son of one of Bryant's teammates. "Mostly they'd hurt their hands from busting somebody in the head, and that would be enough to discourage them from doing it again. It wasn't like gang fights or anything. You'd see boys get into fights in a game and a couple of weeks later drinking Cokes together and laughing."

Bryant confessed to a pretty good whipping at a dance in Hot Springs from "a big red-headed guy. He gave me the worst licking I ever took, man or boy." The boy ended up running a gas station outside Fordyce, and whenever Bryant drove back home from Alabama, he made it a point to drop by and fill up his Cadillac.

If football didn't teach Paul the error of his ways, it at least taught him to change the way of his errors. In his final season at Fordyce, as the unbeaten co-state champion, the Redbugs were nursing a slim lead over Hope High School when Click Jordan took a cheap shot out of bounds and left the game with a sprained ankle. Paul steamed but didn't blow; the game was close, and a retaliatory hit and penalty could have cost the Redbugs an undefeated season and the state title. Toward the end of the game, he went to the official after each play to ask him how much time remained. When he knew it was the final play, Bryant lined up against the Hope player who had knocked Jordan out of the game. Just before the snap, Bryant charged offsides and went straight for the boy's head. The officials pulled him off and ejected him from the game. "Bear had more loyalty than judgment in those days," Click said, but one might argue that on that particular play he showed a little of both. Paul meant to make an impression.[25] He also knew when to back down. For instance, in Fordyce's game against Hope during Paul's junior year, he hurt his knee in the midfield brawl, and after the game, Hope player Charlie Marr came over to the Fordyce bench and jabbed at the knee, saying, "Bear! How's the old knee, Bear?" (Apparently the bear-wrestling story, by this time, had made its way outside Fordyce.) Paul simmered, but he was smart enough to avoid a fight that might further injure his knee. Things worked out for the best: Bryant and Marr later wound up as teammates and friends at Alabama.

JIMMY HARLAND owned a poolroom in Pine Bluff, as rabid a football town as Fordyce. His joint was a hangout for players, fans, and out-of-town recruiters. Harland was a self-appointed scout for Alabama; exactly why he chose Alabama wasn't clear, though it's possible that Alabama alumni had adopted Harland, compensating him for funneling top prospects from southern Arkansas to Tuscaloosa.

Then again, many Arkansas football players didn't need much inducement to go to Alabama. Some chose the University of Arkansas at Fayetteville or Arkansas Tech or Henderson-Brown, a smaller school that in the 1920s was still able to compete with the larger football powers. But for Bryant and numerous other top players, the University of Alabama was what football was all about. It was Alabama that was coached by Wallace Wade, the man called "Bear" by his players—now there was a nickname people remembered—and it was Alabama, not Arkansas or any other southern school, that had gone to the Rose Bowl.

The Rose Bowl! With the exception of some relatively unheralded All-Star contests, there was still no other postseason college football game, and no other school could offer a lure to a potential prospect that compared with the possibility of playing in the Rose Bowl. Other southern colleges could claim it as their goal, but Alabama had been there, three times.

After the Christmas holiday in 1930, Arkansas coach Fred Thomsen, trying to recruit Paul, took him to an All-Star game in Dallas. Bryant left at the half and caught a streetcar back to the hotel to listen to Graham Mac-Namee describe the Tide's 24–0 demolition of Washington State on New Year's Day. Paul wanted to play for Alabama. But did they want him?

In the spring, Alabama assistant coach Hank Crisp, working on a tip from Jimmy Harland, dropped by to see Coach Cowan. Alabama could have pretty much had any football players it wanted, and it wanted Click and Jud Jordan. The university didn't get them—the twins opted to stay in Arkansas. Crisp was disappointed but determined to mine any other available talent; did the Redbugs have any other blue-chip prospects? Cowan said they did, a seventeen-year-old, a big kid, a scrapper whose nickname was Bear. Crisp was impressed. There was a problem, though: the kid hadn't completed enough courses to graduate. Crisp shrugged; that Paul had not graduated from high school was a minor point, one that could be worked around.

Crisp asked if he could meet the kid. When Paul walked into the coach's office, Crisp got up from his chair, extended his hand, and asked him if he wanted to go to Alabama. Paul took his hand and said he sure would.

And that was that.

Chapter 2

You've Got to Be a Football Hero

There ain't nothing to being a football player . . . ,
if you're a football player.

—*W. W. "Pudge" Heffelfinger*[1]

ON A SATURDAY AFTERNOON IN 1869, November 6, if one wants to be precise, a skeptical Rutgers professor stopped his bicycle on the commons, where the gymnasium now stands, in New Brunswick, New Jersey. Fifty young men, students all from the hallowed institutions of Rutgers and Princeton, were fighting over some kind of leather ball. According to John W. Herbert, who graduated in the Rutgers class of 1872 and later wrote an account of the game, neither team wore uniforms, though "some Rutgers players wore stocking caps." The professor watched for a few minutes, then shouted, "You men will come to no Christian end!" and rode away in disgust. Rutgers won the first intercollegiate football game, 6–4, though modern spectators would not recognize the game they played—a sort of hybrid between soccer and rugby—as football. By eight o'clock that night the players of both teams had shaken hands, had dinner, tipped a few drafts, and left for home in good spirits.[2]

The first-known college football writer, an anonymous correspondent for the Rutgers University newspaper, *The Targum*, wrote his assessment of the game: "Princeton had the most muscle, but didn't kick very well and wanted organization. . . . Our men, on the other hand, though comparatively weak, ran well and kicked well throughout, but their great point was their organization, for which great praise is due to the Captain, Legett, '72. The right men were always in the right place." As the years went by, the games would not always be won by the weaker team (though it would always be a useful psychological ploy for a great coach to insist that his men were outmanned but more game), but at least two fundamentals of winning football mentioned in the story—a good kicking game and strong organization—would remain the same from Captain Leggett to Amos Alonzo Stagg to Knute Rockne to Bear Bryant.

Rutgers-Princeton was not, as some historians have identified it, the first football game, or even the first college football game. Football in some form had been played informally on high school and college campuses for several years before 1869. We know that it was played at several eastern schools by the late 1850s. By 1858, football had gotten so rough that town officials of New Haven told Yale students they could not play on the public greens in the center of town. Two years later, Harvard's administration banned football on campus; enthusiastic footballers continued to meet and play off campus. The Rutgers-Princeton match—"match," as some referred to it, because the sport still clung to its rugby origins—was the first between two colleges. The publicity engendered by it sent ripples to the great eastern schools. Harvard lifted its ban on football in 1871.

Critics, though, remained outspoken. "Pig-pile" football, as they referred to it in the 1890s, was a brutal game. Players had virtually no protective padding. To wear a helmet was considered unmanly. As Pudge Heffelfinger explained, "Back in the '90s, we played bare headed—let our hair grow long to prevent scalp cuts."[3] Things hadn't changed much from Pudge's day to that of Riggs Stephenson, who played for the University of Alabama after World War I. Stephenson recalled, "We had mighty bad uniforms. You can tell that from the cauliflower ears I have now. We only had a little piece of leather over our heads. Shoes were heavy and high-topped with big old boards in the front."[4]

In 1873 an attempt had been made to modernize the game when representatives from Princeton, Yale, Rutgers, and Columbia met to establish new rules, some of which helped (such as standardizing the field of play at 140 yards in length and 70 yards in width) and some of which did not (such as restricting scores to balls kicked or head-butted over the goal line and under the crossbars). Football was saved by two things: Walter Camp and the birth of the forward pass. To many football historians, the two are synonymous.

No one knows exactly when or where the first forward pass was thrown in a football game. Pudge Heffelfinger thought it might have been thrown by a Wesleyan player in a game against Yale in the early 1870s, but a more popular story involves the November 30, 1876, match between Yale and Princeton. Grabbed by a Princeton defender, Walter Camp, the legendary Yale quarterback, did something that none of the players had ever seen before: He tossed the ball—either underhanded or sidearm, depending on which story you hear, but in any event, a wobbly, precarious pitch at best—which tumbled end over end into the arms of teammate Oliver Thompson, who was standing perhaps five yards away. Thompson scrambled for a touchdown before the startled Princeton defenders could decide what to do.

A Camp-to-Thompson toss wasn't exactly the same as Joe Montana passing to Jerry Rice, but it got things going. Or, rather, it did after a lengthy debate that involved the players and coaches of both teams and the referee. The ref, nonplussed, decided to settle the dispute the American way: he tossed a coin. Yale won, and the path to Paul Bryant was almost cleared.

In the summer of 1892 William Gray Little returned from Phillips-Exeter Academy in Andover, Massachusetts, to his home in Livingston, Alabama, to attend his brother's funeral. (Gray's intention had been to enroll at Yale for the fall of the 1892 football season. If he had followed through, he would have played on the line along with Pudge Heffelfinger, who became Walter Camp's first-ever All-America selection that year.) Gray brought with him a leather football which was being used in a game that was the craze in eastern schools. His friends, some of whom were attending the University of Alabama, were enthusiastic. At their urging, Gray decided to enroll at Alabama and organize a football team. On the morning of Saturday, November 11, 1892, the *Birmingham Daily News* announced that a "game of football"—as it was now coming to be called—would be played in Birmingham that afternoon between Alabama's "famous" team and eleven players from local high schools picked by a football enthusiast, "Prof. Taylor." The *Daily News* anticipated "a large crowd of ladies, society belles and school girls to wear the colors of their favorites and to applaud the good work of their eleven. Of course, they won't understand anything about the game, but that doesn't make any difference, for they will cheer and enjoy it just as much as if they were critical onlookers."[5] Alabama won, 56–0. So began Alabama football.

The next few seasons were uneventful, except for the formation of the Southern Intercollegiate Athletic Association (SIAA), organized just before Christmas in 1894, a confederation that included Alabama, Auburn, the University of Georgia, Georgia Tech, North Carolina, Vanderbilt, and the powerhouse school in southern football for the decade, mighty Sewanee. The next year Louisiana State, the University of Mississippi, Mississippi A&M (later to become Mississippi State), Tennessee, Tulane, and even Texas would join. That was too many teams spread out over too wide an area for one conference; the SIAA would eventually split into the Southeastern, Atlantic Coast, and Southern Conferences, with Texas joining the South West Conference and Tulane going independent.

Football violence and brutality had become so common that in 1895 the University of Alabama faculty asked the university surgeon to be in attendance at all games. Two years later the administration attempted to reduce the number of serious injuries by cutting down on the number of games, forbidding the football team from traveling to other campuses. That this would have effectively abolished football if other schools had adopted the same policy did not seem to occur to the Alabama administration.

The 1897 team played just one game; the 1898 team didn't bother to show up. "We have seen that it is useless to attempt to put out a football team so long as we are compelled to play all our games on the campus," said the student newspaper.[6] The game on the field had simply become too violent, and behavior among the spectators only slightly less so. No one seemed to have a clear idea how to curb the carnage.* The answer, as knowledgeable football folk gradually came to understand, was the forward pass.

---

* The problem of controlling crowd violence would continue up until the construction of stadiums with staggered seats, which kept more people in their seats, and fences, which restricted them from moving onto the field. As late as 1901, in an Alabama-Tennessee game, the *Birmingham News* reported,

As it happened, representatives of the most prominent football factories, all of them in the Northeast and many of them Ivy League schools, were summoned on January 12, 1906, to the White House by President Theodore Roosevelt, who had been a pupil at Harvard when football was banned and then reinstated. Roosevelt, who loved associating with vigorous outdoor types such as athletes and frontiersmen, immediately saw the virtues of football, particularly college football, as it bred in young boys a love of competition and teamwork. However, he was appalled by the publication in 1905 of statistics on football violence; in that season alone, said the report, 177 serious injuries were recorded, 18 of them fatal. The statistics took on a human face with the circulation of a photo of a Swarthmore player named Bob Maxwell, whose face had been hideously mangled in a 1905 game with Penn. In effect, the president told America's colleges to change the game of football or lose it. Before they left Washington, the representative schools had formed the Intercollegiate Football Association, with Walter Camp as the head of its Rules Committee. A short time later, representatives of twenty-eight more colleges met in New York to establish the "Conference Committee," headed by highly respected Captain Palmer E. Pierce of the United States Military Academy. It was inevitable that Pierce and Camp would meet; before the start of the season, the two organizations had merged to form the Intercollegiate Football Rules Committee. Out of this group, the National College Athletic Association (NCAA) would evolve by 1910.

Most major college teams were playing football with a new set of rules, instituted to make the game both safer and more interesting. Camp inaugurated the concept of a series of downs in which a team could keep possession of the ball by gaining five yards in three downs; the 1906 committee extended the number of required yards to ten (in 1912 the number of

---

After almost every down the spectators would rush across the sidelines and form a compact ring around the struggling teams, preventing beyond a possibility any further play. . . . (Nov. 29, 1901)

Almost every football game played in Birmingham in late years has been more or less marred by the inability of the managers to handle the crowd. Yesterday's game, however, was the worst of its kind ever seen here and it is not surprising that it is looked upon as a failure from a standpoint of clean sport.

The game ended in a tie, 6–6.

downs would be changed from three to four). The playing time of a game was reduced to two 30-minute periods (down from 35 minutes). Most important of all, a neutral zone was created at the line of scrimmage.

Four years later, at Camp's urging, the newly named NCAA added some new rules. The two 30-minute halves were broken up into four 15-minute quarters. The passing game was further refined, with backs and ends identified as the only eligible receivers instead of any lineman who started the play in back of the line of scrimmage.

It wasn't so much the pass as the threat of the pass that changed the game. With the possibility that a player might streak past the defense and score a "cheap" touchdown—cheap because the player received the maximum reward for what some regarded as minimum physical effort—came the understanding that several men must now be kept off the line of scrimmage to defend against that threat. The game of football wasn't quite ready for Joe Namath, but it opened up—at first slowly, then with a rush.

SOMETIME EARLY in the twentieth century Birmingham and Tuscaloosa sportswriters began to refer to the Alabama football team as "The Thin Red Line," an allusion to the poem "Tommy" by the then-most-popular poet in the English-speaking world, Rudyard Kipling ("But it's thin, red line of 'eroe's, When the drums begin to roll . . ."). The red was for the team jerseys (their socks were red with white stripes), the thin because Alabama, like the Princeton team of 1869, was usually smaller than their opponents and proud of it.

Clyde Bolton, a Crimson Tide historian, credits a *Birmingham News* writer named Zip Newman with popularizing the nickname "Crimson Tide" soon after World War I. The name came to him, said Newman, as he watched the Alabama line pound at opponents like "the tide on a seashore." In his history of Alabama football, *The Crimson Tide*, Winston Groom suggests that the name stuck after a game played in Birmingham when the Alabama offense surged to victory on a muddy field. From 1906, the first season played under the new rules, to 1922, the year before Alabama found its first great coach in Wallace Wade, the Tide won nearly 73 percent of its games. Alabama became a major southern power—not quite in a class with the juggernaut at Sewanee, but a power nonetheless.

National recognition was slow in coming, though. In 1913, the year

Bryant was born, W. T. "Bully" Van de Graaff made enough of an impression as far away as Connecticut to be selected by Walter Camp as Alabama's first All-America player. But that was a token. No one considered football outside of the Northeast to be truly first-rate—though that belief was shaken just forty-nine days after Bryant was born. On November 1, 1913, an undersized team from a small Catholic school in Indiana scored the most spectacular upset college football had seen to that time. With quarterback Gus Dorais throwing to Norwegian-born end Knute Rockne, the Fighting Irish of Notre Dame dazzled the greatest football power in the nation, embarrassing Army, 35–13. However, that still meant all the great college powers were north of the Mason-Dixon Line. Or so the complacent eastern press believed.

In 1919, University of Alabama's fourteenth president, George Hutcheson "Mike" Denny, made an unusual choice for coach of its football team, a diminutive Cleveland sportswriter named Xen Scott. Precisely how or why Denny came to offer Scott the job has never been determined, but Scott won 19 of 21 games in his first two seasons at Alabama, with the 1920 team outscoring its opposition 377–35. The star was a sensational athlete named Riggs Stephenson, who would go on to play fourteen seasons of baseball for the Cleveland Indians and Chicago Cubs and compile a career batting average of .336. Scott, who had seen both men play, claimed Stephenson to be "the equal as an athlete to Jim Thorpe."

By 1922, Scott was ill with the cancer that would soon take his life, but he had enough strength remaining to coach Alabama to its most publicized victory in thirty years, the game that put Alabama football on the map. On its first journey north, Alabama was to play the University of Pennsylvania Quakers at Franklin Field on November 4. The Quakers were coached by John Heisman—he whom the trophy would later be named for—and were the favorites of Grantland Rice—then, without question, the most influential and widely read sportswriter in the country—who wrote that Penn would "get a breathing spell that week" and picked the Quakers to beat Alabama 21–0. Before a crowd of twenty-five thousand, easily the largest any of the Alabama players had ever seen, the Tide won a thriller over one of the great teams in eastern football. Scott left the field clutching the game ball. Grantland Rice apologized in his column the day after the game.

The statewide adulation that greeted the Alabama team on its return could not have been easily understood by college football fans in northern states. Alabama papers touted the victory as a revenge for Gettysburg; the score—Alabama 9, Penn 7—was painted on the red brick side of a drugstore on University Boulevard. Locals claim that the score could still be made out on the wall even after World War II.

IN THE twenty-four football seasons between 1892 and 1919, Alabama had thirteen head coaches. For the most part, the selection process was random, as were the methods of payment. One of the coaches, Otto Wagonhurst, completed his duties in 1896 (during which he compiled a 2–1 record) and left the university to pursue other endeavors. In 1926, after Alabama's first victory in the Rose Bowl, the Alumni Association found him working for a rubber company in Akron, Ohio, and presented the astonished Wagonhurst a check for $550, his unpaid salary from thirty years earlier. The senior class, which sponsored the football team, had been able to raise only $200 during the 1896 season.

The prestige of the college coach grew with the complexity and popularity of the game. As the rules and equipment became more sophisticated, football became more exciting and then more popular; administrations simply could not afford to leave such a moneymaking proposition in the hands of college students. As late as the early 1900s, said Pudge Heffelfinger, coaches would not dare to make an important on-field decision without consulting the team captain; by the early 1920s, coaches ruled big-time football. The man who established the prototype for college football coaches was Amos Alonzo Stagg. He was born in 1862 in West Orange, New Jersey, seven years before the first Rutgers-Princeton game, and died in March of 1965, living long enough to see Paul Bryant, the first man to eclipse Stagg's record for total victories, win his second national championship. "Lon," as his friends called him, is credited with, among other things, the huddle (in 1896); wind sprints (also in 1896); the unbalanced offensive line, in which more men were placed to one side of the center than the other (in 1900); and numbering players (1913).* Stagg, who

---

* For good measure Stagg the baseball coach is also credited with inventing the batting cage and pioneering, at least sixty years before Pete Rose, the head-first slide.

He is also thought to be the man who conceived of the "Dead Man" play, in which, according to *College Football, U.S.A., 1869–1971*, "when the ball was snapped, the whole

coached for Springfield in 1890–1891, at the University of Chicago from 1892 to 1932, and at the College of the Pacific from 1933 to 1946, was credited with 314 victories.

"All football," said Knute Rockne, the man who would inherit his mantle and become the most famous football coach in America, "comes from Stagg." Rockne built on Stagg's teachings and took the game of college football to a still higher level. More than anyone else, Rockne showed what football could do for the prestige of a university, taking Notre Dame from a small, unknown Catholic school in the Midwest to international fame.

When President Mike Denny was looking to hire a football coach, he wanted someone who could do for the University of Alabama what Rockne had done for Notre Dame. Denny, a University of Virginia graduate, came to Tuscaloosa in 1911, when enrollment was just four hundred students. He was determined to transform the university from a regional to a national institution that was culturally and ethnically sophisticated. When he retired in 1937, there were more than five thousand students, including northern boys, many from Jewish families, lured by Alabama's football reputation. Denny was one of the first southern university presidents to grasp the importance of a professionally run athletic department. In 1929, the Alabama football team opened its season at the new Denny Stadium; two years later, Paul Bryant, fresh from Fordyce, was working his way through school tending its football field. Forty-four years later, the Alabama state legislature would change the name to Bryant-Denny Stadium. In 1923, a decade before Paul Bryant played his first varsity game, Denny would find his second coach, Wallace Wade, and the first golden age of Alabama football would begin. Wallace Wade was born in Tennessee, named for a national hero of Scotland, William Wallace. A graduate of Brown and an assistant coach at Vanderbilt, he was nicknamed "Bear" for his surly personality. Gone were the easygoing ways of the popular Xen Scott; Wade coached to win, not to be liked. Before he coached a single game in 1923, the *Birmingham News* would report that "the spirit of Wallace Wade is already an institution around the Crimson stronghold. . . . Xen Scott, fine

---

team would run toward the left flank, as though on an end run, except the man who took the pass from center. He flopped on his stomach with the ball concealed beneath him, and played dead. When the enemy players rushed over to stop the fake end sweep, the 'corpse' jumped to his feet and was off to the races. It was a rather unchristian play." (p. 435)

little tutor that he was, was more or less of the easygoing school. Long practices were not the rule under his regime, firm, yes, but in the milder sense of the word. But Wade is different."

Indeed he was. Wade was the first Alabama coach to hire and give authority to strong assistant coaches, Russ Cohen and Hank Crisp in particular. And he was a fanatic on fundamentals. Any player who could not be taught to both block and tackle with perfection did not play on his football team. One of his best players, Al Clemens, described him as "tough as a nickel steak."[7]

Wade served notice on October 20, 1923, that a new order had arrived when Alabama finally overtook, once and for all, its most powerful football rival. In the final two minutes of the scoreless game, Johnny Mack Brown intercepted a pass and Pooley Hubert, who called the offensive signals from the fullback spot, led a forty-eight-yard drive for the game's only touchdown. To many, the 7–0 victory was as significant as the victory over Penn the previous season: Alabama had beaten mighty Sewanee for only the sixth time in nineteen games. They would never lose to them again.

In 1923 and 1924, Wade's teams posted a combined record of 15–3–1. In 1925, led by the running of Brown and the passing of Hubert, they won all nine regular-season games, shutting out every opponent except Birmingham-Southern, whom they scored fifty points against. In an article for the *Birmingham News* printed on December 26, 1925, Wade took time to reflect on what football had come to mean to the South in general and Alabama in particular:

> Sectionalism in football is rapidly disappearing, due to the interchange of coaching ideas. . . . In spite of these conditions Southern football continues to retain some distinctive characteristics. . . .
>
> There is more sentiment in Southern football; the coaches appeal to the affections of the players. . . . The Southern coach holds a higher position in the hearts of his players and of the entire student body than does the coach of the North. Instead of being called by the affectionate term of "Coach," as the Southern coach is, the Northern coach is often called by his first name and is too often treated with very little respect.[8]

Wade's article was intended to cap a glorious season. The Tournament of Roses Committee had selected the Washington Huskies, which had won every game except for a tie with powerful Nebraska, as the West Coast's representative in the bowl game. Eastern powers Dartmouth, Princeton, and Colgate were approached to uphold the honor of eastern football, but all were daunted by the prospect of the 6,000-mile round-trip train ride. The Rose Bowl Committee, growing desperate, sent out feelers to several other schools, including Alabama; Alabama officials were at first wary, wondering how genuine the committee's interest was. Considering the publicity garnered by Alabama's perfect season, the Tide might have seemed like a natural, but the committee was wary of inviting a team from such a poor state—how could Alabama fans possibly come to California in large enough numbers to fill up such an enormous stadium? The 2,800-mile round-trip cost a staggering $250 per person, thereby eliminating the possibility that all but a few students from the wealthiest families could make the trip. With time running out, another feeler was sent Alabama's way, but the Bear-ish Wade was miffed at being a second choice and announced that the Crimson Tide was not interested. Finally, Alabama received an official invitation, and Wade was mollified.

The reluctance of the Rose Bowl Committee to invite Alabama was based on more than economics. In 1932 Erskine Caldwell's *Tobacco Road*, a bawdy melodramatic novel about life in rural Georgia, was published; Caldwell's *God's Little Acre* would follow the next year. The books did not so much create stereotypes of poor uneducated white southerners as reinforce perceptions the rest of the country had held since the time of Reconstruction. Late in 1925, as the Rose Bowl Committee was mulling over the question of what school to invite, a *Los Angeles Times* columnist derided Alabama's players as "swamp students"[9]; a Sacramento editorialist actually wondered if a leading eastern high school team could not be persuaded to play mighty Washington instead of "the second rate team from the country's poorest section."[10] The assumption that Alabama stood no chance was so strong that even Will Rogers got into the act, dropping a line about "Tusca-losers." If Alabama players needed any extra incentive, those passages, read to them aloud by their coaches on the train trip to the Rose Bowl, more than supplied it.

The Alabama team that arrived in Pasadena on Christmas Eve was composed of twenty-two players. In addition to the celebrated Johnny Mack Brown, his brother Tolbert, and Pooley Hubert, the Crimson Tide roster included Lovely Barnes, Sherlock Holmes, and H. S. Dismukes. The game itself was pure football, as neither side had been able to assemble a scouting report on the other. The prejudice against southern football lasted exactly until halftime, with Washington ahead by a seemingly comfortable margin of 12–0.

Wade refused to believe that his boys were as bad as they had looked in the first half. Just before the start of the third quarter, he walked into the Alabama locker room and said in a booming voice, "They told me boys from the South would fight," then turned around and walked out. His players looked at each other in embarrassment, and the apprehension they felt in the first half playing for so many people quickly gave way to anger. In the third quarter, the Tide began to roll. Hubert, whom Wade had inexplicably held back in the first two periods, ran the ball five consecutive times, the last for a touchdown. Then, Brown took in a long pass from Hubert for another. Following a Washington fumble, Hubert passed to Brown for another touchdown. In the final period, the Huskies, regrouping themselves, scored again to cut Alabama's lead to one point, 20–19.

With seconds left to play and Washington threatening again, Brown made a spectacular game-saving one-on-one tackle of Washington's great runner, "Wildcat" Wilson. The Huskies coach was so incensed that he left the field without shaking the hand of his Alabama counterpart. Most of the California fans, however disappointed they were at the outcome, had no qualms about applauding the Tide, particularly the engaging Johnny Mack Brown, whose picture on the front pages of the LA papers helped propel him to a movie career.

The Crimson Tide's victory electrified the South and caught the attention of the entire country, headlining the sports pages of newspapers in Washington, Philadelphia, New York, and Chicago. The team's return to Alabama heralded the greatest statewide celebration since the shelling of Fort Sumter. William Little, who had started Alabama's football program thirty-four years earlier, paid for a special train to greet the team in New Orleans. When the Tide finally reached Tuscaloosa, the players were paraded through the streets in wagons, the horses led by freshmen.

The Crimson Tide also went unbeaten in 1926 and again went to the Rose Bowl, tying Stanford, 7–7. After just three losses in Wade's first four seasons, the seasons of 1927 through 1929 proved to be a letdown with a combined record of 17–10–1. But in 1930 Wade delivered his masterpiece, a perfect 9–0 regular season that included wins over old rival Sewanee and a new rival, Tennessee. The season ended in a devastating 24–0 victory over

Washington State in the Rose Bowl.* More than two decades later, Mel Hein, a consensus All-America for Washington State that season and later a star for the New York Giants, told Pudge Heffelfinger that "when folks talk about the great teams of the past, they never mention that Alabama team, but for my money, they could have licked anybody on that day, including the Notre Dame bunch of the same year." There was no official champion of college football back then, but several polls selected the 1930 Crimson Tide as the best, along with Knute Rockne's great Notre Dame team of the same year.

The hugely popular radio crooner Rudy Vallee apparently held no notion of Alabamians as a race of swamp dwellers. Near the end of the season, Alabama's football reputation soared when Vallee recorded "*Football Freddy*," named for Alabama's best lineman, All-America Fred Sington ("Football Freddy, rugged and tan, Football Freddy, collegiate man"). Vallee's record made it official—Alabama was one of the nation's most recognized football powers.†

THIS WAS the tradition Paul Bryant was about to join as he sat in the rumble seat of Hank Crisp's Ford roadster and crossed the Warrior River, heading for the University of Alabama campus in the summer of 1931. Twenty-seven years later, in an interview for *Sport* magazine, he would recall what it felt like:

> I was riding in Coach Hank's old Ford. I had on a pair of green knickers. Every boy had a pair of knickers in those days. I had a little satchel with nothing in it but an extra pair of britches, a pair of shoes, and a few other

---

* On this Rose Bowl trip, the Alabama players had a bit more time for sightseeing than the squad that had come to Pasadena five years earlier. Johnny Mack Brown, now an established movie star, invited the team to watch him film some scenes with Wallace Beery at MGM. The Tide players, it was recorded, were incredulous that anyone could be paid so much for so little work. Forty years later, another Alabama football star, Joe Namath, would be paid approximately ten times as much for similar work.
† Frank Howard, later to become a successful college football coach, lined up opposite Sington in the 1931 Rose Bowl and tried to distract him by singing, "Football Fred-dieeee . . ." Sington, who eventually became close friends with Howard, later confessed that "his singing didn't distract me at all. Actually, I was kind of tickled pink."

things. They still remember around here the day my trunk arrived. It was one of those old-fashioned round-top trunks. It had no lock on it, so my mother had tied plow line round it to hold it together.[11]

Crisp had shared three national championships with Alabama's first Bear; by the time of his death in 1970, he would live long enough to work for the boy he recruited and help the second Bear win three more national titles.

The University of Alabama that Paul Bryant arrived at was more cosmopolitan than any institution he could have imagined, and football, thanks to Mike Denny, had much to do with that. While eastern universities openly debated the value of a football program, Denny had no doubts: he moved straight ahead, using football profits to upgrade Alabama's academic facilities and recruit new staff. The Rose Bowl victories had given the university spectacular free publicity; Denny followed up by taking out ads in the large northeastern papers, particularly in New York, heralding the advantages in cost, climate, and improved educational opportunities.

In the introduction to a reprint of William Bradford Huie's novel about the University of Alabama in the 1930s, *Mud on the Stars*,★ an Alabama English professor, Don Noble, wrote of the impact of Denny's efforts. Alabama had "no 'quotas,' and it was quotas that were keeping many Jewish students in the Northeast out of some of the more prestigious schools. Jewish students came, 400 in 1926 and 800 in 1927. By 1930, spurred on by the stock-market crash of 1929 and the subsequent Depression, 1–3 of the student body of the University of Alabama was Jewish . . . 60 years later it is not unusual for a professor to ask a Jewish student from Newark how he came to choose the University of Alabama and hear in response: 'My family has always gone to school there.' "[12] While the University of Alabama was solidly segregated against blacks and would remain so for decades, it proved receptive for Jews. At least in some instances, thanks to Mike Denny, there was a progressive attitude. Two Jewish players, Dave Rosenfeld and Andy Cohen, were counted by Wallace Wade among his best players on both offense and defense.†

★ Huie's novel, a best-seller in 1942, was made into a superb but much neglected film in 1960, *Wild River*, directed by Elia Kazan and starring Montgomery Clift, Lee Remick, and Jo Van Fleet.

† Noble writes, "Huie's description of the southern boys' reactions to this 'exodus' is priceless. In the novel, Lafavor [the protagonist] and his Alabama pals linger outside the

Denny's farsighted strategy helped the University of Alabama to blunt the impact of the Depression that was sweeping the country. At a time when many universities were losing students, Alabama's enrollment was increasing. Depression or no Depression, Denny was not going to alter his plan. He was going to send the Crimson Tide nationwide. In 1932 he scheduled games at George Washington University in Washington, D.C., and St. Mary's in San Francisco, and in 1933 Alabama played Fordham in New York City. (He had already sent the Tide to play Wisconsin at Madison in 1928, Alabama's only meeting with a Big Ten team until Bear Bryant would face off against Woody Hayes in the 1977 Sugar Bowl.)

In the fall of 1931, Paul Bryant was less aware of, and less influenced by, the Depression than most of his fellow students. The crash hadn't had much effect on the Fordyce economy by the time he left for Alabama; old timers' accounts scarcely mention the Depression at all. For much of the state, the economic circumstances weren't a great deal different; Alabama was or was close to being the poorest state in the Union before the 1929 stock market crash, and most of the population still lived in rural areas and farmed at least some portion of their food. Birmingham, the steel center of the South and easily the most industrialized area in the state, was hit hard. From a material standpoint, Paul had never had it so good as at the university, even though he still didn't have much. "I think we probably had more fun in those days than boys do now," he said in reflection, "none of us had any money or anything. I didn't have a stamp to write home with, and there was no such thing as a player having an automobile."[13]

If Bryant thought, though, that attending the University of Alabama while playing football was going to be a cakewalk, he was mistaken. The academic standards at the university were not high by the standards of most eastern schools, but it was serious about them. Before he could even gain admission, Paul needed help in the basic areas as well as a language course,

---

Jewish dormitories to hear accents they have never heard and smell odors they have never known. But it is the assimilated Alabama Jews of Birmingham and Montgomery who are the most discomfited. In their efforts to distinguish themselves between German Jews and Eastern Jews, established families and those they call 'kikes.' What a scene of cultural confusion it must have been!" (*Mud on the Stars*, p. xi)

Mel Allen, who was born in Birmingham the same year as Bryant, told me he informed a new Jewish student from New Jersey that "we're a little different here. We call our rabbis 'Bubba.'"

so he studied Spanish, math, and English at Tuscaloosa High for a full year and practiced with the varsity squad—this would later be called "red-shirting," as the nonvarsity players wore red shirts to distinguish them from the other players—while waiting for his college football career to begin.

Later, like many football players of the era, Bryant would talk about his good fortune in getting a scholarship, but the term almost never appears in period literature. The great Riggs Stephenson doubted such a thing existed, at least when he was at Alabama, early after World War I: "We had a training table back then, and some of the players waited on the table. Joe Sewell [who would go on to baseball fame, hitting .312 in fourteen seasons with the Indians and Yankees] and I waited on the table to get our meals. Scholarship? They might have had some, but they didn't offer any to me. . . . But I don't think they had any scholarships at all."[14] "They gave me a job," Stephenson recalled, "sweeping off the stoops of Garland Hall. We got good pay—about $5 a month." Apparently what would later be called a scholarship amounted to a room, tuition, and meal money in exchange for menial work.

In his first year at the University, Bryant cleaned toilets and showers, cleared tables in the dining hall, and did groundswork, including cutting the grass on Denny Field. This gave him enough money to live on but not much for anything else. His sister Louise, in Dallas attending a business college at that time, received a letter from Paul. "He was worried that he wouldn't have enough money to get our mother anything for Mother's Day. He said he didn't even have money for a card. I'd been told by a friend of the family that he had gone to Tuscaloosa without any new clothes, just a few secondhand things, and that he didn't have any sheets for his bed. I borrowed a hundred dollars and sent him a package full of sheets, socks, those sort of things. He said he would pay me back if it took him the rest of his life, but it only took about two years."

Later, on a visit back to Fordyce, Paul enthralled family members with talk of college life in Tuscaloosa. Louise recalls her mother asking her youngest son if he had any money. He told her he had all he needed. Before he returned to school, she went through his pockets, found just three pennies, and slipped in a twenty-dollar bill. A few days after he left, Ida got a letter from Paul with the twenty-dollar bill enclosed. "Paul told our mother that he appreciated it, but that he had plenty of money in his other pair of pants in his suitcase. But he didn't have another pair of pants."

For a while, Bryant roomed with five other players, including Don Hutson, in three rooms converted from three dressing rooms on the first floor of the gym. A nearby Club Room had a pool table and chairs, which was where most of the players hung out when they were not on the practice field or studying.

He didn't do much studying. Melvin Allen Israel, who would become one of Bryant's best friends at Alabama and go on to fame as Mel Allen, "The Voice of the New York Yankees," recalled Bryant as "smart, very smart. There was never a problem with Paul's intelligence, but it was obvious that he just didn't have the background to be a good student."

Despite the extra hours put in at Tuscaloosa High, Paul quickly realized that his academic prospects were hopeless. He had little primary education and had learned to read and write later than most, so there would be few white-collar professions open to him. And what point was there to attending college only to go back to truck farming in Fordyce? It was futile to do anything except try for a degree in physical education. "I wasn't studying anything," he said about his first year in Tuscaloosa. "Heck, I didn't know *how* to study."* In *Bear*, he seemed almost wistful about his limitations. "[Don] Hutson breezed through school. His mother was a schoolteacher and he knew how to study, and the value of it. I wouldn't swap my mama and papa for anybody's, but neither of them had ever been to school, there were never any books around the house, and I was a lousy student. . . . Today, these boys have to fight for their lives in the classroom. My son Paul was a Phi Beta Kappa, and all Mary Harmon had to say was 'Study,' and he'd go to it."

When Paul wasn't attending his makeup classes at Tuscaloosa High, he was mostly practicing football. Many players, even the toughest and most dedicated, hated football practice. Bryant practiced football the way he played football, at full force. "I didn't care if we ever quit practicing football," he told Underwood, "I loved it." In later years, nothing warmed his heart more than a player who loved to practice as much as he did. "I don't know that I was ever that good a player," said Jerry Duncan, who would be

---

* Like many an intelligent man with little formal education, Bryant was sensitive about the subject and often self-deprecating when touching on it in interviews. He once confided to Al Browning, then a reporter for the *Tuscaloosa News*, that he had once had a feeler from Notre Dame but that "they found out I couldn't read or write well enough."

a key player on Alabama's 1965 championship squad, "but I did love to practice, and he loved me for loving it. One of the biggest honors of my life was when Coach Bryant created the 'Jerry Duncan I Love to Practice Award.' Hell, I practiced when I was hurt just cause I knew he was watching me, and I wasn't going to let him down."

When practice was over, Bryant and a handful of friends did their best to get into trouble. Without transportation, the fleshpots of Birmingham were out of reach, so the opportunities were few. Before eight o'clock they could usually be found on the Quadrangle in front of the sorority houses, waiting for their dates. As most of the boys had little money, the dates tended to be simple picnics on the Quadrangle lawn. Occasionally there were dances; Mary Harmon would recall the football players as having reputations for being "the best dancers and the worst risks." The dances, though, were chaperoned, and sometimes Bryant, Hutson, and a handful of other football players would sneak away to a house in the country owned by a friend, Sam Friedman. In borrowed cars laden with players, their dates, and picnic baskets full of food and drink, they enjoyed off-campus afternoons that sometimes extended past curfew. At one point, Hank Crisp—or Coach Hank, as he came to be called—had had enough and raided the players' rooms, confiscating a gallon of corn liquor, which, Paul remembered more than four decades later with a touch of indignation, had cost them six bits. Most of the time, though, discipline problems amounted to nothing more than a player or two sneaking some beers after hours. If a player strayed too far from the line, his teammates would usually straighten him out.

In the summer of 1933, before his sophomore year, Paul strayed so far off the line he very nearly failed to get back across it. Back home in Fordyce on vacation, he got involved in perhaps the worst scrape of his young life. Bit Roland was black and around the same age as Paul. The two had palled around in Moro Bottom, and when Bit proposed a scheme to back a dance band, Paul jumped at it. Getting his stake from his cousin Collins, Bear and Bit had planned to use the same band for a Friday-night dance at a black social club and then take it to a Saturday-night gig at a white country club. Paul was to handle the tickets, and to ease his mind while carrying so much cash, he jammed a .38 revolver (pearl-handled, he claimed, borrowed from the local chief of police—which seems highly unlikely) into his waistband under his jacket. So armed, Paul went to the club on Friday night. Forty-two years later, in his autobiography, he would take complete responsibility for what followed, which is only fair since it was his fault. The dance was advertised at ninety-nine cents a couple. One thrifty fellow put down a dollar and had the temerity to ask for change. "99 cents plus tax," Paul shot back. The man cursed Bryant and demanded his penny. Foolishly, Paul came out of the booth to confront him, only to recognize the penny-pincher as "the toughest guy in town." The man cursed him again, and Bryant hit him, knocking him down the steps.

The man got up and reached for something in his pocket—a knife would be a likely assumption—and Paul made his only intelligent decision that night. Instead of reaching for the pistol in his waistband, he hit the fellow again. This time the man tumbled down the steps, knocking himself cold when the back of his head struck the ground. Paul thought he was dead. As he had so many times in the past, Collins helped him out of a tight spot, hustling Paul into his car and driving him to Pine Bluff, where he stayed with Don Hutson and his family for three days. Hearing that the fellow was up and around—his pal Bit must have filled him in on what was going on in the black section of town—Paul determined to slip back into town to see his mother. At first he was hesitant: To get to his mother's house, he had to pass through the black section of Fordyce. Collins told him not to worry; if he hit any man hard enough, there would be no more trouble. Paul came and went several times after that without any trouble. The incident, though, shook him badly. "Every hour I was awake, for three days solid, I promised the Lord if He let me out of this mess, I'd never have another fight." If he broke his promise, it is not recorded.

No sooner did he get back to Tuscaloosa and start football practice for his first year playing varsity than he received bad news from home: Monroe Bryant died suddenly early in the fall. Paul could not afford to go home for the funeral and was so depressed and homesick that he wrote to Collins and told him he was going to quit school and get a job in a Texas oil field, but his cousin straightened him out. Within a short time, football stopped being a distraction and became Paul's main focus.

BEAR NEVER got to play for Bear. For reasons not made clear at the time, Wallace Wade left Alabama for Duke University after the 1931 Rose Bowl. He never said why until he retired from coaching in 1951, then he explained to an interviewer that Duke, a private university, offered him "greater freedom from interference" in running a university athletic department. Or stated another way, two strong-willed men, Wallace Wade and Alabama president Mike Denny, suffered a clash of egos in determining the future of Alabama athletics. Wade's ego had revealed itself in a legendary encounter with the administration of the University of Kentucky, where, in 1922, he had gone to interview for the job of head football coach. After he answered all their questions, the selection committee requested that he wait outside their conference room while they voted. Instead of voting, however, a debate on Wade's qualifications broke out and dragged on for more than two hours. Finally, the committee cast their votes just as Wade, in a fury, walked into the room and told the committee, in effect, to take their job offer somewhere else. He walked out not knowing that he had been their unanimous selection. Paul Bryant, who later walked out of two college football programs, including Kentucky's, over what he regarded as matters of principle, would have applauded. Wade, while coaching at Alabama, never lost a game to Kentucky.

Although Bryant never played for Wallace Wade, he was acutely conscious of how much he owed him. The first football game he ever listened to was Alabama's victory in the 1926 Rose Bowl, and Wallace's image still dominated Alabama football when Bryant arrived in 1931. Bryant, who would become as awe-inspiring as any coach to ever step onto a college field, never got over his awe of Wallace Wade. In 1976 Bryant invited Wade to attend spring practice in Tuscaloosa, after which the coaches went to a party at the Tutwiler Hotel in Birmingham. Clem Gryska, one of Bryant's assistants, recalls that the two Bears went off in a corner to talk. Wallace asked Bryant how he thought the team would do that season. "It could be good, but to be honest, Coach," said Bryant, "I needed a fullback." "Well, Paul," said Wade—Gryska could recall few coaches who ever addressed Bryant by his Christian name. "Did you not know when you were out recruiting this winter that you'd be needing a fullback?" Bryant, who towered over the older man, replied in a quiet voice, "Yessir, Coach, you're right. I should have done something about that."*

---

* On October 25, 1937, Wade became the second football coach (after Knute Rockne in 1927) to be featured on the cover of *Time* magazine. In 1980, Paul Bryant became the seventh.

THE LOSS of a coach like Wallace Wade might have been expected to devastate a football program, but whatever the nature of Wade's dispute with Denny, he had far too much class to leave the football program in the lurch. "There was a young backfield coach at Georgia who should become one of the greatest coaches in the country," Wade told Denny in his letter of resignation. "He played football under Rockne at Notre Dame. Rock called him one of the smartest players he ever coached. He is Frank Thomas, and I don't believe you could pick a better man." Wade's judgment in selecting coaches was even better than his judgment of football players: he picked a successor who was an even greater coach than he was. Throughout his career, Thomas would compile a won-lost percentage thirty points higher than Wade's.

Denny wanted a coach as smart and tough as Wallace Wade and one with knowledge of the Knute Rockne system to turn the Crimson Tide into the Fighting Irish of the South. Thomas quickly found out how serious Denny was about football on the day he signed his Alabama contract. "Mr. Thomas," the president told his new coach, "now that you've accepted our proposition, I will give you the benefit of my views, based on many years of observation. It is my conviction that material is 90%, coaching ability 10%. I desire further to say that you will be provided with 90% and that you will be held to strict accounting for delivering the remaining 10%."[15] Thomas did not agree with the proportions but had no doubt Denny meant what he said.

"I don't know what a football coach is supposed to look like," said Paul Bryant, the man who arguably looked more like a football coach than any football coach who ever lived. "But Coach Thomas probably wouldn't get a movie role for it." If John Wayne was the ideal choice to play Bear Bryant, Thomas would have been played by a character actor like Thomas Mitchell, who played Vivien Leigh's father in *Gone with the Wind*.

Short, chubby, and generally unsmiling, Thomas inspired respect from his players but not love. For one thing, as Bryant was quick to note, coming from Notre Dame made him a Yankee, not exactly a term of affection in Alabama. But "until I became one of his assistant coaches, I didn't realize that underneath he was like most coaches who have a reputation for being tough; he was a sentimental old man, just like me."

With a little luck, Frank Thomas's name would have been immortalized by Grantland Rice. It was in 1924, after a lackluster 12–7 victory by the Irish over Army, that Rice stumbled on the most famous lead in sportswriting history: "Outlined against a blue, gray October sky, the Four Horsemen rode again."[16] It was Thomas, though, who had led the Irish to a drubbing of Army in the previous season in 1921, and in 1922, Thomas's senior year, he had alternated at quarterback with one of the horsemen, Harry Stuhldreher, and played in the backfield with the other three, Don Miller, Elmer Layden, and Jim Crowley. It was his misfortune not to be starter the day Rice wrote his story.

In 1933, Crowley would become the head coach at Fordham University in Manhattan. Thomas, in keeping with Mike Denny's strategy of making Alabama into a nationally recognized football power, would contact his old Notre Dame teammate and schedule a game at the Polo Grounds in New York. (The following season, Crowley would coach the young lineman named Vince Lombardi and become his mentor at the same time Thomas was shaping Paul Bryant at Alabama.)

Thus, because of Wallace Wade's recommendation, Alabama football took one giant step ahead of almost all other football programs in the South. Graduates from Rockne's program dotted the country; now Alabama had a direct connection to him. Thomas was the first Notre Dame graduate, and the first of Rockne's pupils, to coach at a major southern school. Rockne thought Thomas to be his prize pupil. When he was a senior, Rockne told a sportswriter, "It's amazing the amount of football sense that Thomas kid has. He can't miss becoming a great coach some day."[17]

College football would have boomed without Rockne and Notre Dame, but not as soon. Notre Dame was the first school, even before Alabama, to challenge the hegemony of the great East and West Coast football powers. Notre Dame wasn't the first "national" team; Army, whose cadets came from all over the country, could claim that honor. But unlike Army, the Fighting Irish drew their players from the ranks of working-class Americans, people who regarded themselves as underdogs—in that, they would have a great deal in common with Alabama.

Thomas modernized Alabama football by introducing Rockne's strategy and training methods. His first big change was to discard Wade's offensive formation, which utilized a single wingback and an unbalanced line, and to install the famous "Notre Dame box," which placed the quarterback at a corner of a square in the backfield, with the fullback to either his right or left and the two halfbacks taking the other two corners. The Notre Dame box would become Alabama's standard formation until Bear Bryant became head coach twenty-seven years later. The box was an intriguing mix of basics and finesse. Only a few bread-and-butter plays could be run from the box with effectiveness, but there was an infinite variety of shifts and spins from the backs, and reverses from the ends—the rest of the team would, say, start to the right while the man on the right side of the line would step back and move in an opposite parallel direction, taking a hand-off from the quarterback, or, in an even trickier variation, from a halfback who had taken a handoff from the quarterback—keeping opposing defenses constantly off balance. Football fans with a sense of historical perspective will recognize many similarities between the Notre Dame box and the wishbone formation that Paul Bryant perfected at Alabama in the 1970s. (The major difference was that in the wishbone the fullback and halfbacks would form an inverted V behind the quarterback.)

The single-wing offenses designed by Wallace Wade were essentially power formations; the Notre Dame box put an emphasis on speed and the art of deception. It was ideal for Notre Dame, a small school with a small recruiting base. Strange as it may seem to football fans today, players on the Notre Dame teams of Rockne weighed less than those on the Army team and several other opponents. Thomas installed the Notre Dame box at Alabama for similar reasons. Alabama, like many schools in the Deep South, also had a smaller base from which to recruit and the players were generally lighter than those on teams from anywhere but the Deep South. Alabama had won two Rose Bowls under Wade, but as college football became more popular and more lucrative, recruiting among major schools became tougher. Every year, the top teams got bigger and faster. If Alabama was going to be a national power, then it must stress other qualities to compensate for the lack of muscle. Like the Irish, Crimson Tide teams would win by being better conditioned, better prepared, and more enthusiastic. And, of course, better coached.

"The Notre Dame system I used," Thomas once told sportswriter John D. McCallum, "is just about the same stuff I was taught years ago at South Bend. The shifting of the backs and the flexing of the ends were identical. We had four or five basic running plays that were the same and two or three passes that hadn't changed. In the fifteen years I coached at Alabama, the only thing we added were reverses and spins to bolster the weak-side attack.★ All in all, my Notre Dame offense in 1946 had approximately 20 running plays."[18] Teams that ran their plays from the popular T-formation—a quarterback with a fullback positioned directly behind him and a halfback on each side of the fullback—would often have as many as one hundred plays in their book. Occasionally, Bryant said, Thomas "would have one little new play for the opponent, but basically he preached blocking and tackling and executing."

Paul Bryant was terrified of Frank Thomas. Not terrified as in afraid, but terrified of displeasing him, which is precisely what many of Bryant's players would say about him. Thomas seldom paid him any attention except in practice, where Paul would constantly hear his name barked out in Thomas's nasal Midwestern accent—"Bry-annt!"—so sharply distinguishable from the Deep South pronunciation, "Brynnnt" in one syllable.

One fundamental difference between Thomas and his mentor, Rockne, was that Thomas did not make overtly emotional appeals to his players. He was not a shouter in practice. Practices were tough, but Thomas generally refrained from displaying emotion, at least so long as things were being done correctly. Bryant remembered him as having "a kind of aloof, imperious way. Before a game he would say a few words, then call on Coach Hank [Crisp] or Red Drew, one of his assistants, and they handled the real preaching."

When Alabama lost or otherwise performed below his expectations, Thomas needed no one to speak for him. The worst tirade Bryant ever heard him deliver was after Alabama's loss to Fordham in Paul's sophomore year. It was Alabama's first trip to New York, and Thomas was out to make an impression on the eastern press just as Xen Scott's team had done in defeating the University of Pennsylvania eleven years earlier. Alabama gained more yards than Fordham but seemed dazzled and distracted and lost the game on a safety, the only score. It was the Tide's only loss that season. Bryant learned a lesson from Thomas on how to refocus a football team: practice the week after the Fordham game was torture. "We got the full treatment. If I heard 'Bry-annt!' once that week, I heard it forty times.

★ "Weak-side" simply meant the side of the center that the rest of the backs were not lined up on. In other formations, it would simply indicate the side where the fewest players were positioned. In modern college and pro football, it generally indicates the opposite side of the line from where the tight end, who functions as both a receiver and a blocker on the line, is placed.

Scared of him? You're damn right I was!" The tactic worked. 'Bama rebounded with a 20–0 victory over the University of Kentucky and shut out three of their last four opponents.

Paul didn't realize it yet, but Thomas was giving him a clinic in coaching, particularly in the art of making adjustments during a game. Opponents agreed that Thomas was a wizard at that. Decades later, opponents would say the same thing about Paul Bryant: he may not always have had the best game plan, but no coach was better at adjusting and retooling during a game. And, of course, Thomas had a great eye for spotting talent, not just in football but in other sports. Like Bryant, he was a big baseball fan, and during the summers of the late 1940s, he would sneak up to Birmingham where, according to Bryant, he became one of the first to discover a sensational young centerfielder named Willie Mays.

It's likely that no Alabama team until Bryant's in the late 1970s had as much talent as the 1934 squad. It had to have more talent in order to dominate. The competition in the 1930s had become tougher. Series between regional neighbors had burgeoned into fierce rivalries. The biggest difference in the Southern Conference, which would become the Southeastern Conference in 1933, was the emergence of Tennessee, coached by Brigadier General Robert Reese Neyland, a one-time aide-de-camp to General Douglas MacArthur. Neyland came to Knoxville three years after Wallace Wade started at Alabama, and he was no less ambitious or tough-minded than either Wade or Thomas. The Tennessee Volunteers replaced Sewanee as Alabama's biggest rival, and beginning with Wade's first powerhouse teams, for more than two decades Alabama and Tennessee dominated the South; from 1923 to 1946, the Tide and the Vols either won or shared fourteen conference championships. The Alabama-Tennessee game soon became the biggest annual sporting event in the entire South, one that would dominate the sports pages of newspapers in both states the weeks before and after the game.

Despite the challenge from Tennessee and other schools that were building up their football programs, in his first three seasons Thomas's teams had a record of 24–4–1. The 1934 Crimson Tide would be the first of his three undefeated Alabama teams and the one best remembered by history.

It's a football axiom that the best player on a team never makes a great coach; he relies too much on natural ability and assumes his players can do likewise. Bryant wasn't close to being the best player on the team, nor even the second best. The second best was Quarterback Millard "Dixie" Howell, the best passer the Crimson Tide had had up to that time. The best player, by far, was the great Don Hutson—"the Alabama Antelope," as he was dubbed, though "Arkansas Antelope" would have been more appropriate since he hailed from the town of Pine Bluff. Bryant called him "the class of the outfit," referring to the 1934 national champions, and he meant class both on and off the field. Hutson's father was a railroad man, and thus the Hutson family was on a higher social scale than the Bryants; Paul was impressed by the fact that Hutson, who came from a comparatively well-off family, took the same jobs as the rest of the players. Paul admired him before he ever met him, and they became lifelong friends.

More than Bryant, Hutson was a high school legend. Bryant and his friends would sometimes go to Pine Bluff games just to watch him play; in one game he caught five touchdown passes. He was an incredible all-around athlete, "all-everything in high school," according to Bryant. "In every respect, a complete football player—a good defensive end, a fine blocker, and an intelligent player."

Hutson came to Alabama through the same pipeline as Bryant—Coach Hank Crisp via Jimmy Harland's poolroom. In 1934 he was an All-America player by *consensus*—Alabama's first, really—and would go on to NFL fame with the Green Bay Packers, which signed him immediately after a spectacular performance in the 1935 Rose Bowl. In his autobiography, Bryant said that in his entire career he had never seen a better pass receiver (but at the time, Bryant wrote, he had not yet seen Ozzie New-some). Bryant wasn't the only one Don Hutson made an impression on. In 2000, *Sports Illustrated*'s Paul Zimmerman would put Hutson on his All-Century team along with Jerry Rice.

Bryant only looked slow compared to Hutson. At six feet three inches and weighing 210 pounds by his senior year, he was not so much "the other end" from Hutson, as he would often refer to himself, as what modern football watchers would call "the tight end." All receivers lined up close to the line of scrimmage back then, but Hutson was, in effect, the "split" end—the receiver who could break wide and go deep. Bryant would usually break over the middle of the field into heavy traffic, the normal function of the tight end in today's game. Thomas rated them both highly: "Hutson starred in pass receiving. Bear was a better blocker and a great competitor."[19] Bryant was quick for a big man, and he must have had better hands than he would later claim, or else he would not have been at a receiver's position. Most of all, he had no fear of being hit while going for the ball. Bryant was also a savage tackler on defense, an important point in an era when good players were expected to excel on both sides of the ball. His defensive ability was one of the big reasons he was a second-team All-Conference selection.

Because Hutson and Bryant were two of the team's best players, they had an inflated opinion of their worth to the team. Coach Thomas and his assistants soon gave them lessons in humility that neither would ever forget. Before a big intrasquad scrimmage in the second week of the season, Thomas gave the baseball players on the football squad an incentive to work hard, announcing that those who practiced well would be allowed to leave early and go practice baseball. This was no small thing, as Mel Allen, who had by then become editor of the school paper, *The Crimson and White*, would note: "Baseball practice was fun; aside from Paul, just about everyone agreed that football practice was hell." Hutson, a terrific baseball player, had the good sense to get home early the night before so he would be ready for the football scrimmage against the second team. Bryant and several of his pals did not. One of his teammates rented a riverboat and brought along some wood-grain alcohol to spike the punch as an added inducement to get the girls to come along. They topped off the party with a trip to a local chili parlor, and limped into their rooms about 7:30 in the morning. Hutson, who was up dressed, and ready for practice, greeted them with laughter. On the first play, Dixie Howell threw Bryant a short pass over the middle, and Hutson took out two blockers. Even with a hangover, Bryant was able to lope into the end zone untouched.

Crisp took him out of the game and set him on the bench until halftime. In the dressing room he tore into the other party-going footballers, reserving his worst fury for Hutson, accusing him of dogging it on the football field to save his best effort for baseball. If only, he told the boys, they hustled like Bryant, they might have gotten off the hook to dress for baseball. Hutson and Riley, said Bryant, nearly threw up.

It didn't take Crisp long, though, to catch onto Bryant's extracurricular activities. One night he called a team meeting and walked in with a sack full of women's clothing—silk underwear, scarves—and tossed them at Bryant and his teammates. "Well, dammit, that's all you think about anyway," he said and walked out.

Because Coach Hank was Thomas's designated disciplinarian, the players felt they could take a certain amount of abuse from him without much consequence. But one day, as Hutson and Bryant walked across campus, Thomas terrified them by pulling his car alongside and ordering them in. After driving along in silence for a few moments, he finally told them, according to Bryant, that they had acquired reputations as ladies' men. That wouldn't mix, he told them, with football (actually, the problem was that it mixed too well). They had better decide whether they wanted to play on his team or not.

Unbeknownst to Hutson and Bryant, Thomas had already tipped the local newspaper to his plans. After their automobile ride, they picked up a paper and read that "Alabama will probably have two new starting ends for the big game with Sewanee." Bryant thought it might be a bluff: Coach Tommy might be able to do without "the other end," but surely not without Don Hutson. He was wrong. At Friday practice, Thomas called out the starting lineup, and two second-teamers, Gandy and Walker, were the starting ends. Bryant was stunned; nearly thirty years later, when recalling the incident, he still couldn't believe Thomas had not started Hutson. It made an impact on him.

That Saturday Hutson and Bryant sat on the bench in Montgomery during the opening kickoff for the Alabama-Sewanee game. Bryant wanted to crawl into a hole. Four minutes into the first quarter, Thomas waved his hand, and Bryant and Hutson were out of the doghouse and into the game. They beat Sewanee easily, 35–6, then, the following week, Mississippi State, 41–0. Thomas's message was clear: his best players were not more important than the team. What he was really doing was getting his team ready for Tennessee. They were, and they won, 13–6. General Neyland paid his opponents the ultimate compliment: "You never know," he said, "what a football player is made of until he plays against Alabama."

After the game, Hank Crisp, as usual, walked among the players peeling off tens from a roll of bills, one for each player. Crisp must have thought Paul played very well that day. He came around later and handed him four ten-dollar bills. The money was a reward, not an incentive.

Alabama fans knew what the incentive was—a bid to the Rose Bowl. The entire state buzzed with the talk that the Crimson Tide might once again be invited, and then after eight games, the dream came into focus. Nine years earlier, Paul Bryant, a nearly illiterate kid with no aspirations beyond farming, had been thrilled by the radio broadcast of Alabama's great victory in the Rose Bowl. Now, he was on the verge of playing in that same Rose Bowl against the West Coast's, and perhaps the country's, best team, Stanford. His friends, his family, perhaps even his mother and father would hear his name on the radio, just as he had heard Johnny Mack Brown's. All Alabama had to do was win one more game.

"I remember how cold chills ran up my back, and still do," Bryant recalled for journalist Al Browning, "when I think about a telegram our team received from Stanford before our regular season game with Vanderbilt. The telegram said, 'If you win decisively, where can we reach you after the game?'"[20] Everyone noticed the "decisively" and knew what it meant. It would be enough for a team from the East or Midwest to simply win. A team from the South still had to prove something to the rest of the country. Alabama had to win *decisively*.

Mel Allen recalled that "Paul Bryant was on the field almost the entire game, and I don't think he let up for a single play, including the punt coverages where he was really terrifying to watch. He was running down the field like a demon and flinging himself through Vanderbilt's blockers and on into the guy with the ball."

Late in the fourth quarter, Thomas, not wanting to risk injury to his best players before the most important game of their lives, sent in a substitute for Bryant. As Paul came off the field, the Alabama band was playing "California Here I Come." Alabama beat Vanderbilt, 34–0.

THE TRIP to Pasadena just before Christmas of 1934 was a circus, with the boys singing fight songs and playing cards the entire journey. Along the rail lines, they could see families, dispossessed farmers as if out of the pages of Steinbeck, making their way west in rickety cars and trucks and even on horse-drawn wagons. Before they lost their farms, most of these Dust Bowl victims had been no worse off than some of the players' own families.

The boys inside the passenger cars did not brood over the fate of the Okies. They themselves were lucky, and they knew it. One of Bryant's strongest memories was all the free food. To impress the newspaper people, all the players were decked out in new suits, most of them paid for by grateful alumni. "I think Coach Hank was the man who distributed the money and bought the suits," said Mel Allen. "The truth of the matter is that most of our boys couldn't afford suits—this was in the heart of the Depression, but I doubt if most of them could have afforded suits anyway—and after all of that 'swamp boy stuff' the California papers had written about us in earlier years, nobody wanted Alabama players to go out there and look like a bunch of hillbillies." Jim Whatley, a tackle, recalled that some of the team carried their clothes in paper bags. (Whatley's only suit was sold to him at a discount by Coach Thomas.)[21]

When the train stopped in Houston, Bryant had a reunion with some old pals. In an article for the *Tuscaloosa News* published in 1971, he recalled that in the summer of 1934,

> I worked for a redneck driller, a big guy named Big Boy Williams. . . . I worked hard and Big Boy kind of liked me, I guess. Hutson [Don] and I were playing baseball on the side for extra money, but I got fired from my baseball job. I was trying to con my way through, but I just couldn't play. . . . Big Boy kept me on the oil field job, though.
>
> I remember telling him that I wasn't much of a baseball player, but we [the Alabama football team] were going to the Rose Bowl that year, and I would see him then.
>
> Sure enough, we stopped in Houston about 7 o'clock in the morning, and it was a big thrill for me when I stepped off the train and there was Big Boy and some of my old oil field buddies.[22]

In New Mexico, Johnny Mack Brown boarded the train, armed with scouting reports on Stanford that he had been compiling between movie shoots.

Thomas did his best to keep his team focused on the upcoming game. It was an uphill struggle. With Bryant, though, he knew exactly which button to push. On the train ride, Paul walked into the men's lounge and found Coach Tommy seated with some sportswriters and Louisiana State's athletic director, Red Heard. "Red," he said in a voice loud enough for everyone in the car to hear, "this is my best football player. This is the best player on my team." Bryant did not hold so high an opinion of his football ability to even begin to believe that he was a better player than Howell or Hutson or, to be realistic, half a dozen other players on the 1934 Crimson Tide. Even at that age, he could see that Thomas was using psychology on him, exactly the kind of psychology that he would someday use on many of his players.

And it worked. "He was getting me ready," Bryant told John Underwood, "and I was, too. I would have gone out there and killed myself for Alabama that day."

In Tucson, Thomas stopped the train for a practice and had his players sucking wind from running wind sprints in the thin desert air.

The train was met in Pasadena by a swarm of dignitaries and press. The latter included a now-Alabama-wise Grantland Rice and a cub reporter, Ronald Reagan, who fawned over Frank Thomas for interviews. So many celebrities were at the Alabama practices that Hank Crisp complained that his receivers couldn't run pass patterns. He got so angry with the press he offered his receivers a two-dollar bounty for the first man who knocked one of them down. Needless to say, Bryant was not about to pass up that opportunity. He began his long relationship with the sports media by knocking one of its members senseless on a long pass reception. That night, Dixie Howell, who had thrown Bryant the pass, asked to share the reward. Bryant refused. The next day, Howell refused to throw him a pass. Bryant forked over the buck after practice.

Bryant saw movie stars everywhere. Dick Powell, from the tiny town of Mountain View, Arkansas, had his picture taken with Bryant, Hutson, Charlie Marr, and the other Arkansas boys. Jack Oakie and Mickey Rooney also showed up for photo opportunities with the players. The popular cowboy star Tom Mix brought a pal by to shake hands with Bryant; the pal was a former Southern Cal lineman, Marion Michael Morrison. (Apparently, in the flesh, the young John Wayne made no impression on Paul Bryant, or at least none was recorded.) Distractions abounded. One, he said, was a starlet named Lana Turner. She asked Paul what his plans were. He had no plans— "The only place I could have taken her was to church because I was broke again." Paul did indeed flirt with starlets on that trip, but none of them was Julia Jean Turner, who would have been either thirteen or fourteen, depending on your source, when Alabama came to play in the Rose Bowl late in 1934. Bryant was confusing the trip with the one he would make as an assistant coach for Alabama in 1937, when he did have his picture taken with Lana Turner.

Thomas slapped a hard curfew on the team, but for one boy from Moro Bottom, Sunset Strip was too much of a lure. One night he not only missed curfew but also nearly missed sunrise. The following afternoon, Coach Hank called a few of the worst offenders together and told them that Thomas was on the verge of sending them home. Paul nearly broke down at the thought of losing his dream. He recalled his automobile ride with Thomas in Tuscaloosa and knew that he would be lucky to get a last chance. No more craps, he vowed, and no more Sunset Strip. From that moment to the end of the game he would be all football.

It's highly doubtful that Thomas would have given Bryant or anyone else such a second chance had he known about their escapades. As it turned out, Coach Hank invented the story about Thomas threatening to send them home; in fact, Crisp hadn't known about the broken curfew himself. He just wasn't going to take any chances. The whole experience stood Bryant well decades later when he was confronted with the behavior of Joe Namath and Kenny Stabler.

The diversions seemed to be beyond even Thomas's ability to control. There were press luncheons and interviews with more questions than any of the Alabama players had ever heard before. Paul, for one, didn't mind; he loved every minute of it. He was more bothered by his failure to sell his game tickets. Back then, each player was given several tickets to dispose of as he chose; some doled them out to family members and sold the rest for "walking-around money." But the Rose Bowl seated more than eighty-four-thousand people—approximately seventy-two thousand more than the Crimson Tide was accustomed to playing for in Tuscaloosa—and this was the Depression, so selling them for their five-dollar face value wasn't easy. On the bus to the Rose Bowl, Coach Tommy overheard one of the boys heckling Bryant over getting stuck with tickets. He took the tickets from Paul and handed them to an Alabama cop who traveled with the team with the orders, "Sell 'em for him," which the cop proceeded to do.

Paul, however, had a distraction that even Thomas couldn't help him with. In fact, he dared not tell the coach. He had asked two girls—Mary Harmon Black, a coed from Alabama, and Barbara Dell Simmons from Pine Bluff—to be his "sponsor." (He never specified who he asked first.) Each player picked his own sponsor, from which a select group of sponsors was chosen to attend the coin toss at midfield. (The practice was quite common in southern colleges at that time; Miss Simmons had been Bryant's sponsor for the Alabama-Kentucky game in Lexington that season.) Paul wrote to Barbara Dell's father asking for his permission for Barbara to attend, but hadn't heard back. About a month earlier, he had asked Miss Black, whom he had dated a couple of times, but apparently he expected to be turned down, or, as he phrased it, Mary Harmon "was so popular I had to spread myself around a little just to keep the scales balanced." But Mary Harmon said yes, and she won the sponsor's vote easily. The day of the game, without warning, Barbara Dell Simmons showed up. Things didn't turn out badly, as there were enough Arkansas boys around to keep Barbara Dell occupied. Jimmy Harland, he of the poolroom recruiting connection, was a friend of Barbara's dad and was furious with Paul. It was forty years, Bryant claimed, before Barbara Dell spoke to him again.

New Year's Day, January 1, 1935, would see the birth of the second college bowl game, the Sugar Bowl, but it would be a long while before it achieved anywhere near the status of the Rose Bowl. For all intents and purposes, the Rose Bowl was the second-biggest sporting event in the United States, behind only the World Series—some called it the biggest single day in American sports. "The only way to think about the Rose Bowl back then," says sports historian Bert Randolph Sugar, whose book, *The SEC*, chronicles the history of the conference through 1978, "is to see it as the Super Bowl of the Depression era, with college boys instead of seasoned professionals."

For Bryant and the rest of the Alabama players, the game itself, after weeks of buildup, came as a relief. They approached the game with indignation, feeling that they had been made to "audition" with an extra impressive win over Vanderbilt just to prove they were worthy. They became more indignant in the days before the game when they read they were solid underdogs—some betting lines had Stanford favored by double figures. California sportswriters, blithely disregarding the achievements of Wallace Wade's Alabama teams, openly voiced their contempt for the visitors, stating that the game would be much more competitive had the Rose Bowl Committee invited Minnesota.

The Alabama players probably let themselves get too worked up. Early in the game, Alabama fumbled the ball. Stanford recovered and scored a touchdown for a quick lead. It was the equivalent of a first-round knockdown in a heavyweight championship match. As it turned out, Stanford's touchdown simply knocked the jitters out of the Tide players. As Will Rogers would later quip, that touchdown "just made Alabama mad. It was like holding up a picture of Sherman's March to the Sea."[23] The Tide immediately roared back, scoring 22 points in the second quarter and gaining 256 yards, 150 of them through the air.

One play in particular seemed to define the game for Alabama. Dixie Howell had been bothered the morning of the game with stomach cramps. Thomas substituted a boy named Joe Riley, who wasn't supposed to be nearly as good a passer as Howell. Thomas sent Don Hutson into the game to tell Riley that he wanted him to call a running play; Hutson was to communicate this with sign language, as there was a rule at the time that forbade a substitute entering the game from speaking to any of his team-mates for one play. Riley had not played with Hutson enough to under-stand the sign language and naturally assumed that Hutson was in because Thomas wanted a pass play. To his coach's consternation, he dropped back to throw the ball. Hutson streaked past the Stanford defender, caught the ball in stride at the fourteen-yard line, and glided into the end zone to complete a fifty-yard touchdown pass.

Hutson caught four of Howell's passes, two for touchdowns, and Bryant caught three, one of them setting up a Hutson score. Alabama, after falling behind in the first quarter, won with remarkable ease, 29–13. It was perhaps the most spectacular upset the Rose Bowl had seen up to that time, top-ping even Alabama's 1926 victory over Washington.

Sportswriters from the East, South, and West Coast wrote at the top of their voices, describing the magnificence of the Tide's performance. A West Coast sportswriter, Mark Kelly, wrote, "Open that page once more in the Book of Football Revelations and enter these names: Dorais to Rockne, Wyman to Bastian, Friedman to Osterbaan, add those of Howell to Hutson. And let the last stay in capital letters because it should top the list of two-men combinations in football to make history."[24] A Los Angeles sportswriter, Bill Henry, thought it should have been a three-man combination: "Like arrows from Robin Hood's trusty bow, there shot from Howell's unerring hand a stream of passes the like of which had never been seen in football here on the Coast. Zing, zing, zing. They whizzed through the air and found their mark in the massive paws of Hutson and Bryant, 'Bama ends."[25] Grantland Rice called Howell "the human howitzer from Hartford, Alabama," who "blasted the Rose Bowl dreams of Stanford today with one of the greatest all-around exhibitions football has ever known."

Bryant's only worry came late in the game when he looked down on the ground and saw a small fortune in half dollars, quarters, and dimes—it was the middle of the Depression, and the California fans were throwing change on the field, presumably as a tribute to an underdog Alabama team that had once again whipped the West Coast's best. But whether the gesture was meant as a tribute or insult to the young southerners was irrelevant to them. Bryant scooped up the money as fast as he could, but before he could get it to the bench, Stanford ran a play his way and he was forced to drop it to make a tackle. That and not having enough money to ask Lana Turner out were the only disappointments of the trip.

Having won the 1934 national championship, Alabama happily shared the number-one position with Minnesota. The issue of which team was better would become the topic for much good-natured arguing between Paul Bryant and another great coach who had starred for the 1934 Golden Gophers, Bud Wilkinson.

MARY HARMON Black, the girl who got to be Paul's sponsor at the Rose Bowl, was not, as many would later say, from a wealthy family. The Blacks were well off, and for a boy from Paul Bryant's background, "well off" meant, in the words of his cousin Dean, walking in tall cotton, particularly during the Depression. One might uncharitably suspect Paul of social climbing in his courtship of her, but in truth, given the poverty of his background, almost any girl would have been above his social class. Bryant remembered her as being "just about everything a girl could be at Alabama in those days. Miss U-A, a Cadet colonel, the sweetheart of one thing or another. You name it, she was it. Plus that she was the best-looking gal you or I have ever laid eyes on." And that wasn't all: she had an automobile.*

Paul wasn't everything a boy could be at Alabama, but for a kid who started out on a truck farm in Moro Bottom, he hadn't done badly for himself. He had been voted president of his class in both his freshman and junior years—"Not so much because he was popular," said Mel Allen, "but because he was respected." As a senior, he was president of the varsity letter club; he had been elected to the national honorary men's leadership society, the Omicron Delta Kappa. And, of course, he was a football player, a member of that fabulous 1934 national championship team that had capti-

---

* Mel Allen recalled that in the mid-1930s it was possible to "walk from class to class all day and not see an automobile. When somebody drove a car on campus, everybody would stop to gawk."

vated all of Alabama and much of the nation. It's hard to imagine that a boy from his background could have done much better.

They met the Monday after the Sewanee game in 1934, the one Paul started on the bench because he was in Coach Tommy's doghouse. She spoke to him first, or so he said: "How are you feeling, Paul?" (Her stepfather had taken her to the game, and she saw him limping around on the sidelines.) He knew her, or at least, knew of her. He was surprised that she knew who he was; he would not have been had a song recorded in 1935 been released a year earlier. Hugely popular on college campuses, "You Gotta Be a Football Hero," by Al Sherman, Buddy Fields, and Al Lewis, stated in no uncertain terms that you had to be a football hero to be popular with girls.★ Paul Bryant certainly wasn't rich, but he was handsome, and he was a very good football player. More than that, he loved his mother and he seemed quite serious about bettering his position in life. Up to the time she met Paul, Mary Harmon had, with little enthusiasm, dated a few of the frat-house boys who doted on her; she was about to trade up. A couple of years earlier Paul Bryant would have been well out of Mary Harmon's league. Now, emboldened by his football success, he took his best shot. He asked her for a date; she took out her date book and thumbed through it. "How about January twenty-third?" she said. "I didn't need a calendar to know what that meant," Paul recalled. "I got my back up. 'Shoot, honey, I'm talking about tonight,' and walked away." (This must have been true or he wouldn't dare have said it in his autobiography.) Later that day she called him on the only phone at the gym where he was living, the phone in the coach's office, and told him she was free that night.

IF HIS performance in the 1934 Tennessee game was worth forty dollars, Bryant's contribution to Alabama's 1935 victory over the Volunteers was priceless. The Tide was coming off two disappointing games in three weeks, a shocking 7–7 opening tie with Howard University and a 20–7 trouncing by Mississippi State in week three. Bryant had cracked a fibula in that loss and was ruled unavailable for the Tide's biggest game of the year.

★ To boost sales on campuses all over the country, the song was released with "Patter Choruses" with lyrics specific to Alabama, Army, California, Michigan, Notre Dame, Stanford, Tennessee, Yale, and other schools.

Paul was distraught at the prospect of missing the Tennessee game, but he found some consolation in the company of his Rose Bowl sponsor; he sat out the first and only practice of his college career on the front-porch swing of the sorority house, with Miss Black by his side and crutches on the floor. "I was so excited because Paul told me he would be able to escort me to a dance that weekend," she would remember. "We were a couple of love birds, something Coach Thomas didn't like much, so it was nice hearing I would be first in his life on a football weekend."[26] Indeed, Coach Tommy did not care for the "love bird" stuff and would have been furious had he known the real situation between Paul and Mary Harmon. As for Mary Harmon, she was about to find out that on football weekends—this one and all the football weekends for the next forty-seven years—she would not be first in his life.

At the team meeting on Thursday, Thomas told Paul to travel to Knoxville with the team and get into uniform for moral support. This was Tennessee, Thomas told him, and the team needed all the help he could give.

"I was on crutches and had no idea I'd play against Tennessee," he recalled for Al Browning. "The night before the game, at the hotel in Knoxville, our team physician took off the cast. He said I'd be able to dress for the game, if nothing else, as Coach Thomas wanted. I was a yellowbelly. I asked him if there was any chance of the bone sticking out without the cast on it. He assured me that wouldn't happen."[27]

Thomas knew of Rockne's "Win One for the Gipper" speech. He knew that he couldn't get away with using something like that more than once, and that this was the time to try it. He also knew that he was not the man to deliver the speech, so Coach Hank Crisp delivered it for him. As rehearsed, when Coach Tommy finished his pregame talk, he asked Coach Hank if he had anything to say. He sure did. Cigarette dangling from his mouth, Crisp told the boys, "I'll tell you one thing. I don't know about the rest of you, you or you or you, but I know ol' Number 34 will be after them today."

At that moment, no one knew who "ol' Number 34" was. Alabama, like numerous college teams around the country, gave its players different jerseys almost every week, the purpose being to make a little extra money selling programs to identify them. (Hence, say some old-timers, the expression "You can't tell the players without a program.") It just so happened that at Alabama the man running the program franchise was Hank Crisp. Bryant, like all of the Alabama players, looked around to see who this tiger of a player might be; looking down at his own jersey, he saw the numerals 3 and 4.

Bryant remembered getting goose bumps twice during his playing career. The first time was before the Vanderbilt game, when the Stanford invitation to the Rose Bowl was announced. The second was before the 1935 Tennessee game, when he realized he was the man Crisp was talking about. He was amazed. When he looked up, his coaches and all his teammates were looking at him. Then Coach Thomas said, "Bryant, can you play?" *Could he play?* On Alabama's first possession, Bryant caught a pass, a couple of defenders collided, and he rambled for a first down. A couple of downs later, Alabama ran the same play. Bryant caught the ball, then, as he was about to be tackled, lateraled to running back Riley Smith, who ran for a touchdown. Those plays set the tone for the game; Alabama beat its archrivals 25–0, in the most satisfying victory, next to the Rose Bowl, of Bryant's playing years in college.★

Needless to say, Thomas and his staff made much of Paul and his broken leg to fire up the 'Bama supporters. Ralph McGill, the sports editor of the *Atlanta Constitution*, was skeptical. McGill, a future Pulitzer Prize winner, was no pushover for athletic department propaganda. Before the game he drove from Atlanta to Tuscaloosa, demanding to see the X-rays. Chastened, he apologized to Bryant, who was feeling properly humble: "It was just one little bone," Paul told him. (To which Red Drew snapped, "How many broken bones do you have to have to have a broken leg?") McGill wrote the story confirming that Bryant had played with a broken leg, and Paul got some national attention—"as far as the season is concerned, Paul Bryant is in first place in the courage league."[28] Who could forget a kid with the nickname of Bear who had played and won on a broken leg? When the Crimson Tide took the field against the Georgia Bulldogs in Athens that Saturday, the Georgia fans gave him a hand. Alabama won, 17–7.

★ Bryant may have had a bit of added incentive to play hard. Nearly forty years later, he admitted that the night before the game he and a few of his teammates pooled their change and bet a total of five dollars on the underdog Tide. "We made a killing, about a buck apiece," he confessed in *Bear*.

THERE IS a certain personality commonly found in sports, the type of person who is so driven that he never seems content. His life and career as player and coach appears as one, long, restless quest. In this respect, Paul Bryant stands apart from many of his coaching colleagues, men like Adolph Rupp, Woody Hayes, and Bobby Knight—men who seemed tormented and driven even in victory. Bryant was never one of these men. He often seemed exactly the opposite, amazed and humbled by his own success, deeply and thoroughly satisfied by being able to spend his life doing what he loved best.

In the fall of 1935, Paul Bryant had achieved more than he had ever thought possible ten years earlier on his family's farm in Moro Bottom. He had status, respectability, and a woman he loved. To say he was happy is to greatly understate the case. He didn't want more than this in life; he knew of nothing else to want. As Bryant approached the end of his college playing career, he had only one problem, but it was a major one—how could he hold on to everything he had won? He was good at football, but there were no realistic career options in the nascent pro game. And his five years in Tuscaloosa had not left him qualified for any other profession. One thing was certain: he had no intention of looking for work back in Fordyce.

As the end of the year approached, finding a career suddenly became more important than ever—Mary Harmon was pregnant.

Chapter 3

Coach
in Progress

What is this? It is a prolate spheroid, an elongated sphere in which the outer leather casing is drawn tightly over a somewhat rubber tubing. Better to have died as a small boy than to fumble this football.

—*John Heisman*[1]

BY THANKSGIVING OF 1935, the secret was pretty much out. What friends and family did not know—not even Paul's family and best friends and especially not his coach—was that Paul and Mary Harmon were already married. They had been married the previous June in the tiny town of Ozark, Alabama, slipping away to a justice of the peace to avoid her family and Frank Thomas.*

Mary Harmon was apparently afraid her family would not approve of the match, and with good reason; Paul had no means of support and no clear prospects, on top of which he was far removed from her social class. In truth, the Kilgores back in Fordyce would not even have qualified for

---

* Keith Dunnavant interviewed one of Bryant's best friends, Young Boozer, shortly before he died. Boozer claimed that some time in November of 1934 Bryant let it slip that he was married. "You're not married!" Boozer said. "The hell I'm not. I've got the deed to her!" Bryant responded and proceeded to produce a marriage license out of his truck. (*Coach*, p. 45)

entry into this prospering Birmingham family. The shock of her family when they read of the marriage in the local papers can only be imagined; in all likelihood, had Mary Harmon's birth father been alive, she probably would not have been bold enough to take such a step. But Mary Harmon, like Paul, had her mind made up. And she explained or apologized to no one.

For his part, Paul wasn't worried about the reaction of his family. He was worried about Frank Thomas. Thomas didn't want his players to be married—it interfered with their concentration on football. Paul did not think this unreasonable (he would take precisely the same stand when he became a head coach), but he wasn't about to take a chance on losing Mary Harmon. Even so, he was terrified of losing his job and his spot on the football team. Luckily, by the time Thomas found out, there were only a couple of games left in Paul's college football career. It was life beyond football he was now concerned with.

The problem was he had no definite idea of what life was like beyond football. He did not yet have his degree, and in fact he wouldn't get it until 1939, after working doggedly for it, spending three grueling years holding a full-time job and taking night classes.

The National Football League might have been an option, but outside of his friend Don Hutson and a handful of others such as Red Grange and Bronko Nagurski (all three players were household names in college), no one made much of a living in the NFL. Pro football in the 1930s still ran a poor second in popularity to Major League Baseball, although baseball hardly presented a fortune then to anyone but the great stars. Amos Alonzo Stagg, when he heard the rumor that Nagurski was thinking of playing pro football, said, "Football is not a game you should get paid for." Though Bryant would later claim he was not good enough for pro ball—which was nonsense, since he surely would have been one of the top college prospects in the early years of the pro game and, in fact, had several offers, including one from a Brooklyn team for which two of his Alabama teammates were already playing, earning the eye-opening sum of $175 a game—the truth is that deep down he agreed with Stagg. A part of him always would. He wanted to stay with the college game.

No one knows at precisely what point Bryant began thinking about coaching. His cousin Collins remembered that on a visit home to Fordyce, Paul described his college experience as the best thing that ever happened to him. "'I'm learning things about football from Coach Thomas that I never dreamed.' Thomas, Paul said, would lecture the team one day and then the next day make the players go up to a chalkboard and explain what he said. Paul said almost everybody was scared to death that Coach Thomas was going to call on them and make them diagram plays and explain how they worked. But he said he loved being in that position because he knew the offenses and defenses from top to bottom."

Collins asked him if he had ever thought about coaching. "Yeah, Collins," Paul replied, "that's come to mind a few times." Collins did not remember what year the conversation took place, but it came at a time when Paul was concerned that the family might need him to come back to Fordyce and go to work. His cousin thought this would be a waste of his talent: "I told him it seemed to me his best bet to never have to farm again would be to learn all he could about football. That's the last time I remember hearing him saying anything about quitting the team."[2]

Bryant's work on the blackboards made an impression on Thomas. Though Paul was too insecure to realize it, two years before graduation his coach had spotted a future coaching talent and set about preparing him. In his junior year, Thomas took him to a football clinic at the College of the Ozarks, using him to demonstrate pass receiving and covering punts. ("You go down there and try to kill him.") During a lecture on blocking techniques Thomas had him suit up in full pads to block an Ozark player who was even bigger than Bryant. With Thomas calling signals just before the snap, Bryant shifted his weight and hit the bigger man at an angle, knocking him several yards into the defensive backfield, much to the astonishment of the Ozark coach. Thomas, much pleased, merely commented, "That'll be all, Bry-annt."

As it turned out, Bryant's fear about his coach's reaction to his marriage was unfounded. Thomas shrewdly perceived that a family would help his intended protégé focus more on football, not less. He began to take Paul with him on recruiting trips and to clinics. Bryant got his own private clinics sitting in the backseat of the car, listening to Coach Tommy and assistant coach Red Drew talk about football. On some trips they drove hundreds of miles, occasionally to see Thomas's family and friends back in Indiana. "The more I listened," he would recall in *Bear*, "the more I enjoyed it . . . every mile was a revelation." In Paul's senior year, Thomas recommended that he go to Union College in Jackson, Tennessee, and instruct them on the Alabama—which is to say the Notre Dame—offense. The Union coach, obviously feeling that Paul knew what he was talking about, left him alone to run the practices.

The experience did what Thomas probably intended it to do: it gave Bryant the confidence that he could coach at the college level. From the time he walked onto the high school football field in Fordyce, he had always been intimidated by coaches; they were educated men, at least by Paul's standards—Thomas himself had earned a law degree from Notre Dame—and he doubted he could ever measure up to those standards. He worked up the courage to ask Thomas's advice on playing pro football. Thomas's laconic reply was, "If your ambition is to coach, then coach." For Paul, that settled the issue.

During a recruiting trip for Union, Paul stopped in Tuscaloosa and went to a baseball game with Thomas, a fellow baseball enthusiast. While sitting in the bleachers, Thomas asked him casually if he would like to return to Alabama. Paul was reluctant; Union was paying him good money, and he thought that job might be able to develop into something more substantial. The thirty-odd dollars a month earned by a student assistant at Alabama wasn't going to support his family. But Thomas wanted him as a line coach for the varsity team. Did he want the job? Yes, he did. The salary was $1,250 a year plus housing and transportation, no small concern for a family man. Paul didn't haggle.

One thing that puzzled Paul was how quickly his coach began to warm up to him after his playing days were over. After nearly five years at Alabama and numerous hours on long-distance car trips, Bryant had scarcely had a personal conversation with his head coach. Now, all of a sudden, Thomas began to speak to him as if he were an adult, if not quite his equal. It was similar to what had happened between Paul and Coach Cowan at Fordyce High, though he wasn't quite mature enough to understand the pattern then. A coach and his players were on opposite sides of the line, a line that should not be crossed. When Bryant was no longer a student, he found that the line had vanished. (For the rest of his life, Bryant's relationships with his players would follow the pattern set by Frank Thomas.)

What Thomas had noticed about Paul was that he kept his mouth shut and listened, and when it came time to apply what he had heard, he proved he had paid attention. Bryant was about as unsophisticated as a college football player could be, but he was far from unintelligent, and he was eager to learn. He also had two other qualities that Thomas greatly admired: he loved football, particularly Alabama football, and he was loyal—loyal to Coach Hank Crisp, loyal to Coach Thomas, and loyal to the University of Alabama.

His own players were sometimes astonished in the change in their coach's attitude toward them after they left school. Billy Neighbors was one of Bryant's favorite players at Alabama, a consensus All-America for Bryant's first national championship team in 1961 and a standout in the NFL for eight seasons. He doesn't recall a single personal conversation with his coach all the time he was in school. "I don't think he said fifty words to me the whole time I was playing, except to tell me if I was doing something right or wrong, and I was too afraid of him to try to talk to him. When I was playing in the pros, he wrote me a couple of letters, but I didn't know what to say to him so I never wrote back."

In 1970, nine years after he left Alabama, Neighbors went to Tuscaloosa to see a basketball game. As he walked underneath Bryant's office window, he heard a voice call out, "'Why Billy Neighbors, you're back on campus and you didn't come by to see me?' I thought to myself, 'What in hell is this about?' It was Coach. He called me up to his office, pulled a bottle out of a drawer, poured me a drink, and rattled off a list of things he'd heard about me and games he'd seen me play in on TV. All of a sudden, after ten years, we were instant friends, and I stayed in touch with him for the rest of his life."

FRANK THOMAS knew before anyone else, even Paul, that Bryant was a student of the game. There were other reasons, though, why Thomas took him on as a coach. What Bryant couldn't explain, he could demonstrate *physically*. Once a player got a first-person demonstration from Bryant on how to throw a block in an open field or cut down a pass rusher, he usually absorbed the lesson and did not need another—though he might need an icepack. Even at this point in his career there wasn't much that anyone could teach Bryant about line play; he was ready to do the teaching himself. But there was a great deal more to coaching than blocking and tackling. The most important thing he had to learn was recruiting. In this area, too, Thomas had calculated correctly. Bryant was a natural recruiter. Later, he would come to hate recruiting, but when he was starting out, it was his greatest asset as a coach, and he knew it.

One recruiting trip took Bryant to a West Virginia military school. When he arrived in town, he found out his prospect had left for home. Discouraged and disgusted, Bryant decided to call it quits and head back to Tuscaloosa. Then he remembered something Coach Thomas had told him: coaching is 90 percent material—that is, the ability of the players—and 10 percent coaching. Bryant had heard Thomas say that he did not necessarily agree with those proportions, but that was the way many regarded it, and so recruiting talent was an integral part of the game. Bryant had no way of knowing that his coach's adage had been passed on from Alabama president Mike Denny, but that was beside the point; Paul knew the importance that Coach Thomas placed on recruiting and that's what was important. He decided to pursue this prospect as hard as he could.

He kept going, driving directly to the boy's home. Immediately perceiving that the boy's mother had trepidations about sending her son so far from home, Bryant told her that he understood perfectly, that his mother had had precisely the same fears when he left Arkansas, and that Coach Hank had taken care of him, had driven him to Tuscaloosa, seen that he was settled, and got him started. Her son would be joining a great tradition, he assured her, one headed by a fine president and a coach who would see to it that her boy went to class and maintained his grades. He would help see to that himself. It was a speech Bryant would repeat with only slight variations for the next forty years, and one his assistants would learn from him. It was convincing in part because Bryant was desperate; but he also believed it. The boy's parents said yes. Bryant took no chances on losing his recruit to another school; he had the kid pack up and leave with him that night, driving straight through, rolling the car window down so the cold night air would keep him from dozing off. He had the kid in Thomas's office the next morning, before the coach got in, then left word he was going home to sleep. Thomas, who had not realized Bryant was away, caught him walking out the door and was indignant. "What the hell do you mean, sleep?" Bryant went back to work, trying to look busy. In the afternoon, Crisp told Thomas about Bryant's successful recruiting trip. "Bry-annt, pal," he called from his office. "Nice going. You better go home and get some sleep."

Bryant was willing to do whatever it took to reel in a prospect. In later years, he would expect his assistant coaches to do the same. Twenty-five years after Bryant's soon legendary ride from West Virginia, one of his most able assistants, Howard Schnellenberger, would go him one better, traveling farther and faster than Bryant had to land perhaps the greatest prospect in Alabama history. On another famous recruiting trip, he and Red Drew went to a junior college in Arkansas to try and talk a boy named Sandy Sanford out of playing for the state university. Finally, Drew gave up and went back to the hotel. Halfway to the hotel, Bryant decided, just as he had in West Virginia, that he would not be deterred. He turned around and drove back to the college. Sanford had gone out. Bryant sat in the car for a while, turning the dial on his radio. He sat in the dark, smoked, and waited. About two in the morning, his prospect returned. It took Bryant about ninety minutes to talk him into playing for Alabama. To cement his case and keep Arkansas recruiters from getting to Sanford, Bryant went beyond the call of duty: he helped Sanford with his math homework, though the precise amount of help he was able to offer was dubious. In the morning, they jumped in a car and headed for Dono, Arkansas, to talk to Sanford's parents.

Between Little Rock and Memphis, assistant coach and recruit had an adventure. They were caught in a rainstorm, and water spilled over from Arkansas's White River into the car's floorboards. The vehicle went dead, and Bryant and Sanford had to push it to higher ground. ("It was cold," Bryant recalled, "as a well digger's ass.") Finally, they gave up on trying to get to Dono and headed back to Russellville and the junior college, where Drew was shocked to find that Bryant had bagged Sanford after all. Bryant's extra efforts paid off handsomely. Sanford's field goals were the margin of victory over Tulane and Vanderbilt, Alabama's two closest games of the 1937 season. Quite possibly if Bryant hadn't decided to go back again and make another try for Sanford, Alabama wouldn't have been invited to the Rose Bowl that season.

Usually, Bryant felt, there was no trick to recruiting, just persistence and salesmanship. He was good at it, but he didn't like it because "the boy ought to go where he pleases, and he shouldn't have a bunch of slick-talking salesmen influencing his life or selling him on something he doesn't want." Nonetheless, if Paul Bryant didn't slick-talk a boy—hinting that the boy was certain to get all the playing time he wanted or that alumni would be showering him with gifts—as other recruiters did, Bryant learned at least to outslick the competition. It was understood that blue-chip prospects at the time would be getting some remuneration in the form of cash, free meals, and possibly even cars. But smart coaches like Bryant never upped the ante, they simply let their prospects know in the subtlest way possible that the offers from other schools would be matched. He would tell the boy—and, of course, his mama and papa, but especially his mama— of the long-term benefits of sacrifice and loyalty and applying them to a great tradition. Bryant's primary appeal was to the boy's better side, and if he didn't have a better side, Bryant didn't mind losing him.

Later, when Bryant was at the University of Kentucky, Notre Dame's fiery head coach Frank Leahy accused him of dressing up an assistant in a priest's outfit to influence a prospect named Gene Donaldson. Interestingly enough, Bryant not only didn't deny it, he seemed to relish the story. "Shucks, I'da told him Murphy [an assistant] was Pope Pius if I thought we could get Donaldson that way."[3] If the priest story was true—and Bryant never said it was or wasn't—he didn't regard it as stepping over a line. "Murphy *was* a Catholic," he pointed out, "so we weren't far off. And I believe his brother was a priest."

It wasn't enough, of course, to be good at bringing home prospects; one had to be equally proficient at keeping other schools from grabbing them. Bryant became an expert in finding ways to "hide boys out," taking prospects off on a boating or hunting trip or simply on a long car trip so they couldn't even be contacted by their parents (who, after all, were susceptible themselves to pressures from college recruiters and might try to sway their sons' mind and heart back to another school).

Bryant became a master at "raiding"—the practice of stealing another university's football players, which was still common in the 1930s. Basically it involved talking a kid into a car and driving him to a college where he was expected to play football. The distinctions between this and kidnapping were not always clear, and it was common practice for colleges to raid each other. It happened to Alabama, it happened to schools all over the country, and it was as old as football itself.

Pudge Heffelfinger thought that the most notorious offender before World War I was the United States Military Academy. "Army football teams," he wrote, "were loaded with huskies who had played well and in some cases four years on major college teams."[4] One great Army star, Elmer Oliphant, who would one day be elected to the College Football Hall of Fame, starred at Purdue before coming to West Point in 1914 and went on to make Walter Camp's 1916 All-America team. The legendary John V. McNally, also known as Johnny Blood, admitted to playing at four schools, and some of his teammates speculated that he played for as many as six or even seven—and that included Notre Dame, which kicked him out for playing semipro ball.

Early in his coaching career Bryant began making enemies, not because he broke the rules, but because he was better at breaking them than anyone else. One of his most daring raids was the theft—"in the dead of night," as Bryant phrased it—of three players who were considered the property of the dreaded General Neyland at Tennessee. Raiding any football program could be tough, but choosing to encroach on the general's territory meant all-out war. Thomas knew that attempting to steal a Neyland player would result in a scorched-earth policy, but he also knew that Neyland had no compunctions about raiding Alabama. He dispatched his best man on a mission to Neyland's lair in Knoxville—he sent Bryant. As if in a Hitchcock spy movie, Bryant had his instructions: if caught, he would deny Thomas or the Alabama athletic department had any knowledge of his actions. The mission was a success. Bryant brought back his men, but noted with some irritation that the Tennessee lads "were the eatingest sonsabitches I ever saw. We couldn't drive past a restaurant without them wanting something."

THE TWO sirens whose songs appealed the most to Paul Bryant throughout the first twenty-five years of his coaching career were professional football and California. It's hard to know how real the attraction to pro football was; it's clear that college football was always his first love, and it seems as if the only times he truly considered going pro were when things weren't going right with his college career. California was another matter. On the Rose Bowl trip three years earlier he had fallen in love with California and had often fantasized about getting a coaching job there. Not just California, but Southern California, and not just Southern California, but Hollywood.

The Crimson Tide of 1937 was very nearly one of the school's all-time greats, finishing the regular season unbeaten and outscoring its opposition 225–33 (including a 14–7 victory over Tennessee). The team earned a Rose Bowl bid and once again, before the Christmas holidays, boarded a train to

Southern California. For the only time in his career, Bryant was distracted from football.

The Los Angeles area in 1937, with its palm tree–lined boulevards, Art Deco and Spanish stucco buildings, and smogless skies, was a lovely and seductive place, decades away from Disneyfication and the invasion of strip malls and franchise fast-food restaurants. Much more than today, Hollywood was where the films were made and the big movie stars lived. Americans of all ages regularly traveled there to see Fred Astaire, Bing Crosby, Humphrey Bogart, Joan Crawford, Gary Cooper, Bette Davis, Errol Flynn, Cary Grant, Shirley Temple, the Marx Brothers, and many others, almost all of whom might be seen on a given day on the streets or at a restaurant. (The team visited the set of *The Adventures of Robin Hood*, where they were photographed with a smiling Errol Flynn and director Michael Curtiz.)

It shouldn't be surprising that a poor boy from a small town in the South would dream of getting his big break in Hollywood. After all, John Wayne was born in Winterset, Iowa; Henry Fonda, in Grand Island, Nebraska; James Stewart, in Indiana, Pennsylvania; and Dick Powell in Mountain View, Arkansas, a town smaller than Fordyce. Somewhere along the line, they all had a connection to the movie business, and as it turned out, Paul Bryant had one too. Early in 1938, he came close to consummating his fantasy.

At a time when baseball and college football were the only major team sports in America, Southern California didn't even have a major league baseball team. Hence, football heroes were accorded special status. Paul's head was turned in part by celebrities' fawning over *him*. Back then, movie stars were regularly photographed at college football games the way Jack Nicholson is at Los Angeles Lakers games today. (The agent for Red Sanders, the UCLA football coach who would be Bryant's boss at Vanderbilt, also represented numerous movie actors and screenwriters.) Paul wasn't a celebrity on the order of Johnny Mack Brown, Bryant's and Alabama's first football idol, but he was surprised and flattered by how many actors knew of his triumphs at Alabama.

Johnny Mack Brown escorted Paul and Mary Harmon around the hot spots of Hollywood. On one of their jaunts, Paul connected with someone who arranged a screen test for him at Paramount Studios. Bryant never revealed who got him the screen test, but there is a very good chance it was Dorothy Lamour, the dark-eyed beauty famous for wearing sarongs in the

Bing Crosby–Bob Hope "Road" pictures. Dorothy, a Louisiana girl whose father had graduated from the University of Alabama, had several old friends whom Bryant knew well.

On the day of the screen test, Coach Thomas had scheduled a trip to the Santa Anita racetrack for the coaches and players. Bryant made an excuse and took a taxi to Hollywood without anyone, not even Mary Harmon, knowing. While the rest of the Alabama contingent was betting on horses, Bryant had lunch with Lamour and Ray Milland and then went to the studio, reading some lines with Buster Crabbe, yet another athlete who had parlayed sports into a Hollywood career, and Mary Carlisle, a starlet who played ingénue roles. The secret was blown when a reporter for the Alabama student paper and a gaggle of Alabama coeds on a studio tour peeked through the door and squealed with glee upon recognizing Bear. Paul was nailed; by the time he got back to the hotel, everyone, including Mary Harmon, knew where he had been and what he had been doing. The other coaches ribbed him. Mary Harmon, who had no intention of relocating to California, was furious.

Bryant always recalled his screen test with a mixture of pride and sheepishness: "I knew then, too, that they were trying to make a silk purse out of a sow's ear. They couldn't have cured my mumbling drawl if they'd given me $65 a minute." Actually the idea was not so ludicrous—his drawl was no less thick than Johnny Mack Brown's, and he was just as good looking. Many thought he resembled the character actor Forrest Tucker, who some in California mistook Bryant for and who later became a pal of his.

Bryant was chasing a dream and wanted to see how far he could take it. Just as he would later with pro football, he pursued it as far as an offer—an agent offered him a contract of sixty-five dollars a week, twice what Alabama was paying him—and then backed down. "It was clear to me, as it had always been, that there weren't going to be any short cuts, that I was going to have to work darned hard to be a success at anything."

Alabama didn't lose an assistant coach on the trip, but they did lose the game, to the University of California, 13–0, their only Rose Bowl defeat.

FOOTBALL WAS the only thing Paul Bryant was ever a success at, and football alone never made him a rich man. (Not until his son took over the management of his outside business interests late in his life could he be called wealthy.) On his own, Bryant wasn't much of a businessman. By the time he turned twenty-five, he had made forays into making illegal home brew, managing a black nightclub band, and running a laundry on the Alabama campus. All were minor disasters.

The laundry escapade occurred after the 1937 football season. The entire fiasco can't be laid at the feet of Paul Bryant; Don Hutson, visiting the Alabama campus during his offseason with the Green Bay Packers, was also in on it. Bryant borrowed a thousand dollars for his share, and the two bought a laundry called Captain Kidd's Cleaners, with Hutson's wife as the bookkeeper. The idea was for Coach Hank to funnel business their way, such as a contract for cleaning the team's uniforms. After a victory over Southern Cal in the first game of the 1938 season, the team's new uniforms were sent to Captain Kidd's. Neither Bryant nor Hutson nor their employees really knew much about the craft of laundering, and the uniforms shrunk drastically. ("They looked like doll clothes," said Bryant.) For old time's sake, Coach Hank covered for them and got the team new uniforms. Then, on ROTC (Reserve Officer Training Corps) Day, with the governor about to arrive, Bryant and Hutson dropped by the shop to find stacks of dirty cadet uniforms and a battalion of angry cadets. He remembered in *Bear*, "We served 'em one at a time. Like short order cooks. . . . 'Here, son, try this on. Oh, yes it fits perfect. Perfect fit. You look good. Okay. Next.'"[5]

The problem was obvious. Paul Bryant could never muster the concentration and hence the discipline in his business activities that he could for football. After two years of barely breaking even, Bryant and Hutson sold the place. If they had had to pay for everything they had ruined, Bryant thought, they would have gone to jail.*

---

* Captain Kidd's Cleaners handled more than just team uniforms. Bryant claimed that, through Mary Harmon, all the sorority girls were out drumming up business for them, but Bob Morris, who was at the University of Alabama in the mid-1930s and met my wife at Chicago Bridge & Iron in Birmingham forty years later, claimed that the whole operation was run more like the Mafia. "Bryant and Hutson's friends were everywhere and had prominent positions in several of the social clubs. If you brought your business to another laundry or even, as in my case, you did it yourself, you could wind up ostracized."

———

BRYANT WAS the youngest of Frank Thomas's assistants, and though the thought was now in his head that he could someday be head coach at Alabama, he knew he'd have to prove himself at another school first. After four years under his mentor, he would say he was ready to try his wings, but the truth is he was frustrated.

Early in 1940, Vanderbilt's new head coach, Red Sanders, was looking for a number-one assistant. Mississippi State assistant coach Murray War-math, who would one day win a national championship at the University of Minnesota, had already turned him down. An earlier biographer claims that Sanders had never heard of Bryant before getting a recommendation from Nashville sportswriter Fred Russell. Bryant did claim to have become pals with Russell at the 1938 Rose Bowl and that Russell recommended him for the job, but as with most of the accounts of Bryant's brief stay at Vanderbilt, none of this makes much sense.

By 1940, Paul Bryant had been a second-team all–Southeastern Conference player and had starred on perhaps the greatest team ever in southern football, the 1934 Crimson Tide national champions. He'd been to the Rose Bowl and made newspaper headlines all across the South for having played a game with a broken leg. He was an assistant to one of the most prominent football coaches in the country and had already developed a reputation on the southern football circuit as an aggressive recruiter. It just doesn't seem possible that Sanders could not have heard of him or that he would need the recommendation of a sportswriter when he could have just as easily picked up a phone and asked Frank Thomas himself.

However the connection was made, Bryant eagerly accepted the job, which came with a substantial raise in pay. He tried to sound diplomatic when telling Mary Harmon, asking her if she would enjoy living in Nashville. She would not, and told him so in no uncertain terms. He told her he had already accepted the job. How strenuously Mary Harmon objected is not known; she knew she had signed on to be a football wife, and by 1940 there were few surprises that the life could have still held for her. Years later, she would laughingly tell a TV interviewer who asked if she really liked football, "Well, I like to eat."[6]

In his autobiography, Bryant had only glowing things to say about Sanders—later, when one of his own protégés, Steve Sloan, took the head coaching job at Vanderbilt, Bryant would insist that if anybody can bring Vanderbilt football back to Sanders's level, it was Sloan, surely a generous statement considering Sanders's six seasons at Vanderbilt, which produced a 36–22–2 record. (Sanders would have much more success at UCLA, where he would win 66 of 86 games over nine seasons.)

Sanders gave Bryant a lot of leeway. One of his responsibilities was team discipline, which meant making sure the players met the 10:30 curfew every night. Within a short time, he had the players terrified of him; they posted lookouts near the door to their dormitory who then alerted every room when Bryant approached. He not only knew that his movements were being watched, but also liked the idea that fear of him could clear the hallway. In a short time, the discipline problem on the Vanderbilt football team vanished. He was also there to recruit. "I recruited up a storm." He got an Arkansas boy, J. P. Moore, by winning over the boy's mom: "If the mother's for you, not much can be against you. I'd be in the back room eating cake while coaches from other schools were visiting in the living room."

Bryant, though, upset Sanders by wasting one of the school's valuable scholarships on a player recommended to him by J. P. Moore's brother. "Hell, Bear," Sanders told him, "anybody can look at that scrawny little runt and tell he ain't no football player." If that's true, one wonders how Bryant, who was presumably hired for his recruiting ability and who surely knew as much about college recruiting as Sanders (who came to Vanderbilt from a prep school), could not have known that before offering him a scholarship. Bryant would offer another explanation for why Sanders was displeased with him. In 1940, before a game with an unimposing Kentucky team, Sanders developed appendicitis and turned the game coaching over to Bryant. Paul was so nervous that the night before the game he lost his dinner. In the end he blamed himself for coaching a 7–0 victory over a mediocre Kentucky into a 7–7 tie. He was way too hard on himself. The Commodores, coming off a 2–7–1 season in 1939, were just 3–6 in 1940 without the tie, so there was no reason to assume that Vanderbilt should have beaten anybody.

It's not likely that Sanders, who had given the team a pregame inspirational speech via telephone hookup from his hospital room, was greatly upset about a tie from an emergency substitute coach. If he was really angry at Bryant, it wasn't because of the final score, but because of an incident that occurred late in the game. Bryant was so furious over an official's call that he began moving toward the referee, Bill McMasters. Bryant insisted he only wanted to have his say, but it didn't look that way to Kentucky's athletic director, Bernie Shiveley, who came up behind Vanderbilt's interim coach and put his arms around Bryant to restrain him. After he settled down, Paul said, "I couldn't have been more ashamed."★

Such a display of temper surely would have been embarrassing to a university that bills itself "The Harvard of the South." But it is unlikely that the brief flash of immaturity would have been held against Bryant, a twenty-seven-year-old assistant coaching his first game in a pinch. In any event, Bryant continued coaching at Vanderbilt for another season. Despite their record in 1940, the Commodores had shown definite signs of improvement, losing to Frank Thomas and Alabama by just 4 points, 25–21, in Birmingham. The following year, in Nashville, they scored one of the great upsets in Vanderbilt history, beating Thomas and Alabama 7–0. Surely much of the credit for that victory had to go to Bryant, who helped prepare their defense for Thomas's Notre Dame box offense. Bryant had also recruited several of the key players on that 1941 team. By the end of the season, the Commodores had posted an 8–2-0 record for a won-lost percentage of .800, one they would not match in a full season over the next sixty-two years. (During World War II, they played just nine games over two seasons.) Many Tennessee sportswriters regarded the 1941 squad as the best in Vanderbilt history.

Over the next two decades, Bryant would acquire a miracle-worker reputation for sharply turning around four college programs—Maryland, Kentucky, Texas A&M, and Alabama—but strangely he has never been given any credit for the turnaround at Vanderbilt. Without Bryant, Sanders and Vanderbilt slipped to 6–4 in 1942; from 1943 to 1945 Sanders was away in the service and returned in 1946, with a 5–4 mark. The season of 1948,

---

★ Thirteen years later, after Bryant coached Texas A&M to a Southwestern Conference title, he accepted a speaking engagement in St. Petersburg, Florida. To his horror, Bryant recognized the man who picked him up at the airport as the referee from the Vanderbilt-Kentucky game, Bill McMasters. McMasters invited Bryant to stay at his house and meet his family. After McMasters' family had retired to bed, the two men sat in the den talking football, and McMasters, with a laugh, said, "Say, Bear, you remember that Vanderbilt game when—." Bryant put up his hands in mock surrender and said, "I hoped you had forgotten!" In his autobiography, Bryant referred to McMasters as "a distinguished gentleman."

when the Commodores were 8–2–1, was Sanders only truly successful one without Bryant.

Despite the success of the 1941 team, Bryant never meshed with Sanders, and at the end of the season his contract was not renewed—surely one of the worst football decisions the school ever made. Bryant put all the blame for the failure on himself, though he never exactly said what it was he did wrong. No one connected with the 1941 Vanderbilt squad—not Sanders, not Bryant, not anyone—has ever elaborated on what went wrong between the head coach and his assistant. Some have suggested that it was a clash of egos, which is certainly plausible; the players awarded Bryant the game ball after the upset over Alabama, and the rumor mill had it that Sanders did not appreciate being upstaged.

The simplest explanation is the most likely: Paul Bryant was not cut out to be an assistant coach. The four years under Frank Thomas had prepared him for much more. Twenty-eight seems a little young for the job, but that's what they said about Knute Rockne when he accepted the head coaching job at Notre Dame in 1918 at age thirty.

THE UNIVERSITY of Arkansas concluded its 1941 football season by firing its head coach of thirteen years, Fred Thomson. When Bryant heard the news, he knew exactly what he wanted and exactly how to go about getting it.

Arkansas's biggest sports hero, Don Hutson not excepted, was Bill Dickey, the great catcher who, along with Joe DiMaggio, had helped the New York Yankees dominate baseball over the previous six seasons. An awestruck Bryant had been introduced to the future Hall of Famer by a friend of his family. When Bryant heard of Thomson's firing, he telephoned Dickey. As big a football fan as Bryant was a baseball fan, Bill Dickey knew Bryant's reputation and thought he would be a perfect mix with the state university. (Dickey was born in Bastrop, Louisiana, but made his home in Little Rock when he broke into professional baseball in 1926.) Dickey met with Governor Homer Adkins on Bryant's behalf, then personally escorted Paul to meet with the governor. After three trips, Bryant was convinced that the job was his.

In late 1941, America had finally come out of the Depression, and now it seemed a good time for an aggressive young man to rise in the world.

The future seemed limitless. On Sunday morning, December 7, Paul was headed back to Nashville to collect Mary Harmon and their daughter, Mae Martin. Casually, he flipped the radio dial hoping to hear either gospel music or Bob Wills and his Texas Playboys★ when he heard the announcement that the Japanese had bombed Pearl Harbor. The U.S. Navy would recover from the attack, but Arkansas football has not recovered to this day.

BRYANT DIDN'T wait for the government to act. The next morning, he kissed his wife and daughter and drove straight to Washington to enlist in the navy. He was a college graduate and had coached football at two major universities; that was enough to qualify him for a commission. Lieutenant Commander Paul Bryant was sent to a preflight school in Georgia and then to Norfolk, Virginia, to wait for his overseas assignment.

From Virginia, Paul flew to New York to join the troop ship USS *Uruguay*, which was heading for North Africa. It was Paul's first real chance to see the city (the Alabama football team had just one heavily chaperoned night to itself on the 1933 trip to play Fordham). From LaGuardia Field he went to the New Yorker Hotel, where he bumped into a friend from Alabama, who hailed him as a war hero. He would soon find, like thousands of young servicemen about to be shipped overseas, that there was a backslap and glad hand for him on every street in the city. Armed with introductions from Bill Dickey and Mel Allen, who by now had established himself as the radio voice of the Yankees, he went to Toots Shor's bar. That night, Shor took him on a tour of Manhattan nightlife.

During his three-and-a-half-year hitch with the navy, Bryant never saw

---

★ Bob Wills, a cigar-chomping bandleader, helped change country music in the 1930s and 1940s by combining big-band instruments with traditional country fiddles and steel guitars. His love for black jazz and blues made him something of a rebel in country music and for a while, at least, a pariah among the country establishment. Bryant first became a fan of Wills's music in the early 1930s when he and Don Hutson moonlighted as riggers in Texas oil fields.

Bryant talked to me about Wills in a 1982 interview for *Inside Sports*. I was reading a book about country music, *The Nashville Sound* by Paul Hemphill, at the time. Coach Bryant saw my copy, picked it up, looked at it, and said, "Nothing about Bob Wills in here. He was about my favorite."

combat, but he did see death. He enlisted in the navy without knowing he had a fear of sleeping in a ship's hold: The smell of sick men was bad enough, but there was also fear of a submarine attack, and if the ship was going down, he wanted to be up high. He befriended one of the *Uruguay*'s officers who had the night watch and got used to falling asleep on deck. As it turned out, it wasn't a German sub that got the *Uruguay*, but an American ship. While sailing to North Africa, the *Uruguay* was rammed by another troop ship in the convoy. Bryant, in the middle of a poker game, grabbed his canteen and gun—an automatic carbine, actually, the standard issue for navy officers stationed on land bases—and ran topside. There he found hundreds of terrified soldiers, "praying, and I was leading 'em." There was an order to abandon ship; Bryant thought it was premature and disobeyed, urging others to do the same. The ones who listened to him lived. Two hundred other soldiers and sailors died in the water.

There seems to be some confusion as to whether the *Uruguay* disaster occurred in 1942 on Bryant's first trip to North Africa or in 1943 on his second—for reasons unknown, in 1951 the Department of the Army destroyed all records of ships used to carry troops to their theaters of operations during World War II, and the incident wasn't publicized, as the War Department didn't want to make the crossing routes of troop ships known. Bryant gave the year as 1942 in *Bear*, which was repeated by at least two biographers. But one of his shipmates, Hudson Belcher, recalled the following: "February 12, 1943. It was real foggy and sort of cool outside. I'd been to bed about thirty minutes, I heard that whistle blow unusual, just a few seconds after that we got rammed."[7] The year is confirmed by the daughter of a sailor on the *Uruguay*. Barbara Matthews Wright posted on Guestpad.com, a Web site for sharing military experiences, "My father was on the U.S.S. *Uruguay*, which was rammed by a convoy tanker on February 12, 1943."

The disaster itself was remembered well enough by the men who were there. The *Uruguay* listed but did not go under. For three days and nights the ship bobbed in the Atlantic. "Nobody slept," said Bryant. "A German sub could have taken us with a pocket knife." A U.S. destroyer finally came along and took the survivors to Bermuda; from there they were shipped to Casablanca on a freighter loaded with ammunition, a voyage that gave him more sleepless nights than the first. He made friends with some gunnery officers, who let him stay on deck with them.

Bryant's year-and-a-half tour in Morocco was uneventful, most of it spent as "an errand boy, helping look after the Navy planes on patrol." "The country," he wrote in a letter home, "is about like north Fla., and most of the natives are Arabs. They don't shave, dress in robes, and ride little donkeys and camels. . . . Hope I am lucky enough to bring you a German scalp. In any event I shall give every effort to get the job done."[8]

Bryant wouldn't get close enough to any Germans to take any scalps. In the summer of 1944, shortly after the Normandy invasion, he was reassigned to the navy's preflight training school in North Carolina. The school was located at the university in Chapel Hill; cadets who were training as airmen took advantage of their time to enroll in numerous courses, and physical education was required. With little to do now that his tour of duty was winding down, Bryant immediately saw an opportunity to serve his country while getting a jump on what was sure to be a postwar football boom. He paid a visit to his commander, Admiral Tuttle. "He walked into my office," Tuttle recalled, "carrying a ten pound ham." He was wondering if all cadets-in-training stationed in northeastern schools with any football experience might be assigned to him at Chapel Hill. He didn't need the ham, Tuttle would say later. "I would have done it just because I liked him." But Tuttle kept the ham.

The 1944 North Carolina Navy Pre-Flight School football team, the Carolina Cloudbusters, never appeared on Bryant's coaching resume. Nor, in fact, did anyone think to add its victories to Bryant's total thirty-seven years later when he was approaching Amos Alonzo Stagg's record. Yet, the Duke football archives records that the proud Blue Devils lost to the Cloudbusters, 13–6, on October 7, 1944. Technically, the win was Paul Bryant's first as head coach, and it was enormously satisfying. It would have been even more satisfying had the great Wallace Wade, who would not return from the service until 1946, been coaching Duke. Bryant's squad certainly should have won, as he had several former All-Americas and NFL players on his roster, including Frankie Alberts, who had been an All-America at Stanford, and Otto Graham, the Northwestern star who would go on to win more championships than any quarterback in pro football history.

Bryant drove his players with a fury most of them had not seen from drill sergeants. "We all thought about quitting," said Joe Drach, who played offensive and defensive line for the Cloudbusters. "I mean, we just got beaten bloody every day, and no one said you had to play football to stay in pre-flight training." But to a man they stayed.

Now that he was the boss, Bryant began coaching football with the same desperation he had played it. Mary Harmon was pregnant with their second child—Paul Jr. would be born in December—and Paul had made his jump to head coaching. He had nothing to fall back on, and he had no intention of falling back.

IN 1932, while Paul Bryant was struggling with Spanish and math at Tuscaloosa High School, George Preston Marshall, one of the greatest influences on early-twentieth-century pro football, was fighting to hold his laundry business together during the Depression. Marshall was a man with a vision, and the vision had nothing to do with laundry. He could see a successful professional league emerging out of America's obsession with college football, and this at a time when college football was outdrawing pro football by more than five to one. When given an opportunity to buy into the new National Football League franchise, the Boston Braves (pro football teams back then often took the names of successful American and National League baseball teams), he jumped. After one season, the Braves had lost nearly fifty thousand dollars, and his two partners bailed, but Marshall stuck with it, moving the team to his hometown in Washington, D.C., in 1937 and renaming them the Redskins.

Marshall was one of the men who dragged the NFL into the modern era against the protests of its stodgier owners. It was Marshall who pushed for more liberal offensive rules, with emphasis on the passing game. In this respect, he did nearly as much for pro football as Walter Camp had done for the college game. With Marshall pushing hard, the era of the "fat ball" came to an end; a new slimmer football deemphasized the foot in favor of the arm, and within a few years, college football would follow suit. Marshall also came up with the idea of splitting the NFL into two divisions so a championship game could be played at the end of the season.★

★ Unfortunately, Marshall's progressive ideas stopped there. He was the man who spearheaded the color line in pro football. Blacks had been playing in the NFL since its first season, 1920, but Marshall told his fellow owners that blacks "are bad for business. They are bad for our image. What are out-of-work white people supposed to think when they

Perhaps his greatest contribution to pro football was bringing the flavor of the college game into it. His was the first NFL team to have a college-style marching band and cheerleaders, and he began a radio network that broadcast Redskins games throughout the South. Until the NFL expanded to Atlanta and New Orleans in the 1960s, the Washington Redskins remained the favorite pro football team of most white southerners. As if to return what he borrowed from college football, Marshall gave something back to it: Bear Bryant.

In 1938 Paul and Mary Harmon went to Washington for the wedding of Riley Smith, the Crimson Tide's quarterback in Bryant's senior year, to Mary Harmon's former Alabama roommate. At the time, Smith was playing for Marshall's Redskins; at the stag party, Bryant and Marshall became friendly and eventually Marshall moved the entire party to his house. It didn't take Marshall long to figure that Bryant should be an employee of the Washington Redskins, but still wary of pro football, Bryant suggested instead that he scout for Marshall. Marshall had had good luck with boys from Alabama, and he was about to have more.

In the early years, no NFL team could afford full-time scouts, and about the only way to find talent was to read the papers or pay sportswriters and coaches to scout them for you. Bryant's judgment was unerring, and seven Tide players went on to play for the Redskins. That Christmas, Marshall sent Bryant a check for five hundred dollars—40 percent of his Alabama salary. Eventually Bryant moonlighted for Marshall in the off-season, looking for talent in Texas and Arkansas. When Bryant was stationed in North Carolina, they began to meet frequently.

In the fall of 1945, just after the war finally ended, Bryant went to Chicago to see his friend Don Hutson play in the All-Star game, and Marshall once again tried to entice him into coming to the Redskins as an assistant coach. Bryant didn't particularly want to coach in the pros (he could never entirely articulate the reasons until he was faced with the chance to coach the Miami Dolphins in 1970), and he had no desire at all to be an assistant. Frank Thomas had asked him about coming back to

---

look out on the field and see a bunch of damned negrahs?" Marshall was elected to the NFL Hall of Fame in 1963, a year after the forced integration of the Redskins. (Dent, *Monster of the Midway*, p. 109)

Alabama, and Bryant, wondering what his chances were of getting the head coaching job at Alabama when Thomas retired, was thinking it over.

What did Bryant want, Marshall asked, a head coaching job? Bryant said yes. Marshall left the room and came back shortly, telling Bryant to return to his hotel, the Palmer House, and wait by the phone. The phone was ringing as he came through the door. A voice said it was Curley Byrd, president of the University of Maryland. Would Bryant be interested in being his head football coach? Yes, Bryant would. Byrd asked him how soon he could be there. Bryant told him that he had come to see his good pal Don Hutson play in the All-Star game the following night, Friday, so would Saturday be okay? Byrd told him that if he wanted the job, to be in his office at eight o'clock the next morning. Bryant threw his clothes into a suitcase, took a taxi to Midway airport, hopped on the next plane to Baltimore, and took a taxi straight from the airport to the university. He shaved in a men's room and was waiting for Byrd when he arrived shortly before 8:00 a.m. Bryant left Byrd's office as one of the youngest head coaches of a major college football program in the country.

On September 7, 1945, Paul Bryant signed the contract to be head coach. On September 23, Lieutenant Commander Bryant was honorably discharged from the U.S. Navy. On September 28, Bear Bryant began the greatest coaching career in college football history.

There was little time for the preparation; as they said in the navy, Bryant had to hit the decks running. But because of the groundwork he had laid with his North Carolina Pre-Flight players, his first team was ready to play. On Saturday afternoon in College Park, quarterback Vic Turyn, taking his second snap ever out of the Notre Dame box formation, flipped a short screen pass to Sam Behr—pronounced "Bear"—who broke a tackle and went sixty-four yards for a touchdown. That, at least, is the way Bryant would remember it. Harry Bonk, his first fullback, is pretty sure that *he* was the first, and Turyn, Bryant's first quarterback, swears that *he* scored the first touchdown of Bryant's coaching career "on a quarterback sneak." ("And I have the clips to prove it.") Behr, for his part, says that "I don't really remember, but I swear, Coach Bryant always said he had a newspaper clipping that said *I* scored the first touchdown for him."

Bryant had spent the night before sweating and vomiting; as it turned out, he needn't have worried. The Maryland Terrapins swept past the Guilford Quakers 60–6. A victory over Guilford College might seem unworthy of celebration—Don Hutson, who flew down to see his friend in his first game as a head coach, suggested that if he was nervous about playing Guilford, he might be in the wrong business. Carney Laslie, one of his assistants, chided him for preparing the team as though the Quakers were the Russian Army. Maryland, which had won just five of thirteen games in its previous two seasons, was thrilled with a victory over anyone.

Bryant never relaxed. Early in the game, Jimmy Allen, a halfback, took a handoff from Turyn and darted toward a designated spot between the guard and tackle; when he found a Guilford tackler had penetrated the line, he swerved to the outside and went eighty yards for a touchdown. "You didn't do that back then," said Harry Bonk, the fullback who was blocking on the play. "When Bryant told you to hit a designated spot, you hit that spot whether somebody was there or not." When Allen went back to the sideline, Bryant chewed him out.

Allen, hands on his hips, stared at him in silence. As he walked away, he called back, "But Coach, what did you think of that for distance?" Bryant had to admit that Allen had a point, so he said nothing. "It was one of the few times I ever saw him not reply to a player who talked back," says Bonk. "I figured, 'Well, if I'm ever going to talk back to him, I'd damn well better score a touchdown before I do.' "

Bryant had taken no chances. After accepting the job from Byrd, he drove straight to Chapel Hill and called a meeting of seventeen players and two assistants from his Cloudbusters team to make them a breathtaking offer. He told them that he had been offered jobs at Alabama and Georgia Tech as an assistant coach and at Maryland as head coach. If they would go with him as a unit to one of those schools, he would see that each got a full scholarship in addition to their GI Bill benefits. With a whoop, the players unanimously chose Maryland. Bryant neglected to mention two things to them: first, that he had already taken the Maryland job, and, second, since they had all played at other schools, the University of Maryland, to say nothing of the NCAA, might nix the whole deal and declare them ineligible. (The NCAA couldn't stop them from enrolling at Maryland, but it might bar them from playing football there; no one questioned a soldier's right to enroll at the school of his choice no matter what college he had attended previously, but Bryant was the first to move several servicemen to one school in mass.)

Bryant drove straight from the meeting with the players to Byrd's office.

Byrd, who had coached the Maryland football team from 1912 to 1935, was impressed with Bryant's scheme. He told him not to worry about any eligibility nonsense, "I make the rules here." For his own part, Bryant felt no ethical qualms about the maneuver. After all, he reasoned, most schools were either morally or legally bound to accept any boy who had served his country. Why should service kids who could block and tackle be an exception?★

Having begun his career as part of an excellent staff at Alabama, he understood the importance of putting together an excellent staff. The most experienced of the group and the one who would remain with Bryant the longest was Carney Laslie, who had been a senior on the Crimson Tide when Bryant began playing on the freshman team. Given his seniority, Laslie, as it turned out, never quite got past the habit of calling the younger man "Paul" when everyone else around them referred to him as "Coach." Bryant had met another of his future assistants, Frank Moseley, before the war when Moseley had served roughly in the same capacity for Kentucky that Bryant had for Vanderbilt. The two had made a pact: whichever one got a head coaching job first would call the other with a job offer. Bryant kept his word, phoning Moseley just as the USS *Lexington*, the aircraft carrier he was serving on, reached San Francisco.

The pace was frantic. Bryant sent Mary Harmon, Mae Martin, and Paul Jr. back to Birmingham. He then moved, with his assistant coaches, into the George Washington Hotel and conducted strategy sessions at a Krystal hamburger joint across the street. For the next couple of months, they would eat hamburgers morning, noon, and night.

The Terrapins pass defense improved quickly. It certainly should have: the Maryland football team scrimmaged against the Washington Redskins and "Slingin' Sammy" Baugh, probably the best passer in pro or college football at the time. "The pro guys beat the stuffing out of us," Joe Drach recalls, "but we didn't quit. By the time they finished practicing with us, they knew they had played some football. I got tougher in a hurry."

They all got tougher in a hurry. In practice, Vic Turyn, the quarterback, and Harry Bonk, the fullback, were assigned to block a defensive end

---

★ Nearly thirty years after Bryant's end run around recruiting rules, he was still defending himself in his autobiography. "Some of those seventeen were outstanding young men, too, like Harry Bonk and Red Polling, who are big executives in Maryland. Vic Turyn [his quarterback] became a high-ranking official with the FBI."

(being the quarterback didn't excuse a player on Bryant's teams from blocking and tackling). They did their job: "We pushed the guy right off the field," Turyn said, "then we hear Coach Bryant yelling for the end to bull his way through us, telling him that he wasn't playing it right. That got us mad. We *were* doing it right. So I made what you might call a little mistake. I said, 'Well, why don't you come over here and show us how it's supposed to be done?' I started to lose my confidence when he walked up to the line without so much as a hesitation. At the snap, he tore into both of us. I swear to God, players in the thirties must have had razors on their elbows. He took us both on, and fought us to a standstill. I never challenged him again."

Bryant's players quickly learned something about him: "He didn't measure you by your talent," said Turyn, "but by your desire. To him, the game *was* practice. You practiced harder and better than the other teams, you won. All of us, including the guys who were talking about quitting early in the season, learned that the games were easy compared to the practices. In comparison, the games were fun." It was a sentiment that Bryant's players over the decades would echo.

The games were not all fun, though. As the Maryland players soon learned, Bryant expected his players to play with pain, as he himself had done. Joe Drach broke a bone in his right hand in the tie with West Virginia—like Bryant and his leg in the Alabama-Tennessee game, it was just one little bone—and was writhing in pain. Bryant pulled Drach's hand over to look at it, as if to be sure there really was a break. "He looked like he wasn't too sure," recalls Drach. "He told one of the assistant coaches, 'Tape it up.' I was stunned; I knew that meant that he expected me to play the second half. I said 'Uh, tape it . . . up?' He grabbed my arm and pressed it against the wall and pushed till the bone popped back in place. They told me later I passed out; I really don't remember." In a few minutes Drach had recovered well enough to play the second half, "and damn well, too." Later, Bryant paid Drach the ultimate compliment: "He told me, 'Joe, I had to do that. We needed you. We would have lost without you.' I was still a little sore at him, but when he said that, I swear, I'd have gone out and broken another bone just to show him I could have done it again." Bryant had taken the psychological lessons Frank Thomas taught him and bettered them. Thomas had expected him to play with a broken bone in his leg, but he never grabbed Bryant's leg and tried to push the bone back into place.

Turyn was right, though: the Terrapins were starting to have fun. They were winning. Maryland won its first three games, skidded a bit at midseason with two losses and a tie, then finished the season with three straight victories. Bryant blamed himself for the loss to Virginia Tech and the tie with West Virginia, which the Terps would have won if not for a blocked punt due to an improperly placed blocker. He credited Maryland's only bad performance of the season, an embarrassing 33–14 loss to William & Mary, to the entire team and coaching staff—himself included, of course.

Then came what Joe Drach calls "the first big game of Bryant's career, the one that set the tone for his career." Bryant himself called the game with Virginia, Maryland's archrival, "the biggest of my life to that point, and for many reasons—good and bad—it was unforgettable." Bryant didn't sleep the night before and almost made himself sick with worry. Not only was Virginia unbeaten, but the cocky Vic Turyn, who had become Bryant's favorite player by that point, was injured and unavailable to play. Bryant would later recall that Virginia came in with a sixteen-game winning streak, which was not quite true, though they had won eight straight games extending back into the 1944 season and had twelve wins and two ties in their previous fourteen contests. As would be the case with so many Bryant-coached teams over the years, particularly against teams with better records, the 1945 Terps were outweighed by several pounds per man, but by this point in the season they were in splendid condition, particularly Bryant's preflight ringers, and Bryant had them fired up for the game. As Turyn said, "He had us believing that regardless of our size, we were so good and so ready that we couldn't lose."

They probably should have lost. Down 13–12 late in the game, Bryant called what many thought was an unbelievable play: a pass off of a reverse, with one end, Red Polling, throwing to the other end, Don Gleason, who had to outjump a Virginia defender in the end zone to make a play for the ball. Gleason caught the pass, of a type that Notre Dame would later popularize as a "Hail Mary," to score the winning touchdown, and Maryland fans erupted. The Terps had not only won their biggest game in years, they had beaten Virginia.

Nearly thirty years later Bryant would still be apologizing for the play. "I called a dumb play," he wrote in *Bear*. "It's dumb because in that situation the defense normally will let you reverse all you want. They will just lay back and cover your receivers." But in truth, it was the kind of play that

Bryant loved to throw at bigger, stronger teams when he felt his own boys had the conditioning edge. Late in games, after smaller players had fought the opposition to a near standstill, he would pull out some trick pass play and catch the opposition in football's equivalent of a sucker punch. The reverse pass against Virginia was merely the first of many such plays in big games coached by Bryant.

Of all the reasons why the game was so memorable, Bryant declined to mention in his autobiography the one remembered best by those who were present. "After the game," he said, "so many crazy things happened, I still have to shake my head. Our players had been complaining about getting bitten in the pile-ups, and I hadn't paid much attention. When they undressed, they showed me the tooth marks." What Bryant chose to leave out was that his Virginia counterpart, Frank Murray, ran all the way across the field, pushed a couple of celebrating Maryland players out of the way, and shouted at Bryant, "I want to congratulate you for playing the dirtiest game I've ever seen." Mid-Atlantic football was more of a gentlemanly game in that era, and the Cavaliers took a, well, cavalier approach to Bryant's hardscrabble football. According to one account, Bryant simply replied, "If you weren't such an old man, I'd knock your ass on the ground," and walked away. According to two other accounts, Bryant walked away without a word.

Years later, Bryant's fullback, Harry Bonk, was furious at the accusation that the Terps had fouled the Cavs: "I don't ever remember Coach Bryant teaching us to play dirty," he said. "On the contrary, he always told us that if you were playing dirty, you weren't going to be focusing on the fundamentals and you'd lose your cool. Let the other team play dirty, he said"—even to the extent of taking a few bites—"but don't retaliate. Dirty? We just hit them harder than they'd ever been hit before, and when they got up, we hit them again." Drach also confirmed stories of biting by Virginia players: "In the shower, guys were comparing the bite marks. Coach Bryant should have accused *them* of playing dirty." Accusations of dirty play from an angry coach and a fiery defense from his own players would be heard again in Bryant's career and would one day spark the greatest controversy in college football history.

———

VIRGINIA MAY not have liked Bear Bryant–style football, but Curley Byrd, who had waited a long time to see the haughty Cavaliers and their fans humbled, was ecstatic; this was precisely what he had hired Bryant for. The postgame locker room scene at Griffith Stadium was bedlam. George Preston Marshall, resplendent in an enormous and rather appropriate bearskin coat, was stopped by a security guard who asked him his business, only to be told, "I own the goddamn place." An ecstatic Byrd pushed his way in to announce a banquet to be held that night at the Statler Hotel to honor the 6–2–1 Terrapins.

The night would prove to be the highlight of Bryant's stay at Maryland, and Mary Harmon, who had arrived with Mae Martin and Paul Jr. at midseason, was there to share it with him. Byrd enjoyed showing off; a widower, he arrived, according to Bryant, "wearing a good-looking twenty-two year old girl on his sleeve." Byrd's good friend, Sam Rayburn, the Speaker of the House, the man who would one day help to make Lyndon Johnson the president of the United States, was the evening's emcee. Bryant was indeed impressed, but Byrd was just getting warmed up.

In the middle of the festivities, Bryant recalled, Byrd suddenly shouted out, "Is Bump Watkins here?" *Of course* Bump Watkins was there, and Byrd knew it. Watkins was a building contractor and a Maryland alumnus. Byrd, who had spent the evening building up to this moment, told Bump he wanted him to build the Bryants a brand new house near the chemistry building. Bryant did not know where the chemistry building was, but it sounded fine to him. Byrd was emphatic: "I mean the *finest,* because Bear's got a lifetime contract." Bryant's eyebrows went up; at the moment, he didn't have a contract for 1946, and his future at Maryland hadn't been discussed yet.

Later the party moved to the house of another Maryland alumnus, Don Adams, who invited the Bryants to stay the night. Adams was a restaurant and hotel supplier, and his house was the first Bryant had ever seen with wall-to-wall carpeting. "It felt so good," he said, "I took my shoes off and just wallowed around the floor." The football season being over, Bryant decided to relax and socialize with Adams and take the day off. It was "the only Sunday I can ever remember not working." It may well have been his last Sunday off until his retirement in 1982. The Bryants went home to Birmingham for the Christmas holidays, dazzled by the prospects of their future. Shortly after the holidays when they returned to College Park, they found that the coach's coach had turned into a pumpkin.

The suspension of Larry Cooper hadn't seemed like such a big thing at the time. Cooper, a tackle, was the only holdover among the starters from the previous year's Terps, who had won just one game. On the Thursday before the big game with Virginia, Cooper had been spotted by campus police drinking beer at a local nightspot, in blatant violation of Bryant's curfew. Joe Drach would recall the suspension as "unfair. We were all drinking beer then. What the hell, we were GIs." But Cooper was not a GI. In any event, contrary to his later image, Bryant did not set a great number of rules for his players, but the few he did were strictly enforced, and he may have been using Cooper to make a point.* Vic Turyn had no trouble understanding Bryant's point: "He was very strict, and the rules were clear. He let us drink beer, he just wanted us to be in the dorm by ten. What he told us was, 'Just don't drink in front of the other students. I don't want to give the football team a bad image, and I don't want anybody to say that if we lose a game, it was because you guys were out drinking beer all night.' He would tell us to go ahead, have a couple, you're grown men. He'd say, 'Don't worry. You're not going to lose any game that I coach because you drank beer. I'll run it out of you, I guarantee.'"

Bryant had only three men on the squad who could play Cooper's position, so from a practical standpoint, a suspension seemed foolhardy, particularly before the biggest game he had coached. Yet even as a thirty-two-year-old rookie, Bryant understood that the suspension of a player for violation of simple rules could be hugely effective in pulling a team together. It was exactly the same strategy he would use at Alabama with his biggest stars, Joe Namath and Ken Stabler, in exactly the same situations. As Jerry Duncan, one of his favorite players on the Alabama teams of the 1960s, put it, "He wasn't just saying to us 'You'd better get your ass in line, if I do it to them, I'll sure as hell do it to you.' He was also saying to

---

* Joe Drach claims it was a campus cop who informed on Cooper. "He traveled around with us, drove the bus, sort of served as Bryant's go-fer," Drach says. Apparently Bryant had him on the lookout for violators. If so, why he chose to punish Cooper remains a mystery. It's possible that he was showing favoritism toward the boys he had brought over from North Carolina Navy Pre-Flight. More than likely, though, as Harry Bonk puts it, "He was cutting us a little slack 'cause we'd been in the service and all. If he was ever going to enforce his rules he had to start with someone, so he started with Cooper. He was sending us a message." Drach, though, says, "The hell with that. I kept right on drinking beer."

us, 'If the big stars on this team aren't going to get the job done, I know you boys will suck it up and do it yourselves.'"

When Bryant returned after the holiday, on the way to his office he spotted Cooper on the dormitory steps. He asked Carney Laslie what was going on. "Well," Laslie replied, "the boss just took him back." Bryant simmered but kept his cool. There was an even more upsetting development to deal with. Byrd had fired one of Bryant's assistant coaches, Herman Ball.

Even after just one year as a head coach, Bryant could not accept such an undermining of his authority, whatever the reasons. He would later concede that at this point in his career, "Byrd knew a lot more about football than I did," which was unlikely, but in any case irrelevant. "I also knew if he was going to pull things like this I couldn't coach for him." He calmly gathered the mail that had accumulated while he was away and drove to his new dream-house-in-progress—the one next to the chemistry building. There was no doubt in his mind that either Byrd would reverse both his decisions or Paul Bryant would be leaving Maryland, and as he pondered the options, he knew there was little chance of the former. In his own words, "I sat down and cried like a baby."

After a few minutes, he began to thumb through his mail. A four-day-old telegram jumped out at him: "If you want to be head coach at Kentucky call me collect. Dr. Herman Donovan, President." Well, he had an option after all. Bryant called the head of the Maryland Alumni Association, Don Adams, the man whose wall-to-wall carpets Bryant had been so impressed with. Adams had been a standout on a Maryland team coached by Curley Byrd and knew him well. Bryant asked Adams if it would be worth discussing the matter with Byrd before making his decision; Adams advised him to grab the Kentucky job. Bryant had already made up his mind that that's what he was going to do, but early in his career even Bear Bryant needed some reassurance. He phoned Donovan and accepted the challenge of turning the Kentucky football program around, a job that from a distance looked more imposing than what he had done for Maryland. Bryant, of course, was never daunted by challenges and generally went straight toward them. Also, in the back of his mind was the thought that Kentucky was in the Southeastern Conference and a giant step closer to home.

He was also soothed by the salary: $8,500 a year would go some ways toward mollifying Mary Harmon's misgivings. Donovan wanted to make the announcement within two days: this left Bryant just enough time to meet with Byrd and then with his players. Byrd proved to be far from angry; if anything, his mood was conciliatory. Bryant was his boy, and by God, he meant to keep him at Maryland. Byrd talked money, houses, and a glorious future for Paul Bryant and the University of Maryland, but he did not do the only things Bryant wanted him to do: he never offered to rehire Ball or uphold Bryant's suspension of Cooper.* In other words—and this was the stickler, the point Bryant simply could not accept—Bear Bryant would *coach* the Maryland football team, but Curley Byrd would run it. Bryant, in effect, would be Byrd's trophy. They argued for over an hour. The discussion grew heated. Finally Bryant said, "I'm going." Byrd insisted that he had a legal hold on Bryant, an argument that angered his coach, as he had gone through the holidays without being offered a new contract.

It was after dark when Bryant walked out of Byrd's office. He went straight to the meeting with his players but found they had all gone back to the dorm. Some of them must have been listening outside the door of the president's office because the next morning Bryant awoke to find himself in the middle of one of the strangest protests anyone had ever seen on a college campus. A crowd of students, estimated at between two and three thousand, was picketing in front of the administration building carrying protest signs. There was even a report that someone burned a desk in protest. After an enterprising reporter from the *Baltimore Sun* arrived with a photographer, the story and accompanying photos went out across the country. All of a sudden, millions of Americans were reading about a football coach who had wrestled a bear, been a Rose Bowl star, and played a game with a broken leg. Probably Maryland and certainly Kentucky had never had so much national publicity for a football-related incident; if Bryant had been more mercenary, he could have phoned President Donovan at Kentucky and asked for more money.

Bryant was appalled by the uproar. Though the idea would come as a shock to people who in later years would see Bryant as a symbol of a football program run amok—the popular joke in the 1960s was that "Alabama is building a university that the football team can be proud of"—Bryant

---

* Nor, in fact, did he ever mention a contract. In the opinion of Joe Drach, "Byrd never intended to offer him one. The word that got around was that Byrd wanted to operate on a handshake basis."

had revered the concept of the university since listening to his first Rose Bowl game back in Fordyce. To him, the university and its football team were inseparable, and he never denied for a moment that the president was his boss in all decisions. In this case, he had simply chosen to move on to a university whose president's ideas were more in accord with his own. His differences with Byrd were for discussion only in the privacy of the president's office, not issues to be displayed in newspapers.

Appearing at the rally, he thanked the students for their support and told them he was leaving, and that was final. He also told them that Curley Byrd, who was the object of a score of abusive signs and banners, was their friend. He reassured them that the football players he brought with him would remain. The students would not disperse. It was later revealed that one of the organizers of the demonstration was Frank Sadler, one of Bryant's students from North Carolina Navy Pre-Flight, but Bryant knew nothing of the plans for the protest. "If he had known about it beforehand," says Sadler, "he would have killed me." (Sadler would later become Bryant's team manager at Kentucky.)

Bryant weaved his way through the crowd to the administration building, from which Byrd then emerged. The two hugged each other and begged the students to go back to class. Many of them hung around. Then, says Sadler, "It started to get ugly again. Some of the students marched up to President Byrd's house demanding to know why Bryant was leaving. I thought, 'Damn, I think this is getting out of hand.' " Bryant and Byrd jammed a few hundred of the most vociferous into a gym where Bryant once again reassured the students that he was leaving on his own volition, and slipped out the side door. Years later, he admitted to Frank Sadler that he was afraid of "breaking down right there in front of everyone. I didn't want anyone to see me cry in public."

Then he went to meet with his players. Sammy Behr, one of the candidates for the player who scored Bryant's first official touchdown as a college coach, started to weep. Behr, a Jewish kid from Talladega, Alabama, had a special relationship with Bryant. "We bonded right from the beginning," says Behr. "I played my heart out for him, and he always went out of his way to make me feel special. I went up to him on the practice field and said, 'Coach, I can't play on Rosh Hashanah or Yom Kippur.' He gave me the coach's car and told me to go home and said, 'Just come back tomorrow, nice and early.' " Bryant was so fond of Behr that he asked Sammy to drive back to Alabama with him for Christmas, dropping him off in Talladega on the way to Birmingham. "I'll never forget that trip," recalls Behr, "him smoking those long Chesterfields one after the other, telling me all these great stories about the stuff he and Don Hutson got away with at Alabama. It was one of the best trips I ever took in my life."★

Sam Behr wasn't the only player who felt he had a personal relationship with Bryant. Several others, says Harry Bonk, "teared up." There was some resentment, particularly among the players who followed him to Maryland from North Carolina Navy Pre-Flight School. Bryant, his own eyes swelling, tried to explain to them that he was leaving because of a principle and that they had made a commitment to the university, not to him, that they must keep. Behr begged Bryant to take him along to Kentucky. Bryant told him, "Sammy, I found you here, and I have to leave you here. This is where you belong." He got into his car and drove to Lexington, Kentucky, where, to his amazement, he was greeted by yet another student demonstration, one that included a student with a handmade sign that read, WELCOME BEAR. So they knew who he was. For the first time, his reputation preceded him.

SO MUCH has been written about Bryant's relationships with former players from Kentucky, Texas A&M, and Alabama that his relationships with the boys of Maryland have been overlooked. At Maryland, as Harry Bonk put it, Bryant was "sort of a coach in progress. I don't know that he knew all that much about football then, but what he did know he knew how to communicate to you. And most of all, he knew how to make you feel that you had it in you to be a winner."

"In some ways I think we might have been closer to him than the players on his later teams," says Vic Turyn. "I'd read about how he kept his distance from players at Kentucky, Texas A&M, and Alabama, but it really wasn't possible for him to distance himself from us. We'd all been in the service at the same time, he'd brought us over from North Carolina Pre-

---

★ Behr and the Bear stayed in touch. "In 1954 and 1955, when I was in the ROTC, I was coaching a service team in Anchorage, Alaska. He wrote to me and sent me some of his defenses. I was so touched when he sent a Bar Mitzvah gift to my son—I don't know how he had time to remember things like that." Behr had no idea how extensive Mary Harmon's address book was.

Flight, and he was maybe only ten to eleven years older than most of us. He was more like our older brother. He'd talk to us about personal stuff. I went to him in my freshman year and told him I was going to get married. He spent two hours trying to talk me out of it, then finally he said, 'Well, Vic, if you're going to do this, just make sure she's either beautiful or has some money' "—good advice from a coach who knew. "When my daughter was born during my junior year, he was at Kentucky. He sent her a fifty-dollar savings bond."

Joe Drach, for his part, never entirely forgave Bryant for leaving Maryland. "He brought us down there from North Carolina Pre-Flight," he says. "I was really hurt when he told us. I don't think I've ever quite gotten over it." Nonetheless, says Drach, "He was always reasonable about it when I brought up the subject in later years. But he'd never argue with me about it. He'd just say, 'Joe, I just hated to leave you guys; you've got to believe me about that. I felt I had to do it.'" Bonk was "devastated" by Bryant's decision to leave, but "if I had a family and I didn't have a contract, I think I might have done the same thing."

Vic Turyn, Joe Drach, and Harry Bonk stayed close to Bryant for the rest of his life. For Turyn, the bottom line is, "He didn't ask us to go with him to Kentucky. In fact, he insisted that the right thing was for us to stay when several of us would have happily gone with him. He told me, 'No, Vic, I made a commitment to the University when I asked you boys to come here. I can't break that.' To me that means his decision was based on principle." It could be argued that Bryant stole his Maryland stars from other colleges, though that ignores the players' own part in the decision: they wanted to play for Bryant. In any event, all schools that played big-time football were pretty much engaged in the "stealing" of football players; Bryant would have some of his stolen in Maryland and did not regard it as a breach of ethics. Breaking his word to the university was another matter altogether. Curley Byrd had promised to take the flak for him when he brought the boys in from North Carolina Pre-Flight, and he wasn't going to betray that faith by taking the same players away from Byrd.

Ultimately, the question as to whether Bryant's decision was motivated primarily by principle or ego is irrelevant; he had more than enough of both to justify his actions.

PART TWO

The Bear looks over the shoulder of the Baron, Adolph Rupp.
From 1946 through 1953, Bryant's football teams at Kentucky were
overshadowed by Rupp's basketball program.

Chapter 4

New Kentucky Home

This must be what God looks like.

—*George Blanda upon meeting Bear Bryant*

"AFTER THE WAR, the rat race began," Bryant would say. Throughout Bryant's years as a player and assistant coach, not many southern schools had developed sophisticated recruiting techniques: Arkansas, Alabama, Tennessee, and Georgia Tech, but not many others. "Recruiting was mostly done by mail, and that was kind of haphazard." Bryant was about to end the era of haphazard recruiting at the University of Kentucky, or, as Kentucky football historian Russell Rice would phrase it, "Beginning in 1946, coaches in competition with Bryant were forced to neglect their golf games."

Bryant had coached just nine games in his college career, but he had already succeeded in firing up students on two campuses. The celebration that greeted him as he drove into Lexington was understandable, especially in light of the history of Kentucky football. In the ten years before Bryant, Kentucky had been less than mediocre—a 36–46–4 record from 1936 through 1945. (The Wildcats, like most universities, did not field a team in

1943.) But even that record is deceiving. They had won only five games in the hugely competitive Southeastern Conference over that ten-year span and had not had a winning season since 1941 or an unbeaten season since 1898. They had never contended for the national championship or even won a conference title. Paul Bryant was about to change all that with a swiftness that would shock even those who knew about his turnaround at Maryland.

So dramatically did Kentucky's football fortunes improve that within a short time the question of how Bryant came to Kentucky in the first place would be forgotten. There is no one alive today who knows exactly how Bryant became head football coach at the University of Kentucky, and Bryant's autobiography ignores the most intriguing question—namely, what compelled Kentucky President Herman Donovan to offer Bryant the job at precisely that moment?

The telegram that Bryant found waiting for him at Maryland in early 1946 was four days old, and Bryant did not know of Curley Byrd's interference until he returned from Christmas vacation, so there was no way for anyone else to know about Byrd's action. The reason why Byrd had reinstated Cooper was never really made known; two previous Bryant biographers identify Cooper's father as an influential Maryland politician, but in fact Cooper's father was a policeman. The reason for Herman Ball's dismissal was never made clear either. (He would soon resurface as head coach of George Preston Marshall's Washington Redskins.)

Though he never spoke of it, Bryant must have been having problems with Byrd's hands-on approach to the football program well before the 1945 holidays, and more than likely he had communicated his feelings to his assistant and good friend, Frank Moseley. Moseley, in turn, would have been a likely person to relay those sentiments to *his* former boss at Kentucky. What is strange about Bryant's departure from Maryland is not that another university offered him a job, but that it was the *only* one offered. If it had been public knowledge that Bryant had not signed a contract to coach the 1946 football season at Maryland, there would certainly have been other offers. Somehow, Donovan knew that Bryant had not signed a contract and that he might be available any moment. Stated another way, Bryant had probably foreseen problems with Byrd from the very beginning and was looking out for his and his family's interests.

That Bryant might have prepared a safety net in no way mitigates the breathtaking nerve of his decision to walk out on Maryland. In the winter of 1946, he was just thirty-two years old, not much older than some of the football players at Kentucky and other schools who had just gotten back from the war.* He had been fired from his first job after leaving Alabama and had nothing on his head coaching resume except the 1945 season at Maryland. What mixture of self-confidence, integrity, and just plain stubbornness had gone into his amazing decision to walk out on what most other coaches would have regarded as a dream job?

Only by putting the Maryland departure in the context of Bryant's career does it make any sense. The decision to suspend Cooper was precisely of the kind he would make again and again over the years when a star player violated team rules; the clash with Byrd was uncannily like the one he would have eight years later with Herman Donovan and Adolph Rupp at Kentucky. The only logical conclusion is that even at the outset of his career, Paul Bryant had an unshakable conviction in who he was and what he wanted to achieve, and he was willing to take chances other men simply would not.

IN 1946, Kentucky was known for its lovely bluegrass country, its stately mansions, some untouched by the Civil War, its world-class thoroughbreds, and college basketball. "Football," says Russell Rice, "was something you started to get worked up about early in September. By the end of September, you were already disillusioned and waiting for basketball to start." Later, in retrospect, many would contend that Kentucky's undistinguished football history combined with the state's obsession with basketball put unfair pressure on Bryant to win. On the contrary, Bryant could scarcely have selected a head coaching job with less pressure attached to it. The University of Kentucky had practically no football tradition, and therefore no expectations save those generated by Bryant. Virtually any improvement at all would have been greeted with enthusiasm. Bryant did a great deal more than simply upgrade Kentucky football; for the second time in two

---

* At a pregame dinner that year before the Kentucky-Tennessee game, a waiter refused to serve Bryant coffee, mistaking him for a player. Football players were only allowed milk or tea, and if Bryant wanted coffee, the waiter said, "He'd have to check with the coach."

seasons (or, for the third time in three seasons, if one includes his obvious contribution as an assistant to Vanderbilt's 1941 season), he stopped a losing program dead in its tracks and turned it sharply in a winning direction.

Bryant's first season, 1946, the Wildcats went from 2–8 in the previous year to 7–3, playing just one bad game all year, a 28–13 loss to Georgia at Athens. The other two defeats, 21–7 to Alabama in Tuscaloosa and 7–0 against Tennessee at Knoxville, were as close to acceptable as any loss could ever be to Bryant. (His fourth win of the season, 10–7 over Vanderbilt, was particularly satisfying, as it came at the expense of the man who had fired him from Vandy five years earlier, Red Sanders.) Frank Thomas's last season at Alabama was 1946; suffering from high blood pressure, he would live just eight more years. With Thomas's retirement, General Neyland's Tennessee Volunteers found themselves without a serious rival as the leading power in the SEC, a spot they would continue to occupy until Bryant established himself at Alabama more than a decade later. The next year was even better, capped with a 24–14 victory over Villanova in the short-lived Great Lakes Bowl. The sports world, with no knowledge that the bowl game was the first in a string from the greatest postseason coach ever, paid it little heed, but Kentuckians were ecstatic. Football fever had come to Kentucky. Some thought the 8–3 Wildcats of 1947 were the best team in Kentucky history. They probably were—that is, until the 1949 squad. Nothing before or since has matched the enthusiasm Bryant brought to college football in the Bluegrass State.

It has been said that even Paul Bryant couldn't make football king over basketball in Kentucky, but by 1949 he may well have been on his way to doing just that. The problem was not that Bryant had to overcome basketball, but that he was up against a more firmly entrenched icon: Adolph Rupp, the most renowned college basketball coach in the country. But in the winter of 1949, Kentucky fans were still reveling over their first-ever bowl victory. Bryant loved the fame, the respect, the money, and the bourbon, not necessarily in that order. Mary Harmon, after overcoming her initial misgivings, found life as the wife of one of the most famous men in the state to be quite pleasant and Lexington a fine place to raise children. And Kentucky was in close visiting distance to both Arkansas and Alabama. Bryant regularly chartered planes to Tuscaloosa, where he would visit and talk football with Thomas. During one of his 1946 trips, Thomas may have approached Bryant about succeeding him at Alabama. That's what Bryant claimed, at any rate, though there does not appear to be a source to corroborate it. He certainly would have been a likely choice, but the job went to Bryant's friend, the older and more experienced Harold "Red" Drew. If Bryant was offered the job, it isn't clear why he turned it down. Loyalty to Kentucky is one possibility, his friendship with Drew another. Either reason would have sufficed.

Bryant was very loyal to Kentucky. Over the next eight seasons he would turn down offers from both Arkansas and Southern Cal—refusing the latter haunted him, as he had dreamt about living in California since his first Rose Bowl. He went to President Donovan with the offers, had them matched, and stayed put. In 1951, after Alabama limped through a 5–6 season, he received a feeler about supplanting Drew. He thought it over and finally agreed with Mary Harmon that he couldn't take the job from an old friend.

THE TWIN engines that fueled Kentucky football's rise were talent and discipline. Regarding the second, Bryant knew exactly what the Wildcats' problem had been: politics. Kentucky's previous coaches had been fired for reasons other than losing football games. He was determined that if Kentucky fired him, it would be for just one reason: not winning. This was a roundabout way of saying that up until now Kentucky football had been dominated by internecine squabbling, campus politics, and a failure to capitalize on readily available talent, and that while he was coach, these things would not be allowed to interfere with football.

Before Bryant arrived, it was generally assumed that most of the top-level athletes in the area preferred to try out for basketball. He immediately perceived that this assumption was erroneous; most natural basketball players had different body types than most football players, and even at that, a starting basketball team needed just five players whereas a starting football team needed eleven. Bryant knew something else: just because Kentucky was in the SEC didn't mean that its natural recruiting territory was the less populated southern states. Some southern coaches had an aversion toward recruiting Yankees; Bryant would have recruited Eskimos if he thought they could win for him. With a little extra effort, he could tap into the rich recruiting fields of Ohio, West Virginia, and, most especially, the Pennsylvania mining towns with their tough second-generation boys of Eastern European stock.

One of those Pennsylvania towns, Youngwood, gave Bear Bryant the first great player of his coaching career. George Blanda's freshman year was an example of how the Kentucky football program had wasted its talent. The Wildcats, rudderless, stumbled through a listless season in which they had won just two games. Blanda had heard rumors about how tough a coach Bryant was, and that suited him fine; he wanted to play football the right way, the way he had learned to play in high school, and considered his first season a waste of good time and energy. All that was about to change. When he first walked into Bryant's office, he thought, "This must be what God looks like."[1] Bryant was, as Blanda recalled him from that 1946 season, "a very handsome man, tall and smooth. He was the most energetic man I'd ever seen. He'd walk into the room and you wanted to stand up and applaud. He gives this speech to the student body, and I thought he was going to get elected president."

Blanda had been won over to Kentucky by the promise of a suit—two, actually. "They decided to buy me two suits of clothes," he wrote in his autobiography. "I'd never owned a suit in my life. So I picked out two suits—one blue and one brown." He was also snowed by the fervor with which the Kentucky recruiters sold their program, making talk about going to the Cotton Bowl and the Sugar Bowl. "When you went up East," he wrote, "the coaches and athletic directors didn't talk about a thing except about how great it would be to go to their schools. I said, 'Well, this is the place to go. If they give me two suits and promise me to go to the Sugar Bowl or the Cotton Bowl, I'll go to Kentucky.' "[2]

The son of a coal miner, Blanda had learned to play football with a desperation that might have caused a few players from Fordyce High to balk. At his high school in Youngwood, there was "none of this slipping you $10 for having a good game. They expected you'd have a good game. Nobody ever took you out for a meal . . . we weren't pampered, and that was good training because it got me ready to play for Bear Bryant." Bryant's reputation had preceded him. "I heard all kinds of things about him," Blanda says. "Was I concerned about staying on the football team and staying in college when I heard he was coming to Kentucky? You're damn right I was. I had been on a team that had won just one game the previous year, and I knew, like everybody else, that not too many players from that squad were going to be hanging around. Plus, I had a bad knee. I really thought he might dump me just for that." Bryant did not dump him. He talked to all the players, one at a time, trying to assess their commitment to turning the program around. When he got to Blanda, he looked him in the eye and asked him how he felt; Blanda looked right back at him and admitted his knee was killing him. Bryant saw something in Blanda and decided to take a chance. He got him to a doctor, who advised an operation. Blanda missed school from January to March, then went home to Youngwood to run and get his leg back in shape. "I figured," he says, "that I'd better work because Coach Bryant didn't strike me as the kind who would run an easy practice." He got that right. Blanda came back during the summer and won his starting job back.

COMPLIMENTARY SUITS were the kind of thing you could get away with in the late 1940s when NCAA restrictions on recruiting were still ill defined. Years later, after Bryant was put on probation at Texas A&M, sportswriters would simply assume he had always been disdainful of recruiting rules, but Bryant's players at Kentucky insist he knew exactly where to draw the line. "I got just what the NCAA allowed," wrote Blanda. "Room, board and tuition. One time I thought I should be getting some under the table. I'd heard all these stories. I mentioned it to Coach Bryant. He came up over the top of his desk and grabbed me by my eyeballs. 'You want what?' he yelled. 'Just joking, Coach,' I said and got the hell out of there." To be sure, Bryant had once freely engaged in the common practice of buying recruits, but the NCAA had been cracking down, and in any event, Bryant didn't want a player coming to *him* with a request, and he damned sure didn't want a kid who had already made his deal with the university coming in to renegotiate. After that, Blanda stopped caring about what other football players might be getting: "I was getting my college education paid for, and I was getting help finding summer jobs. So I figured I was damned lucky."

He had no idea. Later he would look back and realize that Bryant had given him the foundation for what proved to be the longest career in pro football history. Blanda played in the NFL for twenty-six years, retiring in 1975 when he was forty-eight years old with 2,002 points, the NFL's all-time leading scorer at the time. "Thank you, Bear," he wrote years later, "for that miserable, instructive background. I think it might have something to do with the fact that I'm still playing today."[3]

Blanda was an unpolished gem waiting for Bryant when he arrived at Kentucky in 1946, but there were still a great many roster spots to fill and, as it turned out, no lack of warm bodies to fill them. The ranks of high school graduates, both those who had signed with Kentucky and those eager for a tryout, had swelled with the publicity that had followed Bryant from Maryland. In addition, there was a swarm of older prospects, former GIs who had played some ball in college and on service teams like Bryant's North Carolina Cloudbusters. This was more talent than any Kentucky coach had ever had to choose from, and, in the words of George Blanda, "It allowed Bear to go nuts with the practices. They were hellish. He must have figured we'd lose two-thirds or more of the potential players. That's what he was aiming at. He wanted the one-third or one-quarter of the best available talent, the ones who were willing to work the hardest."

Bryant would later admit to his mistakes, to mishandling some players and to running off a few good ones. But the majority of his boys were motivated, and they began winning.

Bryant didn't invent the art of college recruiting, but there are those who swear that he perfected it. Decades later, freed from the obligation of soliciting players, a process he came to hate, he would reveal some of the tricks he had used at Kentucky. "We used to hide boys out, what the pros call baby-sitting now, and what they did a lot when they were battling between the two leagues [the National and American Football leagues]. We'd take a few prospects off some place, on boats or on hunting trips, or ride them around until we got them won. That's illegal now." A popular story had circulated—no doubt propagated by one of his recruiting rivals—that Bryant had taken a bunch of recruits on a boat trip, taken them out into the middle of a lake, and threatened to make them swim home if they didn't sign. Bryant called the story "ridiculous because there was no signing. You couldn't register them at sea." He did not say that the idea itself was ridiculous—merely that it was impractical given the existing rules. It's tempting to wonder what Bryant might have done if it had been possible to register players out on the water.

Those who stuck learned fast. They had come to Kentucky from farms and mill towns, but they were now in college; they were football players, and that made them special. For the privilege of being treated as special, they were expected to represent their university as gentlemen. On road games, in fact before all games, Kentucky's football players were expected to wear a coat and tie; those who did not have coats were, as Blanda indicated, provided for and those who did not have ties were welcome to ask their coaches for one. Football players were not allowed to keep a car on campus, so they couldn't miss the curfew. None of this sneaking out to someone's country house with their girlfriends, as Bryant and his pals had done at Alabama. One local sportswriter admonished him for not understanding how young people were "these days." "I understand *exactly* how they are these days," Bryant shot back.

In his own way, Bryant saw that his boys were taken care of, just as he had been at Alabama. He asked Frank Sadler, who went to Maryland with Bryant from the North Carolina Pre-Flight program, to assume the job of team manager. This would prove, in time, to include chauffeuring Mary Harmon and babysitting the two children. Mostly, though, his job was to give out tickets to the players and help them sell them for extra cash. "I'm not sure what the rules were regarding it back then," says Sadler, who runs a successful construction business in Lexington, "but it was widely known that everyone did it. Coach Bryant liked to use the tickets for incentives: so many extra tickets for an interception, a blocked punt, things like that."★

Above all, Bryant demanded that his players attend class. "He didn't demand scholars," said Bob Gain, Bryant's first consensus All-America, "but you damned well better go to class. And don't think he didn't check to see if you had." That Bryant expected his players to attend class didn't preclude clashes with their professors. Bryant lost one of his players when he was ruled ineligible for flunking a course; his assistant in charge of academics, the football team's "brain coach," told Bryant that the boy failed despite having attended every class. "That," said Bryant, "sounded unreasonable to me." He swore to "fix that professor." A couple of weeks later the brain coach informed him that "you sure fixed him good, the University made him head of the department yesterday." One must at least concede that Bryant's petulant response in promising to "fix a professor" was mitigated

---

★ Bryant believed in performance clauses and incentives. As he said in *Bear*, "If I had to do it over, when I went to Alabama I would have had them buy me a twenty year annuity, say for half a million dollars, and if I stayed the twenty years it would be mine."

"Just pay me so much for a win," he told the chairman of the Kentucky Board of Trustees, "and so much for a bowl game, and I will be satisfied." If he had been paid on that basis, Bryant would probably have been a multimillionaire by the end of the 1960s.

somewhat by his willingness to repeat a story in which he wound up as the butt of the joke.

BRYANT'S PRACTICES were savage, unrelenting, and rich with profanity. Walt Yowarsky recalled, "Some days the practices just didn't seem to end. One of the assistant coaches, usually Carney Laslie, who had followed Bryant from Maryland to Kentucky and played the good cop to Bryant's bad cop, would tell us the practices were winding down, and then, before you knew it, Bryant would call for us to pair off against each other in blocking and tackling drills. We'd go at those until either the blocker or tackler dropped from exhaustion. There were nights when I would fall asleep dreaming about that day's practices and wake up from a nightmare dreaming that I was still practicing."

Practices were dry—players were not allowed to drink water. Bryant did not do this, as some would later allege, out of meanness; the belief that water made players soft was indeed a superstition, but a common one at the time among high school and college coaches who had never heard the word *dehydration* and thought that being deprived of water would toughen their players. As Bob Gain said, "He'd a fed us milkshakes if he had thought it would make us play better."

About this same time the NCAA began passing restrictions on the amount of practice time allowed for football. If a coach was ingenious, of course, he could always find ways around the rules. In 1948, after an embarrassing loss to Mississippi, Bryant, simmering to a boil, ordered the team buses to stop late at night on the trip back to Lexington. In a voice loud enough for the team to hear, Bryant instructed Laslie to run out to a field and check it for rocks and holes; if it wasn't in too bad shape, they would stop and practice. Another method of skirting the NCAA's limitation on practice was to take football players to what was euphemistically referred to as a "retreat" or a summer camp on a farm a few miles from the campus. There they would run through conditioning drills and practice plays without a football—technically, Bryant had met the NCAA restrictions on football practice by practicing football without a football.

A player who was late for practice would, according to the late Pat James, be handed a shovel and sent to redistribute cow chips in a nearby pasture for an indefinite length of time. James, who later became one of

Bryant's assistants at Alabama, ran a popular restaurant in Birmingham and loved to tell the story of the day Bryant slept late and showed up fifteen minutes after practice had begun. No one said anything to the Coach; at the end of the practice, James, without saying a word, stepped forward and handed him the shovel. Wordlessly, in full view of the team, Bryant took the shovel, walked to the pasture, and shoveled cow shit. There was no better way to get his point across that his rules applied to everyone.

As James's story indicates, Bryant worked his players and assistant coaches no harder than he worked himself. Younger than nearly all of his coaching rivals, he knew he had much to learn about the on-field strategy and off-field politics of college football. The overtime took its toll. One night after a two-day work binge with no sleep, he and his assistant gorged on a late-night steak dinner. Bryant became violently ill and lost his meal; he had not eaten in two days and had worked himself into a state of nervous indigestion. Bryant's home life languished, and Paul Jr. and Mae Martin became increasingly resigned to seeing little of their father for at least six months out of the year. Bryant tried to compensate by sending them letters and postcards, but sometimes it only increased his and their feeling of loneliness.★ Mary Harmon compensated for her loneliness in part by becoming what Babe Parilli called "a football den mother," bringing the boys into their home, helping to treat their injuries, and keeping up with their families and children after they graduated. In years to come, Bryant maintained an extraordinary number of relationships with his former players, writing them letters and asking them about girlfriends, wives, and kids they didn't know he knew about. The reason he knew about them was Mary Harmon, who kept thick address books.

Such stress wouldn't begin to take a toll on Bryant for the next couple of decades, but for the time being at least, he would beat his rivals through sheer willpower. He would outwork his counterparts. No matter what time rival coaches came to work, he would be there a half hour earlier.

Sometimes, though, the things he wanted done were the wrong things, and he was simply too stubborn to acknowledge the fact at the time. (To his credit, he recognized it years later.) His use of George Blanda, for

---

★ Mae Martin saved a letter written to her when she was twelve, which was contributed to the Paul W. Bryant Museum in Tuscaloosa. It includes the message, "You are still my baby and the sweetest little girl in the world and I love you very much."

instance, whom he first made a blocking back. Though the position was called quarterback in the Notre Dame box formation, it was really a guard lined up in the backfield. Blanda could pass, run, and kick, and his talents were wasted by blocking for others. Blanda didn't object to the work, at least not after Bryant's brutal practices had started to whip him into shape. It was just that he hadn't come to Kentucky to block for someone else. It's an old adage in football that with the game on the line, a winner wants the ball, and Blanda had an abiding conviction that if given the chance with the ball, he would be a winner. "In the last scrimmage of the spring," Blanda recalls, "I changed a play in the huddle. It didn't work, and Coach was furious. He wasn't on the field, I think he was watching from the press box, but he got out and on the field so fast it made my head spin. He grabbed my shoulder pads, shook me and said, 'You little shithead, I'm the coach of this blankety-blank team, and when you get your own football team you can go making up your own plays. While you're here, you run mine or your ass is going to be back in that little Pennsylvania town I can't remember the name of.' "

Bryant's objection to Blanda's improvisation was louder than the one he had to Jimmy Williams's touchdown run in the Maryland-Guilford game, and even more absurd. A running back given an assignment to advance the football should not be told by a coach *how* to do it; he must make that decision for himself once the ball is snapped. A quarterback needs not only freedom to operate within an established framework but also the authority to make necessary changes and have his team believe in his decisions. Bryant did not yet know this; he hadn't yet perceived that football was more complex than it had been when he was playing in the mid-1930s, and that the quarterback needed to be the coach's representative on the field, not his puppet. "I wasn't intimidated by what they did or said after that play," adds Blanda. "I was pissed off. He made me look bad in front of the rest of the offense, which made me a less effective quarterback. I tried to talk to him about that later. I thought, 'Well, maybe he's going to take my head off, but if we're going to win, he's got to know how I feel.' Well, I talked to him, and he wasn't happy about it, but to my surprise he listened. But it took a while to change things."

Finding himself in an angry funk, Blanda moped and Bryant responded by demoting him to the B team. Blanda reacted with ferocity. "Okay, I said to myself, you want to see some action, Coach, I'm going to give it to you." In practice—installed at linebacker, a position he hated—he tore into his teammates with such savagery that, as Bryant put it, "if I had let him go on, he would probably have maimed somebody, or himself." Later, Blanda admitted to Bryant that he had been kicked hard in the face during that scrimmage and was so pumped up that he didn't realize it until afterward. That's how determined he was to make an impression.

Bryant was indeed impressed; while it was too late in the season to start with a whole new offensive scheme, he began 1948 with a T-formation, which put the ball into Blanda's hands for more key plays and allowed him both variety and freedom in their selection. To help him implement the new system, Bryant did exactly what he would do twenty-three years later—he called in a fellow coach who was a friend and asked for some help. Bobby Dodd of Georgia Tech not only came up to lend his expertise, he left his playbook with Bryant upon returning to Georgia. Bryant later admitted, "If I'da done it sooner, George would have made All-America."

Things began slowly, with the Wildcats losing three of their first four games. Then, with the new offensive scheme kicking in, Kentucky shifted into high gear, going unbeaten for the rest of the season. There were two ties, hardly disgraces: one against a powerhouse Villanova team (which had won eight of ten games that season) and the other against Tennessee in Knoxville, the first time Bryant had not lost to the great General Neyland and the Volunteers. The Villanova game was particularly memorable for Blanda's finest moment as a Wildcat. Trailing 13–6 with just over forty seconds left in the game, Blanda shrugged off a Villanova tackler, threw a fifty-six-yard touchdown pass, and kicked an extra point to tie the game. Kissing his sister had never seemed so good to Bryant.

Bryant learned something that season. It did no good to search out and train the best field leader if he wasn't going to let him lead. From here on in, Bryant's quarterbacks would still be kept to a strict game plan, but within that game plan they would be allowed to make their own adjustments and on-field decisions. The next time Bryant got hold of a stud quarterback he would show that he had learned from his mistakes.

BRYANT'S RESPECT for General Neyland was so profound that, according to some observers, the young Bear was often humbled and intimidated in his presence. Bryant did have one opportunity to humble the General. In 1948, the two coaches had made a gentleman's agreement not to prepare for their annual showdown by watching the other's game films. However, three weeks after the Wildcats beat Marquette, a package arrived at the Kentucky athletic department. It was a film of the Marquette-Kentucky game, and it had been mistakenly addressed to the Athletic Department of the University of Tennessee at "Knoxville, Ky."

Bryant simmered but said nothing, resisting the temptation to call Neyland's office and ask him what in the hell was going on. On the afternoon of the game, Bryant arrived early and, without knocking, walked into Neyland's office. "General, here's that film you asked for of the Marquette game," he said, tipping his hat as he slipped out of the office. Kentucky, a big underdog that afternoon, fought the Volunteers to a 0–0 tie.

No MATTER how valiant the ties, Bryant could not countenance a season in which he had won just five games. Most of the 1948 season was frustrating, and not simply because George Blanda was running the team out of a new formation. The relentless pressure Bryant had subjected the Wildcats to in 1946 and 1947 was not producing the same results in 1948. The three puzzling losses to Ole Miss, Georgia, and Vanderbilt, by a total of fifty-five points, were SEC games, and midway through the third quarter Bryant heard the first boos of his collegiate career. He did not respond well. He decided to leave his entire starting backfield home for the road game at Marquette. The Wildcats went on to beat Marquette easily, 25–0, and the following week breezed through a road game at Cincinnati. But Marquette and Cincinnati were not SEC games, and his players may have been responding better to the relative lack of pressure.

Before the Marquette game, Bryant had dinner in Milwaukee with Don Hutson and George Preston Marshall. Hutson told him not to worry about the upcoming game. Marquette, after all, wasn't even an SEC game. Bryant told him he was worried anyway. Marshall told him to forget about Kentucky and to come and work for him, not as an assistant but as head coach.

Bryant was intrigued. The NFL, though still ten years away from the 1958 Baltimore Colts–New York Giants sudden-death title game that would make pro football the country's most popular television sport, was on the verge of turning the corner from minor to major league. Nonetheless, for the second and not the final time in his career, Bryant spurned pro football. He wanted to win in the college ranks where he, and not an owner or star player, could control the game. He wanted to win at Kentucky.*

The 1949 and 1950 Wildcats, benefiting from a stepped-up recruiting pace and from several blue-chippers coming into their own, were to be the greatest football teams in Kentucky history. Two of Bryant's biggest and most talented prospects were Walt Yowarsky and Bob Gain, who had several things in common. Both came from hard backgrounds, both were molded by Bryant and would go on to successful pro football careers, and neither man would ever worship at the altar of Bear Bryant.

Yowarsky, from Cleveland, arrived on campus as a freshman, in Bryant's recollection wearing a zoot suit with narrow trouser legs and suspenders that pulled his pants up above his waistline. His coat came almost to his knees, he had a ducktail hair cut, and he was twirling a long chain around his finger. An assistant coach asked the brash newcomer if he wanted something. Yes, he said, he wanted to see "the Bear." Yowarsky does not quite remember it this way. "Yeah, I dressed kind of funny back then, but I never wore any zoot suit. And believe me, I would have never called him 'Bear.' I was tough, but I wasn't stupid." Yowarsky was, however, what Bryant would call a wiseass, and rather proud of it. "He was always getting in trouble for one thing or another and always running punishment laps," recalls his teammate, Larry "Dude" Hennessey. "He didn't seem to mind them too much, either. He'd run a lap and pass by our freshmen coach, Bill McCubbin, and say, 'McCubbin, I'll be here when you're gone.'" And, as Bryant noted with some surprise, "He was right, too."

Yowarsky was an excellent football player. He would play for six seasons in the NFL, including three with the New York Giants, primarily on

* Two years later, Marshall would ask him again. The second offer was even more tempting: Marshall offered Mary Harmon twenty thousand dollars to help buy a new house if she could talk her husband into signing on the spot. He also offered Bryant an option to become part owner. Bryant claimed to have refused for two reasons, both of which sound plausible. First, he had always been so highly motivated that a purely professional atmosphere, straight-cash reason for coaching was foreign to him. The second, "the real clincher," was what would happen if he didn't get along with one of the team's stars, particularly its great passer, Sammy Baugh. Marshall dodged the issue, assuring him it would never happen. But Bryant knew it could happen and took Marshall's answer to mean that he would knock back the coach if such a dispute were to arise. Basically, that was all Bryant needed to know.

defense. He finished his football career as a scout for the Dallas Cowboys. Two decades after he coached him, Bryant would regret that he had not understood him better. "I could have done a better job."

Bob Gain was a *great* football player. At Kentucky, he was a two-time consensus All-America and, in his senior year, winner of the Outland Trophy as the nation's outstanding lineman. In the NFL, he was selected to go to the Pro Bowl five times and won a championship ring with the 1964 Cleveland Browns.

In his senior year in high school, Gain was the most heavily recruited football player in the football-mad Steubenville Valley, which included parts of West Virginia, Pennsylvania, and southern Ohio. His father had died when Bob was eleven, so at age sixteen he went to work in a coal mine to help support his family. He took a summer job at a strip mine owned by a man named Jimmy Snider, son of a Greek immigrant; history would remember Jimmy Snider as Jimmy the Greek, oddsmaker for, most prominently, CBS-TV. Bear Bryant just happened to know Jimmy Snider; in the absence of any other source to comment on the nature of their relationship, the reader is free to speculate. Bryant had a Greek-American coach, Mike Balitsarsis, on his staff and sent him to Snider to help land Bob Gain. Bryant beefed up the attack by sending in Carney Laslie, but it would take more than reasoned persuasion on the merits of Kentucky football to seal the deal with Gain.

Another school—no one ever said which one—had offered Gain five thousand dollars to sign, an enormous sum for a kid whose mother was a widow and who was destined for the mines. Snider graciously matched the offer, specifying that it was not attached to Gain's going to Kentucky. Mickey Herskowitz, who interviewed Snider years later, said Snider insisted that he gave Gain the money "just because he was a great kid. Jimmy said he gave him the money so he wouldn't feel obligated to go to any school for money." Fortunately for Snider's pal, Mike Balitsarsis, Gain chose Kentucky. Of course, in addition to Gain's relationship with Snider, there was the force of Bryant's personality to consider. Gain was coveted by, among others, Notre Dame, North Carolina, and Pittsburgh. According to Gain, Bryant won "by challenging me. It was masterful psychology—he read me perfectly. The others said, 'We want you. We want you,' but Bryant sort of approached me with an attitude that said, 'I think you're good, but are you good enough to play for me?' I bought it." For his part, Bryant never felt that he "read" Gain perfectly; Gain, he wrote in *Bear*, was someone "I should have handled better."

Bryant never stopped challenging Gain, and a couple of times he came close to challenging him too much. "During one of my first practices, I think it was in '47, he got really pissed off about my having missed a play. 'What's the matter with you, Gain? I wanted you on this team because I thought you were smart. Aren't you smart? A smart man wouldn't have missed that play.' I know it was his idea of challenging me, but the way it came off, it was more irritating than challenging. I know he was trying to appeal to my intelligence, but at the time it seemed to me more like he was challenging it.

"I had a couple of overbearing coaches in high school, but nothing like this. I told him I hadn't missed the play. . . . You couldn't do that with Bear. . . . When I tell you he was shaking when he looked me in the face, I'm not kidding. Dammit, I knew I was in the right, and I stood my ground and faced up to him. I thought he was going to hit me, and so did some of the other guys. It flashed through my mind that that could be the end of my football career at Kentucky, but I thought, 'Well, if it's going to happen, let it happen, but I'm not backing down.

"I don't know whether he saw something in my eye or whether he realized I was right and there was no point in pushing the issue. Whatever it was, he paused, glared at me, and said, 'Well, who the hell were you supposed to get on that play?' I told him what my assignment was. He started calling off the other ten players and asked me, 'Do you know what *their* assignments are, too?' Well, I did. I knew the assignment of every player on that play. I even knew where all four of the backs were supposed to go and who they were supposed to block."

Gain didn't drop it there. He then proceeded to tell Bryant what everyone's assignments were if a reverse had been run off the play. Bryant looked at Gain, exclaimed, "Shit!" and walked away. It was a smart move for more reasons than one. Bryant had seen that Gain wasn't about to back down, but just as important, he saw that Gain knew what he was talking about. He would later admit that he was secretly pleased that his coaching had caught on so well.

Everyone who played on those Kentucky teams has a story about Bear Bryant and Bob Gain. Dude Hennessey's was one of the most popular. After one tongue-lashing, Gain announced to anyone who would listen in the dorm that he was going to "whip the Coach's butt for what he said to him. Some of us kind of egged him on," recalls Hennessey. "We never really thought it was going to happen, but Bob got so worked up that for a while it seemed like it might. We started taking bets. Bob got upset when he saw that everybody was betting on Coach Bryant.

"A bunch of us jumped into some cars . . . and drove to the Coach's house. Bob went up and knocked on the door. Bryant was kind of shocked to see him, 'The hell do you want, Gain?' Bob cracked and said, 'Coach, I was just wondering if I could go home for Christmas this year.'" In Hennessey's version, Bryant is supposed to have replied, "'Yeah, you can go, but don't come back and expect to play in a bowl game.'"

That's Hennessey's recollection. Gain says it never happened. "I'll tell you one that did, though," he says. "The summer before my senior season he took us on a fishing trip. The water wasn't deep, and Coach jumped in trying to land a fish. I was right next to him, and he must have stepped into a hole. He actually went under for a moment. I grabbed him, slipped, and actually went under myself for a split-second. He swallowed some water, and when he came up, he was sputtering. He stared at me and said, 'You tried to drown me.' Well, I hadn't tried to do any such thing, but I could see how it might have seemed like that. I probably should have protested, but instead I just smiled at him and said, 'No, but I could have.'" A few months later, Bryant would find himself in another sink-or-swim situation with Bob Gain.

ALL THROUGH Bryant's career, his critics, supporters, and most of all his opponents misread him as a strategist. He is supposed to have originated the maxim that "three things can happen when you go back to pass, and only one of them is good." (No one really knows who first said this, but Bryant popularized it.)* The one good thing that can happen, a completed pass, began to assume a greater role in postwar football as offensive strategy became more sophisticated.

---

* When I asked Bryant about this in 1982, he was vague. "Well, there are a lot more things than three that can happen when you try to pass. The quarterback can complete the pass, but he can also run out of the pocket for a gain. He can get tackled for a loss or throw an interception, but he can also throw it incomplete. What nobody ever talks

Bryant had seen what a good passer like George Blanda could do to lift a team and knew he should have coached him better. When he heard about Vito Parilli, he was determined to sign him and handle him right. Actually, Bryant had a crack at Parilli the year before his high school graduation and had not handled him at all. Parilli had visited Lexington with a friend of his, a much sought-after running back who eventually signed with Ohio State. He had looked frail next to his friend, and no one on the Kentucky staff seemed much impressed by him. In his senior year in Rochester, Pennsylvania, he was such an extraordinary passer and runner that schools from all over the region were after him.

Bryant and Laslie drove from Lexington to Parilli's home to give him the pitch. Bryant invited him to visit the Kentucky campus; he was surprised when Parilli told him, "Coach, I've already seen it, I was there with a friend last year." Bryant immediately recalled him, as well as how they had snubbed him. Bryant asked for another chance and promised he would make him feel wanted.

"Coach Bryant sure kept his word about that," Parilli recalls. "When it came time to sign, he sent Carney Laslie to pick me up in a limousine. He told me we were going to Pittsburgh, to Forbes Field, to see the Pirates play. Coach Laslie took me and another player, a player from Virginia, John Nestoskie, on a ride straight to Lexington. I don't know how long we were on the road, fifteen or sixteen hours, maybe more. But while we were on the road, there was no chance of any other school getting to us. I think they called it kidnapping back then."

Parilli was tall and wiry, about six feet two inches and perhaps 170 pounds when he started at Kentucky. He was actually best known as a running back who could throw a deadly option pass. Bryant understood that the era when an offense could be built around trick plays was fast closing; Parilli, he thought, was good enough to lead the team and to be a regular passer, and that's how he played him. He remembered Parilli as "the best fake-and-throw passer I've ever seen, so quick and strong with his hands he could pump three times before he threw." "Babe," or "The Kentucky Babe," as he would become known by his junior year, dazzled Wildcat opponents

---

about is how your linemen can get caught with a holding penalty trying to defend their passer. I've never seen any study on it, but it's always been my observation that most of the big penalties on offense came from pass blockers getting caught while holding."

with an amazing total of fifty-four touchdown passes in three seasons and then went on to play for fifteen years with the National and American Football Leagues, ending his career at age thirty-nine as a backup to another great Bryant quarterback, Joe Namath, on the New York Jets.

In an odd twist of fate, Parilli would miss the chance to quarterback for Vince Lombardi and the Packers, leaving Green Bay a year before Lombardi arrived; the Packers' quarterback would become Bart Starr, who had missed the chance to play for Bear Bryant at Alabama when Bryant turned down an offer to replace his friend, Red Drew, in 1954. Drew had his worst season for the Tide, finishing 4–5-2. Starr graduated from Alabama two years before Bryant came back. Starr, who was one of the best fake-and-throw quarterbacks of all time, picked up some pointers from Parilli. Starr's high school football coach at Sidney Lanier High School in Montgomery, Alabama, was Frank Moseley, Bryant's former assistant and close friend. Moseley brought Starr up to Kentucky to meet Bryant and to work with Kentucky's ace passer. Starr very nearly succumbed to Bryant's lure, but changed his mind at the last minute when his sweetheart and future wife Cherry chose to go to Auburn. Starr opted for Alabama because "I knew if I went to Kentucky I would lose her." Bryant came within a wisp of recruiting both Starr and Paul Hornung, two-thirds of the backfield that would win three NFL championships for Vince Lombardi at Green Bay. Parilli, by the way, later taught some of the same fake-and-throw techniques to Super Bowl winning quarterbacks Terry Bradshaw and Craig Morton.

In 1949, the Wildcats—paced by a rock-ribbed defense that featured Gain, Yowarsky, Charlie McClendon, Harry "Wildcat" Jones, and Ben Zaranka and an offense with Parilli's drop-back passing—shut out four of their first five opponents and won nine of eleven games, losing only on the road to Southern Methodist and at home to Tennessee, as usual, 6–0. Invited to the Orange Bowl, the team was to face an unlikely opponent, the University of Santa Clara in California. Everyone figured the Wildcats would beat Santa Clara resoundingly. That judgment wasn't based on logic; Santa Clara, a Jesuit school, had a superb football team. The previous season it had finished 7-2-1, and going into the Orange Bowl against Bryant's Wildcats, its record was 8–2.

The 1950 Orange Bowl was the first big postseason game in Kentucky football history, and in preparation Bryant drove his team with an intensity that a more experienced coach would have tempered. The Wildcats came out throwing and on their second possession moved quickly downfield for a touchdown and a 7–0 lead. In the second quarter, it looked like they would drive with ease for a second touchdown as Parilli hit on two big passes to move the ball inside the Broncos' 10-yard line. Here the drive faltered, but Kentucky kicked a field goal for a 10–0 lead. Midway through the second quarter, it was still all Kentucky. Another near-touchdown drive stalled, but once again the Wildcats salvaged a field goal to give them thirteen unanswered points. Bryant, standing on the sidelines with his hands on his hips, seemed satisfied; things were going almost exactly as he had planned. But the last few minutes of the second quarter revealed the short-sightedness of that plan as Santa Clara took the ball downfield just before the half, moving it with surprising ease on the ground to score a touchdown and cut the Wildcat lead, 13–6 (Santa Clara missed the extra point).

In the second half it appeared as if Bryant's team was wilting, and the third quarter confirmed that impression. The Wildcats managed just two first downs to the Broncos' six, though no points were put on the board. In the fourth quarter, Kentucky collapsed completely, Santa Clara outscoring Kentucky 15–0 to win 21–13.

One wants to give the players their fair share of the blame for losing, but the truth is that the defeat was primarily the result of one of the worst coaching performances in Bryant's career. Two weeks before the bowl game, Bryant had taken the team down to a training facility in Cocoa Beach and worked them out three times a day in the kind of heat that no one in Kentucky saw the entire football season. "It was a damned shame," says Bob Gain. "We were the better team, and by rights we should have won that game by a couple of touchdowns. But we were exhausted before the game started. Bryant had taken it out of us in practice." Bryant's reaction to the loss was childish and petulant. At a post–Orange Bowl banquet he was expected to congratulate his opponents. Instead, he grumbled into the mike, "I'm a win man, myself. I don't go for place or show." He then slumped back down in his chair.

IN MANY ways the 1950 season was a turning point for Paul Bryant. At thirty-seven, he was reaching the age when he was more of a father figure than an older brother to his players, and, despite his embarrassing performance after the Orange Bowl, he was beginning to show signs of maturity. Charlie McClendon, who would later become his assistant at Kentucky and his opponent as head football coach at Louisiana State, was one of Bryant's favorite whipping boys in practice. One afternoon, after a hard one-on-one session, Bryant prepared to square off against him. "I'd had just about enough," McClendon recalled, "and I was ready to let him know it. I loved him, but I wasn't going to let him use me as a practice dummy any more. He looked in my eye and could see that I meant business. He straightened up, slapped me on the shoulder, and said loud enough for everyone to hear, 'Aw, hell, you get the idea.'" That's the way McClendon told the story; Bryant, who loved to tell self-deprecating stories, admitted, "I knew my limits. . . . One day I began to sense old Charlie Mac was getting his back up, and when I got eyeball-to-eyeball with him, I knew I had picked a wrong time. I straightened up and said, 'Anyway, Charlie, we get the idea.'" All of his players were getting the idea. Bryant's Wildcats finally clicked in 1950, playing on all cylinders on offense, defense, and special teams. When he had come to Lexington early in 1946, Bryant had told President Donovan that he had a timetable: "We'll win in five years," he said. His prediction was perfect.

The coaching staff was upgraded with the addition of young Paul Dietzel, who would become one of three assistants to Bryant to win a national championship. Dietzel had been a member of Sid Gillman's staff at Cincinnati. (Gillman, one of the most progressive offensive coaches in college football, would later become the inventor of the so-called West Coast offense popularized by Bill Walsh and his San Francisco 49ers in the 1980s.) Kentucky had beaten Cincinnati in 1949, but Bryant was impressed with the play of their offensive line and lured Dietzel to Kentucky as his offensive line coach.

Dietzel quickly found out that although Bryant wanted coaches who were not yes-men, saying no to him could make for a bumpy ride. At one coaches meeting, a discussion developed around the proper method of blocking the opposing team's defensive end. Bryant gave his theory, and Dietzel, who had learned differently under Gillman, told him, "Coach, I don't agree." "Well,——-it-to-——!" Bryant exclaimed, "So you don't agree." ("Coach Bryant could just come out with the darnedest string of curse words when he got worked up," Dietzel recalls.) He then threw the chalk against the blackboard, shattering it. "He did that a lot," says

Deitzel. "He seldom put the chalk back in the tray. I think he did it just for emphasis."

In the men's room, another assistant coach, Ermal Allen, told Dietzel, "That was great. I haven't seen anybody stand up to Coach Bryant like that." "Well," said Dietzel, "I thought that's why he brought me here." Later, Bryant went up to Dietzel and announced, "All right, we're gonna try it that way." The new blocking plan worked. Bryant turned to Dietzel in a game, smiled, and said, "It works." "That was his way of apologizing," says Dietzel.

Throughout their relationship Dietzel found Bryant quick to anger and—always in his own way, of course—quick to apologize. In 1951, Bryant, once again facing a big game against General Neyland's Tennessee Volunteers, discussed a new blocking plan with Dietzel. Dietzel made his suggestion; Tennessee clobbered Kentucky 28–0. "We had barely gotten into the locker room," remembers Dietzel, "when he said to me 'Pablo'— he always called me 'Pablo' because it was too confusing to have two Pauls on the staff—'What went wrong?'" Bryant always asked all his coaches this question after a loss, but on this occasion Dietzel was the only coach who had an answer.

"I said, 'Well, Coach, we shouldn't have made that change.' He said, 'Well,——-it-to-——, why the——didn't you tell me that before the game?' I got fired up myself and looked him straight in the eye and said, 'Coach, if you didn't think it was a good idea, why did you agree to it?'" The Monday after the game Bryant called Dietzel into his office; Dietzel fully expected to be fired. "'Pablo,' he said to me, 'I want you to go down to New Orleans and scout Oklahoma and Maryland in the Sugar Bowl. You never know, we might end up playing Bud Wilkinson in a bowl game.' That didn't make any sense to me because no one we played a year later was going to have the same team in a bowl game. Then I understood that it was his way of apologizing—he was giving me a vacation in New Orleans for make up for chewing me out."

KENTUCKY WHIPPED their first four opponents of the 1950 season by an average score of 26 to 0, their first six by an average score of 30 to 2.5, and their first ten by 38 to 6.2. (One of those victories was a 28–14 win over Bobby Dodd's Georgia Tech in Atlanta; Bobby Dodd may have regretted leaving Bryant his playbook.) The tenth game was a horrific 83–0 slaughter of North Dakota University in which Bryant yanked his starting players out of the game at the half and sent them to the practice field to start preparing for the following week's game with Tennessee.

The only scare during the first ten weeks came in the opening game against North Texas State, when Babe Parilli took a nasty hit to the groin. "We beat North Texas State by twenty-five points," says Parilli, "but Coach Bryant felt that wasn't good enough, so he wanted to put us through an extra workout after the game. It was the first time that I couldn't do what he wanted me to do. I said, 'Coach, I don't know what's wrong, but I think it's serious, I just can't run.'" Parilli was experiencing pressure from internal bleeding and required surgery to relieve it. On the Tuesday morning following Parilli's injury, Bryant dropped by the hospital and added another story to his ever-growing legend. "He came into the room," says Parilli, "and dropped the playbook on my bed. 'You learn that, Babe,' he said to me. 'The game depends on it.' I thought to myself, 'Is he crazy?' Later, when I got to know him better, I realized that that was his way of saying, 'Babe, I hope you're feeling better.'"

According to Bryant, the coaching staff assumed that Parilli could not play the next week against Louisiana State, but Parilli insisted otherwise. The hospital wasn't conducive toward as fast a recovery as either wanted; the constant parade of pals and well-wishers wasn't allowing him enough rest. It didn't seem to occur to Bryant that his condition might be normal for someone recovering from a groin injury. There being no specific rules against such actions, Mary Harmon picked up Babe at the hospital and brought him home. By Thursday, he had regained much of his strength. On Friday, Bryant decided that Babe could play after all, met with his coaches, and designed a formation to prevent further damage to his still-suffering quarterback. Essentially it involved snapping the ball back to Parilli instead of having him take the ball directly from the center and backpedaling. Later, this would come to be known as the "shotgun" formation, with all eligible receivers scattering in all directions as if from a shotgun blast. The idea was that this would spread the defenders out and keep them from rushing the quarterback.

Pat James, the starting offensive guard, supplemented the new strategy with inspiration. "If you let anyone lay a hand on Babe," he told his teammates on the offensive line, "I'll personally kill you." In the pregame warm-ups, Bryant put his arm around Parilli and told him, "Bigness is in the heart, Babe. You get out there and throw and throw till I tell you to stop." Kentucky breezed down the field and scored on its first possession, passing on all seventeen plays. LSU, an outstanding defensive team, wasn't prepared for this. Its larger defensive players, who outweighed Bryant's boys by ten to fifteen pounds, began to wilt in the heat trying to reach Parilli before he released the ball. With Parilli hitting on key passes early, Kentucky jumped to a 14–0 lead. The Wildcats used up most of the second half running the ball on the ground and chewing up the clock. The 14–0 win was the only game in the first ten weeks in which they failed to score at least 25 points, but it was their most important victory.

By the tenth game, the Wildcats had clinched the SEC title, the first in their history. Many around the country thought the Wildcats were better than just the best team in the Southeast; many thought they were the number-one team in the nation. They already had, in Bob Gain, the most highly touted lineman in college football and, in Babe Parilli, perhaps the best drop-back passer. It was Kentucky's dream season.

But then came the Tennessee Volunteers and General Neyland. In four seasons against Tennessee, Bryant's Wildcats had suffered three close, hard defeats and managed one tie. This seemed to be the year Bryant would break the Tennessee jinx. But playing in a near blizzard in Knoxville—conditions were so bad that Tennessee officials called on the student body to come out on Saturday morning and help remove snow from the tarp covering the field—the Vols managed to escape with a 7–0 victory, the fourth time in five years the Wildcats had failed to score against the Vols and the fourth time in five years they had lost to them by either six or seven points.

Unable to establish any consistent running or passing attack on the slippery turf—neither team could move the ball with any regularity—Bryant called his favorite trick play, the tackle-eligible pass, three times (the offensive tackle checks in with the official as a receiver and then lines up a step back from the line of scrimmage, technically in the backfield). Three times Babe Parilli completed the pass. Three times Kentucky gained a huge chunk of yardage. Three times the officials called a penalty on the play and put Kentucky in a deep hole. Three times, according to most observers on both sides, the officials blundered. (Bryant had alerted them each time before the play that his tackle would be an eligible receiver, just as the rules dictated.)

The loss was devastating. Kentucky still beat out Tennessee for the SEC title and nothing could take that away, but the Wildcats' first shot ever at a national championship had vanished in the flutter of an official's flag. Nearly a quarter of a century later, Bryant's recollection of the game was still fresh. "To this day," he said in *Bear*, "I would tell General Neyland or anybody in the state of Tennessee that the officials took that one. I'm trying to be more humble and all now, but they took it from us. . . . If it had been in Birmingham or Tuscaloosa, I'd have gone out and sat on the ball, but this was General Neyland's territory, and I'd have just got penalized more." It's significant that Bryant did not say, "If it had been Lexington." At that period in his career, he was still in awe of the great coaches of his youth.

IN 1951 there were just four major bowl games: the Rose Bowl, the oldest and most prestigious; the Orange Bowl in Miami; the Sugar Bowl in New Orleans; and the Cotton Bowl in Dallas. The bowl games were still pretty much regarded as postseason rewards rather than as a means for settling arguments as to which was the best college football team in the nation. (The wire-service polls and other organizations that selected the national champion could seldom agree from year to year on whether the bowl games should even be included when voting for the number-one team.)★

The coaches, the players, and sometimes both at the same time had trouble taking the bowl games seriously. A bowl game seldom meant as much as a victory over a school's traditional rival, and if a school wasn't playing for pride, often regional pride, as Alabama had played for so many times in the Rose Bowl, a team frequently turned in a sloppy, dispirited performance of the kind Kentucky displayed against Santa Clara in the 1950 Orange Bowl. Simply put, bowl games were generally anticlimactic. But Bryant did not intend for Kentucky's 1951 bowl game to be that way. All

---

★ There was no NCAA provision in 1950 for a national champion in major college football, and there still isn't. Most college football historians accept the 1992 season, when several conferences and bowls formed the Bowl Coalition, as the first to have an official national champion. The Coalition's first title went to Alabama, coached by Bryant's former player and assistant coach Gene Stallings, who defeated Miami in the Sugar Bowl, 34–13. The Coalition eventually evolved into the Bowl Championship Series system, which is in place today.

through the second half of the season he had been thinking about the Rose Bowl and a match that would be recognized by at least some of the polling groups as a national championship game. For one thing, the 1951 Rose Bowl would be on TV, though the import of this could hardly be appreciated at that time. (The other bowl games were still a couple of years away from being televised.)

It's likely that Kentucky would have been invited to the Rose Bowl if the Wildcats had beaten the Volunteers. Now, what was there to play for? Well, as it turned out, there was still something. While still in Knoxville, Bryant asked his players which bowl they wanted to try for, not knowing if he could deliver any of their choices. To his surprise and chagrin, only a handful of his players voted to accept any of the games he mentioned. Bob Gain, a team captain, spoke up and asked Bryant if the players could meet in private. Bryant knew something was up, and he had no choice but to try and play ball with the player who had faced him down in practice. After raising everyone's hopes, he didn't dare go back to Kentucky without a bowl bid. Bryant and his coaches left the room. Gain knew how his teammates felt; no one wanted to end this otherwise-glorious season with a loss, but none of them was going to put up with the kind of abuse they felt they had taken from Bryant the year before in Florida.

A couple of minutes later, Bryant reentered the locker room. The players would agree to go to a bowl game, Gain told his coach, only if he agreed to their demands. "I told him exactly the way things were," says Gain. "I had nothing to lose, and he knew it. I was a senior, and so were most of the best players on that team. He wasn't going to any bowl game without our consent. We had him, and he knew it." What they wanted from Bryant was an agreement that they would scrimmage just once a week, that there would be just one practice a day instead of the two they had endured before the Orange Bowl, and—if Hennessey's story about Bryant facing Gain down was true, this must have been particularly satisfying to the young lineman—*three days off* for Christmas. Bryant didn't mention any of this in his autobiography, but it happened, and he was smart enough to know when to back down. He agreed to his players' demands.

Yet there was one more. They wanted to play Oklahoma. Bryant was stunned. Playing the University of Oklahoma meant that Bryant would be facing off with Bud Wilkinson. More than Red Blaik and Army, General Neyland and Tennessee, more even than Frank Leahy and Notre Dame,

Wilkinson and Oklahoma were the dominant forces in college football after World War II and symbolized the enormous boom in popularity the game was enjoying. By the end of the 1950 season, the Sooners had been unbeaten for three consecutive seasons and now had a winning streak of thirty-one straight games.

Charles "Bud" Wilkinson was the rising star of college football. Wilkinson had been a celebrated quarterback and guard on Bernie Bierman's great Minnesota Golden Gophers teams from 1934 to 1936; in later years, after he and Bryant became pals, Wilkinson would chide him about Alabama's having been chosen to play in the 1935 Rose Bowl over Minnesota. Wilkinson was suave, well educated, and personable, everything Bryant was not. If Bryant couldn't take his team to the Rose Bowl, he was more than willing to settle for a match in the Orange or Sugar Bowl against Bud Wilkinson and his Oklahoma Sooners. He knew there was no chance of Kentucky winning the national championship so long as the popular Sooners went undefeated, no matter what Kentucky's record was. The major wire-service polls had already announced they would not be taking the postseason bowl games into their calculations, but Bryant knew that most would regard a game between two such highly ranked and highly regarded teams as national championship caliber. What Bryant wanted more than anything else was to settle the issue of which was the best team and, not incidentally, who was the best coach.

The problem was that at this point, after losing to Tennessee, Bryant was no longer sure he could get Oklahoma, and if he couldn't get Oklahoma, said Gain, "then we don't play anybody." Bryant knew Gain was talking for the whole team. Bryant put the players on a plane back to Lexington and left, with SEC Commissioner Bernie Moore and University of Kentucky Athletic Director Bernie Shively, for a meeting at a Knoxville hotel to see if their Sugar Bowl chances could be salvaged. They found a Sugar Bowl official waiting for them with a gloomy look on his face. Other teams, including Miami, were unbeaten and hoping for the Sugar Bowl to call them. Even with the national publicity surrounding Parilli and Gain, Kentucky, with a blemished record, seemed to some a less attractive Sugar Bowl guest. A conference call was arranged; after several minutes of intense give-and-take, the bowl official handed the phone to Bryant and told Bear to talk to them.

Bryant talked to them. "If you give us the bid," he suddenly heard himself saying, "I will guarantee you we will beat Oklahoma's ass. I will guarantee it." Bear Bryant, as the college football establishment was beginning to understand, was a very persuasive man. Kentucky got the bid to play against Oklahoma in the Sugar Bowl.

Why did Paul Bryant make such an outlandish promise? How could he possibly have guaranteed a victory against the defending national champion, the most powerful dynasty in college football, a team that had not been defeated for three seasons? Partly, it was confidence; Bryant always thought he had a chance to win. The better part of confidence, though, was probably desperation. He had now been a head coach for six years and still felt he had not won a big game. If he could live up to his boast, Oklahoma would be the first.

The strategy Bryant would use against Oklahoma had already been divulged to Bud Wilkinson nearly a month before the Sugar Bowl. Early in December, Bryant and Wilkinson went on a speaking tour in Texas designed in part to promote the upcoming game. In the manner of college football coaches of their time, they began to pick each other's brains regarding the other's team and tactics. Wilkinson was happy to tell Bryant anything he wanted to know about Oklahoma's famous split-T formation, then considered college football's quintessential power set, as well as the great All-Americas—halfback Billy Vessels, fullback Leon Heath, and quarterback Eddie Crowder—who implemented it.

Wilkinson then asked Bryant to reciprocate. What defense, he wanted to know, might Bryant use to stop the split-T? Bryant's defensive genius was already becoming legendary; an amazing nineteen times in eleven games that season the Wildcats had stopped their opponents inside the three-yard line. How, Wilkinson wanted to know, did they do it? "Bud," said Bear, "all we do is make 'em pass." The Wildcats accomplished this, he explained, by moving the linebackers and defensive backfield practically up to the scrimmage line, leaving an opposing offense with no gaps to sneak a runner through. "Yeah," Wilkinson replied, "but what if they *do* pass?" Bryant's response was classic: "They're liable to drop it, for one. Or somebody's liable to shoot 'em from the stands. Or they're just liable to screw up. They're going to score anyway if you don't make them pass, so we try to make 'em pass."

In preparing for the Sooners, Bryant utilized some new technology: game films. No one knows who the first coach was to use game films. The idea of using game films to scout an opponent was still relatively new. Bryant's first use of them seems to have been in 1948. Pudge Heffelfinger credited Carl Snavely, who coached at Cornell from 1936 to 1944 and who was famous for having a projection room in his den. "The camera," said Snavely, "reveals flaws the human eye can't see."[4]

As usual, Bryant wasn't the first to do something, but the one to perfect it. Bob Gain had trumped him by demanding lighter practice sessions—very well, then, his players would compensate by spending the extra time watching game films. "It paid off," said Gain, "we felt like we knew every move those guys were going to make before they made it."

It wasn't just Oklahoma's tactics that made an impression on Kentucky. "I almost hate to say this, because Bud Wilkinson was a great man and a great coach," said Charlie McClendon, "but some of his guys played dirty. We could see it in their game films. They punched and kicked and cheap-shotted just about everybody. I'm not saying their coaches encouraged it, but they let them get away with it. We were determined that we weren't going to let them do it to us. We were ready to show them that we couldn't be intimidated."

Bryant knew exactly where to draw the line. A couple of days before the game, says Walt Yowarsky, "Coach Bryant called the seniors together and told us, 'You're not going down there to get into a fight. You hit them as hard as you can, but you do everything within the rules. Just don't forget why we're there.' I think he was conscious of the fact that he was playing Bud Wilkinson and wanted his team to look good for him, but I know he was also thinking that if we started fouling them, we were going to take our minds off the game and make dumb mistakes. And he *hated* dumb mistakes."

Privately, Bryant's confidence grew as he watched the films. His Wildcats weren't as big as Wilkinson's Sooners, but they were bigger than any team Oklahoma had faced in their own conference, the Big Seven. Several college football observers thought that Oklahoma was able to win so many games because of a soft schedule. In his 1954 book, *This Was Football*, Pudge Heffelfinger quoted a Texas fan as saying, "They [Oklahoma] should win. Their schedule is on the soft side year in, year out. Wilkinson doesn't have to keep his squad up week after week, so he has time to rest his players and sharpen them up for the toughies."[5] Bryant would have agreed; more than two decades after the game he told John Underwood, "Bud was used to playing against those children in the Big Eight [the Big Seven at the time] and I wanted him to see some men." In other words, Oklahoma would lose its arrogance as soon as it got a snoot full of Parilli, McClendon, Gain, and Yowarsky.

Bryant had learned his lesson from the previous year. Before the Orange Bowl with Santa Clara, he had worked his team too hard. This time he gave the players a couple of days off before heading for the practice facilities in Baton Rouge. Instead of working them to the last day, he stopped the practices three days before the game. The result was that the Wildcats were chomping at the bit. They were so worked up in the last practice that Bryant called a halt, fearing they would hurt each other.

THE 1951 Sugar Bowl captivated the football-loving public, partly because Bud Wilkinson and Bear Bryant were recognized as the two young rising stars of the coaching profession and partly because their first meeting was the biggest postseason game not played in the Rose Bowl. In fact, the 1951 Sugar Bowl was the first of the other bowl games to overshadow the Rose Bowl.[6]

The Rose Bowl was supposed to be the biggest game in college football, but to cap off the 1950 season Pasadena offered California vs. Michigan, a lackluster match. Even though the Rose Bowl was televised, those who really followed college football were glued to their radios to hear the national broadcast of the Sugar Bowl, played in windy Tulane Stadium in New Orleans before a sellout crowd of more than eighty-two thousand.

For the first time, Paul Bryant had a national stage to work on, and he was determined to shine. Most teams that had faced Wilkinson's Sooners had approached them tentatively, not certain how to attack, like a boxer waiting to counterpunch against a slugger. Bryant had no intention of counterpunching; he was going to take the attack to Oklahoma and let *them* react to his boys. Like a lighter, faster boxer taking the fight to a bigger man, the Wildcats went straight at the Sooners on both offense and defense, keeping them off balance. Using the same strategy Bryant had employed against LSU earlier in the season, they struck quickly through the air. Parilli completed thirteen passes in the first half without being sacked or throwing an interception. Even when the Wildcats did not score, they kept the ball on the Oklahoma side of the field; the Sooners started every one of their first-half possessions at or inside their own twenty-yard line.

Defensively, Bryant did exactly what he had told Bud Wilkinson he was going to do. To the interior part of the line, where Kentucky normally played three linemen, Bryant added the talented Yowarsky, where he became, for all intents and purposes, a fourth lineman. In third-down situations with more than five yards to go, he became the shadow of Bob Crowder, Oklahoma's quarterback. On most downs, Kentucky showed a five-man front and, on several, moved the remaining linebackers and two defensive backs close to the line of scrimmage, creating for all intents and purposes a nine-man line. In this defensive set, only two safetymen remained to pick up a receiver who got downfield or a running back who broke through the line. This was a daring strategy. Bryant knew that physically his team did not match Oklahoma's man-to-man. He was sure his boys would prove to be quicker. He was right. Several times, Gain, Yowarsky, and company pierced the Sooners line and hit their ball carriers almost as they were taking the handoff. In the first quarter, Yowarsky forced a fumble; the Wildcats swarmed on it, and Kentucky had the ball deep in Sooner territory. Three quick passes from Parilli yielded a touchdown. In the second quarter, Parilli moved his team downfield and threw for a second score. Kentucky led 13–0 at the half.

The Wildcats played virtually error-free football. The only mistake was made by their coach, who admitted that he called the game too conservatively in the second half, when he had a chance to go for the jugular. "I lost my guts," as he later put it. (It was a mistake he learned from and would correct in later years.) He nearly got a blowout anyway. Parilli was robbed of a third touchdown pass when an official mistakenly ruled the Kentucky receiver was out of the end zone. In desperation, Oklahoma rallied for a second-half touchdown to make the score 13–7. Twice the Sooners penetrated the Kentucky five-yard line. Twice the Wildcats threw the Sooners for losses, just as they had done to their opponents during the regular season, with Yowarsky stopping Crowder on key plays. Kentucky clung tenaciously to its six-point lead and won, 13–7. Yowarsky was voted Player of the Game.

"I felt like I was in complete control out there," Parilli recalls. "Coach Bryant made me feel he had complete confidence in me, and that made me confident. I was the boss in that huddle, the coach on the field. When I came over to the sideline in a key situation and told him I thought I could hit one of our ends on a third and long play, he just waved his hand and said, 'Go ahead. You know what you're doing.'"★

"I've got to hand it to him," says Bob Gain, recalling the game fifty-three years later. "He delivered what he promised. There were times I wanted to knock him down, and so did several other guys on the team. But he taught us how to play, and how to play together. He coached us to the biggest victory of our lives."

The 1951 Sugar Bowl was the most spectacular upset in college football since the end of World War II. If the game had been televised and if the wire-service polls had chosen to hold their vote until after the bowls, the Wildcats would have been national champs and Bear Bryant would have become, overnight, one of the most famous coaches in America. The final polls still showed Oklahoma ranked at number one, but no one who saw the game had any doubt who was really number one. In 1986, the now-defunct College Research Association studied the 1950 season and concluded that based on schedule toughness and margin of victory, Kentucky was the best team in the country that year. To date, it is the only time in nearly twelve decades that the Wildcats reached that pinnacle.

As important as the game was to Bryant, it may not have been as important as what happened in the locker room afterward. In the midst of the shouting and cheering, Bud Wilkinson walked in and the room fell silent. "It looked," says Parilli, "like that scene in the movie *Gentleman Jim* where Ward Bond's John L. Sullivan walked in to the victory party for Errol Flynn's Jim Corbett and hands him his championship belt." Wilkinson, mustering all the dignity possible for a coach who had just lost his first game in four years, went from player to player shaking hands and congratulating them, ending with a tribute to the Wildcats and their coach. For the first time in his coaching career, Bryant got goose bumps. "Bud Wilkinson taught me something that day," he said. "He showed me the class I wished I

★ Bart Starr would later voice similar sentiments about Vince Lombardi. "Once I understood his system," says Starr, "I felt that I was in charge out on that field. I don't think he sent in nine plays in nine years."

In the legendary Ice Bowl victory over Dallas on December 31, 1967, in perhaps the most famous play in pro football history, Starr, with thirteen seconds to go and the ball on the Cowboys' one-yard line, came to the sidelines and told Lombardi that he thought a "wedge" play with Starr carrying the ball would work. "Then run it," said Lombardi, "and let's go home."

had." Wilkinson taught Bryant that it was possible to bring honor to one's university even, perhaps especially, in defeat. Bryant made a vow on the spot that he would never again be a bad loser. Losses were inevitable, and when they came, he would face them with the same nobility that Wilkinson had shown in the biggest loss of his career—up to that point, at least. Bear and Bud would have one more historic meeting.

Don Hutson and his wife had come down to New Orleans for the game. They went gambling on a riverboat; all shot craps—Bryant won. The next day, early in the afternoon, Bryant walked to a little restaurant near the hotel and met Charlie McClendon (who had to be taken to the hospital after the game with a severe eye gash) and his wife; his cousin Dale Kilgore, down from Fordyce for the game, was there too. They all "looked as numb as I was. Happiness can do that to you."

Before returning to Lexington, Bryant went on a hunting trip with friends on a Louisiana bayou. Exhausted from the big week, he fell asleep and awoke in the dark with a jolt—had he dreamed the Sugar Bowl victory? He couldn't wait to check the newspapers and see the proof in print. But no dream is perfect. When he returned to his office, he found sixty-four unused Sugar Bowl tickets that, considering the hype surrounding the game, would have been worth a small fortune. He had stuffed them in the side drawer for protection and then, in the heat of preparations for Wilkinson's Sooners, had forgotten to take them to New Orleans.

The off-season seemed like even more of a dream. Coaching offers poured in. One night as he was working late, a knock came on his office door. "Hello, Bear," said the man standing there. "I'm Bob Hope." Hope, who was performing at a local show with Jane Russell, had become a fan. Paul couldn't wait to get on the phone and tell his mama that her favorite movie star had just come by to pay him a visit. It was official: Bear Bryant was now famous. Bob Hope knew his name.

Secure in his role as the most exciting young coach in college football and reveling in his new status in one of the most class-conscious of southern states, Bryant turned down all other offers, including the one most tempting to both himself and Mary Harmon, the chance to go back to Alabama and continue the tradition established by Wallace Wade and Frank Thomas. "Shucks, son," he told a reporter who questioned him about the rumors, "I'm gonna live and die in old Kentucky." Herman Donovan rewarded his loyalty with a twelve-year contract. There was just one more hurdle before he reached the top: General Neyland and Tennessee. In reality, his biggest problem would prove to be a basketball, not a football, coach. Technically, Adolph Rupp was not Bryant's boss, but Bryant knew that until he won a couple of national championships, basketball ruled at the University of Kentucky.

"The first thing a football coach needs when he is starting out," Bryant said in reflection, "is a wife who will put up with a whole lot of neglect. The second thing is at least a five-year contract."[7] In Mary Harmon and his new Kentucky contract, Bryant got more than he had ever bargained for. So did the University of Kentucky: after two consecutive national basketball championships in 1948 and 1949, Adolph Rupp's Wildcats won the SEC in 1950, the same year that Bear Bryant produced the best football team in the university's history. Both coaches were given gifts at the annual sports banquet. Rupp got a new Cadillac; Bryant received a cigarette lighter. To be fair, the lighter was engraved. At least, that's the story that Bryant repeated until his death. He either neglected to mention or didn't know that the Cadillac was not from the University of Kentucky but a private gift. (Russell Rice recalls that Bryant's admirers later presented him with a new car as well, though Bryant always failed to mention that when telling the story.) The lighter became part of the Bryant legend, a prop he repeatedly pulled out of his pocket at banquets and interviews as a prelude to the story of why he left Kentucky. Within a few years, Bryant had practically worked the cigarette lighter incident into a comedy routine.

In the winter of 1970, Adolph Rupp invited Bryant to appear on *The Adolph Rupp Show* (and, incidentally, to celebrate the Wildcats' victory over the Crimson Tide in basketball). Bryant launched right into the routine: "Remember when they gave you that big black Cadillac, 75 to 80 yards long? Here's what they gave me." He produced a lighter from his pocket. Rupp, playing the straight man, looked it over and confirmed, "Yeah, that's the original lighter." The camera did a close-up on the lighter; it was a plastic disposable model—the kind that wasn't manufactured until the 1960s.[8]

Nearly all explanations as to why Paul Bryant left Kentucky lead to Adolph Rupp, but in truth the 1951 and 1952 seasons made it clear to Bryant that he had hit a ceiling at Kentucky. The Wildcats were a mediocre 13–8–4 in those two seasons, records mitigated by tough schedules and an impressive victory over Texas Christian on January 1, 1952, in the Cotton Bowl. But there was still Tennessee and General Neyland to contend with—the Volunteers won the national championship in 1951. There was also Georgia Tech, 21–0-1 in 1951 and 1952, and, for that matter, there was Alabama, coached by Bryant's old friend Red Drew.

Most of the best linemen from his great 1950 team graduated, and Bryant was hard put to replace them. To compensate for the change, Bryant installed the Oklahoma split-T formation, which Bud Wilkinson graciously helped him with by sending his quarterback, Darrell Royal, to Lexington to instruct Bryant and his Wildcats on the finer points of the formation. (Twenty years later Royal would help Bryant again by teaching him the intricacies of the wishbone offense at Alabama.) The split-T took much of the heat off Babe Parilli in his senior season, but by the early 1950s, Bryant was finding problems he couldn't solve by changing formations. The biggest problem was increasing competition from the notoriously tough SEC, which had become even more intense in response to Bryant. As Frank Sadler puts it, "He made all the other coaches work harder." As a result, recruiting for Kentucky was now tougher than it had been when Bryant started there right after the war.

Bryant pulled out all the stops when he went after Howard Schnellenberger from Kentucky's most renowned Catholic high school football factory, Flaget, in Louisville. Schnellenberger was regarded by many as the state's best lineman and, if he chose Kentucky, the likely heir to Bob Gain as the school's primary defensive player. But Schnellenberger had already made a verbal commitment to Indiana University when Bryant approached him after the 1950 season. When Bryant's car pulled up in front of the Schnellenberger household, Howard's mother exclaimed, "My goodness, it's Coach Bryant!" A moment later she called out, "My goodness! It's Governor Weatherby!" (Weatherby, a personal friend of Bryant's, was known as "X-1" for his license plate. "There was always a room open for Bear at the mansion," as one of Bryant's former assistants says.) Their argument was direct: no matter what Howard had said to Indiana University, his first duty was to his home state. He should stay put and play football for the greater glory of the state university. So said Bear Bryant and the governor of Kentucky. "Either Coach Bryant or Governor Weatherby would have been enough to impress my father," says Schnellenberger. "I was all set to reverse my decision, but my mama held out. She said,

'Howard, you told Indiana that you were going there. You have to live by your word.' Even Coach Bryant knew better than to argue with Mama about this. He knew exactly when to back off."

He never read Sun Tzu, but Paul Bryant instinctively knew the art of the indirect method in warfare. A week or so later, he dropped in at the Schnellenbergers' home again, this time with an associate more likely to impress a pious Catholic like Howard's mother: the archbishop of the Louisville diocese. The priest and the player's mother went for a brief walk. When they returned, recalls Schnellenberger, "My mother said 'Howard, God wants us to do what is best for you. He will understand if you change your mind and go to Kentucky.'" There were times when it was difficult for those around Paul Bryant to distinguish his will from God's.

Bryant began the 1951 season with more than 130 freshmen. In a tactic that would become infamous in Texas, he bused his new recruits to a spot far from the prying eyes of parents and press, in this case, a military academy in Millersburg, about a half hour from Lexington. There he conducted three grueling practices a day, quickly determining which freshmen had staying power. "In bed at night, you'd hear this scraping sound outside your window," says Howard Schnellenberger. "The first couple of times we got up to look and saw it was guys escaping, sliding down the drainpipes." Schnellenberger stuck it out and became one of the forty freshmen who made the team. In his senior year, he would make All-America.★

By 1953, Bryant had more to worry about than competition from his own conference. The northernmost of SEC states, Kentucky also had to compete with powerful midwestern football behemoths: Woody Hayes's Ohio State Buckeyes, Biggie Munn's Michigan State Spartans (national champions in 1952), and Frank Leahy's Notre Dame Fighting Irish. It was a Louisville boy, Paul Hornung, who was blamed by many for hastening Bryant's departure from Kentucky. Hornung was called a "triple threat," with his abilities to run, pass, and kick. In reality, he should have been described as a quadruple threat, as he was a ferocious blocker too. Or per-

★ Schnellenberger began coaching under Bryant's successor at Kentucky, Blanton Collier, and a few years later joined Bryant at Alabama, becoming perhaps the most brilliant of Bear Bryant's coaching offspring. Schnellenberger was one of Bryant's most celebrated recruiting successes. Ten years later the former player, now an assistant coach, would use the lessons he had learned first hand while observing Bryant to haul in the most famous recruit of Bryant's career.

haps quintuple threat was more appropriate, because he was a superb defensive safety. By the time Hornung was a senior at Flaget, the school that had produced Schnellenberger in 1951, it was widely agreed that he was the best high school player in the state of Kentucky—some thought in the entire Midwest and South. There was also little doubt in Kentucky sporting circles that he would be playing his college ball for the Bear. His versatility and instinct for the big play made him Bryant's type of player. Bryant wanted Hornung so badly that he asked Babe Parilli to go with him to Louisville to help recruit him. The problem was that Hornung's mother could see him going nowhere except to a Catholic university. Notre Dame won out; Hornung went on to win the Heisman Trophy and played on four NFL championship teams at Green Bay, coached by that most Catholic of coaches, Vince Lombardi. Years later at a banquet, Bryant, apparently having exhausted his cigarette lighter story, introduced Hornung as "the reason I left the University of Kentucky." Afterward, Hornung asked Bryant to "please not say that in public any more. I know you're kidding, but I still have to live in this state."

THE SEASONS from 1951 through 1954 were watershed years for college football. The United States Military Academy was shaken by a cheating scandal in 1951 that helped precipitate the decline of Army football. Despite a comeback in the 1952 and 1953 seasons and one more glorious season, 1958, when the Associated Press ranked its team the third best in the nation, Army's half-century run as a major college football power was over. Frank Leahy retired in 1953, and Notre Dame, the leading football power in the nation from the time of Knute Rockne until then, would sputter on and off until Ara Parseghian reinvigorated the program in 1964. In 1954, Pudge Heffelfinger, the first All-America selection and the first man to earn money playing football, died, and his book, *This Was Football*, which summed up more than six decades of the game's lore, was published. In 1954, too, college football went back to a single-platoon team with limited substitution, after easing the replacement rules during and after World War II. This meant players had to put in time on both offense and defense. Still, the unlimited-substitution experiment was a bad omen for traditionalists like General Neyland, who loathed the practice, and for Bear Bryant, who pretty much ignored the liberalized rules altogether and insisted that his players be in good enough shape to play both offense and defense.★ (Though he didn't take chances with a player such as Babe Parilli, who couldn't be replaced; for the most part Parilli stayed on offense.)

At the end of the 1952 season General Neyland retired. Freed from the pressure of having to coach against him, the Bear and the General now became friends. Neyland and his family were regular guests at the Bryants' lake home. "He was more of Coach Thomas's era than mine," Bryant would say later, "but he was a giant and the respect (or dread) Coach Thomas had for him carried over to me."

Bryant's assistants kidded him that he got ill every time Tennessee was mentioned. To Bryant, it wasn't a joke; he admitted to worrying himself sick in the days before Kentucky played Tennessee. Some thought General Neyland had a jinx over him. But "it was no jinx, he was a better coach, and he had better football players—and I couldn't stand it." Bryant never defeated Neyland. By 1953, "I made up my mind I had enough of this Tennessee foolishness. I had five simple plays that were sound and proven. This time I threw everything else out. Just three running plays—an option, a fullback-off tackle, and a counter—and two passes. Our boys knew those good." Pudge Heffelfinger claimed that Neyland had ordered a play run five hundred times in practice before using it in a game; Bryant ordered his five plays to be run more than five hundred times in practice, and in 1953 Bryant finally beat Tennessee, 27–21. It wasn't the same as beating General Neyland, but it sure beat losing.

In the spring of 1954, Frank Thomas died in Tuscaloosa. "How much can a man influence you?" Bryant would ask when recalling Thomas. "I tell my coaches, when they go out on their own, to be themselves, but that doesn't mean not to learn from people who have something to teach you. I used to call long distance to get Coach Thomas's advice"—twenty years after Thomas's death, Bryant was still referring to him as "Coach"—"years after he quit coaching. Even after he got sick—and I hated to see him that

---

★ In *This Was Football*, Pudge Heffelfinger wrote, "It has always been highly ridiculous to me that a young man can't play sixty minutes of football without fatigue. That's why I was happy when they got rid of platoon football. It separated the men from the boys." (p. 181)

Joe Sheehan, the veteran football writer for the *New York Times* and president of the New York Football Writers Association, told Pudge, "Two-platoon football had developed specialization to a ridiculous extreme. Now once again, the 'whole' football player is there." (Ibid.)

way, so scrawny and weak from fighting high blood pressure—I chartered a plane just to go spend a few hours with him. . . . I visited him every chance I got. Just being around him could help you."

One more major change came to college football in the early 1950s, one more important than any revision of rules on the playing field. By that time, most of the major football powers outside of the Deep South were in the process of racial integration. The University of Kentucky, fourteen years ahead of Mississippi, had integrated its student body as early as 1948, but like the other SEC schools, it feared possible reprisals for recruiting black players. "It's difficult now for anyone to understand how hard core racist things were back then," says Russell Rice, "men whom you consider to be good would not speak up about integration of the sports teams. The universities were afraid of the governors cutting off funds, and the governors were afraid of losing votes and political support. The schools were also afraid of being kicked out of the conferences. If you were an SEC school at that time and you were voted out of the conference, it was death to your athletic program."

Bryant, an avid baseball fan, had watched athletes such as Willie Mays play in person, and he was well aware that Jackie Robinson's entry into the big leagues in 1947 had started a process that would never be reversed. Like other Kentucky coaches, he had occasionally gone to games at black high schools such as Dunbar High in Lexington and had fantasized about recruiting some of their top players. Bryant's overtures to the university administration were greeted with embarrassed smiles and silence; he did not pursue the matter, nor did he speak openly to many people at Kentucky about his beliefs on integration. Occasionally, to a trusted friend, he would open up: athletic director Harry Lancaster recalls Bryant telling him that he wanted to play the same role in college football that Branch Rickey had played in Major League Baseball.* In later years, he would speak almost wistfully of the lost opportunity at Lexington. "I wanted to be the Branch Rickey of football when I was at Kentucky," he told B. J. Phillips in a *Time* magazine interview in 1980.[9] In truth, it was only after the publicity surrounding integration at the University of Alabama in the 1960s that Bryant's failure to take more of a stand at Kentucky became an issue. Curi-

---

* The quote was found by David Briley in Lancaster's papers at the University of Kentucky.

ously, sports journalists did not openly criticize the man who really held the power in Kentucky athletics, Adolph Rupp, for *his* failure to push integration.

Things might have been different had Bryant stayed at Kentucky for another few years. In 1955, A. B. "Happy" Chandler was elected governor. While far from an ardent integrationist, Chandler qualified as a southern liberal governor during the Eisenhower era. For one thing, he had offered the Brooklyn Dodgers' Branch Rickey token support in his efforts to bring Jackie Robinson into Major League Baseball, which was more than any previous commissioner of baseball had done. "It's not my job," he was once quoted as saying, "to put blacks in the school, but if they show up, it's my job to see they are protected."[10] Chandler, who integrated Kentucky state parks, and was an avid sports fan and a big follower of University of Kentucky football, would surely have supported Bryant on integrating the Wildcats—which almost certainly would have kept Bryant at Kentucky, Adolph Rupp or no Adolph Rupp. But Chandler arrived two years after Bryant's departure. Between missing Chandler in Kentucky and getting George Wallace in Alabama, Bryant had bad luck with governors.*

"I don't believe that Coach Bryant had a bigoted bone in his body," says his former Kentucky team manager, Frank Sadler. "He had the prejudices he was raised with, we all did. But he was perfectly willing to play any black kid who he thought could help him." In later years, Bryant's critics and supporters alike would echo the sentiment that he didn't care about making a social statement regarding integration, that all he really cared about was finding better football players. Both his critics and his supporters were right. He was a football coach, and he tended to look at men mostly in terms of football.

AFTER THE victory over Tennessee that ended the 1953 season, the Bryants gave a party at their house to celebrate the successful 7–2–1 season. A couple-score sportswriters came to snack, drink, and ogle Mary Harmon

---

* Amazingly, George Wallace asked Chandler to be his vice presidential running mate in his 1968 campaign before he settled on General Curtis LeMay. Chandler was willing, but many of Wallace's supporters were horrified by Chandler's record on integration and Wallace subsequently backed off.

and assistant coach Jim Owens's wife Martha, the twin belles of Kentucky football. Late that night, when the pressmen filed out, Bryant found a handsome brown fedora lying on his bed, the kind of hat, he thought, that an executive might wear. It was to be his signature head wear until the coming of the houndstooth hat.

"SO WE won at Kentucky," Bryant later said, looking back on it all, "and I don't think I would have ever left if I hadn't gotten pigheaded. It was probably the most stupid thing I ever did. I could have had about anything I wanted, and Mary Harmon loved it. We had a social position coaches seldom have—good friends with Governor Weatherby and all—and we lived right there near the Idle Hour Country Club."

Bryant claimed that he and Rupp never exchanged a cross word, and apparently he was telling the truth. "They liked and respected each other," says Frank Sadler, "but they were too much alike to get along in the same athletic department. Both wanted their sport to rule." Actually, the Baron and the Bear got along very well for eight years, but Bryant couldn't stomach incidents like the one that occurred in his first season, when he drove to Harrisburg, Kentucky, on a recruiting mission. When he was introduced at a local function, a town official announced to the crowd, "I'm sorry we couldn't give Coach Bryant the key to the city, but we have given one to Coach Rupp for all the championships he's had. We'll save one for when Coach Bryant wins as many games." Bryant fumed and barely contained his temper. He didn't want a key to the city, and when he won as many games as Rupp, he told them, he would be able to buy the city.

The drive that had propelled Bryant from Moro Bottom to national fame could not be satiated by the kind of limits that Kentucky imposed on him. In 1952, before a game with Texas A&M, a group of sportswriters gathered in Bryant's office to preview the game. Rupp poked his head in the doorway and said, "Don't forget, boys, the real show starts on Monday." It didn't gall Bryant that Rupp said it; Bryant could kid with anyone. What galled him was that it was true, even though the Kentucky basketball team played no games that season because of the NCAA's sanctions.

Rupp, despite his bravado, was blowing smoke, and everyone knew it. Rupp's troubles had begun in 1949 when three players from their national championship team, Ralph Beard, Alex Groza, and Dale Barnstable—the first two were players on the 1948 U.S. Olympic basketball team—were discovered to have conspired with gamblers to shave points in a National Invitation Tournament game at Madison Square Garden on March 14.★ Given the power the NCAA wielded both then and today in today's college sports, no coach's program that is guilty of such infractions could possibly survive. But in the early 1950s, information was difficult to gather and slow to surface. Coaches with powerful friends—and no coach in college basketball had more powerful fans than Rupp—could find ways to weather a storm.

There was more. In 1952, Walter Byers, the first executive director of the NCAA, created a new enforcement division for the rapidly growing organization. Byers was determined to show the organization's power by finding a highly visible athletic program to make an example of, and Rupp's Kentucky basketball, guilty as sin, was perfect. Byers began investigating rumors that the Kentucky basketball program violated recruiting rules by allowing illegal inducements from enthusiastic alumni. In his arrogance, Rupp at first believed he could simply ignore the investigation and bully his accusers into submission. He was wrong; the NCAA and the SEC, working together, suspended the nation's most famous college basketball program for the 1952 and 1953 seasons.

Though Bryant did not mention it in his autobiography, he felt stymied by the regulations passed by the University of Kentucky in large part to control the damage from the basketball scandal. The one that hurt the most was a new recruiting rule that specified that the football team could only award scholarships to five out-of-state players. "That infuriated him," says Frank Sadler. "He knew damn well there was no way Kentucky was ever going to be a major football power with just in-state talent, particularly if

---

★ The Kentucky betting scandal came at what was perhaps the worst period of corruption in college basketball history, following the revelations that several City College of New York players had conspired with gamblers to fix games. Adolph Rupp angered New York sportswriters by implying that the corruption was confined to New York City, saying outright that gamblers couldn't get near his boys with a ten-foot pole.

A few days after Rupp returned to Lexington, an enormous package was delivered to the Baron's office. The contents proved to be an eleven-foot pole. The card read, "Courtesy of the New York Basketball Writers Association."

he couldn't recruit black players." Kentucky simply didn't have enough high schools to draw from.

Bryant had no grudge against Rupp, and in fact sympathized with his plight, but he had no intention of allowing his football program to be scaled back. President Donovan assured Bryant that Rupp would be forced to retire in the near future—or at any rate, that's what Bryant would later contend. Donovan also assured Bryant that Kentucky's football facilities, which were in danger of falling behind those of its SEC rivals, would be upgraded. Bryant seems to have left the meeting with Donovan convinced that Rupp would soon be gone and that Kentucky football would not suffer. In February of 1954, while on a recruiting trip in Alabama, Bryant picked up a newspaper and read that the University of Kentucky had just awarded Adolph Rupp a new multiyear contract. The anger Bryant felt was sharper and more focused than his reaction to Curley Byrd's interference eight years before.

In 1945, Paul Bryant had been a rookie with just one full season of head coaching experience under his belt. Now he had turned two moribund football programs around and established himself as one of the best head coaches in the country. If he would not tolerate Byrd's interference in 1946, he certainly would not accept Donovan's reneging on his promises in 1954. In 1946, shortly after Bryant had accepted the Kentucky offer over the phone, George Preston Marshall had asked him to coach the Washington Redskins. Bryant wavered, but finally turned Marshall down. He had made a commitment and did not feel he could go back on it. Later that year, according to Bryant, after Kentucky played Alabama in Montgomery, Frank Thomas told his former pupil that illness was forcing him into early retirement and asked Bryant if he wanted to take over the Alabama job for 1947. Bryant told Thomas he would take the job, but Donovan found out and told Bryant he was forbidden to leave the campus. Bryant told him he was going.

Donovan got tough, reminding Bryant that he had signed a contract. But Donovan knew enough, too, not to get too tough with his football coach; he raised Bryant's salary to twelve thousand dollars a year and extended his contract to ten years.

It's likely that Bryant could have found a way out of his Kentucky contract if he had wanted to—most coaches can when given what they feel is a justifiable reason. But in this instance Bryant had to acknowledge that Kentucky, by giving him both a raise and an extension, was acting in good faith, so he honored the bargain. Now, seven years later, he felt Kentucky had broken its end of the commitment. As he had done at Maryland, Bryant made up his mind on the spot that he would leave, and damn the consequences. "I don't know," he replied to a reporter who asked him what he would do next, "maybe I'll drive a truck, but I won't be coaching at Kentucky." President Donovan was shocked, or at least said he was; he should not have been, considering that he knew better than anyone else what had gone wrong between Bryant and Maryland. Fans, students, and local press were also shocked; there hadn't even been a rumor of a feud between Coach Rupp and Coach Bryant. They hadn't heard a rumor because there was no feud, but no one would understand that until later.

Donovan was also furious. He met with regents and informed the press that the university would not release Bryant from his contract. Bryant had already decided how to counter that move and called on his good friend, X-1, at the governor's mansion. Weatherby had the sense to understand that there was no point in trying to keep an unhappy Bryant at Kentucky. The damage had been done, and Weatherby knew that once Bryant decided he was leaving, there would be no stopping him. The governor made a conference call to the regents and advised them that it would be a good idea to let Bryant go peaceably. If they did it willingly, Weatherby would not have to order them to do it.

Thinking back on his divorce from Kentucky, Bryant admitted that he had handled the Rupp situation poorly. Given a second chance, he would have simply gone to Rupp and talked things through. Then "he'd have been my friend." Since they wound up as friends, Bryant was probably right. When Bryant needed a public defender after his first tumultuous season with Texas A&M, Rupp gallantly jumped in. In 1973, suffering from cancer and a year after his retirement, Rupp received an invitation from the Bryants to fly to Tuscaloosa for the Alabama-Kentucky basketball game and to stay at their lake house.

No one could see it at the time, not Rupp and not even Bryant, but the truth is that the University of Kentucky was simply not a big enough stage for Bear Bryant, with or without Adolph Rupp to share it. After Bryant left, Kentucky football slowly faded back into mediocrity. Under his successor, Blanton Collier, the Wildcats managed a 19–10–1 mark over the next three seasons, perhaps living off the fumes of Bryant's reputation.*

BRYANT HAD converted a habitual SEC doormat, a team with no football tradition and no first-rate football facilities, into a team that would post a 60–23–5 record over eight seasons and win two of three bowl games. The Wildcats also finished among the nation's top-twenty teams five times. Kentucky had great expectations when it hired Bryant, but it's unlikely that anyone's, even Bryant's, were so high.

George Blanda, his first big star, makes no bones: "I don't think I would've even stayed in football if not for him. He was a huge influence on my life." Blanda's successor, Babe Parilli, says, "He was hard on me, at times very hard, but he made me understand what I was capable of achieving. I can't ever say that he was unfair." Walt Yowarsky, on the other hand, never quite forgave Bryant for that zoot suit remark. "Yeah, he made me a better player. But I respected him a lot more as a coach than as a human being."

Steve Meilinger, who played halfback, tight end, and quarterback for Bryant, had a difficult and complex relationship with his coach. "In my sophomore season," says Meilinger, "I smarted off to one of our assistant coaches. To be honest, it wasn't the first time. I was pretty cocky back then. Bryant sent the team manager to tell me he wanted to see me. He was in front of the mirror fixing his tie when I walked in. Without looking at me, he growled, 'When we recruited you, we thought you were a great football player, but you're turning into a real smart ass, and you're disrupting this team.'

"Then he swung his forearm and knocked me several feet across the room into a chair. I just sat there stunned. I was about as big as he was, but I knew better than to start anything. I knew he had no right to do that, but I also knew something else, which was that I was in the wrong for the way I had acted on the field. Besides, I wanted to see what he was going to do next." Bryant told Meilinger to turn in his uniform and clear his stuff out

* In addition to not being mean, Collier couldn't maintain the recruiting pace required to win at Lexington; he won just twenty-two of fifty games in his last five years at Kentucky before joining the Cleveland Browns, where he would establish a brilliant record, including the NFL championship title in 1964, which put a championship ring on the finger of Bob Gain.

of the dorm. "I didn't argue," says Meilinger. "I got right up out of the chair and walked straight down the hall. About ten seconds later, one of the assistant coaches ran up to me, grabbed my arm, and said, 'Coach Bryant wants to see you again.' I thought, 'Okay, what the hell, I've got nothing to lose, let's see what he's going to do.' I remember asking myself as I walked back to his office if I might hit him back if he hit me again.

"I was rather surprised by what happened. When I went into his office, he was seated calmly at his desk, his hands folded in front of him. He didn't yell at me. 'I'll give you another chance,' he told me, 'but if you screw this one up, you'd better get your ass out of here before I get my foot to it.'" Reflecting back on his encounter with Bryant years later, Meilinger concedes, "I'm not sure it wasn't the best way to handle me. I definitely needed someone to keep me in line, and he certainly did that. I kept my ass in line from then on, and we never had another problem. I've often asked myself if he could have achieved the same results without having to belt me. I don't know, but if he had found a different way he wouldn't have been Bear. Let's just say we worked it out. Yeah, we became friends."

Bryant was so pleased with the way Meilinger fought back that he button-holed Grantland Rice and pressured him to tout Meilinger as an All-America, which might have been possible if Meilinger hadn't divided his time among four positions.* Twenty years after leaving Kentucky, Bryant named Meilinger, Yowarsky, and Gain as players he should have handled better. He handled most of them well enough. "Let's just say we had an understanding," says Bob Gain, "we became friends—after it was all over at Kentucky. To tell you the truth, I think he was still working his way through how to be a coach when he had us. I've often thought over the years how much I would rather have played for him at Alabama."

In 1954, though, coaching at Alabama was not an option for Bryant, and having decided that he could no longer be at Kentucky, there was the imminent question of where he would be coaching next.

---

* Like many of Bryant's former players, Meilinger found a career in law enforcement, becoming a U.S. marshal in Kentucky.

Chapter 5

Gone
to Texas

"I went to Texas A&M, I'm an Aggie."
"Business?"
"Tight end."

—*Billy Bob Thornton to George Clooney,*
Intolerable Cruelty

THE FALLING OUT WITH Kentucky could not have come at a worse time for Bryant. In the last few seasons, he had turned down offers from Arkansas, Alabama, Southern California, and Minnesota, to name just the most prominent schools that had approached him. In the winter of 1954, there were simply no coaching plums to be had; he thought briefly of sitting the season out to see what might develop, but quickly abandoned the idea. He simply could not stand the thought of missing a college football season. One intriguing possibility was pro football. For the third time in his life, Bryant had attracted an NFL offer. Green Bay's president, Emil Fischer, asked Babe Parilli, his quarterback, to talk to Bryant about taking the job. Bryant had met Fischer through Don Hutson and liked him, but the real attraction would have been the chance to work with Parilli again. If Bryant had taken the job, Vince Lombardi might never have come to the Packers and the course of both college and pro football would have been radically altered. But in the end, the combination of leaving the

South and living in the frozen northern tundra of Green Bay, Wisconsin, proved too much for him.

Mary Harmon was not consulted in the matter, which was probably for the best in the case of the Green Bay job; merely the thought that they might move to the tiny blue-collar town with its Arctic-like winters would surely have brought her to despair. As it were, she was distressed enough when she saw what the best-available offer was. The campus of the Agriculture and Mechanical College of Texas—many, including some A&M students, thought the *M* stood for *Military* and referred to their school as "Old Army"—was not one that could be sold by brochure. According to Jim Dent, whose book *The Junction Boys* immortalized Bryant's first year at the school, "The campus possessed all the glamour of a stock show" and "boasted the color scheme of a grocery bag."[1] Texans were fond of referring to it as "Sing Sing on the Brazos," for the nearby Brazos River. The Bryant children didn't find A&M all that unpleasant. As Paul Jr. recalled for Al Browning, "When we arrived at Texas A&M, we were pretty shocked by what we saw. There wasn't much there, at least not to speak of, and Mama was really upset. . . . About all we saw in College Station was a small town and military barracks on the campus. Mae Martin and I had a different position than Mama. My sister was at an age when she liked seeing all the cadets. As for me, I liked seeing the cadets in uniforms and seeing an occasional tank."[2]

To Mary Harmon, leaving the lush bluegrass country of Kentucky for what appeared to her as a wasteland was devastating. Mae Martin's son, Marc Tyson, remembers his mother saying that Mary Harmon's first reaction to Texas A&M was, "Oh my, oh my, what has Daddy done?" The first thing Daddy had done was get a good deal for himself and his family. The day after he made up his mind to leave Kentucky, and knowing Texas A&M had fired its coach, he phoned Jack Finney, a member of A&M's board of directors, and asked to see him that night in Dallas—Dallas, rather than Houston, as Dallas was over two hundred miles from the A&M campus in College Station, thus ensuring secrecy. The meeting was arranged at an airport motel; among the attendees was A&M's chancellor, Dr. Marion Thomas Harrington. When Bryant arrived, they pulled the drapes closed. "Making it out," he remembered, "to be a real hush-hush deal."

Bryant laid his cards on the table. He wanted to make what the heads of the other departments made, no more, no less. To the modern football fan accustomed to seeing college coaches pulling in salaries like those of professional football players, such a position may seem strange. It's important to remember that from the time he began college coaching, Paul Bryant considered himself a teacher serving a legitimate function at the university, and he always measured his economic worth in those terms. Fifteen thousand dollars a year, they told him. Bryant was stuck. He didn't want to earn more than the head of a university department, but he couldn't get any security for his family on that kind of money. One of the Texans, a man named Doc Dougherty, came up with a solution, one that was not uncommon in that era. His company, the Welsh Foundation, would put Bryant on the payroll for ten thousand dollars a year, in return for which he would do off-season promotion for the company, including inspirational speeches and talks. Bryant thought that would do just fine.

He was determined that he would not come cheap. The A&M trustees, stung by inept coaching since World War II, had a policy of only offering one-year contracts. Bryant patiently explained to them that one-year contracts were a big part of the reason why they weren't getting the best coaches. He wanted a six-year deal. At Kentucky, he told them, he had promised a five-year plan, a conference championship by the fifth season. He thought he could win one sooner than that at A&M, but he must have security and they must have patience. The Texans thought it over and reminded each other that Bear Bryant had quickly turned around the Maryland and Kentucky programs in their first year. They gave him the six years. As it turned out, that was not the end of the negotiations but the beginning. There were a few other things. He wanted 1 percent of the football gate—not an outrageous demand, but hardly a typical one. A couple of the board members balked. Why? Bryant wanted to know. Weren't they hiring him in the full confidence that the gate would be increased? If more tickets were sold, what did they have to lose, and if they didn't think he would sell more tickets, why were they hiring him? Okay, they decided after talking it over, that made sense.

There was one more thing. Bryant wanted the rights to the game films for a weekly coach's television show to be aired on the Sundays after the games. Television wasn't much of a factor in college football back then, but who knew that the growing medium would be a valuable tool for a football program and a solid moneymaking proposition for a coach someday? The Texans then gave him the films for a TV show as well. As they shook

hands, Bryant told them he would be back in early February. He returned
to Lexington to clean out his office and then went straight to College Station to get to work. A tearful Mary Harmon stayed behind to move the
family.

Bryant was also sad to leave Kentucky, and in later years would go out of
his way to suggest that he took the Texas A&M job sight unseen. The first
time he saw the campus, Bryant said he, like Mary Harmon, almost got
sick. The suggestion was that they had seen A&M at pretty much the same
time—or at least Bryant not much in advance of his wife. In point of fact,
Bryant had seen the A&M campus nearly two years earlier when he had
taken his Wildcats to College Station to win a close victory over the
Aggies, so it's hard to imagine why he was so surprised when he accepted
the job.

At first, the glamourless, womanless A&M campus seemed like "a penitentiary." There are few more vivid contrasts in college campuses than Texas
A&M and Kentucky in the early 1950s. Kentucky was "a good-time place"
with a lot of temptations. Bryant loved Texas A&M, but he would never
describe it as a good-time place. Some of Bryant's friends thought the
Spartan atmosphere at A&M might have been exactly what he needed after
what they thought was an increasingly frenetic lifestyle. Jones Ramsey,
A&M's public relations man, quickly became close to Bryant. "We were
drinking buddies," says Ramsey. "Shortly after we met, we went over to my
house and went through a bottle of bourbon. We talked the entire afternoon and night away." ("I'm a scotch drinker myself," Bryant admitted in
Bear, "but Jones couldn't beg any in the neighborhood, and he came up
with the bourbon. I made believe I didn't know the difference.")

"I got the impression," Ramsey recalled, "that things were on the verge
of getting out of hand for him at Kentucky. He never actually said so, but I
think the combination of the long hours, unending pressure and the parties
and social life was getting to him. He was getting home too late and up too
early."

The social life may have included affairs. "I never heard anything specific," says Mickey Herskowitz, the *Houston Post* sportswriter who would
become one of Bryant's closest friends after Bryant left A&M, "but there
were stories about Kentucky. You never heard anything in much detail. Try
and picture John Wayne around age forty in an atmosphere like that. There
were a lot of rich, aggressive women in those Lexington social circles, and

they drank as much as the men did. It's obvious that temptation was everywhere, and I'd be amazed if he avoided all of it." According to the strongest rumor, the daughter of a prominent Kentucky horse breeder fell in love with Bryant and confronted Mary Harmon. The story goes that Mary Harmon heard her out and then quietly asked her to leave. No names were attached to this story, and half a century later it remains a rumor.

Ramsey confirms that some people at A&M were hesitant to hire Bryant for reasons unrelated to football. "There were some stories," is all Ramsey will say. Bryant may have been going through a form of midlife crisis around 1954, professional or otherwise. Frank Thomas had once told him that a football coach needs to have made his mark in the profession by age forty. By the time he was forty, Thomas had been at Alabama for eight seasons and had compiled a spectacular 64–8–2 record, won three conference championships, and taken his team to the Rose Bowl twice. One might argue that Bryant's record at Maryland and Kentucky, considering his material, was more impressive than Thomas's, but it didn't look that way on paper and wouldn't look that way to posterity.

"I think it's safe to say that Paul got out of Kentucky just in time to get a grip on his professional and personal life," says Herskowitz. "Texas A&M was a much more difficult row to hoe, but one much more suited to his temperament. There was a lot less—let's say temptation—at A&M. He knew that, and he preferred it that way."

PAUL BRYANT took Jerry Claiborne with him to Texas A&M as an assistant coach. (Claiborne, like Bryant, would one day be head coach of Maryland and Kentucky, and, like his mentor, would one day be elected to the College Football Hall of Fame.) He also brought his trainer, Smokey Harper—not the type of trainer, Bryant noted, who cried over spilt blood.

Bryant was uncharacteristically late in getting to College Station; the airline had to bump him from his flight to Houston, and a sportswriter, Jack Gallagher, from the *Houston Post* would not give up his seat for the new A&M coach. "You don't think," Gallagher asked him rhetorically, "that I'm going to stay behind and let all the other writers from Texas greet you when you land?"

The new head coach wanted to begin work the moment he arrived, and the prestige-starved "Aggies" (short for *Agricultural*) were happy to accommodate him. It was already dark when he reached the A&M campus. He was driven immediately to an outdoor theater where thousands of Aggie students and alumni—a conservative estimate was three thousand, but some who were there claim as many as six thousand—had carefully laid out, according to school tradition, a gigantic bonfire. Some schools called this a "pep rally"; at A&M, says Gene Stallings, a freshman who was in the crowd that night and would one day become Bryant's successor at both Texas A&M and Alabama, "We called it a 'Yell Practice.'" Would the new coach care to address the fans? Hell, yes, he would.

It was also a tradition, Bryant was told before taking the stage, for a speaker to take off his coat when addressing an Aggie crowd. Bryant was happy to comply. As he walked up to the microphone, he took off his hat and tossed it down with a flourish, then threw off his coat and pulled off his tie. Unbuttoning his cuffs, he announced, "I'm Paul Bryant, and I'm rolling up my sleeves so we can get to work." The crowd went berserk. Then he paused and waited for the crowd to grow silent. He held the microphone in both hands and spoke softly into it: "Boys, it's time to win some damn football games."

The crowd erupted again. Several of Bryant's future players were among them. Don Watson, a halfback, was in awe. "I just saw God!" was his first reaction. The Aggies weren't the only ones mesmerized; Bryant had surprised himself with his performance. "It was like voodoo. Those Aggies went crazy. . . . Ten Aggies can yell louder than a hundred of anybody else." Bryant scooped up his coat and tie and walked off the stage. He slapped the Aggies' PR director, Jones Ramsey, on the arm. "I sure as hell lit a fire tonight," he said. "I'd never heard of him until that night," said Stallings, "and he gave me goose bumps. I knew right then and there that things were going to be different."

They certainly were going to be different. Bear Bryant was about to coach the Texas Aggies into the worst season in his or their history.

A&M HAD FIRST come to football prominence after World War I under the leadership of the legendary Dana Xenophon Bible. An Old Testament–quoting son of a classical scholar, he was considered "the first coach to 'civilize' Southwest football," according to Pudge Heffelfinger. The Aggies had won a national championship in 1939 under Homer Norton—who, in his heyday, compiled a good enough record to eventually get him in the College Football Hall of Fame—but they had had just two winning seasons since World War II. Bryant's predecessor, Raymond George, had won only twelve of thirty games from 1951 through 1953.

It was Texas A&M that created the tradition of the "Twelfth Man." On January 2, 1922, A&M was matched against a tiny liberal arts school named Centre College of Danville, Kentucky. The annual clash of southeastern-southwestern powers—and Centre was a football power in 1922 despite an enrollment that was less than half of its current total of nearly eleven hundred—was called the Dixie Classic, from which the Cotton Bowl would eventually evolve. "The Praying Colonels," so nicknamed by Grantland Rice when he saw the Centre team in prayer, were taking it to the Aggies that afternoon so Coach Bible sent for reinforcements. King Gill, who had left the football team a couple of weeks earlier to concentrate on basketball, was summoned from the stands and told by Bible that he might be needed before the game was over. Gill replied that he was ready; players shielded Gill with blankets while he changed into his uniform on the sidelines. As it turned out, Gill was not needed, and the Aggies went on to beat the Colonels 22–14. But the tradition of the Twelfth Man, ready to come out of the stands and fight for Texas A&M, was established. Even today it's not uncommon to see male and female students at Aggie games standing through all four quarters in memory of Cadet Gill.★

With its all-male student body (the school did not become coed until 1964) and military tradition, there wasn't much reason for out-of-state blue-chip prospects—players of the caliber of Bob Gain and Babe Parilli—to consider coming to that part of Texas. As General Phil Sheridan proclaimed after the Civil War, "If I owned Texas and Hell, I'd rent out Texas

★ Aggie spirit, say some older grads, is exemplified by the obscure 1943 film *We've Never Been Licked*, in which a young A&M graduate played by an actor named Brad Craig helps to foil a Japanese plot to sabotage a chemical plant located on the College Station campus—or at least that's what I've been told, as I've never been able to locate a copy of the film. The cast list, though, sounds interesting. A young actor named Robert Mitchum made his screen debut as an Aggie named "Panhandle Mitchell." William Frawley, later to become immortal as Fred Mertz on *I Love Lucy*, plays a Japanese spy. Sportscaster Bill Stern plays himself. Every Aggie in the movie supposedly volunteers for something dangerous at the drop of the hat, thus symbolizing the spirit of the Twelfth Man.

and live in Hell."[3] As Bryant himself put it, "A boy had to want to play football awful bad to go there."

Texas A&M did have one very strong incentive for football players: it was a football school in a way that neither Maryland nor Kentucky had ever been. Aggie alumni were described by their fellow Texans as "invincible in defeat, insufferable in victory"—luckily, Texas sportswriter Dan Jenkins once quipped, "They have had very little opportunity to be insufferable."

If Bryant didn't know already, he soon found that the Aggie spirit was about the only tangible advantage he would have going for him. Aggies "make the worst enemies there are. You get two of them together and you get big talking. Just the sweetest, most obnoxious guys." To most Texas football fans, Aggies were objects of ridicule and scorn; what were called "Aggie jokes" in Texas were generally referred to as "Polish jokes" in other parts of the country. (Sample: "What do they stamp on the bottom of a Coke bottle at Texas A&M?" Answer: "This end up.")★ Aggie fans, the Brooklyn Dodger fans of college football, ignored the insults and cursed right back at their tormentors: "Wait till next year!" Now they had Bear Bryant; now, they believed, next year had arrived.

PART OF BRYANT, and by no means a small part, was proud to be associated with a superb academic institution such as Texas A&M, whose schools of engineering and science were recognized worldwide. The University of Kentucky had lifted him into a social class not usually accessible to truck farmers from country hollers like Moro Bottom, but being on the staff of Texas A&M conferred on Bryant a status he would not have found at almost any other football power in the South—east or west. If Bryant was reassured by his contract and his reception at A&M, much of the school's faculty was not. There was, as Mickey Herskowitz thought, an undercurrent of resentment among them, partly because of rumors about Bryant's salary; the distinction between being paid $25,000 a year by the

---

★ I lived in Texas for nearly two years and found several Aggie jokes that were interchangeable with the ones Alabama fans told about Auburn. Sample: "Texas A&M is a school where the men are men and the sheep are scared shitless." Admittedly, the joke had more sting back before A&M went coed.

university and $15,000 by the university with an additional $10,000 on the side from a wealthy alumnus was not readily apparent.

To mollify the men he hoped would accept him as a colleague, Bryant, while at a conference meeting in Cincinnati, agreed to a radio debate with an English professor on the proper place of athletics in the modern university. The debate—"Is College Football Overemphasized?"—was broadcast back to Texas. It would be remembered in the minds of many as a clash between two entirely incompatible mentalities, one advocating the integrity of scholastic achievement and the other defending the privileges accorded to athletes and coaches.

It wasn't quite that simple. Eager to make an impression at his new school, Bryant strained to be polite and ingratiating. His opponent, Thomas Mayo, was, in fact, a football fan himself, a friend and former roommate of the Aggies' own sainted Dana X. Bible. The discussion centered on whether or not football coaches should be given longer contracts than other members of the university staff. Bryant remembered the debate as being with "some faculty guy who objected to the idea that a coach could get a contract and he couldn't."

The most memorable line was Bryant's. "Sir," he asked Mayo, "how many people watch you give a final exam?" About fifty, replied Mayo. "Well," said Bryant, "I have 50,000 watch me when I give mine, every Saturday."

Recalling the encounter in *Bear*, "I've never felt for a minute that football is the reason an institution exists, or that it is the most important reason. But I don't doubt its importance as a rallying point. It's pretty tough to rally around a math class."

DURING HIS job negotiations at the Dallas airport motel, Bryant wanted to know how many players they could expect to get out of a field of twenty if they offered the same scholarship deal as the University of Texas. Ten, they replied. He had no way of knowing that the Texans were bullshitting him. "I didn't know the Aggies then like I know them now. Old Jack was exaggerating. You couldn't get ten," he would find out. "You would be lucky to get one. The chances were you wouldn't get any. Not then."

In the winter of 1954, however, Bryant chose to accept the Aggies' bravado about their recruiting appeal. He would find to his chagrin that even players who passionately wanted to play for him did not want to play for Texas A&M. At the time, said Bryant, A&M was the toughest place in the conference, perhaps in the country, to recruit for. There were virtually no recruiting advantages to tout to a prospect. He wooed a young quarterback named Don Meredith; Meredith charmed him back by helping Mary Harmon with the dinner dishes one night. But when it came time to choose a school, Meredith burst into tears. "When I saw those tears," Bryant said years later, "I knew I had lost him." He told Bryant, "Coach, if you were anywhere in the world except A&M—anywhere in the world *except* A&M."★

"If we couldn't do anything else," Bryant said, "we could work. You could set your watch by my schedule, beginning with six o'clock breakfast at the Twelfth Man Inn at the North Gate." His staff worked as hard as ever but the results were disheartening. One of his new coaches, a friend from Arkansas named Elmer Smith, was dispatched to the fertile recruiting grounds of Alabama to ferret out some prospects. His first report to Bryant was not promising; there was only one unsigned boy who could play. "Then sign him," Bryant ordered. "Well, Coach, there is one thing. He's only got one arm." "Damn," Bryant responded, "the pickings are slim." However, if the kid really wanted to play, Bryant would give him a shot. Murray Tremble became the first and only one-armed All-Southwest Conference guard. His younger brother Wayne later starred for Bryant at Alabama.

Bryant immediately perceived that the A&M football program, its much-vaunted spirit notwithstanding, had other problems besides a lack of recruiting clout. He had faced interfering alumni at Maryland and Kentucky, but the Aggie crowd was an entirely new species. The football team was riddled with undeserving players who had been handed their scholarships because of contributions by influential graduates. An early Bryant practice was interrupted by a millionaire in a Cadillac who informed the

---

★ Meredith would choose Southern Methodist, where he first won national fame as the Mustangs' quarterback. From there he went to the Dallas Cowboys, after which he acted in television shows and co-hosted ABC's *Monday Night Football* with Frank Gifford and Howard Cosell. He usually managed to work in one good Bear Bryant story on every broadcast.

coach that he had four blue-chippers with him. Bryant cut him off; when he needed "four skinny-assed football players," he said, he'd get in touch.

As if offending wealthy alumni wasn't enough, Bryant risked alienating the athletic department by cleaning house on the football coaching staff. He retained just one assistant from Ray George's staff, William Zapalac, who had played football at A&M. Bryant had fired him before meeting him, but Zapalac simply would not quit without being given a chance to make his case. According to Jim Dent in *The Junction Boys*, when Zapalac finally got his shot, the coach tested him. When he knocked on the office door, Bryant yelled back,

> "Go away, whimp! Come back when you get a gut in your body!" Zapalac's response was to pound the office door. "That's better!" Bryant said, "Open the goddamned door and come in."
>
> Bryant got right to the point. "What would you think," he asked Zapalac, "about winning the Southwest Conference with this sorry bunch?"
>
> "I think it could . . ."
>
> "You *think*," Bryant hollered loud enough to be heard across the street at G. Rollie White Coliseum. "I don't want a bunch of people around here who *think*. Now, goddammit, answer the question."
>
> "Based on what I know about the team, we could. I think—"
>
> "Mister, you've got one more chance."
>
> "Yes, sir, it *will* happen," Zapalac said, jumping to his feet and saluting.
>
> "Now you get your ass out of my office. You're the only coach I'm keeping. So don't screw it up. And *never* salute me again."

Bryant had no patience with what he regarded as military posturing and didn't hesitate to tongue-lash Aggies who saluted him on campus.

After straightening out the coaching situation, he proceeded to try and bring the alumni into line. Dent describes a meeting Bryant called of the "big wallets" at A&M, which included his pal Jack Finney and several Texas oilmen.

> Placing both hands on the table, Bryant assessed each face.
>
> "I think that each and everyone of you is sick and tired of the losing. A&M hasn't won a damn thing since before war and there's a lot of neg-

ative recruiting goin' on. All they gotta do is tell the top recruits that
A&M's got no girls and we've lost the boy."

Bryant dropped a silver spittoon on the table. "I made my commitment when I took this job. Now it's time for you to make yours."

Nobody moved.

"Boys, just think of this as going to church and dropping the dough in
the plate. Let's see how much commitment you got in your hearts."

As Dent relays it, rolls of hundred-dollar bills wound with rubber bands
were dropped into the spittoon. When it was full, the amount was nearly
thirty thousand dollars, enough for perhaps two or three good players.

"Boys, with this kind of money, we might just be able to fix the wagon
and paint the barn."

Mickey Herskowitz doesn't quite buy the silver spittoon story. "The alumni
spent some money," says Herskowitz, "there's certainly no question about
that. But I don't believe Bryant ever saw any of it. Of course A&M gave
money to players; all the Texas schools did, even Rice, which liked to think
of itself as the Harvard of the Southwest. For that matter, I seriously doubt
if there was a major football program in this country whose alumni didn't
get money to its football players one way or the other. But smart coaches
didn't want to know the specifics, they looked the other way. It wasn't necessarily something they could control anyway, and in any event Bryant didn't
try." As Bryant said, "It's mighty hard to turn down something if you've
never had nothin' at all."

Living at the student center while Mary Harmon organized the move
from Kentucky, Bryant conducted a furious spring practice, unlike anything his players had ever seen. There were nearly 120 boys on scholarship;
Bryant thought the number to be ridiculous considering the relative lack
of talent and (he felt) desire in the majority of players. The weeding-out
process had begun. At Bryant's request, Babe Parilli flew in to help Aggie
quarterbacks learn the split-T formation. Darrell Royal, coming to Bryant's
aid yet again, came over from Mississippi State to teach them the proper
method of taking a center snap.

But the Aggie alumni were driving him to distraction. He knew he had
to get his team away from College Station. One of his coaches suggested a

place called Junction, which had been used by the university for orientation for freshman geology and physics majors and was about a six-hour drive from the main campus.

Getting wind of Bryant's intentions, Mickey Herskowitz, who had just gone to work for the *Houston Post*, approached Bryant for an interview. "Coach," he said, "I heard a rumor that there's going to be some dissension." "You're damned right there's going to be some dissension," he replied. "And I'm going to cause it."

BEFORE BRYANT had a chance to do much of anything, even to finish a brief vacation with Mary Harmon, he got devastating news from back home. On August 2, 1954, Ida Mae Bryant died of a stroke in Fordyce. His mother had been ill for some time; two years earlier she had developed a growth on her neck that alarmed her family. True to her beliefs, she refused for several months to have medical treatment. Finally, said her daughter Louise, "We were able to talk some sense into her. 'If God didn't want you to be better, He wouldn't have made a doctor who could operate on you,' we all said. She listened and gave in for our sakes." She had waited so long to have the operation, though, that her iron constitution was weakened. Paul flew up for the operation. Holding her hand at her bedside, he asked her how she could seem so happy. She said that going into the operation she thought that very soon she would be seeing either her son or the Lord, and either one was fine with her. She lived nearly two years longer. When Paul walked into the funeral home and saw his mother, he broke down. Louise recalled him saying, "This is the first time I ever squeezed your hand that you haven't squeezed mine back."

"I don't believe that there was a day in Paul's life when he didn't think about Mama or ask himself if he had measured to what she wanted him to be. She wanted him to be a preacher, but he was too honest to try and convince himself that he could ever be one. Do you know why I think Paul always told his players to go to church and to write home to their mothers? I think it was his way of being as close to a preacher as it's possible for a football coach to be."

WHAT BRYANT did not know was that the facilities at Junction were in disrepair. There was no running water or working toilets, and little more than military-style Quonset huts for sleeping quarters, which made the players feel, as several said, like they were "sleeping in a steam bath." What he also didn't know was that the area had been under severe drought for four years. (In fact, there would be no rain in that part of Texas for another three years.) There was practically no grass for practice. The ground was littered with rocks and cactus burrs. "When we drove in that front gate," Bryant later said, "I wanted to puke."

"I honestly think if he'd have known how bad it was," says Gene Stallings, who Bryant came to refer to as "Bebes" from a childhood nickname, "he wouldn't have taken us there. But once we got there, there was no going back." The die was cast for what would become the most legendary college football training camp ever.

Three busloads of would-be Aggie football players rode out there, their numbers given at anywhere between 90 and 115—Bryant had already lost a few scholarship players before the Junction trip. Only one bus was needed to carry the 29 survivors back to College Station ten days later, after spending eight days at the camp and two days coming and going.

In retrospect, Bryant's behavior that summer seems brutal and cold-blooded. To be sure, even back then some people saw him that way, but taken in the context of the time and place, there is nothing shocking about his coaching methods at Junction in 1954. Nor was Bryant doing anything much different from other football coaches of his time, high school or college. "We had just gone through spring practice with him," says Stallings. "After that, the only thing that was surprising about Junction was that there wasn't any grass on the practice field. Anybody who had played high school football in Texas knew how tough practice could be. At the college level, you expected it to be tougher. Coach Bryant was just a little tougher and a little more thorough than other coaches."

Bryant did what he was hired to do. No school wanted a winning football team more than Texas A&M; Bryant's mission, as he saw it, was to give them that winning team. If it meant running off scores of well-intentioned kids and offending their parents, that was part of the job. The university, he felt, had an obligation to provide physical education for all of its students, but that did not mean that all of those students had an equal right to play on the football team. The football team would be composed of special individuals who were willing to sacrifice more than the average student in order to represent their university—it was that simple. Bobby Drake Keith, a back who was one of the twenty-nine survivors, puts it this way: "We always heard a lot about how the Junction boys were an example of survival of the fittest. Well, I honestly don't think those of us who made it through were any fitter or any stronger than a lot of the ones who quit. We *needed* football more. It was survival of the desperate."

Bryant's Junction schedule may seem insane, but he had his logic. The first session of practice began at five o'clock in the morning in the dark; some players couldn't get much sleep anyway in the stifling heat and were awakened by the chirping of birds and crickets. This session ended in the late morning before lunch; the second one was late in the afternoon, after the heat had abated somewhat, and lasted until supper. Bryant didn't arrange the schedule to make the Junction seem like a military camp— those were the best hours to beat the merciless Texas heat. The only entertainment, Bryant recalled, was a little swimming hole and Mickey Herskowitz.

Herskowitz was a tough, smart Jewish kid, recently graduated from the University of Houston. For his first big assignment for the *Houston Post*, he had the spectacular luck of covering the new Aggie coach. Bryant had a problem unique to SWC coaches: the location of Texas A&M left him without "a big newspaper to defend you. No big city daily like the *Dallas News* or the *Houston Post*. You're stuck out there, and you're fair game."

The *Houston Post*, however, might be cajoled into his corner if he could provide it with good copy. Bryant liked Herskowitz immediately, but while Bryant was the head coach of Texas A&M, their relationship was to be professional. That boundary, of course, was constantly being tested. Bryant knew better than to try and bully Herskowitz—he needed an ally, not an adversary.

The afternoon after Bryant's first practice session at Junction left the cub reporter a bit dazed by the heat, dust, sweat, and blood. There was no Western Union to transmit his story back to the paper, so Herskowitz had to shout his story in over the phone, with his own sweat dripping into the mouthpiece and flies buzzing all around him. By coincidence, the only phone was on the outside wall of the hut the coaches used for their meetings. If you believe Bryant, no one was eavesdropping; Herskowitz's words just happened to be picked up through the thin partition walls. But, Herskowitz recalls, as he dictated his story, "the room got quieter and quieter." His description of the practice was filled with phrases about "bone-crunching tackles," a bit too vivid from Bryant's point of view. Herskowitz was including nuggets about full-scale scrimmages that had players losing their breakfasts.

The Coach waited until Herskowitz hung up, then sent the team manager to inquire if he might have a word with the beat writer. "Now, Mickey," as Bryant recalled the conversation, "you know that story's going to upset a lot of mamas and papas when they read it." Herskowitz was determined not to be cowed, but he was not ready to lock horns with Bryant. "Yes, sir," was all he replied. "And it's so unnecessary," Bryant went on. "That was no full-scale scrimmage. That was no more than a dummy scrimmage. Don't you think you ought to call your paper and tell them what really happened?" Herskowitz thought it over. "I was too young to realize how shrewd he was being," he says. "He could see I was prepared to resist him if he came at me too hard. But the way he did it made me think, 'Well, damn, this guy's won some football games and he knows a hell of a lot more about football than I do. What if he's right?' I was afraid that maybe I just didn't know enough about football to know the difference, so I called my editor and persuaded him to do a little—let's call it 'light'—editing."

As Bogart said to Claude Raines in *Casablanca*, it was the start of a beautiful friendship.

ON THE day of the first practice at Junction, some townspeople rode out to the camp in a small caravan. Aggie fans all, they wanted to throw the team a celebratory barbecue. Bryant was business-like to the point of rudeness: "We didn't come out here to eat, we came out here to play football."

"Play" makes it sound like fun. Bryant was there to *inflict* practices. He broke down the game into a series of basic drills: teaching linemen all over again the proper balance and leverage and how to explode upward by getting underneath the guard of a defensive player, and teaching tacklers to hit a man low rather than high. Like the great coaches who had come before him—Walter Camp, Amos Alonzo Stagg, Knute Rockne, Wallace Wade, Frank Thomas, General Neyland—he emphasized simplicity and precision.

Most of the veterans resented being taught football from scratch and couldn't take the devastating heat, physical pounding, and relentless pressure of the practices. They literally fled in the night, unable to face the coach who had promised them a free ticket home if they would come to him and ask for it. Rob Roy Spiller, a seventeen-year-old clerk in the bus station back in 1954, remembers, "Most of them didn't care which way the bus was going. They just wanted the first bus *out*." Some of the players who stayed weren't sad to see them go—Dennis Goehring, for instance. "I wasn't sad to see any of those guys slipping away in the night. The more who left, the better chance I had of making the team."

"Goehring," said Bryant, "was one of those we took to Junction and hoped wouldn't stay. He was just a little bitty guard"—he was five feet ten inches and weighed about 180 pounds, a ridiculous size for an offensive lineman even in 1954—"and Smokey Harper was afraid he'd get killed." Goehring spat their skepticism right back at them. "I'll be here when you and Bryant are both gone," he snarled at Bryant and Harper. In *Bear*, Bryant noted with pride that Goehring was indeed correct; he later became president of the bank of A&M that counted his former coach among its stockholders.

BRYANT DID not neglect the spiritual needs of his players. On the first Saturday in Junction, he asked, "Tomorrow's Sunday. How many of you boys want to go to church in the morning?" "Some of us still went to church regularly," says Bobby Drake Keith, "and some of us had kind of backslid as we got older. But no matter how we felt about church, we all knew we'd rather be there than practicing." There were about forty players remaining; nearly every hand shot up. Bryant beamed and told his assistant coach, Pat James, to write down the names of all the boys who wanted to go to church. He then informed them that they would leave for church immediately after Sunday-morning practice.

BRYANT WAS telling the truth when he insisted later that the upperclassmen left partly because they knew it was a new regime. They had enjoyed what was pretty much a free ride for two or three years, and now a radical and entirely unexpected change had come. The football program was suffering because a great many juniors and seniors had been granted privileges they hadn't earned. In contrast, Bryant's sophomores were both lean and hungry; eight of them made it through Junction, and, as Bryant was proud of pointing out in later years, five of them, most notably Jack Pardee and Gene Stallings, became coaches.

One of the underachieving upperclassmen, in Bryant's view, was his center, Fred Broussard. Broussard had been voted on the All-Southwest Conference team as a junior, but Bryant, who had counted on him to be a team leader, was disappointed by his lack of hustle in spring camp. Bryant rode him hard, hoping the extra pressure would make him play to the level of his talent. Broussard did not respond the way his coach wanted him to. In his book, published twenty years later, Bryant didn't use Broussard's name but merely spoke of a player he couldn't motivate.

According to Jones Ramsey, Bryant "asked to see me during spring practice. He was short and sweet. 'Jones,' he said, 'if that lazy, fat-assed sonuvabitch makes All-Conference this year without my approval, you can consider your ass fired. You got that?' 'What exactly do you mean, Paul?' (I always called him 'Coach' when in the presence of others, and Paul in private.) 'I mean exactly what I said.' I told him, 'Paul, you know very well that it's my job to see that players on this team get publicity. It's what I'm here for—it's good for the University.' 'It ain't good for the University to have players rewarded for something they didn't earn. I don't want this boy or any other boy on this team getting by on their reputation. If he shapes up and earns it, I'll let you know.'"

But Bryant couldn't motivate the boy. Two days before the end of spring camp, after being blasted by Bryant, Broussard flung his helmet to the ground and stomped off the field. Bryant warned him, telling him to think about what he was doing. When Broussard showed up later at dinnertime, Bryant told him he couldn't eat with the team. Late that night, the Aggies' team captain, Benny Sinclair, came to his coach and begged him to take Broussard back. "Benny," Bryant told him, "I'm not going to take him back. He's quit before, hasn't he?" Sinclair conceded that Broussard had walked away several times. "This is the last time," Bryant said. "We want players we can count on. We've got a long way to go, and we don't want anybody laying down once we get started."

The next morning, the campus—or at least the portion of it obsessed with football, which meant just about the entire campus—was in an uproar. "Several more players, a couple of them friends of Broussard, were ready to walk out in support of him and came to see the coach," says Ramsey. "Coach damn near had a little mutiny on his hands." Bryant defused the mutiny by avoiding a confrontation. He agreed to meet with them, and that was all. And meet with them he did. "Good morning, gentlemen," he said, and then, shaking each boy's hand, he said, "Goodbye, goodbye. Bless your hearts, goodbye."

The rest of the team was stunned. Broussard was the best lineman Bryant had, and now, with the loss of several more players, he was left without a center. At a team meeting he promised his players that everything would work out but that they needed someone to snap the ball. Would someone volunteer to play center?

Bryant had chosen exactly the right ploy to fire up his Aggies. Lloyd Hale, whom Bryant described as "a little old sophomore guard," stood up and volunteered. Bryant proceeded to teach him the position from scratch. By Hale's senior year, Bryant was pushing Ramsey unmercifully to plug Hale to be selected as an All-Conference player at the position. Ramsey finally succeeded. "This means no offense to Lloyd Hale," says Ramsey, "but I'm not sure in terms of ability that Lloyd deserved to be All-Conference. I admit I let Paul pressure me into it. But in terms of heart, nobody deserved it more." Two decades later, in *Bear*, Bryant was still praising Hale as the best offensive center he had ever coached, outside of Paul Crane, his great All-America at Alabama. (In 1979, when Dwight Stephenson, the first black center at Alabama and a consensus All-America, graduated, Bryant would cite him as his greatest player ever at the position.)

Broussard never made it to Junction, but Gene Stallings, who did, insists, "I've never done anything harder in my life, but I don't recall a single instance in which Coach Bryant was unfair."

Some, like Charles Hall, considered quitting not because it was too tough but because they simply could not stomach Bryant himself. "He was the most foulmouthed, profane man I've ever met," says Hall.[4] Some of the other Aggies disagree, suggesting that their old teammate Hall was being, as one said, "a might prudish." Dennis Goehring recalls Bryant's cursing with a chuckle: "I can see how others might have misinterpreted what he was doing, but I never for a moment thought that he was being abusive towards me. That was just his way." Stallings adds, "I don't know what kind of language others might regard as offensive, but I didn't hear anything from Coach Bryant on the practice field that I hadn't heard a lot of other places. He wasn't *that* foulmouthed—he used his words selectively because he wanted to make an impact."

Jack Pardee was another who wasn't offended by Bryant's profanity. "To tell you the truth," he says, "it was kind of amusing. And believe me, there wasn't much else about those practices that was amusing. I kind of got a kick out of waiting to see what cuss words were going to come out of his mouth next and how creative he was going to be in stringing the expressions together. He never let us down." Whatever Bryant's cursing was like, no record of it survives. His Junction boys, to a man, refrain from repeating any of his language for outsiders.

It was also Bryant's way not to allow water breaks during practice. In this he was wrong, but not out of step with most of his peers. The only Junction boy who got water—immediately—was tackle Bill Schroeder after he collapsed during a scrimmage. Jack Pardee was envious. "I almost wished that I had passed out," he says. "Maybe I'da gotten a drink, too." What no one on the field knew was that Schroeder had suffered a heat stroke. Luckily, an assistant coach diagnosed Schroeder's condition and rushed him to a local clinic, where he was packed in ice. A short time later, when he came to, his first words were, "I'm sorry, Coach Bryant. God, I'm really sorry." The next day Schroeder returned to Junction to resume practice. The players heard the news about Schroeder with mixed feelings. "Most of the time," says Dennis Goehring, "we were running around cotton-mouthed. Packed in ice? That sounded pretty good to us. We weren't sure we wanted to have a heat stroke in order to get to the ice, but it sure was something we thought about."

Of all Bryant's methods at A&M, nothing has been more misunderstood than the water deprivation. "Nobody gave you water back then," says John David Crow, who played high school football in Louisiana before coming to A&M. "It may sound crazy now, but all the coaches back then thought that not drinking water during practice made you tougher." Echoing Vic Turyn's comments at Maryland, Crow feels, "If someone could have showed Coach Bryant how giving you Coca-Cola would have made you a better football player, he'd have been handing out Cokes."

Because of the success of Jim Dent's best-seller, *The Junction Boys*, and the attention given the subsequent ESPN movie made from the book, there has perhaps been a tendency to exaggerate how tough Junction was and to view it as an aberration in Bryant's career rather than as an example of his standard operating procedure. For instance, Henry Clark is said to have been hit violently in the head by Bryant during a practice session in which he took off his helmet. The scene is repeated in the film, with Tom Berringer's Bryant smashing Clark not once but twice. Clark says Bryant did butt him, but the incident has been misunderstood. "He didn't just walk up and lay into me," he says. "He was showing me how to make a proper block, and he came up out of the three-point stance lower than I expected and caught me around my mouth and nose with the top of his head. Back then, there were no face guards on the helmets. I had never had proper training as a lineman, or I would have been looking for it. He didn't break any bones, I just got a mouth full of gray hair. Anyway, I got his point. I never let a player submarine me. Bryant running into my head on that day probably saved me from getting a worse beating in the games." Clark is also incensed at the scene in the film, taken from Dent's text, where Bryant kicks a fallen Bill Schroeder. "It never happened. I know. I was standing right there."

Bum Phillips has also gone on record to refute the movie's portrayal of Bryant. "That movie is full of bull," he told an interviewer in 2004. "He's one of the most carin' guys I've ever known. It made me so mad when it showed him kickin' somebody. He wouldn't kick anybody." (Phillips added, "He never would call me 'Bum,' either. He didn't think that was a good nickname. He didn't realize it was just a nickname, it wasn't a description.")[5]

Was the Junction really tougher than Bryant's other summer practice camps? John David Crow, who would start on the varsity team the following season, feels the Junction has been blown out of proportion. "You can't judge it by the fact that there were only 29 players left. It sounds kind of ridiculous by today's standards, where a college team suits up 120 or 130 players for a game, but back then a lot of teams didn't have much more than 50 players. I think that if A&M had showed up on opening day with maybe 10 more players on the team, no one would have thought it so unusual.

"I know most of the guys who were at the Junction personally. It seems to me that the only real difference between what they went through and what the rest of us went through later was the facilities. Sleeping conditions were better on the campus."

Howard Schnellenberger sees nothing unusual in what happened at the Junction. "All that bullshit about what happened at A&M," he says, "for just eight days of practice! We had to put up with him for a month at Millersburg back in Kentucky. I say the Junction was a Boy Scout camp compared to what we went through."

IN THE third week of the season, the Aggies, sporting a 0–2 record, traveled to Georgia for a game with the Bulldogs. A football writer from the *Atlanta Constitution* thought he had been given a partial A&M roster when he counted only twenty-nine names. "You mean these are all the players you got?" he asked. "No, these are the ones who want to play," said Bryant.[6] Bryant's bravado, though, couldn't mask his and Aggie supporters' shock over their first game. On opening day, the Texas Tech Red Raiders administered perhaps the worst thrashing of Bryant's coaching career up to that point, beating A&M 41–9 at College Station. The Aggies fumbled the ball ten times and lost it six.

The crushing loss to Texas Tech hit the Aggies like a collective forearm smash. After the sweat and sacrifice at Junction, it didn't seem possible to have nothing more to show for it than a horrendous thirty-two-point defeat—at home—to a hated foe. Bryant needed some magic to revive his players' spirits. Most of all, he needed to create some team leaders. He reached back into his own past and played off Hank Crisp's "ol' Number 34" ploy. "Gentleman," he said in the locker room after the game, "we're going to have to rely on people who will go all out. Look to those who are proud to wear that uniform no matter what happens. I mean like this skinny old boy right here." He pointed at Bebes Stallings. "I had no idea he felt that way about me," says Stallings. "For him to say something like that after such a devastating loss just made me want to play harder for him. I'd have stood up right there and run into a brick wall for him."

Things did get better, though with agonizing slowness. In week two, A&M lost to Oklahoma State by just eight points; even Bryant had to acknowledge the improvement. In week three, on the road, they blanked Georgia 6–0. The football season was definitely looking up. It was, however, a false dawn—the Georgia game was the Aggies' only victory that season. They would lose their next seven games, leaving all but Bryant's most loyal supporters wondering if the university hadn't made the most colossal mistake in its football history. Bryant's mood was defiant. Near the end of the season, he called Jones Ramsey to tell him he wanted to let the alumni know he wouldn't tolerate any slacking off in their commitment to the footnall team. Bryant said, "Tell them when I started last spring I got a lot of nice alumni coming around asking me 'How's our team doing, Coach?' They still come around, but now they say 'How's *your* team doing, Coach?' Well, I want them to know I accept this team. It's mine now, and I'm proud of every player on it. And if I catch any one of them not giving 100% they will be disassociated immediately from the outfit."

"I was really choked up," Ramsey recalls. "I asked him, 'How did you ever come up with that?' He said to me, 'I didn't come up with it, Jones, I heard Frank Howard say that years ago at Clemson. I stole it from him.'"

Sifting through the wreckage of the 1954 season revealed definite reasons for believing a turnaround was coming. Two of the losses were by the margin of a field goal; one was by a single point; another, by the difference of a touchdown and a conversion. In the final game of the year, Aggie fans had to endure the taunts and insults of the despised University of Texas fans—"Tea-sips," as the Aggies referred to the Longhorns. But the final score, 22–13, gave Texas fans pause; the game had been a battle from start to finish, and the nine-point victory spread for Texas was by no means what the Longhorn fans had anticipated before kickoff.

As the season progressed, there were unmistakable signs that Bryant's style and attitude were beginning to take hold. In the eighth game, against Southern Methodist University, little Dennis Goehring, the boy who Bryant and his trainer had goaded, finally got his shot. In the third quarter, the Aggies' first-string defensive tackle went out with an injury. Goehring was sent into the game in what seemed like a colossal mismatch: his opponent on the other side of the line was Forrest Gregg, who was destined to win a handful of championship rings with Vince Lombardi's Green Bay Packers and be elected to the Pro Football Hall of Fame. Gregg hadn't yet reached his NFL proportions, but at or around 225 pounds he outweighed Goehring by anywhere from 40 to 50 pounds.

Goehring lined up against Gregg, looked him in the eye, and proceeded to jump offside before the snap, landing a forearm to the bigger man's jaw. The game had to be stopped while the SMU trainer tended to Gregg. On the sideline, Bryant, who hated both cheap shots and offside penalties, was furious. Down to his last available defensive lineman, he couldn't yank Goehring out of the game, but he would listen to his explanation. "Coach," Goehring sputtered, "that guy's just too big for me, and I know it. I thought the only way I could handle him was just to let him know right off that he didn't scare me." Bryant simmered, but didn't explode. While he didn't condone Goehring's tactic, he had to admire his determination. "I like a lineman," he said, "who can think on his feet."

LOSSES, THOUGH, are losses, no matter how they are rationalized. The 1954 season was the only losing one a Bear Bryant–coached team ever endured, and the winter of 1955 was the bleakest of Bryant's career. To add to the Aggies' dismal record, he had to live with the comparisons many were making between A&M's season and Kentucky's, where Blanton Collier had coached the Wildcats to seven victories, one of the best records in the school's history. No one at the time understood just how short-lived Kentucky's football glory would be without Bear Bryant.

If there was anything good about the Aggies 1–9 season, it was that it drowned out unpleasant rumors, at least for a while. Texas sportswriters had heard rumblings about a possible NCAA investigation into A&M's recruiting practices. Following the early 1950s betting scandals, member colleges had given the National Collegiate Athletic Association the goal of eliminating the gambling element from college sports (more than half a century later, the NCAA is still trying unsuccessfully to stamp out gambling). What the NCAA did, as the organization's president, Walter Byers, would later admit, was to strictly enforce all rules on outside income to a college athlete—that is, the athlete would increasingly depend on only what the university allowed him in the way of books, board, and tuition. In particular terms, this meant that the era when wealthy alumni could simply buy football players was over. At least, in theory.

"Near everybody was buying players in those days," recalls Jones Ramsey, "and the Southwest Conference was the worst of all. A&M got caught because NCAA investigators happened to be looking our way. Why were we caught? Why were they even lookin' our way? You check all the other football programs in history that have ever been put on probation, and they were all big winners—programs that brought in so much talent that they made people suspicious. Who the hell would investigate a team that was 1–9?" Mickey Herskowitz feels he knows who pushed the NCAA for the investigation. "The very fact of Paul Bryant's presence in the Southwest Conference was upsetting to a lot of the other coaches. The good old boy understandings, the gentleman's agreements were all gone. With Paul Bryant in the conference, there would be no more getting up at eight o'clock and playing a leisurely round of golf before going to work."

In May, Bryant went to Houston for a SWC meeting. With rumors running rampant about A&M's alleged violations, he played poker with, among others, SWC official Howard Grubbs, legendary former Aggies coach Dana X. Bible, Arkansas coach John Barnhill, Rice coach Jess Neely, and former Nebraska star George Sauer, who had been Don Hutson's teammate with the Green Bay Packers (and whose son, George Sauer Jr., would become Joe Namath's most dangerous target with the New York Jets). Bryant kept prodding Grubbs for some kind of information on what everyone knew was about to break; Grubbs simply replied, "We can't discuss any business here tonight." The next morning, the affidavits arrived, and the business was out in the open.

At least two Aggies, Thomas Sestak, an end, and Bob Manning, a quarterback, were discovered to have taken money to play for A&M. Both signed affidavits admitting to having received two hundred dollars apiece along with a promise of an extra fifty bucks per month. (Both boys eventually wound up playing football for other SWC schools.)

Bryant knew the boys were receiving money and freely admitted it. He would later acknowledge that at least four or five others got money as well; he didn't know how much they were getting, he later insisted, and didn't want anyone to tell him. Later, in May, he made an unannounced visit to the NCAA's Infractions Committee, a group headed by Albert "Ab" Kirwan, a pal who had been the faculty representative to Bryant at Kentucky. Bryant claimed ignorance of the NCAA's policy forbidding alumni from giving players money; Kirwan quietly and in no uncertain terms informed him that it was strictly forbidden. Bryant admitted that he had no case to plead and went home.

On his TV show that week, Lloyd Gregory, the *Houston Post* editor and Bryant's co-host, launched into a tirade against the SWC teams that had squealed on A&M. "I want to talk to you Texas and Rice people," he said. I've been in this league 35 years, and everything you're accusing this boy of doing you've done ten to one. You've been doing it, and I know, because I've been a part of it." "Old Lloyd was spittin' fire," remembers Jones Ramsey. "He threw all the hypocrisy right back in all of their faces." Some of the coaches called to complain, particularly Rice's Jess Neely. "Gregor tore into Jess right there over the phone," says Ramsey. (As with so many coaches he clashed with over the years, Bryant eventually made peace with Neely and the two men invested in land together. "It was kinda hard to stay mad at Paul," says Ramsey.)

Bryant's naiveté on the subject of NCAA recruiting rules seems astonishing to the modern fan, who is greeted nearly every week with stories of fresh scandals involving rules violations. But in 1955, the rules, or at least the methods that would be used for enforcing the rules, were still vague and, in any event, seemed to most coaches to be unenforceable. Bryant felt that he had been ambushed, singled out and made a scapegoat. Not quite; scapegoats are innocent, and Bryant and A&M were not. They were guilty of precisely what the NCAA had charged them with. Bryant had allowed the alumni's practices to continue unchecked because, he insisted, players had had offers for money and gifts from other schools as well. All he told his alumni to do was match the competition.* That was why A&M was punished, but Bryant never felt that was why they were charged in the first place.

One leading Texas paper lashed out at Bryant. It was regrettable "that a few A&M people cling to the belief that they are responsible for and honor-bound to support this professional from the scandalized Kentucky campus who had distorted their aims, mocked their spirit, and severed their unity." The story was a scattergun blast of cheap shots, particularly the reference to "the scandalized Kentucky campus," as Bryant had nothing to do with the basketball program.[7] The only spirit he disturbed, insisted Bryant, was the other coaches' peace of mind. "We attacked geographical spheres of influence"—which is a surprisingly fancy way for Bryant to say that he recruited players in areas that other schools regarded as their domains. It was a personal vendetta, he insisted, and he would take it out of his rivals' hides.

"If they had investigated the rest of the conference schools for similar infractions at the time," says Jones Ramsey, "the entire conference would have had to have been shut down that year." As it turned out, A&M would simply be restricted from appearing in bowl games for two years—no one at the time realized that this would keep them from a shot at the national championship in 1956—and scores of letters of intent to prospects were rescinded. Fortunately for Paul Bryant, that wouldn't hurt the status of the best player of any SWC school, who was already a freshman at A&M.

With his spirits lower than they had been at any time in his coaching career, Bryant left for a coaching clinic in Utah. Needing a morale boost, he got one from an unexpected source. He walked into an auditorium and found Adolph Rupp finishing a presentation. Rupp paused and pointed

---

* Bryant, of course, had received additional compensation from alumni, as did most college coaches, but the NCAA has never, then or now, put restrictions on coaches' earnings.

across the room at Bryant. "I want to tell you gentlemen something," he said. "Paul Bryant over there was at Kentucky, and he left us for a lot of money." At this point, Bryant's stomach must have been churning. "You think," Rupp continued, "he's down a little bit now. But I'll tell you, he will win. *He will win.* And you gentlemen in Texas who are playing him, he will run you right out of the business. Five, 10 years from now, he will be the top man, make no mistake about it, and don't forget Uncle Adolph told you."[8]

THE NCAA'S NULLIFICATION of the letters of intent was a brand new punishment, seemingly created for Bryant. The SWC added its own: conference teams would no longer be allowed to use off-campus training sites. That anyone cared what kind of training site a 1–9 team had used is an illustration of how Bryant's mere presence had shaken the conference. But the growing mystique of Bear Bryant, in spite of his devastating first-year record, was stronger than the NCAA's sanctions. NCAA nullification or no, nearly all the prospects Bryant had approached honored their original response to the letters of intent and showed up for spring practice. Despite everything, the Aggies began the 1955 season with hope.

That hope lasted right up until the Aggies took the field in Los Angeles to kick off the season against UCLA. The best that could be said of their 21–0 shellacking was that it was not quite as devastating as the 41–9 loss that had opened the previous season. The loss was especially bitter for Bryant, as it was his first chance to show off in front of the California press in nearly two decades. Melvin Durslaag, who would emerge within a few years as one of the most influential sports columnists in the country, cornered Bryant in the locker room after the game and asked, "Did you really think you could bring a team this inexperienced in here and beat a team like UCLA?" Bryant looked him in the eye and shot back, "Hell, yes. Why do you think we came out here?"

As the season progressed, though, the loss to UCLA seemed less grievous. Coached by Bryant's former boss at Vanderbilt, Red Sanders, UCLA thrashed everyone else far worse than they beat the Aggies. With six legitimate All-America candidates, they were clearly the best team in the nation by season's end and just about everyone's choice for national champion.

———

MICKEY HERSKOWITZ had flown out with the team to cover the game. While waiting for takeoff to fly back to Texas, Herskowitz worked on his story in the back of the plane. Locked in concentration, he lost track of a present he had brought on board, a box of chocolates. After a moment, he glanced up and saw to his horror that the box of candy was being passed back and forth, moving its way down the aisle, slowly, inexorably, toward Bryant's seat. He gritted his teeth, waiting for the inevitable. Suddenly, there was a roar from the front of the plane. Bryant jumped up and shouted, "Who the hell brought this box of crap on this plane?" The players began to turn in their seats in a wave that led back to Herskowitz. Mickey stared and said nothing. Bryant glared, walked to the exit door, and tossed the remainder of the five-pound box.

Years later, when Bryant was coaching at Alabama, he returned to Houston to speak at a football banquet. Mickey paid him a visit in his room at the Shamrock Hilton. They rehashed old times for a half hour or so, and then Herskowitz left. Bryant turned to a friend and said, "I sure did love seeing that little Mickey again, but it sure looked like something was bothering him." Herskowitz, who had stopped at the door, stepped back inside. "Coach, this has been driving me nuts for years, but I've got to tell you. Remember that flight back from UCLA? Dammit, that was *my* box of chocolates!"

Bryant burst out laughing and hugged him.

BACK AT College Station, the UCLA game on film didn't look like the disaster the score indicated. The Aggies had played the Bruins tough for the first half but simply could not sustain any drives and score. One player who had disappointed Bryant the most was the one he had counted on the most. Ken Hall had been one of the top sought-after high school prospects in Texas, having set state high school records with over 4,000 yards rushing and 57 touchdowns. Hall, in the words of Mickey Herskowitz, "was about 6 foot-2 inches, 220 pounds, built like a Greek god, and could run like a deer"—in high school, he was clocked at 9.7 in the 100-yard dash.

On defense, Hall's best position was safety, and he was so quick for a guy his size that he could play it. Bryant thought he should be a linebacker, which was considered the natural defensive position for a guy who started at fullback for offense. Most safeties back then weighed about 180, maybe

185 pounds. Ken was thirty to forty pounds bigger than the average guy who started in the defensive backfield, and Bryant, who usually was a wonderful judge of talent, just couldn't see past the physical stereotype. It was too bad for both men. Bryant rode Hall too hard, thinking he could goad him into living up to his potential. Hall was one of the rare players whom he never quite got across to. Jack Pardee, who saw the mishandling of Hall up close, feels, "If Coach Bryant had a flaw as a coach, it was that he was too set in his ways. At least at that time in his career. I felt he could have adjusted things a little for Ken Hall."

Bryant decided to build his offense around an eager sophomore who had been recruited for him by Elmer Smith and was almost as big and talented as Hall. John David Crow would become one of the greatest players Bryant ever coached. His rise to fame began the following week against Louisiana State, a school he was anxious to beat, having grown up in the small town of Marion and been heavily recruited by the state university before opting for Bryant and A&M.* Bryant was anxious to win too, and not just because he had now lost nine of his first ten games at A&M. LSU had a new coach, Paul Dietzel, his former assistant at Kentucky. It was to be the first of many confrontations between master and pupils.

In the first quarter, John David took a handoff in the backfield and nearly collided with two guards who got their feet tangled together while trying to block to the outside. Crow avoided them, slipped off two tackles before making it back to the line of scrimmage, and then ran eighty-one yards for a touchdown. "He must have shook off fifteen tackles," said Bryant, "the greatest single run I ever saw." When Crow came back to the bench, he patted everybody on the back, telling them what a great job of blocking they had done. The blocking, Bryant thought, had been poor, but

---

* Crow had been heavily recruited for LSU by Dietzel, but Bryant and A&M won out. Apparently Bryant was given the use, for recruiting, of the Louisiana Gas Company's airplane by the president of the company, a Texas A&M grad. Players and families of blue-chip Louisiana players were flown to Texas A&M for the wooing process. Dietzel called his old boss and laid it on the line. "Coach," he said, "don't kid me. I don't care how you recruit at Texas A&M, but I'm not going to let you fly Louisiana high school players out to Texas on a Louisiana Gas Company plane." When Bryant began to protest, Dietzel told him, "Coach, you've got to understand. If I lose players like that to you, I could end up getting fired from this job. You're taking food off my family's plate. I respect you, you know that, but I'll turn you in." "Okay, Pablo," said Bryant, "we won't do it." Dietzel had no more problems with Bryant.

when he heard Crow give his teammates the credit, he knew his boys were on their way. The Aggies breezed past LSU, 28–0, and with startling swiftness suddenly reversed the course of the Texas A&M football program. Though it still meant just two victories in the previous eleven games, everyone could sense the turnaround.

The next week, A&M whipped SWC rival Houston, 21–0. After three more successive victories, the fire had clearly returned to Aggie football. Going into week seven against Arkansas, the defending conference champion, the Aggies were 5–1 and on the verge of becoming a national power. The importance of the Arkansas game, a homecoming at Fayetteville in front of friends and family, had Bryant on tenterhooks all week. On the bus ride through the winding mountain roads that led to Fayetteville, "some of the players," says Herskowitz, "told me that they were looking out the windows and reading signs and old crumbling billboards that had been put up two or three decades earlier. This was backcountry, even for small-town Texas boys. Some of them began making fun of the people and places."

For Bryant, the trip was torture—a long slow bus ride through a landscape littered with signposts of a life he had determinedly fought to escape and of which he was reminded every time he saw a truck farmer selling vegetables by the side of the road. Listening to his players' jokes exacerbated his mood. Suddenly, he stood up and ordered the driver to slow down and pull over. The bus went silent. "All right," he said, "since nobody is interested in playing football against Arkansas, we'll all get out and find a spot to go have a picnic. I'll send our driver into town for some cokes and sandwiches and cookies. To hell with football." The bus went silent. After a minute or so, he said, "Okay, so let's go play some football," and told the driver to get them back on the road. The only sound to be heard for the rest of the trip was the murmuring of players and coaches as they studied their assignment sheets.

When the bus pulled into the parking lot at the Fayetteville stadium, a fan waved for the bus to stop and motioned for the driver to open the door. The man looked down the aisle and asked, "Which one of you is Bear Bryant?" Someone pointed to the Coach. The man, who appeared to have been drinking, held out his hand and announced that he was a distant cousin who had driven from Fordyce. "I'm proud to see you," he told Bryant, "but understand I'm rootin' for Arkansas today." Bryant stood up and gently but firmly shoved him toward the door, guiding him out of the bus. His players heard him mumble, "Ain't nobody who roots for Arkansas getting on this bus."

The Arkansas game was not Bryant's best coaching performance. The Aggies blew two scoring opportunities, leaving the game in a scoreless tie at the half; they would finish in a 7–7 tie. "I don't think I've ever seen him so worked up as he was at halftime," says Goehring. "He went from player to player telling us all how lousy we looked out there. He told Henry Clark"—the boy he had accidentally head-butted in practice— "'Henry, you looked like *dawg*-shit out there.' I'll never forget the look on Henry's face. He said, 'Hell, Coach, give me a *chance*. You ain't put me in the game yet.'"

Clark would get his chance—all the Aggies would. They played well and won their next two games, though in a 13–2 victory over Southern Methodist, John David Crow, trying to impress his coach on a punt return, made a spectacularly bad decision, ran backward trying to elude tacklers, and instead of gaining yardage, lost a whopping thirty yards. Head hung low, he trotted to the sidelines, expecting a much-deserved dressing down. Bryant put one hand on Crow's shoulder and with the other he pointed toward the SMU end zone. "John," he said quietly, "*our* goal is down *there*." It was the last time Crow ran in the wrong direction.

The season finale against Texas was a deflating 21–6 defeat. But at 7–2–1, A&M finished with a number-fourteen rank from United Press International (UPI), easily its best since before World War II. John David Crow was the star of the team, but the backbone was the players who had survived the Junction, especially Gene Stallings, Jack Pardee, Bobby Drake Keith, the "little bitty guard" Dennis Goehring, and a handful of others. Despite the loss to Texas, the Aggies and their fans were now convinced that the program had been turned around. One game in particular stood out and forever cemented Bear Bryant's place in Texas A&M football lore.

The week before the Texas game, the Aggies were in Houston playing the 2–5–1 Rice Owls. Bryant, sniffing a possible upset, rode his team all week, but there was no way that the Aggies could get their minds on Rice and off the archrival Longhorns. Bryant's worst fears were confirmed; his players spent the afternoon playing as if in a fog. With a little more than two minutes to play, Rice led 12–0, and satisfied students and alumni began to reach for their coats and sweaters and file out of the stadium. According to Jack Pardee, "Coach Bryant was never cooler. I've never seen him quite like this before. He was amazing. He told us, 'Men, we've still got plenty of time. We can still win, if you *believe* that we can win. That's what it's going to take: you've got to *believe*.'" Suddenly, the Aggies began to play as if they remembered they were the better team. The kickoff was returned to the forty-two-yard line. On the first play, Lloyd Taylor, a substitute runner in for Pardee, took the handoff, cut to the outside, and ran fifty-five yards before being knocked out of bounds at Rice's three-yard line. It took three plays, but on the third, Taylor went in for the touchdown. With the extra point, Rice's lead was trimmed to five points with less than a minute to play. Rather than give Rice a chance to run the clock out, Bryant decided to try an onside kick; Bebes Stallings, the "skinny old boy" who Bryant had singled out as a leader the year before, grabbed the ball just as it crossed midfield. A&M fans, who now dominated the thinning crowd, erupted. Another Bryant substitute, Jimmy Wright, dropped back and fired a pass downfield. Taylor, who had come out of the backfield, streaked past the Rice safety, caught the ball in stride, and went into the end zone. With the field goal, suddenly—incredibly—the Aggies were ahead 14–12.

What can happen on one side of the ball can happen on the other. Rice still had time to complete a couple of passes and kick the winning field goal. But Jack Pardee intercepted a pass and ran the ball back inside the Owls' ten-yard line. Stunned, the Rice defense collapsed, and the Aggies ran for another touchdown. In approximately 125 seconds, A&M, who had been pushed around all afternoon, had scored twenty points, the biggest comeback in school history. Mickey Herskowitz, who had left the game to prepare his story and was stuck in the elevator when he heard the crowd, or at least the Aggie part of it, go berserk, called it "the most amazing comeback I never saw."

"I'll always believe," says John David Crow, "that one of the reasons we were so flat the next week against Texas was that the final two minutes of that Rice game had taken the fire out of us."

Unable to go to a bowl game because of the NCAA's sanction, it was Bryant's intention to reward his players for their fine season with a postseason game of some sort. He came up with what seemed like a splendid substitute, a game in Honolulu with the University of Hawaii. "If they won't let us go to a bowl," he told Ramsey, "we'll have a bowl. Our own bowl. We'll call it 'The Pineapple Bowl.'" Bryant told the team that the game would be contingent on beating Texas and winning the conference championship, but Ramsey is convinced "he was goin' to take 'em to Hawaii no matter what happened. The way they played that season without hope of going to a bowl game deserved some kind of reward." Somehow, word leaked out. Two days later Bryant awoke to a *Houston Post* headline which read, "Southwest Conference Says A&M Can't Go To Honolulu."[9] "Boy," he wrote later, "I tell you it was brutal. I wound up with a mad-on for every coach in the league."

THE NEXT year, as in "wait till next year," arrived in College Station. In 1956 A&M was paced by two sensational All-America players, Crow and a six-foot-five-inch, 240-pound lineman named Charlie Krueger, the kind of hustling, overachieving player Bryant adored, and quick too. The Aggies won their first three games, allowing just thirteen points on defense. Then came two brutally tough games against two superb teams that defined the Aggies' season. The first, in week four, was a road game against Houston; A&M gained the most yards but had to leave town with a frustrating 14–14 tie. The game ended on a decision that seems almost inexplicable to today's football fans and indeed had many wagging their heads in 1956. On the final possession, A&M drove all the way to Houston's one-yard line. With time left for a single play, Bryant called for a quarterback keeper, and quarterback Roddy Osborne was thrown for a loss as time ran out.

No amount of rationalization is sufficient to justify Bryant's decision. In 1956, goal posts were ten feet farther back in the end zone and field goals were not kicked by specialists but by regular players who often practiced kicking on their own time, so even so-called chip shots were not a sure thing. Still, a one-yard plunge against a goal-line stand defense would have been pretty close to a 50–50 proposition, and a field goal had a much greater chance of success than that. The only explanation for Bryant's choice of plays is that, like many coaches, he had a contempt for field goals, best expressed by old-time Harvard coach Percy Houghton, as quoted in Pudge Heffelfinger's book: "It's a sissy way to score."[10] Six weeks later, with his team on the verge of a national championship, Bryant wished he could have gone back and reconsidered that decision.

In another cliffhanger, the Aggies beat Texas Christian University by a score of 7–6 on a touchdown pass thrown by John David Crow on an option play. Four times TCU drove the ball inside the A&M three-yard line; four times they were stopped. TCU, winning eight of its other ten games, had, in running back Jim Swink and tackle Bob Lilly, a runner and a defensive lineman to match A&M's own Crow and Krueger. A&M won its next four games by a total of seventy-three points, and on the final day of the season it rode into Austin for the game Aggie alumni had been waiting for since the first rumors of Bryant's hiring.

THE NIGHT before the Rice game, Bryant was unable to sleep, as so often was the case before a big game. Slipping out of the house quietly to avoid waking Mary Harmon, he got into his car and drove out into the night. When Elmer Smith arrived at his own office around 5:00 a.m., Bryant was already at his desk. Bryant asked Smith to take a ride with him, and they drove to an old frame house near the campus. Just as they pulled into the driveway, the sun was coming up. A little boy and his mother were sitting on the porch. Bryant went up and put his arm around the boy and talked to both of them. Smith was curious, but didn't ask Bryant for an explanation. Later Bryant told him that when he had been driving around that morning, he hit a dog. Bryant was so upset, he had to go back to tell them what happened. The mother called the athletic office later that day to thank the Coach for the new dog he had sent over.

BRYANT HAD waited three years to take a team this good into a game against the University of Texas, and he knew that his moment had arrived. He had no intention of losing because of bad psychology. Longhorn fans are fond of saying that the school's anthem, "The Eyes of Texas," is worth "two, maybe three points, in any close game."* Texas's usual ploy was to intimidate visiting teams with a rousing rendition of the fight song just before kickoff. As Bryant put it, "The students raise hell, you hear that band, and you wet your pants six times before the kickoff." This time, Bryant held his Aggies in the locker room, refusing to let them go through the tunnel and onto the field until the song had been played. Texas officials sent word down for Bryant to bring his team out. "I ain't heard 'The Eyes

---

* I first heard this from my late friend, the Mississippi-born writer Willie Morris, former *Harper's Magazine* editor and University of Texas grad.

of Texas' yet," he replied, "we ain't coming out till we hear it." A tense five-minute standoff occurred with officials sending a second representative demanding that he send his team out to play. He told them, "As soon as they play that damn song and the Texas team is out there, we'll come." Bryant was deadly serious. "What are they gonna do, cancel the game and send us home?" he told Mickey Herskowitz. Finally, there was nothing the Texas people could do but play their song and get on with the game. When the Aggies finally hit the field, Bryant pulled out the stops. The Texas players "still looked eight feet tall to me, compared with our little boys. But I mean to tell you, we ate 'em alive."

The Aggies stunned Texas, scoring three first-half touchdowns, each big gain punctuated by a roar from their fans. "For a while," says Mickey Herskowitz, "it was as if Texas A&M was playing a home game. The Texas fans were just sitting there with their mouths open." In the second half, with their jaws tightly clenched, the Longhorns gouged out a comeback. They might have made it, but their counterattack was blunted by three spectacular plays by Jack Pardee. After Texas scored to get back in the game, and the momentum seemed to have shifted, Pardee shifted it right back, returning the subsequent kickoff eighty-five yards for a touchdown. Early in the fourth quarter, he took a punt and streaked fifty-four yards deep into Texas territory to set up the Aggies' final touchdown. Then, in the fourth quarter, when Texas was driving for a touchdown that might have cut the lead to six points, Pardee intercepted a pass deep in A&M territory. The Aggies fought off the Longhorn comeback and handily won, 34–21.

After the game, Bryant's players, who had grown up eating guff from arrogant Texas fans, were nearly dizzy with joy. They threw their coach, clothes and all, into a shower. Toweling himself off and grinning as none of his players had ever seen him grin before, Bryant told them, "My limited vocabulary won't permit me to tell you how proud I am of you." He had told them before the game that he didn't want them spending the night in Austin; apparently the sight of all those magnificent Texas coeds might discourage some of them from returning to Sing Sing on the Brazos. Now, Jack Pardee relates, he told them, "I didn't mean it about not staying over. Act like champions. Show some class and have a good time. I'll see you next week."

The A&M victory, combined with the Longhorns' horrific 1–9 record that season, prompted the firing of Ed Price, who had been head coach since 1951. Bryant may have been hated and envied by some SWC coaches and administrators, but his opinion was valued. Some Texas folks asked him for a recommendation to replace Price. Bryant didn't hesitate to offer his opinion, and young Darrell Royal, Bud Wilkinson's former quarterback and the man who had come to Bryant's aid on two previous occasions, was given the job. A couple of years later, says Royal, Dana X. Bible asked him how he had come to get the Texas head coaching position. "I called the two best men I could think of," Royal told him, "and asked them to make phone calls for me, Bud Wilkinson and Bear Bryant." Bible was curious to know how they had responded. "Wilkinson said he'd back me," replied Royal, "and Bear told me, 'Hell no, Darrell, I ain't going to recommend you for that. I don't want you coming in here and whipping our butts.'" Bible was taken aback: "I'm really surprised Bryant told you that." "Naw, that was just his way," Royal assured Bible. "Bear made the call. They never heard from Wilkinson."

Bryant had won the respect of his SWC colleagues. Clearly the Aggies were the class of the league that year, and regional pride dictated that the best team be sent to represent the conference in the Cotton Bowl. Several coaches, particularly Ed Price of Texas and Abe Martin of TCU, spoke up for him. The NCAA, however, declined to rescind the ban despite the protests. Their reason would have drawn a laugh from Bryant had the irony not bitten so deep: A&M's basketball team had been found guilty of recruiting violations, and the football team was to be punished along with them. His football team had been hurt by a basketball scandal at Kentucky when Adolph Rupp was coach. Now Bryant was not only football coach but athletic director too, which Rupp had not been at Kentucky. And the football team was still punished for violations by the basketball program.

That the basketball miniscandal nearly exploded into national news is a story that has never been written. Bryant, in his position as athletic director, felt responsible for building up basketball as well as football. He found a high-profile coach in Ken Loeffler, a jovial, piano-playing basketball fanatic who had won a national championship while coaching for LaSalle College in Philadelphia. He also had professional experience with the St. Louis Hawk of the National Basketball Association (NBA). However, a little more than two weeks after Loeffler arrived in Texas, the A&M basketball program was slammed with penalties. Loeffler flew off the handle and immediately implied that his troubles were the indirect result of the football violations—something Bryant was in no mood to hear.

The investigation revealed that Jackie Moreland, a much-traveled player for hire (who in fact went on to enroll at North Carolina State, where he would become involved in one of the biggest scandals in NCAA history, resulting in North Carolina State receiving a four-year probation, the most severe punishment levied by the NCAA at the time) had received money under the table to play at A&M. It was never proved that Loeffler or his coaches were involved, and it may have even occurred before Loeffler took over, though more than a few Texas sportswriters felt otherwise. More than likely, the culprits were overzealous Aggie alumni. Whoever was responsible, the probation wasn't withdrawn until after Loeffler resigned from A&M, after intense pressure from Bryant.

According to *Sport* magazine, Loeffler was saying out loud that "he had enough goods on Bryant to hang him." Whatever he had, though, was never specified, and after Loeffler left A&M, he said nothing. "I've got a wife and son to think about. I've got friends at Texas A&M who would be caught in the crossfire. I'll save it for a magazine story some day. But if the NCAA really wants to put the blast on the Aggies, it ought to look under the football table."[11]

Oddly enough, later, when Loeffler had his chance to talk while coaching basketball and working as an instructor of business administration at Monmouth College in New Jersey, he had nothing to say about his old charges. "You've got to respect a man who knows what he wants," he told the *Atlanta Journal*'s Furman Bisher, "and is forceful to go out and get it. That's Bryant. If he walked in here now, he would put his arm around me and he would say, 'Ken, I wanted to help you, but you were talking when you should have been listening.' He'd say it real Southern. A big, impressive fellow like that, you've got to respect him."★

Privately, Bryant felt there was a more direct reason why the NCAA was

---

★ In October of 2003, I was at a World Series party at the Yogi Berra Museum on the campus of Montclair State University. I mentioned to one of the college officials that I was working on a book about Bear Bryant. He told me, "My God, you should have known Ken Loeffler. He taught at Monmouth College, not far from here—I think he died about twenty years ago. He used to work for Bryant at Texas A&M. He was always telling Bear Bryant stories, "He's a hell of a guy, what a terrific guy to be around,' things like that."

continuing the probation: it hadn't worked. If the 1954 Texas Aggies were the first team ever to be on probation after a 1–9 season, the 1955 and 1956 Aggies were surely the first team in college football history to go 16–2–1 *after* the penalties. Bryant's 1956 Texas A&M team might have been the best in the nation. Georgia Tech, Iowa, and Tennessee all won top billing in minor polls and could thus, with some legitimacy, claim a share of the national title. Both the Associated Press (AP) and UPI polls chose Bud Wilkinson's 10–0 Oklahoma Sooners, but Oklahoma hadn't played in a conference nearly as tough as Bryant's Aggies. Had Bryant chosen to go for the field goal in the fourth game of the season at Houston, his team would probably have finished 10–0 and perhaps would have beaten out Oklahoma for the top spot in the polls.

The 1956 Aggies produced no Heisman Trophy winner or star quarterback and were ineligible to play in a bowl game. Though they were undefeated, they have been largely forgotten by history. But in several ways they might have been Bryant's most remarkable team and may well be his most quintessential. They won with a slashing running game, sensational punting, and a rock-ribbed defense. Amazingly, they threw just thirty-eight passes all season long, fewer than the average major college team throws in a single game nowadays, but they made deadly effective use of the forward pass: nine of their throws, just under a quarter of their total, went for touchdowns.

No sooner had the season ended than predictions began making the rounds that the Aggies were already the favorite to win the SWC championship again in 1957. But for the second time in his career, Bryant had gotten a whiff of something much larger, and he could no longer be contented with mere conference championships. This time he wanted the *national* championship. He felt his 1956 team had deserved it—or at the very least, the team deserved a shot at it—and that the Aggies would have made it decisive if given the opportunity to play in a bowl game. Counting his 1950 Kentucky squad, it was the second time he felt he had the best team in the nation and had not taken the big prize. Whereas 1956 was the Aggies "next year," in his heart, Bryant felt 1957 would be his.

Mary Harmon did not make the trip to Austin for the big game with Texas because she was recovering from pneumonia. When Paul got back to College Station, he didn't think she was strong enough for a long conversation, so he put off telling her that the night before the Texas game, a delegation from Birmingham and Tuscaloosa had met with him at his hotel. They wanted him to come back to the University of Alabama, as head football coach. He had told them he couldn't think about that just now.

As the 1957 college football season opened, Paul Bryant's optimism echoed that of America's. A year into Eisenhower's second term, the Korean War had already vanished from national consciousness, while Vietnam barely registered as a place where the French had recently been routed. The civil rights movement was gaining steam—Rosa Parks having made her stand two years before—but still seemed removed from the lives of most middle Americans. The Russian launching of *Sputnik* in October would shake Americans from their complacency. But on the whole, 1957 was a great time to be white, living in Texas, and winning.

The Aggies opened their 1957 season in Dallas, defeating the University of Maryland, 21–13. At a postgame press gathering, Curley Byrd, Paul Bryant's first boss in his head coaching career, walked in. As was the case with so many men Bryant had crossed paths with over the years, Byrd bore no grudge. In fact, in the words of Mickey Herskowitz, who was there to witness it, "They took to hugging and laughing and teasing each other about everything that had happened." With a smile on his face, Byrd stood in the back of the hall while the AP's Harold Ratliff asked Bryant if he was really "a genius." Bear kept trying to get him off the subject, says Herskowitz. He started talking about how small and slow his 1957 team really was. "Ratliff wouldn't let him off the hook. 'What's the difference,' Ratliff asked, 'you're a genius, aren't you?'"

"One of Bryant's assistants—Pat James, I think it was—got a little irritated. 'Harold,' he said, 'everyone knows there's no geniuses when it comes to coaching football.' There was a pause, then you could hear Bryant say, 'Pat, are you plannin' on keepin' your job?'

"Everyone in the room broke up, but Curley Byrd nearly split his gut."

Bryant added an important new assistant, former high school coach O. A. "Bum" Phillips, and with a beefed-up staff and the maturing of what he called "my bottle babies"—the first class he had recruited after his first winter at A&M—the Aggies looked as if they could have the greatest team

The Monroe and Ida Mae Bryant family of Moro Bottom, Arkansas, circa 1915. Paul is the blond, barefoot toddler standing next to his father. (Paul W. Bryant Museum, University of Alabama)

REDBUG FOOTBALL FIGHTERS OF 1930

The Fordyce High School Redbugs, 1930 Arkansas state champions. Paul Bryant is in the top row, third from right. (Courtesy of the Dallas County Museum)

Denny Field grass cutters, summer 1934. Left to right, Zeke Kimbrough, Bear Bryant, Chesty Moseley, Jim Whatley, Rayford Ellis, and Joe Dildy. Thirty-one years later, the stadium would be renamed Bryant-Denny. (Paul W. Bryant Museum, University of Alabama)

Alabama's first Bear, and first great coach (1923–1930), Wallace Wade. He was named for the hero of Scottish independence, William Wallace. (Paul W. Bryant Museum, University of Alabama)

Two Arkansas boys who starred on Alabama's 1934 national championship team: number 37, Don Hutson, "The Alabama Antelope," who would go on to an NFL Hall of Fame career with the Green Bay Packers; and number 12, Paul Bryant, who was simply referred to as "the other end." (Paul W. Bryant Museum, University of Alabama)

The 1934 Rose Bowl team visits MGM Studio, December 28, 1934. Alabama players pose with a rising young musical star from Mountainvew, Arkansas, named Dick Powell. (He had just starred in *Gold Diggers of 1933*.) Left to right, Paul Bryant, Happy Campbell, LeRoy Goldberg, Dick Powell, Joe Dildy, Charlie Marr, and Don Hutson. (Paul W. Bryant Museum, University of Alabama)

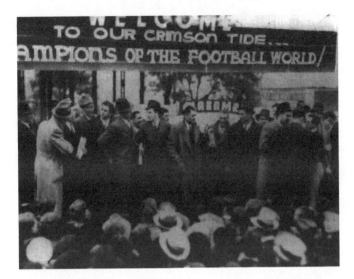

Don Hutson, Dixie Howell, Bear Bryant, and the rest of Frank Thomas's 1935 Rose Bowl champs return home to Tuscaloosa. (Paul W. Bryant Museum, University of Alabama)

Bear Bryant's two favorite cowboy stars: Marion Michael Morrison, the former Southern Cal lineman who was Bryant's choice to play him on the big screen, and Johnny Mack Brown, the Alabama star whose performance in the 1926 Rose Bowl inspired twelve-year-old Paul Bryant to play football. Circa 1937. (Photographer unknown)

Hollywood, 1938. On Alabama's Rose Bowl trip, Assistant Coach Paul Bryant sneaks away for a screen test. He has his picture taken with a young Warner Brothers contract player, Julia Jean Turner, later known as Lana Turner. (Paul W. Bryant Museum, University of Alabama)

The 1939 Alabama coaching staff: left to right, Tilden Campbell, Hank Crisp, Head Coach Frank Thomas, Red Drew, Paul Burnum, and Paul Bryant. (William Stanley Hoole Special Collections Library, University of Alabama)

Lieutenant Commander Paul Bryant, USN, circa 1942. (Paul W. Bryant Museum, University of Alabama)

University of Maryland bobby-soxers protest Bryant's departure, 1945. Photos of the student protests on campus made sports pages all over the country. (Courtesy of the *Diamondback*, University of Maryland)

Paul Bryant, Don Hutson, and Alabama football coach Harold "Red" Drew (left to right) shortly after World War II. While at Kentucky, Bryant turned down a chance to return to Alabama as head coach because he did not want to take his friend's job. (Paul W. Bryant Museum, University of Alabama)

Bryant celebrates the upset of number one–ranked Oklahoma in the 1951 Sugar Bowl with the two-time governor of Kentucky, Albert Benjamin "Happy" Chandler. As commissioner of baseball in 1947, Chandler supported the Brooklyn Dodgers' Branch Rickey in breaking the color barrier in Major League Baseball. If Chandler had been governor while Bryant coached at Kentucky, Bear might well have succeeded in his ambition of becoming "the Branch Rickey of football." (John C. Wyatt/*Lexington Herald-Leader* Photo Collection, University of Kentucky, Special Collections & Digital Programs)

Bear Bryant and his only Heisman Trophy winner, John David Crow, 1957.
(Courtesy of Coach T. J. Troup)

Paul and Mary Harmon, spring of 1958, prior to the start of Bryant's first season as head coach at Alabama. Babe Parilli called her "a football den mother" who kept up with the boys and their families long after they left college.

Four members of Alabama's 1959 Liberty Bowl team—Gary Phillips, Pat Trammell, Bobby Skelton, and Marlon "Scooter" Dyess—arrive with Bryant in Philadelphia. The Crimson Tide played the Penn State Nittany Lions, the first time Alabama had ever faced an integrated opponent. (Paul W. Bryant Museum, University of Alabama)

Sportscaster Howard Cosell and Bryant prepare for an interview before the historic Alabama-Georgia game in 1960. This was Roone Arledge's first televised college football game as an ABC producer, and it became the prototype for his revolutionary sports telecasts. (Paul W. Bryant Museum, University of Alabama)

Alabama All-America linebacker and future Dallas Cowboy All-Pro Lee Roy Jordan (1960–1962). Bryant said, "If they stay in bounds, Lee Roy will get 'em." (Paul W. Bryant Museum, University of Alabama)

Bryant with the quarterback of his 1961 national championship team, Pat Trammell. He couldn't run and he couldn't pass, everyone said—all he could do was win. Trammell died of cancer in 1968. "He was twenty-eight years old when he died," Bryant said in *Bear.* "I still miss him." (Paul W. Bryant Museum, University of Alabama)

The 1961 MacArthur Bowl awards in New York. Bryant is second from the left, then quarterback Pat Trammell, University of Alabama president Frank Rose, President John Kennedy, and (in the background to Kennedy's left) Bryant's college friend, New York Yankees announcer Mel Allen. (Paul W. Bryant Museum, University of Alabama)

Texas sportswriter Mickey Herskowitz gets a boost from Bryant and Lloyd Gregory, former *Houston Post* managing editor and co-host of Bryant's TV show in Texas, at an Aggie reunion in Houston in 1962. (Photograph by Ray Covey/Courtesy of Mickey Herskowitz)

Walter Cronkite led off the August 8, 1963, *CBS Evening News* with "Bear Bryant walked into an Atlanta courtroom today and laid it on the line." Here Bryant arrives to testify in Georgia coach Wally Butts's libel suit against the *Saturday Evening Post.* Bryant and his attorney, Winston McCall, are followed by players Charlie Pell and Jimmy Sharpe. (Paul W. Bryant Museum, University of Alabama)

Bryant, Pat Trammell, and Army football general Douglas MacArthur at the Hall of Fame banquet, winter of 1962. (Paul W. Bryant Museum, University of Alabama)

Bud and the Bear prior to the 1963 Orange Bowl, won by Alabama, 17-0. Bud Wilkinson and Bear Bryant were the greatest college football coaches from the end of World War II until Wilkinson's retirement after the 1963 season. Bryant envied Wilkinson's polished manner and suave appearance. Bryant won both times when they faced each other. (Used with the permission of the University of Oklahoma Athletic Department)

Bryant in his legendary tower. He rarely allowed visitors. "You didn't pass up a chance to go up in the tower with Bear Bryant," said Bill Curry. (Paul W. Bryant Museum, University of Alabama)

Joe Namath and Paul Bryant, the most famous quarterback-coach combination in college football history.

Joe Namath in the air against North Carolina State in 1964. Bryant called him "the greatest athlete I ever saw." Alabama won, 21–0, but Namath sustained a severe knee injury and would never soar this high again. (Paul W. Bryant Museum, University of Alabama)

Bryant with his long-time friend and assistant Charley Thornton, mid-1960s. "Saturday is for the colleges," said the Bear, "Sunday is for the pros—and the Bear Bryant television show." (Courtesy of Golden Flake Snack Foods)

Celebrating the third national championship in five years: left to right, Dude Hennessey, Howard Schnellenberger, Carney Laslie, Coach Bryant, Sam Bailey, Ken Donahue, and Ken Meyer. (Paul W. Bryant Museum, University of Alabama)

Mickey Mantle drops by Tuscaloosa to see his sometime drinking buddy. Dennis Homan and Kenny Stabler look on. (Paul W. Bryant Museum, University of Alabama)

Ken Stabler leads a comeback against Tennessee in 1966 to preserve the Tide's perfect season. Bryant called Stabler "a left-handed Joe Namath." (Paul W. Bryant Museum, University of Alabama)

Alabama's All-America (1970–1971) running back Johnny Musso, whose nickname, "The Italian Stallion," Sylvester Stallone stole. (Paul W. Bryant Museum, University of Alabama)

John Mitchell, Alabama's first black starting player and first black All-America player. Bryant stole him away from his friend and rival, Southern Cal head coach John McKay. Mitchell lettered for the Crimson Tide in 1971–1972 and became an assistant coach for Bryant. He is currently defensive line coach for the Pittsburgh Steelers. (Paul W. Bryant Museum, University of Alabama)

in school history. Bryant later told a Texas sportswriter that he only took on assistant coaches he could learn something from, and that Phillips was one such coach. In turn, Phillips immediately learned something from Bryant. On his first day, says Phillips, "He told me to go organize the quarterbacks and centers. I got there early, and I looked around and there weren't any footballs. I waited and waited: still, no footballs. So I walked up to Coach Bryant and asked, 'You reckon those managers are going to get those balls down here?' And he looked at me and said, 'Well, I don't know. But I'll tell you one damn thing. I ain't gonna get 'em.' On the way to getting the balls, I figured out the difference between the head coach and the assistant coach."

After winning the first four games by comfortable margins, the Aggies had their usual defensive tussle with Texas Christian, though prevailing 7–0—Bryant would lose just one game to TCU in four years, 21–20, and win the other three by just eleven points—before shutting out Baylor 14–0. Then came the return trip to Arkansas, and anxiety time. At a Fort Smith motel the night before the game, Bryant woke up soaking wet, with pains in his chest. He knew immediately that he was having a heart attack, and called Dr. Harrington, the team physician.

"'I don't think you've had any heart attack,' he said. He gave me something to make me sleep. I took it, but I couldn't sleep. I was scared I'd die. I got up and put on my britches and walked the streets the rest of the night. By the time the team bus reached the stadium the next day, I had forgotten my heart attack, and I didn't have time to worry about it during the game." The game nearly caused numerous heart attacks. Arkansas and Texas A&M were bitter rivals in a way that can't be understood today. In 1991, Arkansas would join the Southeastern Conference, but in 1957 it was the only non-Texas member of the SWC. Many Texans regarded Arkansas as the country bumpkin of the league; Texas made jokes about Texas A&M, Texas A&M accused Rice of being "snooty," but everyone else in the SWC made fun of Arkansas. Fan reactions to visiting Texas teams often bordered on the hysterical, and Arkansas fans cut Texas A&M no slack because its coach was a favorite son.

The 1957 game was particularly excruciating. With fifty-five seconds to play, the Aggies had the ball on the Razorbacks' thirty-five-yard line, nursing a 7–6 lead. Bryant called for a "run-the-clock-out play, actually an option pass, where we send one guy out and everybody else is supposed to block while the quarterback runs around using up time." The option pass is misnamed in this kind of situation; it is supposed to *look* like one of the quarterback's options is to throw, but in fact he does not throw because a pass might be intercepted, practically the only way the defense can win that late in the game. But Roddy Osborne *did* throw, to the shock and surprise of nearly everyone in the stadium including, most of all, Bryant.

In doing so, Osborne made a colossal blunder, but he also, unwittingly, supplied Bryant with one of the greatest anecdotes of his career. Rolling to his right, Osborne saw John David Crow break free of the Arkansas coverage and sprint into the end zone. The opportunity was too tempting for Osborne—all he needed to do, it seemed, was simply to shot-put a pass to Crow. An Arkansas defensive back, a boy named Moody, cut in front of Crow, intercepted the ball, and streaked downfield. Osborne, perhaps seeing his entire life pass before his eyes, ran as he had never run before, came from behind, caught up with Moody, and dragged him down on the A&M twenty-yard line. With five seconds left, John David Crow made a spectacular end zone smash into an Arkansas receiver, knocked the ball up into the air, and caught it himself for an interception, miraculously preserving the Aggie's one-point win.

The next morning, Bobby Dodd, who had heard about the bizarre ending to the game, phoned Bryant from Atlanta. "How in the world," he wanted to know, "could a slow guy like Osborne catch a speed demon like that Moody from behind?" "The difference," Bryant replied, "was that Moody was running for a touchdown. Osborne was running for his life."

Later that day, Herman Heap, a close friend and president of the Heap Oil Company, flew Bryant to Houston to get his heart checked.

THE WEEK after the Arkansas game, the Aggies defeated Southern Methodist, 19–6, for their eighth straight victory. They were riding on an eighteen-game winning streak, and were headed for their first national championship since 1939. Their offense starred John David Crow who, by season's end, would become Bear Bryant's first and only Heisman Trophy winner. The defense had not surrendered so much as two touchdowns to any opponent. Bryant had no doubt that his Aggies would be recognized as the best in the country. They probably would have made it if Mama hadn't called.

Frank Rose was a former theological student with the knack for cutting a fine figure. One way to do that at Alabama was to be a football fan, and Rose beamed openly when told of his close resemblance to Alabama's legendary halfback and cowboy movie star, Johnny Mack Brown. Rose had just begun his tenure as president of the University of Alabama in 1958 and was determined to start with a bang. As Thanksgiving neared, Rose could scarcely contain himself. In his exuberance, he let slip to a local journalist that Alabama had just gotten "the greatest football coach in America" to replace the likeable but ineffectual Jennings B. "Ears" Whitworth.

It was Jack Gallagher from Mickey Herskowitz's paper, the *Houston Post*, who first caught a scent of the wind blowing west from Alabama. He broke the news on November 15, the day before Texas A&M's big game with Rice. Though the story was unconfirmed by Bryant, the headline read, "Bear Goes To Bama." Bryant asked Herskowitz to come by his room at Houston's Shamrock Hilton before the game, presumably to discuss his situation. By the time the reporter arrived, the mood was grim. "The only other people there," Herskowitz recalls, were Mary Harmon, Bob Bernath, who sponsored Bear's TV show, and Bob's wife, Kate. We all went down to dinner and ate in almost total silence." An A&M fan came up to the table, extended his hand, and wished Bryant luck; the coach refused to acknowledge the man's presence. Kate Bernath was appalled: "Paul, I've never seen you be so rude." He didn't respond, says Mickey, "He just took a sip from his drink and stared down at the table."

The Aggies, who only one week before had been dreaming of a national championship, spiraled downward. They played in a stupor that Bryant could not pull them out of, fumbled six times, and lost by a point to the Rice Owls, 7–6. Twelve days later, on Thanksgiving Day, they would play even worse and lose to the University of Texas—to Darrell Royal.

HEADING INTO November, the Aggies had seemed to be on track for a national championship. Now their hopes had collapsed. Many blamed Bryant; others looked around for someone else to blame, and Ken Hall was a convenient scapegoat. With a month to go in the regular season and the Aggies ranked number one, Jack Pardee injured a leg against Baylor. Hall, in whom so much faith had been invested, was given a second chance to start. The Aggie fans now had the backfield combination that they had dreamed of in spring practice: John David Crow and Kenneth Hall, side by side. But as the Aggies began their Monday practice in preparation for Arkansas, Hall wasn't there. Bryant was livid, but wanted to avoid any distraction before such an emotional game. When he came home that night, he found Hall waiting for him on his front porch. He pleaded with his coach for another chance. Uncharacteristically, Bryant gave in.

The behavior of both men was puzzling. Bryant seldom gave second chances and never gave third chances. He also hated giving up on a potentially great player—"Don't ever give up on talent," he would write three years later in *Building a Championship Football Team*.[12] Though he never admitted it, Bryant must have known at this point that he was headed to Alabama at the end of the season, and he very much wanted to leave Hall as a legacy to his years at A&M. Mickey Herskowitz felt, "Kenny just couldn't take the kind of pressure that Bryant put on him." Jones Ramsey was more specific: "Kenny cracked." And, "As much as I hate to say it, much of the fault was Bear's. He handled him wrong from the beginning, and he knew it."

"A lot of Coach's toughness and aggressiveness was a kind of pose," says Bobby Drake Keith. "I don't mean he wasn't tough and aggressive, but he could turn it up a few notches to try and test a player, to challenge him. What he was trying to do was bring out his best. Some guys couldn't respond to that, and I honestly don't think that at that point in his life Coach Bryant understood that. He failed to motivate Kenny, and I know he always felt bad about that." Whatever the reason, Hall failed to show up for practice on Tuesday. Again, he waited that night on his coach's front porch. This time, Bryant was adamant. John David Crow went to Bryant and asked him to give Hall just one more shot. "I wish I could do this," Bryant told Crow, "if just for you. But I can't. I just can't." Later he would admit, "I was too pigheaded to let Crow find out what the problem was. Ken Hall was a fine young man, and he was worth saving."

In 1970, someone sent Bryant a copy of a full-page story about Hall in a San Francisco newspaper; Hall had moved to Marin County a short time before. The piece lauded Hall's business achievements and recounted his high school gridiron triumphs back in Texas. To Hall's surprise, he received a letter from Bryant a week or so after the story appeared. "He told me how sorry he was that things hadn't worked out at A&M," says Hall, who is now a retired restaurateur in Fredericksburg, Texas, "and how glad he was that I had succeeded in life. He kept apologizing in his own way—between the lines. I wrote him back and said, 'Coach, I appreciate everything you said. Let's not beat each other up about what happened. It was just meant to be that way.'"

With Pardee and Hall both out of the lineup, Royal and Texas keyed mercilessly on Crow the entire game. The Aggies lost, 9–7. They had dropped the final two games of the 1957 season by a total of three points. Bryant always wondered whether his failure with Hall had cost the Aggies those two games and a shot at the national championship they had richly deserved the year before. But he knew in his heart that the rumors of his resignation had done far more to hurt the team's morale than Ken Hall had.

IN FACT, as late as the Texas game, Bryant's move to Alabama *was* just a rumor. Redskins' owner George Preston Marshall told Herskowitz that in mid-November Bryant had suggested several names for the Alabama job, including Jim Tatum, who had succeeded him at Maryland. Herskowitz asked him why he didn't simply end the speculation by saying he wouldn't be going to Alabama. "I wouldn't want to say that," Bryant said, "because I might do it." "I knew right then," Herskowitz wrote in his memoir, "that A&M had lost him."

The Thanksgiving Day game between Texas and Texas A&M was televised nationally on NBC, and Mel Allen did the play-by-play. On the Tuesday before the game, Allen arrived in College Station and hooked up with his old Alabama classmate. Bryant wanted to talk; he asked Allen to go for a ride with him where they could have a little privacy. "As we drove around," Allen recalled in an interview for *Inside Sports*, "he pointed out where his friends lived on campus, and who had helped him invest money, and how at home everybody had come to make him feel. This wasn't the same situation as Kentucky. It wasn't a question of Paul wanting to leave the job he had. 'Mel,' he said to me, 'I'm gonna feel bad no matter what decision I make. I hate to let anybody down.' 'Well, Paul,' I told him, 'I don't know what to tell you, but it seems to me that what Alabama's doing is asking you to come home. You passed up the chance to go home before. You may never get the chance again.'"

Back in Alabama, the feeling among football fans, which excludes very few in the state, was electric. Well before the rumors reached Texas or the national press, Alabama fans began to assume that Bear Bryant's return was just a matter of time. "I never saw anything like it, the feeling back home for Paul," "Football Freddie" Sington recalled for Alabama football historian Clyde Bolton. "Not just from Alabama alumni, but from the man in the street, too."[13] Columnists in Alabama papers began to write of Bryant's homecoming as a given.

Bryant had never made much money at A&M. Despite the number of close and influential friends he had in Texas, the business deals he chose usually went sour. He made some money from gas and oil investments, but lost on other deals. One business partner, Johnny Mitchell, had, according to Bryant, "more money than a show dog could jump over. He once hit 151 straight wells, missed one, and hit 18 more. But he could lose it as fast as he made it." So could Bryant, who went to Alabama owing money to friends in Texas, including Herman Heap, the man who had flown him to Houston for a checkup after the Arkansas game. But money would not be a motivation in going to Alabama; he would ask for just eighteen thousand dollars, at least seven thousand less than he was being paid by Texas A&M.

He insisted that he was motivated by something much stronger than money. After the Texas game, he revealed it in his office, which was jammed so full of sportswriters that, in Herskowitz's words, "you could identify the brand of deodorant the next guy to you was wearing, if any." "There is one and only one reason," Bryant told them, "that I would consider. When you were out playing as a kid, say you heard your mother call you. If you thought she just wanted you to do some chores, or come in for supper, you might not answer her. But if you thought she *needed* you, you'd be there in a hurry." This was the famous "Mama Called" speech. As Herskowitz wrote, "No one had done so much for motherhood since Al Jolson."

Though Bryant insisted he still hadn't made up his mind, the journalists now understood he was as good as gone. No one has succeeded in pinning down the precise moment he made his decision and informed Texas A&M.

Bryant had eight years remaining on his twelve-year contract. (After winning the conference championship in 1957, Bryant's contract had been extended.) He knew there were powerful men on the Board of Directors who would be angry and resist his departure. As he had done at Kentucky, he appealed to a man of influence at the university, in this case his close friend Herman Heap, probably the most powerful man on the Board. Heap begged him to stay.

"What do you want? What will it take to make you stay?" Heap asked. Bryant told him that he wanted nothing. Just that he had to go, and that he wanted Heap to help him. Reluctantly, Heap told him he would.

Twice before, Bryant had turned down the Alabama job to avoid hurting an old friend. While the rumors circulated about Bryant and Alabama, there was one snag that no one considered. Hank Crisp—the man who had recruited Bryant out of high school back in Fordyce, the man who drove him to Tuscaloosa, whose seemingly endless wad of one-dollar bills had provided Paul with nearly his only spending money in college, and who had given him goose bumps when he called him "ol' Number 34" before the 1935 Tennessee game—was athletic director at the University of Alabama. For Bryant, taking a job where there existed a level of authority between himself and the university president was unacceptable; on the other hand, he couldn't bring himself to displace Crisp. This alone would have been enough reason for Bryant to turn down the Alabama job for yet a third time.

Fortunately for the University of Alabama, someone on the selection committee thought to offer Coach Hank a new job as director of intramural sports. Bryant was not assured by a phone call informing him of this decision, so Crisp drove to Birmingham, boarded a plane for Houston, and met Bryant at the Shamrock Hilton. As Crisp related it to Al Browning, he told Bryant to "get your ass to Tuscaloosa where you belong so we can start winnin' some football games."

That clinched things. The next morning, December 8, 1957, Bryant called a press conference at the Shamrock. He took the podium and delivered a variation of his "Mama Called" speech. He had tried, several times, "to tell my boys. I hadn't had to do that at Kentucky because they were away on vacation. I called them together in our meeting room beside the dining hall, and I tried to tell them, but I never did.

"I would start a sentence and I would choke up. They knew. They knew what I wanted to say, but I couldn't say it. I got to crying, and it got to be like a holy roller meeting, everybody crying. Old John Crow and everybody." The Monday after the press conference, an editorial in the A&M school paper stated that "with his resignation, Texas A&M is no doubt losing the greatest coach in America today."

There was some mild distraction from the gloom that enveloped the A&M campus. John David Crow flew to New York with Elmer Smith to receive the Downtown Athletic Club's Heisman Trophy as "the nation's outstanding college football player." Crow has always believed that Bryant clinched the award for him by telling Texas sportswriters, in a line that would be picked up and run in papers across the country, that "if John David doesn't win the Heisman, they ought to stop giving it." In truth, though, Crow had impressed everyone with his versatility and dedication. The NFL thought so too; Crow became the first player drafted in 1958 and played eleven seasons in the NFL with the Chicago and, later, St. Louis Cardinals, and San Francisco 49ers, closing out his career with just under 5,000 yards rushing, nearly 3,700 receiving, and another 759 passing.

Neither the Heisman Trophy nor John Crow's professional prospects mattered as the Aggies prepared to face Tennessee in the Gator Bowl, their only bowl appearance under Bryant. Nothing he could think of would motivate his players. Bryant, Herskowitz wrote in *The Legend of Bear Bryant*, "did not act like a fellow who had a date to be somewhere else. But nothing he did could fire up his dejected players."[14] Bum Phillips described Bryant's efforts at the Friday meeting before the game. Bryant tore into John David Crow, telling him, "They're saying you don't care anything about this game. They're saying you just want to make sure you don't get hurt so you can sign a big pro contract." To Charlie Krueger: "You know what they're saying about you? They're saying you don't give a damn about this game. All you're worrying about is which all-star game you're going to and how much money you'll make." To Richard Gay: "You're not thinking about football . . . you're thinking about getting married and falling into a fifty-thousand-a-year job." And then, after lambasting nearly everybody, "And you know who *they* are?" After a pause: "Me." His players weren't buying it. "We were flatter than roadkill," says Bum Phillips.

Tennessee kicked a field goal, which was all the volunteers needed to win. It was the first time that Bryant's Aggies had been shut out since the third game of the 1954 season.

Four weeks later, Paul Bryant, Mary Harmon, Paul Jr., "and a crippled old dachshund named Doc, drove into Tuscaloosa in a white air-conditioned Cadillac." Students and alumni were there to greet him, just as at Kentucky and Texas A&M. Mary Harmon had cried when she first saw College Station; she now cried when she left it. "All I did the first year," she told an interviewer, "was look for somebody to ride to Houston with me. Then I began to stay at home more and came to love the place.

"Alabama is the only place Paul could have taken me to get away from there. But let me assure you of one thing: that had nothing to do with his decisions. Paul never listens to me. When he gets ready to go, he goes, and I go along."

And she cried on finally arriving back home too.

"When I drove across that bridge again the other day," Bryant told a sportswriter, referring to the old bridge over the Warrior River he had first crossed in 1931 in Hank Crisp's roadster, "nothing looked the same to me."

PAUL BRYANT had his regrets about leaving Maryland and Kentucky, but leaving Texas A&M genuinely pained him. Seventeen years later, in his autobiography, he would say that he never told Aggie jokes because he still regarded himself as an Aggie. He just couldn't live there.

The career of Paul Bryant raises questions about what exactly a college football coach owes to a university and the boys he recruits to play football. Bryant was criticized then and would continue to be criticized throughout his life as mercenary. From a distance, at least, the charge seems to have some validity. By the time he arrived in Tuscaloosa, Bryant had taken jobs with four different colleges in thirteen seasons. In his first season, at Maryland, he was never offered a written contract by the university president and felt that Curley Byrd had undermined his authority. Byrd did not agree, but held no grudge. There were no hard feelings between the two, and the students and at least the majority of his players sided with the coach, not the president.

The move from Kentucky presents a trickier question. One might contend that even if Kentucky reneged on its agreement to let Adolph Rupp go, Bryant had a written contract and an ethical obligation to stay. But most Kentucky officials and alumni, sorry though they were to see Bryant leave, did not take that position. The prevailing attitude seemed to be that after eight seasons Bryant had kept his promise to transform the football program and win the school a conference championship, and if the University of Kentucky wasn't going to make a more serious commitment to football, then Bryant was justified in finding a university that would. Surely there is something to that argument; would a science teacher be criticized if, after eight years at a university, he left because he felt that the school was not keeping its promise to upgrade his area of expertise?

There are no simple answers to any of the questions raised by Bryant's departures from his first three head coaching jobs. Is, after having recruited a boy, a coach morally obligated to be there for all four or, in the case of "red-shirting" a player, five seasons? If so, then a coach could never leave his school, since he must recruit new players every year. To argue that a coach should never leave a player after recruiting him is to say that a coach must be bound to a school for life, an argument that would seem ridiculous if applied to an English or math professor.

Moreover, the term *mercenary* implies that Bryant changed jobs for better offers. At Maryland he might have stayed had Byrd simply offered him the same salary in writing and agreed not to interfere with the football program. At Kentucky, he might have stayed had Rupp resigned or been fired. His departure from A&M was another matter, and certainly the circumstances were unique. Bryant took less money to coach for his alma mater, a school that had invited him back on at least two previous occasions, and the school, after all, that during his entire professional career he had wanted to return to.

A great many A&M fans and alumni never forgave Bryant for leaving; Bryant knew that would be the case when he made his decision. Nearly forty-five years later, some saw a measure of revenge when A&M lured Alabama coach Dennis Franchione from Tuscaloosa to College Station in 2002. But only a cynic would deny that there are several important differences between Bryant's departure from A&M and Franchione's from Alabama, beginning with Franchione being offered a fatter contract by A&M.

An objective observer cannot be without sympathy for Franchione's plight in the fall of 2002, with the NCAA invoking "death penalty" probations to the football program for recruiting violations—violations that had nothing to do with Franchione. And in truth, Franchione was under tremendous pressure even without the NCAA penalties: he was trying desperately to coach up to a level that Bryant had established. Bear would have understood. What he would not have understood was Franchione's pitching "Accountability—Loyalty—Trust" on his Web site to his players and the alumni, while negotiating a deal with another college. Franchione begged his forty juniors and seniors—all of whom could have transferred to other schools—to stay and hold the team together even though the NCAA sanctions guaranteed that none of them would get to play in a game at Alabama. "I plan on staying at Alabama for the rest of my career," he announced. "I guarantee that I'll be here for you through it all, regardless of what happens." His players believed him, stayed, and played their hearts out to a surprising 10–3 season in 2002. Meanwhile, behind the scenes, Franchione was using the team's success as leverage to get himself more money from A&M.

Paul Bryant kept his word to his players, whereas Dennis Franchione gave his word and then skipped campus in the middle of the night. It's worth noting that when Bryant died in 1983, he was wearing one piece of jewelry—a ring given to him by the Junction Boys, the Texas A&M players who stayed with him through the first training camp in 1954, the ones who he promised a conference championship to if they stuck it out. One wonders how Dennis Franchione's 2002 Alabama team would like to bury him.

The final judgment must come from Bryant's A&M players. Jack Pardee's assessment is typical: "He always stressed being a part of something bigger than yourself. For him, that's what college football meant. I don't think he ever cared much about the pro game because he couldn't feel the same way about it that he did about the college game. He felt college football should get you ready for life.

"He'd say, 'What are you going to do when you're thirty-five and you lose your job and you come home one day and your kids are sick and your wife has run off with the shoe salesman? What are you going to do then? If you quit in the fourth quarter of a football game, what's going to keep you from quitting then?' Well, by the time I was thirty-five all those things had happened to me, except the part about my wife and the shoe salesman. Because of the things he taught me, I was able to fight cancer and win. That was my fourth quarter."

About 5:30 p.m. on December 31, Paul and Mary Harmon checked into the Stafford Hotel in Tuscaloosa and then drove to the Tuscaloosa Country Club for dinner. Bryant couldn't relax; his stomach was churning. He shook a few hands and left. "I couldn't wait to get to work."

Chapter 6

The Second Coming

The blood-dimmed tide is loosed . . .
—*William Butler Yeats*, The Second Coming

IN THE WINTER OF 1958, Paul Bryant did not know that he was returning to the South at what would be the most turbulent time in a hundred years. Coaching at Texas A&M was like working in a military citadel, where he was shielded from the complexities of politics and race. In Alabama, in just a few short years, he would be the center of a maelstrom of social and personal problems. For the time being, though, his only concern was football, and he had plenty to think about.

As he returned to Alabama, he was forced to confront two great regional and national powers: cross-state rival Auburn, coached by Ralph "Shug" Jordan, and Louisiana State University, still coached by his former Kentucky assistant Paul Dietzel. In the two decades since Frank Thomas had been at Alabama, a big change had occurred in the Southeastern Conference, which had become, arguably, the toughest in the nation.

Throughout all of Bryant's days at Alabama as a player and an assistant coach, the biggest game—many would say the biggest in all of the South, and many in the South would have said the biggest in the nation—was Alabama versus Tennessee. Now the archrival was Alabama Polytechnic Institute at Auburn, which Bryant had never played or coached against.

The first match between the two natural state rivals had come on the unlikely date of February 22, 1893 (in Alabama records it was the final game of the 1892 season; in Auburn's record book it was the first game of 1893). The teams met in Birmingham, which, until nearly a century later, would be regarded as a neutral site, thus giving the city the self-proclaimed title of "Football Capital of the South." A special train from Auburn brought more than two hundred fans to the game. More than three hundred came from Tuscaloosa.

It was quickly obvious that the Alabama-Auburn game was something special: "Men and women," read an account in the *Birmingham Daily News*, "who have heretofore jeered at such exhibitions of brawn and muscle were eager to see the contest." Unlike professional baseball, which for the most part did not yet admit women to the games, college football welcomed female spectators. The local reporter noted, "It is hard to decide which of the colleges has the prettiest young women to wear their colors. Both Universities brought a charming lot of young ladies with them."[1] More than eleven decades later, Alabama and Auburn fans still debated the question.

Auburn won the first game between the two schools, 32–22. They went on to play each other ten times in the next fourteen years, with the match quickly establishing itself as the biggest athletic event in the state. But in 1908, the series ended abruptly, and given Alabamians' penchant for holding grudges, it looked like it would never be played again. The real reasons why the series was suspended were soon forgotten, and some of the most colorful myths in the lore of college football sprang up to explain it.

In stories told by fans and reported by newspaper columnists, Alabama and Auburn quit playing because of excessive brutality on the field, fights in the stands, or, in one of the most famous fables, a full-scale riot that took place outside the stadium while the game was in progress. The truth, as Geoffrey Norman wrote in his 1986 history of the rivalry, *Alabama Showdown*,

> is almost embarrassingly humdrum and embarrassing. It turns out that the schools quit playing each other in 1908 because they got into an argument about money. Auburn thought that $3.50 per diem was about right

for the players it would be bringing to Birmingham that year. The players would be staying in a hotel and eating at restaurants, after all, and Alabama was the best team. Alabama thought that was about fifty cents too high. Also, they didn't see the need for Auburn to bring the twenty-two players they said they needed. Twenty, Alabama though, ought to be plenty.[2]

This did not mean, of course, that there wasn't excessive brutality on the field, fights in the stands, or full-scale riots outside the stadium; Alabama folks tolerate such things when they are connected with football, but the people who ran the universities calculated honor in dollars and cents—or, in this case, fifty cents.

For the next forty years, fans and officials of both schools nursed grudges and told nasty stories about the other, until the petty truth about the cause of the feud became lost. Finally, after World War II, a secret weekend meeting was scheduled at a farm about halfway between the two campuses, and, somehow, school officials broke a peace. At last, a game was scheduled for 1948, and a symbolic hatchet was buried in Woodrow Wilson Park, where it apparently still resides.* Auburn didn't need a hatchet to beat Alabama under "Ears" Whitworth. The Tigers had won the last four games before Bryant's arrival by a mind-boggling aggregate score of 128–7, including a 40–0 humiliation in Birmingham in 1957. Under head coach Jordan (pronounced "Jur-dun") the Auburn Tigers had done more than just replace Tennessee as Alabama's archenemy. In 1957, they had done what no Bear Bryant–coached team had yet done: they had won the conference championship and the national championship of college football.

AT 5:30 A.M. on New Year's Day in 1958—four days after the Gator Bowl—Bryant was already in his new office in Tuscaloosa. He had yet to clean out his old space back in College Station, Texas. For the first time in

---

* Woodrow Wilson Park was later renamed Linn Park. The spot where the hatchet was supposedly buried is about a football's throw from the park bench where Tom Hanks, who plays football for an unnamed Bear Bryant in *Forrest Gump*, is seated, telling a disinterested party how "life is like a box of chocolates."

his career he was not merely in charge but in control of a football program, from the recruitment to the press, which at least for the time being, was in his pocket in a way it had never been at Texas A&M.

Later he would say that he had no doubt he would have a winning team at Alabama, but that he didn't know how many years it would take. This is not true; at Kentucky he had established a five-year plan, and surely he knew that given Alabama's greater recruiting potential, it would not take nearly that long. But publicly he would not commit. Benny Marshall of the *Birmingham News*, who would become one of Bryant's leading champions in the Alabama press, tried to corner him at his first conference: "Coach, the alumni are expecting your team to go undefeated next season." "The hell you say," Bryant replied. "I'm an alumni, and I don't expect us to go undefeated." Privately, he had a very clear idea of what he wanted to do and how to go about doing it. Looked at from a certain perspective, Bryant's predecessor had cleared his path by doing everything so spectacularly wrong. What was needed was a complete reversal of nearly every phase of the Alabama football program.

It seems almost unbelievable in retrospect that a university with Alabama's football pride and tradition would have allowed a coach as inept as Ears Whitworth to thoroughly undermine its reputation. Like Bryant, he had been a fine player, an offensive and defensive lineman not only under Frank Thomas but also under Wallace Wade. He had played well and even kicked a field goal in Alabama's 24–0 victory over Washington State in 1931. Like Bryant, he had been released from a contract, with Oklahoma A&M, to go to Alabama, a fact overlooked by critics who still choose to see Bryant's return to Alabama as mercenary. (Not so much attention is paid to where a coach with a losing record goes!)

Whitworth was so likeable that it's hard to find anyone he coached, even today, who will say anything bad about him. Bart Starr, who almost certainly would have been an All-America candidate anywhere else and who would win five National Football League championships with Vince Lombardi's Green Bay Packers, rode the bench in his senior year, as did the rest of the Alabama seniors. (The team was 2–7–1.) Starr, unfailingly polite, will only comment, "I don't know why Coach Whitworth chose to keep us all on the bench that season." Starr revealed that Whitworth was forever prefacing lectures with "Here's what they're doing at Oklahoma"—though whether referring to Bud Wilkinson's Oklahoma Sooners or Whitworth's previous employer, Oklahoma A&M, which won just twenty-two of fifty-one games while he was there, isn't clear.

The problems began right at the top, specifically in deciding who exactly was at the top. Whitworth was head football coach, but he had to answer directly to Hank Crisp, who was his athletic director. Crisp was also defensive coach, which meant that, theoretically, he took orders from Whitworth, the head coach. Who was who in the chain of command was often confusing. Practices were often a mess, with players wasting a great deal of time and energy for no discernible purpose relating to football. Alabama journalist Tom Stoddard, in his book on Bryant's first season at Alabama, *Turnaround*, records one player's frustration: "Damn, Coach, I'm tired, we've run enough of these wind sprints." "Well, golly, guys, I wanted to get you into shape," replied an assistant coach. During practice, writes Stoddard, "After working out for an hour or so, most of the players, as many as 80 or 90 boys, would stand around watching the first and second teams scrimmage. Roy Holsomback, a freshman lineman in the fall of 1957, remembers standing for what seemed like hours. Then finally a coach would grab him and say, 'Get in there.' 'You couldn't hardly move after . . . all that time,' the player said."[3]

Under Bear Bryant, absolutely no one would be standing around doing nothing. At 5:30 a.m. Bryant was in his office; at 7:00 a.m. staff meetings began, followed by study sessions of opponents' game films. The lunch break was often no more than fifteen minutes, and in the afternoon there were at least two solid hours of full-bore practice. After dinner, another staff meeting at 7:00 p.m. sharp. Players—and generally coaches too—were in bed by eleven.

The first week of January passed in a whirl. Bryant released nearly all of Whitworth's staff, taking time to help several of them find new positions. His old end coach, Red Drew, was hired as a scout. Whitworth's trainer, Jim Goostree, who had been hired by Crisp, fretted about his situation and finally cornered Bryant in the hall in front of his office. "Don't we need to visit, Coach?" he asked. "I've been wanting to talk to you," Bryant said. "Let's go to my office." Bryant told him, "Here's the deal. I know a lot about you from Coach Hank. We'll wait till after spring practice, and if you like me and I like you, you've got a job here." "Coach," replied Goostree, "the first half of that is okay. I'm going to get started on the second half."

Bryant filled out his staff of eighteen assistants, including two former

A&M players, Gene Stallings and Bobby Drake Keith, whom he hired as graduate assistants, just as Frank Thomas had hired him. He would always require a big staff, sometimes taking a ribbing from fellow coaches, such as Southern Cal's John McKay, about whose jibes Bryant would remark, "He's smarter than I am, so he should have to make do with less." Every man was chosen carefully for his loyalty and dedication as well as his knowledge of specific areas of football. The head coach at Huntsville High School, Clem Gryska, who had played for Alabama under Frank Thomas, was recruited for Bryant by Gene Stallings. "He figured that I had an open door to every high school in the state," says Gryska. "Before long, Dude Hennessey and I had a recruiting field which extended to anywhere in the country with a high school football team." But there would never be any doubt about whom all those coaches reported to. Years later, Bert Bank, Bryant's radio producer, told him that his assistant coaches were so good that even he, Bank, could have won with them. Bryant replied, "No, you couldn't."

After solidifying his base, Bryant had to make preparations to bring his family to Tuscaloosa, watch films, and make a seemingly endless number of distracting personal appearances. He quickly became exasperated with the rubber-chicken circuit. Morris Childers, a freshman on the 1958 team, recalled a banquet at the Bessemer University Club for the freshman players. Bryant, he says, "was rather insulting. . . . I do remember that he jokingly said that he had never seen anyone celebrate a team that hadn't won a game." The third annual freshman banquet would be Alabama's last.

One thing Bryant was absolutely determined to do was prevent the kind of alumni involvement that had resulted in near disaster at Texas A&M. According to Tom Stoddard in *Turnaround*, Bryant made his position on the subject unmistakenly clear to a group of influential alumni: "I have heard some bad stories. If anything is wrong, come and tell me. If you are giving anybody any money, for anything, I want you to stop right now. I've done it, and I've found out if you pay 'em, they'll quit on you."[4] Presumably, this included even Bryant's old coach and mentor Hank Crisp; the rumor was that shortly after Bryant was hired, Crisp went to pay off a standing bill at Black, Freidman, and Winston, a men's store where players were often sent for free suits. The players were also told not to accept money and to account strictly for the things they did get. For instance, under Whitworth, players had been allowed to help themselves to clothing from the athletic department. Under Bryant, this would cease. Carney Laslie, who had coached for Bryant at North Carolina Navy Pre-Flight, Maryland, Kentucky, Texas A&M, and now Alabama, saw to it that no player would get a clean pair of socks until he had turned in a dirty pair first.★

On January 10, Bryant called a meeting that turned out to be memorable to those who were there and some who weren't. At 1:15 p.m. sharp, Bryant tapped his watch and yelled for his new quarterback prospect, Jerry Gilmer. Someone yelled back that Gilmer wasn't there. Bryant told Carney Laslie to go upstairs and pack Gilmer's belongings. "He's off scholarship." (Gilmer fought his way back on the roster in the fall, but never got to play because of injuries.) The message was clear. The room was tense and silent as Bryant continued. He told his players that he had come to Alabama "for one reason. To build a winning football team. We are going to do two things. We are going to learn to play football, and we are going to get up and go to class like our mamas and papas expect us to. And we are going to win. Ten years from now, you are going to be married with a family, your wife might be sick, your kids might be sick, you might be sick, but you will get your butt up and go to work. That's what I'm going to do for you. I'm going to teach you how to do things you don't feel like doing."

Bryant made it clear that, as he had done at Texas A&M, he was going to clean house of players who had been given scholarships because of political connections. In 1958, the Alabama football team was still segregated according to race, but Bryant was determined that it would not be segregated by class. "I don't care who you are, where you come from, whether you played last year or not. I don't care if your folks are rich or whether they don't own the farm they live on. I want people who want to win and who want to be part of the tradition of Alabama football." This was no small thing to boys from families whose parents never had the opportunity to attend college. Then he shocked them. "I don't have any training rules," he said. The players blinked and stared at each other. "I don't think much of training rules. If you're man enough to come out on the field and give me what I want, then you're welcome to stay out all night messin' around." Having nothing more to say, Bryant left the room. "He never," recalled

---

★ Several players on the 1958 team also confirmed that any player missing a chinstrap would find $1.50 cut from his laundry money. Apparently, this was to deter the players from giving away their chinstraps to their girlfriends, a bit of chivalry particularly common to players in the Deep South.

Marlon "Scooter" Dyess, "told a joke or spoke to anyone one-on-one." Though there would be no training rules, Bryant made one point clear: "When you are out in public, you will remember that you represent the University of Alabama, and you will act like gentlemen. If you don't"—he paused for emphasis—"you will have to answer to me."

Part of being a gentleman meant conforming to a dress code—coats and ties on road trips, hair neatly clipped and combed. Hank Crisp and Frank Thomas had taught Paul Bryant that this was how college student–football players were supposed to look, and it was the way he would have his players look. "It was one of his favorite lines," says Clem Gryska, "that his players would show class in all situations. They were special, they were privileged, and the price of that privilege is that they were supposed to make their families and their school proud of them at all times. By the time the 1970s came around," says Gryska, "he eased up a bit on the clothes and the hair, but he still had this thing about ties. He always had that. In his last season, we played Penn State in Birmingham. The morning before the game he watched our players file into the hotel ballroom for breakfast. When they were all seated, he jumped up and said, 'Nobody in here is going to eat anything until every player is wearing a tie.' Several of our boys didn't have ties, and they scrambled out of the ballroom as if it was an air raid. Some of our fans were in the hotel lobby; it was hilarious to watch the players begging the fans to borrow their ties. I think that's one of the things that upset Coach just a little—the players were supposed to be setting an example for the fans, but the fans were better dressed. I remember my wife, Alice, going into our room and getting my ties out of the suitcase and tossing them down from the second floor into the lobby. I don't think I've ever seen anything that funny, those ties fluttering on down and the boys reaching up to grab them like they were sent from heaven. At least one of our boys couldn't find a tie and actually made a napkin into a tie. One of our quarterbacks—I forget which one—couldn't find anything but a big yellow ribbon, which he tied around his neck. I swear, he looked like Captain Kangaroo. I think Coach actually smiled at that. When everyone was seated, he said, 'Now ya'll look a hell of a lot better, and I think you'll play a lot better because of it.'" Indeed, Alabama beat Joe Paterno's Nittany Lions that weekend, 42–21.

THE RETURN of Bear Bryant to Alabama shook up the SEC even more than his going to Texas had stirred up the Southwestern Conference. In May of 1958, *Sport* magazine featured a profile of Bryant by the *Atlanta Journal's* Furman Bisher. The piece reflected Bryant's growing national fame, but also the hostility he was generating in the southern football establishment. One unnamed SEC coach quoted by Bisher said, "Everybody respects Bear's defenses, but he's a damn poor quarterback on the field the day of the game." Considering that Bryant had not worked in the SEC for four years and that for most of his eight seasons at Kentucky he had faced Tennessee teams with far greater talent, the statement was curious, to say the least. Bisher was never shy about expressing his disdain for what he called Bryant's "professional back-woods Arkansas boy" persona. Bear Bryant had not heard the last from him.

"THE TEAM I inherited when I went to Alabama in 1958," he recalled, "was a fat, raggedy bunch. The best players, the ones with ability, quit us."[5] They would feel pretty ragged after Bryant put them through spring practice, but they would no longer be so fat. "I'm often amused," says Tom Stoddard, "that so much attention has been given to the A&M Junction Boys and so little has been said about Bryant's first practice season at Alabama." Stoddard concedes that the heat of a Texas summer was worse than Alabama's in the spring. "There were a lot of other things about the Alabama practices that made it easier for the players: they were practicing on campus instead of at some remote facility, and in Tuscaloosa you didn't get knocked on the ground and come up with a cockle burr stuck in your elbow." On the other hand, "the weather was milder, so practice sessions at Alabama were a lot longer. One of the assistant coaches, Phil Cutchin, told me that they did the same drills at Alabama that they had done at A&M." Bryant would later admit to his players that he had made the first practices especially tough: "I wanted you boys to take pride in that red jersey because I had worn it."*

As at A&M, water breaks were not allowed. Goostree would later acknowledge, "We all thought—just about everyone thought back then—

---

* Actually, Bryant did not wear a red jersey. In the mid-1930s, Alabama players usually wore white jerseys with red numbers or white jerseys with red numbers and short red stripes down the front and on the sleeves.

that the need for water was a sign of weakness. We just didn't know then how wrong we were." To prevent cramps, players were given salt tablets, which, of course, only exacerbated the desire for water. They bit into sweaty towels so as not to be cotton-mouthed. After practice, they would stand in the shower with their mouths open, drinking the water from the shower heads. It wasn't that Bryant was the only coach who didn't believe in water breaks; it was just that Bryant's relentless drills dehydrated his players more quickly. Bryant made it abundantly clear what he was trying to do. The only solution for the fat that had grown into the Alabama program was to sweat it out. In his words, "My plan was to bleed 'em and gut 'em because I didn't want any well-wishers hanging around." Many of the players couldn't take it, or wouldn't, particularly the ones who felt they had already earned a spot on the football team under Whitworth. Bryant told Chuck Allen, a lineman from Athens, Alabama, "You know, you can quit any time you want to. But the first time you quit is hard. If you're going to quit, I want you to quit on me now, because I don't want you to quit in a game. You know, the next time you quit will be easier. And the next time after that will be even easier."

"We lost about 22 people that spring," Scooter Dyess later told John Forney and Steve Townsend for *Talk of the Tide: An Oral History of Alabama Football since 1920.* "When they were quitting, you kept wondering, 'This guy is a maniac. How is he going to build a team with what we have left?' When we came in, in the evenings, and three of his first-teamers would be gone, he'd move the second ones to the first team. He didn't care. He was going to play with what we had left."[6] Bobby Drake Keith, who had already been through Bryant's routines at College Station, insists Bryant "hated to see kids quit. He felt, though, that if you quit in practice, you'd quit in a game. What he wanted to see was a kid fight, to hang in there, to take what he dished out and come back for more. He wanted to see who wanted that uniform the most."

Whether or not Bryant was always fair or right in his methods of testing players has long been a subject for speculation. In Bryant's fourth season, an unnamed coach in the SEC—perhaps motivated by jealousy, as Alabama wiped out the field in the conference that year—told *Sports Illustrated* that Alabama's practices were so brutal that untalented players had to leave the team. It may have looked that way from a distance, but those who were there insist that Bryant's practices were equal-opportunity punishments for the talented as well as the untalented. Often, it was the more talented players who broke and ran, players such as Benny Dempsey. Some thought Dempsey was to Alabama what Ken Hill had been to A&M, namely, the most talented player that Bryant couldn't motivate. Dempsey was one of the most energetically recruited players ever in Alabama football, so much so that many believed one of his cousins had been given a scholarship by Ears Whitworth just to lure Dempsey to Alabama. Bryant, though, felt that he couldn't get Benny to make maximum use of his natural speed and power. One day, after the centers had been working on their punt snaps in the gym, Dempsey went to pick up his clothes basket and found the dreaded green jersey. At Notre Dame, the green jersey is a sign of great honor, called out only for the biggest games; at Alabama, a green jersey meant a player had been demoted to a lower squad. Dempsey confronted Bryant in his office.

"I was doing," Dempsey told Tom Stoddard, "the same thing the other centers were doing, snapping back as fast as I could snap." "Well," Bryant replied, "you were reported to me for loafing by one of the coaches. As far as I'm concerned, I would have given $10,000 for you as a freshman. I wouldn't give 10 cents for you right now."[7] Dempsey quit. One of Dempsey's teammates later admitted that he thought Dempsey "was probably mistreated. He was one they set out to make an example of because he was so much bigger, a hell of an athlete. I don't know if I could have stayed if I had been Benny." "What Coach Bryant was trying to do with Dempsey," says Clem Gryska, "was challenge him, motivate him. He wanted him to come back and fight harder after that, but it didn't work with Dempsey. Frankly, it was a problem we had with a lot of talented athletes. The ones with too much talent often felt they had other options."

For every Benny Dempsey, though, there were several like Don Cochran, who had been a starter as a sophomore under Whitworth. He had offers to transfer to other schools after the horrible 1957 season but was intrigued by stories of Bryant's toughness. He stayed because he wanted to play for a winner. When Cochran got a chance to talk with Bryant, the Bear went straight at him. "What did you do to get Coach Whitworth run off?" he asked. Cochran was dumbfounded. "Coach, I did the best I could, but"—at this, Bryant seemed to take special interest—"half the time most of us just didn't know what to do." Recovering from the Coach's offensive, Cochran found the courage to say what he had come to say. "All I'm telling you is that you're not going to run me off, no matter how you try. You'll get tired of telling me what to do before I'll get tired of doing it." Bryant, impressed, smiled, and replied, "Well, we'll see. We'll see."[8]

Then there was Gary Phillips, a premed student who desperately needed his football scholarship. On his way to meet with Bryant for the first time, Phillips stopped a teammate who had just come out of Bryant's office and asked him what the Coach had grilled him on. Cars and girlfriends was the answer. Phillips wanted to know Bear's feeling about cars and girlfriends and was told the Coach didn't approve of either.

When Phillips' turn came, Bryant asked him the same questions. He was ready: "Coach, I don't have a car *or* a girlfriend."

"Yeah," said Bryant, "and you ain't too big either." After a pause, as Phillips soaked in this comment, the Bear added, "But one of the best linemen I ever had was Stubble Tremble. And he weighed 185 pounds and didn't have but one hand."[9]

And, then there was Scooter Dyess, who was about five-foot-six and 150 pounds—in his autobiography, Bryant would describe him as "our gigantic 140-pound halfback." It seemed that every time Bryant told a story about Scooter he lost a few pounds. When he finally got his meeting with Bryant, the Coach rubbed his head—"Back then," says Dyess, "everyone wore crew cuts"—and kidded him saying, "What the hell are you, the water boy?" When they sat down, Bryant asked him if he thought he was good enough to make the team. Dyess told him that he would try. Bryant would have none of it: "Let's get something straight right off the bat. We either are or we are not. We're not going to have any triers." "Naturally," says Dyess, "I told him I would make the team."

As if Bryant's practices weren't strenuous enough, he also instituted "voluntary" conditioning. "Voluntary My Ass Practices," as assistant coach Pat James phrased it. James should know as he ran the most notorious one, Alabama's "wrestling" program, in which football players worked overtime building their upper-body strength by throwing each other on a matted gym floor. Some became so exhausted they would climb to the roof of the building and lose their lunch.*

---

* Tradition has it that the room where the football players wrestled was used for off-season workouts by Detroit Tigers ace right-hander Frank Lary, who hailed from nearby Northport. Lary was best known for beating the New York Yankees and earned the nickname "The Yankee Killer," winning twenty-three of thirty-two decisions against them.

ONE MAN, Merrill "Hootch" or "Hootchman" Collins, had been connected with Alabama football longer than anyone, even Hank Crisp. The son of a former slave, he was said to have been born in 1888—no one knew for sure, and Hootch was vague on the subject—and taken his first job for the university, as a janitor, in 1900. He worked numerous odd jobs for the athletic department and the football team through the tenures of Zen Scott, Wallace Wade, Frank Thomas, Red Drew, and Ears Whitworth. When Bryant played on the varsity team, Hootch went along on road trips, keeping track of watches, wallets, and whatever else passed for valuables among Bryant and his teammates. To some of the boys who had been raised in rural, segregated towns, Hootch was practically invisible; to Paul, he was like one of his old neighbors in Moro Bottom. By the time Bryant came back to Alabama in 1958, Hootch's primary function—in fact, his only function, as Clem Gryska recalls it—was to make coffee. Not an unimportant job in the pressure-packed football environment created by Bear Bryant.

Hootch lived in a boiler room in the building alongside the athletic department. Bryant saw that the aging Hootch, who died in 1968, had his meals delivered to him, and often dropped by, occasionally to tip a bottle of scotch. "He was a heck of a guy," says Clem Gryska. "He was one of the few who didn't call Coach Bryant 'Coach.' In fact, he was the only one who called him 'Boy.' I think he was the only one still there who remembered him as a boy."

ONE OF the primary lessons Bryant had learned from Frank Thomas was to regard talent as 90 percent of the game. And so his staff had been chosen largely for their skill and knowledge in locating and luring prospects. Backed by his own reputation as a pupil of Frank Thomas and as a winner at Maryland, Kentucky, and Texas A&M, his assistants would soon prove to be perhaps the most formidable recruiting machine in the nation. For the 1958 season, Bryant would make do with what he had inherited while his lieutenants were out on the front lines assembling the team of the future by recruiting for the freshman class.

Bryant met with his first freshman class in August. First-year players were ineligible for varsity sports back then, but these freshmen were a sensational group "handpicked" by his assistant coaches Jerry Claiborne and Hank Crisp. Bryant would later remember them as "the best freshman group I ever had in terms of character and dedication." He would begin working them into the regular lineup during their sophomore season in 1959, and they would form the heart of his first national championship team. They included future All-America and NFL star Billy Neighbors and Bryant's first star quarterback at Alabama, Pat Trammell. "How many of ya'll have called your mamas?" he asked. He told them all that they should write home to their mamas at least once a week. "Look around at the guys sitting next to you," he told them. "Chances are that four years from now the guy sitting next to you won't be here."

But, he told them, if they worked hard and listened to him, they would be national champions by their senior year. In *Bear*, he recalled his sense that this class was special. He challenged them:

I said, "What are you doing here?" and I waited. It was so quiet in there you could hear a pin drop.

I said, "What are you doing here? Tell me why you're here. If you're not here to win the national championship, you're in the wrong place."

Then I told them what I thought it would take to do it, and they believed me, they believed every word.

They believed it then, and they believed it all the way through school.

Bryant's freshmen were too young to remember when Alabama had been a national power. Stories of the Crimson Tide's great Rose Bowl conquests with the fabled Johnny Mack Brown and "Football Freddy" Sington, of Dixie Howell and Don Hutson, of the great Harry Gilmer, who had carried the Tide to the Rose Bowl after World War II, were as distant as tales recounted from *The Iliad*. It had not occurred to them before now that they could be part of that tradition.

"National champions!" says Billy Neighbors. "I was just stunned when I heard that. We all were. We'd heard so much about this man and what he could do, we all knew how awful Alabama had been before he got there, and here he was telling us that we could be national champions. We would be national champions by 1961 if we did what he told us and believed in ourselves. I got goose bumps. I started believing that very minute." But Billy Neighbors didn't get Bryant's entire message. "What I didn't catch on to right away was that when he talked about commitment to the school, he meant a *total* commitment, as in athletics *and* academics. In my second semester as a freshman, I really began to slack off, and I finally cut classes all together. Coach Bryant asked me to have lunch with him, and I thought, 'Uh, oh, I'm in deep shit now,' except that I really didn't know what the problem was. I had no idea at all that he was paying attention to what kind of grades the players were getting." Bryant had barely scraped through college himself—he would not have made it onto the football team had not the university seen to it that he had supplementary classes at Tuscaloosa High. This did not, however, instill in Bryant the idea that academics were unimportant; on the contrary, it bred in him a lifelong reverence for those who were better educated than he was and a contempt for boys who didn't take full advantage of the generous opportunities offered to them.

When Neighbors showed up for lunch, he had to deal not only with his coach but also with the dean. The conversation began politely; Bryant introduced his prize lineman to the dean and then pulled out an envelope with all of Neighbors's records, which showed exactly how many classes he had cut.

"I didn't say anything," says Neighbors. "I just kept my head down while he talked."

As Neighbors recalls, Bryant's tone became more emphatic: "'I'm talking to you, boy,' he said. 'You look me in the eye.'

"Then Coach spoke to the dean. 'This boy is a good boy, and he has the desire and talent to help us win. But'—he looked at me when he said this part—'if he doesn't start getting better grades, he won't be playing football for us.'

"Then the dean began talking about classes I should be taking and ways to improve my work habits, things like that. I realized what was going on: he was playing the good cop to Coach Bryant's bad cop. Finally, Coach, after listening to the dean and pretending that they hadn't had all this arranged beforehand, said 'Well, okay, on your recommendation I'm going to give him one more chance. But I tell you what I'm going to do—and then he looked at me again—'I'm going to move him into my house and if he pulls stunts like this again I'm going to do with him what I do with Paul Jr. when he comes home with less than a B. I'm gonna' take a dictionary and hit him over the head with it.' I never missed a class again." By September, the squad was down to forty-six players, just seventeen more than Bryant had had with Texas A&M after the Junction.

Alabama was sandwiched between two national champions in 1958, defending champion Auburn and its opening-day opponent, future champion LSU. Alabama fans expected improvement that season, not a miracle. They got a taste of both in the first game, though, when the Tide, battling furiously on defense, led 3–0 at the end of the half. The field goal did not hold up, particularly since Alabama had no genuine offensive weapons to counter LSU's great running back, and eventual Heisman Trophy winner, Billy Cannon. There were jokes to the effect that Alabama's best offensive weapon was the "quick-kick"—on third down, not fourth, when most teams were not expecting it, the center would snap the ball back to a player who had practiced punting and who would then deposit the kick several yards farther downfield than the opposing team was prepared for. You can't score points that way, but you can keep your opponent backed up deep in their own territory and capitalize on their mistakes. LSU went on to win 13–3, but a message had been sent.

The quick-kick is how Alabama beat Mississippi State University, 9–7, in the fifth week of the season. Not all of Bryant's supporters were thrilled with the strategy. When Alabama faced a second-and-one situation on their own twenty-four-yard line, Bryant ordered a quick-kick, which carried a whopping fifty-six yards. Winton "Red" Blount, future postmaster of the United States, a member of the Alabama athletic board, and a huge Bryant booster, was exasperated. "How you gonna win kicking the ball away all the time?" he screamed. Later, when Alabama quick-kicked again on second down, he ejaculated, "Hells bells! We done hired ourselves an idiot!" The idiot's strategy looked a little better when the ball rolled dead inside the MSU five-yard line. On fourth down, Alabama blocked a punt and scored a two-point safety, which proved to be the margin of victory. Blount, along with many other doubters, had to concede that perhaps Bryant knew what he was doing after all.

After a frustrating scoreless tie with Vanderbilt—Bryant's Tide had now gone eight full quarters without scoring a touchdown—Alabama began the greatest twenty-five-year run of any school in college football history. This new era commenced, not with a rousing win over Notre Dame, Southern Cal, or Tennessee, but with a 29–6 victory over little Furman. Alabama fans weren't so much exhilarated as relieved. The next week, at Knoxville, the Tide played tough but lost a 14–7 decision to hated Tennessee. Then, for the first time since Red Drew had been coach, the Tide started to roll, winning three of its last five games, including a 17–8 upset over Bobby Dodd's heavily favored Georgia Tech and a heartbreaking 14–8 season-ending loss to Auburn, in which Alabama penetrated to the Auburn twenty-eight on the final drive before sputtering when end Jerry Spruiell narrowly missed making a spectacular end zone catch as the ball was tipped by an Auburn defensive back.

Paul Bryant wasn't the same man who had behaved like a petulant child when his Kentucky team lost to Santa Clara ten years earlier; now he knew when his outgunned team deserved some praise. In the locker room, Bryant knelt down in front of Spruiell and quietly told him, "You tried. There'll be another day." To the rest of the team, he said, "You played as hard as I believe you could. And we came awfully close. I'll make one vow. It will be the last time we lose to those sonsabitches ever again." Bryant was blowing smoke, and his players knew it; there was no way he could keep a promise never to lose to Auburn again. Though over the next twenty-four years it would often seem to Auburn fans as if he had kept that promise; Auburn, which had been the dominant team in the SEC before Bryant took over coaching at Alabama, would never again win a conference championship under Shug Jordan. Alabama's 5-4-1 record in 1958 did not quite merit a bowl invitation, the only time that was so in Bryant's quarter century at Alabama.

Before the season was over, Mary Harmon and Paul Jr—Mae Martin was now married and gone from home—moved out of the Stafford Hotel and into a house on Lakeshore Drive in Tuscaloosa, "a big, solid brick one, with a look of permanence about it. J.B. (Ears) Whitworth, my predecessor, hadn't gotten around to buying a house. He had rented. I wanted them to know I wasn't thinking about going anywhere." The house, nestled in a grove of pine and oak trees, had eight rooms and a game room the size of a small auditorium, where the Bryants entertained. "Naturally," said Bryant, "I had it air-conditioned."

Bryant had the university's football offices gutted and remodeled. He brought two air conditioners with him from College Station and bought several more in Tuscaloosa, all for his assistants. On his office wall, Bryant proudly displayed a sign: "Winning Isn't Everything, But It Beats Anything That Comes In Second."

———

PAT TRAMMELL was the son of a Scottsboro doctor (and would eventually earn his own medical degree). He was not, as so many of his teammates were, desperately in need of a scholarship. Coming from a middle-class background, he was an unlikely candidate to become Bear Bryant's all-time favorite player. Perhaps what impressed Bryant the most was that Trammell, who didn't need football as much as most of his teammates, *wanted* to win so much.

One story told by several of Trammell's teammates has now become a part of Alabama lore, so that makes it true. Details vary, but supposedly in his freshman year, Trammell walked into a room where the freshman quarterbacks were all sitting at a table. Pulling out a switchblade, he flipped it into the tabletop, and while the others could still hear it quivering, Trammell announced in a loud voice, "I aim to be the quarterback of this team. Does anybody else here think they're quarterbacks?" No one answered, so Trammell became the quarterback. It may have been a show of bravado; it may not have happened at all. In a sense, it's irrelevant whether it did or not. That so many were willing to accept the story as true told you what you needed to know about Pat Trammell.

It would be said of several of Bryant's quarterbacks, "He can't pass and he can't run; all he can do is win." That was said more about Pat Trammell than any of the others, and it was the least true about him. In fact, at six foot two inches and around 195 pounds, Trammell was a superb athlete who could both run and pass very well; in high school he was recognized for achievement in basketball as well as football. Though perhaps not gifted with as strong an arm as a coach might prefer in a classic drop-back passer, he nonetheless set three school passing records in 1961. Bryant's habit of diminishing Trammell's athletic ability was his way of praising his commitment and desire. Numerous times throughout his career, Bryant was quoted as saying that Trammell was "the greatest leader I ever saw." Several of Bryant's close friends and coaches claim Trammell, of all of Bryant's players, was his favorite. Many described their relationship as father and "surrogate son."* (It is not known what Mary Harmon's reaction was to the line

---

* Bryant did relate that Pat and Paul Jr. became friends. "Both," said Bryant, "wanted to be historians, and they'd get together and talk about the Civil War and the Roman Empire and always go past bedtime. They decided they'd wind up starving to death on that route, however, so Paul went into business school and Pat into medicine."

in her husband's autobiography where he called Trammell "the favorite person of my entire life.") Trammell "was always early for practice. Most of the time he came by my office first, like Lee Roy [Jordan] and John Crow and Babe Parilli did. Just came by to talk. I loved that." Bryant apparently did not know that a great many of his players would have liked to come by to talk to him but simply didn't know how. Billy Neighbors, for instance, his first All-America lineman at Alabama, says, "I just had no idea how to start a conversation with him." Bob Baumhower, an All-America for Bryant in the 1970s, says, "As much as he meant to me, there was never really a time when I was able to talk to him. I guess I never stopped being in awe of him."

"I think Coach Bryant was always a little in awe of people who weren't in awe of him," says Clem Gyrska. "Pat loved him, but he wasn't in *awe* of him." On one occasion, at lunch, Bryant walked into the dining hall and over to Trammell's table. "Pat," he said, "I was thinking about going over this play in practice. Maybe trying to work it into this week's game. Why don't you take a look at it?" Trammell, scarcely raising his head, gazed intently at the playbook for a solid minute. He then glanced upward. "Coach, I think it's crap. It'll never work." Bryant nodded, smiled, gathered up his playbook, and walked back to his table. In 1959, Trammell became what Bryant called "the bell cow of the whole outfit. . . . The Alabama players rallied about him like little puppies. He could make them jump out a window to win. We didn't have any bad practices when he was there because he wouldn't let it happen."

If Trammell was the field general, then Darwin Holt was the master sergeant. While at Texas A&M Bryant had first scouted him at a high school near the Texas-Oklahoma border. The Coach had gone there to see his brother, Jack, a star running back, but came away more impressed by Jack's little brother, who was a good 40 pounds smaller. Bryant signed Darwin to A&M, and in 1959 he transferred to Alabama to play for Bear. (Jack would wind up playing for Bud Wilkinson at Oklahoma.) At about 152 pounds in his senior year in high school, Darwin was ridiculously small for almost any position on a football team, and at 167 pounds at Alabama he was small even for the late 1950s and even for a Bear Bryant–coached team, whose players were invariably smaller than those on opposing teams. In the words of Coach Gryska, though, "He ran like a panther and hit like an express train." He had something else too: the ability to motivate himself to exceed the apparent limits of his physical talent. "I've always been proud that Coach Bryant spotted that in me," he says. "You'd hear so much over the years about what a great motivator he was. But I always thought that what he was really good at was spotting the self-motivators."

Holt was Pat Trammell's opposite number, the signal caller for the defense. Rules back then allowed one substitution at the end of each series of downs, and Holt would replace Pat Trammell, not because Trammell wasn't capable of playing defense, but because Bryant didn't want to lose his most valuable offensive player to injury. Perhaps more than any other player, even Trammell, Darwin Holt symbolized Bryant's early Alabama teams, and his aggressiveness on the gridiron would help to initiate the most controversial episode in Bryant's football history.

AL "BUTCH" Browning of Andalusia, Alabama, was a third grader at East Three Notch Elementary School when Alabama began the 1959 football season. Urged on by his family, all fanatical Alabama fans, Little Butch sent a letter to Coach Bryant with the hope that it might be read on *The Bear Bryant Show* one Sunday. Two Sundays after mailing his letter, his father appeared in the backyard, pulled him off the swings, and dragged him into the living room. "I knew something was up," recalled Browning, "when I saw my aunts and uncles and cousins all sitting around the television set smiling, looking at me and waiting for *The Bear Bryant Show* to begin. It was like it was a surprise party or something, and they were waiting for it to start."

After a commercial break for Coca-Cola and Golden Flake potato chips—"Great pair, says the Bear"—it came time to read the weekly question. Suddenly, as if in a dream, Browning heard Bryant's rough bass baritone reading his question. "When Alabama is on defense, who calls the signals?" "Butch," the Bear said, "that would be the middle linebacker."

Later that week, Browning received a child-sized Crimson Tide football uniform. He sent Bryant a thank you letter; Bryant sent him back an autographed picture. A follow-up letter brought him an Alabama football brochure from the sports information desk. Still another letter got him an invitation from Bryant to "come and see us." In 1982, after spending ten years at the *Tuscaloosa News*, Browning, sitting in the Coach's office, reminded Bryant about their correspondence twenty-three years earlier. "I remembered that 'bout ten, eleven years ago when I met you," said the Bear. "I remembered your name from back then." Browning wanted to know: With all the letters you got in those years, you remembered mine? "Hell, yes," said Bryant. "You kept writing back. You were persistent. I admire persistence."

THE 1959 season did not start all that well. Auburn and LSU were the favorites to win the SEC title going into 1959. Jordan's Auburn Tigers had won twenty-three consecutive games and had now beaten Alabama for five straight years. The previous season LSU had won both the conference and the national championship. Other SEC contenders' prospects improved after Alabama opened with a resounding 17–3 loss to the University of Georgia at Athens. (The surprising Bulldogs, led by quarterback Fran Tarkenton, would go on to win the conference championship with a perfect 7–0-0 record.) The next week marked Bryant's return to Texas, with a shaky 3–0 victory in Houston. It took the Tide three weeks to finally score a touchdown, in the first half against Vanderbilt. The team would not score another in the game and settled for an exasperating 7–7 tie. Two weeks later, Bryant failed once again to beat Tennessee, with another frustrating tie game, 7–7. There was no denying reality: Alabama was going to need considerably more than some surprise quick-kicks to reach the top rung.

After victories over Mississippi State and Bobby Dodd's Georgia Tech Yellow Jackets, the biggest game of the season rolled around, the game the entire state of Alabama had planned its fall around. The previous season Auburn was undefeated; it wasn't that good in 1959, but going into the last week of the season its record was 7–2 to Alabama's 6–1-2. Bryant wanted to win this game desperately, not merely to establish state supremacy but to accelerate Alabama's national reputation with a lucrative bowl bid.

"I couldn't believe how hard he drove us in preparation for that game," says Billy Richardson. "He kept drilling it into us that it was the most important that we had played at Alabama so far, and that we would turn the corner against Auburn. I thought I was going to be nervous when we finally got on the field against them. I learned something that day. I wasn't nervous at all, I was just excited. Playing the game was the easy part. We were so well prepared, there was no way Auburn was going to beat us." As was their pattern that season—they scored more than fourteen points only once—the Alabama offense produced little that afternoon. But the Tide defense smothered the Tigers, and Alabama won, 10–0, in a game that was not nearly so close as the score indicated. One point, at least, was firmly established: Bear Bryant's Alabama teams could play defense. After the opening loss to Georgia, no team scored more than a touchdown against the Tide all season.

Alabama was 7–1–2 and ranked tenth in the final Associated Press poll. The team merited a bowl invitation, Bryant's first at Alabama, and the game would be an historic one. Alabama had more than one invitation. The Tide had been invited to play in the Bluegrass Bowl in Kentucky. Instead, Bryant chose the Liberty Bowl against Penn State, which would be played in mid-December in Philadelphia. Several of the players were not enthusiastic about his choice and had to be talked into it. It didn't help matters that there was a great deal of grumbling throughout Alabama about the Crimson Tide playing an integrated team—one member of the Alabama Board of Trustees was vocal about his dissatisfaction with Bryant's bowl choice, and there were rumors that several others found excuses to boycott it. Alabama's president, Frank Rose, received a telegram from the chairman of the Tuscaloosa Citizens Council that read, in part, "The Tide belongs to all Alabama, and Alabamians favor continued segregation."* Black Alabamians were not consulted on the issue.

For some unexplained reason, Governor John Patterson, who had beaten George Wallace in the 1958 Democratic primary with the support of the Ku Klux Klan, assured Bryant that he had his support to play in the Liberty Bowl. Perhaps seeing an opportunity to use Bryant and a winning football team to showcase the virtues of segregation, Patterson not only approved but also traveled to Philadelphia for the game.

Bryant's choice was not arbitrary. An important reason for his wanting to play in the Liberty Bowl was national recognition: he wanted Alabama once again to be perceived as a national, not a regional, power. (No doubt

---

* Keith Dunnavant quotes from a telegram Rose received after the announcement that Alabama would play in the Liberty Bowl. "Don't [sic] you realize the consequences of a most certain repetition [sic] of trouble and a very probable unhappy return of such trouble to your doorstep. . . . May God have mercy on you at this Christmas season and the days to follow." (*Coach*, p. 252) The apparent reference to "a most certain repetition of trouble" was to the violence that occurred in February 1956, when Autherine Lucy attempted unsuccessfully to register at the university.

he was remembering Alabama's legendary trip to Philadelphia in 1922 when the team played the University of Pennsylvania.) He knew this was impossible without recognition from the northern press. Second, the 1960 Liberty Bowl would mark the first time an Alabama team took the field against an integrated squad, as Penn State had five black players. "They had a really good black lineman named Charlie Jenrett," says Billy Neighbors, "and he lined up against me. He was one of the best players I ever faced. All Coach Bryant said to me about playing against a black guy was, 'Now, Billy, a lot of people are going to be watching us and watching how you behave yourself. You play hard, you play clean. You knock him down, you hold out your hand and help him back up.'"

The game would not change the homefolks' minds overnight, but it was a start.

As feared, the weather was bad, so bad that Bryant decided against flying. For many players, it was the first train ride of their life. "We rolled into Penn Station [in Philadelphia]," recalled halfback Billy Richardson, "and, of course, none of us had ever been in a place that big in our lives, and we'd get off the train and start gawking and looking for the people meeting us, but there was no press to be seen anywhere." The terrible weather had discouraged many eastern journalists, so Bryant took it upon himself to stir up some news. At the next day's practice, he showed off his "chair drill." "We had 11 chairs lined up in the offensive position," says Richardson, "and 11 in the defensive position, just plain old folding chairs. We sat down on the chairs, and Trammell would call a play and a snap, then we would point to the chair that was in the position we were supposed to be playing and then go to it. It was a mental drill. Well the next day, we got the headlines in the Philadelphia papers. None of those guys had ever seen anything like Coach Bryant's chair drills. The point of the drill was to show that in any situation on offense or defense we knew exactly where we were supposed to be. And we did know."

On a field so covered with snow the officials could barely see the markers, Penn State scored a touchdown off a fake field goal and won, 7–0. At the game's end, a young Penn State assistant coach came over to shake hands with Bear Bryant for the first time. Forty-one years later, Joe Paterno would become the first Division I-A coach to surpass Bear Bryant's career record for victories. At a postgame party, Charlie Jenrett walked up to Bryant to shake hands and congratulate him on his team's sportsmanship.

"Charlie," Bryant replied, "I don't know how to take that. I think I'd rather you told me they were mean and ugly. Maybe we'da won." For the team, one of the side benefits of the Liberty Bowl trip was a visit to New York City and a dinner courtesy of NBC at Mama Leone's. Mel Allen was the host, and before the night was over, he had regaled the awestruck Crimson Tiders with stories of the team's legendary past, some of which involved their coach. The trip to New York also gave Bryant a chance to drop by Toots Shor's and renew some old press contacts.

As soon as he got back to Tuscaloosa, Bryant began beefing up his coaching staff. He called Larry "Dude" Hennessey, his former player and assistant coach at Kentucky, and now a high school football coach in Louisville. Dude and his wife were watching television the night he got the call. "The first sentence out of his mouth," says Hennessey, "he offered me a job. 'At Alabama?' I asked. 'I'll take it. When do I leave?' 'Now, Dude,' said Bryant, 'Don't you want to talk about money? And how do you know you're gonna like it here? You've never seen Tuscaloosa.'" Hennessey didn't care; he took the job without even discussing the terms. Not until he got his first check did Hennessey realize he was making about two hundred dollars less per month than he had received for coaching high school ball in Kentucky. Hennessey shrugged, stuffed the check in his coat pocket, and went back to work. The pay cut was worth it to be working with Bear Bryant.

SOMETIME DURING the winter, Tommy Brooker, a player from the Class of 1958, slipped away with some friends and teammates to a Tuscaloosa movie theater to see Howard Hawks's *Rio Bravo* with John Wayne. As they were leaving the theater, they were startled to see their coach, hat in hand, walking out the door. They tried to avoid being seen— "Coach Bryant just kind of intimidated you, no matter where you saw him," says Brooker—but Bryant turned to look at them. "Just wanted to see," he grumbled to Brooker with what appeared to be a sheepish grin on his face, "this guy who everybody says reminds them of me."

IN MAY 1960, George McAdams was ten years old. His older brother, Clayton, had just graduated from the University of Alabama with honors with a B.S. in Business Statistics, and Lieutenant Colonel McAdams had brought his wife and youngest son for the graduation. After the ceremonies, they attended a tea at the President's Mansion. Colonel McAdams noticed a tall man off to the side, smoking an unfiltered cigarette, one foot on a chair, his elbow resting on his knee, looking somewhat bored. "George," he said, "there's Alabama's new football coach, Coach Bryant. Go over and introduce yourself." (The McAdams family had been stationed in Taiwan for over two years, so Bryant was the "new" coach to them.) George, all of four feet four inches and weighing eighty pounds, walked over and introduced himself. "Coach Bryant, I'm George McAdams. My father is Colonel McAdams, and we are here because my brother Clayton just graduated, with honors." Bryant took his foot off the chair, reached out, took the boy's hand in a firm but careful grip, and shook it. "It's a pleasure to meet you, George," Bryant said. "Do you play football?" George replied that he had just returned from Taiwan, where they mostly played soccer, but, yes, he did know how to play football. "Can you run fast?" Bryant asked. Yes, George could run pretty fast.

Bryant glanced backward to the President's Mansion, then out toward Denny Chimes and University Avenue. "You know," he said to George. "I bet you are fast. I'll tell you what I want you to do. I want you to run as fast as you can to that sidewalk down there and come back here, as fast as you can." George was dressed in his Sunday suit with polished shoes that hadn't been broken in. Ordinarily, sprinting in that outfit would have been unthinkable, but "there was something about Coach Bryant—when he asked you to do something, you wanted to do it. I wanted to impress him." George ran down to the sidewalk and back as fast as he could. "George," Bryant told him at the finish, putting his hands on the boy's shoulder. "That was pretty good. But I think you can do better." He then proceeded to give George a few tips: take off his coat and tie—and be sure to put them on a nearby table in case his mother was watching—and "run harder this time, don't run quite so far past the sidewalk. Just touch it and head on back." Bryant took out his watch and held it up to time the second run.

"Now get ready . . . go!" Unfettered by coat and tie and heeding Bryant's advice not to overrun the sidewalk, George was positive he had beaten his first time. When he finished, Bryant told him to "come over here and tell me some more about yourself." What were George's hobbies, Bryant wanted to know. What were his favorite subjects in school? While they were talking, Colonel McAdams approached. "Coach Bryant," he said, "I see you have met my son, George." He also introduced Bryant to his older son, Clayton. Bryant shook hands and said it was a pleasure to meet them. "Colonel McAdams," Bryant said, "you have every right to be proud of Clayton, but he has just graduated, he can't do me any good." Glancing at the younger son, he said, "I still might have a chance with George." Bryant shook George's hand again, told him to keep running to increase his speed, and come and see him some day if he ever tried out for football. George McAdams opted for a degree in political science and eventually graduated from the University of Alabama in Birmingham. For the rest of his life, he took with him the satisfaction of knowing that he had been recruited by Bear Bryant.

MORE THAN a thousand miles from Bryant's Tuscaloosa office, decisions were being made that would forever change Bear Bryant's image with the American public—or, rather, they would help establish Bryant's public image. Though he had been profiled in the 1950s in national publications such as *Look* and *Sport* magazine, he had yet to attain the status of genuine celebrity outside of the Southeast and Texas. He was known, loved, feared, respected, and hated within his profession. But, in terms of national recognition, his profession limited his fame. Thanks largely to the Johnny Unitas–led Baltimore Colts, pro football was on the verge of establishing itself as America's most popular television sport, but college football, which had the jump on the pros by several decades, had yet to drove itself as an important staple of television sports.

Part of the problem was that college football was by nature feudal compared to the centralized pro game. Fans living in almost any part of the country could instantly identify with the Green Bay Packers or Baltimore Colts or Dallas Cowboys simply by tuning in to national telecasts, but it was far more difficult for fans in one part of the country to relate to football passion in another. Interest in college football was generally confined to local traditions and rivalries, with most fans only paying attention to their own schools. For decades, the only college that transcended regional appeal was Notre Dame, which played a national schedule—Army in New York, Michigan in the Midwest, Southern Cal on the West Coast, and so on—and benefited from a large Catholic following spread out across the country. It was difficult for football fans in, say, the Northeast or on the West to care or understand why local rivalries such as Ohio State–Michigan or Texas–Texas A&M or Alabama-Tennessee were so special.

Roone Arledge would show them why they should care. Arledge didn't invent the idea of college football on television, but he invented it as we now know it. As late as the early 1950s, the widespread belief in college football circles was that television hurt the game by offering fans something for free that they had previously been inclined to pay for. And in fact, early returns bore this out: in 1950, for instance, the Pacific Coast Conference had broadcast thirty games and found that the revenue it lost in terms of reduced ticket sales and related concessions cut revenues by more than 10 percent—or slightly more than the conference had earned in television fees.

But Bear Bryant, who had become enamored with college football before playing his high school game, understood what officials of the NCAA (which kept a tight clamp on all television rights) and officials of the big Northeast and West Coast schools did not. In most of the country, interest in college football transcended the students and alumni of the colleges, and—especially in the South, Midwest, and West—college football was not a sport just for the upper crust, but one with a fanatical following among the common people. He understood something else. Television would help create *more* paying customers. And, long before most of his rivals, he grasped the power of television as a recruiting tool. The boy who had discovered the Alabama Crimson Tide through a radio broadcast in rural Arkansas was quick to see the possibilities of putting boys on television for all their mamas and papas and girlfriends to see. Clem Gryska, who saw the impact of television on Alabama's recruiting clout firsthand, says, "After 1960, every young man who was serious about football wanted to be on TV, and any young man we approached knew that we would always be on TV, every year. That gave us a tremendous edge in going after almost any boy we wanted."★

Arledge could have cared less about the recruiting power of television. He was twenty-nine years old when he was hired by ABC's Edgar Scherick

---

★ Gryska had come to play for Alabama from Steubenville, Ohio, without ever having seen a college football game. "Coach [Frank] Thomas told my parents that he'd look after me, that I'd get my education. That's all they needed to know."

on the strength of an unsuccessful pilot. (Arledge's pilot was an entertainment show aimed at the *Esquire-Playboy* men's audience; Scherick didn't care for the idea, but liked the way it was produced.) When Scherick made him an offer, to head up the new division that would become ABC Sports, Arledge was producing Shari Lewis's "Lamb Chop" puppet show for NBC. Scherick was a visionary, or perhaps he was simply desperate; in the later 1950s, the American Broadcasting Company was known derisively in the television industry as the Almost Broadcasting Company. Sports, it seemed to Scherick, was a vast untapped resource with an already massive audience. All that was necessary was to connect sport and the audience with the medium.

Arledge rejected the notion that sports could not be established as big-time television programming—in his famous phrase, "Sport is unscripted drama," and he knew instinctively how to convey that drama to the masses. One of his ideas involved the use of new technologies, "shotgun" mikes that could pick up sounds several feet away and handheld cameras that brought an immediacy to off-the-field action. He soon hired a director who added yet another potent mixture to the brew: sex.

"He called me in California and told me to write him a letter about ideas I had for college football broadcasts," says Andy Sidaris, who would one day gravitate to a lucrative career as a soft-core porn filmmaker. "I wanted women on camera—women in the stands, coeds, girlfriends, cheerleaders. It always pissed me off when I'd watch games on NBC, and the camera would pass right over the cheerleaders like they were hardly there. When I found out we were going to do a game in Alabama, I thought, 'Hot damn! Are we going to get some honey shots down there!'" Arledge liked the way Sidaris thought; he hired him for a healthy three hundred dollars a game as a freelance director.

Bear Bryant would have admired Arledge's work habits: "Roone's day was just getting starting when everybody else was going home. And he did it deliberately," said one aide. "He had more time to think. He did not clutter up his day with administrative bullshit."

When Arledge died in December 2002, he was widely recognized as the man who created ABC's *Wide World of Sports* and *Monday Night Football*. Not enough mention was made of the fact that he made college football into a major TV attraction. As stated by Marc Gunther and Bill Carter in *Monday Night Mayhem: The Inside Story of ABC's Monday Night Football*:

Arledge began by questioning the very purpose of sports television.

His first heretical idea was that sports television did not exist to televise sports. Television was not in the business of selling tickets, or of telling viewers to turn off their sets and come to the ball park because there were still great seats available.

Sports television, Arledge decided, was like the rest of television. Its job was to entertain the audience at home. That led him to the belief that television had to do more than just document the game.

It became the Arledge credo: the show, not the contest, is what counts. It was a simple idea, but one with revolutionary implications.[10]

In a legendary memo to Scherick, Arledge wrote,

Heretofore, television has done a remarkable job of bringing the game to the viewer—now we are going to take the viewer to the game!!

We will utilize every production technique . . . to heighten the viewer's feeling of actually sitting in the stands and participating personally in the excitement and color. . . .

We must gain and hold the interest of women and others who are not fanatic followers of the sport. . . . Women come to football games . . . to sit in a crowd, see what everyone else is wearing, watch the cheerleaders and experience the countless things that make up the feeling of the game. Incidentally, very few men have ever switched channels when a nicely proportioned girl was leaping into the air. . . .

We will have cameras mounted in jeeps, on mike booms, in risers or helicopters, or anything necessary to get the complete story of the game. We will use a "creepy-peepey" camera to get the impact shots that we cannot get from a fixed camera—a coach's face as a man drops a pass in the clear—a pretty cheerleader just after her hero has scored a touchdown . . . all the excitement, wonder, jubilation and despair that make this America's Number One sports spectacle.[11]

In other words, Roone Arledge and ABC Sports were going to take America to an Alabama football game. Leaving nothing to chance, Arledge arrived in Birmingham several days early to scout out his territory. He had no personal stake in the contest to come: "Unless the Almighty has a grudge against the Bulldogs," he wrote in his memoir, *Roone*, "Georgia, which had won the last Orange Bowl, was going to crush Alabama, which had lost the last Liberty Bowl. So long as there was drama in the crushing, that was fine with me."[12]

On the Friday night before the game, Bryant invited Arledge and his crew out to dinner at what-was-then Birmingham's poshest restaurant, The Club.* He introduced them to some patented Bear Bryant "poor-mouthing." "Least I can do," he said, "is to take you folks out to dinner, see-ing's how my po' boys are going to embarrass themselves on your first show and all." After the dinner, some serious drinking began, and with it, a debate on football strategy between Chuck Howard, at the time one of the lowest-ranked men on the ABC crew, and Bryant. Voices were raised, heads began turning, and Arledge was horrified to think that his initial venture into college football might be shot down by a squabble between one of the most celebrated coaches in the game and one of his crew. "Will somebody get Chuck the hell out of here?" Arledge pleaded. "The funny thing," says Sidaris, "is that Roone didn't understand that Bear was getting a huge kick out of the whole thing—this Yankee smart-ass coming down there and lec-turing him on football."

On Saturday, September 17, 1960, rookie Roone Arledge, age twenty-nine, climbed out of his mobile-unit truck in front of Birmingham's Legion Field to produce his first live sports telecast. ABC had just paid an eye-popping six million dollars for its college football TV package, and this game would establish the pattern. Arledge's professional life was on the line. Just to add a little pressure, all of ABC's top executives were in attendance that afternoon. Arledge's instincts were uncanny. He had picked the right part of the country, the right school, the right announcer (Curt Gowdy, who had his first big break broadcasting Bud Wilkinson's Oklahoma Soon-ers and who had worked with Bryant's old Alabama classmate, Mel Allen), the right matchup, the right cheerleaders, and, most of all, the right coach. Alabama was out to avenge the previous year's season-opening humiliation from Georgia. To do so, they would have to stop the Bulldogs' amazing scrambling quarterback, Fran Tarkenton.

---

* The Club was built atop Red Mountain near Birmingham's famous statue of Vulcan, the forger of the gods and symbol of Birmingham's once-proud steel industry, which overlooks the city in the valley below. The Club hangs almost directly above my mother's house on Birmingham's Southside.

Arledge knew that the game would hook the entire southeastern audience as well as many hard-core fans throughout the country. What he wanted was everyone else. Relaying his thoughts to Gowdy and his co-commentator, Paul Christman, Arledge, according to Gunther and Carter, told them "to emphasize the developing story of the game, the contrast between the Bryant-drilled unit of Alabama and the soaring individual ability of Fran Tarkenton for Georgia." Arledge instructed his cameramen to focus on "the calm concentration of Bryant on the sideline before an important call, the youthful elation of Tarkenton after a scrambling first down, the sweet exuberance of Alabama cheerleaders, and the anguish of a rooter with a Georgia pennant."[13] There was a great deal of the latter that day as the Alabama defense shut down Tarkenton in a convincing 17–3 victory; Bear Bryant had no intention of losing what he would come to regard as his real national television debut. It was the start of a beautiful relationship.

"We always knew at the start of the football season that we'd be doing at least one Alabama game," says Sidaris, who became a producer for Arledge. "I think I probably did twenty-five or thirty games in Birmingham and Tuscaloosa over the years, and at least that many Alabama games on the road. Bear Bryant became one of our television stars. I guess considering how long he was there and how many of his games we did, you might say he was our biggest star. It was like a party every time we went to Alabama." Roone Arledge must have thought so too, particularly when Bryant later introduced him to his future wife, Ann Fowler, a former Miss Alabama.

"Most other coaches hated us getting so close," says Sidaris. "Bear loved it. I always thought he had a third eye for the camera; he seemed to always know when it was on him. In all the years we broadcast Alabama games, he never showed his temper on camera. When things got scary, he just gripped that rolled-up paper in his hand a little harder. He was a hell of a lot of fun to be around. When we'd start setting up for a big game, I'd see him and yell something like, 'Bear, your team sucks, you're going to get the shit kicked out of you today! But you got *great* cheerleaders!' He'd say, 'Andy, you old sonuvabitch, you don't know shit about football, and you ain't got manners enough to serve grits to a bear. I would have thought that all these years of watching me you woulda learned somethin', but you haven't learned shit. It's really nice to have you down here.'"

Prior to the national television explosion in the early 1960s, college football coaches were revered figures in American sports, but somewhat akin to medieval barons in terms of national fame. Except for Notre Dame's Knute Rockne, who achieved immortality not just through winning national championships but by dying in a plane crash, the great coaches ruled their universities, their states, and sometimes even their regions, but they did not achieve national acclaim. Roone Arledge and ABC would change all that. In the 1960s, Ohio State's Woody Hayes, Texas's Darrell Royal, Southern Cal's John McKay, Michigan State's Duffy Daugherty, Notre Dame's Ara Parseghian, and, most of all, Alabama's Bear Bryant would become national television stars and reach a level of fame unknown to General Neyland, Red Blaik, Frank Leahy, and even Bud Wilkinson.

IF PAUL BRYANT had a fondness for players "who weren't awfully talented but who didn't know it," that didn't mean he wasn't ready to accommodate players who were very talented but still played as if they had something to prove. In 1959 he recruited such a freshman, Lee Roy Jordan, from the tiny town of Excel, Alabama. By 1960 Jordan was a varsity standout, a weapon both on offense, where he played center, and especially on defense, where he became the most savage tackler most observers had ever seen. Bryant said two memorable things about Jordan. One was at a press conference after the January 1, 1963, whipping of Bud Wilkinson's Oklahoma Sooners in the Orange Bowl in which Jordan made a mind-boggling thirty-one tackles. "Lee Roy," Bryant said, "will get 'em if they stay between the sidelines." The other quote was, "Lee Roy is the best football player I've ever had," this line coming much later, in reflection. In 1962, he merely called him "the best linebacker in football, bar none." Bryant said that, or something close to that, about several of his players, but he was probably closest to being right about Jordan, who would become a perennial All-Pro with the Dallas Cowboys.

With two bona fide All-America players—a lineman, Billy Neighbors, and a linebacker, Lee Roy Jordan—Alabama needed only a reasonable offense to have a great team in 1960. Pat Trammell provided it. After the opening win against Georgia, Alabama stumbled into a tie with Tulane and then lost just one game—a humiliating 20–7 drubbing by Tennessee at Knoxville—the rest of the season. The final game was a brutally played, 3–0 victory over Auburn, the second year in a row the Tide had shut out the Tigers. In the Bluebonnet Bowl, Bryant once again failed to beat his younger friend, Darrell Royal, as Alabama played to a 3–3 tie against Texas. The defense had allowed more than six points in only two games all year and had shutout *six of ten* regular-season opponents.

One game from 1960 stands out and has worked its way into Alabama folklore. In the eighth week of the season, against Bobby Dodd's Georgia Tech, the Tide found itself shockingly behind Georgia Tech at halftime by a score of 15–0. As the players filed into their locker room, they were dejected by their own poor performance. To a man, they expected a severe dressing down from their coach—"We thought it was going to be all fire and brimstone for fifteen minutes," says Billy Richardson—and Bryant, if he thought it would have worked, would have been happy to give it to them. Instead, Richardson had an inspiration. "Where are the Cokes?" were the first words out of his mouth when he stepped up to address the team. "Let's get some Cokes in here!" Then, "Now, this is great, this is great! We got 'em right where we want 'em! They're gonna see what we're made of now."

"We were shocked," recalls Billy Neighbors. "I mean, we were sipping Cokes and looking at each other, and wondering what in the hell has gotten into him?" Having decided that the only thing wrong with his team was that they had temporarily forgotten how much better they were than their opponents, Bryant figured that the best way to get his boys back in the game was to simply remind them of who they were. He played it cool and told them of a few adjustments for the second half, making it clear that all that was necessary for them to win was to go out there and just be themselves.★

The third quarter was a scoreless standoff. In the final period, the Tide staged one of the most furious rallies in its history. Pat Trammell was forced out of the game with a leg injury, and Bobby Skelton, the quarterback whose job Trammell had taken, led Alabama on two heroic touchdown drives. The first drive became legendary: four times Alabama was faced

---

★ Vince Lombardi used the same psychology in one of the Packers' most famous comebacks. In 1965, Green Bay was getting whipped by its bitter rivals, the Detroit Lions, 21–3 at the half. According to David Maraniss, "Lombardi's players were furious as they clattered into the dressing room at halftime. Surprisingly, they were more upset than their coach. Rather than vent his frustration on his players, Lombardi stepped atop a footlocker and delivered an oration on pride and loyalty. 'Win, lose or draw, you are my football team . . . and you have your pride!'" Several players, says Maraniss, began "misting up." (*When Pride Still Mattered*, pp. 371–372) In the second half, Bart Starr threw three touchdown passes and ran for a fourth as the Packers rolled over the Lions, 31–21.

with a fourth-down situation, and four times the offense converted. Failure on any one of the four would have cost the team the game. After the first touchdown, Bryant ordered an onside kick. Alabama recovered the ball, and then scored on the next possession. With about a minute to play, everyone in the stadium thought that Alabama would try another onside kick. But with astute attention to clock management, Bryant had been able to mass all four of his timeouts, and now he used them. The Tide kicked off and the Yellow Jackets took the ball on their own twenty. The Alabama defense jammed Tech on its first three plays, after which Bryant ordered a timeout. With seconds left, Tech punted, and Alabama took the ball on the Jackets' forty-five-yard line. Skelton threw a sideline pass to halfback Butch Wilson, who was skirting the sideline around the Tech thirty-five and got knocked out of bounds. The officials, though, didn't see him cross the line. Wilson stepped back on the field, caught the ball, and ran it to the twelve-yard line, with Alabama fans screaming their throats raw.

There was time for just one more play, a field goal try—a chip shot for the Tide's regular field goal kicker, Tommy Brooker. The problem was that Brooker was hurt and out of the game; he couldn't walk back on the field under his own power. Bryant turned to his substitute kicker, Richard "Digger" O'Dell, a junior. Slapping him on his backside, Bryant told him casually, as if it was practice, to go out and kick a field goal. With seconds left to play, Digger O'Dell calmly got into place, with his eyes fixed down on the ball, and prepared for the first field goal attempt of his Alabama career.

The result was not an aesthetic triumph. Bryant thought it looked like a knuckle ball: "It went this way and that way. But it went through the goal posts and barely over the bar. It might have even grazed the bar." But in the record books, the kick was right down the middle. Alabama won in its most sensational victory so far in Bryant's tenure, 16–15. It was not only the first but the last field goal attempt for O'Dell in an Alabama uniform.*

A few days later, while discussing other matters with Bryant, Bobby Dodd suddenly changed the topic of conversation. "We've been friends a

---

* In *Talk of the Tide: An Oral History of Alabama Football since 1920,* John Forney, the long-time Alabama radio announcer, revealed that the play-by-play crew had not noticed that O'Dell had gone in for Brooker as the substitute kicker. "Everybody at home thought Brooker had kicked the field goal because that's how it was announced on the radio, and when we got back home to Tuscaloosa, everybody mobbed him." O'Dell never received the adulation he deserved for one of the biggest kicks in Crimson Tide history. (p. 91)

long time," Dodd told Bryant, "and you really embarrassed me over there, coming from 15–0 to win that game. But dammit, that Wilson was knocked out of bounds on that pass. He came back into catch the ball. We saw it in the movies." Bryant said, "Yeah, Bobby, I saw it, too. What's wrong with that?" Bryant laughed at his own quip, but did not record Dodd's reaction.

The season-ending tie with Texas was a disappointment—Bear Bryant still had not won a bowl game with Alabama. But there was now a clear feeling in the SEC that the future would belong to Bryant and his Crimson Tide. Alabama would own the 1960s as no college team had ever owned a decade before. They would win by the book: the book Bryant himself had written.

IN THE 1960s, the Crimson Tide won the most games, had the highest won-lost percentage (.836), was invited to ten consecutive bowl games, won three national championships, should have won a fourth, and came within a point of winning yet another. Together, Bryant and Alabama established college bowl games as prime-time television fare, and produced the decade's most celebrated college player, the man who would change pro football. Bryant also became the most famous coach in the game, found himself embroiled in the biggest scandal in the sport's history, and wrote a book, *Building a Championship Football Team*, which was published in 1960 in time for the Christmas holidays. Bryant dedicated it to numerous friends and colleagues who had influenced him over the years, including his Fordyce High football coach, Robert Cowan; Frank Thomas; H. R. "Red" Sanders, the man who had fired him at Vanderbilt; Jim Tatum, the coach who had begun coaching at Maryland after Bryant left and who he had recommended for the Alabama job; and the colorful former Yale football coach, Herman Hickman.*

---

* Bryant was a fan of the legendary Hickman, who had been an All-America lineman at Tennessee under General Neyland when Bryant was playing for Alabama. (Hickman was so good that Grantland Rice put him on his all-time college football team.) Known as the "poet laureate of the Great Smokies" and "The Tennessee Terror," the stocky Hickman was described as looking like "Friar Tuck in a high school production of Robin Hood." General Neyland once described him as "the greatest guard football has ever known." Hickman, who idolized his Yale predecessor, Pudge Heffelfinger, insisted he was only second best.

Written with the assistance of Gene Stallings, *Building a Championship Football Team* states its case in the first chapter. "Football is a drama, music, dignity, sorrow. . . . Football is the memory of Red Grange, the Four Horsemen, and the Seven Blocks of Granite."[14] The book contained primers on game strategy with suggestions on "When To Kick" ("when in doubt" and "early on a wet field; let the opponents handle the ball"), "When Not To Pass" ("when the opponent expects a pass" and "when backed up and you are ahead"), "When To Try and Score In One Play" ("when you have mental edge on opponent following a blocked kick, a recovered fumble, or an intercepted pass in the opponent's territory"), and "When To Run Your Best Ball Carrier Behind Best Blockers" ("when you must have a first down," but "do not use him first play after a long run").

Only a coach who had played football at a major college and had turned several football programs around could have written *Building a Championship Football Team*. For the first time in his life, Bryant put his professional principles and beliefs on paper. In the first chapter, "Why Football," he wrote,

Not only is football a great and worthwhile sport because it teaches fair play and discipline, but it was also the number one way of American life—to win. . . . It is not the mere winning of the game, but the teaching of boys to win the hectic battle over themselves that is important. Sure, winning the game is important, and I would be the last to say that it wasn't. But helping the boy to develop his poise and confidence, pride in himself and his undertakings, teaching him to give that little extra effort are the real objectives of teaching winning football.

If I had my choice of either winning the game or winning the faith of a boy, I would choose the latter. There is no greater reward for a coach

---

Hickman lectured on Rudyard Kipling at Yale and, when coaching the football team, would fire up his players with a popular period oration, "Spartacus to the Gladiators" by one E. Kellogg—"Ye call me chief, and ye do well to call me chief. If ye are men, follow me! . . . If we must fight, let us fight for ourselves. If we must slaughter, let us slaughter our oppressors! If we must die, let it be under the clear sky, by the bright waters, in noble, honorable battle!"

Having concluded his oration, Hickman would snap his fingers and say, "Whaddya say, Men, let's go chew up those Harvards!" (McCallum and Pearson, *College Football U.S.A., 1869–1971;* Yale University Archives)

than to see his players achieve their goals in life and to know he had some small part in the success of the boy's endeavors."*[15]

In his book, Bryant didn't hesitate to name the most important position on a football field. "All outstanding football teams have two distinct characteristics in common—a great fighting spirit and a great quarterback. A smart capable quarterback is the greatest single asset a football team can possess." He believed that there were basically three types of quarterbacks, and since he didn't want to waste time with the first two, we shall go directly to his third: "The one every coach is seeking. He directs his team to maximum results. He is a student of the game. He is logical in his thinking, and bold in his action, when necessary to win the football game. He is confident, which in turn gives his team confidence in him and the offense. He is a winner through preparation, and he will give you winners through action and leadership."[16]

He is George Blanda, Babe Parilli, Roddy Osborne, Joe Namath, Steve Sloan, Ken Stabler, Scott Hunter, Richard Todd, Gary and Jeff Rutledge, Steadman Shealy, and Walter Lewis. And in 1961, he was Pat Trammell.

By the time of the Auburn game at the end of the 1961 season, Pat Trammell had become so confident of his own leadership that he surprised his coach by calling for a quick-kick on second down with the ball near the fifty-yard line. When Trammell came off the field, Bryant inquired as to

---

* Noting that "you can never be absolutely certain about a boy because you cannot see what is inside of his heart," Bryant cited one particular boy who showed up at the first practice session at Kentucky in the fall of 1948. "His appearance literally stopped practice. He had on a zoot suit with the trouser legs pegged so tightly I am certain he had difficulty squeezing his bare feet through the narrow openings." This unnamed player must be Walt Yowarsky, though Yowarsky always insisted that he never wore a zoot suit.

Identified by Bryant only as "Smitty," the boy, his coach figured, "wouldn't have the heart for our type of football and would eliminate himself quickly from the squad." But, "despite Smitty's outward appearance, he had the heart of a competitor and the desire to show everyone he was a good football player. He worked hard and proved his point. In his senior year, he was selected the outstanding player in the 1951 Sugar Bowl when we defeated the University of Oklahoma. . . . I shall always have the greatest respect for him." (Bryant, *Building a Championship Football Team*, p. 15)

Clearly, Bryant was trying to make the point that the smart coach learns to accommodate nonconformists if they have the proper desire and ability. Precisely why he failed to identify Yowarsky by name isn't apparent; perhaps he still felt a bit embarrassed by his failure to win Yowarsky's full affection at Kentucky.

what in hell he thought he was doing. "Coach," he replied, "we're just not blocking anybody worth a crap, so I figured I'd see what our guys can do on defense." Bryant shrugged his assent; he had reached a point in his career when he knew simply to go with a good idea.

IN THE opening game of the 1961 season, the Georgia Bulldogs scored a touchdown against the Alabama defense. No one was shocked at the time, but if they could have foreseen the rest of the season, they would have been. The Crimson Tide would surrender just two more touchdowns (one on a punt return)—and, in fact, just four field goals—all season long. The touchdown scored by Georgia in the opener would prove to be unique in two respects: it was the only sustained drive for a touchdown scored against Alabama, and it was the only touchdown scored against Alabama's first-team defense, during the entire season. Alabama recorded six shutouts, prevented eight of eleven opponents (including Arkansas in the Sugar Bowl) from scoring a touchdown, and held nine of eleven to under seven points. After thrashing North Carolina State 26–7 in the fourth week of the season, the Tide allowed just one touchdown over its last seven games. The team beat Houston 17–7 in week six, and did not give up another point the rest of the regular season, for a total of sixteen consecutive shutout quarters. After the Houston game, the Tide did not allow another touchdown through the end of the Sugar Bowl—a total of twenty consecutive touchdown-less quarters.

It was one of the greatest defensive performances college football had ever seen. "We feel," Bryant had written in his book, "if we do not permit the opposition to score, we will not lose the football game. While in reality, most teams actually score on us, we still try to sell our players on the idea that if the opposition does not score, we will not lose."[17] In 1961, Bryant was wrong—most teams did *not* score on Alabama. The Tide defense allowed just twenty-two points in eleven games. In the more than four decades since then, no college team has come close to matching that feat.

The Alabama offense wasn't so bad either. With Trammell passing, running, pitching the ball on the option, and leading brilliant, controlled drives, Alabama scored twenty-four or more points in seven games and won every regular season game by at least nine points. The team defeated old foes Georgia (32–6), Tennessee (34–3), Georgia Tech (10–0), and, in the last game of the regular season, Auburn (34–0), before recording a 10–3 victory over Arkansas in the Sugar Bowl, which secured Alabama as number one in the country by the Associated Press, United Press International, and MacArthur Bowl voters.

Though Bryant never said it in so many words, his 1961 national championship team was probably his favorite. Not only did it have as its core the 1958 freshman team, led by Trammell, but it featured several more of his favorite players, including Darwin Holt and Lee Roy Jordan. It also included some—Bill Battle, Mal Moore, Bill Oliver—who would become highly respected coaches. Nearly one hundred boys had gone out for freshman football in 1958. To the eleven who stuck it out for four years, Bryant made good on his promise of a national championship ring. In a 1970 ABC poll of coaches and sportswriters to determine the best college football team of the decade, the 1961 Alabama squad finished a close second to Woody Hayes's 1968 Ohio State Buckeyes.

IN JANUARY 1962 Bear Bryant treated a jubilant Alabama to a special edition of *The Bear Bryant Show* that reviewed the season's highlights. Many years later, Roone Arledge and ABC would give Bryant a shot at doing football commentary. It didn't work, and the 1961 highlights show illustrates why. Even back in 1961 Bryant had a problem recalling players' names.

After one play sequence from early in the season, Bear told viewers, "Watch little Billy Neighbors lower the boom and carry him into the end zone . . ."—little Billy Neighbors weighed in excess of 250 pounds—"I mean Billy Richardson, of course . . ."

"You'll see Little Billy [Richardson] make a fine play here. No, that's Butch Henry . . . I mean Butch Wilson . . ."

"I think I made a mistake on who made that last play. I think it was Bill Oliver. Sometimes I get their names wrong, but as long as I call out all the names, that's the important thing."

From the Auburn game: "I believe it was Price [for Auburn] on that tackle. I usually don't try to identify the other team's favorites because I get ours wrong half the time, so it really doesn't matter all that much."

Reviewing the Tennessee game: "That's Mal Moore. Is he from Dozier? I think he's from Dozier. . . . [On that play] our guys are lookin' around instead of knocking someone down. We don't recommend that."

BRYANT, WHO had probably been the best coach in college football during the 1950s, had never won the coveted Coach of the Year award. The award had been started by the *New York World-Telegram and Sun*'s sportswriter Joe Williams and was voted on by the American Football Coaches Association. In 1961, at the end of Bryant's seventeenth season, he finally won it—it was long overdue. Several of Bryant's friends, including Bud Wilkinson (in 1949), Jim Tatum at Maryland (1953), one of his former bosses, Red Sanders at UCLA (1954), and one of his former assistants, Paul Dietzel at LSU (1958), had already won it. In the spring, a special dinner was given in Bryant's honor back in Fordyce. Football writers from around the country attended, including the *New York Times* Joe Sheehan. One of Bryant's friends decided to organize a pilgrimage to the Bryant family home in Moro Bottom. After several curious writers insisted, a reluctant Bryant finally agreed to go.

When they got out to Moro Bottom and saw the clapboard house, there was some embarrassed silence. Sheehan spoke first, "Why, Bear," he said, "I've been hearing for years that you were born in a log cabin." "Naw, Joe," Bryant shot back. "That was Abraham Lincoln. I was born in a manger."

PART THREE

The Bear in a familiar stance, leaning against the goalpost.

(Paul W. Bryant Museum, University of Alabama)

Chapter 7

Bear
Accused

How much is a year of a man's life worth?

—*Bear Bryant*

"YOU WOULD NATURALLY THINK," Bryant said in reflection, "the happiest years of my life were those that followed. Our boys won national championships and three SEC championships, went undefeated twice, and played in seven bowl games. . . . But those years weren't the happiest of my life."[1]

In his seventeenth season, Bryant had finally won the national championship that had eluded him in 1950 and 1956. Yet, to some of his friends, his postchampionship mood was a bit subdued. Talking on the phone with Jones Ramsey back at College Station in January 1962, he hinted, "There are some problems I'm going to have to deal with down the road." One of those problems was the sudden end of his long friendship with Georgia Tech coach Bobby Dodd.

In 1961, Atlanta had not yet become what many in the South, and particularly those in envious blue-collar Birmingham, would soon call it: "New York's southern branch office." Professional teams—the Braves, the Falcons, the Hawks—were still years away. Georgia Tech football was the city's major sporting attraction, and it was covered by the largest and most influential press in the Southeast. Along with Auburn, Tennessee, and Louisiana State, Tech was one of the traditional southeastern powers that Alabama had to subdue to regain the top rung in the conference, and Bryant's friendly rivalry with Bobby Dodd added even more spice to the game. The 1961 game took friendliness out of the equation forever.

Late in October, a story in *Time* magazine proclaimed Bear Bryant "the most controversial coach in America." *Time* could scarcely have been more timely.[2]

Less than a month later, the Crimson Tide, in its next-to-the-last regular-season game against Georgia Tech, was leading the Yellow Jackets 10–0 in the fourth quarter. Billy Richardson went back to return a Yellow Jacket punt. One of his blockers, the fiery Darwin Holt, was supposed to take out the man on the end of the Georgia Tech line and create a corridor for Richardson as he headed upfield with the ball. The Tech punter made a weak kick, and Richardson, coming up to receive it, realized that he was moving right into the Yellow Jackets' coverage. While running forward, he waved his arm to signal fair catch. Holt, with his back to Richardson and perhaps ten to fifteen yards away, did not see his teammate's signal. Tech's Chick Graning, however, did see Richardson's arm go up and relaxed his guard.

Holt's forearm slammed into Graning's jaw and cheek. "I caught him with my flipper [forearm], which is a legal play if you keep your hand on your chest, which I did. I was aiming for his chest—he was about three or four inches taller than me—and that's exactly where I would have hit him if he hadn't started to duck and come down low." Graning's face exploded, and he collapsed as though shot with a dumdum bullet.

Today, helmets have face guards constructed to prevent such accidents, but in 1961 most players wore just a single bar above the chinstrap. (Graning says that better suspension headgear was available, but "there was no good way to fasten it to the helmet—the helmet wouldn't support the extra gear.") Graning says, "I never saw him coming, and I never ducked. The whistle had blown, and as far as I was concerned, the play was dead." Graning left the field on a stretcher.

A grainy black-and-white tape of the play, more than forty years old, does not reveal whether or not the referee blew the whistle. The tape does show clearly that Richardson called for a fair catch, that Holt's back was to Richardson and therefore he could not see him raise his arm, and that Graning does not seem to notice Holt rushing toward him. Further, Holt appears to collide with Graning at precisely the same moment Richardson catches the ball, which means that fair catch or no, the ball was still in play—if Richardson had fumbled the punt, it would have been a loose ball and Graning or another Tech player might have recovered it.

Graning, though, maintains that the possibility of a fumble was irrelevant. "He left his feet to hit me," says Graning. "He hit me high. Bear Bryant always coached his players to hit low, to knock opponents off their feet. There was very little above-the-waist blocking back then." Holt, for his part, maintains, "If I was trying to tackle him, I would have hit him lower, but I was trying to block him, and the angle I started out at would have been proper had he not pulled his head down"—Graning, again, says he did not pull his head down. No foul was called, but whether that's because the referee did not see the play or regarded the hit as legitimate was never made clear.*

Holt, a retired insurance salesman living in Birmingham, contends to this day that he never meant to hurt Graning. "It was unfortunate," he says, "but it was entirely legal. We were always taught by Coach Bryant never to let up until we heard the referee's whistle end the play. There was no whistle. There probably should have been a whistle when Billy's arm went up for a fair catch, but there wasn't." Graning, for his part, believes, "Darwin crossed the line. There's a difference between clean, hard football and cheap shots. It was a cheap shot." Graning is also very clear on another very important point: "I never said that the play had anything to do with the way Coach Bryant coached football. The play was Darwin's fault, not Coach Bryant's."

But the Atlanta newspapers quickly jumped on Holt *and* Bryant. "Holt forfeited the right to play college football when he intentionally smashed his left forearm into Chick Graning's face," wrote one columnist for the

---

* At least on the Alabama game tape. Darwin Holt says he has seen the Tech film: "You can see an official looking at Billy. You can see him looking in the direction of my play, too. He sees Chick go down, but does not call a penalty on me." Georgia Tech did not respond to my request for a copy of its game tape.

Atlanta Journal.[3] Graning's father poured fuel on the fire when he told a reporter from the *Atlanta Constitution,* "I believe Bryant is encouraging such tactics."[4]

For his part, Bryant steadfastly insisted that he did *not* encourage such tactics. Gang-tackling, yes, as hard hitting as possible, but no cheap shots, and never anything that would draw a penalty flag. For what it is worth, his players backed him up: "The idea that Coach Bryant encouraged a cheap hit on Chick Graning is ridiculous," says Lee Roy Jordan, who played against Georgia Tech in that game. "The injury was due to an unfortunate combination of circumstances, but it was part of the game. I can tell you from personal experience that nothing would get you tossed out of the lineup quicker than taking a cheap shot in a game that he was coaching."

Bryant appeared nonplussed by the incident, and even thirteen years later, in his autobiography, was unsure of what stance to take. "There was no doubt," he told *Sports Illustrated,* "he [Darwin] fouled Chick Graning and the officials should have penalized us, which they didn't, and I probably would have disciplined him my own way if those Atlanta sportswriters hadn't set out to crucify him."[5]

But did Bryant really believe that Holt had fouled Graning? If he did, he should have disciplined him immediately; in fact, given his oft-stated distaste for foolish penalties, he most certainly would have disciplined him, penalty or no. Given the damage to Graning's face, it's doubtful that Bryant would have protested vehemently had Holt been penalized by the official; occasional injuries are a part of the game, and so are occasional penalties. Bryant must have felt that Holt had not hit Graning in the face intentionally—which is not to say that he did not feel Holt hadn't hit him correctly, too high rather than too low. But this is just speculation; outside of his remark, "There's no doubt that Darwin did not mean to hurt Chick Graning," he never commented on whether or not the hit was made correctly.

What is puzzling in retrospect is why, if Graning was so severely injured, he was not taken to a Birmingham hospital immediately. Instead, the Tech staff waited until the next day when the team was back in Atlanta. The Sunday papers in both Atlanta and Birmingham gave little mention to the collision; it wasn't until Monday that the seriousness of Graning's injuries was revealed. Tech's team physician, Dr. Henry, told reporters that it was the worst facial injury he had ever seen in football.

The *Atlanta Constitution* reported the diagnosis: "(1) Fracture of alveolar process (cheek and other facial bones); (2) five missing upper front teeth and the majority of remaining front teeth broken; (3) fracture of nasal bone; (4) fracture of right maxillary sinus and sinus filled with blood; (5) fracture of right zygomatic process (the bone just underneath the right eye); (6) cerebral concussion; (7) possible fracture of base of skull."[6] Wire services picked up the story, and it appeared in newspapers all across the country, given even more attention because the victory had boosted Alabama into the number-one spot in the wire-service polls.

Bryant probably erred in not going to see Graning right after the game to, at the least, express his and his team's wishes for a swift recovery. Like many southerners, Bryant reveled in opportunities to display his gallantry. Such a lapse in this circumstance might be explained by his not understanding how badly Graning had been hurt, which in itself might be explained by the Tech staff's initial failure to grasp the extent of the injuries. Tech assistant coach and later Southeastern Conference commissioner Tonto Coleman stopped by the Alabama dressing room to shake hands after the game and made no mention of Graning at all.

On Sunday night, Bryant went to New Orleans with President Frank Rose to talk with the Sugar Bowl committee, apparently still without knowing how badly Graning was hurt and how much the press was making of it. After all, this was decades before twenty-four-hour talk radio and sports television, which make incidents like the Holt-Graning hit instant controversies.

By the time Bryant got back to Tuscaloosa on Tuesday, it was impossible to ignore headlines that were appearing in sports pages throughout the country—not to mention two heated letters from Dodd, one to Bryant and the other to Frank Rose. Even at this point, though, Bryant refused to act contrite. Perhaps that was his intention when he called Dodd on Tuesday afternoon. Both coaches became agitated, and Bryant hung up. Then, Bryant did something he would later regret. He had an assistant take the game film and play it for the Alabama writers, pointing out all of Tech's violations. Dodd was furious. On reflection, Bryant didn't blame him. "It was a small thing," he would say in *Bear*, "and showed no class. If I had it to do over, I wouldn't, but our people thought the Atlanta writers were trying to destroy me."

Bryant was perfectly justified in pointing out that it had been an extremely rough and bitterly played game, and that the Tech players had been doing their best to hit as hard as the Alabama players. *How hard* the players were hitting, though, was not the point; the point, or rather the points, were whether or not Holt's hit was justified and whether or not Bryant should have made some gesture of regret, if not an apology, to Chick Graning.

As for the Atlanta writers trying to destroy him, future events would indicate that Bryant was not entirely paranoid. From his perspective, part of the problem was that there was no national sports media to appeal to at the time—no ESPN to rerun the play from several different angles and no *USA Today* to print his side of the story. Bryant felt it was a question of the Atlanta papers' interpretation of the Holt-Graning play versus the one taken by the Alabama papers, and in 1961 that was no contest.

Dodd, Bryant felt, "might have made an effort to stop it if he had known how it was going to be blown out of proportion." Bobby Dodd, of course, knew what the Atlanta papers were writing: he was the source of much of it. At any rate, within a couple of days, there was no more question of stopping it. The bad publicity, generated by the Atlanta sportswriters and picked up by the northeastern press, began to take on a life of its own, and the volume of the debates got louder as Alabama drew nearer to the national championship.

Georgia Tech, with higher academic standards than most of its SEC rivals, was finding it harder and harder to compete in what was probably the nation's toughest football conference. In Georgia, Florida, and Auburn, Tech could count on three bitterly intense football rivalries each season, and with the coming of Bear Bryant, Dodd found that he now had four that he could not reasonably hope to defeat. The Georgia Tech game was always big to Alabama—the Alabama fight song has a line bidding the Crimson Tide to "send the Yellow Jackets to a watery grave"—but the game wasn't quite as traditional to Georgia Tech as those with its nearer geographical foes. Dodd did appear to be looking for an excuse to pull out of the conference and may well have used the 1961 Alabama game to that end.

Two years later, Tech left the SEC and became independent. After losing to Alabama, 24–7, in 1964, the Yellow Jackets did not play the Tide again until 1979, when the Tide routed the them 30–6 on opening day in the first step to another national championship. Bear Bryant and Bobby Dodd had patched up their friendship by then, but Tech has never rejoined the SEC. In 1965, Notre Dame's Ara Parseghian was the head coach for the Eastern All-Stars in the Coaches All-America game, held that year in Buffalo. Before the game, Bryant, who was an assistant coach for the East, approached Bill Curry, one of Dodd's favorite players, and said he wanted to talk. "He asked me how Coach Dodd was doing and if I was in touch with him," says Curry, who was preparing for a pro career with Vince Lombardi's Packers and, later, with Don Shula's Baltimore Colts. "I told him he was doing fine and that we kept in regular touch. Coach Bryant said to me, 'Bill, when you talk to him, you say hello for me.' Then he asked me if I wanted to go to an Alabama alumni meeting with him in upstate New York. I jumped at the chance. I had always wanted to get to know him, and I finally had the opportunity."

Ten years later, Curry, working as a National Football League scout, attended an Alabama practice. As he was walking near Bryant's famous tower, he heard a voice: "Bill, come on up here and see something." Curry climbed up. "You didn't pass up a chance to go up in the tower with Bear Bryant. When I got up there, he said, 'Bill, you ever see Coach Dodd?' I told him I did, all the time. 'Well, me and Bobby are too old to be feudin'. You tell the Coach that I'd be happy to sponsor Georgia Tech for the Southeastern Conference.' I went home and called Coach Dodd and told him. I think it was too late for Georgia Tech ever to get back in the SEC, but I'd like to think I had something to do with getting Alabama and Georgia Tech back on the schedule four years later." When Bill Curry became Alabama's head football coach in 1987, he felt that "there were still a lot of Alabama fans who couldn't accept me because I had played and coached for Georgia Tech."

Darwin Holt left his native Texas and settled in a Birmingham suburb. "Not a week goes by," he says, "when somebody, somewhere, no matter where I am, doesn't hear my name and say, 'Are you *that* Darwin Holt?'"

Years after the fateful play, Holt's daughter was trick-or-treating. "Is your daddy Darwin Holt?" she was asked by a neighbor. She replied that he was. "Your daddy is the meanest man in the world," the man said to the little girl. Holt never asked if the neighbor was an Auburn fan.

Chick Graning moved back to the state of Mississippi and currently lives in Natchez. He says he bears no ill will for Darwin Holt. "We got together some time after the game and we got along well. I feel he is a good man.

But to this day, he has never actually apologized to me. If he had just said, 'I made a mistake,' I think the whole thing would have gone away."

EVEN THOUGH a far more serious cloud than the Holt-Graning incident was looming over Alabama football, most white Alabamians were clearly unaware. Throughout the 1961 season, Bryant had relished the thought of taking his magnificent team to the Rose Bowl, scene of so many legendary Alabama triumphs and of his own glory as a player on New Year's Day in 1935. When time came for the Rose Bowl committee to choose, though, they opted for Murray Warmath's Minnesota Golden Gophers—fitting revenge, Minnesota fans felt, long having believed they were shafted at the end of the 1934 season when Alabama was invited instead of Minnesota and its fine quarterback, Bud Wilkinson. Bryant and much of Alabama, however, took the snub as an indication that the Rose Bowl was no longer going to tolerate segregated football teams.

Bryant was not alone in this opinion; Jim Murray and several other West Coast writers had similar sentiments. In fact, Bryant felt that Murray had almost single-handedly cost Alabama the Rose Bowl invitation. In several columns written during the 1961 season, Murray openly questioned whether a team from a segregated school should be invited to play in the Rose Bowl. Bryant regarded segregation and the Ku Klux Klan—two of Murray's favorite points when discussing Alabama football—to be "unrelated" to sports. Such things were "unrelated" only if one considers the football team a university fields as being unrelated to the outside world; Bryant was fully aware that the Alabama headquarters for the Ku Klux Klan was, in fact, in Tuscaloosa, just minutes from Denny Stadium.

Privately, Bryant expressed to some of his friends a hope that the snub would get home folks to think about changes that would have to be made. But, not wishing to put a damper on his team's spirits as they prepared for the Sugar Bowl, he said nothing. "We were in a cocoon when it came to race and politics," says Alabama lineman Steve Wright. "It was like we weren't going to have contact with events in the world outside of football." But events outside the world of football would soon be having contact with them.

Wright had come to Alabama from Manual High School in Louisville, Kentucky, where he spent four years hearing three of his coaches, one of whom was Dude Hennessey and all of whom had played for Bryant at the University of Kentucky, call him the best football coach in the world. "'You can get an education anywhere,'" they told me, "'but if you want to play football, there's only one place to go, and that's where Bear Bryant is— at Alabama.' So, when they gave me a scholarship, I went."

For reasons no one, not even Wright in his 1974 memoir *I'd Rather Be Wright*, was ever able to pin down, Bryant and Wright could never connect. The root of the problem may have been that the talented Wright did not practice football with the desperation Bryant demanded, though Wright insists he practiced very hard. "I came from an upper middle class family," he wrote, "where you are taught to do the right thing, respect others, work for your living, get paid for what you do, get a house, raise a family, and do the best you can." But, "I just wanted to play football. I was going to put everything into it. But I expected to be treated like a human being because that's how I was taught to treat people. I found out that it didn't work that way [at Alabama]."[7]

Wright's biggest problem was with Bryant's assistant coaches, particularly Pat James, "who would grab you by the face mask and jerk your helmet up and down. I got fed up with that real quick. When any of the coaches would do that, particularly James, I'd knock their hands away, and they'd just glare at me."[8]

Darwin Holt remembers Steve Wright "as an okay guy. He just couldn't take Coach Bryant's brand of discipline. Coach Bryant thought he was challenging Wright; Steve just didn't see it that way. It was like they talked in different languages."

In three years at Alabama, Wright never started a single game, but, almost incredibly considering his bitter feuds with the coaching staff, he was drafted by Vince Lombardi and played on three of the Packers championship teams in four years as well as five seasons with other NFL teams. "To this day I have no idea how I got into the NFL," says Wright. "Later I found out that I had lettered my last two years at Alabama. I didn't know that, no one ever told me."

One wonders why the Packers would have bothered with him if he had gotten a bad recommendation from the Alabama coaches. In other words, why would Vince Lombardi have taken a chance on a player whom Bear Bryant gave a thumbs down to? "I don't know what Coach Bryant said to the Packers about Steve Wright," says Dude Hennessey, "but I imagine it was something along the lines of 'The boy's got a lot of ability, and we just couldn't get to him, but maybe you'll have better luck.'"

Wright did not like Bryant and never got to know him well, but he tells at least one story about him that is illuminating. Wright's best pal on the Alabama team was a running back named Joe Sisia. "He was a real cocky kid, an Italian kid from New Jersey, the kind of guy that didn't think he had to go to Alabama and apologize for which side won the Civil War. The coaches were always on his butt. One time Charlie Bradshaw, I think it was, smacked him in the head, and Joe didn't think that he had to take that. He started chasing Bradshaw down the field. We all looked up at the tower, and saw that Bryant was coming down. Everybody froze, even Joe, who stood there with his hands on his hips, breathing hard while Bryant shuffled over to him. He was in no mood to take any more crap from any coach, even Bryant, and to his credit, I think, Bryant could see that. We were all waiting to see what Bryant would say. He put his arm on Joe's shoulder and said, 'Now, Jo Jo, you really got spirit. You got real enthusiasm, and that's something I like to see in a player, but we can't have players treating coaches like that.' He gave him some extra laps to run, things like that, as punishment." On this occasion Bryant's calm and restraint were primarily the best solutions to a potentially explosive situation.

Sisia, though, didn't last at Alabama. He was caught copying a term paper and had his scholarship taken away. "That was bullshit," says Wright. "There must have been a dozen other guys who did the same thing, but they chose to punish Joe. Then they did something really strange. One of the coaches told him that they expected him to come out and try for the team again. That's the way they were, they wanted you to beg for a second chance."

It may have been strange psychology, but Bryant's handling of Sisia was consistent with his handling of other players: He was willing to make adjustments for individuals within the system, but the player had to learn to live and to play within that system. He would challenge a boy to the point of pushing him over the edge, but the reaction he wanted was not anger or resentment but a strong determination to show the coach that he could do better. (Whether or not the boy liked him was of no particular importance; Bryant preferred to be liked because it made his job easier, but his intent was to motivate.) Bryant's methods may have seemed inexplicable to those raised in a different environment, but if he picked on a particular player, it was invariably because he saw something in that player he thought would benefit from a challenge. He was incapable of understanding those who didn't respond as he himself had responded to such challenges.

One of the things that Wright most resented about Bryant was what he regarded as preferential treatment for the kid who was Alabama's quarterback from 1962 through 1964. "Namath," says Wright, "was Bryant's boy. Joe did what he wanted to do, and he got away with it because he was a great football player. He was maybe the greatest football player I've ever seen." Namath was also the greatest football player that Bear Bryant had ever seen—though that needs to be qualified. "I don't classify quarterbacks as players," he said. "I think of them as coaches on the field."

Bryant *did* let Namath get away with things he would not have let an ordinary player get away with—unless the ordinary player displayed the desire and dedication of a Joe Namath. Not even Namath, though, was allowed to get away with anything on the football field. In 1962, against a mediocre Vanderbilt team, Namath, after a poor series of downs, was yanked out of the game by Bryant. Walking to the sidelines, he flung his helmet to the ground and then watched in horror as it bounced, rolled, and landed at Bryant's feet. "He looked at it calmly," Namath told Mickey Herskowitz, "without any expression, and then he came over and sat down next to me on the bench and draped an arm around my shoulder. There were fifty thousand fans in the stands, and it must have looked as though he was giving me some fatherly advice, or cheering me up. But what he was doing was squeezing the back of my neck with one of those big hands of his. He was saying, 'Boy, don't ever let me see you coming out of a ballgame like that. Don't ever do it again, or you're gone.'"[9]

Bryant was a stickler for seeing that his players attended class and kept up their grades, yet with Namath he looked the other way. "A lot of kids have high IQs," he said in his autobiography, "and aren't good athletes. That's obvious. Others who aren't so smart in a classroom find something like football easy to pick up. Billy Neighbors was like me. It would take us five years to pass an English course, but football was easy. Namath could have made As in school, but he didn't study. Nothing came easier for him than football. He could sit down and listen to some football concept for the first time, and, snap, snap, he'd have a mental picture of every phase of it."

Those who point to Bryant's indulgence with Namath as an indication of his attitude toward academics and football are missing the point. Bryant understood the moment he met Namath that Joe was destined to be a football player and that no amount of prodding or guidance was going to turn him into a scholar. Rightly or wrongly, Bryant was content with making Joe Namath into the best football player he could be.

Namath had the toughness of mind and body that Bryant admired in Pat Trammell. The difference between the two quarterbacks was that Namath was a far superior athlete with a fantastic throwing arm. Though no one knew it at the time, Namath would prove to be the prototype of the modern NFL passer: big and mobile with quick feet and a fast release that made him almost impossible to blitz. With Namath at quarterback, the Alabama offense took on a whole new dimension. No longer was it necessary for the Tide to move the ball downfield on controlled precision drives. Defenses always had to be aware that with Namath in the game, Alabama could score from anywhere on the field. In the 1962 season opener, he dazzled the Georgia Bulldogs by throwing for 179 yards, most of them in the first half, allowing Bryant the luxury of keeping the ball on the ground and running the clock out in the second half.

"If we'd needed him to," says Gryska, "he'd have thrown for twice that many yards. Easily. I remember the first pass he threw like it was yesterday. It was a national TV game on ABC, and that was Joe's element. He faked to the fullback on the first play from scrimmage and threw a bomb to Richard Williamson. Williamson ran right past the Georgia defensive backfield, caught the ball in stride, and went into the end zone untouched. I think it was fifty yards." (It was fifty-two.) Bryant had not had a passer like that since Babe Parilli at Kentucky. "Pat Trammell could throw," recalls Billy Richardson, "but he couldn't throw like that. I'd never seen anybody who could throw a football like that."

Behind Namath's three touchdown passes (to go with one touchdown running), Alabama coasted to an easy 35–0 win. At the time, no one knew that that game was destined to become the most controversial in Alabama and possibly in college football history, one that surpassed even the 1961 Alabama–Georgia Tech game.

THE YOUNGEST of five children, Joe Namath was born of Hungarian parents in the rough steel-mill town of Beaver Falls, Pennsylvania, where, as

Bryant noted in *Bear*, "Many of his friends were black." His father left home when Joe was young, and his mother did the best job she could raising the family. She couldn't keep Joe away from pool halls and gamblers, but then his father probably couldn't have either.

His father did make one important contribution to Joe's life: when he was eleven, he took him to the steel mill where he worked. He didn't say much to his son; he didn't have to. The mill did the talking. "It was terrifying," Namath is quoted as saying by Mark Kriegel in his 2004 biography. "The noise, the heat, the molten metal. I vowed I would never work in such a place, and to this day I'm convinced that's why he took me there."[10]

Namath was a natural at football, baseball, and basketball, and played both sand-lot and organized games with integrated teams. He very nearly chose professional baseball as a career, but his mother wanted him to go to college, which meant football. He received good instruction in high school—his football coach, Larry Bruno, had learned the art of ball handling, including the fake and throw, from Bryant's ace at Kentucky, Babe Parilli. By his senior year, Namath was one of the most sought-after quarterbacks in the country.

Penn State seemed like a logical choice, but Joe Paterno, the Nittany Lions backfield coach, didn't think he was a good enough student. Joe's mother, a devout Catholic, pushed for Notre Dame, but the school showed little interest in him and Joe wasn't thrilled at the prospect of attending a school without girls. He intended to enroll at the University of Maryland, but his SAT score, which was in the low 730's, fell short of the required 750.[11]

One of Joe's coaches called a friend at Maryland who knew Charlie Bradshaw at Alabama. Alabama bit; Bryant was hooked after Clem Gryska and Dude Hennessey returned from a trip to Beaver Falls, where they had watched several reels of Namath's high school games, narrated by Coach Bruno.

"Alabama?" Namath responded when he heard the news. "That's Bear Bryant, isn't it?"[12]

Namath wasn't sure he wanted to play for such a coach. He had heard of Bryant's reputation as a taskmaster. Bear Bryant *was* sure he wanted Namath so he sent his best recruiter, Howard Schnellenberger, to Beaver Falls. Schnellenberger had become for Bryant what Bryant had been for Frank Thomas.

Schnellenberger had an edge over the others who were after Joe; he had known Frank Namath, Joe's older brother, at Kentucky. (Frank was a freshman in Schnellenberger's senior year and was coached by Schnellenberger when he returned to Kentucky as an assistant coach.) "Frank hadn't played for Coach Bryant," says Schnellenberger, "but he got to Kentucky just in time to know his reputation, so that was a big plus. I'm not sure we could have landed Joe without Frank's help. I think Frank was convinced that his little brother needed a good ass-kicking, a straightening out, and that Bear Bryant was just the man to do it."

Having watched the master work up close, Schnellenberger knew an important rule in recruiting: court the mother. Rose Namath was convinced that her boy would be well taken care of at the University of Alabama. "She made us chicken and dumplings for dinner," recalled Schnellenberger. "I thought to myself: we've got him."

The Schnellenberger-Namath recruitment was to become part of Alabama lore, a modern version of the wild rides Bryant had made as an assistant coach. Not wanting to take a chance that Maryland might have second thoughts or that some other school might make a pitch, Schnellenberger wanted to whisk Joe out of Pennsylvania and down to visit the campus at Tuscaloosa as soon as possible. Short on cash, Schnellenberger didn't want to wait for money to be wired from Bryant's office. "I'd rather have faced a judge for writing a bad check," he says, "than to go back and face Coach Bryant without Joe Namath." He wrote a check, despite insufficient funds, for their plane tickets to Birmingham, but they missed their connection in Atlanta, and Schnellenberger was forced to write another bad check for a hotel room. Up before dawn, Schnellenberger had just enough change left in his pocket to buy Namath a cup of coffee. "I was hoping like hell he didn't want ham and eggs," he recalls. When they walked into Bryant's office, Schnellenberger's fellow assistants had a good laugh. "It looked like he'd been wearing the same shirt for a week," says Hennessey. "He looked like a hobo."

Namath looked like a grungy hipster, wearing a straw hat with a blue hatband and a toothpick jammed in his teeth. He sullenly shook hands with Bear Bryant. "He wasn't the kind of boy we were used to recruiting, I can tell you that," says Gryska, "but Coach Bryant made a little smile when he first saw him, like he understood him. He understood him better than the rest of us could." A poor kid from the wrong side of town who was raised by his mother, hung out in pool halls, palled around with black kids, acted cocky to hide his insecurity, and saw football as a way out—oh, yes, Paul Bryant understood Joe Namath very well.

Several of Bryant's staff were appalled by Namath's appearance and joked about the can of whup-ass the Coach was going to open on this smart-aleck Yankee kid. They didn't understand, but Dude Hennessey did. "If I was you," he told them, "I wouldn't say anything bad about this boy. He'd trade five of you for him." Before long, the Coach's staff and everyone else would get Bryant's message in no uncertain terms; Joe Namath became the first player ever to be invited up into Bryant's tower. They would become the most celebrated player-coach pairing since Knute Rockne and George Gipp. Bryant would mold Namath into the greatest player in football; Namath would help make Bear Bryant the most famous football coach in the country.

The cultural adjustment was not easy. At first, Namath, as Bryant put it, "didn't speak the language. For a long time, he was a loner." Within four years, he had cultivated a drawl and earned a nickname. Joseph William Namath left the University of Alabama as Joe Willie, with, in Bryant's words, "more of a southern accent than me."

FOR THE first eight games of the 1962 season, sportswriters were asking not if Alabama was the best team in the country but whether or not it was better than Alabama's 1961 national champions. The Tide defense allowed an average of just four points a game, while the offense scored just under twenty-nine points per game. Tennessee, no longer the daunting presence it had been for Alabama in General Neyland's years, went down meekly at Knoxville, 27–7. A shot at a second national championship in a bowl game seemed to be a foregone conclusion.

A couple of weeks before the annual meeting with Georgia Tech, Bryant and the Tide were blindsided. The October 20 issue of the *Saturday Evening Post* led off its contents page with a story bluntly titled, "College Football Is Going Berserk." "A game ruled by force," read the subtitle, "needs a house-cleaning." The article was by the *Atlanta Journal's* sports editor, Furman Bisher, the man who had first skewered Bryant in *Sport* magazine in 1958.*

---

* Bisher, who still writes for the *Atlanta Journal-Constitution*, declined to be interviewed for this book.

"College football," he wrote, "appears to have gone absolutely silly on 'hitting,' even at the expense of clever execution. A new term, 'hardnosed,' is about as common in the conversation of football savants as punting, passing, and praying. . . . But far too often, it seems to me this aspect of the game has been glorified to the extent that players are being blocked and tackled not simply out of the immediate play but right out of the game—often on a stretcher." Bisher then went on to describe the Holt-Graning hit, "such a devastating blow to the face that for days afterward Graning looked like Joe Louis the morning after his knockout by Rocky Marciano." Bisher claimed to have been at an Alabama practice four days before the game and seen Holt, wearing a sweatshirt, "prancing about on the practice field among a squad otherwise dressed out in full gear. Paul Bryant, the head coach, explained, 'He's so tough we don't let him scrimmage during the week. He's liable to hurt somebody.'" (Bryant would later say, "That was either a misquote or he took a kidding remark and twisted it to his own purpose. Either way, it came out wrong." Holt says, "Coach Bryant was always kidding about me like that to reporters.")

Bisher also claimed that Bryant told him that Holt came to him and said he was "all broken up" about the hit and that he "didn't know why" he had done it. But Bryant never admitted to saying this to Bisher or anyone. Holt says Bisher's Bryant-attributed quote is "fiction." Most of the rest of Bisher's story was a capsule history of violence in college football, beginning with Teddy Roosevelt's alarm over the eighteen fatalities among college players in 1905, and leading up to . . . Bear Bryant. Even Auburn coach Ralph "Shug" Jordan, according to Bisher, was getting into the act with "this new hell-for-leather, helmet-bursting, gang-tackling game." "Since Bear Bryant had come back to Alabama," Jordan told Bisher, "it's the only game which can win." Jordan apparently was not asked why SEC football, which had been famous for hellacious hitting football back around the turn of the century, needed Bryant's presence to revive the tradition. Tech's Bobby Dodd joined the chorus: "At Georgia Tech we're hitting harder in practice now than we were in games eight or ten years ago. . . . You play tough football or you get eaten alive nowadays." Apparently Dodd's Tech teams were not hitting as hard as they could when they were slaughtering Alabama's teams before Bear Bryant returned.

Coaches, said Jordan, were now sending out recruiters to bring in a far bigger, fiercer athlete, "the kind equipped to handle himself in hand-to-hand combat."

"Bud Wilkinson," Bisher wrote,

> built his reputation at Oklahoma on speedy, hit-and-run, brush-blocking teams that were a delight to watch. A few years ago, he took one of these teams to play Notre Dame while Frank Leahy still coached there.
>
> Oklahoma lost the game by a close score but took a physical beating from Leahy's bigger, tougher, harder hitting team that Wilkinson went home vowing never to subject players of his to another such mat-grinding without proper physical preparation. He began bringing in the bigger, more rugged player and emphasizing the kind of conditioning required to win beachheads; and as the idea spread from Oklahoma, toughness sometimes got out of hand.

The main culprits, Bisher wrote, were Bryant, Forest Evashevski (who coached at Iowa from 1941 to 1960), Woody Hayes, and the late Jim Tatum. All, he said, coached football that "demanded Marine Corps conditioning."[13]

Bisher's argument was flawed. It was true that during the 1950s, as substitution rules became more liberalized, more and more specialized players began to appear—players who could afford to be bigger and heavier because they didn't have to spend as much time on the field. Linemen, in particular, on both offense and defense, became dramatically larger than the backs they blocked for and tackled. Offensive ends evolved into pass receivers, split wide from the interior line. (In today's game, they are seldom referred to as ends at all, but simply wideouts.)

But Alabama's players were most certainly not part of this evolution; if anything, Bryant's teams were a throwback to the kind of football Bryant had played in the 1930s, precisely the kind of "speedy, hit-and-run, brush-blocking teams" that Bisher thought were such a delight to watch. In 1962, when Alabama opened the season against Georgia in defense of its national championship, the Bulldogs outweighed the Tiders by an average of about twenty pounds a man. Darwin Holt, the "linebacking specialist" whom Bisher had observed in sweats at the Alabama practice, weighed perhaps 172 pounds, surely making him the smallest linebacker on any major college team in the country. For that matter, though it was irrelevant to the appropriateness of Holt's hit on Chick Graning, the average Alabama player was outweighed by his Tech opponent by perhaps twenty pounds. In other words, by any standards, Bryant's Alabama teams were the "light, fast, and tricky" teams that Bisher was praising. As for the "Marine Corps conditioning" Bisher derided, Bryant would have been the first to admit that was precisely what he was striving for. How else, Bryant surely would have replied, could small scrappy teams like his beat the big fellows except by being in better shape?

As Bryant has moved about the country, Bisher charged, he had left a trail of "discarded athletes" at Maryland, Kentucky, Texas A&M, and Alabama. "'Riff raff,' he [Bryant] calls them."[14]

Bisher's use of "riff raff" incensed Bryant. He had used the word, he admitted, but there were extenuating circumstances. "We'd lost our first game that year," Bryant said in explanation, "and I had gone on television and said there would probably be some rumbling, but this was my team now and the best thing about getting beat was that you always get rid of the 'riff raff.'" Bryant said he wasn't talking about his players: "I was talking about people, and I'll say it again if we lose a couple of games this fall. We'll get rid of the riff raff, the hangers-on, the few people who take up your time getting in your way and who would turn on you in a minute. We have them, Notre Dame had them, everybody does."*

Those who made it through this type of toughening process were better prepared to survive the season, but that meant they were also trained to deal out punishment in an increasingly violent game in which more boys would be injured—"some of them fatally."[15]

This was a strange argument. What football program did not leave behind a "trail of discarded athletes"? And what decent football coach would want any player who didn't meet his 120 percent demand for conditioning? And precisely how did conditioning lead to "excessively rough football"? How, exactly, did top conditioning result in football fatalities?

---

* Kentucky and A&M had them too. In 1953, when Kentucky was losing to Rice, at halftime Bryant charged into the dressing room to address his players and, according to Frank Sadler, demanded, "Get the riff raff out of here!" After the disastrous start at A&M, said Jones Ramsey, "Paul got tired of the people who had called it 'our team' before the season and 'your team' to the Coach when we were losing. He said to me, 'Well, there's one good thing to be said about losing—it sorts out the riff raff.'"

Surely most football coaches would have insisted that top conditioning *prevented* fatalities.

In the last couple of paragraphs, Bisher got to his point, that the players who were in top physical condition must "acquit themselves on the field as sportsmen rather than bully boys" or be subject to "public indictment."

"In the revolution that developed after the season of 1905, Dr. Charles W. Eliot, president of Harvard, made this observation: 'Death and injuries are not the strongest argument against football. That cheating and brutality are profitable is the main evil.' That statement is still applicable fifty-seven years later.[16]

Conditioning, then, was not really the issue at all. The issue was coaches who taught cheating and brutality, and university presidents who condoned such coaches because they won football games. Bisher's example was Paul Bear Bryant and, by implication, University of Alabama President Frank Rose.

Bryant was furious when he saw the *Saturday Evening Post* with Bisher's story. The piece, he believed, was reckless and poorly argued. It almost seems surprising in retrospect that the *Post* allowed the story to run as it was written. Perhaps an editor did not anticipate that the story would invite a lawsuit, but that's exactly what happened on January 4, 1963, when Bryant filed a libel suit against Curtis Publishing, the parent company of the *Saturday Evening Post*, for $500,000. One wonders what Bisher's and the *Post*'s defense would have done if Chick Graning had been called to the stand and made the same statement that he had made forty years later—that the hit put on him by Darwin Holt was *not* the result of the coaching methods of Bear Bryant. Graning never got the chance to testify. The *Saturday Evening Post*, Bear Bryant, and the world of college football would soon be caught up in a trial that put the Darwin Holt–Chick Graning incident on the bench.

Bryant would insist for the rest of his life that if he hadn't sued the *Post* for the first story, there would never have been a second story. He was correct.

No one wanted to say that Alabama was distracted by Bisher's story, but the attendant publicity certainly served to fire up Georgia Tech. Namath was intercepted three times in the 7–6 loss, his worst performance at Alabama. Bryant blamed his own play calling, but it was Namath who had called most of the plays. Tech fans were fired up too: Bryant was hit by at least two whiskey bottles and had to dodge several others. He walked off the field wearing a football helmet for protection. He went straight to the Georgia Tech locker room and shook hands with the team captains, congratulating them. He then shook hands with Bobby Dodd, mumbled a compliment, and left. In the next game, the Tide took out its frustration with a hideous 38–0 beating of Auburn in Birmingham.

Alabama's 9–1 record and fifth-place national ranking got the team an invitation to the Orange Bowl, where Bryant would face his old friend Bud Wilkinson and the Big Eight champion, the Oklahoma Sooners. A defensive struggle was anticipated, with the Tide a three-point betting pick. But Alabama came out throwing, and with Namath calling a near-perfect game, led 14–0 at the half. In the third quarter, Namath brought Alabama downfield for a nineteen-yard field goal. Just as in the legendary 1951 Sugar Bowl game against Kentucky, the Sooners twice drove down to their opponent's ten-yard line but couldn't crack Bryant's defense. The 17–0 win was Bryant's second in as many tries over Wilkinson. In the Alabama locker room, a photographer asked Bryant how to spell his quarterback's name. "That's Namath, boy," he responded. "N-A-M-A-T-H. Don't worry about it. I guarantee you in a couple of years you'll learn how to spell it."[17]

President John F. Kennedy flew to Miami for the game and stopped by the Oklahoma dressing room to wish Wilkinson and his boys good luck. Bryant did not say so in his autobiography, but those who were there recall that the Coach was miffed. Lee Roy Jordan, who would have a memorable afternoon that would impress his future pro team, the Dallas Cowboys, said later, "When President Kennedy went to their dressing room and didn't bother to come visit us, it gave us a little added incentive." It was a little spur-of-the-moment psychological edge just before kickoff. Kennedy's snub of Alabama may not have been intentional. The former Harvard football player knew the value of having perhaps the nation's best-known football coach—and a Republican one at that—on his side and had courted Wilkinson to lead the President's Physical Fitness Program.

And then again, perhaps the snub was intentional. Oklahoma was an integrated team, and there were already grumblings from the East and West Coast presses that Alabama should not be gunning for a national championship with a segregated team. Kennedy was already locked in a battle with George Wallace over civil rights in Alabama, which was about to explode as a national issue. In fact, the 1963 Orange Bowl game marked the first recorded moment of racial tension in an Alabama football game, though nothing was to come of it except a story that reflected the bigoted, racial humor of the era. According to Lee Roy Jordan, Alabama's Charlie Pell and Digger O'Dell had agreed on a defensive signal. Pell would shout, "Look out, Digger!" when a play was coming in O'Dell's direction. At the half, Jordan informed Bryant, "Coach, Pell's going to get us thrown out of the game." "Thrown out . . . what the hell?" replied a stunned Bryant. The official thought Pell had been hollering, "Look out, Nigger!" at the Oklahoma lineman on the opposite side of the line from O'Dell.*

During the game, Kennedy was observed to have a little more "vigah" than some Alabama fans thought the occasion called for. Perhaps as a show of impartiality, Kennedy invited nineteen-year-old Alabama cheerleader Martha Campbell to his red-carpeted box on the fifty-yard line. "Your team," the president told her, "is doing mighty well, isn't it?" Miss Campbell was so excited at meeting the president, she began to cry.

Bryant kept his chagrin over Kennedy's deference to Oklahoma to himself. Luckily so, since in about two months he would need a Kennedy for a friend.

The 1963 Orange Bowl victory over Oklahoma was important to Bryant for many reasons, but none more so than the respect in which he held Bud Wilkinson. It was to be their second meeting on the field, and as it turned out, their final meeting. Bryant wanted to make an impression so much so that he became obsessed with finding out how Wilkinson planned to dress for the game; aware that the president was going to attend, Bryant was concerned that the head coach of the University of Alabama not come off as a country bumpkin. Bryant talked to sportswriter Bill Connors and asked him to do some spying: "I don't want to look bad in front of the President. Do you think you could find out what Bud's going to wear?"† Connors asked, but Wilkinson just smiled and shrugged. Bryant told Connors, "I'll just send Mama [Mary Harmon] down to one of those Palm Beach stores and let her try to guess what kind of Florida clothes Bud would wear." On game day, Wilkinson showed up in a white short-sleeved

---

* The incident was related by Al Browning in the 1987 edition of his book, *Bowl, 'Bama, Bowl: Sixty-one Years of Crimson Tide Glory*. Browning later told me, "Bryant was horrified at the idea that Wilkinson or Kennedy would have thought one of his players would be shouting 'Nigger.'"

† Bryant also said to Connors, "He [Wilkinson] always looks like he just came out of the barbershop."

shirt and tie. Bryant appeared in a long-sleeved shirt, a light blue sweater, and a new sport coat. "In the Miami heat," said Connors, "he [Bryant] just looked like he was burning up."[18]

SOMETIME LATE in January of 1963 Mickey Herskowitz got a call from his good friend Dan Jenkins of *Sports Illustrated*, one of the most celebrated football writers in the country. Jenkins asked if Mickey had heard the incredible rumor that the *Saturday Evening Post* was about to publish a story detailing how Bear Bryant and Wally Butts, a former Georgia coach and the current athletic director, had conspired to fix the 1962 Alabama-Georgia game.

Herskowitz was dazed. "I felt like somebody had just punched me. I never thought even for a second that such a thing was true—I'd never known anyone in my life who I could less associate with a football fix than Bear Bryant. But the thought was so hideously ugly that it almost caused me to physically recoil. I was confused for a moment. What exactly did Dan want from me?"

As it turned out, the article in the *Post* was in the works, and all Jenkins and *Sports Illustrated* wanted to know was if Bryant knew about it. And, if yes, "How strong is his denial?" Herskowitz hesitated. "I told him, 'Dan, I'm just not going to ask Coach Bryant to deny it. That would be like a breach of faith.' I knew there was just no way that that story could be true.

" 'Try this,' Jenkins asked. 'Just let us know what his reaction is when you call. It looks like the *Post* is going ahead with the story, so we may want to do a brief tip on it. It might help him if he has a strong reaction in print ahead of the *Post* story.' "

Herskowitz, his heart pounding, picked up the phone and called Bryant in Tuscaloosa. "I knew there was no point in talking around it," he recalls, "so I just put out all the cards on the table. I told him that even if he knew about the story, he should probably know that news about it was already getting around." Bryant was both polite and blunt. He told Mickey he appreciated the call, but that he had already been informed. Alf Van Hoose of the *Birmingham News* had heard the rumor while covering spring training in Florida; so had Mel Allen, who was with the Yankees in Fort Lauderdale. Allen told Bryant that if need be, he would contact the celebrity trial lawyer Louis Nizer for him.

Bryant told Herskowitz, "I haven't figured on exactly what my reply is going to be, the way it's going to be worded. I want to make sure I have time to go through it with my lawyers first." Herskowitz phoned Jenkins back and repeated the conversation with Bryant as he remembered it. The next week, *Sports Illustrated* printed a short item about an upcoming story that would cause an upheaval in the SEC. The *SI* story grossly understated the impact the *Post* story would have; for a while, it seemed as if the entire world of college sports was on the verge of being shaken.

GEORGE PRICE BURNETT, a forty-two-year-old insurance salesman, had no idea of the role he was about to play in college football history when he picked up his phone at the Foundation Life Insurance Company on September 13, 1962. Through a technical foul-up (the industry term was a *cross-connect*), Burnett heard the voice of Wally Butts on another line. Butts was a director of Foundation Life, and Burnett had seen him at the office but had never met him. He quickly recognized the voice of the other party on Butts's call—one only had to hear Bear Bryant once on TV or radio.

Burnett was a casual football fan, not an expert in its terminology. He did know that Alabama would be Georgia's opening-day opponent for the 1962 season. His curiosity was aroused, particularly by what he remembered as Bryant's opening line: "Do you have anything for me?" The next thing he heard, according to hastily scribbled notes he made while listening in, was Butts calling Georgia linemen "the greatest in history." Butts, said Burnett, then went into detail in his discussions of Georgia coaches, players, and tactics.

Occasionally when Bryant would ask a question, Butts's response was usually, "I don't know." Bryant would then ask him if he could find out, and Butts would respond, "I'll try." The call lasted approximately fifteen minutes. Finally, Bryant asked Butts if he would be at home on Sunday, Butts replied he would, and Bryant said he would call him at home. Burnett was unsure as to specifically what he had overheard, but he claimed to be positive on one point: Butts was giving Bryant information on the Georgia football team, and Bryant was not reciprocating with information about his own.

Through a remarkably convoluted path that has never been completely traced, Burnett's story and his handwritten notes worked their way to the *Saturday Evening Post.* There is no doubt that Butts and Bryant had a phone conversation at precisely that time; both phone records and the testimony of the coaches confirm it. There is also little doubt that Burnett prepared his notes on the spot; two of Burnett's friends and business partners later testified to this. In other words, either Burnett overheard a conversation or he was being insanely creative. The question was precisely what Burnett had overheard and how accurately he had reproduced it by hand.

Apparently Burnett decided to forget the matter. He stuffed the notes in a desk drawer and forgot about them until ten days later, when Alabama thrashed Georgia 35–0 in the first game of the season at Birmingham's Legion Field. In light of the charges that would be made about the game, it is of interest to note that Bryant's new star, Joe Namath, threw a touchdown pass early in the third quarter to put the Tide ahead 28–0. On Alabama's subsequent possession, Namath fumbled away the ball at the Georgia seven-yard line. Bryant then sent in the team's second quarterback, who engineered a final touchdown drive. By the end of the game, Alabama was playing its third team. It appeared to just about everyone watching the game, including Georgia fans, that Bryant was being merciful, that Alabama could have won by any score it chose to. Burnett did not see the game, but 35–0 appeared to be lopsided enough to qualify as a rout, particularly in the early 1960s game of limited substitution. Georgia had made just seven first downs all afternoon and totaled a ridiculous 116 yards on offense.

Afterward, a reporter for the *Birmingham Post-Herald* reported that the new Georgia coach, Johnny Griffith, "was a picture of complete dejection . . . the disconsolate coach kept his eyes on the ground and virtually whispered his [postgame] answers." Butts, in his capacity as athletic director, offered a puzzling assessment to the press: "Potential is the word for what I saw, unlimited potential." Precisely what potential Butts saw in a game in which the Bulldogs never came close to scoring, and in which the winning touchdown was scored on Alabama's first play from scrimmage, was not specified.

Led by Joe Namath and Lee Roy Jordan, Alabama ripped through every opponent that season except Georgia Tech, losing 7–6 and missing a second national championship by the margin of a two-point conversion try. Burnett thought nothing more of the overheard conversation until early January, after Alabama had beaten Bud Wilkinson's Oklahoma Sooners

17–0 in the Orange Bowl. Shortly after that game, Burnett had some sort of change of heart. At a regional meeting for the Foundation Life Insurance Company in Atlanta, he struck up a conversation with Bob Edwards, a Georgia fan who happened to be a friend of Coach John Griffith. As he later described the conversation, Burnett asked the man, "Bob, I want to get something off my chest. Does Georgia have a player named Wood-something; maybe 'Woodruff'?" Edwards told him yes, the Bulldogs had a safety named Brig Woodward.

Per Burnett's account, he then proceeded to tell Edwards the entire story of the phone conversation, adding a remark from Butts that Woodward tended to "commit" too fast from his safety position. (As the safety is the last line of the defense, to "commit," used in this context, means that he would come up too quickly to stop the run and leave his team vulnerable if a pass receiver should move into his vacated area.) Edwards commented that Woodward did indeed commit fast, and that "he was very poor on pass defense."

If Edwards made this remark, it is somewhat puzzling, as it begs the question of why a safety who was poor on pass defense would be playing the position at all; it's a bit like calling a centerfielder in baseball "poor on fly balls." In any event, an angry Edwards urged Burnett to get together with Coach Griffith and tell him the full story of what he had heard. On January 24, Griffith, in Atlanta to attend an SEC meeting, met with Burnett in his hotel room. Burnett recalls that Griffith, after seeing his notes, commented, "This looks like our game plan. I figured someone had given information to Alabama." Burnett's notes went through the Georgia coaching staff and university officials like wild fire, immediately undermining Wally Butts's already tenuous position as Georgia's athletic director.

WALLY BUTTS was fifty-five in 1962 and had reached an unhappy end to what had been, at times, a glorious coaching career. Butts had been the head coach of the Bulldogs from 1939 to 1960, winning four SEC championships, taking them to eight bowl games, and producing twelve All-America players, including two men, Zeke Bratkowski and Fran Tarkenton, who achieved fame in the NFL. In 1942, Frank "Fireball Frankie" Sinkwich, "The Croatian Crusher," a player recruited by Butts out of Ohio, became the first SEC player to win the Heisman Trophy.

Butt's career record was 140–86–9, but this included a string of losing seasons from 1954 through 1958 when Butts found it increasingly difficult to squeeze enough money from the university to field a competitive football team—or at least that's what Butts maintained. Other Georgia officials and more than a few alumni thought Georgia's football problems were increasingly due to Butt's old-fashioned strategies (he was one of the last coaches to stick with the T-formation). There were also disturbing rumors about Butts's personal life.

In 1959, Butts's Bulldogs rebounded to a surprising 9–1 record, but in 1960 they slipped back to 6–4, giving him a losing record, 29–34–1, for his last six years. Georgia had had enough; in view of his longtime service to the school, he was kicked upstairs as the school's athletic director, and one of his assistant coaches, Johnny Griffith, who was just thirty-two years old, was given the job of head coach. Although Butts had hired Griffith and even loaned him money when he moved to Athens, Griffith began to distance himself from his mentor as soon as he assumed the top spot.

Griffith excluded Butts from all strategy sessions and did not consult him when formulating the Bulldogs' game plans. In this matter, Griffith had the backing of the university's president, O. C. Aderhold, who told Butts they didn't want him involved in football matters—a strange order to give a former head football coach and current athletic director. Clearly there were people at the University of Georgia who had suspicions about Wally Butts well before his phone conversation with Bryant, which, it was later discovered, had been charged to the university.

Butts responded to his new restrictions with rancor, making frequent criticisms of Griffith in football circles where the word was sure to get back to the administration. More seriously, many felt that he had discouraged football-devoted alumni from making donations by telling them that Griffith was receiving greater financial support than he had ever been given. In the summer of 1961, Butts clashed openly with Georgia officials when he was refused expenses for traveling to Tennessee for the funeral of General Neyland. Clearly, the University of Georgia was sending a message to Wally Butts that he was not accepting.

Butts had painted himself into a corner through a combination of bad business investments—investments in Florida orange groves and real estate had not panned out—and by flaunting a mistress and charging her travel expenses to the university. To the school's embarrassment, Butts brought her to football games against Alabama and Florida and was seen in public with her by Georgia players, some of whom complained to the athletic department that she should not be traveling on the team plane.

Some of Butts's business associates had questionable dealings. One was Louis Wolfson, a Georgia alumnus, whose illegal stock transactions eventually led to his imprisonment for violating federal security laws. The stock was in a company called Continental Enterprises, which both Butts and Bryant had heavily invested in, though apparently neither man knew of any illegal activity on Wolfson's part (Bryant, after all, had a long series of bad business investments). Another of Butt's associates was Frank Scoby, a Chicago beer distributor and known gambler, whose bank loaned Butts six thousand dollars as late as 1962.[19] In the words of Professor James Kirby, the SEC's official observer at the subsequent trial, "By the fall of 1962, Butts was on a collision course with disaster. Personally, professionally, and financially, his life was a shambles. He was reckless and vulnerable. His actions were totally out of character for the devoted family man and disciplined, dedicated professional who had ground out winners for Georgia between 1938 and 1959."

On January 30, Butts was in Philadelphia attending a friend's funeral when he got a call from John Carmichael, who knew both Butts and George Burnett. Carmichael told him that Burnett had taken his story and his notes to Griffith and the University of Georgia. Butts took the news calmly, apparently unaware of the maelstrom that was building around him.

Back in Athens, the executive committee of the Georgia Athletic Board had chosen one of its members, an attorney and former FBI agent named Cook Barwick, to act as both its counsel and investigator. Barwick met with Burnett, recorded a statement from him, and administered a lie detector test. Burnett, Barwick was convinced, was on the level. He reported his findings to President Aderhold, who then took over the investigation himself. Aderhold, along with the executive committee, then met with SEC commissioner Bernie Moore, who evaluated the evidence and suggested that they all meet with Wally Butts.

Butts was not informed as to the purpose of the meeting; Aderhold and the committee wanted to see the effect that the news had on him. But Butts must have expected something from the time Carmichael had phoned him in Philadelphia. When confronted with Burnett's notes, Butts, according to Bernie Moore's written recollections, "did not show any surprise or emotion . . . he did not deny the conversation [with Bryant]. His first statement was that 'Mr. Burnett and you gentlemen have placed the wrong interpretation on this conversation and on the notes that Mr. Burnett was supposed to have taken.'" Butts did say several times that he would never do anything to hurt the University of Georgia, but otherwise the meeting was indecisive. Nonetheless, the following day Butts resigned as Georgia's athletic director.

Later, after Butts left the meeting, the same group met with Burnett. Burnett was asked if he might have "simply overheard two coaches talking about general football." Burnett said he did not think so, as Bryant had not exchanged information with Butts on Alabama's strengths and weaknesses. From Burnett's point of view, though, the meeting took a sour turn when a member of the Board of Regents, a friend of Butts's, produced information on Burnett's financial situation, which included several bad checks. Burnett left the meeting suspecting that the University of Georgia was out to discredit him and decided to consult an Atlanta lawyer, a friend named Pierre Howard.

Events had been moving faster than Burnett knew, and he was confused as to what his next move should be. Apparently, the aggressive action by Butts's friend on the Board of Regents had unnerved him. What should he do? Howard advised him to tell the story exactly the way he remembered it before someone else got a hold of it and distorted it. Up to that time, Burnett had no intention of selling the story for publication and had even told Coach Griffith, after giving him the notes, that he wanted no further involvement. Now, he changed his mind.

The traditionally more folksy *Saturday Evening Post* may have seemed an unlikely candidate for this kind of story. In October 1962, however, Clay Blair Jr. was appointed editor-in-chief of the *Post*, having persuaded the president of Curtis Publishing, Matthew Joseph Culligan, that he had a radical plan to turn around the company's flagship magazine. In 1961, Curtis, which included *Ladies' Home Journal, American Home, Holiday*, and a children's magazine, *Jack and Jill*, lost in excess of four million dollars, with the *Post* accounting for about three of that four million. Blair was determined to change that.

Years later, after the debacle of the Butts-Bryant trial, Alabama fans quipped, "The *Saturday Evening Post* was begun by one great American legend"—Benjamin Franklin—"and ended by another"—Bryant. This wasn't entirely true, but there were some truths to both halves of the joke. The *Post* was a successor to several publications that began with Franklin's *Pennsylvania Gazette* in 1728. By 1962, the circulation was more than six and a half million. But there were storm clouds in the *Post's* future. James Kirby quoted Otto Friedrich, a *Post* editor himself and author of *Decline and Fall*, about the magazine's demise, as stating that by the early 1960s, "the *Post* was widely considered to be old and stodgy, edited by the old and stodgy, to be read by the old and stodgy. In fact, despite the healthy-looking circulation numbers, the *Post* had been in steady decline for more than a decade, particularly in comparison to its more upbeat competitors, *Life* and *Look*, and had actually fallen behind them in circulation."[20]

Blair's plan was to remake the *Post* into "a high quality reading magazine for influential people, more of a competitor to the *New Yorker* than to *Life* or *Look*." The Norman Rockwell covers chafed his editorial sensibilities: "We've got to have covers that have something timely to say," he told his staff. (In fact, the most infamous issue ever of the *Post*, the March 23, 1963, story about the alleged Butts-Bryant fix, featured the magazine's first cover on the beginning of the Vietnam War.)

Bard Lindeman, who wrote for the Blair-era *Post*, recalls, "It was an exciting time. The *Post* moved out of Philadelphia to New York and began hunting for the best new people. They hired people from *Time*, from *Newsweek*, from everywhere. The top people." One of the top people was Roger Kahn, who had written for *Sport*, *Newsweek*, and nearly every other prestigious sports magazine in the country. Blair challenged Kahn and his other editors to make the magazine "compelling" and to seek out "hard-hitting articles that are timely and mean something." Furman Bisher's 1962 story on brutality in college football seemed to be exactly what Blair was looking for. Perhaps someone a bit less ambitious would have seen Bryant's subsequent lawsuit as a warning sign. Instead, the *Post* saw the Butts-Bryant story as a milestone.

Burnett's story made its way to the *Saturday Evening Post* via a Birmingham native, Roderick Beddow, who was an attorney for Curtis and who knew Pierre Howard. Shortly after Burnett met with Howard, Dave Thomas, the *Post's* managing editor, was conferring with Kahn and executive editor Don Schanche on how to proceed. Kahn, apparently, was skeptical. He had worked at *Newsweek* and seen numerous rumors of big-time fixes come and go, all of them impossible to pin down.

According to Kahn, Schanche and Thomas wanted to push the story forward. George Burnett, it was agreed, would receive two thousand dollars for his story as an advance and an additional three thousand upon publication. Milton Flack, Burnett's business partner, and Pierre Howard, his lawyer, also received money from Curtis Publishing.

A well-respected freelance sportswriter named Frank Graham Jr., son of the renowned sportswriter Frank Graham, was chosen to write the story for the *Saturday Evening Post*. Graham's editor, Roger Kahn, had told him that "Furman Bisher would be the logical choice, but we are being sued because of that earlier piece he wrote. It would make us look vindictive if he came right back with this one." Graham had flown in from New York the day before to talk to Howard (exactly how Graham made the connection between Burnett and his lawyer is not known, though it was probably from Graham's having spoken to Burnett's colleagues, John Carmichael, and Milton Flack). Graham was clear in his purpose: he had heard a rumor about a phone call which indicated that Wally Butts and Bear Bryant had conspired to fix a football game, and he wanted to write the story.

Almost from the outset, the *Post*'s exposé seemed doomed—as Frank Graham Jr. recalled years later, "As in a classic disaster, the wheels, once set in motion, could not be stopped. A sense of excitement of inebriated delight in pulling off a coup, held together those who were in the know."[21] There had been no semblance, Graham felt, of the fact-checking process that is routine in the office of every magazine. Graham was told that he would receive Burnett's notes on the Butts-Bryant phone call by mail, but for reasons never made clear—they were in the possession of the University of Georgia administration—the notes were never sent to him. As Graham was to find out later, the notes had been impounded by Georgia's attorney general. Graham was forced to write the story without seeing the primary evidence.

That was one mistake; another, perhaps just as serious, was when the *Post* asked Furman Bisher to do some research to corroborate Burnett's story. "Bisher's attempts," Graham wrote later, "to gather more telling quotes in the South had largely failed. He sent me several comments, but the people he talked to had little of significance to add, or, as in Alabama, they refused to discuss the game at all."[22] At the very least there should have been an acknowledgment that Bisher's relationship with Bryant was, to put it mildly, adversarial. Bisher interviewed Georgia players and coaches (though, apparently none from Alabama) and phoned in quotes to Graham at his Brooklyn apartment. When Graham's story was edited, Bisher received a copy and was asked if he had any corrections. He did not. In fact, he used Graham's story as a basis for his own article, which was supposed to appear in the *Atlanta Journal* at the same time the *Post* hit the stands.

In his autobiography, *A Farewell to Heroes*, Frank Graham would accuse the *Post* of "excessive haste and secrecy" in the entire affair; there was a compulsion to "pull off a stunning scoop."[23] If the story of the fix had been true, it would have been a stunning scoop. It was indeed a bombshell, but as it turned out, the bomb would fall on the writer and the magazine.

PAUL BRYANT shook hands with a great many political figures in his lifetime, but he almost never sought them out. Some time early in February 1963, just before the *Sports Illustrated* item by Dan Jenkins appeared, Bryant made a phone call and flew to Washington, D.C., for perhaps the most extraordinary meeting of his life. In his book he claimed he went to Washington "for a clinic."

While talking politics, Bud Wilkinson, his old friend, told Bryant how impressed he was with Attorney General Robert Kennedy. Bryant, who had been telling friends of a growing interest in politics, asked him to set up a meeting. It finally came about just as the rumors of the fix broke. In his account, Bryant wasted no time getting to the point:

So I went in to see Mr. Kennedy, and I think he is one of the most impressive men I have ever met. We started to talk, and I said, "Mr. Kennedy, before we go further, if you've seen the morning paper, they're talking about *me*. What they're hinting at is that Wally Butts and I fixed a game."

He said, "Well, what the heck could Wally Butts do for you?" I said that's a good question. He said he thought there was nothing to it, because he hadn't heard anything. Something that big would have come by his desk. So we had about a half-hour visit, and later, when the story broke, people found out I'd been there, and I read where a writer asked Mr. Kennedy what we talked about. He said, "Well, I think you should ask Coach Bryant." I appreciated that.[24]

The passage is far more interesting for what is unsaid than said. There was no recorded mention before 1963 of Bryant having an interest in politics, although two years later, in *Look* magazine, he talked about it at some length. But if Bryant was considering politics, what office could he possibly have been seeking? Surely not senator, which would require him to live and work in the alien world of Washington (and surely not mayor of Tuscaloosa, which he was, de facto). The only logical assumption, which Bryant never even hints at, is that he was thinking at some point of running for governor of Alabama. What is truly fascinating about his description of the meeting with Bobby Kennedy is that there is no mention of the fact that almost precisely at the time he was meeting with Kennedy, the attorney general was locked in a furious battle on the subject of integration with George Wallace and the University of Alabama. About four months after Bryant met with Kennedy, Wallace made his infamous stand in the doorway of the university, attempting to block the registration of two black students, Vivian Malone and James Hood. Joe Namath, who had registered just minutes before, watched in silence from perhaps ten feet away. Bryant was not there. Scheduled to appear at a coaching clinic out West, he was making a stopover in Chicago. At a restaurant near the airport, he left his name on a waiting list; when it was announced, heads raised to see the man who coached the championship football team from the university that George Wallace was making notorious that very day. Trying to make a good impression, Bryant left a sizable tip. A scornful waiter—white, Bryant noted—told him, "I don't want your money," and walked away.

We will never know precisely what was discussed in the attorney general's office that day—if only Kennedy had been taping all his meetings. But how was it possible that the attorney general—lest we forget, a rabid football fan—could have been sitting in his office with, if not the most famous football coach in the country, certainly the most famous coach of an *all-white* football team in the country, and not discuss the subject of integration? The question is all the more intriguing because, as we would discover later, Kennedy was in constant direct or indirect contact with Bryant's boss, University of Alabama President Frank Rose. Yet, more than a decade after his audience with the attorney general, and even well after George Wallace's fall from power, Bryant was reluctant to discuss the details of their meetings beyond them involving a handshake in Kennedy's office and a pleasant dinner in Tuscaloosa (a dinner, by the way, which must have infuriated Wallace).

A slightly different version of Bryant's meeting with Kennedy appeared in Mickey Herskowitz's memoir, twelve years after Bryant's book was published. (According to Herskowitz, Bryant talked to him at length about the meeting on June 7, 1968, the day after Robert Kennedy was assassinated.) "When the first blind item ran in *Sports Illustrated*," wrote Herskowitz, "and was picked up by newspapers across the country, he [Bryant] flew to Washington and arranged through a friend to meet secretly with Robert Kennedy."[25] No mention is made of Bud Wilkinson's having arranged the meeting.

It was a disturbed Paul Bryant who was ushered into the solemn offices of the Justice Department. The story had not yet broken fully into print, but the first hints had appeared that a scandal in college football was brewing. Two Southern coaches were said to have rigged a game. After a few minutes of small talk, Bryant asked Kennedy if he had seen the morning papers. He said that he had.

"I was one of the people," said Bryant, the words coming hard, "they were accusing."

The Attorney General had his coat off, his shirt sleeves rolled up, his tie loosened at the knot. He looked him in the eye. "Why don't you tell me about it?" he said. And Bryant did.

When he finished, Kennedy leaned across his desk and said that his department had already run a check on the rumors. He was satisfied that Coach Bryant, and Wally Butts, were not guilty of the charges. Bryant said, "I know that. I just wanted to be damn sure you knew it."

Robert Kennedy offered his help, if and when it was needed. Bryant didn't call on him again. He had the assurance he had gone there to get.[26]

There probably could be no greater testament to Bryant's innocence on the charge of fixing a football game than his meeting with Kennedy. Reflecting back on his conversation with Bryant, Herskowitz feels, "Bryant was not a political man, at least not in the sense that politics indicates ideology. He admired Bobby Kennedy largely for his tough stance on organized crime, and would sometimes chuckle over the way Kennedy tenaciously pursued Jimmy Hoffa. 'I sure hope he nails that bastard,' Bryant once said to me. He said he was prepared to shock people in Alabama by supporting Kennedy for president in 1968, although he said it wasn't his way to campaign for someone. He said he was going to support Kennedy 'privately,' whatever that might mean. But there was no doubt that he was a Kennedy fan, and that included Kennedy's doggedness in integrating the University of Alabama."

When Bobby and Ethel visited Tuscaloosa in 1968, Bryant made a show of being seen with them in public. The Kennedys and Bryants dined with Dr. Rose at his mansion, and both couples spent the night at Bryant Hall.

"It might surprise a lot of people," says Herskowitz, "to find out that Paul Bryant's politics were not predictable. He once told me that he 'never trusted Nixon.' He said, 'I shook hands with him once, and his palms were sweaty.'"

AT THE end of February, SEC commissioner Bernie Moore met George Burnett in Atlanta and heard his story firsthand. Moore then met with Alabama president Frank Rose and Georgia president O. C. Aderhold. In the second week in March, a friend of Bryant's, whom he never named, procured for him a copy of the page proofs of the *Saturday Evening Post's* story and drove it from Birmingham to Tuscaloosa. At about four in the morning, Bryant met him in front of the football offices. Not waiting to take the story inside, he held the pages up to his car's headlights and read "The Story of a College Football Fix."

The preface, signed "the editors" but actually written by Roger Kahn, stated the case:

> Not since the Chicago White Sox threw the 1919 World Series has there been a sports story as shocking as this one. This is the story of one fixed game of college football.
>
> Before the University of Georgia played the University of Alabama last September 22, Wally Butts, athletic director of Georgia, gave Paul (Bear) Bryant, head coach of Alabama, Georgia's plays, defensive patterns, all the significant secrets Georgia's football team possessed.
>
> The corrupt here were not professional ballplayers gone wrong, as in the 1919 Black Sox scandal. The corrupt here were not disreputable gamblers, as in the scandals continually afflicting college basketball. The cor-

rupt here were two men—Butts and Bryant—employed to educate and to guide young men. How prevalent is the fixing of college football games? How often do teachers sell out their pupils? We don't know—yet. For now we can only be appalled.[27]

Graham's story ended with words more damning than the introduction:

The chances are that Wally Butts will never help any football team again. Bear Bryant may well follow him into oblivion—a special hell for that grim extrovert—for in a very real sense he betrayed the boys he was pledged to lead. The investigation by University and Southeastern Conference officials is continuing; motion pictures of other games are being scrutinized; where it will end no one so far can say. But careers will be ruined, that is sure. A great sport will be permanently damaged. For many people, the bloom must pass forever from college football.

"I never had a chance, did I?" Coach Johnny Griffith said bitterly to a friend the other day. "I never had a *chance*."★

When a fixer works against you, that's the way he likes it.[28]

THE NEXT day, Bryant called his players together—he wanted them to hear the *Post* story from him first. He came to a part of the story which insinuated that Alabama's knowledge of Georgia's offensive plays had enabled the Tide defense to hold the Bulldogs to just thirty-seven yards of rushing. Bryant stopped in midsentence and stared at the text. "Hell," he said, "did we give up that much on the ground? That's too many yards to give them regardless." The players broke up laughing, and Bryant turned to stare at them. He hadn't been joking.

ON MARCH 15, eight days before the *Post* hit the newsstands, Wally Butts and the grim extrovert, Paul Bryant, held separate press conferences in which they emphatically denied the charges. Both their attorneys announced publicly that the information contained in the *Post* story was

---

★ Later, under oath, Griffith admitted he never said that and that the line was "pure fiction."

false and would be addressed with immediate legal action. But the *Post* issue containing the story had already been printed and was ready to be shipped—there was no going back.

The *Saturday Evening Post* featuring the Bryant-Butts story was dated Saturday, March 23. On Sunday morning, much to the dismay of Frank Graham Jr. and the other *Post* editors, the *Atlanta Journal* did not carry the expected supporting story from Furman Bisher. As Graham later said, the *Journal* was supposed to "carry the public relations burden." No explanation has ever been offered as to why the Atlanta paper backed off the story. The nation's leading sportswriter, Red Smith, then of the *New York Herald-Tribune*, wrote that the story did not live up to its promise of exposing a "Black Sox"–type scandal. There was, said Smith, "no suggestion of misbehavior by players. If it were established that one embittered man had done the old school dirty, this would hardly constitute evidence of widespread corruption. . . . Nothing more has been charged than unseemly conduct between two men."[29] (The *Birmingham News* reprinted Smith's column.)

Alabamians came home from church, ate Sunday dinner, and anxiously waited for 4:00 to hear Bear Bryant's denial on his TV show. Bryant did not know how he was going to pay for the TV time. Representatives of his sponsors, Sloan Bashinsky of Golden Flake Potato Chips and Preacher Franklin of Coca-Cola, assured him that he could go on the air to give his statement without any commercials and their companies would foot the bill. Viewers were mesmerized; most had never seen Bryant except on his Sunday football show or on an occasional news interview, where he was usually jovial because Alabama usually won. This was a different Bryant, an angry Bear who spit the words defiantly into the camera. "I have been accused in print," he said, "of collusion or attempted collusion, with the athletic director at the University of Georgia to fix or rig"—the sneer in his voice as he pronounced those two words was especially palpable—"the game we won against the University of Georgia by a score of thirty-five to nothing. . . . I want to take this opportunity to deny these charges with every force in my command." On the screen, Bryant looked into the camera like John Wayne facing down the bad guys in *Rio Bravo*, but immediately after the telecast he slumped down in his chair, exhausted. Attendants rushed to him, Cokes in hand, patting him on the shoulder and telling him what a great impression he had made. But Bryant knew, if they didn't, that things were going to get a lot worse before they got better.

The state of Alabama mobilized behind Bryant, but, ominously for Butts, there was no public show of support from the University of Georgia or anyone else in the state. To the contrary, the quotes from Georgia head football coach John Griffith in the story made it clear that whether or not there was any fix, Butts had indeed given information to Bryant.

The story seemed to progress in waves. Burnett, then Butts and Bryant, took separate lie detector tests; all passed. On April 8, two weeks after the *Post* story appeared, *Sports Illustrated*, which had obtained copies of Burnett's notes, ran a story in which "The Scandalous Notes" (as the title phrased it) were submitted to a panel of football experts. The experts' conclusion was pretty much unanimous: there was nothing in any of the notes that could be regarded as "secret," and nothing that any well-coached football team wouldn't already know about. Again, for Butts, there was an ominous note in the story. Two of the experts felt that the information in Burnett's notes was "indiscreet"; if Butts had indeed divulged the information to Bryant that Burnett's notes suggested, "He was guilty of [at most] a profound indiscretion." "Maybe," said one member of the *SI* panel, "we [college football coaches] talk too much to each other. I know we all try to con one another a little bit, but if I had to be one of the two men in that conversation, I would rather be the listener than the speaker."[30] The *Saturday Evening Post* would have done well to submit Burnett's notes to that panel of experts before printing Graham's story.

Butt's ten-million-dollar libel suit against Curtis Publishing went to court first, on August 5, 1963, in Atlanta. According to Dan Jenkins in *Sports Illustrated*, the case generated more heated anticipation than anything since the Scopes' ("Monkey") trial of 1925. Butts surprised observers when he appeared in court with his wife and three daughters. Barbara Eggleston Kirby, the widow of James Kirby, the official legal observer for the SEC, recalls that Butts's daughters, who were all married, "looked very pretty, like simple country girls. I believe the youngest one had on a gingham dress." Burnett was the first witness called to the stand. Cross-examined by Butts's lawyer, Bill Schroder, a former coach of the Georgia freshman football team, Burnett testified that the *Post* had paid him five thousand dollars to supply the information for the story. Things quickly went bad for the defense when Burnett admitted that the very first line of Graham's story was incorrect, that their conversation was on September 13 rather than the stated September 14. In and of itself, the detail was insignificant, but it did establish a pattern of disregard for details that would catch up with Curtis Publishing.

Then came a second blow to the defense: Burnett denied one of the quotations attributed to him by Graham. The article alleged, "Butts also said to Bryant that [Georgia quarterback] Larry Rakestraw tipped off what he was going to do by the way he held his feet. If one foot was behind the other, it meant he would drop back to pass. If they were together, it meant he was setting himself to spin and hand off." Heads in the courtroom turned; if Burnett had never said this to Graham, from where had Graham gotten it? The incorrect quote pointed at the sloppiness of the *Post's* editing process. Apparently Bryant had spoken to Butts about one of his quarterbacks who tipped his plays by how he set his feet, but he was not referring to the 1962 game, he was talking about the 1954 Texas A&M–Georgia game, a 6–0 victory that was Texas A&M's only victory that year. Both coaches, it appeared, were chuckling over an otherwise forgotten game.

Quickly, the *Post's* case began hemorrhaging. Coach Griffith admitted on the stand that the secrets which the *Post* called "significant" weren't really secrets at all but were common knowledge about Georgia players and formations. He did, however, acknowledge that two of the offensive formations found in Burnett's notes had been used by Georgia in closed practices. The intimation was that fix or no, Butts had been trying to slip information to Bryant. More errors in the *Post* story were revealed: Alabama defensive players were alleged to have taunted Georgia offensive players by telling them, "You can't run 88-pop on us," suggesting that Alabama defenders recognized signals for Georgia's plays. But Griffith testified that Georgia had no such play. Precisely where Graham had come across the term "88-pop" was never revealed; why Furman Bisher, who checked the text for the *Post*, never questioned the play designation was also not revealed.

The defense rested on August 7, 1963. The next day, the prosecution ran the legal equivalent of a trick play: Paul Bryant, who had not been expected to testify for several days, walked into the courtroom, wearing a seersucker jacket and dark slacks. He looked, in the words of SEC observer Kirby, "grim and preoccupied." On the witness stand, he started out in his trademark grumble; Schroder, the defense lawyer, asked him to speak up. It turned out to be the only time such a request would be necessary. "He rose to the occasion," Kirby wrote later, "and was soon relishing his role." Asked about his defensive preparation for the game, Bryant regaled the all-male jury with a lengthy lecture on game preparation, complete with blackboard diagrams. "Few persons in the room," wrote Kirby, really understood what Bryant was talking about, "but all were impressed."

When Burnett's notes were given to Bryant, he said, "I don't have my specs. I left them on the plane," and had to borrow Butts's glasses. He then gazed over Burnett's notes, which he apparently saw in the courtroom for the first time—though, at the very least, he had seen the excerpts that appeared in *Sports Illustrated*. His reaction to the notes, wrote Kirby, "was casual, almost flippant. It was as if he was seeing them for the first time and did not consider them important. Taking them one by one, he flatly denied that he and Butts had ever discussed during any telephone conversation any of the information in them except for player Ray Rissmiller, whom Bryant had tried to recruit. He insisted that most of the notes would have been of no help to him." Which was probably true, but not necessarily to the point. What if Butts had been *trying* to supply him with information that might have hurt the Georgia football team? When grilled about a supposed piece of information on the Georgia defense contained in the notes, Bryant shot back, "If I didn't know that, I oughta be bored for a hollow head."

Then, Bryant was asked about one of the notes which indicated that the Bulldogs' safety, Brigham Woodward, "committed too quickly," meaning that when a play was run to his side, he came up too quickly, leaving him vulnerable to a pass receiver who moved into his zone. Bryant testified that he did not know this, and that if he had known it, he "surely would have taken advantage of Woodward" by having his quarterback (Joe Namath) roll out to Woodard's side of the field and throw a long pass. This was curious testimony for two reasons. First, because Griffith, the Georgia coach, had already testified that Woodward's tendency to commit too fast "was common knowledge"—though why, if it was common knowledge, did Griffith not instruct him to stop doing it? Second, because if it was common knowledge, Bryant, as he readily admitted, most certainly would have taken advantage of Woodward, but he did not.

Asked about the purpose of the call from Butts, Bryant responded that he couldn't recall specifics, but supposed that he and Butts had talked about football in general, including such mundane matters as tickets, scheduling, and conference rules on roughness, which, after the Holt-Graning incident, he had apparently taken a greater interest in. As to the question of whether or not he had had the phone conversation that seemed to be recorded in Burnett's notes, Bryant simply denied it. Schroder then asked him point-blank whether the information would have been of any help to him in formulating a game plan. "Sir," Bryant replied, "there may have been a couple of things I would have rather known than not known, but those notes, as far as I am concerned, would not help me one iota. As a matter of fact, all it would do is get me confused. Things I want to know weren't in the notes."

Apparently having been prepared for just such an eventuality—the defense should have expected Bear Bryant to come to a showdown prepared—he went to the blackboard and outlined a number of things he would like to know when preparing a game plan, stressing what the opposing offense tended to do on first down—first down, he said, is anybody's guess. He also stressed the importance of knowing what an opponent tended to do "on the five or seven big plays" between the twenty-yard lines. "If you would tell us what they are going to do field position-wise, and what they are going to do on first down, and what they are going to do on these big downs, five to seven of them, then we have a game plan, and if you can't win then, why, you are playing somebody that is an awful lot better than you are. Does that," he said, looking Schroder in the eye, "answer your question?" The former freshman football coach replied that it did.

At the end of his direct examination, Schroder read the editorial introduction to the *Post* article, pausing to emphasize the words "fix," "sell out," and "corrupt." Had he, Paul Bryant, and Wally Butts fixed the game? Bryant was full of restrained fury. "Absolutely not," he said without hesitation, "and if we did, we ought to go to jail, and anybody that had anything to do with this ought to go to jail, because we didn't. Taking their [Curtis Publishing] money is not good enough."

On cross-examination, the defense's attorney, Wellborn Cody, seemed to be intimidated by Bryant. At several points, recalled Kirby, he seemed "visibly taken aback by the ferocity of Bryant's answers." Cody completed his cross-examination in ten minutes. As Bryant walked from the witness stand, he stopped, looked around, and asked, "Can't I wait for my boys?" Two Alabama players, Jimmy Sharp and Charlie Pell, were getting ready to testify. A chair was brought in so their coach could sit and watch them. The jury ate it up. That evening, Walter Cronkite began the *CBS Evening News* with the words, "Bear Bryant walked into an Atlanta courtroom today and laid it on the line."

Kirby, writing about the trial nearly thirteen years later, said Bryant's testimony was "a virtuoso performance, and its effect was enormous. Bryant's denial of guilt could not have been more forcefully delivered." Kirby, who had formerly been dean of the Ohio State University College of Law, vice president and general counsel of New York University, and, finally, a professor of law at the University of Tennessee, called Bryant "the single most awesome figure this writer has ever seen in a courtroom, including lawyers and judges." It would later be acknowledged that Bryant's testimony essentially won the suit, though there were some sideshows still to come.

Georgia defensive coach John Gregory, while leading the jury through a film of the game, grew demonstrative when a Larry Rakestraw pass was intercepted: "The *Saturday Evening Post* story says our moves were analyzed like 'rats in a maze.' The truth is that Rakestraw wasn't rushed at all and should have run for a first down." In other words, Gregory was saying, the Alabama defense wasn't keyed to the Georgia plays. (Judge Lewis R. Morgan warned Gregory to keep his statements less emotional.) Schroder asked Alabama tackle Charlie Pell, could a football game be rigged or fixed without the players knowing it, without the players participating in it? "No, sir," replied Pell. This was an interesting point, one that, perhaps, was not pursued enough. How could a game be fixed without the players knowing about it, and if they were in on it, how could there not have been some hint or rumor? As Joe Namath commented many years later, "There's no way that game could have been fixed without me knowing about it, because I called almost all the plays."

Alabama's Pell and Jimmy Sharpe were so well groomed in appearance and articulate in their comments that after their testimony, Judge Morgan asked them if they intended to pursue college coaching. "Yes, sir," they both replied modestly, and both eventually did become coaches. It soon became apparent that Curtis Publishing was firing blanks. Much to the surprise of the prosecution, the jury, and the attending press, neither the author of the *Post*'s story, Frank Graham, nor the Atlanta sportswriter who was closest to it, Furman Bisher, were called as a witness for the defense.

It was probably lucky for Wally Butts that he was called to take the stand *after* Bryant; he was also lucky that none of the questions touched on his private life. Butts began his testimony calm and composed, but when Schroder asked, "Does this editorial [the one that preceded the *Post* story] contain any truth?" he began to reply and broke down in sobs. Then, to the dismay of almost everyone in the courtroom, while crying openly, he got up and stumbled over to the table where his attorneys were sitting. Judge Morgan allowed a recess. Those present in the courtroom seemed to feel that Butts's breakdown was the result of weeks of accumulated stress; a few minutes later Butts had composed himself and the trial resumed. (It was observed that some of the spectators in the courtroom were drying their own eyes.)

While under cross-examination, Butts was asked about a quote from the article, presumably from him, which read, "Don't worry about quick kicks. They don't have anyone who can do it." But two witnesses had testified that Georgia did in fact have a player, Jake Saye, who was skilled in quick-kicking, and in fact opponents knew about him. Regarding the Georgia safety man, Woodward, who was said to commit himself too soon, Butts reinforced the point that "if I were an opposing coach and knew this, I would fake a running play and throw over Woodward for a touchdown." But as Bryant had pointed out, Alabama had not done this.

Other witnesses, including Charlie Trippi, who many regarded as Georgia's all-time greatest player,★ testified that wherever Burnett's notes had come from, the information in them could not have given Alabama an advantage. Similar testimony was given by the Dallas Cowboys' Lee Roy Jordan, who had mopped up on Georgia in the 1962 game. Four Georgia players testified that they saw nothing in the notes that suggested Alabama had any special information on their game plan.

The most damaging testimony probably came from the defendants' own side. Though none of the editors or writers who worked on the story testified in person, they admitted in their depositions that they were not accusing the two coaches of betting on the game. Justifiably, this mystified many in the courtroom, particularly jury members who must have been wondering why, if the coaches had not bet on the game, the *Saturday Evening Post* had published a story accusing them of having fixed it. Curtis's lawyers were left to argue that Butts, bitter over having been removed from his position as head football coach, wanted revenge on Griffith, who had once been his assistant (and to whom, it was revealed in the course of the trial, he had given some

---

★ Trippi, a star halfback, had finished second to Glenn Davis in the 1946 Heisman Trophy vote and had just resigned from a position on Johnny Griffith's staff to take a job in the NFL.

small financial assistance). This, however, was practically an admission from Curtis Publishing that it could not prove that the game was fixed.

After emotional closing arguments from both sides, there was only one conclusion for the jury to reach, and deliberations took less than a day. On August 20, in Tuscaloosa Bryant told his secretary, Linda Knowles, that he was going down to Druid Drug for a cup of coffee. He instructed her to call over to the store when she heard that the verdict came in. Knowles got the call and alerted Bryant, who returned to his office and waited to hear from Butts. Butts phoned Bryant with the news: he had been awarded "general damages" of sixty thousand dollars and "punitive damages" of three million. That was fine, said Bryant, but what had happened to the rest of the ten million Butts had sued for? The award was later reduced to $460,000. Judge Morgan described the article as "clearly defamatory and extremely so," but ruled, for reasons not made clear, that $400,000 was the highest sum that could reasonably be awarded. The award for "general damages in the amount of $60,000.00," said Morgan, "to remain undisturbed." According to the law, Butts had no right to appeal the sum; his only choice was to risk everything in another trial. He accepted the sum.

For most journalists the decision was the end of the story, but the entire incident would have an afterlife that would take years to play out. The *Post* subsequently filed three motions for a new trial. The first was quickly denied by Judge Morgan. The second motion was based on new evidence and was denied by Morgan under the traditional rule that new trials would not be granted on the basis of new evidence if that evidence was in existence at the time of the first trial. Moreover, it was ruled that the new evidence was tangential to the case.

Frustrated, the *Post* filed yet a third motion for a new trial based on the landmark decision in *The New York Times Co. v. Sullivan* on March 9, 1964, which, in the words of James Kirby, in his 1986 book on the trial and its aftermath, *Fumble: Bear Bryant, Wally Butts, and the Great College Football Scandal,*★ "revolutionized First Amendment law governing libel actions by public officials." An Alabama jury awarded Sullivan $500,000; the defen-

---

★ The case, in a nutshell, revolved around the lawsuit by a Montgomery, Alabama, police commissioner, L. B. Sullivan, who sued the *New York Times* and several signees of an ad that appeared in the *Times* and charged that nonviolent civil rights protesters had been denied their civil rights.

dants appealed to the Supreme Court, which ruled that, according to the First Amendment, a public official suing for damages for "damnatory falsehoods" relating to his official conduct must prove that the statements were made with actual malice. (Otherwise, the court reasoned, public debate on important issues would be impaired.)

Precisely how this could have related to the Butts case was tricky. According to James Kirby,

> The instructions given the jury in Butts's case were not based on this new standard. Butts's lawyers had only two ways to avoid a new trial under the *New York Times* rule. One was to argue that the *Post*'s lawyers had waived the right to rely on this defense because they had not raised it in their pleadings. The second was to convince Judge Morgan that Wally Butts, as athletic director, was not a "public official" within the *New York Times* rule.
>
> Judge Morgan did not consider the first argument and went directly to the second. Reasoning that Butts was more analogous to a university faculty member or employee than to a public officer, he ruled that Butts was not a public official.
>
> As a final reason for denying a new trial on the basis of *New York Times*, Judge Morgan declared that even if the ruling applied, the evidence against the *Post* would have justified a jury in finding that the defendant acted in reckless disregard of whether or not the article was false.

So the proceedings in Morgan's court ended. The case, on later appeals in other courts, went through a dizzying series of decisions and opinions all the way to the Supreme Court. In June 1967, the Court ruled by a five-four vote that public figures as well as public officials must prove that defamatory falsehoods were made with reckless disregard for truth in order to collect libel damages. The majority opinion was encapsulated by Chief Justice Earl Warren, who wrote that the *Post*'s story "constituted an extreme departure from the standards of investigation and reporting ordinarily adhered to by any responsible publishers."

FOR BRYANT, the ordeal was far from over. "Oh, my," he said in *Bear*, "the nightmares." Many a night he would wake up in a cold sweat, his pajamas soaked through. After a while, he began to sleep alone. "I didn't want

Mary Harmon to know what I was going through." Innocence was no guarantee that his reputation would not be smeared forever. Every night he went to sleep with the knowledge that he might lose everything he had been fighting for since he left Fordyce. No, since he left Moro Bottom.

Though Bryant never knew it, he had good reason to be worried: Curtis Publishing was indeed out to get him. Bard Lindeman, a career journalist who lives today in Georgia, was a talented freelancer in 1963 when Bill Emerson, an editor at the *Saturday Evening Post*, called him and said, "Get to Lexington. We're going after the Bear." Lindeman and James Atwater (who would later head the school of journalism at the University of Missouri and had previously worked for Bud Wilkinson during his stint as chairman of the President's Council on Physical Fitness) were dispatched to Kentucky to find any dirt they could on Bryant's past. "We were told to spare no expense," says Lindeman.

They found nothing except an occasional rumor. "We heard a couple of stories about Bryant and a woman, but to tell the truth it was impossible to say whether there was anything to it, or if it was just somebody still pissed at Bryant for leaving Kentucky," Lindeman recalls. He also found that Bryant still had a lot of supporters there. "I tracked down one guy who knew about all the gambling in Lexington. I told him I was after anything I could find on Bear Bryant—had he bet on football games or basketball games when he was at Kentucky? The guy told me, 'I ought to punch you in the nose!'"

Bryant didn't know Curtis Publishing was sniffing into his past in Kentucky, but he did feel somebody was out to get him in Alabama. After the first *Saturday Evening Post* story came out, the Bryants' house was broken into while he and Mary Harmon were away for the Auburn game over Thanksgiving weekend. Somebody, it was never determined who, rifled through the desk and dresser drawers. The house had been ransacked.

In the months that followed, Bryant was visited by a representative of the U.S. Senate McClellan Committee, which was investigating gambling in college sports. Then, the IRS sent a man in, presumably looking for signs of unreported income. (Bryant had to supply the agent with an office to work out of, a fact which seemed to afford him more amusement than irritation.) On one occasion, Bryant invited him over to his house for a drink; it's not known whether or not he accepted.

It took Curtis Publishing nearly five months to decide that it should settle with Bryant. Francis Hare Jr. was working for his father, a specialist in libel law whom Bryant described as "a mean one who knew libel law backwards and forwards . . . a tough son of a gun." "Daddy told Bear, 'They're offering $360,000. I don't think they have a prayer of winning in court, if that's where you want to let this go.' Bear thought about it for a moment, and said, 'Francis, I've done a lot of things I shouldn'ta done in my life. Sometimes I drink a quart of whiskey a night. I gamble, and a lot of people know it. I've been to Las Vegas and I go to racetracks, and I've played some card games for a thousand bucks a card. What if they get a hold of that information and twist it the wrong way? It could make me look bad. Besides, this is putting a big strain on Mary Harmon, on the University, and everybody. Let's settle.'" There was another reason too. Bryant was in no financial condition to afford a protracted legal battle; as he would later admit, he had had a bad year in the stock market.

Hare called Curtis to advise that his client wished to settle. "For $360,000?" the Curtis representative asked. "Yes," replied Hare. "The check will be on the next plane to Birmingham." The details that settled the suits were worked out in less than five minutes.

"ONE THING I always loved about Coach," says Mickey Herskowitz, "is that he could focus on something with both eyes and still find a third eye to be looking at himself while he was doing it." On August 30, after Curtis Publishing's settlement with Wally Butts, Bryant was still nervously awaiting word on how his own case would be resolved. He was also about to begin the new football season. He still found time to write Herskowitz about a project that the two of them had been discussing for some time. "At that point, Bryant had been considering himself as legend fodder for a couple of years. Every now and then he'd say something and then pause and remark, 'I've gotta remember to use that in my book.'★ Just before the opening game, I got a letter from him. He wrote, 'I believe we should think of the book in terms of a date two years from now, possibly immediately following the '64 season. This is *strictly, strictly confidential*, but if everything went right, what would you think of the possibility of a movie autobiogra-

★ Because of the series of articles Bryant worked on with *Sports Illustrated*'s John Underwood in 1966, Underwood, not Herskowitz, would become Bryant's coauthor.

phy type of thing?' His one worry was that if it was going to be done, 'We should do it before John Wayne gets too old because he would probably be the only one who could do the job.'"

THE LAWSUITS brought by Wally Butts and Bear Bryant against the *Saturday Evening Post* and Curtis Publishing are among the most publicized legal actions of their kind in American sports history. Today, the details are only dimly remembered, and then only to cite another spectacular victory for Bryant. At the time, the results were not seen as quite so decisive. Bryant did not boast of his settlement; whenever he did speak of it, such as in his autobiography, he sounded almost grim. "How much is a year of a man's life worth?" he asked rhetorically in *Sports Illustrated*. "I don't know, but the *Saturday Evening Post* took ten years off my life, and I billed them ten million for it. I guarantee you, if I had collected that much, which I didn't, it would not have paid for the suffering they put me through."[31]

Wally Butts said little about the case after the settlement. He lived quietly and was never known to be involved in any scandal or engaged in unseemly conduct for the remainder of his life. Still, there were suspicions about him even before George Burnett overheard his conversation with Bryant, and the subsequent notoriety of the trial ended his career in football. He made overtures to other teams, college and professional, but no one hired him. (One Georgia sportswriter wrote that Butts found "all doors were closed to him" even though he won his case.)

When Butts died in 1973, Furman Bisher, who was still sports editor of the *Atlanta Journal*, praised him as a "Bona Fide Coach." Bisher's only reference to the *Saturday Evening Post* story in his tribute to Butts was to say that "I was stretched beyond all bounds of imagination by a young sports editor"—presumably he meant Clay Blair Jr.—"just employed by the magazine attempting to break in with a big noise." Bisher made no mention of his part in the *Post* scandal story or that he had been asked to check Frank Graham Jr.'s work before publication. "One of life's little ironies," Graham wrote,

that cropped up in the affair's aftermath was that many people refused to believe I had written the story. This was especially true in Alabama, where Furman Bisher was repeatedly fingered as the villain, and Bryant nourished the suspicion in magazine articles and in his autobiography. The story persisted for so long and interfered so seriously with Bisher's football assignments in Alabama that a dozen years after the event, he asked me to write a letter affirming my authorship of the article.

"They still don't believe it over there," Bisher told me not long ago. "Time after time, I'll be introduced to someone in Alabama, and this person will say to me, 'Oh, yes. You're the fellow who wrote the Butts–Bryant story.'"[32]

Bear Bryant's reputation was damaged by the two *Post* stories, but not by the trial. He went back to work, and after winning successive championships at Alabama in 1964 and 1965, his stock grew higher than ever.

The *Saturday Evening Post* was not, as many people thought, destroyed by the lawsuit, but Otto Friedrich, who worked there during the suit and later chronicled the magazine's demise in *Decline and Fall*, wrote, "The intangible damage was hard to assess, but it was substantial. The *Post* had lost a dangerously large part of its reputation for accuracy and responsibility, the reputation on which all its other stories had to rest. . . . From that point on, even the most implausible suit against the *Post* became news, and the news stories surrounded the magazine with an aura of scandal mongering and sensationalism."[33] The *Saturday Evening Post* lasted until 1969; a subsequent version of the magazine was launched, but it had less connection with the previous magazine of that title than that one had to Benjamin Franklin's *Gazette*.

Friedrich, in *Decline and Fall,* laid the blame for the *Post* disaster squarely on Clay Blair; the problems with the story's preparation, said Friedrich, were due to a combination of aggressiveness and in-house secrecy that characterized Blair's brief tenure (for example, articles editor Bill Emerson's being excluded from the editorial process). In other words, Blair wanted the *New Yorker*–type prestige without the *New Yorker*–type attention to detail. Blair failed miserably in his attempt to make the *Saturday Evening Post* into a rival of the *New Yorker* and was fired by Curtis seven months after the settlement with Bryant. Later, he picked up his career and carried on, among other accomplishments coauthoring the autobiography of General Omar Bradley.

Roger Kahn went on to write perhaps the most praised of all baseball books, *The Boys of Summer,* and has written best-selling sports books into the twenty-first century.

Frank Graham Jr. was given a full-time job by the *Post* and went on to write books, including—in an irony that must have caused Bryant to shake his head—*It Takes Heart*, a collaboration on notable sports events with Bryant's old friend and University of Alabama classmate, Mel Allen. Graham, who declined to be interviewed for this book, seemed to grow increasingly disenchanted with big-time sports and later became editor of *Audubon* magazine. He and his wife, Ada, have written several books together on the subjects of ecology and nature, as well as six books for the National Audubon Society. Graham mentioned that after he completed a book on conservation, a publisher's distributor noticed his name and insisted on having the manuscript reviewed by legal counsel. The law firm that charged his publisher a fee for reviewing the book was Pepper, Hamilton and Scheetz, for which Philip Strubing, the Philadelphia lawyer who handled the Bryant case for Curtis Publishing, was employed.

Graham's career was apparently not hurt by his association with the *Saturday Evening Post*, but it could have been. Bard Lindeman says, simply, "Frank's editors at the *Post* treated him like shit on that story. They hung him out to dry."

If there was an unacknowledged victim in the whole story, it was George Burnett, who did not seem to have any motive to hurt either Wally Butts or Bear Bryant or anyone else, and except for an extraordinary series of coincidences, would never have overheard the phone call, related it to a friend who passed the information on to the University of Georgia, or, finally, made a deal with Curtis Publishing Company. What became of Burnett's notes is not known; they were reproduced in Kirby's *Fumble*, but it is not known where the originals are today. Burnett was vilified by both Georgia and Alabama fans, many of whom sent him letters threatening physical harm and even death. He eventually moved to Texas, where he apparently lived a full, happy life, selling insurance and raising a family. At least one report claimed Burnett became a millionaire. One of his sons, according to James Kirby, graduated from West Point and became a lawyer, while another graduated from the Air Force Academy and became an officer. I do not know what year George Burnett died, and so far his final years have resisted my best efforts at investigation.

FUMBLE, THE book on the trial by James Kirby, was largely ignored by most of the sports press. It was treated with considerable derision in most newspapers in the South that took notice of it. Today, the book is almost impossible to find, and with the conclusiveness of the verdict, the temptation is simply to pretend it was never written. Considering, however, the possible importance of what Kirby had to say on the character of Paul Bryant as reflected by the affair, I think it's necessary to address and deal with *Fumble* in some detail.

To begin, Kirby felt that

> if Butts's case were tried today [1986] he [Butts] would unquestionably be considered a public figure, and the *Post* would get the true benefit of the *New York Times* rule. The attempt of four members of the Supreme Court to apply separate standards to "public officials" and "public figures" died after Butts's case; a single standard for all public officials became the rule. In this sense his case was unique; he won four of his five votes in the Supreme Court under a relaxed *New York Times* test that was never applied in another case.
>
> Under *New York Times,* as it has evolved, the *Post* would not have had the burden of proving the truth. Instead, Butts would have had the burden of proving falsity. He would also have to prove "actual malice." An early formulation of the Supreme Court's standard for actual malice was that the plaintiff must prove that the defendant acted with "a high degree of awareness . . . probably falsity" (*Garrison v. Louisiana,* 379 U.S. 64. [1964]). A more recent formulation is that the plaintiff must prove by "clear and convincing evidence" that the defendant knew that his statement was false or that "subjectively entertained serious doubt" as to its truth (*Bose Corp. v. Consumers of United States,* 466 U.S. 485 [1984]).
>
> The jury instructions under *New York Times* would have been very different from those given by Judge Morgan, as two justices of the Supreme Court noted at the time. How important are jury instructions? Former Israeli defense minister Ariel Sharon against *Time* magazine shows how a conscientious jury can follow instructions and find for the plaintiff on falsity but for the defendant on the malice issue. General Westmoreland's libel case against CBS was abandoned when his lawyer learned that the judge planned to give an unfavorable instruction on the weight of evidence required.

Kirby makes a convincing argument, I think, that had the *New York Times* standards been applied in the Butts trial, the legal strategies would have been much different. In effect, the situations would have been reversed, and Butts's and Bryant's lawyers would have had to prove the falsity of the article. Kirby did not believe this was possible; he believed that in fact Butts and Bryant conspired to fix the 1962 Alabama-Georgia game.

To touch on the essential points of his argument, Kirby believed the appeal on the basis of new evidence should have been allowed. The new evidence was a letter dated February 28, 1963, to University of Alabama president Frank Rose from Bryant and found by the *Post*'s lawyers during their preparation for the trial of Bryant's suit against them. In the letter, Bryant stated that he remembered his call to Butts on Sunday, September 16, "very well." If that was true, then Bryant—and for that matter, Rose—gave false testimony at the Butts trial when he swore that he had no specific recollections of what was said during the call. (It should be recalled that Judge Morgan denied the motion for a new trial because the new evidence was in existence at the time of the first trial and could just as well have been used then. No reason has ever been given for why the *Post*'s lawyers failed to either find the letter or use it for the Butts trial.)

Kirby also felt the overall evidence indicated that everything George Burnett testified to was, if not always correct, at the very least truthful, that Burnett did overhear the conversation and did take his notes while listening to Butts and Bryant discuss the Georgia football team. "My personal conclusion," wrote Kirby, "is that it is highly probable that Butts and Bryant had the conversation reflected in Burnett's notes." The jurors, he said, "avoided the task of deciding who was lying by concluding that even if the *Post* article told the truth about the phone call, the game simply was not fixed."

There is among the evidence, Kirby admitted,

no smoking gun to show that the play of the Alabama-Georgia game was affected. . . . It is safe to say that nothing Butts told Bryant caused Georgia to lose. And it is unlikely, though not inconceivable, that their conversation was responsible for Alabama's more than doubling the point spread, enabling gamblers who bet on the Tide to win handily.

This does not mean that Bryant would not have listened if Butts called with information that had any chance of being helpful. Considering

Bryant's drive to win games and championships and Butts's bitterness and vulnerability, such a phone conversation was something both men were capable of at that time.

There was but one hypothesis, Kirby concluded, "that is consistent with all the known facts. It answers the troublesome questions of motive and the effects of the call on the game." Bryant's motive, he decided, was easy to identify: "His powerful will to win had motivated him on more than one occasion in the past to resort to means less defensible than listening while an opposing athletic director talked about his team." Bryant might have gambled on the game, but "there is little need to speculate on gambling as a motive because winning the game and winning it big was reason enough for Bryant." As for Butts, his

bitterness towards the Georgia Athletic Board and John Griffith may have been sufficient motivation for him. Some suspect that Butts still hoped to regain his coaching job. As for gambling, his financial troubles were severe, and a winning bet would have helped. His financial difficulties are the key to another motive, however. He had received financial help from businessmen all over the country and would have been vulnerable to pressure from them.

It should be remembered that Burnett said Bryant was the aggressor in the conversation. He had opened it by saying, "Do you have anything for me?" indicating that he was expecting the call and that it was for his benefit. For the most part, Butts did not volunteer information; in the statement recorded in Barwick's [Georgia Athletic Board member Cook] office, Burnett said: "Butts sounded like he didn't know what he was doing. He sounded ashamed. On several occasions he answered, 'I don't know.' Bryant kept drawing him out. He asked, 'What about this defense and this offense?' He also asked where the weakness on the pass defense was."

Though Butts avoided outright denials of Burnett's charges prior to the trial, he repeatedly insisted that he would never do anything to hurt Georgia. When Carmichael called to inform him of Burnett's disclosures, his response was that Georgia had not been hurt by any call Burnett may have overheard. When first confronted with the notes in Barwick's office, he admitted, according to some, that Burnett could have overheard such a conversation but had "misconstrued" information that did no harm to Georgia.

In this regard, there was a part of Bryant's testimony that may not have been fully appreciated at the time. At one point early on, Bryant volunteered, "He [Butts] is for Georgia, and I am for Alabama. . . . If he would give me something on Georgia, the first thing I would think is they weren't going to use it." . . . Could this comment have been inspired by what actually happened?

Bryant's clear indication that he was expecting a call for his benefit, his aggressive questions, and Butts's reluctant replies all suggest that Butts was not the principal architect of whatever scheme was at work. Nor is it likely that Bryant would have taken the initiative in approaching Butts for information. Was it possible that a third party who bet on the game had put pressure on Butts to assist Bryant with whatever information he could get on the Georgia team?

The third party, Kirby suggests, was Frank Scoby, the Chicago beer distributor and gambler whose bank, on Scoby's endorsement, had loaned Butts money in 1962, and whom Butts had called fourteen times in September of 1962, including one call close in time to his call to Bryant.

Considering the absence of proof that the play of the game was affected by the call, it is possible that Butts sought to satisfy this third person by furnishing Bryant with such a mixture of valid, commonplace, harmless, and even inaccurate information that he could honestly believe he had done nothing to hurt Georgia.

It is also possible that Bryant sensed what was happening and distrusted or disregarded the information; he may even have sympathized with Butts's predicament.

It is not possible to prove the third-party theory with any degree of certainty. It has the advantage of being consistent with all known facts and exculpating both Bryant and Butts to some extent.

In 1986 when *Fumble* was published, I phoned Kirby for a brief interview for the "*Jockbeat*" section of the *Village Voice*. After reading his book, I found most of his conclusions valid or at least plausible. But after the interview, I felt a vague sense of uneasiness about many of his points and decided not to write the piece. Rereading his book and reviewing his argument eighteen years later, I see more clearly now what disturbed me then.

For one thing, Kirby expressed some doubt that Bryant's lie detector test was legitimate, a point he emphasized in his book. The test, he said, was administered by Fred Nichol, the public prosecutor in Tuscaloosa; an FBI man, Kirby thought, should have been present. I don't know whether or not the FBI thought it had sufficient reason to send a man to Tuscaloosa for the test, but a check of the record revealed that the man who hired Kirby as observer for the trial, SEC commissioner Bernie Moore, was present during the test. Kirby seemed surprised by this when I told him, and there was no indication in his book that he knew it. As Kirby did not hesitate to vouch for Moore's integrity, the question of whether or not the lie detector test was entirely legitimate should be laid to rest. Whether or not Bryant was guilty, it certainly seems like a stretch to suggest Bryant, the Tuscaloosa prosecutor's office, and the SEC—which, after all, had a stake in getting to the truth of the matter—would rig a lie detector test to support Bryant.

Another problem I had, though, with Kirby's conclusion was the new element of a third party. Kirby seemed to feel that this was the only theory that tied the loose ends together and answered all the questions. After reviewing the material, I'm convinced there is another, far more likely explanation.

Kirby did not try to build a case that Bryant actually bet on the game, "even though he was a gambler"—which was wise, as not even the Curtis lawyers tried to make that case. Nonetheless, Kirby refused to dismiss the idea. I believe, first, that that point should be dealt with. Bryant—as pointed out by numerous friends and acquaintances, ranging from his old Maryland quarterback-turned-FBI-agent Vic Turyn, to his attorney's son, Francis Hare Jr.—was not adverse to a high-stakes poker game.* Nor did he refrain from bringing up the fact that he participated at the craps table when he went to Las Vegas. It is an enormous stretch, however, to go from card games and dice to betting on football games, let alone fixing them. Not only had there

---

* "Insinuations were made about a lot of things," Bryant said in *Bear*, "and my gambling was one of them. I've never tried to hide that. I'd be a fool if I did. I'd tell anybody that wants to know I've cashed checks at race tracks and in Las Vegas and I've played the stock market."

never been any evidence of Bryant betting on a football game, there was never even a rumor. (The *Post's* own investigative reporters turned up nothing on Bryant when they checked out his past in Kentucky.)

If Bryant did not bet on the game, then what exactly would his motives be for helping to fix it? His friendship with Butts? A moment's thought on this reveals its obvious absurdity: Bryant would have risked his entire career—everything he had worked for since hauling produce on his mother's mule cart in Arkansas—to help Wally Butts achieve . . . exactly what? Revenge against Butts's former assistant? And how much of a revenge would it have been, really? That Georgia and Johnny Griffith would lose the game by a few more points than they were expected to lose by anyway? (Surely no one but Butts thought that Georgia would hire him back as head football coach.) If Butts had still been Georgia's coach and fighting for his professional life and had asked Bryant to hold the score down, some sort of agreement might have made sense. But what special motivation could Bryant possibly have had to impel him to risk everything for a few more points in a game he was playing on his own home turf and expected to win handily anyway?

There are several problems with Kirby's "third-party" theory, the first one being that any professional gambler could conceivably think that a football game could be fixed by a head coach and an athletic director, particularly an athletic director like Butts, who was known to be out of favor with his own university and banned from the team's practices (though apparently he attended one). What special knowledge or inside information could any gambler have thought Butts could provide?

Another more serious problem with the third-party theory is it doesn't explain how anyone thought Bear Bryant would cooperate with a fix. As far back as Maryland, Bryant had had a reputation as a coach who would not hesitate to bench a key player who was out of line; he would continue to have this reputation at Alabama, as Joe Namath and Ken Stabler would find out to their chagrin.

Yet another problem involves the point spread and the final score. Alabama was favored, according to two sources, by seventeen or eighteen points, a not unreasonable spread considering that Alabama had won by twenty-six points, 32–6, in the 1961 game played in Athens. In other words, Alabama would have been reasonably expected to beat Georgia by at least thirty points on its own home field the next season, and probably would have been expected to win by many more if everyone had known how good Joe Namath would turn out to be. The reason, of course, why Alabama was not favored by that many points in the betting line is that no one would take a bet of thirty points or more in a game between two traditional rivals; even if Alabama was ahead by a significant score late in the game, tradition and gallantry would dictate that the winning coach replace his starting team and ease up on his rival so as not to embarrass him. In fact, Bryant had a reputation for doing exactly this throughout his career; he repeatedly put his second- and third-team players in the second half of a game, refusing to roll up the score when a touchdown or two might have made a big difference in the voting polls. (Of course, it should be remembered that Alabama's second team was generally capable of beating most opponents' first teams.)

And that is exactly what Bryant did in this game: with Alabama ahead 28–0, about midway through the third quarter he took Namath out and by the end of the game was playing most of the players off the bench. If Bryant had conspired with Butts to win by more than the eighteen-point spread, he was taking a ridiculous chance. Though it is enormously unlikely Georgia could have done anything to win the game at that point, it is not far from the realm of possibility for a desperate team to throw a couple of long passes in the fourth quarter, or block a punt, or run a kick back, for the points that would have resulted in a loss that at least covered the point spread. If Bryant was participating in an agreement to cover the eighteen points, how difficult could it have been in the third quarter, and who would have blamed him, to have Joe Namath fake a running play and loft another long touchdown pass over the head of the Georgia safety—in fact, precisely the kind of play that was named in the *Post* story and later discussed at the trial. But no such play occurred. In fact, the opposite occurred: through his conservative play calling, Bryant actually set up precisely the situation by which Georgia could have scored a couple of fourth-quarter touchdowns and finished within the point spread.

But, of course, you can win two ways in gambling—you can also bet that a team will finish *under* the point spread. This is how most gamblers make their money. Most fans in most situations, however, will bet on their favorite team to beat the point spread, though Alabama was often an exception to this rule because so many of Bryant's teams won without exceeding the spread. This was the area in which it would have been easiest to spot some kind of fix. If on downs that were considered a "passing" down—say, third down and six—Bryant called an excessive number of running plays of the kind that don't normally net six yards and Alabama was forced to punt, the score would have been lower and eyebrows might have been raised. (And unless the quarterback, Joe Namath, was in on the fix, which is not plausible, Bryant would have had to call those plays from the sideline, sending in new players with them in each instance. This alone would have seemed a bit suspicious.)

If Alabama had scored two touchdowns and a field goal and missed an extra point, beating Georgia by just 16–0, there might have been some disgruntled bettors asking why the Tide had not "covered the spread." Again, though, what happened in the game was pretty much what was expected to happen: Alabama ran the ball most of the time, passing early and often enough to get a lead and forcing Georgia to play catch-up. Simply put, there wasn't a play in the game that seemed out of the ordinary for a Bryant-coached team. So if Bryant was cooperating with Butts in an attempt to fix the game, precisely how was he cooperating with him?

I do not challenge James Kirby's assumptions that smarter lawyers and a better legal strategy and an application of *New York Times v. Sullivan* might have changed the verdict in Curtis Publishing's favor. They well might have.

As Graham wrote in *A Farewell To Heroes*, Kahn, in his introductory box, "by equating this case with the Black Sox Scandal, surely made implications about Bryant that were not supported by facts in the article itself. But the lawyers had a ready answer: if he listened to Butts, then he was part of the conspiracy."[34] But "conspiracy" exactly to do what? And if there was no fix, then what exactly was the conspiracy?

I'm not essentially interested in what a different legal strategy or interpretation of "actual malice" might have accomplished. What I'm essentially interested in is whether or not Paul Bryant fixed or cooperated in the fixing of a football game, and I can't see the slightest evidence that he did. Neither, apparently, could Attorney General of the United States Robert F. Kennedy. It seems inconceivable that Bryant would have paid a visit to Kennedy had he been guilty of fixing a football game.

Yet, I am left with a nagging, unanswered question: If Wally Butts and Paul Bryant were not fixing a football game in the conversation overheard by George Burnett, what exactly *were* they doing? And I think the answer to what they were doing is exactly what they seemed to be doing: they were talking about the University of Georgia football team and its weaknesses. I don't know what other reasonable conclusion one can reach without falling back on the notion that Burnett invented the story out of whole cloth. There is no need to bring gambling into the scenario; I think Bryant's entire career argues that the margin of victory, *any* margin of victory, was completely unimportant to him. I believe that the notes Burnett took of the conversation proves that Butts was telling Bryant things about the Georgia football team and Bryant was listening. Surely Bryant knew that Wally Butts would know virtually *nothing* of any use to him; surely a meticulous planner like Bryant would know that a man who had been to only one Georgia football practice could not tell him anything substantial on which he could base a plan. How could Bryant possibly have put faith in anything Butts observed in so short a time?

Does this mean I believe that Bryant lied under oath when he said he did not recall the contents of the call? This is a difficult question. Yes, probably he lied, which is to say it's hard to imagine that he could not have remembered at least some of the specifics of the phone call. How does that square with the fact that he passed a lie detector test? Very simple—the questions asked during the lie detector test concerned a fix, and there was no fix. When Bryant took the stand in Atlanta, he was defending himself against a charge that he knew was unfair, the charge that he had conspired to fix a football game. If he lied about not remembering the specifics of his conversation with Butts, he was acting in the time-honored tradition of great American men—from football coaches to presidents—who believe that it is no sin to lie about a question that no one had a right to ask you in the first place.

This conclusion, I think, is supported by the fact that in the game itself Alabama showed no signs of having made adjustments based on Butts's confidences. Not one of Bryant's players gave any indication that plays or strategies had been changed during practices. As Bobby Kennedy had shrewdly pointed out in his rhetorical question, what could Butts possibly do for Bryant?

Why, then, was Bryant listening to Butts? I believe for the reason that Butts wanted to tell him what he thought would be helpful: it fed Butts's desire for revenge and made him feel important. I believe Kirby inadvertently hit upon the truth when he wrote it was possible "Bryant sensed what was happening and distrusted or disregarded the information; he may even have sympathized with Butts's predicament"—not a predicament with gambling, of which no real motive or evidence has ever been found, or really a predicament at all, but a late-life crisis for a man who thought he had been unjustly passed over. There is no evidence I see that the phone call involved anything more.

Chapter 8

High Tide

Luck is the residue of design.

—*Branch Rickey*

THE ALABAMA CRIMSON TIDE would be housed in a new athletic dormitory for the 1963's football season. The state legislature had no problem agreeing on a name: Paul W. Bryant Hall. Not surprisingly, the vote was unanimous. The players were overwhelmed by the luxury in the dorm, which had wall-to-wall carpeting and color TVs. They even had phones in their rooms. In the dining room, the players could not only order a steak, but order it cooked the way they wanted it. Jerry Duncan, who was a freshman in 1963 and would play on two Alabama national championship teams, liked the food. "It was one of the best kitchens in Tuscaloosa," he says. There were guest rooms for visiting parents of the players, most of whom had never been in a building anything like this one.

Bryant was no spendthrift; he was in fact a fiscal tightwad who abhorred waste and saved money wherever he could in the athletic department. He was a stickler about showing a profit. But the football team paid not only for itself, but for a great many other things at the university as well, and the boys, *his* boys, who brought in the money were going to be treated as if they were special. This was not privilege, at least not in the usual sense of the term. It was a reward for the extra sacrifice and work the players had put in.

Bryant Hall wasn't merely an athletic dorm, it was an antebellum-style sanctuary from the turbulent life on the outside. "Every now and then," says Jerry Duncan, "you'd hear about some Klan demonstration nearby, and sometimes some Klan guy would yell 'Roll Tide!' like we were some kind of symbol of what they were marching for. It galled Coach Bryant to hear that." Bryant didn't want his boys mixed up in *any* kind of demonstration. "He told us flat out," says Duncan, "if I ever hear of any of you boys mixin' with that stuff, you're going to have to answer to me." The problem was that Bryant had to answer to Frank Rose, and Frank Rose had to answer to George Wallace.

GEORGE CORLEY WALLACE'S rise to power bore some eerie parallels with Paul Bryant's. On the surface, the two most famous men in Alabama had several things in common. Both were born, despite Wallace's famous pronouncements for the great Anglo-Saxon race, of Celtic ancestry. Both had grown up poor, both had been raised primarily by their mothers, and both found the University of Alabama to be their ticket to a higher social strata. Both, to a degree, were outsiders, lower-class boys who had to fight for acceptance in a caste-driven college society. Both, in college, made friends with northerners, and occasionally Jews, more easily than with southern students. But the side of university life that Wallace experienced was a bit different from the one Bryant knew. As Marshall Frady phrased it in his 1968 biography *Wallace*, "The campus of the University of Alabama is like a farm club for the future politicians of the state, or a meadow where yearlings are put out to frisk and test their mettle. Personal coalitions are formed there which last for decades afterwards. If the Battle of Waterloo was won on the plains of Eton, many an Alabama governor and senator has been born in the dorms and dining halls and sidewalks of Tuscaloosa."[1]

Bryant had gone through school knowing little of these kinds of politics and caring less. A life in which social and economic success revolved around football fostered the comfortable illusion that football was a metaphor for life, and therefore that life was a more or less fair contest in which hard work, teamwork, leadership, and fair play were ultimately rewarded. Up to this point in his career, Bryant had found it easy to maintain these illusions. His political relationships at Kentucky had been limited to downing scotch and shooting a few rounds of golf or spending an afternoon at the racetrack with the governor. Bryant had not been so big a fish in the far larger pond of Texas football, but to the degree he had experienced politics and politicians, it had been in much the same vein as Kentucky—backslapping, handshaking, and fund-raising banquets.

George Wallace was a different matter altogether. He wasn't gregarious and scarcely drank. "He was a model of sobriety," wrote another biographer, Dan T. Carter, "but it didn't take much to send him out of control"[2]—and in truth, and this was positively deviant in a white Alabamian male of his time, he really didn't care all that much about football (his sport was boxing). To the outside world, both men seemed powerful, but Bryant's power was an illusion compared to Wallace's. Wallace stood directly in Paul Bryant's path and could destroy everything he had won in life.

Below the surface, there were a great many differences between the two men, differences that were perhaps more profound than the two men's similarities. Bryant's mother had given her children a secure home life, and Bryant remained close to her until she died. Wallace's mother was responsible for whatever home life her children knew, but as she told Marshall Frady, "My boys and I don't spend much time together. I hardly even talk to them on the telephone." Though Wallace's family had come upon hard times as he was growing up, his background was middle class compared to Bryant's. Both of Wallace's parents were educated. His mother had been a student of classical piano and a graduate of a Mobile prep school for women; his father had attended Southern University and became the only doctor in the town of Clio. His mother struggled to introduce what Carter called "refinement" into her children's lives, buying them such books as *Tom Swift* and *Robinson Crusoe*. Wallace was probably better educated when he left high school than Bryant was when he left college.

Perhaps the biggest difference between them might not be apparent to those outside the South and even many in it. Wallace grew up in the so-called Black Belt, which had been dominated by the slavocracy that ruled plantation life. Bryant's relatives were of independent yeoman farmer stock whose political instincts and interests were markedly different from those farther South. While they had no love for or even understanding of black people, neither did they have any particular attraction to segregation fanatics. Nor, during the formative years of his political career, did George Wallace. In point of fact, in temperament both Wallace and Bryant were close to Governor "Big Jim" Folsom, "the little man's big friend," who dominated Alabama politics for more than a decade after World War II. A notorious drinker and womanizer whose administration was so corrupt it often shocked even his own supporters, Folsom, who stood nearly six foot eight inches and weighed over 270 pounds, was, for all his massive faults, a liberalizing influence in Alabama politics, a staunch New Deal advocate and part of what Franklin D. Roosevelt had called "a new generation of Southern political leadership."[3]

Wallace had been Folsom's protégé and had run his South Alabama gubernatorial campaign in 1954. As a district court judge, he had actually acquired something of a reputation for fairness to blacks.* All that changed in 1958 when Wallace, despite Folsom's backing, lost the Democratic primary, and hence the governorship, to John Patterson, who had exploited the uneasiness of white Alabamians as the civil rights movement gained momentum. Stated simply, Patterson had the backing of the Klan, whose center of power in the state was Tuscaloosa. "I'll never," Wallace is supposed to have said after losing the election, "be out-niggered again." Wallace's relationship to Folsom in politics was roughly the same as Bryant's with Frank Thomas in football, but as Marshall Frady put it, "Bryant followed his best instincts while Wallace denied his and gave into the dark side."†

On June 11, 1963, George Wallace stood in the doorway of Foster Auditorium and attempted to block the registration of two black students, Vivian Malone and James Hood, at the University of Alabama. University

---

* Dan T. Carter, no Wallace admirer, notes in *The Politics of Rage*, "Every black attorney who argued a case in Wallace's Clanton courtroom was struck by his fairness and by his refusal to engage in the kind of first-name familiarity that most white southern judges used in dealing with black lawyers." "George Wallace," said a black attorney from Selma, J. L. Chestnut Jr., "was the first judge to call me 'Mr.'" (p. 236)

† In an interview in December of 2003, Frady told me he had finally come to feel that "Wallace's poison was not racism but a lust for power, which blinded him to the evils of racism. He gave in so thoroughly that his own worst instincts took hold and overwhelmed him."

officials, including President Rose, watched the proceedings nervously from Paul Bryant's office.* (The football coaches, says Clem Gryska, were away on recruiting trips. "It was sort of implied to us that we shouldn't be on campus for June registration, and since that was the time of year for recruiting anyway, it didn't seem unusual.") Rose had good reason to be nervous; in an interview with Dan Carter years after the fact, he revealed that Wallace had reminded him of the financial power he wielded over the university and had told him point blank, "I'm not going to ask the Alabama legislature for money to run an integrated school."[4] Rose was in constant contact with Robert Kennedy through Burke Marshall, the Kennedy administration's assistant attorney general for civil rights. According to Carter, both Marshall and Kennedy took elaborate precautions to ensure that news of Rose's cooperation did not leak back to Alabama. Cryptic written communications, worthy of a James Bond film, passed between the attorney general's and Rose's assistant, Jeff Bennett. Both parties reserved substantive discussion for furtive meetings held in Washington, often when the university president was in the capital on other business.†

No one doubted that George Wallace was vindictive enough to use his power to hurt anyone who got in his way. In the first legislative session after becoming governor, Wallace canceled millions of dollars in road construction projects in his opponents' districts; not a man doubted he would do something similar to the University of Alabama if anyone, even someone as popular as Bear Bryant, opposed him.

BEGINNING WITH an easy 32–7 victory over Georgia at Athens, the Crimson Tide breezed through the first three games of its 1963 schedule before losing to Florida, 10–6—it was the first time Bryant lost a game at Denny Stadium (and the last one he would lose there until 1982). After crushing Tennessee 35–0 and avenging the previous season's loss to Georgia Tech with a 27–11 victory, the Tide was back in contention for a national

---

* This was revealed for the first time, to my knowledge, by Hoyt Harwell of the Associated Press in a piece written nearly twenty years later, June 6, 1983. "I always wondered why they gathered in Bryant's office," says Harwell, who is now retired. "I think they felt it was the calmest place they could retreat to."

† Carter feels that Wallace, "unlike Bryant, had no compunction about hurting his alma mater if it served his political interests." (*Politics of Rage*, p. 112)

championship. All such thoughts came crashing to the turf when Alabama played horrendously and lost to Auburn, 10–8, Bryant's first loss to its intrastate rival in five years. The Southeastern Conference championship went to Mississippi, who was unbeaten despite two ties and was to be Alabama's opponent in the Sugar Bowl.

If Alabama had not lost to Auburn, and in particular if a Joe Namath fumble hadn't been instrumental in the defeat, Bryant might have been in a more forgiving mood, but with a season-ending nationally televised game against the Miami Hurricanes coming up, he felt something needed to be done. Rumors about Namath's off-field antics had been swirling for some time, but nothing had been substantiated. (Years later, in President Rose's files, a copy of a reckless driving citation issued to Namath was discovered.) A few days before the final game, Bryant heard a rumor he couldn't ignore. Apparently Namath had been involved in an altercation in a parking lot in front of a convenience store. Bryant, who was preparing to fly to Tennessee on a recruiting trip, went instead to the dorm looking for Joe. He was seated in the dining room drinking coffee when Namath came in; Bryant asked him back to the room he kept at the dorm for private conversations. Whatever exactly Namath did, according to Bryant he admitted it. In later years, Bryant would insist that Namath's offense wasn't major, but "I believe if you have rules you abide by them. You can't make exceptions." What he did not know for months, he later admitted, was "that other players were involved. They let him take the rap alone." Namath never mentioned the names of the other players who were with him.

Bryant told Joe he was suspending him. How many days? Namath wanted to know. Until the end of the year, was the answer, "or forever." Or until Joe proved something to him. He would help Namath go to another school if he wanted to, or help him get into the Canadian Football League, or allow him a chance to get back on the team if he stayed in school and proved that his transgression was just a bad mistake. The choice was up to Joe. Bryant then called a meeting of his coaches and told them of his decision. All of them, except one, argued for finding a way to keep Joe on the team; a few of them might have been considering the extra bonuses they would receive—which amounted to about a month's salary—if Alabama won its Sugar Bowl game, an unlikely prospect without Namath. The lone dissenter was Gene Stallings. Bebes was unyielding: "If it had been me, if I had been the player, you would have fired me, wouldn't you?" he asked his boss. Bryant had to admit that he would have. "Then let him go," said Stallings.

Bryant politely dismissed his aides and sat in his office for two hours, ruminating. Finally, he called Namath and Assistant Coach Sam Bailey into the office. He told Namath, he would give his right arm not to have to do it, but if he didn't, he would be hurting both Namath and the team. He told him the university could reverse his decision, but if they did, he would resign. This was Bryant's own account, and it sounds like hyperbole to any-one who did not know his history, anyone who did not know that he had done precisely that at Maryland under precisely the same circumstances—or that he would later do it again at Alabama.

Namath teared up and begged his coach not to consider resigning. He had a favor to ask: would Coach Bryant call his mother and tell her before the news hit the papers? Of course he would. Mrs. Namath cried over the phone and begged Bryant to reconsider, but he told her his decision was final. That night, unbeknownst to Bryant, Namath had dinner at the Bryants' home with Paul Jr. and Mary Harmon, who tried to comfort him. Some credit Mary Harmon with saving Namath for Alabama. "I sent for him," she revealed some years later. When he arrived, she hugged him and said, "Joe, what happened? You couldn't do anything bad. You're just too good a boy to do anything bad." What Joe had been doing, according to at least one source, was not only drinking but directing traffic in downtown Tuscaloosa—not exactly a low-profile pastime for Alabama's most easily recognized football player.

As usual, the press gave Bryant carte blanche: "We know none of the background," wrote a columnist for the *Birmingham Post-Herald*, "of Bryant's sudden action against his quarterback, and we aren't really inter-ested. We are confident it was justified."[5] But for the first time since com-ing to Alabama, Bryant took heat from the fans. As they had supported him a couple of months earlier during the Butts trial, Alabama fans now felt free to openly disagree with him on his treatment of their quarterback. Letters, telegrams, and hand-delivered petitions showed up at the football office, including one from Beaver Falls, Pennsylvania, that seemed to be signed by the entire town. Bryant would not relent. He had not done a good job with Joe, he would later admit. But if he had let him go unpunished another year, the team wouldn't have come together.

As it turned out, the suspension of Joe Namath was to set the stage for one of Alabama's and Bear Bryant's most legendary improbable finishes. At first, the loss of Namath seemed like a devastating blow. Bryant's players did not doubt that he had done the right thing, but at that moment no one could see how they would get through the games with Miami and Ole Miss. The team pulled together in large part because Namath accepted the suspension—at least, he made no public complaint. According to Butch Henry, Namath's roommate who was quoted by Mark Kriegel in his biography, Namath came out of the dorm after his meeting with Bryant in tears and threatened to leave.

Miami wasn't very good, but its quarterback, George Mira, was regarded by many as a passer almost in a class with Namath. Bryant handed the ball to a nervous sophomore named Steve Sloan, and on national television the Crimson Tide eeked out a 17–12 win, winning, as Bryant said, "without really beating anybody."

The Sugar Bowl against unbeaten Ole Miss was another matter. "I didn't think we had a chance to win the game after we had disciplined Namath," Bryant said to Al Browning. "I had no idea we could ever win."*[6] Neither did much of the press. "Alabama has about as much chance of beating Mississippi as it has a chance of snowing in New Orleans on New Year's Eve," said one Crescent City sportswriter.[7] Bryant woke up at four in the morning on New Year's Day and looked out the window of his New Orleans hotel room to see the streets covered in snow.

Bryant was on edge from the combination of pregame stress and anxiety about how the litigation with Curtis Publishing would play out. If he had known that his team would not score a touchdown that day against Ole Miss, he would have been even more miserable. Remarkably, a touchdown wasn't needed. Sloan, who had played at least well enough to win the Miami game, was given the nod as starting quarterback. He was nervous before the game and never stopped being nervous during the game; on an option play, he pitched the ball back not to a teammate but to an official. "To this day, I'm just thankful he didn't catch it," says Sloan. "I'd have never lived that down." Alabama outgutted and outhustled a bigger and more talented Mississippi team. The defense shut out the Rebels until the fourth quarter, and Tim Davis made four field goals, including two boomers of

---

* Browning had a knack for getting Bryant to admit things on reflection that he would never otherwise acknowledge.

forty-six and forty-eight yards for a 12–7 victory. "It wasn't the national championship," says Sloan, "but it was sweet."

DURING NAMATH'S suspension, Jimmy Smothers, a reporter for the *Gadsden Times*, interviewed Bryant in his home. "Is there anything I should have asked you," he wanted to know, "or something you wanted to talk about?" There was. "I have decided to let Joe Namath back on the team," Bryant said, "but I haven't been able to reach him." Smothers knew where Namath was: he had been staying in the basement of Bryant's house, courtesy of Mary Harmon. She had told Smothers one night during one of the weekly sessions Bryant held for the press at his home; after the session, Bryant and several of the sportswriters would sit around, drink, and talk, but Smothers, who did not drink, would go into the kitchen and help Mary Harmon clean up, and they became good friends. After the interview, Smothers left Bryant's house, went straight to a telephone, and called Mary Harmon to tell Joe he was back on the team.

THE 1964 season, when Alabama *did* win a national championship but finished on a sour note, made for an interesting contrast with 1963.

Namath, now officially listed as "Joe Willie" in the Alabama press guide, came out roaring, completing sixteen of twenty-one passes and running for three touchdowns in an easy 31–3 season opener over Georgia. By the time the Crimson Tide was ready to host North Carolina State in the fourth week of the season, Alabama had outscored its opponents 91–9. The game was uneventful midway through the second quarter, with Namath completing seven of eight passes while the Tide rolled. Then, it happened.

On a sprint to his right, Namath found his receivers covered and, rather than put the ball up for grabs, decided to run. Suddenly, without being touched, he went down as though he had hit a trip wire. Somehow, Joe had found an unfamiliar and unfriendly chunk of turf in Denny Stadium and twisted his knee. One of the first to reach him was North Carolina State defensive back Tony Goldmont, one of Joe's teammates at Beaver Falls High. Then, from the Alabama sideline came trainer Jim Goostree and Bryant. Bryant did not call for a stretcher. This was Alabama, and any player who could rise and leave the field under his own steam, particularly who had not been hit, was expected to do so. Namath got up, the crowd cheered, and Joe limped off the field with Goostree at his side. In the third quarter, his knee wrapped in ice, Joe hobbled to the sideline to watch a cautious Steve Sloan guide the Tide to a 21–0 win. The injury would eventually be diagnosed as torn ligaments and cartilage, and though no one knew it at the time, the little cleft of turf at Denny Stadium would have almost the same effect on football history as the drain pipe in Yankee Stadium had on baseball history—Mickey Mantle stumbled on it and twisted his knee in the 1951 World Series. Like Mantle, Namath would always be remembered partly for what he did and partly for what he might have done.

Namath put in an appearance the following week, subbing for his own sub, Steve Sloan, in a 19–8 win over Tennessee at Knoxville. In the next game, he was subpar in a 17–14 victory over Florida, a performance that caused Bryant to comment for the *Tuscaloosa News*, "He moves like a human now. He did move like a cat." At the time, no one knew how much pain Namath was playing with—Joe just gritted his teeth and won. After eight weeks, Alabama was unbeaten and fighting for a share of the national championship with equally unbeaten Notre Dame, which was enjoying a resurgence under rookie head coach Ara Parseghian. In week nine, Alabama traveled to Grant Field in Atlanta to face a superb Georgia Tech team, which had won seven of its nine games. On the bus trip to the Atlanta Biltmore, Bryant was edgy. The bus driver was giving the Alabama team a friendly tour, pointing out landmarks, when he was cut off by Bryant: "Thank you, but we got the tour when we came over here in 1962. Just get us to the hotel."

Remembering the whisky bottles that had been flung at him two years earlier when the Tide played there, Bryant wore a football helmet for the 1964 Georgia Tech game and came out of the tunnel to fans screaming such epithets as "Go to hell, Alabama!" ("That," recalled Bryant, "was the nicest one.") Like Muhammad Ali playing off a hostile crowd, Bryant walked around Grant Field for several minutes pretending to check the condition of the grass and the chalk lines, but in reality letting the Tech fans get a good look at him. They shouted out insults; he ignored them and went about his business. Finally, he walked over to the Alabama side of the field and exchanged the red helmet for his lucky brown felt hat.

The Georgia Tech fans put up more of a fight than their team. After taking the Tide to two touchdowns in less than a minute and a half, Namath sat out the second half and let Steve Sloan and the defense wrap up the 24–7 victory. In the dressing room after the game, Pooley Hubert, who had starred for Alabama in its first nationally acclaimed victory over Penn in 1922 under Xen Scott, cried and embraced Bryant.

This was one of the odd years when the major wire services chose not to hold off their national championship vote until after the bowl games, which meant Alabama had just one slim chance to win the title. They needed to first beat Auburn and its All-America fullback, Tucker Frederickson, on Thanksgiving Day, and then hope that two days later number one–ranked Notre Dame would lose to Southern Cal in *their* annual grudge match. For Alabama's part, defeating Auburn was no easy task. Though the Tigers were just 6–3 going into the game compared to Alabama's 9–0, the yearly contest had evolved into a match in which, as local sportswriters like to say, "you can throw all previous scores out the window." This proved to be the case in 1964 at Birmingham's Legion Field when thousands of Alabama fans gasped collectively as Steve Sloan went out of the game with a knee injury and a still-limping Namath was forced to take the field late in the second quarter. Namath threw a dazzling twenty-two-yard touchdown pass that proved to be the difference in the game.

Two days later, the team gathered in the dorm to watch Notre Dame and Southern Cal on national television. For three quarters, a cloud of gloom grew thicker as the Irish built up a 17–0 lead. Then, suddenly, almost unbelievably, Southern Cal rebounded to win 20–17 in the closing moments. The Crimson Tide partied that night, unrestrained by its coach, knowing Alabama would be voted national champions the following Monday.

Later, no one would want to say that Alabama wasn't quite ready for the Orange Bowl match with Darrell Royal's Texas Longhorns. But, says Jerry Duncan, "Things were just a little more slack, a little more unfocused than we wanted them to be. If the national championship had been on the line, I think we'd have had everything together. But with the game being kind of anticlimactic, it just took a while for us to get emotionally up for it." It took almost three quarters, actually.

With the national championship already wrapped and Namath, his knee in bandages, hobbling around on the sidelines, the Crimson Tide seemed to be in something of a stupor. The Longhorns came out roaring, and in the first quarter Texas's star running back, Ernie Koy, who, at 220 pounds, was bigger than most of the Alabama linemen, swept around the right end and went seventy-nine yards for a touchdown. Alabama reacted like a fighter who had just been straightened up with an uppercut. On the Longhorns' next possession came the right cross: George Sauer Jr., who in just four years would hook up with Joe Namath to win the most famous Super Bowl ever against the Baltimore Colts, broke free from the Alabama secondary to take in a sixty-nine-yard touchdown pass. The national champions found themselves down 14–0.

On the sidelines, Bryant fumed. If his team wasn't taking the game seriously, he certainly was. The January 1, 1965, Orange Bowl was the first bowl game televised in prime time, and NBC, with its dramatic and pioneering use of color, was showcasing the game to send a message to ABC and Roone Arledge that they weren't the only ones who knew how to stage college football. The pregame show started at 7:30 p.m. EST, preempting Bob Hope and Jack Benny, two of the network's biggest attractions, and Jackie Gleason was chosen to toss the coin. The combination of Bear Bryant, Alabama's number-one ranking, and the national publicity surrounding Namath (despite rumors that he might not be able to play) guaranteed the largest TV audience to ever watch a bowl game. Now, in front of that audience, Bryant was watching his uninspired team get trounced.

With less than ten minutes to play in the half, inspiration arrived. Sensing that now was the time, Bryant sent Namath, wearing soccer shoes so his cleats wouldn't catch on the turf, in for Sloan. Namath's sudden appearance in the game caught the Longhorns by surprise; Darrell Royal's grapevine had assured him that Namath was hurting too much to play. Dropping back and releasing the ball so quickly that the Texas pass rush couldn't reach him, Namath proceeded to move Alabama eighty-seven yards with six pass completions—two to the speedy end, Ray Perkins, and finally one to halfback Wayne Trimble for a touchdown. But Texas came back to score again and took a 21–7 halftime lead.

The television drama intensified in the second half. Alabama played like a national champion, shutting down the Texas offense and putting ten points on the board, the touchdown coming on a pass from Namath to Perkins. Late in the fourth quarter, Namath drove the Tide to the Texas six-yard line, with a first down and goal to go. After three consecutive running plays with fullback Steve Bowman, Alabama found itself a bowtie's length from the winning touchdown. Namath called his own number on a quarterback sneak and carried the ball into the line himself. Gaylon McCullough put a good block on Texas's consensus All-America linebacker Tommy Nobis, and Namath wedged right beside him. "I know he made it into the end zone," said McCullough, "because he was lying right on top of me, and *I* was in the end zone. I said to myself, 'Damn, that's it! We did it, we win!' I pushed Joe away, got to my feet and started celebrating." One official's hands went up; Alabama players exploded in jubilation and mobbed Namath. But after several seconds, both sides realized that the referee had signaled no score. After conferring, the officials placed the ball down on the very edge of the goal line.

An exasperated Namath headed to the bench, drank from a cup of water, and spat. A member of the Orange Bowl committee leaned over and yelled in his ear that he had been voted the game's most valuable player. Namath merely muttered, "Yeah," and threw the paper cup on the ground. As the clock wound down, the dejected Crimson Tide left the field. Namath caught up with Bryant, telling him out loud that he had crossed the goal line. Bryant stopped and softly replied. Later, Namath would reveal that Bryant told him that it made no difference whether he had or not, that "if you can't jam it in from there without leaving any doubt, you don't deserve to win."

Bryant and the rest of the Alabama players had the national championship to console themselves; Namath had a bit more. Much of the pregame publicity surrounding the Orange Bowl involved a bidding war for Namath by the two professional teams that had selected him in their drafts, the St. Louis Cardinals of the National Football League and the New York Jets of the upstart American Football League. Before the game, Sonny Werblin, the Jets' flamboyant owner, had become antsy after hearing rumors that the Cardinals were making a push to sign Joe, and had asked Bryant to intercede on his behalf; Bryant told him that if he had Joe's word, "That's all you need." The day after the game, Bryant and Namath met with Werblin, and Namath signed a contract for the astronomical sum of $427,000, making him the highest-paid professional athlete in America. Werblin would later reveal that he had talked to Namath the day before the Orange Bowl and had offered him a Coca-Cola. Werblin told Mickey Herskowitz that Joe had refused the Coke: "Coach Bryant told him he was not to accept a damned thing until the game had been played."

There can be no greater indictment of the process for selecting "The Outstanding College Football Player in the Nation," which is how New York's Downtown Athletic Club labels its Heisman Trophy selection, than the fact that Joe Namath, the most sought-after college player in the nation, did not win it in 1964. In fact, Namath did not finish in the top ten. Even before Namath's injury, Bryant had simply not given him enough playing time to build up the statistics needed to impress the Heisman voters—Bryant did not believe in running up the score on a beaten opponent to impress anybody. Namath would go on to football immortality, leading the AFL to its first Super Bowl victory in 1969. The man he had to beat out for the Jets' starting job was the 1964 Heisman Trophy winner, Notre Dame's John Huarte, who never threw a pass for the New York Jets and threw just one touchdown pass in twenty-four NFL games before retiring after the 1972 season.

PAUL BRYANT was now officially Bear Bryant, without question the most famous college football coach in America. There were still some skeptics, though, most notably Jim Murray of the *Los Angeles Times*. "So Alabama is the 'national champion,' is it?" he wrote in his January 2, 1965, column, titled "Bama In Balkans":

> Ha!
>
> "National" champion of what? The Confederacy?
>
> This team hasn't poked its head above the Mason-Dixon line since Appomattox. They've almost NEVER played a Big Ten team. One measly game with Wisconsin back in 1928 is all I can find. They lost.
>
> This team wins the Front-Of-The-Bus championship every year—largely with Pennsylvania quarterbacks. How can you win a "national" championship playing in a closet? How can you get to be "No. 1" if you don't play anybody but your kinfolks? How do you know whether these guys are kicking over baby carriages or slaying dragons? . . .
>
> . . . You can't be "Numero Uno" in the bull ring slaughtering cows. They have to be certified bulls and they have to fight back. When 'Bama beats these, THEN we'll give them the ears and throw flowers in the ring. Until then, don't make me laugh.

Murray, along with Red Smith, was generally regarded as one of the two leading sportswriters in America, but his column on Bryant and Alabama was a collection of cheap shots with one legitimate punch.

For instance, the notion that Alabama never played anyone outside the South. Murray, of all people, should have remembered how Alabama regularly shocked West Coast teams—teams that were precisely as segregated as Alabama—in the legendary Rose Bowl clashes of the 1920s, 1930s, and 1940s. He might have also noticed that only two years before, Bryant had blanked Bud Wilkinson's integrated Sooners in the Orange Bowl.

The charge that Alabama did not travel far to find its opponents was true, but most major powers did not travel far out of their own regions to find opponents in 1964. (If SEC teams did not schedule games against Big Ten teams, it was equally true that Big Ten teams did not schedule games against SEC teams.) One of the notable exceptions was Notre Dame—which had pretty much always been a notable exception. The Irish, not playing in a conference, had always played a national schedule because it recruited nationally. But as late as 1964 Notre Dame was scheduling no teams in either the Southeast or the Southwest and for years had been padding its schedule with the relatively weak service academies, Navy, Air Force, and Army (the latter of whom, after years of domination, had fallen on hard times). In 1964 Notre Dame played both Air Force and Navy, who won just seven of their twenty games. In fact, the Irish played only three teams all season with winning records—Purdue, Stanford, and Southern Cal—and Stanford was 5–4 not counting its match with Notre Dame. In truth, most college football teams at the time were bound to a fixed schedule with traditional foes and were limited in their outside choices by the expense of transportation. All that would change within the next few years, but it could hardly be said in the early 1960s that Alabama was guiltier of Balkanization than other major powers. Murray might also have mentioned that in 1966 Notre Dame's national championship team featured just one black starter, defensive lineman Alan Page.

Still, on the issue of segregation, Murray was right on target and was saying what sportswriters in Alabama and the rest of the Deep South would not say. But Murray had to know that he was committing a foul by pinning the race card on Bryant. Because Murray was a sportswriter, he was focusing on a football coach, but surely he knew that Bryant no more set policy for the University of Alabama than Southern Cal coach John McKay set policy for his school. In any event, Murray would soon have no cause for complaint that Alabama was winning national championships by slaughtering cows instead of bulls.

———

EARLY IN 1965, Darrell Royal made a list of coaches to be invited to the White House for the annual presentation of the Coach of the Year Award. "I wanted to get a mix of people who would reflect the diversity in our profession," says Royal. "Ara Parseghian, who had just led Notre Dame back to prominence, John McKay, and, of course, Coach Bryant. I said to my wife, 'I can't wait to see Bear Bryant and President Johnson together in that Oval Office.'" Johnson, knowing a good photo opportunity when he saw it, had, in fact, expressed an interest in meeting Bryant, perhaps wishing to grease the wheels of integration in Alabama. "Now here's the guy I want to meet," said Johnson. "You're a big one, ain't cha?" said Johnson with a grin as he shook hands. Bryant grinned right back at the president and replied, "You're a pretty big sonuvabitch yourself."

THE 1964 Alabama national championship team had a few outstanding players and several others who, judged solely from the standpoint of talent, were average. As Bryant was proud of saying, the team just didn't know it. Wayne Freeman had made most All-American teams, and, of course, there was Namath, but Joe was hurt for much of his senior year. The Tide would not have won without Steve Sloan, who had chosen Alabama despite the knowledge that he would be playing in Namath's shadow for two years. Gene Stallings had recruited Sloan out of high school in Cleveland, Tennessee. He was sought after by several other schools, including Tennessee. The courting process became too intense at one point; he excused himself, left the recruiters alone in his living room, and "went out to pray for guidance." When he came back a half-hour later, he had been guided. "I want to thank all of you. I appreciate it, and I'm flattered. But I'm going to Alabama."

The 1964 team had scratched out four come-from-behind wins, but, said their coach, "the 1965 group was even more amazing." The players did not look that amazing in the opening game of the season, losing to Georgia 18–17 on a controversial "flea-flicker" touchdown pass late in the game, when the Georgia receiver's knees either touched the ground or were close to doing so when he lateraled the ball back to another Georgia receiver.

The following week, says Jerry Duncan, "He tore us a new one in practice. A couple of the new players had never seen him like this, and it was

more than they could take and they quit." The players responded by beating Tulane 27–0, but Bryant wasn't satisfied. During a practice for the Ole
Miss game, Bryant decided he needed to shake things up. "Coming down
from the tower," says Duncan, "he told the team, 'If I don't see some change
here, there's gonna be some different jerseys in the starting lineup.'" Later,
he had the team manager summon them out of the showers, announcing,
says Duncan, a 5:30 a.m. practice. Bryant remembered it a bit differently—
he said he told them to be on the field at "six o'clock tomorrow morning,
because we're going to get this thing done." (A practice at 5:30 sounds
more like Bryant.) Any player who was late would be off the team; any
coach who was late would be fired. Everyone showed up on time.

Bryant's recollection of his pre-practice speech sounds a little tame:
"You're here to go to school, to get an education, but you're also here to
play football. It works both ways. You promised to give your best. Now, if
you don't like this, go on home. Tomorrow morning you're going to give
your best or you're going to quit." Duncan remembers a slightly different
speech: "He said, 'Y'all looked like shit out there. You should be ashamed to
hold hands with your girl friends.'" The practice didn't last more than
twenty minutes, but according to Duncan, "We got the message."

Or perhaps not. At halftime, the Tide found itself trailing a good Mississippi team 9–0. Having failed with the bad-cop approach, Bryant decided
to switch tactics and play good cop. "We expected a real chewing out,"
says Sloan, "but I guess he figured that would just distract us from our goal
at a point when we needed focus. I've never seen him as calm at a game as
he was giving us our halftime instructions. He was almost friendly. He
pointed out on the blackboard where we had made some costly mistakes,
but, he said he was confident we'd get them straightened out, and that
we'd win—in the fourth quarter." With just under six minutes left in the
game, Alabama was down 16–10 with a first down on its own eleven-yard
line. "I'll never know how we came back," says Sloan. "Three times we
had to make a fourth-down play in order to keep the ball. Each time we
made it." Sloan scored the winning touchdown with less than a minute
left. Afterward, Bryant told his team, that it was "the gutsiest performance
I've ever seen."

The comeback against Ole Miss put the season back on track for
Alabama, despite one big bump in the road in the fifth week against Tennessee in Birmingham. Late in the game, with the ball on the Tennessee

two-yard line and the score tied 7–7, Ken Stabler, in for Steve Sloan, threw a pass out of bounds on fourth down. Bryant was so angry that he knocked the dressing room door off its hinges. He then cooled off and apologized to everyone, blaming the screwup on himself and saying, "If I had to do it over, I would have stayed home and just sent you boys to Birmingham. You would have won if I hadn't been there. That was the most disorganized bench, the most disorganized game plan, the most disorganized everything I've ever seen." But, he told them after a pause, he thought they still had it in them to be national champions if they wanted it badly enough. And, he told them, he thought they did.

With a loss and a tie in their first five games, the players may not have believed Bryant, but they played as if they did, and the Tide roared back, winning five straight games, scoring thirty points or more in the last three, and posting two shutouts. Alabama finished the regular season strong with a 30–3 shellacking of Auburn. What Bryant was banking on was that this season the national championship would be decided in the major bowl games, as the wire services had agreed to delay their final vote until after January 1, 1966. Michigan State, seeded number one, was slated to play UCLA in the Rose Bowl, while Arkansas, number two, was to play Louisiana State— whom Alabama had already beaten 31–7 at Baton Rouge—in the Cotton Bowl. That left Alabama, number four, against number-three Nebraska in the last game, the Orange Bowl.

To motivate his players, Bryant outlined the scenario on a blackboard: UCLA, he told them, would defeat Michigan State—no small task, as the Spartans, coached by Bryant's friend Duffy Daugherty, were unbeaten and favored by more than a touchdown. LSU, also an underdog, would upset Arkansas. Simple, he said. All that left was for his boys to go out and beat Nebraska, a team that had a 10–0 record to their 8-1-1, that had outscored their opponents by an average of twenty-three points per game, and that outweighed Alabama by at least twenty-five pounds a man—and perhaps as much as thirty-five pounds on the offensive and defensive lines. Simple. Oh, and there was one more thing. Before the game, Bryant took his starting quarterback, Steve Sloan, aside and said, "Steve, I've thought this through, and we're not gonna win the national championship if we only win by a point or two. We're gonna have to win big. We're gonna play this whole game like we're coming from behind, like we're behind by fourteen points."

Earlier that day, incredibly, events began to unfold as Bryant had told his players they would. LSU slipped by third-ranked Arkansas, 14–7, in the Sugar Bowl. The Rose Bowl, which was in the second quarter, would take care of itself; all the Crimson Tide needed to do was go out and beat Nebraska. Alabama took the field in a fury.

As he did so often over the years before an important game, Bryant radically changed his game plan to fit the situation. Fifteen years earlier at Kentucky, against a bigger, stronger Oklahoma team, he had ordered Babe Parilli to come out throwing to keep the Sooners off balance. Now, against Nebraska, he did the same thing. After studying Alabama's game films, Nebraska coach Bob Devaney was convinced the Tide would play the kind of conservative, ball-control attack it had used all year. The Tide could pass; Nebraska knew that. In Sloan and Stabler Alabama had two superb quarterbacks who could strike from anywhere on the field. Ray Perkins and Dennis Homan, two All-America wide receivers, were capable of making big catches against, if need be, double coverage. But for most of the year, Alabama had used the pass as a secondary weapon. On this night, it took center stage. On the first play from scrimmage, the offense ran Bryant's favorite trick play, a tackle-eligible pass to Jerry Duncan, a play in which the offensive tackle reports to the official as an eligible receiver and lines up a step back from the line. The play caught Nebraska flat-footed and gained thirty-five yards. "I was so nervous," says Duncan, "that I just stood there when Steve [Sloan] called the play in the huddle. I thought, 'Damn, I can't believe this. We're playing for the national championship and they're going to throw the ball to *me*?' Then I caught it and rumbled downfield, and I got hit, and it felt good. I got up thinking, 'Damn, that was great. Let's run that play again!' And you know what? We did. Steve called it *again*, and *again* I caught it, and *again* we got a first down. There was no stopping us after that."

Nebraska's defensive line featured two future NFL draft choices, Walt Barnes, who weighed in at over 240, and Tony Jeter, who was about 230. The offensive guard who was switched back and forth on both of them was John Calvert, who weighed 178 pounds. Like a middleweight swarming all over a heavyweight, the Alabama linemen slammed into their Cornhusker opposites, taking just enough heat off Steve Sloan to allow him time to get the ball to Perkins and Homan, breaking free in the Nebraska secondary. Bryant pulled out all the stops; ahead 21–7 just before the half, he called for an onside kick, which his kicking team snatched out of the hands of the shocked Nebraska kick-return unit. Sloan quickly moved Alabama into position, and the Tide kicked a field goal just before the half ended, to take a 24–7 lead at halftime. In the locker room, Bryant broke the news to his boys: the UCLA Bruins had scored a shocking 14–3 upset over the top-ranked Spartans in the Rose Bowl. Alabama was just thirty minutes from its third national championship in five years.

What Bryant didn't tell them was that the news would also fire up Nebraska, which stood now as the only unbeaten team in the nation. In the second half, recalls Jerry Duncan, "Nebraska came at us with everything they had. We came right back at them. If we hadn't, if we had slacked off one bit, we would have lost." The Huskers scored three touchdowns in the second half, but Alabama came back with two more, actually wearing down the far larger Nebraska defense and rushing for more yards in the fourth quarter than Nebraska did the entire game. As the score kept increasing, Bryant turned to his offensive coordinator, Howard Schnellenberger, and said, "Isn't this the damnedest way to win a football game? I promise you this will never happen again." Bryant had no way of knowing that within a couple of years, games like this would be the norm.

The final score was 39–28. Alabama had gained an extraordinary 518 yards, 296 of them through the air; Perkins in particular had embarrassed the Cornhuskers, catching ten passes. The Tide scored thirty-nine points against a Nebraska defense that had given up just ninety points all season.

Bryant loved the 1965 team—Jerry Duncan, Cecil Dowdy, Johnny Calvert, Bruce Stephens, Jimmy Carroll, Steve Sloan, Ray Perkins, and all the rest—for their spirit and flair. "I don't think," he would later say, "any team of mine ever enjoyed themselves more in a game. Just wild, reckless fun." Pudge Heffelfinger, who had once voiced his admiration for southern players for their "reckless abandon, a wild fanaticism," would have appreciated the team.

In the jubilation of the Alabama locker room that New Year's night, no one could have known that it was the end of an era. The 1965 Alabama Crimson Tide was not, as is often said, the last all-white team to win a national championship. That distinction would fall on Darrell Royal's 1970 Texas Longhorns and would escape the notice of future historians, largely because Texas was not associated with church bombings or public officials hosing black demonstrators in the streets. Many people have thought it was the last all-white college championship team because it was *Bear Bryant's* last all-white championship football team. Seventeen years later, in his eulogy for Bryant, Howell Raines, who would later become the top editor of the *New York Times*, wrote,

> In preparing that team [1965] for an Orange Bowl game with an integrated Nebraska team, Bryant provided an example of simple decency around which the state could rally. He enforced a rigid discipline of sportsmanship on the team that went beyond a ban on dirty tactics and racial taunts. The Alabama players' insistence on helping fallen opponents to their feet bordered on the comic. But the intention was not to humiliate or patronize their rivals. It was, as everyone in Alabama knew, to show the national sports audience that the state's football team was more civilized than its governor. Alabama played with a kind of desperate politeness. . . . If Bryant had refused to confront Wallace, his team had at least shown that Alabamians were capable of sane conduct in a racially charged environment.[8]

IN 1965 the Reverend Billy Graham spoke to a crowd of more than eighteen thousand at Denny Stadium. One of the topics was civil rights, and the audience was perhaps the largest integrated gathering seen in Alabama up to that time. A storm broke as Reverend Graham delivered a message about racial tolerance; lightning struck the stage, sparking the microphone.

Graham immediately sat down and leaned over to make a comment to Bear Bryant, who was also scheduled to speak: "Coach, you'd have stopped, too, if that lightning had hit you like that."

Bear was adamant: "No, sir!"

"Why not?"

Bryant replied, "When I'm down on the one-yard line, I don't stop until I score."

At that, Reverend Graham returned and completed his message.

BY THE MID-1960s, Bryant, having done it for over twenty-five years, had grown to hate the recruiting process and resented the amount of time it took away from actual coaching. But Pat Dye, who joined the Alabama coaching staff in 1965, still regards Bryant as "the greatest recruiter I've ever seen. When he set his mind to it, he got just about any boy he wanted."

His name was Joe Kelley. A much sought-after quarterback from Ozark, Alabama, he attracted coaches from all over the country, including Nebraska's Bob Devaney, Michigan State's Duffy Daugherty, and, of course, Auburn's Shug Jordan. Dye drove with Bryant down to Ozark to find the rival coaches already in the Kelleys' living room making their pitch. Bryant walked in smiling and shook hands with all the Kelley family and friends, then greeted all his fellow coaches, who looked at him warily as they smiled back. After the introductions, Mrs. Kelley announced that she would be serving snacks to everyone. Bryant spoke up immediately: "Mrs. Kelley, you just stay put. I'll be happy to get you something. Would you like a cookie with your coffee?" "Coach Bryant went right into the kitchen," Dye recalls. "When he called back to her and said, 'Mrs. Kelley, how do you like your coffee?' the other coaches just stared. They knew they had lost that recruiting battle."

Despite his dislike of recruiting, Bryant never lost his knack for knowing how to reel in a blue-chipper. Even as late as 1974, eager to land Barry Krauss, he put in a personal appearance at the Krauss's home in Pompano Beach, Florida. "I walked in," says Krauss, "and there was the greatest coach in football standing, waiting for me, with his hat in his hand. The fact that he had his hat off in our house made a big impression on my mother. She took his hat from him and put it on her head and had her picture taken with him. Afterwards, she said, 'Coach, I love this hat. Do you mind if I keep it?' But Coach Bryant wasn't taking any chances. He told her, 'Mrs. Krauss, I'm afraid the NCAA wouldn't allow that.'"

Look magazine, which had emerged as one of the principal rivals to the fading *Saturday Evening Post*, featured a profile of Bryant, "The Bear of Alabama," by senior editor Gerald Astor. Astor, a veteran journalist, painted a picture of Bryant as "a successful executive [who] finds himself smoking more now (two to three packs a day) and enjoying life less. During the fall, the Coach's appetite drops off. Friday, the one day he does not rise at 5:30 am for meetings, he takes a sleeping pill at that hour to force rest." There was a suggestion in some of Bryant's responses that the enormous strain of the job was starting to get to him. Before the first game of the 1965 season, Bryant told Astor, "I'd like to be behind a plow, just working up a good sweat."

Other responses, though, indicated that Bryant was willing to talk about some subjects that Alabama journalists were simply not asking him about. For instance, race. "We're not recruiting Negro athletes; that's a policy decision for others to make. But Negro players in Southeastern Conference games are coming." The statement startled many Alabamians,★ some of whom took it as a direct slap at Wallace. There was renewed talk of Bryant's interest in politics: "If you hear of me running for office, you'll know something's gone wrong." And then, "All those people urging me to go into politics, they make it sound good. But then I think how they cut you up in politics." But he wasn't saying no.

Frank Rose, in *Look* magazine, credited Bryant with being one of the "campus leaders" who helped "prepare the climate" for the "close to 100 Negroes we have on campus." Because of the contributions of Bryant and others, Rose said, the transition to integration was made without violence. "He talked to his boys about their responsibilities," Rose was quoted as saying, "and he talked to alumni, quietly. He's committed to the total university."[9] Rose sounded very much like a man who knew which way the winds were blowing but was afraid of too much wind too soon. Clearly his best and perhaps his only public relations weapon against George Wallace was Bear Bryant.

FOR YEARS, the rules restricting substitutions had been whittled away; by 1964 there were no longer any limits on the number of substitutions a coach could make, and by 1965, coaches were beginning to understand how radically the game had changed. Exactly why college football headed in this direction in the 1950s has never been satisfactorily explained. Howard Schnellenberger, who would eventually become head football

---

★ I have a vivid memory of being with my father in a Mobile truck stop as four men poured over the article on the counter, drinking coffee. Someone read the headline from the story, "Negro Players in Southeastern Conference Games Are Coming." There was silence for a moment, then, finally, one of the men said, "Well, I hope there're some Negro linebackers available. We need linebackers."

coach at the University of Miami (and help accelerate the evolution of college football into a junior version of the pro game) insists, "It didn't happen by design, the game just evolved that way. It was the inevitable pull towards pro football. Pro football got their players from college, and when the players came back from the pros to coach in college they taught pro techniques and strategy."

The elimination of substitution rules immediately manifested itself in the expansion of rosters and the heights and weights of the players. With no limits on substitutions, coaches began to recruit more and more talent. Stamina was no longer as important as it once was; you could send in a fresh player to spot a tired one at any time. A 260-pound lineman who might not have been able to carry that much weight through an entire game no longer had to; he didn't even have to carry it for *half* a game. And the combination of advances in nutrition and weight training put those 260-pounders over 290. At the beginning of the 1960s, many major college teams dressed no more than sixty players for the varsity team, but by the end of the decade nearly every major college team featured over 100 players and some as many as 130. Specialization was inevitable. From the early to late 1960s, football players went from being football players to being running backs or outside linebackers or free safeties—not players who played those positions much of the time, but players who played those positions *exclusively*.

Bear Bryant's initial response to the era of unlimited substitution was to ignore it. Like every other major power, Alabama doubled the size of its roster within a few seasons and the Tide's offensive and defensive game plan became more sophisticated. But in terms of size, Alabama's 1966 team looked like an average high school team today. To watch Alabama in 1966 was to watch a team fighting desperately against history and winning.

Bryant never called the 1966 team his favorite, but he always insisted that it was "the best I ever had and got done in by the ballot box. We were locked out of the national championship by Notre Dame and Michigan State, who got more attention by playing a 10–10 tie." But Bryant wasn't being entirely honest. He knew very well that it wasn't Notre Dame or Michigan State or even the sportswriters in one wire-service poll or the coaches in another that deprived the Alabama football team of the 1966 national championship. Alabama lost the title that year because of George Wallace.

FOR ALABAMA FANS, the 1966 season began with a surprise. The August 15 issue of *Sports Illustrated* showed Bryant not in the familiar lucky brown fedora that had been left at his home in Lexington by a Kentucky sportswriter many years before, but a black-and-white checked hat in a style referred to as "houndstooth."★ No one knows exactly where or from whom Bryant got the hat; a good bet would have been Charlie Finley, the flamboyant controversial owner of the Oakland A's and its Birmingham farm team, also called the A's. Within a year, though, Bryant benched the hat in favor of a style with bigger checks and a red feather. There is better evidence as to the person who gave him this model; in *Bear* there is a photo of his granddaughter, Mae Tyson, fitting the new checked hat on his head as a smiling Sonny Werblin, owner of the New York Jets, looks on. The houndstooth hat would become Bryant's trademark, but by the time he actually wore it during the football season he had already been coaching for twenty-one years and won three national championships.

Bryant's lucky houndstooth hat brought him and the Tide no luck at all in 1966, which would prove to be the most controversial and closely followed season in college football history. It was the football equivalent of a pennant race, with three monster teams battling it out each week in the wire-service polls and in the nation's sports pages. There were four teams, actually, as Nebraska was very nearly in a class with Alabama, Notre Dame, and Michigan State, though the Cornhuskers were to falter late in the season.

Alabama was the preseason favorite in most polls, not merely the defending national champions but the champions for two straight years. But nearly as many had favored Duffy Daugherty's Michigan State Spartans, who had very nearly won it all in 1965, going unbeaten in the regular season and losing in the Rose Bowl to UCLA and its much-heralded quarterback, Gary Beban, who would win the Heisman Trophy in 1967. Some held out for Notre Dame and its brilliant coach, Ara Parseghian, who, in Bryant-like fashion, had immediately reversed the fortunes of the Fighting Irish when he took over in 1964.

If Bryant made a mistake in the 1966 season, it was in not starting a

---

★ The cover story, "I'll Tell You About Football," was the first of a series of autobiographical articles, a collaboration between Bryant and *Sports Illustrated*'s John Underwood.

week earlier. The Spartans opened on September 17 with a 28–10 victory over North Carolina State and early the next week found themselves sitting atop both the Associated Press and United Press International polls, as they had for most of 1965. Alabama opened its season the following week, beating Louisiana Tech 34–0, but on the same day Michigan State trounced Penn State, 42–8, winning over eastern voters. Also on September 24, Notre Dame opened its season, announcing in grand fashion that it would be a three-way race by beating traditional rival Purdue and its fine quarterback, Bob Griese, 26–14, in a televised game. By October 15, Michigan State had established an average margin of victory of 20.5 points against its opponents, compared to Notre Dame's 25 and Alabama's 23.3.

Then, in the fourth game of the season, in Knoxville, Alabama stumbled. Tennessee was just a shade behind the top teams that season; the Volunteers would lose three games, all to fierce SEC competition, by a total of eleven points and go on to win the Gator Bowl against a Syracuse team with the running back combination of future All-Pros Floyd Little and Larry Czonka. On October 15, the Vols came within a wisp of beating Alabama. On a miserable gray, wet afternoon and on a muddy field, Bryant started things off in uncharacteristic fashion by choosing to accept the opening kick. Normally under bad playing conditions he would choose to kick off and put the pressure on the opposing team's offense, but for some reason in this game, he let his assistants talk him into receiving first. On the first snap fullback Mike Kelley fumbled the ball. Tennessee recovered and went in for a "cheap" score. Tennessee got another gift on the subsequent kickoff when the Tide, shockingly, fumbled the ball away again. This time, the Alabama defense stiffened, but the Vols kicked a field goal for a 10–0 lead at the half. "We went into the locker room expecting to get our butts handed to us," recalls Jerry Duncan. Instead, a funny thing happened: "Coach came in smiling, whistling 'What A Friend We Have in Jesus.' He started patting us on the back, telling us we'd played well but had made a mistake here and there, and that we needed to correct this or that in the second half, and that he was confident we were going to come back to win. It was really strange. By the time we went out for the second half, we had started to believe him." Slowly, in the third quarter the Alabama defense began to assert itself, and the Tennessee offense disappeared from the game until late in the fourth quarter.

So, too, did the Alabama offense—until the last twelve minutes in the final period. By then the field was in such horrendous condition that officials could scarcely see the yard markers, and Tennessee's 10–0 lead seemed insurmountable. Then and there, Ken Stabler redeemed himself for throwing the ball out of bounds on fourth down in the previous year's Tennessee game, and stepped forward to claim his place among the great Crimson Tide quarterbacks, running and passing on Alabama's only touchdown drive of the day. Bryant then made a gutsy decision. Reasoning that Alabama could count on just one more offensive possession, he chose to play for the win rather than the tie. The team would try for a two-point conversion—which had, at best, a 50–50 chance for success—instead of kicking the extra point, which was not a sure thing on a slippery field but which stood a much better chance than a run or pass. If successful, the Tide would be down by two points. Bryant was thinking ahead to the next kickoff, feeling certain his defense would stop Tennessee, force a punt, and give Alabama the ball in good enough field position to claw its way into place for a field goal; if the time left only allowed a try for a field goal, Bryant wanted that field goal to be for a win rather than a tie. The down side was that if Alabama failed on the two-point conversion try, it would be down 10–6 and need a miracle touchdown to win in what was almost certain to be the final minute.

Stabler got the two points, faking the ball to a runner and then firing a quick pass to Wayne Cook in the end zone. Alabama kicked off, the defense held, and with about four minutes to go Stabler and Alabama started on their own twenty-five yard line. As the rain came down harder, Stabler put together a Johnny Unitas–type drive, controlling the ball with short runs and then stretching the Tennessee defense with big passes, including a twenty-yard strike to his All-America wide receiver Ray Perkins. From the Tennessee twenty-six-yard line, Stabler kept the ball himself, rolling to his left and gaining eleven yards. Alabama gouged its way through the mud to the Tennessee one-yard line, where, on fourth down, kicker Steve Davis put the ball through the uprights, and Alabama led for the first time in the game, 11–10. The Alabama bench exploded in jubilation, but Bryant, remembering all the heartbreak he had suffered over the years at the hands of football players in orange and white uniforms, was not ready to celebrate.

Forced to do in the final minute what they had not been able to do the entire game, the Vols completed two long passes—the first from quarterback Dewey Warren and the second a steal of a classic Bryant maneuver, a surprise pass from halfback Charlie Fulton—and were down to Alabama's thirteen-yard line. Tennessee then moved to a first down on the Alabama two-yard line with sixteen seconds to play. All the Vols had to do was what Alabama had done about two minutes earlier: make a chip-shot field goal. As he had done so many times in his career and would continue to do, Bryant pulled an ordinary player out of the ranks and willed him into being a star. Donny Johnson, the son of a Birmingham preacher, had impressed Bryant in practice with his uncanny ability to get his hand on place kicks. Now he was called off the bench and asked to do it in the biggest game of his Alabama career. Ray Perkins threw in some extra incentive: "You block that kick," he told Donny, "and I'll give you my tickets the rest of the year."

Johnson did not block the kick, but his maddened rush from the left side of the Tennessee line forced the kicker to go at a right angle. The ball went high, over the right upright—for one incredible moment, no one in the stadium had any idea whether the kick was good or not. The next moment, the moans of fifty thousand Tennessee fans were drowned out by the hysterical cheers of a few thousand Alabama fans as the official signaled wide right. Though Johnson had not touched the ball, Bryant gave him credit for securing the win: if it had been straight, he said, Donny Johnson would have blocked it. Ray Perkins agreed; he gave Johnson the tickets.

ALABAMA BEAT Tennessee, in its only close contest all season, but lost in the polls as Notre Dame beat North Carolina 32–0, a victory that vaulted the Fighting Irish into first place after the Spartans, also playing on a wet field in Columbus, Ohio, squeaked by their traditional rivals, the Ohio State Buckeyes, 11–8. Now it was Notre Dame, Michigan State, and Alabama. On October 22, all three teams won impressively. Alabama beat Vanderbilt 42–0, but Notre Dame and Michigan State beat tougher opponents. The Irish trounced Oklahoma in Norman, 38–0, and the Spartans, playing at home, thrashed Bob Griese and Purdue even worse than Notre Dame had on opening day, 42–20. And so all three maintained perfect records until the weekend of November 19, when the Fighting Irish went to East Lansing to take on the Spartans.

The 1966 Notre Dame–Michigan State game was perhaps the most hyped contest in college football history. Ara Parseghian had pumped new enthusiasm into Notre Dame fans across the country; for its October 28 issue, *Time* magazine chose Notre Dame's sensational sophomores, quarterback Terry Hanratty and split-end Jim Seymour, for its cover, making them the youngest football players ever to appear on the cover of the magazine. The Irish had several consensus All-America players, including a dazzling half-Irish, half-Mexican halfback and kick returner, Nick Eddy, linebacker Jim Lynch, and defensive end Alan Page, and at least a dozen other players who eventually made it to the NFL. The Spartans also had several All-Americas, including halfback Clint Jones, wide receiver Gene Washington, roverback/linebacker George Webster (voted by some as the college football defensive player of the 1960s), and, the most hyped of all, 290-pound defensive lineman Bubba Smith.

Fans and sportswriters across the country debated which team should be number one, but no one thought that Alabama was in the same class with Notre Dame or Michigan State in overall talent. The Tide had several All-America candidates, including offensive tackle Cecil Dowdy, who weighed under 210 pounds, defensive back Bobby Johns, and wide receivers Ray Perkins and Dennis Homan. Kenny Stabler would eventually prove to be a better quarterback than either Hanratty or Michigan State's Jimmy Raye, but Bryant didn't allow him to throw enough passes to make a serious All-America bid. Man-for-man, the Tide didn't appear to belong in the same comparisons with the Irish and Spartans. Nonetheless, the Tide stayed on the heels of the Irish and Spartans throughout the fall. Alabama fans' attitude was best summed up by a cartoon by Murray Olderman, which ran in the *New York Post* on Tuesday, November 15, four days before Notre Dame and Michigan State played. The cartoon depicted a colossal Notre Dame player, holding a flag that represents his school, racing to the top of a mountain peak labeled "No. 1." On the opposite side of the peak, a colossal Michigan State player, carrying his school's flag, is running to the top. To the right of that peak is another, just as high as the "No. 1" peak but with no number. A little guy in a football uniform with the letters "'Bama" written across his chest, stands with his hands on his hips, exclaiming, in a clear tone of indignation, "I could knock both of them off!"

The result Alabama fans wanted most to the Notre Dame–Michigan State game was a tie. The last thing in the world they expected was to get one.

Notre Dame played without an injured Nick Eddy, and early in the game lost its center, George Goeddeke, and then Terry Hanratty to injuries from hits by Bubba Smith. With a second-string diabetic quarterback named

Coley O'Brien, the Irish fought back to tie the game 10–10, and just missed winning in the last few minutes when a thirty-seven-yard field goal attempt went wide. This left number-one Notre Dame with a record of 8–0-1, number-two Michigan State with one of 9–0-1, and number-three Alabama at 9–0. Michigan State's season was over, but Notre Dame had one more game to play. In *Sports Illustrated*, Dan Jenkins assessed the situation: "Alabama's best chances lie ahead. So do Nebraska's. Both teams could wind up undefeated. And, should one beat the other in a bowl game, the winner would have an 11–0 record to glisten against the 9–0-1 of Notre Dame and Michigan State, neither whose schedules was *that much* fiercer than Alabama's or Nebraska's." Jenkins also noted that "there was mounting dissatisfaction with Notre Dame's policy of shunning bowls while at the same time gunning for a national championship, and with the irritating Big Ten rule that forbids a team from going to the Rose Bowl two years in a row. So long as Notre Dame and the Big Ten teams keep these policies, they perhaps deserve to be outpolled by an Alabama—as punishment."[10]

The week after the epic tie, the Irish went to Los Angeles and humiliated Southern California 51–0, leaving their All-America back Nick Eddy in the game just long enough to score the touchdown that would make it 44–0. Clearly, Ara Parseghian was out to impress the pollsters. One week later, on December 3, Alabama had a chance to do likewise at Birmingham's Legion Field against Auburn. But Bryant was out to make a different impression and seemed to be holding his team back, as if to say that 34–0, the game's final score, was bad enough, and that if he had to run up the score on a beaten opponent to impress voters, then the voters could go to hell.★ The week after the Alabama-Auburn game, the voters of AP and UPI told Alabama to go to hell, telling the only unbeaten, untied team in the country—the only team with ten victories, that it was only third best. Then, the wire-service polls added insult to injury: because Notre Dame and Michigan State, their number-one and number-two teams, could not play in bowl games, they would declare the voting over for the 1966 season. Once again, the bowl games would be irrelevant.

★ The 1966 Alabama-Auburn game was the first I attended. I will never forget the frustration of Alabama fans who were repeatedly calling for passes on third-down situations while Alabama stubbornly ran the ball up the middle. The father of my good friend Robert Studin, Sid, kept shouting, "C'mon, Bear, just one more touchdown! 41–0 will look great to the voters!"

———

WHAT IRKED Bryant the most was not so much losing the national championship as the manner in which Notre Dame had won it. Late in the Notre Dame–Michigan State game, with the ball on the Notre Dame thirty-yard line, facing into the wind with a diabetes-weakened second-string passer leading the team, Parseghian elected to have his quarterback fall on the ball and run out the clock, preserving the 10–10 tie rather than risking an interception. Notre Dame, he reasoned, had superior clout in the wire-service polls, and would almost certainly stay ahead of both Michigan State and Alabama. Parseghian knew the Irish still had the Southern Cal game on its schedule and that a victory would cement Notre Dame's first-place ranking. He was right, but the decision struck many, particularly Bryant, as cynical.

Eight years later, in *Bear*, Bryant had changed his mind, but only a little. If Notre Dame won the championship, Ara must have made the right decision. Bryant was being diplomatic, of course. He would no more have played for a tie to win the national championship than he would have run up the score on a beaten opponent to secure the top spot. Bryant knew something else too, which was that his drinking buddy and poker pal Duffy Daugherty had also turned down a chance to play for the win on the Spartan's last possession, when, on fourth down, and on his own home field, he chose to punt the ball away to the Irish. Michigan State was, after all, the number-two team, and Daugherty surely knew that if the game ended in a tie, the voting would favor Notre Dame. He was as obligated to try for the victory as Parseghian, but he chose to punt. History unfairly remembers Parseghian as the coach who settled for the tie, which only proves that if you don't want to be blamed for a tie, don't wind up as the last coach with the ball.

The 1966 season was a landmark in the history of college football. The controversy generated by the final vote stirred changes within college football's upper echelons. Within a couple of years, Notre Dame, which had not played in a postseason game since the 1927 Rose Bowl, dropped its ban on bowl games. The Big Ten eliminated the baffling rule that kept a team from going to the Rose Bowl in consecutive years; it also lifted the restriction that kept its other teams from going to other bowls.

The Notre Dame–Michigan State face-off also shook up television.

Because both schools had already had their one appearance per season allowed by the NCAA, the game was not initially scheduled for broadcast. As game time came near and lawsuits were threatened, ABC came up with a compromise: the game would be shown live in the East and Midwest and on tape delay in the rest of the country after the Tennessee-Kentucky game. Many fans in Alabama turned off their radios (just about the only way to get an early college football score back in 1966) so they could watch the game without knowing the outcome.* The public's response was an indication of the TV drawing power of college football: the Irish and Spartans drew more viewers than the first Super Bowl game between Green Bay and Kansas City, which would be played two months later.

The controversy created by the game was not lost on the pollsters. From then on, the major wire-service polls agreed to include the bowl games and would wait until after they were played to determine the final rankings. This did not placate Alabama fans, many of whom to this day are rankled over the injustice of the final 1966 vote; in sports bars and luncheonettes all over the state, one can still see faded bumper stickers which read "Notre Dame Plays Politics, 'Bama Plays Football" and "To Hell With AP and UPI—'Bama's No. 1!" The argument over the need for a college football playoff began in earnest, one that still has not been resolved.

With their size and strength—Notre Dame's defensive front four outweighed the front four on the NFL champion Green Bay Packers—the Irish and Spartans were the wave of the future in college football, especially the Spartans, whose major stars—Bubba Smith, George Webster, Clint Jones, Gene Washington, and Jimmy Raye—were black. Alabama, with its undersized, all-white team, was a relic of the past. Alabama fans who had always seen football as a distraction from the politics of everyday life now grumbled over the politics of college football, acting as though the prob-

---

* My family was in transit from the Northeast the day before the game. On Saturday afternoon, driving past Atlanta, we listened to the game on the Mutual Network, which broadcast the Notre Dame games nationwide. Just as we pulled into Birmingham, Notre Dame missed its attempt at a winning field goal. Unaware of the tape delay, I ran across the street to the home of a neighbor, Charlie Reagan, who (though an Auburn fan) had been waiting all month for the game, and proclaimed, "Mr. Reagan, you'll never believe what happened! They tied!" "Allen!" he exclaimed. "Now why did you have to go and ruin that for me?!" To my astonishment, the game had just started on TV.

lems of the outside world would never intrude on college football. The unspoken message of the 1966 final vote was unmistakably clear: segregated teams would no longer be welcome among college football's elite, even if they were coached by Bear Bryant.

Two years earlier, Alabama had played a bowl game for nothing but pride and had lost by inches. This time it would be playing for pride again, and Bear Bryant was determined to show the country what that meant. All season long the Nebraska Cornhuskers had been itching for a rematch with Alabama to avenge the previous season's Orange Bowl debacle. Nebraska was unbeaten through its first nine games and had outscored its opponents by 133 points. Then, on the last day of the regular season, the team lost a heartbreaker to its own archrival, the Oklahoma Sooners, 10–9, and were all but out of the national championship race. Again with a team outweighed by more than thirty pounds a man, Bryant fell back on the same strategy that had won him the national title the year before: pass early, run late. As it had in the Orange Bowl a year earlier, Alabama began the Sugar Bowl on a big play. On the first snap from scrimmage, Ken Stabler hit Ray Perkins with a forty-five-yard bomb to the Nebraska twenty-seven-yard line. The Nebraska defense never recovered. Alabama gouged out twenty-seven yards on seven plays, and Les Kelly scored the touchdown. Before the first quarter was over, Alabama led 17–0. At halftime, the score was 24–0, with three different Alabama players taking the ball into the end zone.

The previous year, Nebraska had mounted a furious second-half comeback, but this time it went down meekly, smothered by the Alabama defense. Alabama won the second half, 10–7, spending most of the final two periods on the ground controlling the ball. As in the Auburn game, it appeared that the Tide could have easily scored one or even two more touchdowns to impress the voters, but again Bryant was stubborn. His team, he seemed to be saying, was the best in the country and if the voters could not see that, then they were voting on something besides football. Stabler, who was voted the game's Most Valuable Player, riddled the Nebraska defense, completing twelve of seventeen passes for 218 yards, but threw just three passes in the second half. Nebraska coach Bob Devaney made no bones: "They are better than the score indicates. Alabama is the best football team I've ever seen."

In consecutive bowl games Alabama had now beaten two Nebraska teams, two very much larger Nebraska teams that had otherwise won nine-teen of twenty games, their only loss coming to their closest rival, Okla-homa, on their home field, by a single point. And Alabama had beaten those two Nebraska teams by a combined score of 73–35. If Jim Murray was ready to proclaim Alabama "Numero Uno" for slaughtering "certified bulls," he failed to say so.

Not every sports columnist outside of the South failed to acknowledge the Crimson Tide as the best. Bud Collins, writing in the *Boston Globe* on November 22, 1966, commented, "The US would be better off by trading the state to Europe for Spain or Switzerland, but until the deal can be made, we may as well recognize that our best team is located in Tuscaloosa."* In *Sports Illustrated* Dan Jenkins agreed emphatically. "Be truthful now, Notre Dame and Michigan State," he wrote in the January 9, 1967, issue,

Would you *really* want to play Alabama? Would you honestly care to spend an afternoon trying to swat those gnats who call themselves line-men and swirl around your ankles all day long? Why, heavens to Bear Bryant. Nobody ought to want to play Alabama unless it just plain enjoys going to football clinics, which is what last week's Sugar Bowl was—a clinic with the Bear instructing the nation on what a top team is sup-posed to look like.

The New Orleans game bore the only resemblance to a contest of importance as the collegiate season finally ended last Saturday and Mon-day with five bowl attractions. Alabama went into its game wanting to prove that it was as good, or better, than either Notre Dame or Michigan State by defeating a big, talented Nebraska team convincingly. It did exactly that, 34–7, with Bryant's second-and-third-stringing it through-out the damp afternoon. Had he not substituted mercifully, the score might have gone much higher. . . . No fewer than 12 different Alabama backs darted through and around Nebraska's huge but outquicked line

---

* In 1991, I met Bud Collins at the apartment of Marvin Miller, former executive direc-tor of the Major League Players Association. I reminded him of his remark back in 1966 and asked him what foreign country Boston deserved to be traded for in 1975 when white citizens, enraged over busing, threw rocks at school buses in which black children were riding. "South Africa," he replied.

anytime yardage was needed on the ground. Overall, Alabama's mistakes could have been charted on a postage stamp.

Jenkins composed a "best and worst of the bowls" chart. His All-Bowl Team featured Ray Perkins at end, Cecil Dowdy at offensive tackle, Jimmy Carroll at center, Ken Stabler at quarterback, Charles Harris at defensive end, Louis Thompson at defensive tackle, Bob Childs at linebacker, and Bobby Johns at defensive back. The best player in the bowls, he said, was Stabler. The best defender, Bobby Johns. Best kicker, Steve Davis. Best strategy was "Alabama's mixing inside traps with a wide variety of passes." Best offense was "Alabama, particularly in the first quarter." Best team was "Alabama, easy victor over Nebraska." Last laugh: "Bear Bryant on the country."

Chapter 9

Ebb Tide

Martin Luther King Jr. preached equality. Coach Bryant practiced it.

—*Ozzie Newsome*

THE FUTURE OF COLLEGE FOOTBALL would be shaped by a more sophisticated passing game, and it arrived with a bang in Alabama's first game of the 1967 season. In 1966, the Tide had led the nation in scoring defense, allowing just thirty-seven points during the regular season and recording six shutouts in ten games. On September 23, Florida State, with its pro-style, pass-and-catch combination of quarterback Kim Hammond and end Ron Sellers, stunned Alabama by putting up thirty-seven points, as many as the Tide had given up in all ten games the season before. At one point, Bryant became so frustrated with his defense's inability to contain Florida State that he yelled for his defensive coaches to put in a tackle named Ron Durby, whom he remembered as a pretty good pass rusher. "I want Durby in the game!" he shouted. "Somebody get Durby's ass in there." Pat Dye, who had joined the team just two years before, ran up and down the Alabama bench calling frantically, "Durby? Where's Durby?" Finally, says Dude Hennessey, "One of us worked up the nerve to tell Dye to tell Coach that Durby had graduated three years before." Bryant stood there with his hands on his hips and stared at Dye. After a moment, he said, "I don't give a damn if he *has* graduated. *I want his ass in the game!*"

Florida State's strategy was the one underdogs would increasingly employ when taking on the big boys: use bigger offensive linemen, the kind better suited for protecting the passer than blocking for the runner, then add more receivers, spread them out, and throw. The combination of liberalized passing rules and the more sophisticated offenses that followed in the wake of "two-platoon" football made the pass less of a risk, and teams that couldn't match Alabama's depth would increasingly attack the Tide through the air. Fortunately for Alabama in 1967, its own passer, Kenny Stabler, was probably the best in the nation.

Ken "Snake" Stabler—he earned the nickname when his coach at Foley (Alabama) High School said, "That boy runs like a snake!"—had been considering both Auburn and Alabama, but Bryant snared him without trying too hard. He came to dinner at the Stablers' house in Foley, near the Gulf Coast, and talked about hunting and fishing. Ken was hypnotized.

Stabler was the second coming of Namath, a left-handed version, Bryant thought, of Joe. The similarities were uncanny. Like Namath, he had a rough childhood and a shaky relationship with his father, Leroy "Slim" Stabler, who suffered from the lingering effects of trauma from combat in World War II, particularly during the Anzio invasion. One day he arrived home from high school to find the rest of his family backed into a corner by his father, who was brandishing a shotgun. Kenny had to wrestle the gun away from his dad.★ Like Namath, he was a fantastic high school athlete, recruited by Major League Baseball; he turned down twenty thousand dollars from the Yankees. (He was in pitching duels a few times with the ace for Pensacola's Tate High School, Don Sutton, including a memorable 1–0 win, the only decision Sutton lost in high school.) At Alabama, in his sophomore year, he spent as much time at safety as he did at quarterback, and some felt he tackled well enough to have a future on the defensive side of the ball. Much like Namath, he caroused and womanized his way into

---

★ On his Web site (www.snakesplace.com/rookiehistory/asp), Stabler pays tribute to his dad, saying he taught him to love "sports, fast cars, and music." He also credits his father as having "swayed him to football in the ninth grade with a fast 1954 Ford. A tough critic because he knew his son had the ability, he pushed him to be his very best."

sections of newspapers that didn't cover sports. Like Namath, he took Alabama to an undefeated season, and like Joe, he sustained a near-crippling knee injury that would eventually cut his pro career short. Like Namath, he would go on to win a Super Bowl, with John Madden's Oakland Raiders in 1977, and, like him, he would be the subject of a headline-making suspension.

That would come in his senior year, 1967. Long before that, there was a difficult period of adjustment. From his tower Bryant saw every mistake his young players made, and when they failed to correct them, he would come down and let them know in terms harsher than their high school coaches had used. In *Snake*, Stabler remembers thinking Bryant would end up killing them.

In his first game, Stabler, per the game plan, called for a pitchout, but before he could toss the ball to the running back, he spotted Ray Perkins breaking free from his coverage. He fired the ball to him, and Perkins took it in for a touchdown. Kenny went to the sidelines expecting Bryant's praise for thinking on his feet. "One thing you should know, son," Bryant said to him, "is you can never trust left-handed crap shooters and left-handed quarterbacks."[1] It was Bryant's way of saying, okay, good job, but don't get too used to winging it. Stabler didn't quite get the message. In the next game, he changed a play Bryant had sent in. Stabler's call resulted in a first down which set up a touchdown, but on the sidelines Bryant said to him, "When I send in something, you don't have to call it. Run what you like—but you make goddamned sure it works!"[2] Stabler had no way of knowing that Bryant's attitude had evolved a great deal since a game at Maryland twenty years earlier, when he chewed out running back Jimmy Allen for scoring a touchdown after hitting the wrong hole.

Bryant's attitude also showed maturity after Stabler's most famous blunder, the out-of-bounds pass on fourth down that left Alabama tied with Tennessee in their 1965 meeting. When Stabler came to the sidelines after throwing the pass, Bryant walked up to him, hand on hips, and inquired about his sanity. After the game, Stabler followed Bryant to the visitor's locker room at Neyland Stadium to get his chewing out. The door was still locked, and Bryant was in no mood for the key. He hit the door with his right forearm, knocking it off its hinges, and told all the assistant coaches and nonplayers to leave. Stabler's heart was pounding. But instead of chewing out his players, Bryant took a deep breath and proceeded to apologize for "not preparing you people well enough to win the game today. It was us, not you, who lost that game. I'm sorry." Stabler held back his tears: "No wonder we all loved that man."[3]

In spring practice before the 1967 season, Stabler tore a cartilage in his knee. He was the best player on the team, and Bryant knew it; taking no chances, he told Kenny to sit out the rest of the spring drills. Depressed at the possibility of his future going down the drain, Stabler began cutting classes and eventually went back to Foley and rehabbed with beer, hot rods, and girls. Bryant had no objection that, but had no patience with players who didn't attend class, particularly quarterbacks. Kenny thought he had gotten away with something until, getting out of bed late one morning at his mother's house, he received a telegram: "You have been indefinitely suspended. Coach Paul W. Bryant." Stabler got the message. And if he didn't, he certainly got it when he received a second telegram a few hours later from Joe Namath. It was three words long: "He means it."[4]

Stabler decided that Bear Bryant and Alabama football could go to hell and embarked on an intense campaign of partying. Jimmy Sharpe, recruiting in Mobile, ran into Stabler and tried to talk some sense into him. (Clem Gryska suggests that Bryant may have dispatched Sharpe to Mobile precisely for the purpose of "accidentally" bumping into Stabler.) Sharpe couldn't change Kenny's mind. Fortunately for Stabler, his father was smart enough to realize that the war in Vietnam was reaching its height and that an unmarried college student without a scholarship was draft fodder. Slim Stabler asked a lawyer friend to fake a letter from the draft board stating in no uncertain terms that if Ken was not back in school by the fall, he would be eligible for induction.[5] Stabler returned to Tuscaloosa, got a job loading trucks, and went to talk to Sharpe and another assistant coach, Pat Dye. "We told him," says Dye, "that the first thing he better do is get his butt back in school and then go and tell the Coach that he'd done it." Stabler immediately enrolled in summer school, signing up for one more credit than he needed (though, he says, two of the courses were "Modern Dance" and "Marriage and the Family"). After he enrolled, he went to Bryant's office and told the Coach of his intention to return to the football team. Bryant just stared at him. Finally, after a long drag on his Chesterfield, Bryant told him, "Stabler, you don't deserve to be on my football team." Stabler hesitated, but finally told Bryant, "Well, Coach, I'm coming out anyway."[6] Stabler left Bryant's office assuming he was off the team. As he was packing his suitcase, Jimmy Sharpe came up to tell him that his determination had won Bryant over—he would get his chance. Elated, he bought a case of beer and drank every can on the way back to Foley, throwing the empties at stop signs.

When Stabler showed up for the first day of preseason practice, the most valuable player of the 1967 Sugar Bowl found he had been given not a red jersey, which signified first team, or a white jersey, worn by the second team, or any of the other colors used to distinguish different levels of the squad. In his basket Stabler found a brown jersey—the only one handed out in that color. Stabler did not need a professor to help him figure out what it symbolized. The next couple of weeks were rough, but "I never considered quitting," says Stabler. "He challenged me, and I was going to let him know that whatever he put in my way, I intended to be the starting quarterback of that team when the season began."[7]

He wasn't. In the opener against Florida State in Tuscaloosa, Joe Kelley started at quarterback. Stabler, helmet on his head and hands on his hips, stood on the sidelines and said nothing. On the second series, Bryant waved him in. It was none too soon for either one of them.

ROONE ARLEDGE sent an ABC crew to Birmingham the week of the Alabama–Florida State season opener to shoot footage for a documentary—*Coach Bryant: Alabama's Bear*—narrated by Chris Schenkel. The timing was unfortunate; for the first time in his Alabama career, Bryant did not seem to be fully in charge of his game situations, and his players, mirroring their coach's confusion, did not perform with the usual snap and verve. There were other unfortunate choices, particularly the use of a country song, "The Ballad of the Bear" ("It's the ballad of the Bear, you can hear it everywhere"), which Bryant hated. The best part of the show was a trip back to Fordyce with carefully staged "accidental" meetings between Bryant and several old friends and family members. In Kilgore's General Store, cousin Dean cheerfully related stories of Paul's clumsiness serving customers as a teenager, while Bryant grinned in the background. On the street, Bryant "accidentally" bumped into his old English teacher: "How are ya, Sweetie?" "Bear, you want to come back to English class?" "I need to," he responds.

As he was about to walk into the Kilgore store, Bryant delivered a telling ad-lib. With his third eye on the camera, he tells everyone to "be sure to watch my mule there. I'm afraid I might have to go back to plowing this afternoon."

EVEN WITH Stabler's offensive fireworks, Alabama was lucky to escape with a tie against Florida State. The Tide won its next three games, but in week five, against Tennessee, the cracks showed. The 24–13 loss at the hands of the Vols was the most thorough licking Alabama had taken since losing to Tennessee, 20–7, back in 1960—but that game had been in Knoxville, and this one was in front of the home folks in Birmingham. For the first time since 1961, an Alabama team faced a November without national championship implications. It could have been worse than that. On the last day of the season, Alabama played its traditional game with Auburn in Birmingham. In the fourth quarter, with about eleven minutes to play, Auburn punter Tommy Lunceford couldn't field a low, wet snap from the center, and Alabama recovered the ball at Auburn's forty-seven. "Kenny Stabler stood in the middle of the muck in the middle of Legion Field," said Birmingham News's Benny Marshall, "and at this moment, this was Auburn's football game because John Riley had kicked a 38-yard field goal in the third quarter and because Auburn had been master of the day, which grew darker and wetter and windier."[8] Stabler took that moment to make the most famous play of his college career. Rolling to his right on the option—not the easiest play for a left-handed quarterback—he saw that the running back who was trailing him was covered, kept the ball, turned the corner, skirted forty-seven yards down the sidelines, and scored the game's only touchdown.★

Stabler's career at Alabama ended on a sour note. With an 8–1–1 record, Alabama accepted an invitation to the Cotton Bowl. Bryant had wanted a match with the 8–2 Nebraska team in the Liberty Bowl, for the third matchup between Alabama and Nebraska in five years. He called Bob

---

★ It was the most spectacular play I have ever seen live in a football game. My mother had driven me to Legion Field to buy some souvenirs for cousins visiting from out of town, and as I jogged through the rain up to the souvenir stand at the gate, I realized the gate was wide open. I decided to go in just as the security people, hot dog vendors, and everyone else yelled and ran toward the end zone. I had a bird's-eye view of Stabler streaking down the sideline, and thousands of fans leaving their seats as he ran past them—perhaps the first version of "the wave" ever seen at Legion Field.

Devaney in Lincoln to set it up. "Bob," he told him, "neither of us are good enough to get one of those big bowl game bids, so why don't we try to get together again?" Devaney was wary after having seen his Cornhuskers thrashed by Alabama on New Year's Day after both the 1965 and 1966 seasons. "I told Paul that sounded good to me. That's when I called the Sun Bowl and told them Nebraska would accept an invitation to play down there. At that point, Paul Bryant had hooked me enough."

The 1967 Southwest Conference champion, and Alabama's opponent in the Cotton Bowl, was Texas A&M, which, since 1964, had been coached by Gene Stallings. Bryant had a ball trying to upstage his former player and assistant coach at pregame functions. At a press conference two days before the game, Bryant appeared in a checked sports coat, charcoal gray slacks, white shirt, and a blue-striped tie. Stallings walked in looking as if he had just come from practice, in a sweat-stained A&M baseball cap, muddy khaki pants, and hunting boots. At the press conference the next day, Stallings wore a tuxedo. He walked into the pressroom to find Bryant already there, dressed in a cowboy shirt with a bandana and a ten-gallon hat, and his trousers tucked into cowboy boots.

Answering questions from the press, Stallings, trying to out "poor-mouth" Bryant, suggested that A&M had recruited well that year, although "we recruited a bunch of kids who couldn't play for Alabama." Without missing a beat, Bryant lobbed back, "Well, hell, Bebes, we still have some you recruited. *They* can't play for Alabama either." So similar were the teams in style and strategy that one wise-cracking reporter asked Stallings if they both said the same team prayer in the locker room. "Yes, we do," replied Bebes. "It's called the Lord's Prayer."

Bryant's good-natured gamesmanship was aimed at getting a mental edge on his former pupil, to keep him off balance and a bit unfocused. But in the game itself it was Alabama that was unfocused, losing 20–16, as several of Bryant's old A&M players—John David Crow, Jack Pardee, Charlie Krueger, and Dennis Goehring—stood on the sidelines rooting against their old coach for the first and only time in their lives. With about twenty seconds left, A&M intercepted a pass from Stabler and walked off with the win. Bear and Bebes met at midfield and embraced. Foregoing the handshake, Bryant reached down and lifted Stallings up onto his shoulders and, in full sight of millions watching on national TV, unsteadily carried him off the field. Stallings grinned, but looked relieved when Bryant finally put him down.

Alabama finished the season as it had played much of it—slightly out of kilter. Bryant, for one, felt that in some not-quite-definable way he had lost his handle on the team. It began with Stabler. His failure to be firm with Kenny had a bad effect on the team's morale. But as Bryant would say in his autobiography, "I don't blame Kenny." Nor did Stabler blame Bryant. "He saved my ass," Stabler said later. "It's as simple as that. I never would have had a pro career without him." Stabler was drafted by the Oakland Raiders. In 1970, he found himself fighting to take the first-string job away from Daryle Lamonica. The third-string quarterback was a forty-three-year-old veteran playing out a Hall of Fame career, George Blanda, and he and Ken Stabler had some great Bear Bryant stories to swap during their golf games.

Bryant's problems at Alabama were a great deal more complex than a rebellious quarterback, and he knew it. "I'm the chairman of the board. I'm the one who's responsible." The 1960s had finally arrived in Alabama.

THE 1967 SEASON was only a disappointment by the standards of the previous six, which, to be sure, were ridiculously high, but 1968 was a disappointment by the standards of many, and 1969 and 1970 were disappointments by the standards of most. In an end-of-the-decade NCAA-conducted poll, the nation's coaches, athletic directors, and PR people overwhelmingly selected the Crimson Tide as the team of the decade and Bear Bryant as the coach of the decade. However, for all intents and purposes, "the decade" meant 1960 through 1967. Bryant had shaken up the game and dominated it, but college football had changed, and Bear Bryant had not changed with it.

In 1968 the Crimson Tide took the field with another smallish, all-white team featuring an extraordinary straight drop-back passer, Scott Hunter, and little else. After eeking out two unimpressive victories, they sputtered to a 10–8 loss to Ole Miss, whipped Vanderbilt, lost a 10–9 squeaker to Tennessee at Knoxville in week five, then proceeded to win five straight games by the uncomfortable margin of less than eight points per contest. Alabama fans will usually concede that whatever else happens, any season in which Alabama beats its three major rivals—Tennessee, LSU, and Auburn—cannot be counted as a bad one. But 1968 tested that thesis. Alabama accepted a bid to the Gator Bowl against Missouri, and for the second year in a row gave a flat postseason performance, losing 35–10 to an underdog Tigers.

No one in Alabama was ready to openly criticize Bryant; every coach and team has a down period. Give him a season or so, the home folks felt, and Bear would recruit a new batch of studs, and they would be right back on top. But things got worse. In 1969 and 1970 Alabama won just twelve of twenty-three games, losing in consecutive years to Tennessee by ugly scores (41–14 in 1969 and 24–0 in 1970), to LSU twice (20–15 and 14–9), and, worst of all, to Auburn (49–26 and 33–28). The 1969 defeat by the Volunteers was particularly galling to Bryant. John Forney, the Alabama broadcaster, later admitted that Alabama had looked so bad that he spent some airtime in the second half talking about airplanes flying over Legion Field on the way to the Birmingham airport so he wouldn't have to comment on the game. In the *Birmingham News* on October 19, Tennessee's All-America linebacker, Steve Kiner, was quoted as saying that the Alabama players he faced "didn't seem to have pride in that red jersey anymore."

The 1969 Liberty Bowl against Colorado was a horror, a 47–33 loss to a stronger, more talented team. Many dared to say aloud that Alabama didn't deserve to be playing in the Liberty Bowl, that it was only there because of recent achievements and Bear Bryant's reputation. They were right.

The next year, 1970, was no better, featuring such humiliations as a shutout by Tennessee and a loss in Birmingham to LSU. What particularly stung was that both defeats came at the hands of Bryant's former pupils, who were beginning to fill out coaching ranks throughout the South. Charlie McClendon had started at LSU in 1962; Bill Battle had taken over the reins at Tennessee that season.

The season was capped off by a sloppy 24–24 tie against a not particularly distinguished Oklahoma team in the Astro Bluebonnet Bowl. The only saving grace was that against the Sooners Bryant got his first up close look at the wishbone formation.

From 1968 through 1970, the Alabama defense recorded not a single shutout. There was just one memorable game during the entire three-year span, and, victory or no, it was not the kind of game Bear Bryant ever wanted to see one of his teams play again. On October 4, 1969, at Legion Field in the third game of the season, Scott Hunter and Archie Manning squared off in a nationally televised game that came to be known as "The Shootout." Hunter threw twenty-nine passes and gained 300 yards; Manning, with less run support, threw fifty-two times and gained 436 yards. "It was one of those games," recalls Clem Gryska, "that seemed like it was going to be decided by whichever team had the ball last."

Leading 26–21 early in the fourth quarter, on a third-and-fourteen play, Manning dodged a tackler and completed a pass for twenty-five yards and a first down. Bryant tossed his Chesterfield to the ground and stalked the sidelines looking for defensive coach Ken Donahue. "Dammit, Ken, what coverage were we in on that play?" Before Donahue could mumble an answer, Bryant told him he was fired. Scott Hunter, who had been talking strategy with another assistant coach, Jimmy Sharpe, was stunned. "Coach Bryant just fired Coach Donahue!" he whispered to Sharpe. Sharpe glanced up from his clipboard and told Hunter, "Don't worry about it. He's already fired him twice this half."

Hunter threw the winning touchdown pass after some confusion on the Alabama sideline. Neither Bryant nor Jimmy Sharpe nor Steve Sloan, who was trying to coordinate the passing attack from the press box, could come up with a play. As Hunter ran from the sidelines to the huddle, he heard Bryant yell, "Run the best thing you got!" It was good advice; Hunter passed to end George Ranager on a comeback pattern close to the goal line; Ranager caught the ball about knee high, spun around, broke through the grasp of the defensive back, and fell into the end zone for the go-ahead touchdown. Manning very nearly had the Rebels set up for a winning field goal try at the end of the game.

Chris Schenkel, who did the play-by-play for ABC, called it "the greatest duel two quarterbacks ever had." In an article written for *The Crimson Tide: An Illustrated History of Football at the University of Alabama*, Hunter recalled walking out on the field after the final gun and looking for Manning, "thinking what I could say to him, and when we finally met I realized there was nothing to say. How do you console a quarterback who just had one of the best games in college football's history and lost? We looked each other in the eyes and shook hands and both knew we had shared something so special that nothing needs to be said."[9] Special it was, but it was not Paul Bryant's kind of special. The nearly 750 yards gained through the air and sixty-five points scored made it seem more like basketball than football.

SHORTLY BEFORE noon on September 3, 1970, nine days before the Alabama football season began against Southern Cal, Bryant received a phone call from his friend and assistant, Charley Thornton. "Coach," said Thornton, "I just thought you'd want to know, Coach [Vince] Lombardi died up in Washington." Bryant paused for a moment, then said, "Well, that's a shame. I'm awfully sorry to hear that." Then, says Thornton, there came a longer pause. "You know what's really a shame, Charley?" Bryant asked. "It's a shame he didn't last long enough to do anything in his life outside of football." "What do you mean, Coach?" "I mean, there could have been a lot of things in life he wanted to do. People he never got to spend time with." Now it was Thornton's turn to pause: "Well, Coach, that is a shame." "Yes, it is." Neither Bryant nor Thornton had any way of knowing that shortly before Lombardi's death from cancer, he woke up in his hospital bed and called out, "Joe Namath! You're not bigger than football! Remember that!" Lombardi had always been an admirer of Namath's ability and fantasized about coaching him, but he was skeptical about Namath's brash attitude. He needn't have worried, though, about Namath thinking he was bigger than the game; Bear Bryant had long ago drummed that lesson into Joe.

Thirty-four years later, Thornton was still a little puzzled by Bryant's response. "In all the years I knew him," he said, "I never heard him voice any regret over the time football took up in his life. It was just that one time, when Vince Lombardi died. It kind of made him think. It made me think, too, that even though he was surrounded by people who loved and admired him, in some ways he was a lonely man."

JOAN PERRY worked as an assistant on *The Bear Bryant Show* from 1962 to 1973, which aired at four o'clock on Sunday afternoons. "It was a fun job," she says, "but some days it could be harrowing. The show was broadcast on Sunday afternoons from the Channel 13 studio on Red Mountain, near the famed Vulcan statue which looks over all of Birmingham." A plane was chartered to take the game films to Memphis for processing and then fly them back to Alabama. "On more than one occasion," she recalls, "we were still editing the film when the show started." Bryant and Charley

Thornton, Alabama's longtime sports information director and Bryant's co-host, would come in early to review the films before the show.

"Coach Bryant was a wonderful man, but thank God for Charley Thornton. We didn't use a script, and Coach Bryant was not, and I hope you'll excuse me for saying this, very good at following directions. If you told him he had plenty of time, he'd tend to run out of things to say too soon. Charley would pick up the ball, so to speak, and talk until we were ready for a break. If you told Coach Bryant that time was running short, he tended to talk too much, and Charley had to break in and get him to stop. We had all kinds of accidents in the early days when we were on live. Once, Coach Bryant ripped open a package of Golden Flake Potato Chips, the product of one of our sponsors [the other was Coca-Cola] and missed the bowl. The chips spilled all over the floor. But he and Charlie just laughed, scooped them all up, and kept right on talking. No one seemed to care, because it was Coach Bryant.

"To be honest, he did drink, and some days were worse than others. The better days were when Alabama won. If we won, he'd come right in and start chatting with everybody. If we lost, he'd go straight to the screening room and start watching the game films. Of course, Alabama didn't lose very often."

By the late 1960s, the show was taped. Assistants would gather to watch the show in Bryant's office, which had the best television in the athletic department. Dude Hennessey, who was known for his excellent impersonations of Bryant, would amuse his colleagues while the show was in progress. One Sunday afternoon, as Hennessey sat with his feet propped on Bryant's desk, he heard, "Dude, can I have my chair back?" Hennessey, in his best Bryant growl, replied, "You can have it all right, when I'm finished with it." Hennessey was startled to discover a moment later that Bryant himself was standing there; no one had bothered to inform the coaching staff that the production had been switched from live broadcast to videotape.

When the show changed to videotape, Bryant had to be in Birmingham by 9:00 a.m. One Sunday morning he had unexpected delays, so Bryant and his driver, Billy Varner, didn't get started until around 8:30. As the car roared down Highway 11 toward Birmingham, it attracted the attention of an Alabama state trooper. Varner told the trooper who his passenger was and asked him if he could take care of the matter on the way back to Tuscaloosa. The trooper looked inside and then waved for Varner to follow him. The Coach got a blue-light escort to Red Mountain.

1969 Alabama Sports Hall of Fame inductees: left to right, Johnny Mack Brown, Joe Louis, Coach Bryant, Don Hutson, and Ralph "Shug" Jordan. (Paul W. Bryant Museum, University of Alabama)

The Coach's granddaughter, Mary Harmon Tyson, fits the Bear with a new hat given to him by New York Jets owner Sonny Werblin. The hat replaced Bryant's lucky brown fedora, which he had worn since a sportswriter left it at the Bryant home after a Kentucky victory party. (Photograph by Tom Self, the *Birmingham News*, 2005. All rights reserved. Reprinted with permission.)

For nearly two decades, George Wallace and Paul Bryant were the two most famous men in Alabama. The public wasn't aware of the tension between the two, as Wallace resisted integration of the Alabama football team for years. This picture was taken sometime after 1972, after an assassination attempt left Wallace paralyzed. Following integration of the football team, the two men were more at ease around each other. (Note Bryant's hair, the shaggiest of his career.) (Paul W. Bryant Museum, University of Alabama)

The Crimson Tide is back! Coach Bryant and his good friend Southern Cal coach John McKay walk off the field at the Los Angeles Coliseum, September 10, 1971, after the Tide's 17-10 upset of the Trojans. It was the first integrated Alabama team and the first to use the new wishbone formation. (Photograph by Tom Self, the *Birmingham News*, 2005. All rights reserved. Reprinted with permission.)

Bart Starr, the Alabama quarterback who never got to play for Bear. Starr won five NFL championships with Vince Lombardi's Green Bay Packers. (Paul W. Bryant Museum, University of Alabama)

Notre Dame coach Ara Parseghian and Bryant stir up the traditional café brûlot at Antoine's Restaurant before the 1973 Sugar Bowl in New Orleans, "The Greatest College Football Game Ever Played." (Paul W. Bryant Museum, University of Alabama)

Bryant with grandson and fishing pal Marc Tyson in the early 1970s. "He was the greatest grandfather I can imagine." (Paul W. Bryant Museum, University of Alabama)

John David Crow, Bryant, and longtime Alabama assistant coach Clem Gryska at a golf tournament, circa 1975. Gryska played at Alabama under Frank Thomas and Red Drew and then spent thirty-one seasons as a recruiting coordinator and assistant for Bryant, Ray Perkins, and Gene Stallings. He is currently an administrative aide at the Paul W. Bryant Museum. (Paul W. Bryant Museum, University of Alabama)

"The Wizard of Ozzie," Alabama's all-time greatest receiver, Ozzie Newsome. Ozzie lettered 1974–1977, was a consensus All-America player, and went on to become an NFL Hall of Famer. He is currently general manager of the Baltimore Ravens. (Paul W. Bryant Museum, University of Alabama)

Bryant and Kent Waldrep, the Texas Christian player who was paralyzed in a 1974 game at Legion Field in Birmingham. "They raised more money in Alabama than TCU ever spent on me," Waldrep says. (Courtesy of Kent Waldrep)

Bryant gets in a zinger at his former quarterback during Dean Martin's Celebrity Roast for Joe Namath in 1974 (left to right, Martin, Bryant, Namath). (Paul W. Bryant Museum, University of Alabama)

Joe Namath (in the New York Yankees shirt) visits Tuscaloosa and his old coach. On the right is Alabama quarterback Richard Todd, who would become the second Crimson Tide quarterback to start for the New York Jets. (Paul W. Bryant Museum, University of Alabama)

Bryant and longtime rival, Auburn head football coach Ralph "Shug" Jordan. The two men were friends; they might have been the best of friends if not for the intensity of the football rivalry between their two schools. (Paul W. Bryant Museum, University of Alabama)

Bryant visits his old Kentucky Wildcats quarterback Babe Parilli at the New York Jets training camp at Hofstra University, Long Island, 1976. The tower in the background looks like the one Bryant used in Tuscaloosa. (Paul W. Bryant Museum, University of Alabama)

Former Michigan lineman Gerald Ford tries on one of Bryant's trademark houndstooth hats at a 1976 rally in Mobile. Bryant's favorite president was Harry Truman, but he was always happy to shake hands with any chief executive. (Paul W. Bryant Museum, University of Alabama)

Reggie Jackson describes one of his home runs to baseball fan Bear Bryant at a charity game between the New York Yankees and the Alabama Crimson Tide baseball team in 1978. (Paul W. Bryant Museum, University of Alabama)

College football's winningest coaches— Alabama's Bear Bryant and Ohio State's Wayne Woodrow "Woody" Hayes—before the 1978 Sugar Bowl. Alabama won, 35–6. (Paul W. Bryant Museum, University of Alabama)

Bryant's surprise 65th birthday party in Birmingham, September 11, 1978. Left to right: Actor Dale Robertson (who Bryant tried to recruit at Texas A&M); Bryant; president of the Birmingham Touchdown Club, Jake Reiss; Michigan State coach Duffy Daugherty (in back of Reiss); and Joe Namath. Howard Cosell and Don Meredith interrupted *Monday Night Football* to say happy birthday. (Courtesy of Jake Reiss)

1979 taping of the *Bob Hope Show* in Tuscaloosa. Left to right, Joe Namath, Bob "Thunderfoot" Hope, and Coach Bryant. (Courtesy of the Bob Hope Estate)

Paul Bryant and Penn State coach Joe Paterno before the 1979 Sugar Bowl game for the national championship. Paterno would eventually break Bryant's record for most victories by a major college coach but failed to beat Bryant in four head-to-head meetings. (Paul W. Bryant Museum, University of Alabama)

Ardelle Krauss, Barry Krauss's mother, tries on the famous houndstooth hat during a recruiting visit from Bryant in December 1974. She wanted to know if she could keep the hat; Bryant told her he didn't think the NCAA would approve. (Courtesy of Barry Krauss)

"The Most Famous Defensive Play in College Football History." Former Alabama and NFL linebacker Barry Krauss sits beside his painting of the goal-line stand from the 1979 Sugar Bowl victory over Penn State. At the left is the trophy for the Miller Digby MVP Award from that game (he is the only defensive player ever to win it). On the table is the helmet he wore in the game, and the 1978 national champion- ship ring is on his right hand. A photograph of Coach Bryant's picture hangs on the wall over Krauss's left shoulder. (Courtesy of Barry Krauss)

Billboard erected on Route 202 outside Philadelphia by the Alabama Boosters Club of Bridgeport, Pennsylvania, following the Tide's victory in the 1979 Sugar Bowl. Penn State fans were not appreciative. (Courtesy of Johnny Nicola)

Bryant at the twenty-fifth reunion of his Texas A&M Junction Boys with Billy Granberry (left) and Dennis Goehring. The commemorative ring they gave him at the reunion was the only jewelry he was wearing when he died. (Copyright, Photo by the *Birmingham News*, 2005. All rights reserved. Reprinted with permission.)

Bryant on the *Dick Cavett Show* in 1980. Cavett: "There's something bear-like about you. By that I mean, you know how a bear is a nice friendly-looking creature. . . . Are you easily moved to violence?" (Courtesy Dick Cavett/Daphne Productions)

Walter Lewis, Alabama's first black starting quarterback, gets a pat on the back from his coach, circa 1980.

Cotton Bowl, 1982. Bryant with the ever-present, rolled-up roster sheets in his hand.

The Coach and 315, a painting by Daniel A. Moore commemorating the victory over Auburn, November 28, 1981, with which Bryant passed Amos Alonzo Stagg's record to become the winningest coach in college football history. (Used by permission of artist, Daniel A. Moore)

Congratulatory phone call from President Ronald Reagan after Bryant broke Amos Alonzo Stagg's record of 314 career victories, November 28, 1981. (Paul W. Bryant Museum, University of Alabama)

Paul Bryant, Bob Hope, and Billy Graham at America's Tribute to Paul "Bear" Bryant, March 1982. (Paul W. Bryant Museum, University of Alabama)

December 15, 1982. Bryant announces his retirement. "Scarcely anyone in Alabama could believe it.... People pulling out of their driveways on the way to work stopped their cars to listen; those already at work sipped coffee and huddled around radios." (Paul W. Bryant Museum, University of Alabama)

Liberty, a painting by Daniel A. Moore, depicts Bryant carried off the field after his final game, a 21-15 victory over Illinois at the Liberty Bowl in Memphis, December 19, 1982. (Used by permission of artist, Daniel A. Moore)

Paying their respect, an estimated quarter of a million people—perhaps one out of twelve in the state of Alabama—gathered along the fifty-five-mile route from Tuscaloosa to Birmingham as Bryant was carried to his final resting place.

Thousands of mourners fill Elmwood Cemetery at Bryant's funeral.

Giant reproduction of the Bear Bryant commemorative stamp outside the Paul W. Bryant Museum in Tuscaloosa. Its first day of issue was August 7, 1997. The painting for the stamp is by renowned Alabama artist Daniel A. Moore. The numbers on the players' helmets, 3 and 23, represent the number of Bryant's career victories. (Kent Gidley, University of Alabama)

The affection of Alabama state troopers for Bryant bordered on the mystical. College football fans around the nation, of course, were familiar with the sight of Bryant walking off Legion Field or the turf at Denny Stadium surrounded by troopers. On one occasion, says Mal Moore, "Billy Varner, Coach Bryant, and I were coming back from a recruiting trip in Montgomery, and the Coach was taking a nap while Billy ignored the speed limit getting us home, and we got nailed by a state trooper. Coach woke up when Billy started to slow down and asked what was the problem. Billy told him they were about to get a ticket. Coach took off his houndstooth hat and put it in the back window and went back to sleep. The trooper never stopped us."

BY THE end of the 1968 season, Paul Bryant was a very tired man. The combination of the stress of the *Saturday Evening Post* incident and the ongoing pressure of the integration issue had aged him beyond his fifty-five years. Friends would later say that in this period the smoking and drinking got worse and that Paul and Mary Harmon were now sleeping in separate bedrooms. Bryant didn't need more bad news at this point in his life, but the week after the Auburn game he got some. A call to his office informed him that Pat Trammell was in the hospital in "very serious condition." In late November 1967,[*] Trammell, who had graduated from medical school and gone into private practice in Birmingham, had phoned his old coach in Tuscaloosa to tell him he had a tumor. "My stomach turned over," Bryant recalled. "If I had been standing up I'd probably have dropped to my knees." Trammell was going to the Ewing Clinic in New York for treatment; Bryant said he would go up with him. "Well, dammit," Trammell replied, "that's what I was calling to ask you."

Trammell and his wife Baye (who Bryant had once described as "cute as a speckled pup") flew to the clinic in New York. Ray Abbruzzese, an Italian kid from South Philadelphia who was a teammate from the 1961 team, and Joe Namath, now in his third year with the Jets, met Pat and Baye at the airport and drove them to the clinic. Trammell put on a game face and ribbed his friends. Bryant came up a few days later, and he and Trammell opened a bottle of Jack Daniel's Black Label and talked late into the night.

[*] In *Bear*, Bryant mistakenly places this call the week of the Auburn game in 1968.

The next day, the doctors operated for testicular sarcoma; Bryant and Baye Trammell were told that all the cancerous tissue had been removed.

Trammell went back to his medical practice and early the next fall took his son, Pat Jr., to Tuscaloosa for a three-day stay in the Pat Trammell Room at Bryant Hall. His former coach thought the length of the stay was "unusual, as though he didn't want to go." As Trammell was leaving, he took Bryant aside and told him that the tumor had reappeared. The week of the Auburn game, Bryant met Pat in Birmingham and invited him and his son to ride with the team on the game bus to Legion Field. Alabama won, 24–16. Mike Hall, the Tide captain, presented Pat and Pat Jr. with the game ball. A week later, Trammell was back in the hospital. On Sunday morning, Bryant was headed for a golf game at the Indian Hills Country Club; suddenly he decided he didn't want to play golf, he wanted to see Pat. He turned onto Highway 11 and drove to University Hospital in Birmingham. When he walked into the room, Trammell began chiding him—shouldn't he be out recruiting? The next night, Trammell slipped into a coma, and the following morning, Bryant got the inevitable call.

Bryant escorted Pat's mother to the funeral; Mary Harmon supported Pat's father. Ralph "Shug" Jordan, the Auburn coach whom Trammell had beaten three times, was there with several of his former players. President Richard Nixon sent a telegram of condolence; George Wallace sent flowers. Bryant wept unashamedly. "Pat Trammell," he later said, "was everything known to man. Everybody loved him. He was twenty-eight years old when he died. I still miss him."

Shortly after Trammell's death, Bryant helped establish a charitable foundation to assist the families of former University of Alabama athletes, particularly with medical expenses and educational needs. The "A" Club Educational and Charitable Foundation was incorporated on December 31, 1968, by Tommy Brooker, Jimmy Sharpe, Joseph Sims, and Billy Neighbors. More than seven hundred children have attended college because of the foundation. Among the beneficiaries is Pat Trammell Jr. "The only negative thing about the scholarship," he says, "is that once a quarter I had to take my grades to him. I wasn't as smart as my dad, and if I made B's and C's, he'd get mad at me and tell me my dad never made a B the whole time he was in college."

During this period, Bryant's drinking got worse. In the winter of 1969, he was in New York for the Hall of Fame dinner when Joe Drach, his former Maryland player, ran into Bryant and a friend from Birmingham at the 21 Club. "Both men had had quite a bit to drink," recalls Bonk. The loyalty Bryant inspired in his first players came back to help him in a completely unexpected way. "With all the New York press guys hanging around 21, I didn't want any of them to see him like that." Drach phoned Vic Turyn, Bryant's first quarterback at Maryland who lived on Long Island and was still working for the FBI; Turyn had two agents go by the club and quietly "arrest" Bryant and slip him back to his hotel.

Little more than a year later Bryant suffered another personal loss. On January 23, 1970, Henry Gorham "Hank" Crisp was going to be inducted into the Alabama Sports Hall of Fame. Before the ceremony there was a reception at the Birmingham Museum of Art attended by, among others, Bryant, Mickey Mantle, Joe Garigiola, and the running back Crisp had helped coach into a Rose Bowl star, Johnny Mack Brown. A few minutes after arriving with his family, Coach Hank collapsed with a heart attack. He died before the paramedics could arrive. Johnny Mack Brown cried so hard he almost collapsed himself and had to be helped into a chair. Waiting for the ambulance, Bryant gripped the hand of the man who had driven him from Fordyce to Tuscaloosa four decades earlier. Crisp, who was seventy-five years old, had retired in 1967, but was still active in football affairs. There was, Bryant said in his autobiography, "no man in my football life I was closer to. As a player I worshipped him, and for years after, he was the man I went to." The last remaining link from Xen Scott to Bear Bryant was gone.★

The losses seemed to pile up. In September of that year, Bryant lost another old friend from his A&M years when Smokey Harper died at age seventy-three. Smokey had never been much of a medical man and wasn't much use as a trainer in an era of more sophisticated techniques, but Bryant found a job for him organizing and maintaining Alabama's game film library. A couple of weeks later, in the wake of a horrendous 24–0 loss to Tennessee, Mickey Herskowitz got a letter from Bryant. "I really need Smokey now to tell me what a great coach I am," he wrote.

─────────

★ Visitors to the campus can visit the Hank Crisp Indoor Facility, which houses tennis courts, offices for the tennis coaches, and a tennis lounge.

ON JULY 2, 1969, the Afro-American Student Association at the University of Alabama filed a lawsuit in federal court against Bryant, the university, the Board of Trustees, and Alabama's new president, David F. Matthews. (Frank Rose had retired earlier in the year.)★ Stated simply, the suit charged that representatives of the University of Alabama athletics department—and by definition this meant Paul Bryant—had not recruited black athletes with the same diligence it had shown in the recruitment of white athletes. There is absolutely no question that the charge was true.

Pressured by the need to integrate the team, Bryant was also becoming increasingly disillusioned with some of the changes the game on the field had been taking. Two-platoon football had expanded rosters so much that Bryant had far less time for personal contact with his players. "Around this time," says Clem Gryska, "you'd hear him grumble things like 'I coach coaches so much, I ain't hardly coachin' football no more.'" There was something else: the newer breed of players Bryant was recruiting didn't have the same fire as the three generations he had known as a player and coach. Increasing affluence had made boys less dependent on football scholarships; more and more, the top athletes went out for football with an eye toward the National Football League. This was a process Bryant himself had accelerated with the professional success of Billy Neighbors, Lee Roy Jordan, and, most of all, Joe Namath, who had practically put the younger American Football League on the map. The new direction in which the game was going seemed to baffle Bryant, who began to adopt an attitude that he was better off joining what he couldn't beat.

In January 1969, about six months before the lawsuit was filed, Bryant decided to leave the University of Alabama and coach the Miami Dolphins of the NFL. For years, Bryant had been tempted by professional football. After the 1966 season, Charlie Finley, who owned the minor league Birmingham A's as well as the major league parent team in Oakland, began talking publicly about getting a pro football team for Birmingham. Finley bragged that he could get Bryant a ten-year contract good for a hundred thousand dollars a year as well as 35 percent ownership of the team. Bryant felt that Finley was overplaying his hand, particularly since it was obvious that the flamboyant and controversial baseball owner would want to retain

★ Robert Finch, secretary of Health, Education, and Welfare, was also named in the suit.

at least 51 percent of the team for himself. Bryant had another reason for not buying into Finley's optimism: he didn't believe that NFL commissioner Pete Rozelle would let an owner into the league who also owned a Major League Baseball team. Bryant asked Mickey Herskowitz to do some checking with NFL insiders and see what Finley's chances were. Herskowitz's sources did not equivocate. "Pete Rozelle had no interest in expanding to Birmingham," says Herskowitz, "for the simple reason that there wasn't a big enough TV market to go with it. The Atlanta Falcons were already bringing in most of the new viewers that a team in the Southeast was going to provide for the NFL." And there was another reason: "The NFL just wasn't going to tolerate Charlie Finley. He was a maverick who consistently defied the commissioner of Major League Baseball, and Rozelle wasn't going to let anyone like that into a league where absolute control by the commissioner was the operating norm. I passed that information on to Coach, and he said to me, 'Mickey, that's all I need to know. Charlie's a pal of mine, but when it comes to these deals, sometimes his eyes are bigger 'n his stomach.'"

A couple of years later Bryant attended a Jets game in New York as the guest of Sonny Werblin. Representing a group of Alabama investors, Bryant went to Werblin with an offer: would he take ten million dollars for the Jets? Werblin didn't want to sell, but he advised Bryant that they could buy the Miami Dolphins, a team that had only been in existence since 1966, particularly if Bryant would be the head coach. Bryant decided not to move on the deal, but in the winter of 1969, when the Dolphins' managing partner, Joe Robbie, approached him, he finally gave in.

Bryant and his attorney, Winston McCall, met with Robbie in a Birmingham hotel room. Having never succeeded in achieving financial independence, Bryant decided to shoot the works: he wanted a five-year contract for $1.7 million, a house, automobiles, and stock options. He even asked for cash to be set aside for Mary Harmon to travel from Miami to Tuscaloosa. Robbie agreed in whole, but they continued to negotiate the details.

Meanwhile, Bryant met with Joe Namath, who assured him that in quarterback Bob Griese, receiver Paul Warfield, and running back Larry Csonka, Miami had the best core of young talent in the league—better, Joe had to concede, than the Jets. Bryant then consulted Howard Schnellenberger, who was working for the Los Angeles Rams, and his former lineman and assistant coach backed up Namath's assessment. Bryant told Robbie he'd take the job.

All that remained was to clear it with President Matthews and the Board of Trustees. Bryant had ten years left on his contract, from which he was now asking to be released. He would later claim that he thought the trustees might be glad to see him go—that's how badly the 1969 and 1970 seasons had shaken him. Bryant was surprised to find that, in fact, Matthews and the Board members not only didn't want him to go but were rather stunned to find that he wanted to. After some discussion, the Board members, most of whom had gone to school with Bryant, were willing to release him if he could find a suitable replacement. The only coaches in Bryant's class and age group were Texas's Darrell Royal, whose Longhorns would win the national championship in 1969, his old assistant Charlie McClendon at Louisiana State, and John McKay, the head coach at Southern Cal. McKay would win Coach of the Year in 1972, the year after Bryant won; McClendon would share the honor with Darrell Royal in 1970. But he knew that Royal would not leave Texas, or McClendon, Louisiana State. He called McKay in Los Angeles; the Trojans' coach said he would think about it on the way to Mobile, where he was to coach the Senior Bowl. Bryant told him he needed an answer on the spot. McKay declined.

At six o'clock the next morning he called Matthews and asked if it was too early for a cup of coffee. Matthews had been up since five and had already had his first. Bryant dropped by his office and admitted he would never be able to find a replacement as good as him.

Late that night, John David Crow, Bryant's Texas A&M golden boy who was coaching Alabama's running backs after a distinguished stint in the NFL, got a call from his boss. Bryant wanted Crow to come over to his house immediately. "When he told me he'd agreed to take the Miami job, I was stunned," says Crow. "I didn't know what to think. He asked me to run the office for him for a couple of days while he got things in order. His intention was to fire everybody and rehire them with Miami." If his assistants had chosen not to go to Miami, Bryant knew the university would happily take them all back. The next morning, Bryant walked into the Memorial Coliseum and into Crow's office. "He said he had changed his mind," recalls Crow. "He hadn't told anyone yet, but he had made up his mind he wasn't going to Miami. I was as stunned as I had been the night before, but I was also a little bit relieved."

Later that day, Paul and Mary Harmon were in Mobile and, while waiting to greet some friends at the airport, encountered a perturbed Joe Robbie, who had gotten wind of Bryant's change of heart—which was what
the decision ultimately boiled down to, as Robbie well knew. Robbie
stayed on a day in Mobile, dining, drinking, and joking with the Bryants
and John McKay and his wife. Taking his failure to land Bryant good
naturedly, Robbie left without holding a grudge. The Dolphins did okay
for themselves; Robbie was already considering the young coach of the
Baltimore Colts, Don Shula, if he couldn't get Bryant, and in little more
than a year Shula joined the Dolphins and went on to become the winningest coach in NFL history. Afterward, Bryant felt guilty. He tried to tell
himself that the challenge was what intrigued him—no coach had ever
been able to win in both college and professional football. But in the end,
it was the money, money for better houses, country clubs, luxury cars,
"things I didn't need or already had."

Bryant wasn't being entirely honest. He was comfortable but far from
wealthy, and had never been paid anywhere near his market worth. Nor
would he use the occasion of the professional offer to try to renegotiate his
contract with Alabama, maintaining his personal policy of a salary one dollar lower than that paid to the university president. His concern for his
family's future was one of the primary reasons he considered the pros in
the first place.

At any rate, in the winter of 1969, Bear Bryant's flirtation with professional football was at an end. "It was ridiculous. And I knew it. Never
again."What seems ridiculous, in retrospect, is that Bryant would have tried
so hard to convince himself that pro football could ever mean as much to
him as the college game. His game was *college* football, not pro. He was fond
of quoting John McKay: "Whoever heard of the University of the Rams?"
It meant something to a college football fan, he felt, "to know that these
kids represent you, and the school you attended. And are in it for more
than just a big salary and a fancy pension plan."

After twenty-five years he still got a kick "out of the antics and enthusiasm of college kids. Cheerleaders hopping around, and bands playing, and
the alumni up there whooping and hollering and raising hell. I still get
chills when they play those old fight songs and the Alabama alma mater. If
that's corny, then I'm corny."

Unless his boys were playing, though, he didn't much care for the pro game, where the same plays were run time after time and it was simply a matter of which team executed them better. No better argument for the difference between pro and college football has ever been made.

Still, there was room enough in the football universe for the game at all levels. "Our feeling in Alabama," he said in *Bear*, "has always been that weeknights—Thursdays and Fridays—are for the high schools. Saturday is for the colleges, Sunday is for the pros—and *The Bear Bryant Show*."

Having decided that now and for the rest of his career he would be a college football coach, Bryant determined to rebuild the Alabama football program. Calling his assistant coaches together, he told them, "I know I can get another job if I need one. Now, if you don't go out and get us some better football players, you're going to find out if *you* can get another job."

THE SOCIAL issues of the 1960s hit Alabama, it might be stated, a little later than other places. Around 1970, they reached the University of Alabama. Campuses around the country, said Bryant, "were going through a rebellion in those days. It hadn't seemed to touch us at Alabama, and I suppose I got complacent. It wasn't until I was up to my nose in it, and discovered that at least part of our problem was drugs, that I snapped to attention."

In early 1970, Bryant began to hear disturbing rumors about drug use by some of his players. "The idea of recreational drug use bewildered him," says Clem Gryska. "He simply could not understand how a boy fortunate enough to be going to college and playing football would need drugs in order to feel good about himself."

"He didn't hesitate to cooperate with the state and federal investigators," says former assistant coach Jack Rutledge. "If there was going to be some kind of scandal, he wanted to be on top of it."

There was no scandal, though the sad story of Robin Parkhouse a couple of years later indicates that there might well have been if Bryant had not taken personal action. On a late March afternoon, Bryant gathered his coaches in the projection room of Memorial Coliseum and told them, "We've got some things going on around here that are illegal, and they're going to stop, today." With trainer Jim Goostree leading the search, Rutledge, Gryska, Ken Donahue, and other coaches conducted a military-style sweep of the athletic dorm. What they found—marijuana and pipes, hallucinogenics, and, most shocking of all, a few needles—were tossed in boxes and hauled out. Seven boys were discovered to be using drugs. Bryant phoned each one's parents and told them he wanted to set up a meeting. Two of the boys' parents expressed indifference and did not show up for the meeting. Bryant was stunned. The next day, players and parents gathered at Bryant's office; all seven were told that they would either face the law's punishment or resign. All seven withdrew from a Crimson Tide roster none too deep to begin with. The local papers carried no mention of the incident.

"I suppose I could say that never happened here," Bryant would later reflect, "because nobody knew it. But it happened."

"To be honest," recalls Gryska, "most of us were more upset than angry. We just didn't know what to think about all of it. Coach Bryant was adamant in his resolve to eliminate drugs, but I think mostly he was bewildered, saddened, and amazed that such a thing could be happening, right under his nose."

Bryant's problems with drugs at Alabama were not yet over. After the season opening loss to Southern Cal in 1970, Robin Parkhouse, one of his best defensive players, was so upset that he threatened to quit the team and missed practice the following Monday. Several Alabama assistant coaches begged him to reconsider, and Parkhouse, after taking a night to think it over, showed up early on a Tuesday morning to ask Bryant for a second chance. Bryant decided to suspend him for four games but, echoing his words to Ken Stabler four years earlier, told him, "Robin, I think it's the biggest mistake I've ever made." Bryant was right—it was a mistake. Parkhouse was a troubled young man who had been using marijuana and LSD for nearly two years. Parkhouse lasted long enough to be a star on the 1971 Alabama comeback team, but less than two years later he was arrested in El Paso, Texas, with a trunk full of marijuana he had bought in Mexico City. Bryant was disgusted with Parkhouse's behavior and his own failure to correct it. But Robin was a spark plug on the 1971 team, and that counted for something. Francis Hare Jr. relates that through his father's legal skills and some old political friends in Texas, Bryant was able to have the case remanded to a federal court in Birmingham. He was well aware, says Hare Jr., that just about any judge in a Birmingham court was going to be a little more sympathetic toward a former Alabama All-America. Parkhouse served nearly five months at a correctional facility at Elgin Air Force Base in

Florida. Almost a decade later, Parkhouse returned to prison on the charge of trafficking cocaine. He eventually returned to his hometown of Orlando, became a born-again Christian, started his own business, and credited his former college coach with saving his life.

OF FAR less importance but equally bewildering to Bryant was the hair issue. In the fall of 1970, Bryant was watching the Texas-Oklahoma game and was astonished to see the length of the Texas players' hair. Bryant told Royal, "I noticed some of your players had hair that was stickin' down under their helmets. What's going on? From what I just saw, yours is getting a little shaggy, too." "Coach," Royal replied, "my players are wearing their hair the same length as the other students. If you don't let them do that, they're going to feel like they're discriminated against, and they're going to resent you for it." Bryant paused for a moment, then said, "Well, I never thought of that." "And, Coach, there's something else," Royal went on, "the girls like it long, and there's nothin' you can do to change *that*. You make them resent you because they lose their girlfriends and you're really going to have trouble on your hands."

Bryant was slow to see the wisdom in Royal's new philosophy. He was approached by Johnny Musso, who had been chosen by his teammates to ask the Coach to relax the hair rules. Perhaps overstressed by more important issues, Bryant was in no mood to negotiate and turned him down. Jimmy Sharpe remembers "a three-hour meeting on hair. Coach finally got a little exasperated and said, 'We're just spending too damn much time talking about hair.'" Jack Rutledge went to his own barber shop and came back with a picture book of hair styles, "a big old thing with pictures of hairstyles for both blacks and whites. Coach didn't care much for most of them. He just took a marking pen and exed out the styles that wouldn't do." Finally, Bryant designated trainer Jim Goostree as his "hair coach." "If Jim says it's too long, then they cut it." Bryant summoned Musso back to his office. "I don't know why in God's name," he said to him, "you want your hair hanging out of your helmet." Musso stood his ground, explaining to his coach how important it was to the players. Bryant still didn't understand, but decided it was more important to them than to him.

Slowly but surely, the hair of the Crimson Tide players reached the players' collars. Within a year, Bryant, too, literally began to let his hair down. "I called him after the 1973 Sugar Bowl with Notre Dame," said Royal, "and said, 'Coach, what's the matter? You don't have any barbers in Tuscaloosa?' 'Aw, Darrell,' he told me, 'I've been busy lately. I'm going to get it cut just as soon as the recruiting season is over.'"

"Coach was a lot more flexible than most people think," says Rutledge. "It took him a while to catch up on some things, but when he thought things through, it was surprising how much common sense he could show. He knew exactly when *not* to come down on people too hard." In the mid–1970s, Bryant was faced with the possibility of a minor revolt from the other end of the social spectrum, when, according to Rutledge, some players who were active in the Fellowship of Christian Athletes began to get the mistaken idea that they were playing football exclusively for the Lord. "Coach handled it beautifully. He called in a friend of his, a preacher he respected, and asked him to talk to the boys and explain that decimating themselves to the Lord also meant they were playing for their family and their school, and that meant relegating themselves to authority on earth." Contrary to the many jokes that circulated throughout Alabama, Bear Bryant never confused himself with God, and when it came to football, he wanted his players to understand that when they played for Alabama, by God, they would render unto Caesar.

IN APRIL 1970, Craig Fertig, now a college football analyst for Fox Sports West, but then an assistant coach for John McKay at Southern Cal, got a call from his boss. McKay wanted Fertig to pick him up and drive him to LA International for a meeting with his friend, Paul Bryant. "We went into the Western Airlines Horizon Room," says Fertig, "and ordered drinks. When we sat down, Coach McKay glanced at his watch and said, 'Bear will be here inside of five minutes.' About four minutes later, Bryant walked in." Bryant had traveled out West, ostensibly to play golf in the Bob Hope Desert Classic, but he had something else on his mind.

"Paul," said McKay, "what can I do for you?" What Bryant wanted was for McKay to bring the Trojans to Birmingham to open the coming season. McKay needed just a moment to think it over. "Paul, how about this?" he replied. "We'll play you in Birmingham, and we'll give you $100,000 more than you give us if you'll agree to play us in Los Angeles to open next year."

"Coach McKay was thinking of how much bigger the LA Coliseum was than Legion Field," says Fertig. "He thought an attraction like Alabama

could sell thousands of tickets more than anyone else we could have scheduled. They had a drink, shook hands, and got up to leave." It did not occur
to Fertig at the time that he was "sitting in on a historical moment. Coach
McKay and Coach Bryant both understood what had just happened, but I
didn't catch on right away. They had just agreed to play the first integrated
college football game in Alabama."★

On September 12, 1970, for the opening game of the season, Alabama
and Southern Cal met for the first time in a quarter of a century. John
McKay's University of Southern California Trojans inflicted one of the
worst and perhaps the most famous defeat of Bear Bryant's career, smashing
the Crimson Tide 42–21 at Birmingham's Legion Field. The sellout crowd,
sullen and mostly silent after the first quarter, watched Bryant's outweighed
and outmanned white boys get steamrolled and humiliated in front of a
national sports press, Southern Cal's great fullback Sam "Bam" Cunningham shredded Alabama's defensive line for 135 yards, overshadowing a fine
performance by another fine black running back, Clarence Davis. Davis,
who scored two touchdowns against Alabama, was born in Birmingham.
He would go on to stardom with the Oakland Raiders and in 1977 would
win a Super Bowl ring playing in the same backfield with Kenny Stabler.
"The point of the game," wrote Jim Murray in his dispatch to the *Los
Angeles Times*, "is not the score, the Bear, the Trojans; the point of the game
will be reason, democracy, hope. The real winner will be Alabama."[10] In a
very short time, Alabama would come to see how true that was.

A wealth of folklore has been built around the game, a process Bryant
greatly contributed to when he was quoted as saying, "Cunningham did
more for integration in Alabama in sixty minutes than Martin Luther
King, Jr."† Many of the stories are myths, though some were not without a

---

★Actually, it was not. The previous season the Tennessee Volunteers had thrashed Alabama
41–14 at Birmingham's Legion Field with a team that featured two black stars, linebacker Jackie Walker and receiver Lester McLain. Exactly why history has chosen to
ignore this game and focus on the 1970 Alabama-USC game has never been adequately
explained. The only explanation I can offer is that Alabama newspapers completely
ignored the significance of the black players on the 1969 Tennessee team, whereas
Bryant's actions in orchestrating the 1970 game with Southern Cal forced national
attention on Alabama's program.

†This quote is often attributed to Bryant's former assistant, Jerry Claiborne, but Claiborne told me that he first heard it from Bryant.

hard kernel of factual basis. First among the myths is that Bryant scheduled the game in Birmingham to shame Alabama's hard-core segregation-
ists into submission. "Coach Bryant never scheduled a game in his life in
order to lose it," insists Clem Gryska. "He knew that a two-game series
with Southern Cal would give us terrific national exposure and highlights would be picked up for broadcast on national television. Coach
McKay was a good friend, and Southern Cal had a national reputation on
a par with ours." (The Trojans had won the national championship in
1967 and narrowly missed winning it in 1968.) On the other hand, Bryant
must have had a fairly good idea of what the game would expose about
his 1970 team. If Alabama was going to lose, he surely understood that a
resounding defeat at the hands of an integrated team would accelerate the
process of integration that had already begun.

Another great myth about the 1970 Alabama–Southern Cal game has
been harder to dispel: Bryant, after the game, went to the USC locker room
and escorted Sam Cunningham to where the Alabama players were changing. "Gentlemen," Bryant is said to have said to his beaten players, "this is
what a football player looks like." The story has made its way into so many
books and articles over the years that it almost seems like it has to be true.
Did Bryant actually do it? Before the 2003 Southern Cal–Auburn game,
Neal McCready of the *Mobile Register* did a thorough job of punching holes
in the myth in a story that appeared August 24, 2003. McCready could not
find a single Alabama player or coach who remembered Bryant bringing
Cunningham into their locker room. Scott Hunter was emphatic to
McCready: "It never happened. I didn't even hear about it until some time in
the mid-1970s. I've never talked to a teammate or coach who remembered
seeing Sam Cunningham in our locker room." Jack Rutledge, an assistant
coach at the time, insisted to McCready, "Coach Bryant would have never
done that. That wasn't his character at all." Another assistant, Mal Moore (currently athletic director at Alabama), said that Bryant would often go to an
opponent's locker room to congratulate the coaches and players, but had no
recollection of Bryant bringing Cunningham back with him. Clem Gryska
simply denies the story. "We all knelt down and waited for Coach Bryant to
come in and speak. He did *not* bring Sam Cunningham into the dressing
room. I don't know where or how the story got started, but it's a myth."

It's a myth, though, that has some supporters. John McKay, who died in
June 2001, was quoted as saying that Bryant came to him and asked if he

could borrow Cunningham. "To his players," McKay said, "Paul pointed to Cunningham and said, 'Gentleman, this is what a football player looks like.'"[11] Craig Fertig says, "I have a definite memory of Bryant asking if he could 'borrow' Sam. Sam was still in his girdle pads when Bryant came in and walked him out of the locker room. I heard Coach Bryant say, 'Ya'll listen up now. This is what a football player is supposed to look like.'" But, says Fertig, "I wasn't right there with him, I heard it at a distance." To further confuse matters, the man who is at the center of the story, Sam Cunningham, told McCready, "I don't remember a lot. I don't remember clearly. Coach Bryant was very polite and very, very strong in his belief that we did something special that evening. For the sake of history, I was taken in. I kind of think it didn't happen. I think I would remember, but I don't want to be the guy who said it didn't happen." Curiouser and curiouser.

What seems undeniable is that Bryant did go to the USC locker room. That he "borrowed" Cunningham is more difficult to verify. How could it be that not a single Alabama player or coach remembers seeing Cunningham in their locker room or hearing their Coach say something like, "This is a football player"?

The only credible explanation of the story I have ever heard, one that fits most of the known facts, came from the late Al Browning, who was then a reporter with the *Tuscaloosa News*. First of all, Browning once told me, "Bryant would not have humiliated his own players by parading a victorious player in their locker room. There would have been no purpose. The Alabama players were already predisposed towards integration.* What Coach Bryant wanted to do was make sure that some sense got knocked into the heads of some people connected to the university who wanted to drag their feet on integration. I believe he had invited a few of them down into the locker room. As much as he hated to lose that game, I think he got a particular kick in presenting Sam to them. Watching Cunningham perform on the field and then seeing him in the flesh right in front of them jolted them more than any lecture ever could have. I believe Bryant said something to them on the order of, 'Gentlemen, this is a football player,' but he wasn't going to embarrass them publicly by telling anyone what he had

---

* Scott Hunter, the Alabama quarterback, told the *Mobile Press Register*'s Neal McCready, "I had no problem with recruiting blacks. I thought we had put ourselves at a disadvantage without them on the team." (Aug. 24, 2003)

said to them. I think some people who were there overheard it, and over the years the story evolved into Bryant having said that to his players." For his part, Bryant never mentioned the story in any form in his autobiography.

John Papadakis, a linebacker for Southern Cal that year, along with former teammate Mark Mouska, wrote a screenplay with the working title of "The Turning of the Tide." In preliminary reports, Bryant not only says the famous words in the Alabama locker room, he says them while pointing to Cunningham, who is standing on a bench. To paraphrase the reporter in John Ford's classic, *The Man Who Shot Liberty Valance*, "When the legend becomes fact, print the legend."

The reason why so much legend grew from this game is better understood when one listens to the players describe the tensions that surrounded it. "The blacks on our team had a swagger," recalled John Papadakis. "They knew they were playing in a place where they were highly accepted and promoted, based on their athleticism. Our best players had been black players, at least some of our best players. In any case, they had a swagger and they were loose and they weren't short on words.

"Well, I could tell once we announced the Alabama game, and especially in the fall practices when we gathered, the blacks grew tighter and tighter. You know, like you tighten a drum. They were extremely fearful about going down South. When the team's plane landed in Birmingham, you could hear a penny drop on the ground. When we got on the buses, there was absolute dead silence and the guys staring every which way, just looking deeply. The [hotel] marquis said, 'Welcome USC Trojans.' Well, it could just as well have said, 'Welcome USC Niggers' because there were crowds of people there waiting for the team and gawking, pointing at and almost being in shock at seeing these black players coming off the bus in coats and ties and going into that hotel. The black players themselves weren't loose and fluid in their motion. They were huddled together like Japanese tourists in Disneyland. They got their keys quickly and started going across a pedestrian bridge that went over a pool. There were kids playing in the pool, and the kids started screaming, 'Look at the niggers! They're coming into our hotel!' A group of black players ran at a sprint to their rooms."

Papadakis also recalled some kids knocking on the players' doors, wanting to get a closer look at them. One asked him, "Are there any USC niggers in there?" "Yeah," Papadakis replied, "I got one in here. He's right over here," and introduced him to his roommate, Kent Carter. The child reached out his hand to Carter, who picked the boy up, "took the kid's hand, and ran it down his face. The kid was shaking. He was making contact, skin contact, with a black man. Kent said, 'Black is beautiful.' The other two kids were shocked. They said, 'What am I going to tell my parents?' I said, 'Tell them the truth. You came looking for a black man, and you found one.'"[12]

By the end of the game, Craig Fertig began to understand the significance of what had just happened. "I walked with Coach McKay across the field where he shook hands with Bryant. In the middle of the field we found Bear Bryant, with, swear to God, a smile on his face. His team had just gotten whipped by three touchdowns, and here's the man who John McKay had always told me hated to lose more than any man on earth and he's got a smile on his face. I'll never forget what he said. He said, 'John, I can't thank you enough.'"

The 1970 Southern Cal game was the worst opening-day defeat of Bryant's career, but he had a nice fat payday to console the university with. He also had the knowledge that by scheduling USC that year, he had pushed the timetable for the complete integration of Alabama football ahead by perhaps a couple of years.

"When the action is over," John McKay wrote in his autobiography,

> it's sometimes an emotional strain to cross the field and shake hands with the rival coach, if he's my friend. I found this out with Paul "Bear" Bryant of Alabama, Duffy Daugherty, when he was at Michigan State, and I certainly find it difficult with Washington's Jim Owens, whose team we play every year. But the handshake is one of our profession's rituals, so I do it.
>
> But sometimes when I walk over to see a friend, we relax each other with a quip or two. In 1970 we opened at Alabama, the first time I'd ever played my best buddy, Bear Bryant. We jumped ahead 32–7 and coasted to victory, 42–21. When I met Bear at midfield, he looked me in the eye and said, "Damn, John, we just ran out of time."[13]

ONE MYTH about the 1970 Alabama–Southern Cal game that is easily exploded is that it finally integrated the University of Alabama football team. Watching the game in the stands that day was a talented receiver, later to turn running back, from Ozark, Alabama, named Wilbur Jackson. Jackson was already on the Alabama freshman team, and in the next season he would play a key role in leading the Tide back to national prominence. Exactly why it took a coach with as genuinely integrationist sympathies as Bryant's so long to integrate—in fact, why Alabama waited until six other SEC schools had fielded a team with black players—isn't easily explained.

Before the start of the 1967 season, Bryant spoke with his old Kentucky team manager, Frank Sadler, who congratulated him on the Tide's 11–0 record in 1966 and commented on the injustice of the number-three spot in the final polls. "You know, Coach," said Sadler, "that they're going to give you a tough time until the team is integrated." Integration would come soon, Bryant told him, "but I'll tell you, Frank, when I sign my first black player, he's going to be a great one, he's going to be a black Ray Perkins." (Perkins had been drafted by the Baltimore Colts and was about to begin his first pro season.) But Bryant would have to wait until 1974 to get his black Ray Perkins.

On April 6, 1967, a front-page article in the *Tuscaloosa News* announced, "Bryant checks Negro hopefuls." Five black players—Arthur Dunning, Melvin Leverett, Andrew Pernell, Dock Roan, and Jerome Tucker—went out for Alabama football; all but Tucker were Alabamians. Tucker, a Georgian, would prove to be academically ineligible. All five were nonscholarship players, "walk-ons" in football parlance. The chance of a walk-on making the team in almost any major college football program is slim; the odds of a walk-on making the team in a program like Alabama's is miniscule, no matter what color the player's skin. "Coach Bryant told us," says Ken Stabler, "that we were to treat them exactly as we wanted to be treated ourselves."*

Pernell, a running back, and Roan, an offensive guard, made the cut for the annual A-Day intrasquad spring game. They lasted on the squad until fall practice before being cut. Two years later, testifying in the lawsuit brought by the Afro-American Student Association, Bryant would say that he liked Roan and respected him, that he thought Roan might be able to help the team, though probably not as a starter. The problem, Bryant said, was Roan's academic failures, which resulted in his being drafted into the military. Roan, apparently, came close to being Alabama's first black football player. David Briley, assistant professor of political science at East Tennessee

---

* In an interview for *ESPN Classic Sports Century*, Stabler recalled three black players trying out for the team. (Dec. 13, 2002)

State University, in assembling material for a book on the integration of the Alabama football team, has come to the conclusion that "Bryant was probably sincere in giving Roan and the others a shot at making the team. But the fate of five walk-on players does not get into the question of the University of Alabama's lack of commitment in recruiting black players."[14]

In his biography of Bryant, Keith Dunnavant contended that after discussing the matter with several important alumni—mostly notably George Wallace, who was a presidential candidate at the time, not the governor, but still very much the power in Alabama politics—Bryant told his staff to begin recruiting black football players. No source for Dunnavant's claim has been found, but the scenario seems plausible. Wallace was still the power who had to be dealt with in the state, but as his presidential aspirations became more serious, his stand on segregation had to soften. Bryant sensed the change coming some time before that. In a memorandum to President Rose dated March 3, 1967, and entitled "Colored Athletes," Bryant admitted, "Finally, we do not plan to recruit colored athletes from out-of-state at this time, but certainly would be interested in any that qualify within the state."[15] From a certain perspective, this made sense. Alabama produced a rich crop of black football players every year, and it made little sense for Bryant and his staff to spend their time and resources focusing on out-of-state players when there was so much talent to be had right there at home. Also, it would hardly appease Alabama's black leaders if the Crimson Tide football team was integrated by an athlete who wasn't a native son. Bryant spent a great deal of time in the mid-1960s attending football games at black high schools and had nothing to show for it but a long string of recommendations made to coaches in other parts of the country.*

For that matter, Alabama's failure to integrate was costing the team white talent as well. Richmond Flowers Jr. referred to himself as "the fastest white boy alive." This was not an idle boast. In April 1965, two months before graduating from Montgomery's Sidney Lanier High School, Bart Starr's old high school, Flowers, competing in the Gulf Coast Relays in

---

* Including to his friend Duffy Daugherty at Michigan State. At the surprise party for Bryant's sixty-fifth birthday in 1978, Daugherty wryly announced, "I got out of coaching when Bryant started recruiting black kids."

Mobile, ran the 120-yard hurdles in 13.5 seconds, a new national high school record. The following month, competing in an open meet in Modesto, California, he beat Blaine Lindgren, the silver medalist in the 120-yard high hurdles at Tokyo in 1964. Bryant was thrilled at the prospect of Flowers playing on the same team with his speedy ends, Ray Perkins and Dennis Homan, but was jolted when Alabama's hottest football prospect chose to accept a scholarship at Tennessee.

Richmond Jr.'s attitude toward Alabama had changed sharply during the Mobile meet when his father was heartily booed after being introduced at a pregame ceremony. Richmond Sr. had been the state's attorney general since 1963 and would remain so until 1967. "The hatred that Flowers Sr. stirred among many white Alabamians illustrates how tough it was to be a racial moderate in Alabama in the sixties," says Diane McWhorter, whose 2001 history of the civil rights movement in Birmingham, *Carry Me Home*, won the Pulitzer Prize. "Flowers's crime was urging compliance with federal anti-segregation laws—in other words, doing his job. He had the guts to prosecute the Ku Klux Klan at a time when all other state agencies were conspiring to lay off them. They burned crosses on his lawn and sent death threats to his family, but he never backed off." Flowers's crowning insult to George Wallace was seeking the Democratic nomination for governor in 1966, which went to Wallace's wife, Lurleen. (Alabama governors were not allowed to succeed themselves.) A large portion of the white electorate never forgave Flowers. "I really wanted to get out of Alabama and get it behind me," Richmond Jr. told an interviewer in 1977. "I didn't want all that heavy stuff laid on me about politics and segregation and civil rights. I was a kid who wanted to be a kid." But he was also a kid who, though he respected Bear Bryant, was glad to stick it to the football team of George Wallace's alma mater. In 1968, Flowers scored the winning—and in fact the only—touchdown of Tennessee's 10–9 victory over the Tide. Richmond Flowers Jr. had the distinction of being the only white football player from Alabama in the 1960s to go out of state and become an All-America.★

To lose black blue-chippers to northern schools was one thing, but to lose a white player like Richmond Flowers Jr., perhaps the most sought-

---

★ Another factor in Flowers's decision to go to Tennessee was the school's superior track program. He would also become an All-America in track.

after prospect in the country, and to lose him to, of all schools, Tennessee was, to Alabama fans, intolerable. If nothing else, the anger generated by Richmond Jr.'s defection caused at least a few white Alabamians to consider what their stand on segregation was costing them on the football field.

"BRYANT," SAYS David Briley, "was a racial moderate who understood the politics of his state and insisted on a go-slow incremental approach to integrating his football team." The evidence would seem to back up Briley's conclusion. Bryant's insistence that he wanted to be "the Branch Rickey of football" needs to be put in context. Rickey took great pains to find precisely the right black player to integrate Major League Baseball, one who was talented enough to win over skeptics who doubted a black's ability to compete at a big-time level, but he also wanted the kind of man who was temperamentally suited to withstand the taunts and jibes of bigots.* This seems to be exactly what Bryant, who, after all, had been close to Commissioner of Baseball Happy Chandler, was looking for. In fact, Bryant would find two such players.

In July 1969, when the lawsuit against the university was filed by the Afro-American Student Association, Bryant was at a coaching clinic, but a sports information spokesman told the local paper that Alabama had offered scholarships to three black players the previous fall, but that all three had chosen other schools. To add insult to injury, one of those three, James Owens, would become a star at Auburn. Why wasn't there more publicity

---

* Bryant believed in 1970 that the time was not yet right for a black quarterback at Alabama. Condredge Holloway, one of the most sought-after quarterbacks in the nation, grew up in Huntsville in North Alabama and was very much desired by Bryant. But Holloway wanted to play quarterback. Keith Dunnavant reports,

> On his official visit to the campus in Tuscaloosa, Holloway was shocked by Bryant's candor. "He said, 'I'd love to have you at Alabama, but Alabama's not ready for a black quarterback.' A lot of the other coaches, when I asked them about playing quarterback, they'd hem and haw. They'd dodge the question, but Coach Bryant was honest. He knew it would be awfully tough for a black quarterback at Alabama at that time. I really respected that. He didn't have to be honest with me. He could have signed me and then made me change positions, which is probably what a lot of schools would have done." (*Coach*, p. 259)

Holloway ended up starring for the University of Tennessee.

about Alabama having offered scholarships to three blacks? The likely reason is that Bryant didn't want it revealed that Alabama was now aggressively pursuing black prospects but the black prospects didn't want to come to the school. "I really think this is something that Coach hadn't counted on," says Clem Gryska. "I really think that he figured that once he began offering scholarships to the best black players, they would forget the George Wallace years and line up to play for Alabama. But it wasn't that easy."

Whatever Bryant's feelings, there were a growing number of skeptics in his own backyard. In the July 8, 1969, issue of the *Crimson-White*, an editorialist asked rhetorically, "How conscientious they"—the "they" meant the athletic department and ultimately Bryant—"were in the recruitment of black athletes. With all the resources available to their department, it is quite unrealistic to think that no blacks can be found to play football for the Crimson Tide. . . . The Afro-American Association, whatever the outcome of the case, has rightly filed suit against the athletic department. The Association is to be complimented for its dignity in all its efforts so far. The suit filed at Birmingham should indicate that blacks on this campus want full equality in all phases of university life."

U. W. Clemon of the Birmingham law firm of Adams, Baker and Clemon served as counsel for the plaintiffs in the suit and was concerned about what appeared to be foot dragging at the top of the chain: "Shortly after I took the case, we filed the lawsuit. We did quite a bit of discovery. We talked with a fair amount of black coaches who told us that Bryant was not serious in the recruitment of black athletes. We took his deposition. He was a very gracious guy . . . he equivocated a lot in his deposition. We were prepared to show that the contacts with the black coaches were superficial and they were convinced he was not really serious. What really incensed the group and Ed Nall [president of the Afro-American Student Association] was that the Owens guy had gone down to Auburn and they were apparently serious in recruiting black athletes and Alabama was not."[16] The Crimson Tide basketball team had already been integrated earlier in the year with the signing of Wendell Hudson, but to break the football color barriers, Bryant wanted his own Owens or, depending on one's point of view, his own Jackie Robinson.

On August 28, 1971, the University of Alabama Student Government Association received a letter from Bryant that included a list of black football players who had been recommended for Alabama football scholarships.★ Four players were named; in addition, Bryant and his coaches were keeping a close eye on six more players who might be worthy of scholarships. One was a receiver from an all-black high school in Ozark, D. A. Smith, named Wilbur Jackson. Pat Dye had spotted Jackson when he had gone down to Ozark in Jackson's junior year to scout two other players. Dye came back with a glowing report; the boy was not only fast but also tough and seemed to have the right maturity and attitude. He certainly had Bryant's kind of mama and papa: "His daddy," Bryant noted proudly, "was a railroad man, at the same job thirty-five years." Dye thought Jackson's natural position might be running back. Bryant sent another assistant, Richard Williamson, down to offer Wilbur a scholarship. Jackson was understandably hesitant to sign with Alabama, but after talking to Wendell Hudson, "I got favorable reports. He was convinced that Coach Bryant wasn't interested in token integration. The black players were in the same dorm with the white players. 'It's tough,' Wendell told me, 'but it's changing.'"

Jackson met Bryant on his first recruiting trip in his senior year, coming straight to Tuscaloosa from a game with Eufaula. "I was a little nervous, but he smiled and reached out to shake my hand, and I felt better. I was surprised and a little unnerved: he already had a report on the game. He knew we had lost. 'That shouldn't have happened,' he told me. 'You guys were better than they are.' All right, I said to myself, he's serious. 'Wilbur,' he said to me, 'I'm not gonna lie to you and tell you that you won't have problems here. All I can tell you is that when you do, before you go to anybody else with them, you come to me.'" On December 13, 1971, in his parents' living room, Wilbur Jackson signed a grant-in-aid to become the first black scholarship player for the Alabama Crimson Tide.

But he was not Alabama's first black *varsity* football player. In the spring of 1971, Bryant and John McKay got together again, this time at the Bob

---

★ The letter was not sent to the University of Alabama chapter of the Afro-American Student Association, but the Student Government Association, which represented the entire student body. Why Bryant wrote to this group is not clear, but David Briley feels that the members of the group wanted to back Coach Bryant, "but were concerned about the possible negative implications that resulted from the pending litigation." Apparently Bryant wanted to reassure them that genuine efforts were being made to recruit black players.

Hope Desert Classic golf tournament. Sitting in the clubhouse and discussing the rapid integration of college football in the Deep South, McKay made an uncharacteristic blunder—he bragged about a great new prospect he was on the verge of signing, a young linebacker from Mobile, Alabama, who was playing for Eastern Arizona Junior College. McKay said something to the effect that Bryant would be seeing him up close in a few months when Alabama took the field against Southern Cal to open the season in Los Angeles. He would be right, but not in the way he thought. "I got a call from Coach Bryant in Palm Springs," says Clem Gryska. "He said John McKay just told me about this terrific black linebacker from Mobile playing in a junior college in Arizona (it was Eastern Arizona Junior College). He told me, 'See if he's signed yet, and if he hasn't, get after him.'" It was the last time McKay or any other football coach would be so loose-lipped about black prospects around Bear Bryant.

Bryant's approach to integration was paternalistic; he never pretended otherwise. For years, he would later admit in *Bear*, he had delayed recruiting black players. The time wasn't ripe in Alabama, he maintained, but he would help place promising black players at other schools in the mid-1960s because Alabama was "still two or three years away." By 1971, Bryant felt the time had arrived, and he pounced on John Mitchell.

He picked a lucky moment to call the Mitchell home in Mobile. John was home from Arizona on a break, and Bryant had a chance to make his pitch to father, mother, and son at the same time. John was immediately intrigued: "Growing up in Mobile, I'd always been a big fan of Alabama. Alabama won, Bear Bryant won. I wasn't put off by the fact that the teams were all white. That just made me want to be a part of them even more." Unlike Jackson, who was younger and had never played in a college game, Mitchell had two years' experience at the junior-college level, and Bryant thought he might be better prepared to deal with the historical importance of his playing for Alabama. "John," he told him, "you'll be the first black ever to start for Alabama, and that should mean something to you." "It did," recalls Mitchell, who is currently the defensive line coach for the Pittsburgh Steelers, "I liked the idea of the challenge. Coach Bryant liked the idea that I liked the idea." Mitchell's attitude gives credence to those who insist that Bryant was not so much a genius at motivating so much as a genius at finding players who could motivate themselves.

Bryant assured Mrs. Mitchell, "John and I have talked this thing out, and the problems that might arise, but you just trust me." White family or black family, Bryant understood the psychology of recruiting in 1971 as surely as he had back at Kentucky when he took Howard Schnellenberger's skeptical mother for a walk and convinced her that her son was meant to play for him: "As I've always said, the best thing you have going for you in recruiting is a boy's mother, and I made a friend out of Mrs. Mitchell. And she got a friend in old Papa."

On September 10 at the LA Coliseum, Alabama won the coin toss against Southern Cal and elected to kick off. John Mitchell, playing on the kicking team, tore downfield and smashed into Southern Cal's return man. The era of integration at Alabama had begun.

WHAT, THEN, is Bear Bryant's record on integration? By nearly all accounts, he was ahead of most southern whites of his generation in his attitude toward race. Nearly every comment that can be gleaned from his friends and associates over the years indicates that he was for the integration of the football teams he coached. He was certainly no radical, and the evidence for calling him a progressive is slight—though Richmond Flowers Sr. went on record as calling him that.★ It is easy to dismiss his intentions toward integration as attempts to stock his football teams with more talent, but there would be two answers to that charge. The first being that Bryant was, after all, a football coach, and that it was perfectly reasonable for him to see black kids as potential football players on the same terms with whites. He admitted as much in *Bear*. Speaking of his early probes at integration, he replied rhetorically to his critics, "You say, well, you were being selfish. You were just trying to get good players. That's right. I was. I wanted to win, and there was a couple of black boys then who could have helped us a lot." The second response would be that, after all, a great many other football coaches could also have been helped by black players, and the overwhelming majority of them were *not* in favor of integration. So therefore, it must be said that on this issue, Bryant stands out.

At least, that is, in his personal feelings. On the more important issue of acting on them, of taking the lead in integration, Bryant did little. Paul

---

★ Dunnavant thought, "Bryant was a progressive in the race issue. We talked about it several times, and it was clear to me that he was all for integration." (*Coach*, p. 249)

Finebaum, the outspoken sports radio talk show host, is not prepared to give Bryant a passing grade in this area. "I don't buy the argument that Bryant couldn't have done more," he says. "He had more power than any football coach in the South, maybe in the country, and any public declaration from him would have helped enormously. I honestly wish he'd have forced integration a couple of years earlier. It would have enhanced his legacy." Finebaum is right. Even allowing for the pressure Bryant was under from George Wallace—and this should not be underestimated, as Wallace was more than another bigoted southern governor, he was the most powerful symbol of segregation in the entire twentieth century—it is disappointing that Bryant did not do more or at least attempt to do more to become, in his own words, "the Branch Rickey of football." One sees the beginning of such attempts in his statement to *Look* magazine in 1965 that "Negro players in Southeastern Conference games are coming," a bold declaration for that time and period and one that surely must have angered Wallace and made Bryant's own university president squirm. Perhaps one also can see his desire to make a change in his Hamlet-like considerations about running for governor. But ultimately, he never acted on his beliefs.

Bryant was a University of Alabama man. For better or worse, and in some cases it could be argued for the worse, he believed sincerely that the highest good he could achieve was to serve the university that had given him the opportunity to make a life for himself. Rightly or wrongly, he felt that forcing integration prematurely would have hurt Alabama, and there is some evidence that he was right. As Wayne Flint, professor of history at Auburn, says, "The University of Alabama was George Wallace's flagship for segregation. He didn't try to block any doorways at Auburn." This is not a defense of Bryant's failure to do more to integrate, but an attempt at an explanation that fits the known facts.

That being said, Bear Bryant's record on integration did not end with his failure to make a public declaration prior to the signing of Wilbur Jackson. Surely he also has a right to be judged on the second half of his coaching career at Alabama, which began officially on September 10, 1971, in Los Angeles. Ozzie Newsome later made a controversial remark that angered those who felt Bryant was not forceful enough on integration. "I said, 'Martin Luther King Jr. preached equality. Coach Bryant practiced it.' I'm not saying he couldn't have done more to integrate the football team faster, but when I was there there were no complaints from black players about unfairness from Coach Bryant. I can tell you that the man practiced what he preached."

"Nothing changed over the weekends of either the 1970 or 1971 Alabama–Southern Cal game," remembers Professor Flint, "but you could see it start to change. As Churchill said of El Alamein, it wasn't the beginning of the end, but it was the end of the beginning."

PART FOUR

Coach Bryant and Assistant Coach Sylvester Croom, 1982.
The Crimson Tide's first black offensive lineman and an All-America
player in 1974, Croom became an assistant coach at Alabama in 1976,
went on to the NFL, and, in 2004, became the Southeastern Conference's first black head coach, at Mississippi State. (R. D. Moore)

Chapter 10

Bear
Redux

There are no second acts in American lives.

—F. Scott Fitzgerald

F. Scott Fitzgerald never met Bear Bryant.

—Mickey Herskowitz

ON THURSDAY, SEPTEMBER 9, 1971, Bear Bryant was smoking a Chesterfield in his Los Angeles hotel room when he received a call from his old friend Darrell Royal. "You think McKay knows?" Royal asked. "Naw," replied Bryant. "I don't think he has any idea."

Bryant guessed correctly. On the following afternoon on national television, the Alabama Crimson Tide, an eleven- to fourteen-point underdog, depending on your source, lined up and began a radical new era in the school's football history. And John Mitchell made his presence known during the first play, slamming the Southern Cal kick returner to the turf of the LA Coliseum. John McKay must have winced, still stung by his naiveté in discussing an unsigned Mitchell in front of Bryant. But that was nothing compared to the shock McKay and his staff got a few minutes later when, following a Trojan punt, Alabama came out of the huddle and lined up over the ball. In back of quarterback Terry Davis, the three running backs were set in an inverted V-shaped formation—the fullback was directly behind the quarterback, and each halfback to either side in back of the fullback. The Southern Cal coaches knew immediately what it was: the "wishbone" formation, which had been used at both Texas and Oklahoma. Darrell Royal had made spectacular use of it with the Longhorns, going undefeated and winning the national championship for the 1969 season (after gouging out a tough 21–17 victory over Notre Dame in the Cotton Bowl) and had very nearly ridden it to a second consecutive national championship (before Notre Dame Coach Ara Parseghian devised a defense that stopped the wishbone cold in the 1971 Cotton Bowl). "They got us," says Craig Fertig. "We had exchanged game films from the previous season, but of course all of theirs showed them running the pro-set. We didn't have a clue about the wishbone." In fact, Alabama had used the wishbone in a few circumstances that season, "mostly," says Johnny Musso, "when we were down close to the goal line, inside our opponent's ten-yard line." Scott Hunter recalls having used it for a long-gainer in the famed "Shootout" with Archie Manning and Ole Miss. "But it was only for one or two plays," says Hunter. "We caught them by surprise. It wasn't like we thought of the wishbone as an important part of our offense."

Throughout most of the first half, USC's talented but befuddled defensive players pointed fingers at each other or stared toward their coaches with "What's up?" gestures, trying to figure who was supposed to be where doing what to whom. Paced by slashing runs from Johnny Musso, the All-America runner who had been one of the few high spots on the 1970 team, Alabama jumped to a 17–0 halftime lead. The Trojans regained their composure in the second half, partly because of veteran players such as Sam Cunningham, and partly because Bryant, still feeling out his new offense, played it a bit close to the vest when a long pass or two might have broken the game open. But Southern Cal came up with no more than ten points in the final two quarters, and Alabama left the field with one of its all-time great upset victories. It was the two hundredth win of Bryant's coaching career, and it came the day before his fifty-eighth birthday. Back in Birmingham and Tuscaloosa, Alabama fans partied all night. The integration of the Alabama football team had come off without a hitch, and Bear Bryant had given notice that he was back, with a vengeance.

Later, after Darrell Royal's retirement, Texas would scrap the wishbone formation, and Alabama under Bryant would be the school most identified in the minds of fans with the most exciting of all college football offenses.

Legends would build up around how he first came to adopt it, but what is certain is that Bryant first saw the wishbone up close at the end of the 1970 season when the Tide played to a desperate 24–24 tie with Oklahoma in the Astro Bluebonnet Bowl. Larry Lacewell, the son of his old Fordyce pal, Chink, was then an assistant coach with the Sooners, and Bryant picked his brain about the finer points of triple-option football. "I think one of the things he liked about it," says Lacewell, "is that it was a *college* football formation. It was exactly the kind of thing they wouldn't run in the pros because the quarterbacks had to do too much running and they might get injured. I think that putting the integration problem behind him took a lot of pressure off and that discovering the wishbone made football fun for him again."

OFFICIAL CREDIT for developing the wishbone must go to Royal's assistant, Emory Bellard. "I was still running the split-T we used under Wilkinson," Royal says. "Emory's idea looked intriguing. In some ways it was a throwback to some of the old formations—it had some of the same qualities as the split-T and what they used to call the 'Notre Dame box' in the way it gave you several options on a single play and capitalized on the confusion it caused in opposing defenses—it forced them to make decisions in a split second after the ball was snapped." But the wishbone was more than just a throwback to the old days: it had some unique features that Bryant was quick to spot and the first coach to exploit.

Early in 1968, Royal had called Bryant to tell him about his new offense, one that utilized *four* running backs—this at a time when college football was moving more and more toward a wide-open passing game. After describing it in detail, he told Bryant, "Don't say anything. We're going to pull it on Houston." It didn't work well against Houston, who tied the Longhorns on opening day, and it didn't work all that well against Texas Tech, who beat Texas in the second game. But after that, the Longhorns began to gel with the wishbone, winning the rest of their games, including a thorough whipping of Tennessee in the Cotton Bowl. Bryant monitored his friend's progress from afar. From the third game of the 1968 season to the last game in 1970, Texas didn't lose a game.

In the spring of 1971, Bryant flew to Austin to meet with Royal. He was so anxious to get started on learning about the wishbone that he arrived for the first session before Royal and his staff. Jones Ramsey, his old friend and drinking buddy from the A&M years, was the first to show up. (Bryant had recommended him for the PR job at the University of Texas.) "I found him sitting on the steps," Ramsey recalls, "looking like a racehorse chomping at the bit. Most of our staff was just getting out of bed. I said, 'Goodness, Paul, what are you doing up so early?' He said, 'Damn, Jones, don't they take their football seriously around here?'"

The Royals, who were having their house remodeled, were living in an apartment near the Texas campus. The apartment soon became crowded; Bryant moved in and Royal had a projector and several reels of game tapes sent over from the office. After one day of watching Texas steamroll opposing defenses, Bryant told his friend that he had seen enough—he had made his decision. Before returning to Tuscaloosa, Bryant extracted a promise from Royal. Could Bryant call him at any time during the accelerated practice sessions he was going to initiate? "I told him, 'Coach, when I'm not on the field, I'm yours.'"

Alabama held a coaching clinic every summer in Tuscaloosa, and Bryant decided he could kill two birds with one stone by inviting Royal, Bellard, and other Texas coaches to speak in Tuscaloosa. After the Texans gave their talks to the assembled high school and college coaches, Bryant brought them together with his offensive staff for a private crash course in the wishbone while he and Royal went out to play golf. The session was held at a local hotel; Bryant didn't want to take a chance that some visiting sportswriter would recognize Bellard commiserating with the Alabama offensive coaches and start rumors.

Less than a week before fall practice was scheduled to begin, Bryant called a meeting of his coaches. "He told us, 'I'm not going to go on this way,'" recalls Jimmy Sharpe. "'I made a decision. We're going to sink or swim with the wishbone. This isn't going to be a trial or anything. This is going to be a commitment. Is there anyone who has any objections?' We were caught off guard," says Rutledge. "Some of us said things like 'Well, Coach, don't you think this is a little sudden? Do you think we really have enough time before the season to make this work?' He said, 'This is what we're going to do. Anyone who doesn't agree, I'll be happy to help you find new jobs.' We said, 'Coach, I think we can make this work.'"

A short time later, Bryant walked into the squad meeting and informed his players that the pro-style passing game they had used the previous two years was a thing of the past. They would start the season against Southern Cal using the wishbone. The players looked at each other and kind of shrugged. Nobody objected, but they couldn't help wonder what they were getting themselves into. Their coach reassured them. "Trust me, if I didn't think you could do this, I wouldn't be asking you to try." Of course, Bryant wasn't *asking* them, he was telling them.

Why was Bryant so taken with the wishbone? First of all, as he stated clearly in *Bear*, "Formations don't win football games, people do. But they can give you an edge, and that's what coaches look for." Bryant called the wishbone "a glamorized split-T." But, he added,

It's the best formation I've ever seen. In the first place, the fullback is always in the same spot and it's easy for the quarterback to get the ball to him. In the old split-T, with the irregular line splits, the quarterback was reaching a lot of the time. . . . Two, in the old split-T, when the quarterback moved out to option on the defensive end, he had to pitch the ball blind or blind *behind* him to the trailing halfback. With the wishbone, the halfbacks line up a little deeper and closer into the fullback, . . . the halfback winds up about 4 yards wider when the quarterback makes his pitch, and the quarterback can *see* him. It's so much easier.

Bryant was the first coach to grasp the true advantage of the wishbone. To the average fan, the wishbone at work was a thrilling sight: the quarterback could hand off to the fullback on a straight-ahead run or he could fake a handoff, stick the ball in the fullback's belly and then pull it out again and roll out. This gave him plenty of time to gauge the defensive pursuit. If the quarterback was a good runner—and all wishbone quarterbacks were good runners or they wouldn't be wishbone quarterbacks—he could cut to the inside or sprint around the end for a gain, depending on his pursuers and his blockers. If he saw a linebacker coming at him, he could pitch the ball back to the halfback "trailing" on the right (if the play was run to the right side of the field) or on the left. Bryant would add many more wrinkles to the wishbone attack over the years, but those were its bread-and-butter plays.

Bryant saw how those possibilities could result in an even bigger payoff. He preferred quick, agile offensive lineman, "run" blockers who could fire off the ball and strike opponents first. With the straight drop-back passing game, though, this advantage in quickness was negated. Defensive linemen didn't need to look for the run as often and could come straight across the line at the quarterback. It was a simple case of strength on strength, and in many cases Bryant's smaller linemen simply could not hold back their more powerful opponents.

The wishbone changed all that. After watching a couple of hours of Texas's running plays with Royal, Bryant had asked him to "play the tapes that show your pass blocking." "There aren't any, Coach," Royal replied, "you block the same way for the pass as you do for the run." That had sold Bryant, who liked the idea that with the wishbone "you get one-on-one coverage *every* time. Then it's just a matter of whether you can hit the receiver." It took five men, Bryant figured, to defend against the fullback, meaning, usually, the four down linemen and perhaps a middle linebacker moved up close to the line, or a middle guard. That left three defensive players on each side, one to key on the quarterback, one to key on the back who might take the pitch, and just one to cover the pass receiver. Other coaches noted that important fact before Bryant, but no one would exploit it with such success.

While some coaches and football writers scoffed at the wishbone as a "Model T" offense, Bryant understood that it had the potential to be incredibly high-powered. More than any of the great coaches of the running offense, more than Woody Hayes or Darrell Royal or Joe Paterno, Bryant understood the importance of creative passing, and in the wishbone, more than in the split-T or the Notre Dame box or even the pro set, Bryant saw the possibility for breaking a game open with a long pass. Bryant's wishbone regularly averaged around twenty yards per completion, much more than even the best pro-style college passing attacks.

BRYANT'S PREPARATIONS for the season opener against Southern Cal show what he would have been like had he chosen a career in the military rather than football. He sent one of his players, a boy who had spent one season under John McKay before transferring, over to pay a courtesy call on the Trojan staff and instructed him to look around and see if Southern Cal's defense was scrimmaging in preparation for a wishbone offense. (It wasn't.) Doug Layton, who hosted the Alabama pregame radio show, was stunned to get a call from Bryant telling him that "under no circumstances was I supposed to say anything about Alabama using the wishbone. I thought to myself, why would he care? The farthest west you could pick up the Alabama broadcast would have been New Orleans, and we went on the air just fifteen minutes before game time. But then I realized, he figured some Southern Cal grad in Louisiana might hear, phone coach McKay, and the USC coaching staff would start to formulate some defense they could install after the first half."

John Forney, who did the Alabama play-by-play broadcast, was instructed to say nothing to his Southern Cal colleague, Mike Walden.* "After exchanging pleasantries," said Forney, "we did a little information swapping, or at least that's what we presumed to do. Mike asked me if Alabama had made any changes or if he could expect to see pretty much the same thing from Alabama as he had in 1970. With as much innocence as I could muster, I told him there had been no changes, that the offense and defense would be basically the same, and added that we hoped Terry Davis would turn out to be the kind of passer we needed to run the offense."[1] The Southern Cal announcers had watched Davis up close during an Alabama practice session and didn't think much of him; he couldn't throw nearly so well as his predecessor, Scott Hunter, who had gone to the Green Bay Packers. What they didn't know is that for that practice session, Bryant had his team working out in the old pro set; as soon as the press and Southern Cal people left, it went back to practicing the wishbone. When the Alabama offense lined up in the wishbone, the Southern Cal crew realized they'd been had and stared daggers at their Alabama counterparts.

Late in the game, faced with a fourth down and two yards to go and not wanting to give Southern Cal's great punt returner Lynn Swann a chance to tie the game, Bryant elected to go for the first down. Johnny Musso was hit by a Trojan tackler in the Alabama backfield but regained his balance and slashed forward for four yards to seal the victory. In the press box, Forney and Layton were joined by a popular black disc jockey from Birmingham known as Tall Paul. The black man and the two white men from Alabama had a victory toast and did a victory dance right there in the

---

* Forney was the Alabama play-by-play man for more than three decades and an invaluable source for information on several stories I wrote on Crimson Tide football over the years. In 1981 he published a book of short fiction, *Crimson Memories, Golden Days and Other Short Stories*, which included a foreword by Mary Harmon Bryant.

broadcast booth to celebrate a new era. The Trojan's play-by-play man, miffed by the behavior of the boisterous southerners, asked the three to tone it down. Back in Alabama, the joy was unconfined.

Sunday morning, in the lead paragraph of the game story in the *Los Angeles Herald-Examiner*, Bud Furillo wrote, "Paul (Bear) Bryant, the world's best college coach, has reached the stage in his life where he'd like to get things done in a hurry, even if he does talk slow. The Bear is getting high on hours, as his 58th birthday today makes clear. So he didn't mess around waiting long for his 200th coaching victory. Bear reached out and grabbed it from a USC football team favored by a dozen points."[2]

THE ALABAMA wishbone steamrolled its opponents for the next seven weeks as no team in school history had ever done, averaging better than thirty-eight points a game. After a 40–6 win over Ole Miss in week four, *Sports Illustrated*—perhaps referring back to the remarks made by Tennessee linebacker Steve Kiner two years before—headed a feature on the Tide resurgence: "Pride in a Red Jersey."[3] Tennessee found out the hard way in week six when it was beaten 32–15, the first Tide victory over the Vols since 1966. Not until week nine, against Louisiana State in Baton Rouge, did the Tide face a stiff challenge, winning by just one touchdown, 14–7. Alabama rolled into the final week of the season unbeaten and in the middle of the fight for the national championship.

Since Bryant's return to Alabama in 1958, the Alabama-Auburn game had begun to pull even and then ahead of the Tennessee game in importance to Tide fans. By the mid-1960s Alabama's number-one priority had become beating Auburn. But the 1971 contest was unique—for the first time ever, both schools went into the game unbeaten. Both had a nationally acclaimed star: Auburn had quarterback Pat Sullivan, who would become the first player in the school's history to win the trophy named for former Auburn coach John Heisman, and Alabama had consensus All-America Johnny Musso, who was nicknamed "The Italian Stallion," five years before Sylvester Stallone copped the name for *Rocky*.

Musso very nearly missed the biggest game in Alabama-Auburn history. The week before the game, in practice, he injured his foot. Bryant almost held him out of the game, not because Musso had asked him, but because he thought the injury would keep him from being the workhorse he needed him to be against Auburn. John David Crow was convinced that Musso "was 90 percent physically sound, and he'd make up the last 10 percent with heart." Musso, who started the week on crutches and did not suit up for the Friday pregame workout, played and gave 110 percent, tearing up the Auburn defense for 167 yards and two touchdowns. Still, the game was tight, 14–7 in favor of Alabama, going into the fourth quarter. Finally, the relentless Tide pressure broke the Tigers down, for a 31–7 rout.

The regular season for Bryant's new model Crimson Tide began and ended on a spectacular note. After losing nine games in the previous two years, Alabama had rebounded to Bryant's fourth undefeated regular season since 1958. Unfortunately, there was still a bowl game to play. Alabama fans, the memories of their 1966 and 1967 thrashings of Nebraska still warm, couldn't wait to get at the Cornhuskers for the third time in six years. But this was a different kind of Nebraska team, one that, even as the season ended, some observers were calling the greatest in college football history. A more accurate assessment would have been "the greatest up to that time in the era of unlimited substitution," because the 1971 Cornhuskers, who went unbeaten, including against their archrivals, the equally unbeaten Oklahoma Sooners in *their* annual showdown, were stocked with pro prospects. The team was the prototype for the monster college teams of the 1970s and 1980s. "Nebraska," wrote Dan Jenkins in *Sports Illustrated* after the Cornhuskers defeated the Sooners, "was a muscled-up bully, reflecting the personality of [coach] Bob Devaney."[4] Bryant began to suspect as much after Bud Wilkinson gave him the lowdown just before the Orange Bowl. "I'm going to tell you, Nebraska has more great athletes than have ever been on one team." The Cornhuskers had All-America candidates on both sides of the ball: quarterback Jerry Tagge, tailback Jeff Kinney, linebacker Willie Harper, middle guard Rich Glover, and, most spectacular of all, Johnny Rodgers, the receiver, kick and punt returner, and all-around "scat back" whom everyone knew was the best player in the nation in 1971 but, because of a lingering prejudice against juniors getting the Heisman, had to wait until the following season to get the award.★

★ Curiously, not one of the great college players from the Nebraska 1970–1972 teams ever became a major professional star. No satisfactory reason has ever been offered for this, though some blame the intensive Nebraska weight-training program for burning out its players too early. Rodgers, who set NCAA records with eight punt returns and

The Cornhuskers began the early 1970s with a remarkable run. In 1970, with just a tie to spoil their record, they had won the national championship after Notre Dame upset previous number-one Texas in the Cotton Bowl; at the end of the 1972 season, in the Orange Bowl, they would clobber Notre Dame 40–6. At the end of the 1971 season, in the Orange Bowl, they faced unbeaten Alabama. Late in the first quarter, with the game scoreless, Alabama lost the ball after a fumbled punt snap in its own territory. The Cornhuskers jumped to a quick 7–0 lead on a touchdown run by Kinney; a few minutes later Rodgers, building his portfolio for the Heisman race, took a punt and ran seventy-seven yards for the second Nebraska touchdown. Shaken, Alabama then fumbled during the ensuing kickoff, Nebraska recovered the ball at the Tide twenty-seven, and moments later, the score was 21–0, and that was pretty much it. Alabama lost, 38–6. Even without the bad breaks, the Tide was probably overmatched. Terry Davis was a terrific wishbone quarterback, but in third-and-long passing situations he did not have the arm to consistently hit his receivers on the big passes downfield. A more basic problem, though, was that Bryant was still trying to win with undersized linemen; center Jimmy Grammer weighed about two hundred pounds and simply could not control Nebraska's bearlike middle guard, Rich Glover, who outweighed him by nearly forty pounds. In an earlier era, Alabama might have been able to whip bigger, stronger teams through stamina, but now, with a team able to substitute as often as it liked, size and strength assumed greater importance, especially in line play.

"When we played both ways," said Bryant, assessing the Nebraska game two years later in *Bear*, "we could take a guy like [Jimmy] Sharpe, 194 pounds, hone him down, have him so quick, and he'd go out and beat a guy who weighed 240. They used to ask me what I thought about little players. I said they looked as good to me pitching the ball to the official behind the goal as the big ones do."

But two-platoon football changed all that. Just ten years earlier, Alabama linemen averaged about six feet in height and about 200 pounds in weight;

---

nine kickoff returns for touchdowns, probably had the best shot at NFL stardom. But after being drafted in the first round by the San Diego Chargers in 1973, he bypassed the NFL to play in the Canadian Football League. He didn't make it to the NFL until five seasons later, and by then his hamstring and knee injuries all but ended his pro football career.

now Alabama's opponents up front were six feet four and six feet five inches tall and weighed usually more than 250 pounds, and Alabama was forced to match them. Bigger linemen and a more effective passing game were needed if Alabama was going to make it back to the top rung of national powers. A second-place finish in the United Press International poll and a fourth place in the Associated Press poll after the 1972 bowl game were not enough. Bryant would make the needed adjustments, and the Tide would be back on top.

THE YEAR 1972 looked like the one. Johnny Musso was gone, drafted by the Chicago Bears, but Wilbur Jackson moved from receiver to running back and became an integral part of the Tide offense. Big John Hannah came of age. Hannah, from Albertville, Alabama, had the requisite quickness for a Bear Bryant offensive lineman combined with pro-style size and strength; in his senior year of 1972 he stood about six foot three inches and weighed nearly 275. Bryant thought him the greatest college lineman he had ever seen, and his subsequent success with the New England Patriots, nine Pro Bowl appearances, and a plaque in the Pro Football Hall of Fame, supported that judgment. The man who would play alongside Hannah in 1972, Sylvester Croom, was Bryant's first black offensive lineman. He had grown up in Tuscaloosa hearing stories of the Klan's power and wondering if his football future would be in Alabama or away from home. Like Paul Bryant and so many other boys who played for the Tide, he knew that football was his ticket out. "My father worked in a sawmill," Croom says. "He told me, 'I know it's a rough game, but you play football or you go to work.' And I knew there wasn't any future in that saw mill." Like John Mitchell before him, Croom wanted to play with the best and was attracted to the challenge of playing for Bryant. "I saw that people did things either out of fear of him or to prove to him that you were better than what he thought. With me, it was a little of both. Whatever the reasons, I was better for him than I thought I could be. He was the only man I ever knew who could kick you in the butt and make you like him for it." Bryant needed a center and asked Croom if he would make the switch. "I'd played a couple of different positions for two years, but I kind of avoided playing center, not because I didn't think I could do it, but because I felt it would make me look like a failure at the other positions. Coach Bryant called me into his office one day and asked me if I'd move to center for the good of the team. He didn't tell me, he asked me, and that impressed me. I only had one question for him: 'Coach, do you think I can do it? Do you think that's my position?' He looked me in the eye and said, 'Yes, Sylvester, I do.' That was it. That was good enough for me." For the next two years, Croom was the center.

In 1975, Croom graduated with a bachelor's degree in history and a minor in biology; he signed with the New Orleans Saints as a free agent. After graduation, Bryant stopped him in the hall and surprised Sylvester just as he himself had been surprised by Frank Thomas forty years before. He put his hand on Croom's shoulder, "If things don't work out for you in the NFL, come back and see me." "I was really surprised," says Croom. "I hadn't realized that he thought about me as a possible coach. Outside of football, we hadn't talked all that much while I was a player." He played for one year with the Saints, then returned to Alabama to become the school's first black assistant coach. (Croom also went back to school and earned his master's in educational administration from the university in 1977.)

Terry Davis's passing limitations notwithstanding, the Alabama offense was overpowering through the first ten games of the 1972 season. After beating Virginia Tech 52–13 on November 18, the Tide was averaging just under thirty-eight points per game. The only hitch came against Tennessee at Knoxville in the sixth game of the season. With less than three minutes left to play, Tennessee led 10–3 and seemed to be on the verge of a spectacular upset, just as it had been in 1966. And just as in 1966, its roof caved in. Davis completed two quick passes for forty-six yards, followed by a Wilbur Jackson touchdown run. This left Bryant with the option of kicking the extra point for the tie—a sure bet with his fine kicker, Bill Davis—or the riskier option of playing for the win by running or passing for the two-point conversion from the Tennessee three-yard line. Bryant chose to go for the tying kick and, for the first time in his career, aside from the Georgia Tech game following the Holt-Graning incident, was greeted by a chorus of boos from opposing fans. But Bryant had a plan, or rather, he listened to one of his coaches who had one. Pat Dye figured that "with our timeouts remaining, we could get twenty to thirty yards and give Bill Davis a chance to win it with a field goal." But luck, as Branch Rickey said, is the residue of design, and Alabama's attacking-style defense brought it a huge bonus. On second down, John Mitchell and Mike DuBose stuffed Tennessee's runner in the backfield for a six-yard loss. On third and sixteen, Condredge Holloway—the black quarterback who had wanted to play quarterback for Bryant at Alabama—dropped back to pass, probably with the intention of throwing the ball out of bounds if he couldn't immediately spot an open receiver, but DuBose and Woodrow Lowe hit him before he could bring his arm forward, Holloway fumbled the ball, and John Mitchell recovered it at the Tennessee twenty-two with less than ninety seconds to play. Many coaches would have tried to kick the winning field goal right there, but Bryant wanted more and had the confidence that his team could get it. On the first play, Terry Davis rolled to his right and saw orange uniforms rush to cover Wilbur Jackson, who was to receive the pitch. Davis decided to keep the ball and went all the way for the winning touchdown. Alabama had scored the tying and winning touchdowns in a total of thirty-six seconds.

As the jubilant Alabama players and staff left the stadium named for Bryant's old nemesis, General Neyland, a drunken Tennessee fan shouted to Bryant, "Bear, you may be good, but you're the luckiest sonuvabitch I've ever seen!" "Mister," Bryant replied, "I think you are right on both counts."

Three weeks later, Alabama won a 35–21 thriller against McClendon's LSU Tigers in Birmingham. This year the Tigers had future NFL star Bert Jones at quarterback. Alabama was unbeaten, ranked second; LSU was unbeaten, ranked sixth. The score was just 7–7 at the half, but in the third period, Terry Davis, taking advantage of an LSU defense drawn up close to stop the wishbone offense, threw touchdown passes of twenty-five and twenty-seven yards to end Wayne Wheeler, to break the game open.

The 1972 season was supposed to end with Alabama wondering who it would be playing for the national championship. Instead, the season ended in perhaps the most bizarre game of Bryant's career. The outmanned Auburn Tigers put up a stiff fight on defense, but were helpless to score. With about six minutes to play, they were trailing 16–0—Alabama had missed an extra point after its first touchdown, which seemed meaningless at the time. On fourth down deep in Alabama territory, Shug Jordan elected to go for a field goal—a seemingly absurd decision, as it left Auburn virtually no chance of winning other than stopping Alabama twice on consecutive possessions and then scoring two touchdowns against almost ridiculous odds. And that is precisely what happened, though even Auburn fans in their wildest dreams could not have predicted exactly how. With approximately five minutes to play, Auburn linebacker Bill Newton spotted a hole in the Alabama blocking and soared through to block the punt;

defensive back David Langer scooped the ball at the twenty-five and ran it into the end zone for a touchdown. The Auburn fans came alive: there was still hope, however little, with the score 16–10 and four minutes to play.

It was rare enough to see an Alabama punt blocked, but no one could remember the Tide having two punts blocked in a game since Ears Whitworth had been coach. Once again Alabama was forced to kick, and once again, someone up front blew a blocking assignment. Thirty-three years later, Sylvester Croom still will not say who. "I'm not going to say whose fault it was. Teams lose games as teams." Once again Newton roared through the same hole and blocked the punt, once again Langer scooped it up, this time having to run only twenty yards for the touchdown. Auburn went ahead 17–16, and that's how the game ended.

Bryant was so devastated that he refrained from ripping into his players with the usual ferocity; perhaps he realized how devastated they were. Perhaps, too, he felt a tad guilty for an ill-advised remark that helped fire up the Tigers. Before the game, responding to a comment that Auburn was supposed to be a "cow college," Bryant reportedly had said, "I'd rather beat that 'cow college' than beat Notre Dame."* The exact source of the "cow college" quote has been difficult to pin down; most feel that Bryant was actually intending some sort of compliment, but Auburn fans, after years of humiliation, jumped on any chance to motivate their players.

Alabama had held Auburn to the incredible total of just eighty net yards from scrimmage—and still lost the game. It was the only regular-season defeat that Alabama would suffer from 1971 through 1974.

"Sometimes before I go to sleep at night," says Croom, "I stare at the ceiling thinking about the end of that game. I just go, 'Damn!' You know why people really remember it so well? Because Auburn didn't win another game against Alabama for the next ten years. That's all Auburn fans had to cheer about for ten years." After the loss to Auburn, the air seemed to leak out of Alabama's balloon. Heavily favored against Darrell Royal's Longhorns in a battle of wishbones in the Cotton Bowl, Alabama jumped to a 7–0 lead on a dazzling thirty-one-yard touchdown run by Wilbur Jackson and led 13–3 at the half. Then, says Croom, "We just lost our fire, our spirit, our concentration." Texas scored in the third quarter to make it 13–10, and then,

---

* Bryant probably didn't know this, but in the 1920s it was common for the eastern powers to insult Notre Dame by calling them a "cow college."

in the fourth quarter, Longhorn quarterback Alan Lowry ran thirty yards down the sideline for a touchdown, to make the final score 17–13.

IN 1973, Alabama's basketball team was invited to play in the National Invitation Tournament in New York, a plum in the time before the National Collegiate Athletic Association relegated the NIT to the status of backwater. Tide basketball coach C. M. Newton, a former Kentucky player under Adolph Rupp, invited Bryant, Alabama's athletic director, to come and watch his boys play Manhattan at Madison Square Garden; Bryant, never one to miss a chance to take a trip to New York, was enthusiastic. The rules about who could sit on a team bench were fairly strict, but Newton did not have the heart to tell his boss that he couldn't sit with the team. Newton was even more abashed to find out that Bryant had asked his friend, New York Jets owner Sonny Werblin, to join him. Enjoying himself immensely, Bryant good-naturedly kibitzed the referees about the "penalties"—the basketball term is "fouls"—they were calling on Alabama. Once, an errant pass came to the Alabama bench and Bryant instinctively stood up and caught it. The Tide should have been called for a technical foul, but instead the referee came over to the Alabama side and calmly explained to Bryant that he could not touch a ball that was still in play. Bryant promised not to do it again. The Crimson Tide beat Manhattan by a point. After the final buzzer, the referee went over to ask Bear Bryant for his autograph.

BY 1973 Bryant had found the right linemen, running backs, and passers. The right defense too. Before the 1973 season, John Mitchell was asked to join the Alabama staff as defensive line coach. The integration of the Alabama football team had been a tortuous process, but the integration of the coaching staff was accomplished with surprising swiftness and no controversy. The first black player to take the field for Alabama became the first black coach.★

★ Mitchell coached at Alabama for four years before leaving, with Bryant's recommendation, for a six-year stint at Arkansas with Lou Holtz. In 1990, he became the first black defensive coordinator in the Southeastern Conference at Louisiana State, and in 1994 he joined the Pittsburgh Steelers' coaching staff.

Bryant came very close to calling the 1973 team his best team ever—as close as a missed extra point. "I tell you, I have never been around another team like that one we had in 1973. We really put it together on the field and off the field; we enjoyed being around each other. Black, whites, the rich, the poor—there was some kind of togetherness. . . . We had a feeling in 1973 that's impossible to describe. And we accomplished so much. We came from behind to win at Kentucky, won in that scorching heat against Florida, beat Louisiana State to win the Southeastern Conference championship in a hard hitting game, and whipped Auburn to pay them back for those two blocked punts the season before."

Wilbur Jackson blossomed as a runner, and Bryant found two splendid quarterbacks to run the wishbone. In later years, Richard Todd would be referred to as the "passing quarterback" and Gary Rutledge the "running quarterback," but people were projecting Todd's professional success with the New York Jets back on his college career. In point of fact, Todd was a superb runner and Rutledge a more-than-capable passer, and both gave the wishbone more sophisticated dimensions than it had had against Nebraska in the 1972 Orange Bowl. Opposing defenses had no idea how to defend against Alabama; the 1973 Tide averaged better than forty-one points per game and totaled over 4,000 yards rushing, an NCAA record. The quarterbacks didn't pass often, but when they fired, they aimed to kill: the 1973 Tide averaged an eye-popping 24.8 yards per completed pass, the highest average in the nation. A few of the games seemed surreally unfair. In beating Virginia Tech 77–6, Alabama gained 828 yards of total offense, twice what a very good team averages on a normal day. Four Alabama runners, led by Wilbur Jackson, gained over 100 yards, another NCAA record. In beating the California Golden Bears on opening day, 66–0, Bryant used seventy-three players, and eight different runners scored touchdowns. The Tide offense rushed for 405 yards and passed for 262 more. Todd and Rutledge threw two touchdown passes each. In the newspaper, the game seemed a shameless mismatch, but Cal had as much front-line talent as Alabama. The Golden Bears had two quarterbacks who went to the pros, Steve Bartkowski and Vince Ferragamo, who would take the Los Angeles Rams to the 1980 Super Bowl; a running back, Chuck Muncie, who starred with the San Diego Chargers; and a wide receiver, Wesley Walker, who in a few years would be catching touchdown passes from Richard Todd for the New York Jets.

Alabama scored 154 points in winning the next five games. LSU blitzed like mad, attempting to spill into the Alabama backfield and disrupt the wishbone; Alabama quarterbacks settled down, spotted the single coverage on their wide receivers, and burned LSU on long passes for a 21–7 win. Angered all season long by bumper stickers on the cars and pickup trucks of Auburn fans which read, "Punt, Bama, Punt," the Tide got revenge, methodically destroying the Tigers 35–0 in Birmingham. "Believe me," says Gary Rutledge, "when I say the only reason that game wasn't 56–0 or something like that was Coach Bryant's respect for Coach Jordan. We could have made that score whatever we wanted it to be."

Richard Todd, who many thought could throw as well as Joe Namath or Ken Stabler, got most of the attention, but Rutledge, nicknamed "Rooster" by his teammates for his red hair, was one of the two players who best exemplified the spirit of the new Crimson Tide. The son of a former minor league ballplayer, Rutledge was regarded by some as too skinny for big-time college ball when he played for Birmingham's famed football factory, Banks High School. (One of his backfield partners was Johnny Musso.) As a red-shirted freshman, he spent a season playing "dummy" quarterback, getting knocked around by All-Americas John Mitchell and Robin Parkhouse. By 1973, he was ready to help lead Alabama to a national championship. So was Woodrow Lowe, who, like Rutledge, didn't seem to be big enough for big-time college football. When he graduated from Phenix City's Central High School in South Alabama, Lowe was five feet eleven inches tall and weighed about 185 pounds; some questioned whether he was big enough to play defensive back, let alone linebacker. "I didn't have too many schools interested in me," he recalls. "My parents couldn't afford to send me to school, so the only way I could go was on a scholarship. If I didn't get one, I had already decided to join the Navy. In fact, I had already taken the test to get in."[5] Pat Dye, the linebackers coach, was impressed with his speed and determination and wanted him; Bryant, when he finally met him, was equally impressed. Lowe was one of the new breed of black athletes, one who reminded Bryant of the scrappy white kids of his youth, boys who played football not for a shot at the pros but for scholarship and school. No one could have guessed at the time that the undersized kid *would* get the scholarship *and* the pro contract (Lowe played eleven seasons with the San Diego Chargers). Bryant liked the way Lowe streaked downfield and slammed into blockers on the kickoff team. Since the NCAA had okayed the use of freshmen on varsity teams, Lowe was eligible to play and showed so much enthusiasm against Duke in the opening game in 1972 that he was named captain of special teams. Before the 1973 season began, Bryant paid him the ultimate compliment: "Woodrow Lowe might be as good as Lee Roy Jordan before the season is over." When Lowe read Bryant's words in a local newspaper, he was confused. Lowe, who was eight years old in 1961, knew Lee Roy Jordan as a star with the Dallas Cowboys and did not realize Jordan had once starred on an Alabama national championship team.

At the end of the 1973 regular season, Nebraska, which had won the national title in 1970 and 1971, and Southern Cal, which had won it in 1972, faltered, leaving three teams unbeaten and at the top in both major polls: Alabama ranked number one; Oklahoma, number two; and Notre Dame, number three. Oklahoma had one tie in its season record and was ruled ineligible for postseason play by the NCAA because of recruiting violations. That left two super teams to play for the mythical national title. The country was electrified by the likelihood of the first-ever meeting between the Fighting Irish of Notre Dame and the Alabama Crimson Tide; "It's doubtful," reported *Sports Illustrated*, "that any college bowl game ever featured two teams with such an itch to get at one another."[6] Great matchups on paper seldom result in great games on the field, but at the Sugar Bowl in New Orleans on New Year's Eve 1973, Alabama and Notre Dame played the greatest game in the history of college football.

THAT'S HOW a great many people who saw the game—fans of the winning team, fans of the losing team, and just plain fans—still remember it. For some unexplained reason, a tape of the game has never been made available to the public or replayed on any sports classic channel. Until it is, you'll simply have to trust the words of the people who saw it.

Alabama brought some issues into the game, as many fans were still smarting from the 1966 snub—many a pickup truck from the Gulf Coast to the Tennessee border still had a faded bumper sticker that read, "To hell with AP and UPI, Bama's Number One!" Notre Dame had some issues too, including resentment over talk that the Irish had not really earned the national championship in 1966, and the knowledge that Bear Bryant had been highly critical of Ara Parseghian's strategy of playing for the tie against Michigan State. Many Notre Dame fans also held a lingering belief that the mostly Protestant fan base of Alabama harbored anti-Catholic sentiments. Some sportswriter speculated openly about possible ugliness between Irish and Tide fans; it probably helped that the game would be held in New Orleans, the Deep South's quintessential party city, which was largely Catholic. Given the two schools' football traditions—and who besides a few misguided Tennessee or Michigan or Southern Cal fans would argue that Notre Dame and Alabama did not have the two greatest traditions in college football?—it was amazing that they had never faced each other on the gridiron.

In addition to issues, Notre Dame brought a sensational football team to New Orleans. The Irish offense, while not so explosive as Alabama's, was equally well balanced, featuring both power and speed and the pinpoint passing of quarterback (and future Buffalo Bills offensive coordinator) Tom Clements. Perhaps its best all-around player was future NFL Hall of Famer Dave Casper, a fine blocker and capable receiver from the tight end position who made several All-America teams. The Irish also had a defense that was even stingier than Alabama's, allowing just sixty-six points in ten games. Most of all, they had a head coach in Ara Parseghian, who was probably a more brilliant strategist than even Bryant. It was Parseghian who first conceived of a plan for stopping the wishbone offense, sometimes inserting an extra linebacker or safety to shadow the quarterback and trailing halfbacks on rollouts, "mirroring" the wishbone attack. Of course, when Notre Dame won its famous upset over Texas in the 1971 Cotton Bowl, it had not faced a wishbone offense with as many dimensions as Alabama's, and certainly not one with a passer as good as either Richard Todd or Gary Rutledge. All in all, the Sugar Bowl game looked like perhaps the greatest intersectional grudge match college football had ever seen.

Enthusiasm for the game reached fever pitch by New Year's Eve Day, with scalpers asking and getting over two thousand dollars a ticket. The anticipated TV audience was so huge that Roone Arledge talked a reluctant Howard Cosell into doing the play-by-play. Cosell knew virtually nothing about college football except that it provided players for professional football; when Notre Dame took the field, Cosell gaped at its odd offensive formation—a variation of the T-formation with one wide receiver and a halfback flanked out on the opposite side as a wing man—and exclaimed, "Oh, this college game is *something else!*" It certainly was, with Notre

Dame's T-wing and Alabama's wishbone providing a more varied contrast in offensive styles than one could see in a month of watching pro games.

Bryant's team took the first punch. Clements completed three passes to end Pete Demmerle for fifty-nine yards on the opening drive, setting up a short touchdown run by fullback Wayne Bullock. On the sidelines Bryant and his coaches quickly made adjustments, and Clements and Demmerle would connect on only one more pass that night. Early in the second quarter, the Tide got on track, mixing option runs with short passes and marching downfield, where halfback Randy Billingsley scored from the six-yard line. Notre Dame had missed the extra point on its opening touchdown drive; Alabama made its, to give the Tide a 7–6 lead.

The ensuing kickoff resulted in a jaw-dropping play. Halfback Al Hunter, Notre Dame's fastest player, ripped through Woodrow Lowe and the much-heralded Alabama special-teams coverage for a ninety-three-yard touchdown. It was Notre Dame's first kick return for a touchdown all season, and the first one Alabama had allowed. The Irish lined up at the Tide's three-yard line to go for the two-point conversion; Clements faked a hand-off and flipped a short pass to Demmerle for the score. It was their last connection of the game. Unshaken, Alabama regained its poise and moved into Notre Dame territory for a thirty-nine-yard field goal. The score was 14–10 at the half, and the lead had already changed hands four times.

Early in the third quarter, it looked as if Alabama had finally solved the complex Irish defense and taken control of the game for good. Pinned to its own seven-yard line, the Tide ground out ninety-three yards for the go-ahead touchdown, the final five yards coming on a run by Wilbur Jackson. But near the end of the third quarter, Notre Dame's penetration into the Alabama backfield forced a fumble, with the Irish recovering the ball at the Tide's twelve. Wingback Eric Pennick, starting from a slot on the right side of the field, ran to his left and took a handoff from Clements while the entire Notre Dame line moved to the right. For once, the Alabama defense went to the wrong direction, and Pennick swept untouched around the left end for a touchdown, making the score 21–17. But Alabama was capable of forcing fumbles too, and recovered one at the Notre Dame thirty-nine-yard line early in the fourth quarter. Then, Bryant, sending in a play from the sidelines, made one of the most daring calls of his career. Todd pitched the ball to Mike Stock, a halfback from South Bend, Indiana, who had chosen Alabama over Notre Dame because he wanted to play for Bear Bryant.

Stock rolled to his right and then lofted the ball back to his quarterback, Richard Todd, who carried it into the end zone as the stunned Irish defenders looked on. That made it 23–21, Alabama. Now, though, it was Alabama's turn to miss an extra point. On the sidelines, Bryant grimaced in pain; Notre Dame might now win the game with just a field goal.

Clements, who had been stopped for most of the second and third quarters, now marshaled the Notre Dame offense for a long drive, seventy-seven yards, the big play coming on a thirty-yard completion to Casper. For a moment, it looked as if Notre Dame would take the ball in for a touchdown, but the Tide defense stiffened at the two-yard line. Kicker Bob Thomas made a wobbly kick and the ball barely made it through the uprights. The score was 24–23 with Notre Dame ahead and just minutes left to play. The lead had now changed hands six times.

Then came two series of plays that are still argued about. Alabama moved close to midfield before it was forced to punt, which in this situation was far from fatal. Bryant's intention was to pin the Irish deep inside their territory, possibly inside the five-yard line on one of the Tide's famed "coffin corner" kicks, and force them to punt, an exchange, he hoped, that would put Alabama in position for the winning field goal. The kick went exactly as Bryant had planned, only better, rolling out of bounds at the Notre Dame one-yard line. Notre Dame was called for roughing the kicker, but Alabama declined the penalty and accepted the play. In the broadcast booth, Howard Cosell was appalled, informing the nation that Bryant had made a mental blunder in not taking the penalty that would have given Alabama a first down—or so he thought. Actually, it was Cosell who blundered: in pro football, roughing the kicker was an automatic first down, but in college ball the penalty still would have left Alabama with a fourth down and five yards to go. Notre Dame tried two off-tackle runs, but the Tide defense was unyielding, allowing just two yards, leaving the Irish with a third-and-eight at their own three.

To understand how daring Parseghian's next call was, one must go back decades in time. In today's wide-open game, college teams will pass in any and all situations, but in 1973 teams seldom passed inside their own five-yard line. For Clements to pass in this situation meant the likelihood of an end zone sack for a safety, which would have given Alabama two points and the lead; or an interception, which would have given the Tide the ball deep in Irish territory; or an incomplete pass, which would force the Irish to punt from the back line of the end zone and almost certainly give Alabama the ball just a play or two out of winning field goal range. The usual strategy would have been to run the ball into the mass of the line, settle for perhaps a two-yard gain, and hope for a long punt. But Parseghian, perhaps thinking to redeem himself of charges of having been too conservative in 1966, called for Clements to fake the ball to his fullback and fade back into the end zone. From there, he lofted a high-arching spiral toward the left sideline. Amazingly in retrospect, it was not aimed for either Demmerle or Casper but toward a freshman tight end named Robin Weber. A step or two from the sidelines Weber made the grab and went out of bounds, perhaps ten feet from where Bear Bryant, ashen-faced, was standing. Notre Dame fans erupted. A few seconds later, the Irish had run out the clock and the game was over—24–23, the margin of victory being Alabama's missed extra point. Robin Weber hadn't just made the biggest catch of his Notre Dame career, but his only catch. The next season he was injured and never played another down in a Notre Dame uniform.

In the press box, Herbie Kirby of the *Birmingham Post-Herald* filed his last story, which began, "Call it luck, call it a leprechaun, but the issue in the fortieth annual Sugar Bowl classic was settled here Monday night by a cool Notre Dame quarterback named Tom Clements, who dared to throw from his own end zone with only two minutes left in the game against No. 1-ranked Alabama."[7] Moments after filing the story, Herbie collapsed with a heart attack and died in the press box.

A Japanese sportswriter watching his first American football game began his story with, "I am not sure what was happening on the field, but I know it was something exciting and something good."[8]

In the Alabama locker room, the boys hung their heads unashamedly and wept as a team. Sylvester Croom, Gary Rutledge, and Woodrow Lowe all sat on the stools in front of their lockers and cried as if in unison. Bryant, his own eyes misted and red, told his boys that they had nothing to be ashamed of, that they had played their hearts out and lost to a great team because of their coach's mistakes. When they heard the last part, some of the players wept even harder. It was a great season, he told them; they had whipped Tennessee, beaten a previously unbeaten LSU team to win the conference championship, and taken fearful revenge on Auburn. They had set national records. On the strength of the toughness of their schedule and their performance, they had already been voted half the national championship from the UPI voters. Then, summoning up all the dignity he had seen Bud Wilkinson display nearly twenty-three years before, Bryant walked into the Notre Dame locker room and headed straight for a jubilant Tom Clements. A hush fell over the boisterous Irish players. To the tradition-rich Notre Dame players, it was almost like Knute Rockne had just walked in. The moment would not have been complete without a Bryant malapropism. "Is this Mark Clements?" asked Bear, confusing the Notre Dame quarterback with an Alabama reserve defensive back. Clements was too shaken to correct him. "Yes, Coach, it is," he replied. "Well, son, you're a great quarterback. I just want you to know that."*

Two weeks after the game, Bryant received a letter from Ara Parseghian, the only one he ever received from a coach who beat him. "He said how much his group had enjoyed playing us, how wrong the impressions were beforehand. (They pictured us as a bunch of rednecks, and we had some thoughts about them, too.) He said how much everybody got out of the game, and how great it was for college football that we now had a series going. It was very gracious, Ara's letter. One I'd love to have written him." Relations between Alabama and Notre Dame were no longer strained; in fact, friendships blossomed. That spring, the president of Notre Dame, Father Theodore Hesburgh, was spotted at spring practice in a spiffy new houndstooth cap. When asked where he got it, Hesburgh beamed that it was a gift from his good friend Bear Bryant. Of course, Bryant probably didn't mention to Hesburgh that he had gone into business with his friend Butch Baldone selling houndstooth caps, and that Hesburgh seen wearing one in public was great advertising.

There have been higher-scoring championship games than the 1973 Alabama–Notre Dame clash, but none greater. The match was a once-in-a-century meeting of great football schools, brilliant coaches, and great players. The game was a near-perfect balance between offense and defense, between running and passing. Notre Dame, with the "passing" offense, threw twelve passes; Alabama, with the "running" offense, threw fifteen. The two teams combined to gain 738 yards, yet both defenses played heroically in key situations. The game had spectacular plays, and inspired great performances from the established stars and even produced an unlikely storybook hero in the star-crossed Robin Weber.

* Bryant also misnamed Tom Clements as "Mark" in his autobiography. (*Bear*, p. 315)

Bryant never quite got over losing the 1973 Sugar Bowl. "I don't really consider it a loss. We just ran out of time." Perhaps—and though, as Parseghian had put it, there were no losers in the game—it stung Bryant that he had lost the biggest, most publicized football game of his career. The 1973 Sugar Bowl was a supergame, and most coaches, even great ones, went through their whole careers never getting to coach in a supergame. In 1973, Bryant turned sixty. At his age, who knew if he'd ever get such an opportunity again?

TO AMERICA, it mattered not at all that Alabama's kicker had missed an extra point in the Sugar Bowl or that Alabama had only won the national championship on one of the wire-service polls. Bear Bryant was a national celebrity, and the offseason was filled with banquets, speeches, interviews, and television appearances. In the spring he taped a Dean Martin Roast for Joe Namath. Shortly afterward, he gave a talk at the convention for the American Football Coaches Association in San Francisco. While there, Bryant finally got to swap stories with the man he had long ago selected to play him if a movie of his life were made. John Wayne was to receive an award; Herschel Nissenson remembers them sitting on a couch, laughing, both getting a little looped. Charlie McClendon recalled, "John Wayne was talking to Coach Bryant about a movie where he had played a football coach. I don't remember what movie it was." That would have been *Trouble along the Way*, a 1953 film directed by Michael Kurtiz and costarring Donna Reed. In the film, Wayne's coach says, "Winning isn't everything, it's the only thing," which was later mistakenly attributed to Vince Lombardi and sometimes to Bear Bryant.

It is intriguing to wonder whether America's best-known football coach told Wayne about his brief flirtation with Hollywood, or whether America's most popular movie star told Bryant about his undistinguished college football career.

NEW YORK Yankees principal owner George Steinbrenner met Paul Bryant at coaching clinics in the mid-1950s when George was an assistant football coach, first at Northwestern and then at Purdue. He liked Bryant immediately and kept in touch over the years.* On October 26, 1974, Steinbrenner was Bryant's guest, along with Oakland owner Charlie Finley, whose A's had won the World Series just nine days earlier, at the game in Birmingham between undefeated, fourth-ranked Alabama and the hopelessly outmanned Horned Frogs of Texas Christian University. No one could have guessed that they were to witness a great personal tragedy. On what seemed like a routine play en route to an easy 41–13 Alabama win, TCU running back Kent Waldrep took a pitch from his quarterback and headed toward the right end. Waldrep took a clean hit from two Tide defensive backs, but an Alabama defensive player who had already been knocked down was starting to rise behind Waldrep at the moment he was hit. Waldrep went over backward and landed on his head, snapping his spine. As Waldrep was taken off the field on a stretcher, Bryant seemed stricken. There was no controversy about this play as there had been with the Holt-Graning hit thirteen years before; no one thought for a moment that the injury was the result of anything but a clean hit and an accident. This was irrelevant to Bryant, who spent most of the following Sunday, Monday, and Tuesday at the hospital trying to check in on Kent and console his parents. On Monday, he brought Steinbrenner and Finley by to meet Waldrep and offer hope for his recovery. It was not to be. Tests soon revealed that Waldrep would be paralyzed for life.

"It was a side of him I never knew existed," recalls Steinbrenner. "He kept saying, 'George, George, God help me, this can be a really rough game.'" "He came in and would act like nothing was wrong," Waldrep later said. "And then Mom and Dad years later told me he would go out in the hall and cry with them." In September the following year, TCU stopped paying Waldrep's medical bills. Bryant started a fund to cover his medical expenses as well as the cost of a specially equipped van (both Steinbrenner and Finley made contributions).

Another famous Alabamian unexpectedly came to Waldrep's aid. George Wallace sent Waldrep the doctors who had treated him after he was para-

---

* One of Bryant's most hardnosed players, Butch Hobson, a defensive back and punt returner from the early 1970s Crimson Tide, played for Steinbrenner's Yankees in 1982. Hobson, who had a reputation for never calling a fair catch on the football field, shortened his baseball career considerably by smashing into fences and crashing into the stands for pop fouls.

lyzed by Arthur Bremer's bullets in 1972. Later, Wallace provided a plane to move Waldrep from Birmingham to a hospital in Houston.

"They raised more money in Alabama than TCU ever spent on me," says Waldrep. "Coach Bryant had no responsibility for me at all. No one in my family expected anything. He assumed the responsibility that my own university did not. He did it from the heart." Waldrep was inducted into the Alabama Lettermen Association, and the next year talked TCU into returning to Birmingham for the annual game rather than have Alabama make a trip to Fort Worth. The reason was simple: TCU had trouble selling out their games, and Bryant knew that every Tide home game would have no empty seats. The extra money would benefit Waldrep. Waldrep went on to establish the Kent Waldrep National Paralysis Foundation in Dallas, raising over $21 million to research a cure for paralysis. He also wrote a biography, *Fourth and Long*. He has become the leading advocate for providing health care for college football players, and in the late 1980s finally persuaded the NCAA to provide catastrophic health care insurance for football players. In Waldrep's home there are no mementos from TCU, but the walls are adorned with paintings and photographs of Bryant as well as personal letters.

Of those who knew him well, Bryant appeared to mellow after turning sixty. "I think the Waldrep accident changed him," says Mickey Herskowitz. "I think he began to reflect back on how many such accidents like that might have happened over the years and didn't, and considered himself blessed. His general philosophy didn't change—he was still as doggedly committed to winning as ever, but he began to consider more humane ways of doing it, as well as understanding the ways in which he might be asking too much from some of his players." Jimmy Bryan, who covered sports for years for the *Birmingham News*, thought, "After Kent Waldrep got hurt, Bryant started to think more and more about how he would be remembered." As he got into his early sixties, he seemed to care more that the boys who played for and against him regarded him as something more than just a disciplinarian. "Coach Bryant had always been there for boys to talk to," says Charley Thornton, "but by the early 1970s he was making more of an effort to let them know that his door was always open for them and that he would make time to help them with their problems." It pained him, though, that many didn't take advantage of his open-door policy. He told Mickey Herskowitz, "I encourage my players to come in and see me if they have a problem. But the young ones, they don't. I wish they would. They would flatter me if they came in. I may not be helpful, but I'd surely listen."[9]

When the need arose, though, Bryant did not hesitate to come down hard. After Alabama lost its 1976 season opener to Ole Miss, 10–7, the team rebounded the following week to slaughter Southern Methodist, 56–3, in Birmingham. Barry Krauss, then a sophomore, recalls his teammates' elation at getting back on the winning track. "We were whooping it up, celebrating our first win, and Coach Bryant apparently thought we had gotten too smug. 'You boys stunk it up out there,' he told us. 'You were just better than Southern Methodist, but you didn't *play* better. You were sloppy and unfocused. If that's all you're going to put into it, I don't see the point in playing the rest of these games. So I can call the NCAA tomorrow and cancel the rest of the season if that's what you want.' We were shocked. We had just won, and he was telling us that we weren't that good. And he was right. Two weeks later, we were humiliated by Georgia, 21–0. It was the worst game we played while I was at Alabama. I had to admit he was right. We weren't focused."

Krauss and his roommate hadn't gotten the message Bryant sent after the SMU game. They decided to go out drinking one night in defiance of curfew. "It was just our luck," recalls Krauss, "that this would be the one night when Coach Bryant himself would do the bed check. I knew we were in deep." His roommate was kicked off the team. Krauss was shaken; he went to Bryant's office to plead for another chance. "They had this real soft sofa in there. I hated it; you'd sit on that damn sofa and you'd sink lower and lower while trying to look at him at eye level. God, I hated that sofa.* Anyway, I started crying, 'Please, Coach, give me another chance.' He didn't yell at me, he just kind of looked away from me, like he wasn't listening. Then I realized I had to up the ante. I took crying to another level. I begged, I sobbed, I shook. I told him, 'Coach, if you throw me out, if I lose my scholarship, my mother will be crushed.' I think that got to him. He just looked at me and said, 'Son, you better straighten out.'"

Krauss got his second chance. Later in the season Alabama was getting whipped soundly by Notre Dame at South Bend when a Tide linebacker

---

*Years later, Barry Krauss would pay his first visit to the Paul W. Bryant Museum and saw the furniture from Bryant's office. "I couldn't believe it," says Krauss. "There was that same damn sofa!"

missed an open-field tackle. "If you did that," says Krauss, "he'd take you right out of the game. He took him out and said, 'Krauss, get in there.'" Krauss intercepted a pass and helped spearhead a Tide comeback that should have won the game, but Alabama lost, 21–19. Krauss started against Auburn, then became the MVP of Alabama's Liberty Bowl win against UCLA. He would go on to play eleven years in the NFL, crediting his entire career to the mercy he had begged for which Bryant had granted him as he sank into the sagging couch. A year after graduating, Krauss was back in Tuscaloosa and seated near his former coach at a banquet. Bryant started talking to him as if they were old friends. "He said more to me that day than he had in all the time I played," said Krauss. "It was like we had been friends for years." Bryant and Krauss would be friends until Bryant's death.

OFF THE field, Bryant was living harder than ever. The off-season binge drinking continued; in fact, to some of those who observed him from a distance it seemed that the drinking got heavier. One year, Mickey Mantle came to Birmingham for an Alabama Sports Hall of Fame banquet. The Bear and the Mick had always been friendly, and on this occasion they got even friendlier, so much so that by late that night, friends of both men were alarmed. "You heard a lot of stories from people who ran into Bear Bryant after five o'clock," says Jimmy Bryan, "and more than a few provided him with a sofa for the night."

His smoking got worse. "He bummed thousands of cigarettes off people," says Bryan. "I gave him a filtered cigarette, and he looked at it in disgust, ripped the filter off, and called me a sissy." There were rumors of womanizing; many of his friends are now gone, the ones who survive offer no details, and the press back then regarded the Coach's private life as strictly off-limits.

"The truth," says Clyde Bolton, who covered Alabama football for the *Birmingham News*, "is we didn't care about Coach Bryant's personal life so long as we won." And Alabama continued to win. The 1974 Crimson Tide was much like the 1973 Tide. They won all their games easily and went into the Florida State game with the longest regular-season winning streak, fifteen games, in the nation. The Seminoles, conversely, had the nation's longest losing streak, sixteen straight. And yet, shockingly, Florida State, with five and a half minutes to play, was leading the unfocused Tide, by the odd score of 7–5. With Gary Rutledge injured and Richard Todd having his worst game in crimson and white, Bryant elected, as he did so often in his career, to put the game in the hands of untried players off the bench. Unknown quarterback Jack O'Rear fired a wobbly pass to a black freshman receiver named Ozzie Newsome. Newsome slapped the ball out of the air, hauled it in, and stepped out of bounds at the Florida sixteen-yard line. With thirty-three seconds to play, kicker Bucky Berrey won the game with a field goal. After the game, Bryant would chortle, "Great catch by the kid!" It was the first of many great catches the kid would make over the next four seasons. Newsome was big—slightly taller than six feet three inches and around 215 pounds as a freshman—super fast, blessed with sensational hands, and supremely coachable. His specialty was the acrobatic catch, either hauling in a low pass while on his knees or tipping a high pass out of the air and reeling it in against Florida. "I thought I could have stayed in bounds and gone for the touchdown," he recalls, "but Coach Bryant told me before the play that my job was to catch the ball and get out of bounds, so that's what I did. I did what the man told me to do."

The Tide coasted through the next five games, including an impressive 30–0 win over LSU, before a showdown for the SEC title with an Auburn team nearly as tough as the unbeaten squad it had fielded in 1971. Alabama prevailed, 17–13, in a game that was brutal both physically and emotionally. (The Tigers lost only one other regular season game and would go on to whip Texas in the Gator Bowl.) In the Orange Bowl, Alabama once again drew Notre Dame as an opponent, an Irish team that had won nine of eleven, losing a humiliating season-ending match with Southern Cal in which it had given up forty-nine unanswered points. It looked like the year for Alabama's revenge on Notre Dame, but this time the Tide was inexplicably flat—or perhaps the Irish, fired up by the announcement that this would be Ara Parseghian's last game, was exceptionally sharp. Notre Dame jumped to a 13–0 halftime lead before Bryant, once again using the soft-sell approach at halftime, was able to rally his boys. With Richard Todd doing much of the work at quarterback, Alabama scored eleven points in the second and third quarters and seemed headed for the winning field goal in the final minute when Todd, from the Notre Dame twenty-eight, threw a bad pass that was intercepted by the Notre Dame safety to end the game. Alabama had lost the national title by two points.

The loss set some home folks to grumbling. With amazement, sports columnists throughout Alabama noted that Bryant had now gone eight years without a bowl victory. If the defeat by Nebraska in the 1972 Orange Bowl was understandable, the next three bowl defeats were less so: *three losses by a total of seven points.* From 1971 through 1974, Alabama had been on a dazzling regular-season roll. Playing most of its games in what was almost certainly the toughest conference in the country, Alabama had won *forty-three of forty-four games,* the only loss coming against Auburn in the "Punt, Bama, Punt" game. Perhaps, some timidly suggested, Bryant's teams put too much emotional investment in their traditional regular-season rivalries and ran out of gas before the postseason bowls. Or perhaps Bryant wasn't cracking the whip hard enough.★

"WHAT DOES a man like that have to do with higher education you may ask," wrote Roy Blount Jr. in the September issue of *Esquire.* "Well, look at it this way, what if people were educated, in, say, sociology as hard as they are in football? Pretty soon either there wouldn't be any more sociologists or they would be worth something. . . ." But, "at a time when colleges can't seem to stay solvent . . . over the last twelve years Alabama football has not only supported itself and the rest of the athletic department without any state money but also has contributed some $1,700,000 of its revenues to the university. And the Bear has given $171,871 of his own money to set up a nonathletic scholarship fund. That's not the only way it benefits the university. 'As long as the football team is winning,' says an Alabama English professor, 'those politicians are a lot less likely to be looking for Communists in the wood pile.'"

Blount recalled a 1972 *Sports Illustrated* story in which a copy of Phillip Roth's *Portnoy's Complaint* was spotted on a bookshelf in Bryant's office.

Ever since then I have wondered what if Bear Bryant is some kind of closet modernist? Or at least, what if he surreptitiously maintains a lively interest in contemporary fiction?

★ Gary Rutledge does not think so. "The practices were harder than anything I could have imagined. In comparison the games were not only easy, they were fun. I don't know why we didn't play as well in a couple of those bowl games as we should have, but it wasn't because the practices weren't hard enough."

After all, he shows in his own book a feeling for language, character, and peculiar episode. "Our guys are scratching for every yard, playing like their lives depended on it. Scooter Dyess got hit and when he came off he kind of fell into my arms—he only weighed about 140 pounds and I could pick him up like a child—and I looked into his eyes and they were crossed."

What if you got to talking with the Bear and writing and he started saying things like "This Thomas Pynchon. Now there is a man who writes like he never has hunkered down with enough folks and talked. I believe if I was going to take thirteen years to write a book and call it *Something Happened*, something would." We could use a Bear Bryant of criticism.[10]

THE 1975 football season kicked off with the long-awaited publication of *Bear: The Hard Life and Good Times of Alabama's Coach Bryant*, or, as Alabama-born writer Michael Swindle cracked in the *Village Voice*, "The New Testament." The book was developed out of the stories that Bryant and Underwood had collaborated on for *Sports Illustrated* back in the mid-1960s; apparently the reason it had taken so long to get the full story between hard covers was that Bryant's schedule was just too busy to allow much time for reflection.

Bryant was an avid reader of books about his favorite baseball heroes, and he had enjoyed Ted Williams's autobiography, *My Turn at Bat*, which Underwood had coauthored. The two met, hit it off, and began working on the book in snatches, sometimes meeting in the Florida Keys where Bryant would vacation at a friend's house, sometimes at the Bryant retreat at Lake Martin, and sometimes in Las Vegas, where Bryant blew off steam. On one occasion they were killing time at the crap tables when Underwood heard a commotion and turned to see a man's face pinned to the table, his nose buried in a pile of chips. Bryant's right hand was on the man's neck. The fellow was a pickpocket; in his right hand was Bryant's wallet.

After the Vegas trip, Underwood accompanied Bryant to a coaching lecture at Pepperdine University in Malibu, California, an area of the country Bryant never failed to appear in when invited. "He was worn out," Underwood told Al Browning, "looking drained, and I was a little worried that he wasn't up to the challenge. I knew he wasn't feeling good."[11] In the middle of what Underwood would recall as a marvelous talk, Bryant began growling in an even lower voice than usual as the coaches in the audience strained to hear him. Then, he went silent. After a few seconds, he mumbled, "I don't know how to say this, but is there a doctor in the house?" and collapsed. Headlines in the national papers indicated that Bryant had had a heart attack. Underwood rode to the hospital with him in the back of an ambulance. Bryant handed Underwood his wallet and asked him to hold it for him; there was a wad of one-hundred-dollar bills in it, perhaps as many as forty—the coach's winnings from the previous day. The heart attack story proved to be premature. Bryant was suffering from nervous exhaustion.

"Part of the problem with his health," says John Underwood, "was not that he partied too much. On the contrary, he had a fierce and powerful work ethic. The problem, I think, was that he worked so hard, that when the time came to let off steam, he would let off too much too fast." Before the annual Hall of Fame banquet, Underwood was supposed to meet Bryant in New York at Patsy's restaurant. The flight was delayed, and Underwood, deciding that midnight was too late to go out on a cold and rainy night, went to his hotel and turned in. Just as he got in bed, the phone rang. "The hell are you?" asked a familiar growl on the other end of the line. "I'm in bed," said Underwood. "It's late, and the weather is shit. What in hell are you doing out?" "I'm sittin' here with Frank Sinatra," Bryant replied. "You better get dressed and get your ass on over here." "Yeah, right," Underwood said. "Frank Sinatra. Is Bing Crosby there with him?" "No, Frank says Bing's in Palm Springs. Hold on a moment." Another highly recognizable voice then came on the line. "Is this John? This is Francis Albert Sinatra. The Bear is here, and he's pissed off. He says for you to get your ass over here." Then Bryant was back on the phone. "You see?" said Bryant, chuckling on the other end. "What'd I tell you?"

IN 1975 the Tide lost the opening-day game 20–7 to Missouri at Birmingham, one of the team's worst performances in five years. It rebounded the next week to beat Clemson, 56–0, in the first game played in Tuscaloosa since the state legislature had renamed the field Bryant-Denny Stadium. More than forty years after he had been a groundskeeper there, Paul Bryant walked out onto the field of the stadium named for himself and the other man who had done the most to establish Alabama football.

The Tide then proceeded to win all its remaining games, including sound whippings of Tennessee (30–7), LSU (23–20), and Auburn (28–0). The slaughter of Auburn was not as satisfying to Bryant as it might have been; it was Shug Jordan's last game as Auburn's head coach. The season had been a miserable one for the Tigers, who had won just four games, and there were those who felt that Bryant had pulled in the reins on his horses to keep the final margin of victory to four touchdowns. Jordan, who was three years older than Bryant, was a devout Catholic and, Bryant not excepted, the most beloved figure in Alabama sports. (As Jimmy Bryan recalls, "People are awed by Bear, but they loved Shug."). Bryant liked and respected Shug, but had never gotten as close to him as he had to several out-of-state coaches, hard-bitten Irishmen like Duffy Daugherty, John McKay, and Bob Devaney. Bryant and Jordan would sometimes hunt together and were often seen having drinks, but there was always a slight tension between the two men, a gulf created by the enormous emotion generated by the Alabama-Auburn rivalry. Jordan had had the state of Alabama in his pocket when his Tigers won the national championship in 1957, but a year later Bryant arrived at Alabama, and although Jordan won a thriller over Bryant in their first meeting, for the rest of his career Jordan had to be content with running a sideshow. In Alabama it was often said, though never written, that Shug was simply too nice a guy to compete with Bear. It was all symbolized by a story that may have been apocryphal but that Bryant often repeated and Alabama fans took as gospel. Sometime in the 1970s, Bryant was supposed to have called the Auburn athletic office around six in the morning, trying to reach Jordan. The cleaning lady answered and explained that she was the only person in the building at that time of the morning. "Ma'am," Bryant is supposed to have said, "don't you people at Auburn take your football seriously?" Bryant may have concocted it to tell at banquets, but on the other hand, the story doesn't *sound* false; one recalls that in 1971 when Bryant flew to visit Darrell Royal at Texas, his friend Jones Ramsey found him sitting on the steps of the athletic building early in the morning waiting for the coaches to arrive, with Ramsey quoting Bryant with the same question he is supposed to have asked the Auburn cleaning lady.

In the Sugar Bowl, on New Year's Eve, in the first game played in New Orleans's opulent new Superdome, Alabama ended its puzzling eight-year bowl drought by beating a tough Penn State team, 13–6. Richard Todd was the game's MVP and assured himself of a lucrative NFL contract with the New York Jets (where he would replace Joe Namath at quarterback) by completing ten of twelve passes for 210 yards.

The 1975 season had started with some distractions. Details were never made known when eight players were dismissed for disciplinarian reasons, two of them permanently. The other six were assigned to a work program at the Veterans Administration Hospital in Tuscaloosa. Three would earn their way back onto the squad; Leroy Cook and Wayne Rhodes made the All-America team, and the third, Connley Duncan, would make the All-SEC team.

On the plus side, a remarkable sophomore came of age and would make Alabama, and later, NFL history. Back in 1967 Bryant had told a friend that he wanted the player who integrated Alabama football to be a "black Ray Perkins." It's too bad for Bryant that Ozzie Newsome Jr. hadn't come along a few years earlier; he was all that and more. At the end of the decade, readers of 'Bama magazine voted for an all-time Alabama team. The offense had only ten players: Newsome got the most votes at both wide receiver and tight end. (In his NFL Hall of Fame career with the Cleveland Browns, Newsome would catch more passes than any tight end in pro football history, though he would often line up at the wide receiver spot.) In 1980, fans voted for the Crimson Tide's "Player of the Decade." The leading vote-getter for the school with perhaps the most sensational decade college football had ever seen was Ozzie Newsome. "People used to tell me," says Newsome, "'Man, if you'd gone to some other school where they threw the ball more, you could have set all kinds of records.' Well, I'm happy with the numbers I had at Alabama. And I got to learn football from Coach Bryant."

Newsome had been recruited out of Colbert County High in North Alabama, a school that had been integrated in Newsome's freshman year, 1970, and had produced several more great athletes, including Phil Gargis, who would quarterback for Auburn, and Leon Douglas, who would become one of Alabama's all-time best basketball players. An all-around athlete, Newsome had grown up watching *The Bear Bryant Show* on Sunday afternoons. In his senior year he had thoughts of heading for Auburn, where he could team up on the gridiron with his high school battery mate, Phil Gargis, until Bryant dispatched John Mitchell to reel Newsome in. Mitchell caught two prizes: fullback Johnny Davis, who would be Newsome's roommate, and Ozzie himself. "By the time John Mitchell had finished talking up Bear Bryant and Alabama to me," says Newsome, "there was no way I was going anywhere else." Bryant lost his temper with Newsome just once in four years. "When I was a freshman," Newsome says, "all the black guys would sit together, and I think it maybe upset Coach Bryant a bit because he thought all of us, black guys and white guys, should be mixing it up together. It wasn't anything, you know, it was guys palling around with guys they knew, but Coach Bryant thought that we were maybe kidding around too much and that we were losing some focus on the game. After four games in 1974, we were 4–0 and we were thinking, 'Man, nobody's going to beat us this year.' And that's exactly the mentality that Coach Bryant hated. Before the Florida State game he was saying to us, 'Now, you boys better understand that just because they haven't won a game doesn't mean that we can just show up and expect to win. You better get your minds on football.' He was right. There was no concentration during that game whatsoever. We were lucky to win that game, and I really learned something that day." Newsome redeemed himself when his thirty-two-yard catch set up the winning field goal, and the legend of "The Wizard of Ozzie" was born.

At the end of his freshman season, Ozzie knew he had made the right choice.

BRYANT'S FIVE-YEAR run from 1971 through 1975 was remarkable, fifty-four victories in sixty games. During the regular season, they were 53–2. In what was by consensus the toughest conference in college football, Alabama, over that five-year span, was 35–1; the 1972 "Punt, Bama, Punt" game, a one-point loss, *was the only conference defeat over five seasons*. Bryant's status as an American folk hero was secure. His fame had spread beyond the South and the boundaries of football. Bud Wilkinson was long retired, and Vince Lombardi had been dead for five years; Woody Hayes of Ohio State was the only football coach, college or pro, whose image was even remotely as recognizable to the average American as Bear Bryant's. James Michener, while researching his 1976 book, *Sports in America*, at first concluded,

Nebraska must surely be the football capital of the world.
But then I went to Alabama, where the first eleven people I met— businessmen, professors, housewives, took me aside to assure me confi-

dentially that "Bear Bryant is the greatest man this state has ever produced." . . . I doubt if there's any sports figure in America who comes close to dominating his community the way Bear Bryant dominates Alabama.[12]

Few Americans, Michener concluded, truly understood the pressures that a big-time college football coach worked under:

No other member of any faculty is subjected to the close and constant scrutiny which the coach experiences. He is written about in the papers, criticized on radio and television, and reviewed constantly by the alumni who pay the bills. If he is of a sensitive or retiring type, he has no place in coaching.

Nor is any other faculty member subjected to the rigorous performance-evaluation which a coach must undergo. If he is deficient, a crowded stadium witnesses his failure and he is not allowed to remain deficient very long. An ordinary faculty member can get away with murder for decades without detection.

Few other members of the faculty exert the degree of constructive leaderships manifested by the coach. The testimony in this point is overwhelming; perhaps athletes are several degrees more simplistic than non-athletes are and thus predisposed to absorb the leadership their coaches exert. But too many athletes have testified to the moral importance of their coach to deny that it exists.[13]

At a dinner in Birmingham, Michener told Bryant how embarrassing it was that his new novel, *Hawaii*, was being outsold in Alabama three-to-one by Bryant's autobiography, *Bear*. "Hell," Bryant later told a friend, "it should have been fifteen to one."

THE YEAR 1976 would prove to be the only "bad" one of the decade, a 9–3 record with two conference defeats (including an embarrassing 21–0 loss to Georgia at Athens) and a heartbreaking 21–18 defeat by Notre Dame in the Tide's first-ever trip to South Bend. But the season had to be counted as a success: Alabama still beat Tennessee, LSU, and Auburn, and on December 20, in the Liberty Bowl, a larger and more talented UCLA team that had lost just one game during the season. Bryant pulled out all the stops. The Tide came out with Jeff Rutledge, younger brother of Gary, throwing to Ozzie Newsome to set up a first-quarter field goal. Shortly after the ensuing kickoff, tackle Charles Hannah, John Hannah's younger brother, deflected a UCLA pass into the hands of linebacker Barry Krauss, who took it in for a touchdown. The favored Bruins went down, 36–6. When asked by a reporter if he was surprised at the one-sidedness of the game, Bryant shot back, "Hell, yes, weren't you?"

UCLA coach Terry Donahue not only got a lesson in football from Bryant, he received a crash course in poor-mouthing. Before the game, Donahue went on and on about Alabama's great tradition and how coaching against Bear Bryant left him in awe. Bryant would not surrender the underdog card. "When I heard who we were playing," Bryant said at a pregame conference, "I thought they meant the University of Central Louisiana. When I found out what UCLA really stood for, it almost scared me to death." No California football coach should have ever dreamed that he could out poor-mouth Bear Bryant.

BY THE MID-1970s, Bear Bryant was finding ways to be for his grandchildren what he had never been to his own children. "The pressures of being the son and daughter of Bear Bryant weren't on me," says Marc Tyson, Mae Martin's son. "People say to me 'What was he like?' and all I can tell you is that he was the greatest grandfather I can imagine. Some of my happiest memories as a boy are of my Mom and Dad loading up the Christmas presents and driving to Gran and Papa's big house in Tuscaloosa."

Freed from the burdens of recruiting in the off-season, which he increasingly delegated to his staff, Bryant would take his grandchildren fishing. His favorite was brim fishing on Lake Martin; he always fished with a cane pole baited with crickets, just as he had done as a boy in Moro Bottom. "He had no patience for fly fishing," recalls Tyson. "He couldn't bother with casting and untangling the line in the reel." Bryant took pleasure and pride in attending Tyson's Friday-night football games at the Montgomery Academy, but he had even more fun sharing Marc's passion for baseball. In the spring of 1977 Bryant asked his grandson which three major league ballparks he wanted to see; Tyson chose Yankee Stadium, Fenway Park, and Riverfront Stadium, home of the world-champion Cincinnati Reds. Marc was treated to a grand tour at each. At Yankee Stadium, they were the guests of George Steinbrenner, and at Fenway Park they visited with Bryant's former defensive back, Butch Hobson, who was playing for the Red Sox. The biggest thrill came in Cincinnati. "The Reds were my favorite team," says Tyson. "It was such a thrill to meet Johnny Bench, George Foster, Joe Morgan, and especially Pete Rose, who made a big fuss about my grandfather. I wish other people could have seen him like that, having fun, relaxing, enjoying himself. It would have tempered a lot of people's image of him as this gruff, unyielding man." Tyson, though, has no illusions as to how others must have seen Bear Bryant. "When we rode to games on the team buses, everybody wanted to ride on the bus with my grandmother. They all knew they could have fun on the bus with Mary Harmon. On my grandfather's bus, scarcely anybody made a sound."

BY 1977, the Bear had outlasted nearly all his contemporaries—all but one.

In the second half of the 1970s, Bryant could no longer maintain the fiction that his teams weren't as big, as fast, or as talented as most of his opponents. It was true that in games against top teams the Crimson Tide was still, man-for-man, outweighed, with several positions filled by the hustling overachievers that Bryant had always favored. But early in the decade Bryant's teams were more and more spearheaded by extraordinary talents, most of them among the finest players in the nation. Most writers who covered the team generally conceded that the only reason the Tide lost some blue-chip recruits is because they knew that at Alabama no single player would dominate. They might not have as much opportunity to win at other schools, but they would have a better chance to show off their skills. Alabama's offense was well balanced between running and passing, and the running was divvied up among several good backs. At the quarterback slot, Bryant usually had two and even three strong athletes. "I believe we were the last championship team to do this," says Clem Gryska. "We could say to any recruit, 'If you come to Alabama, you'll get to play.' What we couldn't say is, 'Come to Alabama and you'll get a chance to win the Heisman Trophy.'" Gryska is right. There is probably no single fact about Bryant's quarter century at Alabama than this: despite an unparalleled record of success, Bryant's Alabama teams never had a serious Heisman Trophy contender. Even Joe Namath, who at his peak was regarded by many as the greatest passer in the game's history, did not finish among the top-ten Heisman candidates in his senior year. In today's game, it's taken as a given that a coach will leave a Heisman Trophy candidate in a game to pile up meaningless statistics on a beaten opponent just to impress the media. In contrast, Bryant's policy of sending in reserves after taking a commanding lead seems like a forgotten chivalric code of a bygone era.

The Crimson Tide teams in the second half of the 1970s were loaded. From the Class of 1976, Charlie Hannah went on to play for the Tampa Bay Buccaneers for six years, then with the Raiders for six more, and Bob Baumhower went on to play for ten years with the Miami Dolphins, making the Pro Bowl in five of them. The 1977 team would send Johnny Davis to the NFL for ten seasons with the Bucs, 49ers, and Browns.

The 1977 squad might have been the most talented in Alabama history. Ozzie Newsome was probably the team's best player, but there were numerous candidates for the honor. The primary quarterback was Jeff Rutledge, a terrific runner and a good enough passer to last thirteen seasons in the NFL. The best running back was Tony Nathan, who would go on to play in two Super Bowls with the Miami Dolphins, with whom he averaged 4.8 yards a rush and caught 383 passes in nine seasons.* In 1977 Nathan was joined in the backfield by a sensational freshman, Major Ogilvie, who would become the only running back to score a touchdown in four consecutive New Year's bowl games.† On defense, Alabama had so many outstanding players that they often tended to cancel each other out in All-America voting. The defensive line was particularly outstanding. Byron Braggs, E. J. Junior, and Marty Lyons would all go on to professional success (Lyons became one of the New York Jets' famed "Sack

---

* Rutledge and Nathan were probably the two most celebrated high school football players in Alabama in their senior year, 1974. Rutledge attended Banks High School and Nathan attended Woodlawn High School; the schools were fierce rivals and the Birmingham area's foremost football factories, high school equivalents of Alabama and Auburn whose annual meeting at Legion Field could draw over twenty thousand spectators. The legendary duels between Rutledge and Nathan are still part of Birmingham high school football lore.

† Ogilvie, whose professional chances were curtailed by a back injury, still holds numerous rushing records at my old high school, Mountain Brook.

Exchange" in the early 1980s), as would linebackers Rich Wingo (who played five seasons with the Green Bay Packers), Barry Krauss, and defensive back Don McNeal (who joined Tony Nathan on two of Don Shula's Super Bowl teams at Miami). Probably the best player on the team, if not Newsome, was center Dwight Stephenson, who finally supplanted Paul Crane (of the 1964 and 1965 national championship teams) in Bryant's estimation as his best center. In 1998 Stephenson would become Alabama's first black player to be inducted into the Pro Football Hall of Fame. Considering the talent available, it might be argued that Alabama, through the first four games of the 1977 season, was that rarity of rarities: a Bryant underachiever.

In the second week of the season, against a fine Nebraska team at Lincoln, Alabama's season hit a road block. Jeff Rutledge, who had become starting quarterback when Jack O'Rear was injured, could not control his passes in the swirling winds that whipped over the Nebraska plains, and threw five interceptions. The Tide outgained the Cornhuskers but could not overcome the handicap of the pickoffs and lost, 31–24. Spoiled Alabama fans bombarded Rutledge with abuse; according to older brother Gary, "Jeff promised he was not going to throw another interception all year," a promise which, amazingly, he kept. In week five, the Tide went to Los Angeles to play Southern Cal, who, under John McKay's successor, John Robinson, were unbeaten. Alabama rolled to a 21–6 lead, fought off a furious fourth-quarter Trojan comeback, and won 21–20 when defensive end Wayne Hamilton and linebacker Barry Krauss stopped a last-minute two-point conversion attempt. After that, Alabama built up a head of steam and would not relinquish it through the Sugar Bowl. By season's end, Alabama was ranked number three behind number-two Oklahoma and unbeaten number-one Texas.

The situation was similar to the one in 1965—for Alabama to win the national title, Texas would have to lose to number-five Notre Dame in the Cotton Bowl and Oklahoma would have to lose to number-six Arkansas in the Orange Bowl. Both possibilities seemed unlikely. Oh, yes, Bryant reminded his players, there was one more thing: Alabama had to beat number-eight Ohio State in the Sugar Bowl. The Irish, led by Joe Montana, were solid six-point underdogs to a Texas team that featured Heisman Trophy running back Earl Campbell. As for Arkansas, it was already touchdown underdogs when Coach Lou Holtz suspended six players before the game, after which the oddsmakers took the game off the board, assuming it would be a route. And it was, but not the one expected, as the Razorbacks won a shocker, beating Oklahoma 31–6. Bryant was confident that Alabama would beat Ohio State, and if Notre Dame could beat Texas, in a Cotton Bowl that was being played at the same time as the Sugar Bowl, then Alabama's path to the national championship was clear. The 1978 Sugar Bowl, though, would not be remembered as a game that decided the national championship. It would be remembered as the only game Bear Bryant coached against Woody Hayes.

All through the 1960s and 1970s, Bryant and Wayne Woodrow Hayes were compared and measured against each other. Hayes, like Bryant, was born in 1913 (eight months before Bryant). Like Bryant, he served in the navy during World War II. Like Bryant, by the end of the 1977 regular season he had won four national titles.* He was even credited with originating some of the same phrases as Bryant, such as "There are three things that can happen when you pass, and two of them ain't good." He had produced almost as many successful protégés as Bryant: Lou Holtz, Earl Bruce, Rudy Hubbard, Bo Schembechler, and Bill Mallory were among the most prominent. Like Bryant, he was a perfectionist with a near-fanatical attention to detail. Before they faced each other in the 1978 Sugar Bowl, Bryant's career record was 272–75–16, tops among major college coaches, while Hayes's was 231–67–9—practically a wash considering that until 1972 Hayes's teams only played nine regular-season games and in most of those seasons they were not allowed to play in bowl games. (The Big Ten was contractually tied to the Rose Bowl and for many years did not allow its teams to play in any other.)

Perhaps a more accurate comparison is to take them both from 1951, Hayes's first year at Ohio State. From 1951 to the end of the 1977 season Bryant's record was 225–60–13, to Hayes's 198–56–9—which is also pretty close. But Bryant coached at three schools from 1951 through 1977 and had to restart two moribund programs at Texas A&M and Alabama, while Hayes coached at Ohio State the entire time. If we consider Bryant and Hayes from Bryant's first year at Alabama, 1958, Bryant starts to pull away, with a 180–44–8 record compared to Hayes's 150–41–7. If we are

* Five, actually, if one includes the National Football Foundation award given to his 1970 Ohio State Buckeyes.

generous and allow Bryant one season at Alabama to kick-start the program and take the comparison from 1959 through the end of the 1977 season, Bryant wins by more than a stride: 175–40–7 to Hayes's 144–40–5. Even if Hayes had played the same number of regular-season games and the same number of bowls as Bryant, he could not have matched Bryant's record in that period. From 1959 through the end of the 1977 regular season, Bryant had the same number of defeats as Hayes while winning thirty-one more games. Nonetheless, to the endless debates about which man was the greatest coach in college football, the 1978 Sugar Bowl would add a fascinating chapter. The game would be historic for other reasons as well—it was the first meeting ever between the great northern and southern football powers, and just the first game Alabama had played with a Big Ten team since Wisconsin in 1928. Both coaches seemed to relish confrontation. At a press conference in New Orleans on December 31, Bryant joked about the sports media's focus on the coaches. "I'll agree to stay at the hotel and watch the game on television," he told reporters, "if Woody will do the same thing." To which Hayes responded, "Oh, no, not for a minute. I'll be on the sideline because I want to see it up close." Hayes probably should have watched the game from his hotel room, or perhaps from the hotel's bar.

For all the similarities between Bear Bryant and Woody Hayes, there were two significant differences. One was temper. Bryant, as the years went by, had learned to control his. Hayes had not. In the following year, 1979, Bryant and his staff would watch with incredulity as Hayes, his team losing to Clemson in the Gator Bowl, came off the sidelines to punch a Clemson player. It was Hayes's last game and a sad end to a great career. The other difference was imagination, particularly as it manifested itself in the passing game. (The phrase "three yards and a cloud of dust" was generally associated with Hayes's Buckeyes.) Hayes favored enormous linemen, and given Ohio State's recruiting clout, he was generally in a position to get them. His offense for much of the 1960s and 1970s was an uninspiring I-formation that usually featured at least thirty thrusts per game from a star tailback. (Archie Griffin, Hayes's star runner, won the Heisman Trophy in 1974 and 1975, the only runner ever to do so.)

The difference between the two teams manifested itself immediately on the opening drive. The Alabama team, a meager one-point favorite, took the field with a fury, knowing that it was playing not only for a possible national championship but also for its coach's honor. Led by center Dwight Stephenson and offensive tackle Lewis Green (who played the game with pictures of Ohio State defenders in his socks)*, the smaller Crimson Tide linemen hit the massive Buckeyes from so many angles that it must have seemed like there were more than five of them leading the charge. Taking the opening kickoff, Alabama drove down to the Ohio State three-yard line, where it faced a fourth down with goal to go. Bryant then made his biggest mistake of the game, electing to go for the touchdown instead of the sure-shot field goal. As it turned out, Bryant's impatience would have no effect on the outcome of the game. The Tide defense jammed the Buckeyes on three consecutive plays, forcing a punt. Jeff Rutledge quickly moved the offense to midfield, where, spotting single coverage on Ozzie Newsome, he drilled a pass between two Buckeye defenders for a twenty-nine-yard gain. It was immediately obvious that whatever else between the two teams was near equal, Ohio State had no equivalent of or answer to Ozzie Newsome, and the only hope for containing him was double coverage. This was tantamount in boxing to lifting your hands to cover your face and exposing your midsection. A minute after Rutledge's pass to Newsome had stretched Ohio's defense, Alabama ran it up the gut with Tony Nathan, who dove over the one-yard line behind the right guard to score. Again, Ohio State failed to move the ball against the Alabama defense, and again Rutledge, starting from the twenty-four-yard line, engineered a touchdown drive—Alabama's second consecutive seventy-six-yard march. From Ohio State's twenty-seven, Rutledge, faking a handoff, spotted the double coverage on Newsome and immediately threw to Alabama's other receiver, Bruce Bolton, for a touchdown. Alabama missed the extra point, about the only luck Woody Hayes would have that day.

The only consolation for Hayes and Ohio State was that they were down 13–0 instead of 16–0 or 20–0 at halftime. That consolation lasted exactly as long as it took Alabama to take the ball sixty-seven yards on thirteen plays during its first possession in the third quarter, scoring a touchdown and a two-point conversion. Ohio State came alive, briefly, taking the ball downfield for its only sustained drive of the game, but it was the Buckeyes' last score of the game too. Later in the quarter Major Ogilvie ran

---

* "I wanted to put the pictures on my helmet," Green said later, "but I thought that might look trashy."

for a touchdown. Alabama led 28–6 and coasted to a 35–6 final score. Rutledge played only three quarters but completed eight of eleven passes for 109 yards and two touchdowns, and was voted MVP. At the postgame press conference, Bryant played down the crashing victory over his fellow future Hall of Famer: "This isn't about Woody and me. This doesn't mean Woody isn't a great coach. Woody is a great coach. And," he added, almost as an afterthought, "I ain't bad myself."

The national championship payoff for the 1977 Alabama Crimson Tide never arrived. Alabama had been so focused on beating Ohio State that the players gave little notice to what was happening in the Cotton Bowl at the same time. Joe Montana and Notre Dame had upset unbeaten Texas, 38–10. When the votes were tabulated early the following week, the Irish had slipped ahead of the Tide for the number-one spot. Alabama fans were shocked and angered, and several players publicly commented, "No one else but Notre Dame could have gone past us" (from number five to number one). That wasn't entirely fair. Notre Dame did go from fifth to first, but number-two Oklahoma and number-four Michigan both lost, so this left, logically, a choice between Alabama and Notre Dame. Both teams finished with the same 11–1 records. But while Alabama had beaten the eighth-ranked team, Notre Dame had scored an equally impressive victory over a much stronger opponent, the unbeaten Longhorns. In truth, a fair solution would have been for the Tide and Irish to split the championship, which both would have been amenable to. In fact, the national title would be split the next season. But early in January 1978, Alabama fans were left feeling that, when in doubt, the voters tended to choose someone besides Alabama.

IN MARCH 1978, Bryant's good friend George Steinbrenner agreed to bring the Yankees to Tuscaloosa for an exhibition charity game against the Crimson Tide baseball team. Bryant enjoyed himself immensely, being photographed by New York photographers with Reggie Jackson and other Yankee stars. The morning of the game, Steinbrenner, Jackson, and Bryant were taking a leisurely stroll across campus while Bryant pointed out the historic sights. A group of Alabama students spotted them and began cheering. Grinning, Jackson stopped to tip his hat to the students.

"Reggie," Steinbrenner put his hand on Jackson's shoulder, "That's not for you."

IT WAS a toss-up as to what did the most damage to Paul Bryant's health. Whiskey and cigarettes probably would get the most votes from those who knew him, but some might opt for the cream gravy. "My grandfather's eating habits weren't the best," says Marc Tyson. "On days when he had time, he'd indulge in those big country breakfasts—lots of fried food. On days when he didn't have time, he'd go for Krystal hamburgers, not exactly the Atkins choice." Probably, it was the combination of fried food early, whiskey late, and cigarettes in between, mixed with the never-ending stress of the job that shortened his life. In the spring of 1977, while visiting a friend in Florida, Bryant collapsed in the shower; he was still unconscious when paramedics arrived. The diagnosis was congestive heart failure. Several months later, after the big win over Woody Hayes and Ohio State in the Sugar Bowl, he checked himself into an alcohol rehabilitation clinic in Shelby County, near Birmingham. "He was a binge drinker," says Clyde Bolton. "He was kind of like Ulysses S. Grant. He never drank while working and never let it affect his job, but when the pressure was off, he tended to let loose, and it became harder and harder to get back to normal speed." Charles Land, who covered Bryant for years while at the *Tuscaloosa News*, said, "You'd walk into his office and see all those pill bottles on his desk and stare. When he'd catch you staring, you'd try to look the other way real quick."

In September, his friends held a surprise sixty-fifth birthday party for him at the Kahler Plaza (now the Radisson Inn) in Birmingham. Duffy Daugherty, Bryant's old poker buddy who was long retired from Michigan State, led off his part of the tribute by announcing, "I'm the illegitimate son of Bear Bryant." "There was a bit of edge to Duffy's remark," says Jake Reiss, who was then president of the Birmingham Touchdown Club and who organized the event. "Duffy was two years younger but actually looked about *ten* years younger than Bryant. In fact, many of the people there were Coach Bryant's contemporaries, and some of them were older, but most of them looked younger than Coach Bryant."

Among the guests were Joe Namath and actor Dale Robertson, whom Bryant had tried to recruit for Alabama in the late 1930s but who instead had chosen Oklahoma and then an acting career, starring in TV's *Tales of Wells Fargo*. At a prearranged time, a television set that had been hidden by a blanket was uncovered and switched on to ABC's *Monday Night Football*. Don Meredith, who nearly a quarter of a century earlier had cried when he told Bear he was going to Southern Methodist instead of Texas A&M, and Howard Cosell gushed out their tributes to the Bear. Cosell did not take the occasion to apologize for second-guessing Bryant in the 1973 Sugar Bowl.

Daugherty got off the second-best line of the night. "Paul," he said, "I don't know if you were the best coach in the world, but you sure as hell caused the most commotion." Bryant had the best: "If I'd known you were going to do this, at least I'd have dressed up some. This is what I always thought my funeral would look like, with a bunch of football people."

No one knew how little of Bryant's career was left. They would have been amazed to know that Bryant's greatest achievements were still ahead of him.

Chapter 11

The Bear
in Winter

There is little difference between man and man.
But superiority lies with him
Who is reared in the severest school.
— *Thucydides (quoting King Archidamus of Sparta)*

THE FIRST GAME OF the season is a little early for a defining moment, but for the 1978 Crimson Tide it came in the second quarter of the season opener against the Nebraska Cornhuskers. The game, televised nationally by ABC, was so eagerly anticipated that, Jimmy Bryan remembers, "Kirk McNair [Alabama's director of sports information] said he was glad the *New York Times* was on strike because he couldn't have fit them into the press box."

Alabama played a sluggish first quarter and trailed Nebraska 3–0 at Birmingham's Legion Field in a game that was supposed to avenge the previous season's loss. A Nebraska punt had stopped just inches short of the goal line; a fumble or interception could dig Alabama a hole from which it might not be able to emerge against a team as good as Nebraska. Calmly, behind the jackhammer blocking of Jim Bunch, Buddy Aydelette, Dwight Stephenson, Vince Booth, and Mike Brock, the Tide began the most impressive scoring drive it would have that season, moving ninety-nine yards in sixteen plays, consuming nearly twelve minutes. Fullback Billy Jackson made the first big play on a surprise run on third down from the Alabama three; he caught the Cornhuskers expecting a pass and carried the ball up the middle for the eight yards needed for a first down. Fifteen plays later, on a fake to Jackson, Jeff Rutledge flipped a ten-yard scoring pass to Major Ogilvie, who was playing with cartilage damage to his left knee from which fluid had to be drained every Friday. The Huskers would net just sixty-five yards through the air all afternoon and never came close to another score. Rutledge scored a final touchdown with a little more than two minutes left in the game, and Alabama had a stunningly easy 20–3 win, its third victory in five games with mighty Nebraska.

In the next game, Bryant's Tide faced a fine Missouri team that had shut out Joe Montana and Notre Dame just the week before. With Alabama trailing 20–17 at the half, Bryant did not choose to use his famous "this is great we've got them where we want them" speech. Coming off the emotion of the Nebraska game the week before, the team had played sloppily and deserved to be behind. "Coach had a genius," says Clem Gryska, "for knowing when to be nice. He also knew when not to be nice." On this day, he did not choose to be nice and gave his team a verbal pasting. It worked. In the third quarter E. J. Junior swatted down the ball during a Missouri punt, and later in the quarter the Tide would recover the ball after a Missouri fumble. In a matter of moments, Alabama was back on top, 31–20, and won by eighteen points.

The following week the Tide would play the fourth game in an odd series with Southern Cal in which the home team lost all four games. This year the game was in Birmingham. In a match of national title contenders—and as it turned out, national champions—the Tide suffered a crippling blow on the first play when defensive end Wayne Hamilton, the star of the previous year's victory over the Trojans, went out of the game with an arm injury. The game would be remembered for a great rushing performance by Charles White, who would win the Heisman Trophy the following season, but the big play came in the third quarter when Alabama's most sure-handed defender, Don McNeal, looked up at the Alabama twenty and found himself directly in the path of a ball thrown from USC quarterback Paul McDonald intended for receiver Kevin Williams. Tide fans roared as McNeal went up for the interception; the cheers became a collective groan a second later when the ball went through McNeal's hands and into Williams's, who took it into the end zone. Rutledge later threw a forty-one-yard touchdown pass to put Alabama back in the game, but a rare fumble by Tony Nathan and an even rarer interception of a Rutledge pass sealed the 24–14 Southern Cal victory.

The game against the Trojans was the only regular-season loss for Alabama over three years—from the September 17, 1977, Nebraska defeat to November 1, 1980, when the Tide lost to Mississippi State. Equally impressive, it was the only home game Alabama would lose between September 8, 1975 (against Missouri), and November 1, 1980 (Mississippi State). At the postgame press conference, Bryant would blame the loss on a fool of an athletic director who had scheduled three brutally tough games in successive weeks. (Nebraska, Missouri, and Southern Cal would finish the season a collective 28–6 against all their other opponents.) Who, asked a visiting rookie sportswriter, was Alabama's athletic director? "Our AD," said Bryant's publicity director, Charley Thornton, "is Coach Bryant."

The next week, though, Alabama was right back in the national championship race when number-one Southern Cal, still glowing from its victory over Alabama, was soundly whipped by Arizona State, 20–7. Alabama plunged back into its brutal schedule, which included eight teams with winning records. In the fourth game of the season, the Tide was once again sluggish, leading perennial Southeastern Conference doormat Vanderbilt by just three points with fifteen minutes left to play. The subpar performance elicited boos from the fans. Bryant was furious and afterward made his only recorded criticism of home fans: "All I can say is that they'd better be booing me and not my players. Anyone who boos a college football player isn't a college football fan, and we don't need them around our program."[1] Of course, Bryant was well aware that he could always direct criticism of the team back to him because no Alabama fan would dare to boo Bear Bryant. "The booing really hacked him off," says Marty Lyons. "It bothered him more than us." Thirty-one fourth-quarter points washed away the boos.

There were still cobwebs in red-and-white helmets as late as the fifth game of the season at Washington, when Alabama was down 10–7 against the defending Rose Bowl champion Huskies. This time, Bryant reverted to a variation of his "this is great we've got them where we want them" approach, and once again his players responded. E. J. Junior blocked his second big punt of the season, setting up a Tony Nathan touchdown that keyed a 20–17 win. West Coast sportswriters were then treated to a first-hand dose of Bryant's press conference persona. At a postgame press conference held on the team bus, some of the scribes, particularly the ones from California papers, were indignant that they had not been allowed to talk to the players in the locker room. They had no way of knowing that this was a violation of a strict Bryant policy. They also had no way of knowing that in Alabama, Bryant held tight rein over the press. Bill Lumpkin, a veteran *Birmingham Post-Herald* sportswriter recalls a meeting with Bryant where the coach informed him, "Hall's injured; I don't think he's gonna play . . ." "Coach," replied a puzzled Lumpkin, "who's Hall? I don't think he's on the roster." "Dammit," Bryant exploded, "if I say Hall's not gonna play, then Hall's not gonna play!"

The West Coast writers, however, had no reverence for Bryant or any other coach and wanted to know what went on in the Alabama locker room. "Bear," one of them asked, "what did you tell your players at halftime to make them come back and win?" Bryant stared toward the back of the bus where the writer was seated and said, "I don't ask you what you and your wife talk about in the morning when you're taking a crap and she's putting on makeup, do I?" The stunned journalist stammered back, "No, I don't guess so, but we're talking about football players, not my wife." "It's the same thing," said Bryant. "Some things are private. What goes on at your house in the bathroom is private. What goes on between me and my players in the dressing room is private." The writers ate it up, realizing that Bryant was giving them better copy than if they had been allowed access to the players.

IN 1978 Bryant involved himself in a foolish political controversy. Forrest H. "Fob" James Jr., a former Auburn football player, was running in the Democratic primary for governor of Alabama. (At that time, whoever took the Democratic primary in Alabama was guaranteed to win the governor's chair.) Bryant was worried that having an Auburn man as governor would hurt his university, and so, against the advice of friends, he endorsed James's leading opponent in the primary, Bill Baxley. Worse, he did it at one of his weekly press conferences during the football season.

Paul Bryant was apolitical in temperament, but Democratic in sympathy. He had deviated from this path two years earlier, when, as a goodwill gesture, he had attended a rally in Mobile for Gerald Ford, where he presented the president with a houndstooth hat. The photo was widely distributed, and many Alabama fans, including some of Bryant's most ardent supporters, were angered. Now Bryant was publicly favoring a candidate, apparently not for political reasons but because Baxley had graduated from Alabama's law school. It wasn't much of a reason, and some of Bryant's friends and colleagues in the Alabama faculty and administration were not shy about letting him know it. "I don't think," said Charley Thornton, "that Coach thought this one through." Fortunately for Bryant, and, for that matter, the University of Alabama, Fob James, who eventually won the primary in a runoff with Baxley and went on to the state's highest office, didn't hold a grudge. Then, James knew what side of the cornbread to butter and had no intentions of being on the bad side of Bear Bryant.

A meeting was arranged at a Tuscaloosa hotel where Bryant had the team staying the night before Homecoming. When James walked into Bryant's room, he found the Coach lying in bed, fully clothed, watching television.

"Hello, Coach," James offered.

Bryant's gruff response was, "How old are you?"

"I'm forty-four," the governor replied, "sir."

"Well, then," said Bryant, sitting up and reaching out to shake James's hand. "You're old enough not to believe all the crap you read in the papers, aren't you?"

The University of Alabama suffered not at all from an Auburn grad as governor.*

AFTER THE Washington game, the Tide shifted into national championship gear, winning its final six contests by an average of over twenty points a game, including a 34–16 win over Auburn in which the team roared back from a 13–10 deficit in the second quarter. Its record was good enough to win the number-two ranking in both wire-service polls. First place was occupied by the unbeaten Nittany Lions of Penn State, coached

---

* Thornton says the story of Bryant's meeting with James was related to him by the governor's brother, Cal.

by the rising young star of college football, Joe Paterno. Bear Bryant was about to get the second supergame of his career, thanks to the backstage machinations of Aruns Callery of the Sugar Bowl committee. Paterno's first choice was the Orange Bowl, partly because it was the last game of the day and would be played at night for an undivided audience, and partly because it would give his much-heralded defense a crack at Oklahoma's Heisman Trophy winner, running back Billy Sims. Callery wanted the game for New Orleans and the Sugar Bowl. He coaxed Bryant into phoning Paterno. Recalling the conversation for Al Browning, Callery said,

> Paul told Joe they had played a great game in New Orleans in 1975, that both programs were national names, and that it was time for them to get together again. Then he offered the clincher. He said, "Joe, it's only right that one of us win the national championship this season, so let's get the players together on the field and let them settle the issue."
>
> After a few minutes, Paul hung up the telephone, smiled, and said, "Aruns, ol' boy, you've got your match."[2]

But Billy Varner, who was at the house when the Sugar Bowl deal was made, told Al Browning, "What Mr. Callery didn't say is it took about five calls to Joe Paterno to get the game arranged. I think the final convincing statement by Coach Bryant came when he said, 'You know, Joe, we aren't worth a lot, really, and somebody is going to beat us. I'd like for it to be a good team like yours to do that when it happens.' Joe Paterno bit the bait."[3]

JOE PATERNO, like Vince Lombardi, was born of Italian parents in Brooklyn. Thirteen years younger than Bryant, he quarterbacked for "Rip" Engle at Brown University, and in 1950 went with Engle to Penn State, where he put in fourteen seasons as an assistant. (He was on the Penn State staff when the Lions beat the Tide 7–0 in the icy 1959 Liberty Bowl in Philadelphia.) Considered by many as the most brilliant college football coach to come along in the 1960s, Paterno was one of the leading defensive strategists in the game; his specialty was his coaching of linebackers, where he had helped to earn Penn State the moniker of "Linebacker U." (Jack Ham, one of the leaders of the Pittsburgh Steelers "Steel Curtain"

Super Bowl teams was a Paterno protégé.) Paterno had led Penn State to perfect seasons in 1968, 1969, and 1973, but had become increasingly frustrated by the lack of respect his teams got from the wire-service polls. In 1973, the Lions had gone 11–0 but sat and watched as Alabama and Notre Dame slugged it out for the national championship. After a tough victory over LSU in the 1974 Orange Bowl, he had national championship rings made for his players. "Whose poll did you win?" asked a sportswriter. "The Paterno poll!" he snapped back. "We took it in the locker room after the game."

Paterno was determined to establish Penn State as one of the major national football powers in the eyes of the nation, and in 1978 he had the horses to do it. There was a lingering prejudice among teams in other parts of the country, particularly the South, about eastern football, not so much about Penn State, which had beaten teams from all over the country in bowl games, but their opponents. "Who did they play?" was a regular refrain among Alabama fans and players. ("An SEC school like LSU," Joe Namath would tell any northern sportswriter who would listen, "could whip a dozen schools like Pittsburgh.") That prejudice would last only until Alabama linemen got a snoot full of Millen and Clark. Matt Millen and Bruce Clark were usually described in newspapers as "the Lions' lion-like tackles"; together, they made it virtually impossible for teams to run up the middle against Penn State. Both were consensus All-America players in 1979, the only teammates on any college team to be honored at that position in the 1970s. They would go on to play a combined twenty years in the NFL.

Penn State had other All-America players too. At safety, there was Pete Harris, younger brother of former Penn State and then Pittsburgh Steeler Franco Harris. On offense, guard Keith Dorney made just about everyone's All-America team, as did quarterback Chuck Fusina and long-range kicker Matt Bahr. Penn State's list of All-Americas didn't even include the player some regarded as Penn State's best, fullback Matt Suhey, who would gain more than five thousand yards running and receiving in his ten years with the Chicago Bears, starting on the great 1985 Bears Super Bowl championship team. "Anyone who thinks Penn State doesn't have a bunch of great football players doesn't know much about football," Bryant said at the Football Foundation and Hall of Fame dinner in New York. "Of course," he added, "we got some pretty good plow hands, too." Indeed he did.

Defensive tackle Marty Lyons and linebacker Barry Krauss both made several All-America teams, while defensive ends E. J. Junior and Wayne Hamilton, offensive tackle Jim Bunch, safety Murray Legg, and center Dwight Stephenson had made the All-SEC team. (Both Bryant and Paterno thought Stephenson should have been All-America.)

The problem with evaluating Alabama's talent is that the Tide was so deep, most of its best players were shuttled in and out of the lineup. Both Jeff Rutledge and Tony Nathan were second-team SEC choices, but everyone knew they were even better than that. Rutledge, operating Alabama's complex triple option with ruthless efficiency, was regarded as a "running" quarterback, but he had actually thrown more touchdown passes that season than Penn State's Fusina. And NFL scouts were as aware as the Penn State coaching staff that Nathan was one of the best backs in the nation.

Both teams had tremendous power, speed, and depth; both had superb special teams; and both had rock-ribbed defenses—probably the two best in the nation. Penn State was a little bigger; Alabama hoped it was a little quicker. Both had great head coaches and staffs. If the national championship wasn't enough incentive, both teams had plenty to get worked up about. For Penn State, it was the biggest game in the school's history; for Alabama, it was a chance to win on the field what most of the players had taken away from them by the polls the previous year. If there was a substantial difference in coaching philosophies, it was pinpointed by former-Arkansas-coach-turned-ABC-commentator Frank Broyles in a pregame analysis: "On offense, Joe Paterno tends to be a little too conservative, and a conservative offense won't make a nickel's worth against Alabama."[4]

KEITH JACKSON, the greatest of all college football announcers, called it "the greatest game I ever saw in person." In a December 2002 poll by ESPN.com, the 1979 Sugar Bowl was voted the greatest college bowl game ever. Alabama's Marty Lyons and Penn State's Bruce Clark would later say that no hit they ever took in the NFL was as hard as the licks they took in the game. Frank Broyles, who did the telecast with Jackson, called it "the cleanest, hardest-hitting football game I have ever seen. Up in the booth, my teeth were shaking from the hits down on the field."

Penn State's defense was ranked number one in the nation and had allowed just fifty-four yards rushing per game during the season, but it had not faced a team that ran from a wishbone formation—let alone one that could quickly shift out of the classic wishbone to several different offensive sets, as Alabama could. Bryant feared though—and rightly so, as it turned out—that the Lions had a cure for Alabama's offensive complexity in Millen and Clark. One of the virtues of the wishbone, Bryant observed, was that the fullback alone had to be contained by five men up front, but with Millen and Clark in the middle of their defensive line Penn State could afford, in many situations, to get by with just a four-man line, leaving an extra linebacker to be placed where Paterno thought best.

It was Joe Paterno's best defensive team, and it instantly won Alabama's respect. "We were throwing the kitchen sink at them," says offensive tackle Buddy Aydelette. "We kept moving the ball in their territory, and every time we did I thought, 'This is it, we're going to bust this open.' But each time they sucked it up and stopped us." Alabama's defense did an even more thorough job on the Penn State offense. Neither Suhey nor running back Mike Guman could reach the line of scrimmage without an arm, shoulder, or helmet hitting them, and nearly every time Fusina dropped back to throw, he was hit by someone. Penn State, dressed all in white, would line up and snap the ball, and almost immediately streaks of red would stream through its blockers. Most of the game was played on the line where "the big uglies," as Jackson called the interior lineman, played, and it was a savage standoff.

With a little more than three minutes left in the first half, the Tide forced a punt and took over with good field position, at its forty-seven-yard line. Rutledge connected with end Bruce Bolton for a fifteen-yard gain, then, rolling to his right, threw back to his left on a screen pass to Steve Whitman for fifteen more. It looked as if Alabama had at last established its offensive rhythm, but on second down, as Rutledge rolled to his right and dropped back to throw, Bruce Clark came crashing in and forced him to throw the ball higher than intended. The ball tipped off Whitman's hand and was picked off by linebacker Rich Millot, who swept back to his right and down the sideline, with no red shirts in sight. Major Ogilvie, running diagonally across the field, managed to catch up with Millot at the Alabama thirty-seven and knocked him out of bounds. Penn State now had its own chance to break the deadlock—it was already within Matt Bahr's field goal range. But on third down, in the biggest defensive play of the game for Alabama up to that point, Byron Bragg broke up the middle and sacked Fusina out of field goal range.

With one minute, thirty-two seconds left in the first half, the game was still scoreless. The Tide started from its own twenty. On first down Ogilvie gained two yards, but Alabama then became the unexpected beneficiary of a Penn State timeout. Paterno was gambling that his defense could stop Alabama, force it to punt from somewhere around its own ten-yard line, get the ball in good field position, then complete a pass to set up a tie-breaking field goal by Matt Bahr. The plan backfired. On second down Rutledge flipped a short pass to Tony Nathan for six yards, then Whitman blasted straight ahead for four yards and a first down, stopping the clock briefly with about a minute to play in the half. All Paterno had done was give Bryant another chance, and he jumped on it. On the first play, Nathan broke free, streaking for thirty yards down to the Penn State thirty-seven, the first down temporarily stopping the clock. Nathan got the ball again and gained seven more yards, to the Penn State thirty. If it had been Paterno, Matt Bahr would have come in on that spot for a field goal try— but Bryant wanted a knockdown punch. Huddling with Rutledge and offensive coordinator Mal Moore, Bryant decided that it would be safe to give his quarterback a shot at the end zone—Rutledge was instructed to throw the ball away if his receiver wasn't open. He delivered, zipping the ball between the Penn State defensive back and safety and into the hands of a diving Bruce Bolton for thirty yards and a touchdown. The Tide led at the half, 7–0.

Alabama had been the better team in the first half. Against the number one–ranked defense in the nation it had rolled up 214 yards, 129 on the ground, while holding Penn State to −7 yards in rushing and just 21 yards overall. Rutledge had even outpassed Fusina, 85 yards to 28. But every time the Tide had penetrated into Penn State territory the Lions had stiffened and thrown them back—every time except near the end of the half. In the third quarter, Alabama's Alan McElroy missed a seemingly easy field goal that would have made it 10–0. Now it was Penn State's turn to land a punch. Paterno made some adjustments on defense, and the next time Rutledge tried to pass downfield, Pete Harris came up from his safety spot and intercepted, returning the ball to the Alabama forty-eight. A few plays later, Fusina finally connected with his fine end, Scott Fitzkee, for seventeen yards and a touchdown, Fitzkee making a great leaping grab before tumbling out of the end zone. Suddenly the game was tied, and the momentum had shifted. The Lions' defense shut the wishbone down on the next possession, giving Penn State the ball close to midfield. Bryant responded with a daring countermove: on third down, he called for a safety blitz. Murray Legg sacked Fusina before he could throw the ball downfield.

Over the years, the Crimson Tide was saved time and again by relative unknowns, unheralded players who stepped up in key moments to make big plays. Now it happened again. Major Ogilvie had been Bryant's primary punt returner, but now, on a hunch, Bryant decided to use Lou Ikner, a senior who had seen limited playing time during the season. Taking the Penn State punt at the twenty-three-yard line, Ikner saw a mass of red shirts, led by Byron Braggs, forming down the left sideline. He followed it, cut back to the middle, and raced all the way to the Penn State eleven-yard line before being dragged down. The sixty-two-yard return stunned Penn State. On third and goal from the ten-yard line, Bryant and Mal Moore had correctly guessed that Penn State would be looking for a pass. Rolling to his left on the option, Rutledge pitched the ball back to a trailing Ogilvie just before Matt Millen slammed the quarterback to the ground. Ogilvie, without breaking stride, snatched the pitch out of the air, skirted the sideline, and went into the end zone untouched. With only seconds left in the third quarter, Alabama was up 14–7.

Following a Penn State punt, Alabama took over at its own twenty-two with just under eight minutes left in the game. At this point, it was Paterno's turn to gamble. He had his linemen shoot the gaps, diving into the Alabama backfield trying to disrupt a handoff or pitch to the running backs. They did: Rutledge was hit while attempting to pitch back, and white uniforms scrambled for the ball, recovering it at the Alabama nineteen. Fired up, the Lions' offensive linemen blew the red uniforms away on the first play as Suhey ripped up the middle for eleven yards and a first down, safety Jim Bob Harris and defensive back Murray Legg combining for a touchdown-saving tackle at the Alabama eight. On first down, tailback Mike Guman ran off tackle for two yards. On second down, Fusina rolled to his right and fired a short pass to Fitzkee, who, running parallel to Fusina, caught the ball around the four-yard line and started to turn toward the end zone. Watching the replay a quarter of a century later, it still seems impossible that Fitzkee did not score—when he turned toward the end zone after the catch, there was not a red shirt in front of him. It seemed as if all Fitzkee had to do was fall into the end zone. Then, seemingly out of nowhere, cornerback Don McNeal, who just an instant before had been tangled up with another receiver in the end zone, came up and collided with Fitzkee just inside the one-yard line, knocking him out of bounds. Keith Jackson called the play immediately, and Roone Arledge's crack ABC unit replayed it as Jackson described it: "I want to tell you, folks, that was one whale of a defensive play by Alabama's Don McNeal, because Fitzkee had momentum and McNeal simply would not let him get in." Fitzkee would say after the game, "I don't know where the Alabama defensive back came from."

In all great football careers there are a handful of plays that define a coach's personality and philosophy. McNeal's play did that for Bear Bryant. In the chapter on defense in *Building a Championship Football Team*, Bryant wrote, "The corner man should line up 'in his regular position' about four yards wide and two and one-half yards deep, with his feet parallel and even about 18 inches apart pointing directly towards the offensive quarterback. He should be in a good football position, weight on the balls of the feet, arms cocked, etc. He should not rest his hands on his knees. From a good football position he can rotate quickly and properly, or he can come forward and meet the play if it comes toward him."[5] McNeal performed as if Bryant's text was in front of him. As Fitzkee caught the pass under the coverage, McNeal was in perfect position to rotate, shift his weight, and come up to make the hit. He did not have the proper angle or the momentum, but, surging low and then pushing upward into Fitzkee from the side, he used the receiver's momentum against him, forcing him out of bounds. "It was," said the secondary coach, Bill Oliver, "one of the greatest individual efforts I've ever seen. I mean ever."[6]

"We feel," Bryant wrote in the chapter "Planning for a Game," "we can do a better job of planning after we have a fairly clear understanding of what our opponents are likely to do."[7] Bryant knew exactly what Joe Paterno was likely to do in this situation: run the ball straight at the heart of the Alabama defense. "There was no doubt in our minds that we could stop them," says Marty Lyons. "I don't mean that we were cocky or that we took it as a given. I mean we were confident because we had been told in these situations what Penn State's tendencies were, and we felt we were prepared to stop them."

On third down, Suhey hurtled into the middle. Finding no hole in the line, he tried to leap over it; Curtis McGriff, playing at middle guard, and Rich Wingo, coming up from his linebacker spot, threw him back. As the mass of red and white separated, Chuck Fusina anxiously searched for the ball. "How far is it?" he asked Marty Lyons. "'Bout a foot," Lyons said. A couple of seconds later the referee placed the ball on the ground; it was almost exactly between the one-yard line and the end zone stripe. Looking the Penn State quarterback in the eye, Lyons advised, "You better pass." But everyone knew that Paterno and Penn State would not pass.

From the beginning of his career Bryant had believed in the importance of stopping an opponent inside the five-yard line, but what made him a great coach was the ability to make his players believe that "when the opposing team has the ball inside our 3-yard line, they aren't going to score—they can't score—they must not score! If a team believes this, it's almost impossible for the offense to score."[8] Bryant's players believed.

"Could be for the whole ball of wax," Jackson said as the two teams lined up for the fourth down. There was a momentary pause when the roar of the crowd, amplified by the stadium's dome, necessitated an official's timeout. Then they lined up again. Someone—some Alabama players thought it was Murray Legg—yelled, "Gut check! Gut check!" Byron Braggs would later say, "There was an excitement in the huddle. We were telling each other *this* is Alabama football. This is all about what Coach Bryant had taught us. The one moment we'd worked for and sweated for, coming down to one play. It was all those winter days in the lower gym." At the snap of the ball, the Penn State line surged forward in a white wave, and Alabama surged back like a crimson tide. In the backfield, Suhey led the charge left of center. Guman took the handoff from Fusina and plunged into the mass. In his book, Bryant stipulated that on a goal line defense the defensive tackles "aim for a spot one yard deep in the offensive backfield behind the inside foot of the offensive tackle. Each tackle is responsible for the hand-off play to his side, making the tackle or forcing the dive play to the inside so our middle linebacker can make the tackle." They are responsible, he said, for "sealing off the middle of the line, and for keeping the offensive center from blocking the middle linebacker. They aim for a spot about one yard behind the offensive center's position. They must get to this spot using a low, hard submarine charge." If the tackles and the other linemen carried out their defensive assignments, "using a low, hard charge . . . we will form a wall."[9]

For a split second, it appeared the white wall had overcome the red one, but the red wall coming from underneath was forcing the white one up. "The middle linebacker," Bryant wrote, "is responsible for making any play that occurs between the offensive tackles."[10] "Coach Bryant hammered into us," recalls Barry Krauss, "the idea that we wanted to reestablish our line on *their* side of the line of scrimmage. Anyone who could make the tackle on the ball carrier, of course, was supposed to, but basically the point for the defensive lineman was to clear away interference so the linebackers could make the tackle." Penn State center Chuck Correal immediately moved through the hole as if to hunt out an Alabama linebacker, either Wingo or Krauss. David Hannah, moving to his left, cut Correal off. Krauss, seeing Guman heading straight for the off-tackle spot, moved forward to meet him just as Guman tried to go over the top. Murray Legg, moving in behind Krauss, added his momentum to the play. "I don't think I could have kept Guman from scoring if Murray hadn't been right there," says Krauss.

A picture of the collision between Mike Guman and Barry Krauss would appear later that week on the cover of *Sports Illustrated*, and would be immortalized on the walls of thousands of Alabama restaurants, bars, and dens. "He didn't make it!" exclaimed Jackson, just loud enough to be heard over the roar from Alabama fans. "What an unbelievable goal line stand by Alabama!" As the jubilant players in red ran off the field, one form remained motionless on the turf: Barry Krauss.

Krauss was able to leave the field under his own power, but did not regain full control until a few minutes later on the bench. He had played with a pinched nerve in his neck since his junior year, and the pain was sometimes excruciating. The head-on crash with Guman had given Krauss such a jolt that he was temporarily paralyzed. When things came back into focus, his team was once again in a desperate situation. There was still five minutes left in the game and Penn State was full of fight. On fourth down, from his own end zone, Alabama's punter, Bobby Umphrey, made a terrific grab of a low snap that bounced in front of him. His punt, though, was weak, soaring out of bounds in the vicinity of the Penn State thirty-yard line. But back in the end zone, an official had flagged Penn State for having twelve men on the field. Alabama got another chance, ran more time off the clock, and punted deep into Penn State territory. With twelve seconds on the clock, Mark Clements intercepted a Fusina pass, and one of the greatest of all college bowl games was over, 14–7.

If the game had ended in a tie, Penn State might still have won the national championship with a 10–0-1 record, or, perhaps, have won in at least one of the wire-service polls—probably the Associated Press, the sportswriters' poll, which Alabama ended up winning. In a strange turn of events, Southern Cal, which won a controversial victory over Michigan in the Rose Bowl, went from third to first in the United Press International, the coaches' poll. Alabama, number two before the game, was given no credit by the coaches at all for beating the number-one team. Most Alabamians didn't begrudge USC its share of the glory, as the Trojans had whipped the Tide during the regular season and finished with the same 11–1 record, but it certainly did appear that Bryant had a few enemies among coaches who voted in the UPI.

But if the game had ended in a tie, Alabama would not have won either poll. The goal line stand can legitimately be called the most important series of plays in Alabama's season—some would say in Bryant's entire career.

The 1979 Sugar Bowl stand would haunt Paterno throughout the years. In 1988, while delivering a speech at the Republican Convention in the Superdome in New Orleans, he made mention of having lost the national championship at that very spot. In his autobiography, *Paterno: By the Book*, published ten years after the great game, he reflected, "What a perfect moment! There, steeled against us, the great Red Tide, and we—*we are Penn State!*—perennial winners, until now, never the acknowledged champs.

"There was Bear Bryant. Here was Joe Paterno. In this play I go hand to hand, my destined chance to outcoach a legend." Paterno called a timeout and told his coaches he wanted to call a play-action pass: Chuck Fusina would fake a handoff, which would freeze Alabama's linebackers, and flip a short pass to the tight end. His assistants were against it. If the offense couldn't move the ball a yard, they argued, the team didn't deserve to win the national championship. Paterno's instincts told him, "That's a lot of crap. This is the time to surprise them and throw the ball."

In such a situation Bryant would have listened to his instincts; Paterno listened to his assistants. The result was,

To this day down in Alabama, anywhere you go you can find their blown-up photo: an army of crimson defenders stopping Guman cold.

I have talked about getting angry with myself when I lose. Nothing of the kind compared to this loss. I beat up on myself not only immediately but for months afterward, halfway into the next season. . . . I let my anger turn against the staff and against the team, even though the decision was purely mine. . . . Writers and fans said, for all to hear, that Paterno couldn't win the big one at the critical moment. Even former players said openly, "He should have won that one."

It got to me. It hammered at my ego. *When I stood toe to toe with Bear Bryant, he outcoached me.*

Some time during the next season, as he was brooding to himself about the game, his wife leaned over and said to him, "Joe, the Alabama game is over! It's just another game you lost."[11] Paterno would get over it, four years later, when his Nittany Lions finally won the national title, beating Herschel Walker and Georgia in the Sugar Bowl, but the man who would eventfully pass Bear Bryant in all-time wins lost two more times to him.

Immediately after the game, in the euphoria of Alabama's locker room, the *Birmingham Post-Herald*'s Bill Lumpkin asked Bryant how far from the goal line Penn State had come on that final play. "Bill," Bryant replied, "about the length of your talleywhacker."

Barry Krauss was the focal point of perhaps the most famous college football play ever, but he had no illusions about his role in it. "I was just there, where the play happened to be. Anyone of us could have made it, and as far as I'm concerned, we all did."

BY THE late 1970s it was common for writers and journalists to make pilgrimages to Tuscaloosa in search of the "real" Bear Bryant. In the spring of 1979, novelist Richard Price, author of *The Wanderers* and *Blood Brothers*, traveled to Alabama to profile the Bear for the October issue of *Playboy*. Perhaps because it was written by a skeptic, an outsider, Price's story offers perhaps the best contemporary look at Bryant and the Alabama program in its silver age.

"Because I grew up in a multiethnic environment in New York City," Price wrote in "Bear Bryant's Miracles," the South has always conjured up some bad news reactions on word-association tests for me: Klan, lynch, redneck, moonshine, speedtrap towns and death . . . lots of death.

As the years have passed, I've started hearing some flip sides. . . . I've heard that, despite the headline horrors, Southerners get along racially better than Northerners. And that foreign blacks prefer the upfrontness of the South to the hypocritical liberal bullshit of the North.

But despite all my revisionist thoughts, the only good images that have held up in my head are Southern novelists and the University of Alabama football team. The novelists because they are good or great and the Crimson Tide because, like Notre Dame, they are the New York Yankees of college football. I don't give a rat's ass about football, college or otherwise, and I'm not crazy about regimentation. But I do admire winners.

And as ignorant as I am of the "real" South and football in general, even *I* know that the man behind the winning tradition at Alabama is a magnetic, scary John Wayne type named Paul "Bear" Bryant. I would see him every few years on a televised bowl game, standing on the sidelines, craggy-faced, in that houndstooth hat. I figured he was some kind of coaching genius. I also got the notion that he was somebody I was very glad not to have as a teacher in any course I was flunking.

Escorted by Alabama's sports information director Kirk McNair, Price first visited Bryant Hall, which he found to be "a cross between a dorm and a housing project. The place looks like shit. Off the lobby is a TV room and the dining room. Players walk by: Some are mammoth, with roast-beef shoulders and ham-hock thighs, and they walk sway-backed into the dining room; others aren't much bigger than I am. Alabama opts for quickness over bulk; consequently it's not that big a team." Price, at first, didn't hear anybody mention Bryant's name: "He doesn't have that much personal contact with his players. He's got a huge staff of coaching assistants who get down in the dirt with them. But he's there. He's in that room. He *is* the team, and everybody knows it."

Finally, "It's my day to interview Bear, and, to be honest, I'm scared. I consider giving myself a haircut with nail clippers. . . . Everybody walking around is named Coach. It's like sitting in a room with the tall, stately aging cowboys of Hollywood. A room full of Gary Cooper-Ben Johnson look-alikes, all nodding to one another. 'Mornin,' coach.' 'Hey, coach.' 'Nice day, coach.' If I were to scream out 'coach!' there would be a ten-way collision. And everybody looks like Bear Bryant." Price found Bryant

cordial, patient but distant. He has been interviewed six times a week since coming to Alabama.

He looks all of his 66 years—his face is like an aerial shot of a drought area. His eyes are glittering hard. His hands are huge and gnarled. He needs a haircut himself. . . . All in all, I like the guy, though I couldn't see being in a sensory-awareness class together.

"Coach, you're pretty much an American hero these days. I was wondering who *your* heroes are."★ . . . He pouts, shrugs. "Well, my heroes are John Wayne, Bob Hope, General Patton . . . I suppose you'd like me to say Einstein."

"Nah, not Einstein."

But Price was interested in knowing what it was like to be a football player in the late 1960s

when regimentation was so reactionary—when long hair and a taste for dope were de rigueur. I know that Bryant's worst years since coming to Alabama were 1969 and 1970. Is there any connection?

"I did a real poor job of recruiting and coaching," he says. "Every youngster in America was goin' through a rebellious period. Nobody wanted anybody to tell 'em anything. I remember a boy sittin' right there an' tellin' me, 'I just want to be like any other student.' Well, shit. He can't *be* like any other student. The players have to take pride in the fact that football means that much to 'em. That's where the sacrificin' comes in. That they *are* willin' to do without some things. Without havin' some things other students have, to be playin' football, to win a championship."

Price interviewed several players, including senior quarterback Steadman Shealy, whom he finds "isn't much bigger than I am, but he's a lot blonder and tanner. He also has a firmer handshake, better manners and a neater appearance." Shealy talks to Price "of Bear's father image, of how the

---

★ In the article, Price inserted in parentheses, "Please don't kill me."

coach applies football to life (another thing I'll hear again), of what it takes to win. All hokey stuff in the abstract—but not to Shealy and the others. The guys talk about these bland notions as though they were tenets of radical politics."

Price found Byron Braggs "a little less awestruck, more blasé. . . . 'A lot of guys are scared of him [Bryant], they're in awe of his presence, but I just look at him like anybody else. I'm just happy he can remember my name. He mixes up a lot of names and faces, but two minutes later, he'll remember and apologize." Price reminds him that ten years ago Alabama was segregated. "When I ask Braggs if prejudice lingers, he just shrugs. 'It doesn't bother me,' he says, 'there were times when things looked shaky, but there were no major problems.'" Braggs says that a few years before he came to Alabama "'it was mainly white. I didn't even *know* about Alabama. I would watch Notre Dame, USC with O.J. Simpson. I didn't really notice Alabama until they beat USC out there. That was the first time I knew they had a team. And since they had black players, a lot more people became fans of the team. My folks and others follow the team now. In my hometown, people have become real fans.'" (Braggs was born in Montgomery four years after Rosa Parks refused to give up her seat on a bus.)

In the middle of their interview, Bryant told Price a joke. Price failed to laugh "because I can't understand a damned thing he says. He sort of mutters from his diaphragm in his artesian-well deep Arkansas drawl, and it's like listening to a language you studied for only a year in high school." Days later, he found,

I'm still smarting about that missed joke. I feel I understand something then about why this man is successful. There is something about him— about *me* in that moment when I blew being an appreciative audience— that goes beyond past embarrassment. I fell like I let him down. I feel like I could have pleased him by laughing, made him like me for a moment, could have broken through the interviewer-interviewee roles for a few seconds in a way that would have made me feel like a million bucks *because it would have given him pleasure*. There is something in Bear's subdued dignity, his cordial distance, that got to me. He is a man of *character*. I could see myself having done Mexican tailspins during that interview to get his admiration. Or just his acknowledgment. And this was just a magazine assignment. If I were one of his five-year players, I could see myself doing 90 mph through a goal post to get a pat on the back. And, frankly, I can't define motivation, either, but whatever it is that he lays on his boys, I got a tiny ray of it myself. The man could literally crush you by letting you know you were a disappointment to him. Shit, maybe I've just seen too many John Wayne movies.

ON MAY 18, Bryant boarded a private jet and headed for one of the most desolate parts of Texas to revisit his past. The Junction Boys, the A&M players he had put through the brutal 1954 trial, were staging a twenty-fifth anniversary reunion. Time had softened their memories of the ordeal; it had also softened the landscape, which, with a change in rainfall and better irrigation, had grown green and lush. Middle-aged men in business suits now walked across the grassy strip of land and joked about how a bunch of sweaty boys in football pads had rolled around the same field covered with rocks and sand spurs.

When Bryant arrived, he was apprehensive, and he had every right to be, knowing that the men he was about to see still had reason to harbor resentment. He gazed out over the field. Dennis Goehring went up to shake hands: "The first thing he said is, 'Well, damn, it just shows what a little rain can do for a place.'"

"He got kind of misty-eyed as he approached the group," says Goehring. "He said, 'Dennis, please don't let me embarrass myself. Kinda whisper their names to me, I don't want to get anybody's name wrong.'" But Bryant recognized everyone. A few of the old faces were not there. Gene Stallings, an assistant with the Dallas Cowboys, and Jack Pardee, head coach of the Washington Redskins, could not get away, but almost all of the rest of the team were there. "I've never had a team I was more proud of," he told them. "I came here today to apologize to ya'll. I shouldn't have done what I did twenty-five years ago. If somebody'd done that to me, I would have just walked off. Quit, I really would have."[12]

Early in April one of Bryant's old Aggies had phoned the house in Tuscaloosa and asked Mary Harmon what the Coach's ring size was; she did not know. A picture of Bryant's hand was presented to a ring maker, and the craftsman correctly guessed that Bryant wore a size twelve. At the Junction reunion, Bryant was presented with a commemorative ring. He wore it till he died.

———

IN SEPTEMBER one of Bryant's heroes, Bob Hope, came to Tuscaloosa to tape a television special. "I want to congratulate Alabama for being the number-two team in the country," cracked Hope, referring to UPI's snub of the Tide in favor of Southern Cal the previous season. The line drew good-natured boos from the crowd. "Tuscaloosa," he went on, "sounds like an Italian elephant with a dental problem." Tuscaloosa "is easy to spot from the air. All the empty beer cans spell out B-E-A-R B-R-Y-A-N-T." "He's like a god around here. He's the only coach I know whose play book is carved on stone tablets." And so on. Then came what everyone had been waiting for: Bear Bryant's network comedy debut. A voiceover explained, "We take you now to the nerve center of the University of Alabama—the office of its football coach, Paul 'Bear' Bryant." (A big sign on Bryant's wall informs us that "Winning Is Never Having To Say You're Sorry.") The sketch opens with Bryant at his desk, wearing an Alabama windbreaker, on the phone apologizing to the university president for a kicker who missed an extra point. "Sir, it's hard to get a good kicker these days. . . . I will *not* cut his foot off! Who do you think you are, the Ayatollah?" (Between the time the show was taped and when it was aired in the late fall, the U.S. embassy in Iran was taken over; NBC executives, fearing that the Ayatollah line would seem in bad taste, cut it from the sketch.)

Joe Namath, by now two years retired from pro football, drops in to tell his old coach about a fantastic place kicking prospect, Bob "Thunderfoot" Hope. Namath then calls in Thunderfoot. Hope enters dressed in what looks like an outfit from a Depression-era football movie; his right foot is the size of a yeti's. The Bear is unimpressed. "But," says Namath, "Howard Cosell called his toe 'the prodigious digit.'" Bryant gets to deliver the zinger: "You sure he didn't mean his nose?" This coach finally relents and offers Thunderfoot a scholarship. "Sign your John Henry right there," he tells his new recruit. Namath, acting as Thunderfoot's agent, tells Bryant that his man "has some reasonable demands." One of them is "no more than five TDs a game so he won't have to overtax his foot." Bryant replies, delivering the sketch's biggest laugh-getter, "Well, it won't be easy, but we'll try."[13]

———

THROUGH THE first eight games of the 1979 season, the Tide averaged nearly thirty-eight points per game until it faced a tough LSU team on November 10 at Baton Rouge. The entire game was played in a driving rainstorm. The game was memorable for two reasons: First, Alabama won 3–0, the only game all season in which it did not score a touchdown. Second, on the first play of the game, Major Ogilvie nearly knocked Bryant senseless. Driven out of bounds by two LSU tacklers, Ogilvie did not realize he had crashed into his coach until he was informed so by trainer Jim Goostree after the game. At first Ogilvie was afraid to go into the training room, but, as it turned out, the Bear still appreciated a good lick, no matter under what circumstance it was delivered. On Monday, it was revealed that Ogilvie had received a perfect 100 score on Bryant's rating system.

Alabama's only real scare came against Tennessee, when, inexplicably, the Tide found itself down 17–0 in the second quarter. There are times when a coach helps his team by simplifying matters. This was one of those times. At halftime, Bryant's assistant coaches had been frantically diagramming Tennessee's plays and Alabama's proposed adjustments for them on the blackboard; Bryant walked over to the board and erased everything. His strategy for Alabama's second-half comeback was a model of clarity: "Just go out there, hang on to the football, and knock 'em down, and we'll be all right." Defensive back Ricky Tucker opened the second half by intercepting a pass and returning it to the Tennessee thirty. Six plays later, Major Ogilvie ran for a touchdown, and the score was 17–14. On Alabama's next possession the Volunteers wilted; quaterback Don Jacobs engineered a classic wishbone drive, seventy yards in fourteen plays, with Ogilvie scoring from six yards out. In the fourth quarter, Jacobs did it again, this time going eighty yards and running the ball in himself. Alabama scored the last twenty-eight points of the game and won by eleven. The win over Tennessee gave Alabama a comfortable lead in the AP poll and second place behind Southern Cal in the UPI one.

Two weeks after the Tennessee game, a 24–7 win over Mississippi State was notable only in that the Bulldogs were coached by Emory Bellard, the inventor of the wishbone. After the game, Bellard commented, "Alabama's personnel is really no better than ours and certainly not Tennessee's. Alabama is a great team because they are mentally tougher and they do the little things better than any of the rest of us. That man drills it into them that they are champions, and they believe it." What Bryant was really drilling into everyone's head was the idea that these late 1970s Alabama teams didn't have the talent that many other schools had, that they won through toughness and preparation. That was half true; Alabama *did* win on toughness and preparation, and fifteen of the team's twenty-two starters were home grown. But the 1979 team had enormous talent, paced by Dwight Stephenson, Byron Braggs, E. J. Junior, Major Ogilvie, Don McNeal, and many others, all of whom had played for the 1978 team that won the national title and the 1977 team that should have. The 1979 team had talent, depth, maturity, and cohesiveness. It may have been his best; that it isn't widely regarded as such is probably because its alternating quarterbacks, Steadman Shealy and Don Jacobs, weren't pro-type passers or even All-America candidates, but dedicated workmen who could run, pass, and work the wishbone's tricky option. Shealy was a bigger, stronger version of Terry Davis, the wishbone quarterback Alabama had started the decade with, but with a better throwing arm and playing behind bigger blockers.

The first ten victories would have meant little had Alabama lost to Auburn in the season-ending showdown. Or as Bryant put it, "I'da as soon go back to plowin' than go to a bowl game if we lose to Auburn." Auburn fans, who hung on Bryant's every word, determined to use the remark against him. He walked onto Legion Field that afternoon to chants of "Plow, Bear, Plow!" He responded by extending his arms behind his back while Charley Thornton, his hands on Bryant's wrists, pretended to push him forward. Even the Auburn people had to laugh.

They weren't laughing an hour later when Alabama, keying on Auburn's great running backs James Brooks and Joe Cribbs, led 14–3 at the half on a touchdown pass and a touchdown run from Steadman Shealy. The Tide defense had given up just 13 points in the second half in its ten previous games while scoring 193, so at halftime Alabama fans began arguing over whom their team should play for the national championship. A powerful Southern Cal team that would finish 10–0–1 was out of the question, as the Pacific 10 Conference was contracted to play the Big Ten winner in the Rose Bowl. That took care of Ohio State, also a contender. Nebraska, Florida State, and Houston, all of which had shared the November 12 cover of *Sports Illustrated* with Alabama, were definite possibilities. The Alabama players must have been giving thought to the question too, because their minds weren't on Auburn, as they proved by fumbling *five* times in the third quarter. Auburn recovered four, and after allowing a fifty-five-yard touchdown pass in the fourth quarter, the longest given up by the Tide secondary all season, Alabama found itself behind 18–17. This time, the players did not need either the good-cop or the bad-cop speech from their coach. Everyone knew what had to be done. Starting from its eighteen-yard line, Shealy guided the offense eighty-two yards for what would prove to be the winning touchdown, in a 25–18 victory. This year it was the AP's turn to slight Alabama; early the next week, Bryant and his coaches switched on the radio in his office to hear that Alabama was comfortably ahead in the UPI poll but trailing Ohio State (which finished the season unbeaten while both Nebraska and Houston lost games) in the AP poll. The Tide would need some extra help to sweep the final polls.

JOHN NICOLA JR.'S brother-in-law, Tony Chiccino—"Chick" to his friends—had played for Bear Bryant at Kentucky, where he had become pals with Larry "Dude" Hennessey. It was from Chick that Johnny acquired his love of SEC football—"There's no football anywhere like you'll see in the SEC," Chick had told him, "and no coach anywhere like Bear Bryant." Both men transferred their loyalty to Alabama when Bryant went there and in 1970 started a booster club in their hometown of Bridgeport, Pennsylvania, a little town about twenty minutes outside Philadelphia. Every year they would lead a group to Birmingham or Tuscaloosa to an Alabama game. In 1973, the club voted in a bylaw: when Alabama won a national championship, they would put a congratulatory billboard on Route 202. Billboards went up in 1973, 1978, and 1979. After the 1979 Sugar Bowl victory over Penn State, the Alabama Booster Club's billboard attracted national attention when the AP put a photo of it on its wire service. It also garnered much hostility from the mostly pro–Penn State citizenry. But, said Nicola, "There was no insult intended to Penn State. We were just Alabama fans."

Nicola's greatest thrill in football was being in New Orleans for the 1979 Sugar Bowl, which he calls "the greatest game I ever saw, pro or college or anything." At halftime, he and another booster club member sat with Mary Harmon, who was thrilled to see the two Yankees. "She said, 'I hope ya'll are having a fine time in New-ah-lens. The boys look like they're playing mighty well today.'"

A few months later, Nicola traveled to Tuscaloosa for spring practice. Bryant came over to shake hands and thank him for the club's support. "Is there anything I can do for you?" he wanted to know. "Coach," Nicola replied, "if you can find time in your schedule to come up and give us a talk in Bridgeport, it would be about the biggest thing that ever hit our town." After checking his schedule, Bryant told him, "You know, Johnny, I do have a couple of days before Christmas, and I'd love to come up to your neck of the woods."

On December 18, the town of Bridgeport was in a tizzy in anticipation of the arrival of Bryant, along with Mel Allen and New York Jets quarterback Richard Todd, both of whom were coming in from New York. "But a snowstorm hit our town you wouldn't believe. We had sold over six hundred tickets, and my phone was ringing off the hook with people asking, 'He can't possibly make it, can he?' I called Coach Bryant and told him how bad the weather was. He said, 'Johnny, I promised you I was going to come, and if I can get there, I'll be there.'" Todd and Allen got stuck in Manhattan; Bryant, along with Hennessey, his friend Aruns Callery, and a Birmingham nightclub performer named Bob Cain, boarded a private plane and headed into the maelstrom. The flight was horrendous, but the Alabama contingent made it in time.

Bryant spoke for just under an hour. "He told jokes, he told stories, he told us anecdotes about presidents and movie stars, and then he shook hands and signed autographs for everyone who was there." The club had university presidents, football coaches, and baseball stars speak to its members over the years, but, says Nicola, "There was never anything as memorable as the day Coach Bryant came to Bridgeport." Bryant gave Nicola one of his houndstooth hats, which he took to New York and had bronzed and mounted on a plaque.

About a year after Bryant's death, Mae Martin wrote Nicola a letter telling him how much her father had enjoyed seeing the boosters every year. "She wrote me that he would brag to people when we were in town that 'my Bridgeport boys are here.'"

ALABAMA'S OPPONENT on New Year's Day would be none of the likely teams. Arkansas had lost just once, a 13–10 thriller with Houston, and shared the Southwest Conference championship with the Cougars. Given its outstanding season, Arkansas would face Alabama in the Cotton Bowl. The year before, the Razorbacks had scored one of the biggest upsets of the decade, defeating heavily favored Oklahoma in the Orange Bowl after suspending seven of their best players for disciplinary reasons. Bryant knew that their coach, Lou Holtz, was capable of doing it again and, with the national title on the line, had no intention of letting his team get complacent. "When he read us the scouting report," recalls Bryant's offensive coordinator, Mal Moore, "he came across a line, 'They've got a great young coach in Holtz, very smart . . . ' He paused for a moment, then looked at us and said, 'I just *love* coaching against smart coaches.'"

Bryant also had smart coaches like Moore, who for this game added wings to the wishbone—double wings, that is, with the running backs split out wider on each side. "Our play selection wasn't different," says Moore, "but it *looked* different and put Arkansas off balance." Don McNeal surprised everyone by fumbling the ball on the opening kickoff. But when the Tide defense held the Razorbacks to a field goal, the players chose to take it as a moral victory and an omen. It was both. Shealy then drove Alabama eighty-two yards, with Major Ogilvie scoring on a twenty-two-yard run. A few minutes later, the Tide's great defensive ends, E. J. Junior and Wayne Hamilton, forced a fumble at the Arkansas twenty-four, and ninety seconds later, Ogilvie had his second touchdown and Alabama was up 14–3. In the fourth quarter, with one mighty effort, the team put the game, and the national championship, away. Leading 17–9, the Tide took the ball at its own two-yard line and drove it ninety-eight yards for the last score. The game ended 24–9.

Alabama got the extra help it needed from Southern Cal, which beat Ohio State 17–16 in the Rose Bowl. The Tide had the only 12–0 mark in the nation, and won the national championship by comfortable margins in both wire-service polls.

The 1979 Crimson Tide was Bear Bryant's last national championship team. Excepting the LSU game, for which the field conditions were horrendous, Alabama had scored 25 or more points in every game and averaged just under 36 per game for the season. But it was defense that separated the team from all other contenders. In 1979 Southern Cal outscored Alabama over the season by 6 points overall, 389 vs. 383, but allowed a whopping 171 points on defense, 104 more than Alabama. This sounds impressive enough, but it needs to be put in proper perspective. Twenty-five years after the 1979 season, in 2004, Southern Cal astonished the nation by averaging 38.2 points per game, or exactly 7 more than

Alabama's 1979 team, but the 1979 Alabama team not only averaged over 30 points per game, its wishbone triple-option attack ruthlessly controlled the clock while doing it, leaving relatively little time for opponents on their possessions. (Southern Cal's 2004 national champions, by the way, allowed 169 points overall.) Alabama allowed just 67 points in twelve games, shutting out five opponents.

In the 1970s, Alabama had an incredible end-of-the-decade run. From 1977 through 1979 the Tide won thirty-four of thirty-six games. One of the two losses was to Southern Cal, with whom they shared the national championship in 1978 and who they had beaten the season before; the other loss was to Nebraska by seven points on Nebraska's home field, a loss the Tide avenged by beating the Cornhuskers 20–3 the following season. Alabama won three consecutive bowl games and two national championships and should have won a third. Though no one saw it that way at the time, the 1979 season, in retrospect, seems almost like Bryant's farewell tour, his swan song.

BILL LUMPKIN recalls having been at a press conference some time in the mid-1970s when he first became aware of "The Record." Bryant made mention of coaching long enough to break Amos Alonzo Stagg's record for victories, which, Bryant said, was 314. Lumpkin turned to Benny Marshall, of the *Birmingham News*, and asked, "Did you know that Stagg held that record?" Marshall replied something along the lines of, "I didn't even know there *was* a record."

The number 314 wasn't a hallowed sports record such as Babe Ruth's 714 home runs or Joe DiMaggio's streak of hitting safely in fifty-six consecutive games. In fact, scarcely anyone in college football knew Stagg had won that many games or that it was a college record before Charley Thornton alerted the world. "I don't remember exactly when it was that it came to me," says Thornton. "We were in a car going somewhere. Billy Varner was driving, and I was flipping through some college football records. I came across some information on the career of Amos Alonzo Stagg and started doing some arithmetic. I realized that he was the winningest coach in college football history, which was no big surprise considering what a legend he was. But the surprise was that Coach Bryant was within striking distance of his record. I mean, it was surprising because we hadn't really thought about it before." Thornton wasn't the first one to figure out that Stagg had won 314 games, but he may have been the first to publicize it, and he was definitely the first to point out that Bear Bryant was within striking distance.* In a few years, the entire world of college football and then much of the American sports media would be talking about it.

Bryant's transformation from regional to national icon was complete. Slowly, grudgingly at first, the intellectuals began to accept and finally respect him, first for his straightforward, unsophisticated intelligence, and, eventually, as a symbol of values he represented that they perceived to be disappearing. Before the 1980 football season began, he flew to New York to tape *The Dick Cavett Show*. Cavett was known for swapping witticisms with the likes of Groucho Marx, Hugh Heffner, and David Susskind; Truman Capote was an Alabamian more in tune with the sensibilities of Cavett's audience than the football coach who had made his nickname by wrestling a carnival bear. But the hour went well, with Cavett and Bryant proving to be surprisingly simpatico.

> CAVETT: "There's something bear-like about you. By that I mean, you know how a bear is a nice friendly-looking creature, but you have a feeling that it could play you out with one blow. Are you easily moved to violence?"
> BRYANT, smiling and shaking his head: "Nooo."
> CAVETT: "What's the last time you decked anyone?"
> BRYANT: "No way! I'm a peace-loving person."[14]

Relaxing in the company of the Nebraska-born New York intellectual, Bryant was candid about how his job had changed over the years—"I don't coach football any more, I coach people"—and how the rough handling of his players was the result of his own insecurity—"I made the poorest grades of anyone who ever went to Alabama, I cut more classes, I did all the things I wasn't supposed to do, and I tell them that that's why I'm not going to let them do it."

---

* Clyde Bolton of the *Birmingham News* says he was always aware of Stagg's total. "I just never heard it talked about much till Coach Bryant looked like he was going to surpass it."

These were themes he stressed more and more in interviews as he got older, as if he felt an increasing need to justify or at least explain the harshness of the methods for which he had been criticized for decades. In the cover story of *Time*'s September 29 issue, "Supercoach," the man who was "unquestionably the dominant figure in college football today" all but apologized for his harshness during the Junction period at Texas A&M. "I don't know if what I did was good or bad. I will never know. It was just the only thing I could have done—at that time, knowing what I knew then. I wouldn't do it now because I know more than I knew then, more about resting players, letting them drink water, more about other ways to lead them. They had to put up with my stupidity, I believe if I had been one of those players, I'd have quit, too." He never forgave himself for his responsibility in getting Texas A&M put on probation. "All the other schools were doing it, so we did it too. I was real bitter about it at the time—I cried all the way home from the meeting where they put us on probation—but looking back, it may have been the best thing that ever happened to me. After that, I always lived by the letter of the game. Never won a game anything but the honest way."

"I don't have time to coach individuals any more," he lamented to *Time*. "I organize my assistant coaches."

Time quoted Alabama governor Fob James, "who is far less famous than Bryant in the state," as calling the Bear "larger than life." Bill Baxley, Alabama's former attorney general—and though *Time* failed to note it, Bryant's choice for governor of Alabama—"calls Bryant 'the number 1 asset of the state.' He is certainly treated as though he were: two uniformed state policemen act as bodyguards and chauffeurs on game days. Bryant has achieved a pop-hero status, his face appears on T-shirts and bumper stickers, and there are even post cards showing him strolling on water. The inscription: I Believe. Small wonder that former governor George Wallace says: 'He never got into politics, but if he ever did, he could have had anything he wanted in the state.'" Except, perhaps, black football players while George Wallace was in office.

Time got some things right, most notably Bryant's status as a pop culture hero in Alabama, though it would have been more accurate to say throughout the entire South, and maybe throughout the world of college football. By 1981 much of that was due to the collective business acumen of his financial advisor, Paul Bryant Jr., and the marketing skills of his former

player and coaching opponent, Bill Battle. Bryant began the decade represented by IMG, a sports and lifestyle management and marketing firm,
which today is the world's largest. "They're the best in the world at what
they do," says Battle, "but Coach told me, 'They're not doing anything for
me.' I told him it probably wasn't their fault; they just didn't know how to
get around the 'regional' thing. You could sell Bear Bryant as a hero just
about anywhere in the country, but you couldn't sell him as being *from*
anywhere in the country. You had to find a way to capture what he was
about, the values that he represented to common people."

Battle was one of the first to understand "the regional thing." In 1981,
Battle was president of a division of Circle S Industries that manufactured
high-performance commercial aluminum windows. But another subsidiary
of Circle S was Golden Eagle Enterprises, which handled licensing rights
for a variety of products, from Jack Nicklaus Golden Bear golf gloves,
socks, and accessories to Chris Evert ladies' eyewear.★

When Bryant mentioned to Battle that he would like to change agents,
Battle proposed that Golden Eagle serve in that capacity. "We agreed
shortly thereafter to serve as Coach Bryant's exclusive agent and sought to
develop an organized licensing/merchandising program, and to manage his
endorsement and speaking engagement opportunities." Battle and his company helped turn Bryant into a marketing gold mine. Early in 1981, Bryant
taped several spots for South Central Bell. In the most famous of the spots,
the best line was an ad-lib from Bryant. "Have you called your mama
today?" said Bryant, repeating a question he had been asking his players for
more than thirty years. Bryant had gone through perhaps thirty takes with

---

★ Through a series of buyouts and mergers, today Battle's firm is the Atlanta-based Collegiate Licensing Company. It is the nation's leading collegiate licensing and marketing
representative, assisting collegiate licensors in protecting and controlling the use of their
logos through trademark licensing. When Battle began working on Bryant endorse-
ments, they went to the University of Alabama for permission to use its signature "A"
and found that not only did the University of Alabama not have an organized licensing
program, there was really no collegiate licensing program in existence. Alabama became
the first university Battle and his group signed. Battle credits several University of
Alabama people for their assistance with developing the concept of collegiate licensing,
especially Finus Gaston of the university purchasing department, who represented the
university's interests in the negotiations. Today , the CLC consortium includes more than
two hundred universities, bowl games, conferences, the NCAA, and the Heisman Trophy.
They also represent some thirty-five universities abroad.

the fastidious New York crew. Then, without indication, he said his line and added, "I sure wish I could call mine." At first, it caught the crew by surprise, but they loved it. The commercial was a smash success.

So was a whole line of commemorative Bear products including teddy bears in houndstooth hats, matchbooks, plaques, silver medals, coins, and even crimson-and-white vans with houndstooth seat covers. In banks, restaurants, and stores throughout Alabama, one can still see telephone face plates honoring his 315th victory, as well as Bear Bryant Coke bottles.

As the new decade began, Bryant had more to think about than just his place in college football history. The previous year he had called his quarterback from the 1965 national championship team, Steve Sloan, one of the most openly religious of his former players. "It was a strange call," recalls Sloan, who at the time was head football coach at Ole Miss. "He was at a coaching clinic in Washington and wanted to know if I could fly up to Dulles Airport to meet with him the next day. Coach didn't tell me why, so I didn't ask." What Bryant wanted was what Sloan describes as "a frank discussion on the concept of grace. He was very concerned about being forgiven for all the sins he had committed in his life; he didn't feel he had earned forgiveness from all the people who he had hurt. I tried to explain to him as best I could that true forgiveness is something that can only come from God, and that He alone could decide if you were really worthy of it. That seemed to calm him."

In April 1980, Bryant met Shug Jordan for a drink at a Birmingham lounge owned by Bryant's former player and assistant coach, Pat James. Jordan was suffering from leukemia and was scheduled to check into University Hospital in Birmingham the next day. Patrons saw the old warriors laughing and draping their arms around each other throughout the evening, but afterward, James found his old coach depressed. "Pat," he said, "I don't think Shug's gonna be around long." Bryant was right; Jordan died three months later, on July 17. Bryant attended the funeral at a small chapel in Auburn and sat in the back of the chapel; during the service, Evelyn Jordan, Shug's widow, spotted him and motioned for him to come up and take a seat with the family. David Housel, the sports information director at Auburn during Jordan's last years, recalls, Bryant "seemed to be walking slower, more deliberate, and had a somber, almost ashen expression on his face."

"I think when he saw Coach Jordan's casket, he realized his own mortality. I think it put some of those competitive juices both men had for years in perspective."[15]

James thought that Jordan's death had a sobering effect on Bryant—literally. "It was right about the time that Shug was so sick," James recalls, "that Coach made an effort to cut back on the drinking. Cigarettes, too." In August, diagnosed with fluid in his lungs, Bryant spent a week in the hospital on special medication. Some thought the stay helped his appearance as well as his health, as he lost more than twenty pounds. "It didn't hurt his vanity none," says James. "With all the talk of him closing in on Stagg's record, more and more photographers were following him around, and he didn't mind looking a little better for them."

But Bryant's health problems were more serious than could be resolved in seven days. Mickey Herskowitz asked him what his doctors said the problem was. "They say it's eighty-five percent smoking, poor diet, and the pressures of coaching," Bryant told him, "and fifteen percent booze and other things." After a pause, he added, "I wish it had been eighty-five percent booze and other things." Once, when Herskowitz was visiting in Alabama, Bryant excused himself to go for a long walk, an exercise prescribed by one of his doctors. Mickey offered to go with him. "He said, 'Naw, that's okay, I'll go by myself.' I thought, 'Well, he has a lot of things to think over and wants some time to himself.'" When Bryant returned from his walk, he told Herskowitz, "Sorry, but I try and walk alone. It's about the only time I can smoke without somebody fussin' at me about it."

His friends seemed to think that Bryant was making more of an effort to relax and enjoy life outside of football a little more. He always enjoyed golf and hunting with his friends, though, as his business partner Jimmy Hinton told Mickey Herskowitz, "half the time he never fires a shot. He mostly just likes to ride a horse and watch the dogs work." He had never been a big television watcher except for baseball, particularly when the Yankees were playing, and college football, though he did have his favorite shows. "*Sanford and Son* was his favorite," grandson Marc Tyson recalls. "He loved Redd Foxx. I don't think I ever saw him laugh harder than when he was watching Redd Foxx." Bryant was not overly fond of watching pro football unless one of his boys was playing. Al Browning was with him on an autumn Sunday as they followed the fortunes of Bob Baumhower, who had become an All-Pro nose tackle for Don Shula's Miami Dolphins:

"Hey, that's a good tackle by Bum-hower," Bryant said.

"Baumhower," Mrs. Bryant said.

Bryant remained fixed on the game.

"It looks like Bumhower was offsides on the play."

"Baumhower," Mrs. Bryant said.

Bryant sort of grunted, sipped on a Coca-Cola, and said, "Mary Harmon, I'll call him what I want."

"It's Baumhower, not Bumhower," Mrs. Bryant said.

"Well, Bumhower wasn't offsides," Bryant said. "Their offensive line drew him offsides."

Bryant talked about Baumhower. He said, "He's a good person, a fine player, too, and has helped us recruiting in south Florida for years."

"Who?" Mrs. Bryant said.

"Bumhower."[16]

FROM SEPTEMBER 23, 1978, when it lost to Southern Cal, to November 1, 1980, the Crimson Tide did not lose a football game, a string of twenty-eight consecutive victories. Since losing to Nebraska in the second game of the 1977 season, Alabama had won thirty-eight of thirty-nine games over four seasons. Seven games into the 1980 season, Alabama fans were living in anticipation of unprecedented glory; the Tide had won consecutive national championships in 1978 and 1979—and, as everyone knew, that should have been three straight, including 1977—and now looked well on the way to winning another. After crushing Southern Mississippi 42–7 on October 25, the Tide was 7–0 and beating its opponents by an average of better than four touchdowns a game. In that stretch, the Tide stumbled only once, and it was against the unlikeliest of opponents.

"I first learned there was a Rutgers when I read it on the schedule before the season started," said Alabama kicker Tim Clark. In truth, since helping to invent football in 1869, Rutgers hadn't done a great deal to advance the game. It wasn't clear to a great many people why the match between the nation's number-one college football program and the New Jersey school that had been struggling for football respectability for decades had been made in the first place. For Bryant, apparently, it was a matter of money and public relations with the New York sports media, the last point being best expressed by E. J. Junior, who said "It's exciting to play in New

York . . . the press can see you in real life and a good performance can be convincing when it comes to poll time."

Sometime in the mid-1970s Bryant had been enjoying a weekend with Sonny Werblin at his home in Golden Beach, Florida, when Werblin showed him an architect's drawing for a new stadium at the Meadowlands in New Jersey, which would become Giants Stadium, not far from Rutgers, the state university of New Jersey for which he served as a trustee. "I can't wait to see Alabama play Rutgers in this stadium," he said. "You've got to be crazy," Bryant replied. "Our schedules are made up fifteen years in advance." "Well, I know nobody would be stupid enough to turn down a game in front of 78,000 people at ten dollars a head." Bryant: "Say those numbers again." And so, Alabama's first appearance in the Northeast since the 1960 Liberty Bowl was arranged.

It was almost as if, as his career wound down, Bryant was determined to make a pilgrimage to every mecca of college football. On the Thursday night before the game, he got together with Ray Perkins, who was now the coach of the New York Giants. The next morning, he loaded his team and staff onto three buses and sent everyone on a tour of New York. The Polo Grounds, where his 1933 Crimson Tide had lost to Fordham 2–0, was no longer there. "That was the first time I'd been to New York," he told a local sportswriter, "and it was a big deal for me. We came up on a train, and I got to see a little of the town. I'd never seen a town bigger than Birmingham, and not much of that. When I got to New York, I couldn't stop staring at the large buildings." His players were awed by the George Washington Bridge, the United Nations building, and, finally, the Statue of Liberty. "What they really noticed, though," said C. D. Tatum Jr., the business manager for Alabama athletics, was "winos with their bottles and the drunks lying in the gutter. They'd seen all those things in pictures and the movies, but they thought that was just play acting."[17]

On Friday night, Bryant met with Joe Namath and Sonny Werblin; George Steinbrenner had sent a limousine to bring him to the Yankees-Royals playoff game at Yankee Stadium, but at the last minute Bryant declined. He was a little worried about Rutgers. As it turned out, he had reason to be. Rutgers had won all four of its games before facing Alabama and would win seven of the other ten games on its schedule; on paper, at least, the Scarlet Knights had one of the best rushing defenses in the nation—though, as Alabama sportswriters were quick to point out, their opponents up to that point had been Temple, Cincinnati, Princeton, and Cornell. As it turned out, they had a very good rushing defense on the field. Rutgers scored first on a forty-four-yard field goal—it was the first time all season that Alabama had been behind in a game. Late in the first quarter, the Tide drove to the Rutgers six, but could not drive the ball in and settled for a twenty-three-yard field goal by Peter Kim, a native of South Korea who had kicked for the University of Hawaii and who paid his own way to come to Alabama and play for Bryant. Midway through the third quarter the Tide found itself clinging to a 10–6 lead, and Bryant decided to take matters into his own hands. He sent in successive pass plays to quarterback Don Jacobs, who completed them both to end James Mallard for seventy-two yards and a touchdown that made the score 17–6. But later Jacobs fumbled on the Alabama twenty-four, and two plays later, to nearly everyone's surprise, Rutgers scored to make it 17–12.

It very nearly got worse. Midway through the final period, Alabama's usually reliable punt coverage broke down, and the Rutgers return man sprinted forty yards down to Alabama's thirty-three—some thought that only a shoestring tackle by defensive back Mike Clements prevented a game-winning touchdown for Rutgers. On third down, though, the Tide defense recorded its sixth sack of the game, and Alabama escaped.

Alabama had been caught looking ahead to Tennessee. The following week, on national television, Alabama won back any prestige it might have lost in the Rutgers game by shutting out the Volunteers 27–0. But there were chinks in the Tide's armor, and as the weeks went on, they began to show. Alabama had lost to graduation nine of eleven starters on offense from the 1979 national championship team. Major Ogilvie, the team's best runner, was hobbled by injuries and carried just six times against Rutgers. The week before, in a 45–0 victory over Kentucky, he had carried just once. Don Jacobs was a scrappy prototype of the early wishbone quarterback, but he could not pass with the authority of a Richard Todd or Jeff Rutledge, or even Steadman Shealy. Against Kentucky, Bryant had shuttled five quarterbacks and sixteen running backs in and out of the lineup, numbers that helped to conceal the team's genuine lack of offensive stars, and special team lapses like not covering the punt return by Rutgers were a definite indication that Alabama didn't have the same depth of talent it had had the previous year. In the eighth week of the season, the chickens came home to roost: Mississippi State beat Alabama 6–3 at Jackson, Mississippi, without scoring a touchdown. Worse than that, it stopped Alabama at the one-yard line late in the game to do it.

What had happened? There were whispers that rival coaches were telling blue-chip recruits that while they might get a chance to play for Bear, he probably wouldn't be there for all four of their years at Alabama. Who knew how many more years Bryant would coach? There were other stories, too, suggesting that Bryant's attention to detail was slipping. Not in print, of course, not just yet.

Alabama's loss to Mississippi State took some of the wind out of what was billed as the biggest regular-season matchup of 1980. In 1976 Bryant had taken the Tide up to South Bend to play Notre Dame; now, for the first time ever, the Fighting Irish came to Alabama. Bryant's teams had lost three heartbreakers to the Irish by one, two, and then three points; this would more than likely be his last crack at them. Like Alabama, Notre Dame was unbeaten through the first seven weeks, and the November 15 game at Legion Field looked as if it might have national title implications. Then, the week before playing Alabama, the Irish, having offensive problems of their own, stumbled to a 3–3 tie against a second-level Georgia Tech squad in Atlanta. Nonetheless, the Notre Dame–Alabama game proved to be the highest-rated regular-season televised contest.

Excitement in Alabama was heightened when a local rumor suggested that the latest single by the pop singer Blondie, "The Tide Is High," had some connection with Alabama (which, if true, would have been the second reference to the Crimson Tide in a rock song in three years, including Steeley Dan's "Deacon Blue"). Actually, "The Tide Is High" was Blondie's remake of an old reggae song, but it was fun for Alabama fans to pretend otherwise. Just before the record's official release, an enterprising deejay secured an advance copy, thought it made a promising anthem, and played it over and over for nearly three hours. The stunt earned him a phone call from Blondie's lead singer, Deborah Harry. Harry, whose knowledge of football was probably equal to Bryant's of new-wave rock, wished the Crimson Tide "good luck" and said she "really wished we could make it to the game."

Alabama, though, didn't need an anthem, it needed a quarterback. Once again, the Tide defense was superb, stuffing Notre Dame for just 192 total yards on offense (56 fewer than Alabama gained). But in the second quarter, Alabama fumbled the ball at its three-yard line, Notre Dame got a cheap touchdown, and that was the game's only score. It was the first time

Alabama had been shutout since the Georgia game in 1976, a span of four years and fifty-three games. It was only the second time it had been shutout in 121 games, going back to 1970 against LSU. There was a bright side, though it was difficult for Alabama fans to see it at the time. In the second half, Bryant put in a dazzling freshman quarterback named Walter Lewis, who came close to pulling the game out for Alabama. He would become the Tide's first black starting passer, and the last great quarterback of Bryant's career.

The season ended positively when Alabama beat Auburn 34–18. With a 9–2 record, the Tide did not receive its usual Sugar Bowl bid, which went to unbeaten Georgia and its sensational running back, Herschel Walker. But a Cotton Bowl bid did nicely. On New Year's Day, Alabama played its best game of the year. The Baylor Bears had won ten of eleven games and were ranked fourth in the nation in total offense, but the Tide held them without a touchdown and won easily, 30–2. It would be Bryant's last major bowl game victory.

Things weren't merely changing in Alabama, they had already changed. Pat Dye, who had coached at Wyoming for the 1980 season, phoned his old coach to tell him he had been offered the head job at Auburn. Bryant paused when he heard the news, then advised him against taking it. "Pat, you know you ain't gonna beat me." Dye told his mentor politely that he appreciated his concern, but that "Coach, you know you're not going to be at Alabama forever."

Bryant had always had a fondness for Dye, having witnessed his spirit and tenacity firsthand when Dye played against the Tide for three years while attending Georgia. Dye had been eager to learn from Bryant and approached him for a job after Gene Stallings left Alabama; Bryant told him, "If I ever get around to considering a young, eager, inexperienced coach, I'll consider you." In June 1965, Bryant kept his promise and offered Dye a job at Alabama. He stayed until 1974, when he left for East Carolina, which he coached for six seasons, and then spent one season at Wyoming. What Dye wanted at first was the head coaching job at his alma mater, Georgia, but jobs like the one at Auburn didn't come around very often. Bryant told Dye that he had thought of him as a possible successor at Alabama, but Dye didn't know when that would be or what his chances would be among so many promising candidates. What made it tough to accept the Auburn job was that he and Bryant had grown closer over the years. "I loved him and respected him, but we weren't that close. He kept his distance from his assistant coaches. It was only after I left that we became friends." For nearly three decades, Bryant had been coaching against his own former assistants, but never had one so close to home.

ON A trip to New York, Bryant took a night off for one of his favorite yearly traditions: a night out on the town with Joe Namath. Broadway Joe had been appearing in a production of *Damn Yankees* at Jones Beach in Long Island. Afterward, Joe took the cast and his coach to Mama Leone's for dinner. Bryant took a good-natured jibe at Namath, who was seated across the table, when an actress in the show who couldn't penetrate Bryant's drawl leaned over to ask Namath what he had said. Bryant overheard and called, "Hey, Joe, you tell her I teach diction at Alabama."

WITH BRYANT just nine victories short of Stagg's record, the 1981 season seemed like one long distraction from start to finish. In the spring, the state legislature, without alerting Bryant, approved a special bill allowing him to coach past the age of seventy, the mandatory retirement age for state employees. It was signed into law by the former Auburn halfback, and now governor, Fob James. The bill was insurance that in case he didn't break the record in 1981 and 1982, Bryant would be around long enough to do it. The legislators who initiated the bill intended it as an honor, but Bryant was embarrassed and irritated, first, because it implied that he needed extra help to break the record, and second, because it gave him a special privilege not accorded to other University of Alabama staff. Bryant issued a press release stating in no uncertain terms that he did not know the bill was being proposed and had nothing to do with it. "I would like to ask that the entire matter be dropped." It was too late; the law had been amended, and Bear Bryant could now coach to age seventy, if he wanted to.

According to his friends, Bryant wavered between pride at breaking the record and annoyance that he was allowing it to take up so much of his time and attention. Now that he was getting close to it, Bryant, who always respected his elders and felt humbled by the great tradition of college football, wasn't entirely certain that he wanted to surpass Stagg. "Coach Stagg was the Babe Ruth of college football," he said in an interview. "To me, he is on a pedestal. You can't compare what he did years ago with football of today. In those days he didn't have a large staff. I've heard his wife scouted games for him, and both of them mended uniforms. It was a completely different game then."[18]

Bryant was right. The game Stagg had coached was far different from his—though, incredibly, their coaching careers overlapped by two years, 1945 and 1946. Stagg, who was born ten months before the Battle of Gettysburg in West Orange, New Jersey, began coaching at Springfield College, Massachusetts, in 1890; he coached at the University of Chicago for forty-one years from 1892 to 1932 (Bryant's freshman year at Alabama); retired by Chicago because he was seventy, he then went to College of the Pacific and was retired by them when he was eighty-four. He went to Susquehanna University to coach with his son, Amos Alonzo Stagg Jr., until he was ninety, and then coached punters at Stockton Junior College until he was ninety-eight. He cashed in his own life insurance policy, which he had taken out when he was thirty, and died at age 102 in 1965, the year Paul Bryant, who would first break his record, was winning his third national championship at Alabama.

"Charley," Bryant told Thornton just before the start of the 1981 season, after a long interview with the New York Times, "I swear to God, there are times I'm beginning to wish you hadn't brung this thing up. I think it's really gonna hurt our football team." Again, he was right. After an easy opening win against LSU, the Tide suffered one of the most eye-opening defeats of Bryant's career in Birmingham when Bill Curry's Georgia Tech team upset Alabama 24–21—not only did Tech win, it overcame a 21–14 Alabama advantage in the final quarter, scoring the last ten points. To Alabama fans, this was almost unthinkable. For years, it had been a statement of faith for them to say "the fourth quarter belongs to us."* It was to be the only game Tech would win that season. Bryant was flabbergasted, but he knew where the fault lay: his full concentration had not been with his team. For the first time since the dark days of 1970, discipline had become an issue. Before the opening game with LSU, linebacker Thomas Boyd had been demoted from the starting lineup for disciplinary reasons; Boyd had still not

---

* In 1974 Amerigo Marino, conductor of the Birmingham Symphony Orchestra, got a huge laugh from his audience when he stopped a performance and reminded everyone, "Remember, the fourth coda belongs to us."

gotten the message the following week, missing curfew, and after the shocking loss to Georgia Tech, Bryant suspended him. Things got worse. At Kentucky, where Alabama struggled to a 19–10 win over a weak Wildcats team,
running backs Charley Williams and Linnie Patrick were ordered to report
for treatment at the training room but failed to show. When they got back to
Tuscaloosa, they found that Bryant had thrown them out of the athletic
dorm. Williams quit the team but then thought better of it and came back
to ask for forgiveness; in his time-honored fashion, Bryant took him back.
Later, Linnie Patrick would be allowed to return to the dorm, but Bryant's
problems with him were never quite resolved.

Hailing from the coal-mining town of Jasper, Alabama, Linnie Patrick
was bit smaller and a little faster than Herschel Walker, but many coaches in
the Southeast thought he compared favorably to the Georgia star, who had
set national high school records. Bryant had always done his best work, as
he was fond of saying, "with boys who come from good mamas and papas."
In the 1970s, this proved to be as true with his black recruits as it had been
with his white ones; Bryant knew good parents were his allies, not his
antagonists, in maintaining discipline. But Patrick was one of the first major
black talents at Alabama. He was brought up by his mother, who thought
that Linnie needed a father figure and that three or four years with Bear
Bryant would help get him into line.

But by 1981 Bryant was too old to be a new father and, with rosters that
swelled to upward of 120 players, had little time to devote to reforming
prodigal sons. Patrick ruffled feathers almost from the outset. In the summer of 1980, at the Alabama High School All-Star game, Patrick, who had
committed to Alabama, told a reporter, "I'll win three straight Heisman
Trophies." He even hinted that he would be in the running for it as a freshman. Bryant liked his players brash; he did not like them selfish. If Patrick
did not know that he would not get the ball often enough to win a Heisman while playing for Bear Bryant, he should have.

At a preseason practice Bryant suddenly decided to test Patrick. "He had
gotten fed up with Linnie," recalls one of Patrick's teammates. "I heard him
call to Coach [Mal] Moore, 'Run him again. I wanna see how he responds.'
The play was a sweep to the right where the quarterback pitched the ball
to Linnie, and he followed his blockers. It was brutal. The defense knew he
was coming, and they hit him pretty hard. They kept calling the play over
and over, I think we ran it six times. After the last time, Linnie was crying."

Patrick walked off the field. This was not the reaction Bryant was hoping for. Moving faster than he had in years, Bryant came down from the tower as practice came to a halt. Walking up to Patrick, Bryant grabbed his face-mask and chewed him out in front of the team. Patrick did not rebel but submitted to authority and did his extra running without complaint, but he would never entirely give himself over to the Bear. Bryant would always classify him with Ken Hall back at Texas A&M as a great player he could never quite reach.

The difference between Hall and Patrick, though, was that Patrick was black, and up to now Bryant had never had any significant problems with a black player. It was inevitable that someone would write the story, and in October the *Atlanta Constitution* finally did. Unidentified team members were quoted as saying that Bryant's 1981 Crimson Tide had both "morale" and "racial" problems, all at least partially the result of Bryant's disciplinary action against Patrick, Williams, and Boyd. Herschel Nissenson of the Associated Press was in Tuscaloosa working on another story but felt he needed to at least find out if there was anything more to the *Constitution*'s story. "Sit down, boy," Bryant snapped at Nissenson, who was forty-seven at the time. "I'm through tip-toeing around, and I'm through pussy footing around," Bryant growled at him. "I'm going back to being Paul Bryant, and anybody who doesn't like the way Paul Bryant does things can get out of here." Nissenson, who knew Bryant well, remembers thinking, "What in hell is all this about? Who does he think this act is fooling?" As it turned out, Bryant knew he wasn't fooling anyone. After going on for a few minutes, Bryant stopped and smiled sheepishly at Nissenson and said, "Aw, hell, I don't really know what I'm trying to say."

"He gave me a story," says Nissenson, who is now retired and lives on Long Island, "but I got the feeling that he wasn't entirely sure of how he was going to deal with these new problems. There had never been charges of racial problems on his football team, and he was very upset by them. He knew he couldn't bluff or bluster his way through them. I also got the impression that he felt some of it was his fault because he hadn't had the proper time to address some of his players' problems."

Boyd made no bones about his punishment being deserved, and Williams asked for and got a second chance, but Patrick sulked and continued to be a problem. In November, Bryant defused another potential problem when another black player, Kenny Simon, was arrested for the illegal possession and firing of a shotgun. Bryant's own investigation indicated that Simon was innocent, and he jumped at the chance to make a public statement in favor of his player. "I am proud," he told the *Birmingham News*, "to stick by him like any father would stick by his son."[19] The charges against Simon were vague and were eventually dropped. Whatever Bryant's investigation revealed, the coach had made a shrewd public relations move with his black players by coming out so openly on Simon's side.

After the listless win over Kentucky, Alabama won two more games, picking up a head of steam. That left five wins to break Stagg's record, but it was abundantly clear Alabama was not headed for a national championship. In the sixth week of the season, the Tide collided with an excellent Southern Mississippi team at Birmingham and, Bryant felt, was lucky to come out with a 13–13 tie. It was no disgrace, as the Golden Eagles would win nine of their other eleven games that season, but Alabama fans had come to regard a victory over Southern Miss as a preseason assumption. It was unthinkable for Alabama not to beat Southern Miss *because* confusion on the defensive team resulted in an inexplicable Alabama timeout that gave the Southern Miss kicker a relaxed shot at the game-tying field goal. A 38–19 win over a fine Tennessee team the next week eased much of the soreness from the Southern Miss game; then, it was Rutgers's turn to come to Alabama and experience the realities of big-time college football. This season, the Tide was not looking ahead to a match with Tennessee, and it beat Rutgers soundly, 31–7. The Tide's old wishbone instructor, Emery Bellard, brought Mississippi State to Tuscaloosa the next week. Bellard had one of the best Bulldog teams in years; it would finish with eight wins against its other ten opponents. The Tide struggled but prevailed, 13–10, only after a familiar Alabama scenario was played again. Peter Kim, the regular kicker, had injured his leg making a tackle, and Bryant had to call on a freshman, Terry Sanders, who had never kicked a field goal in an Alabama uniform. Sanders's twenty-eight-yard field goal was the winning score for Alabama. Two wins to go.

The next game figured to be the toughest of the year. On November 14, Bryant took what looked like an outmanned Crimson Tide to State College, Pennsylvania, to face Joe Paterno's powerful Nittany Lions, which had lost only one game, a 17–14 thriller to a fine Miami team coached by Howard Schnellenberger. With the New York media descending on the Pennsylvania college town, Bryant was determined to put on a good show.

It would be the Tide's most impressive performance of the season, as Walter Lewis picked the Penn State pass defense apart, and the Tide defense made yet another great goal line stand. Two, actually, as a fourth-down penalty gave Penn State first down at the one-yard line, and the Tide defense had to do it all over again. By the time the offense raced back on the field, Alabama's defense had stopped Penn State on six plays that began inside the one. Alabama won handily 31–16.★

Immediately after the game, Penn State fans accorded Bryant an honor that Alabama fans who were present had never seen the likes of. Hundreds of them lined up on both sides of the grandstands and applauded Bryant as he walked off the field and into the tunnel. Bryant was so moved that in the first couple of minutes after leaving the field he could not speak.

Bryant had now tied Amos Alonzo Stagg with win number 314. Appropriately enough, the chance to break the record would come the final day of the season against one of his favorite former assistants and Alabama's bitterest rival. He would not have had it any other way.

BRYANT RETURNED home to find Birmingham and Tuscaloosa besieged by journalists. Every morning a stack of new newspaper and magazine articles about him was left on his desk. Most of them got little more than a passing glance, but one caught his attention and aroused his anger. *Sports Illustrated*'s Frank Deford had been down during the summer to interview Bryant. The result, a cover story which appeared at the end of November, featured such reportorial gems as, "Like a lot of old men, [Bryant] has weak kidneys." (On a trip to Birmingham, Bryant reportedly asked his driver, "Billy, have I passed all my pissin' places?")

According to Charley Thornton, Bryant simmered at a passage that read,

It is certainly illuminative of his nature that the Bear took no lead whatsoever in the matter of integration. His defenders will claim that Wallace

---

★ In his book Joe Paterno said he should have disavowed the advice of his assistant coaches in the 1979 Sugar Bowl and called for passing the ball on fourth down when they were on the Alabama one. This time, Penn State did pass on two of the six plays but couldn't complete either one. Bryant was so proud of his defensive team he grabbed each man and shook his hand as he came off the field.

kept his hands tied, that the Bear wasn't even allowed to schedule teams with black players, much less dress any of them in crimson, and there may be a measure of truth in that. But given the Bear's surpassing popularity, he had it within his power to assume a burden of leadership. Yet he held back on race and let other—and less entrenched—Southern coaches stick their necks out first. Only after Southern Cal and Sam (Bam) Cunningham ran all over the skinny little white boys in a 1970 game, only when it was evident that the Tide couldn't win any longer lily-white, only then did the Bear learn his civics.[20]

Thornton said that Bryant would not talk about the article. Thornton thought what angered Bryant was that Deford had not discussed the issue of integration with him. "If he had," Thornton felt, "he would have gotten a few facts right. Coach Bryant did schedule games with integrated teams—the Liberty Bowl against Penn State in 1959, for instance, and the bowl games against Nebraska—precisely to help focus on the need for integration. Deford didn't seem to know or care that Bryant had arranged the 1970 Southern Cal game, and he seemed completely unaware that Wilbur Jackson had already accepted a scholarship and was, in fact, in the stands that day. He also forgot to mention how quickly and thoroughly Coach Bryant integrated our coaching staff."

What angered Bryant the most, though, was the following: "Understand, if the university is a football factory, that isn't the Bear's fault. He isn't to blame that the woebegone library languishes, that professors in the English department didn't have telephones until seven months ago." (That the library was woebegone and the English department lacked phones was indignantly denied by faculty and administration.) The implication, of course, was that the emphasis on football was responsible for these ills, though the Alabama football program had been making money for the university since Mike Denny's tenure in the 1920s. Bryant, a notorious bean counter with the athletic budget, had always been enormously proud of the financial contributions his teams had made to the university. According to Thornton, Bryant never finished reading it. "When he got to the part about there being no telephones in the English department, he crumbled it up and threw it across the room."

FROM THE beginning of November until the Friday before the Auburn game on November 28, the athletic department was besieged. "We just weren't equipped to handle the requests for press credentials and tickets," said Charley Thornton, who had done much to set the media ball rolling. "The hardest part was trying to accommodate all of Coach's family and friends, folks from back home in Arkansas, friends he'd made over the years from New York, Pennsylvania, Kentucky, Texas, California, even friends from his one year at Maryland."

Bryant paid special attention to his old players. He invited Joe Drach and Harry Bonk, two of his favorite players from his first Maryland team, for the big game. "We were in a motel in Birmingham," recalls Drach, "and the phone rang at five in the morning—no, it was about ten till five. It was Coach. He had just driven over from Tuscaloosa to Birmingham, and he wanted us to meet him for breakfast in half an hour.

"I said, 'Coach don't you ever sleep?' He said, 'Hell, Joe, we got to get started. I got a football game to play this weekend.'"

The game at Birmingham's Legion Field was a sellout before the season started; Alabama-Auburn games always were, but this time the demand for tickets bordered on the insane. Outside the gates, hawkers were already selling "I Was There for Bear's 315th" T-shirts. Auburn fans, as if in anticipation, were wearing "I Was There for Bear's First Try at 315" shirts.

Auburn was a much more formidable opponent than it appeared on paper. The Tigers had been just 5–5 that season, their first under Pat Dye. But after losing three of their first four games, they got the hang of the newly installed wishbone formation and won four of their last six. Dye had no intention of rolling over for his old boss. This was the opening shot in the war for football supremacy in the state, and Dye was not there to play a supporting role to the Bryant legend.

His team was aggressive from the opening series. Having seen the Alabama wishbone up close for several seasons, Dye knew how to coach against it. After Auburn's defense stopped the Tide on its first series, the Tiger's Chuck Clanton ran a punt back fifty-five yards to the Alabama ten-yard line. On the Auburn sideline, the players were ecstatic. They let out a collective groan three plays later when their kicker missed what appeared to be an easy field goal. "It was one of those games," said Alabama quarterback Walter Lewis, "where you're sky high coming out of the tunnel, feel yourself drained moments later, then you get all pumped up again. It didn't feel like half the crowd was for Alabama and half for Auburn; each time we did something good, it sounded like everyone in the stadium was yelling for Alabama, and every time they did something good, it sounded like everyone was yelling for Auburn. It was back and forth, back and forth."

On its next possession Auburn came right back and drove to the Alabama eight, looking as though its offense could not be stopped. Alabama came right back on the next play when defensive back Tommy Wilcox intercepted a pass at the one-yard line. The Tigers, who could have been up 10–0 at that point, still had not scored. On its first two possessions, the Alabama offense had played tentatively, as if surprised by the Tigers' fervor; the Tide finally came alive when quarterback Alan Gray faked a pitch and ran sixty-three yards down to the Auburn one, then took it over the goal line himself on the next play, for a 7–0 lead. But Alabama could get nothing more going offensively, and with less than four minutes to go in the first half, Auburn fullback George Peoples headed into a gaping hole in the left side of his line and went sixty-three yards for a touchdown, tying the game at 7–7 at the half.

In the locker room, Bryant was calm and matter of fact. He knew his boys had class and told them he was sure it would show before the day was out. All they had to do, he said, was to play like they were capable of playing and make a few simple adjustments. "He was so cool, you'd have never thought," says Walter Lewis, "that this was one of the biggest games of his life."

In the third quarter, Alabama was at its own forty-five-yard line when Bryant, almost as if teasing Pat Dye, called for a play out of the past. Ken Coley, Alabama's third quarterback, dropped back to throw; Jessie Bendross, Alabama's fastest receiver, had lined up in the tight end's spot, and now stepped back and ran parallel to the line of scrimmage in the Alabama backfield. Coley flipped him an underhanded "whoopee" pass—that was Bryant's favorite term, though it was often identified as a "shovel" or "Utah" pass, for some obscure historical reason. Bendross cut back and raced right up the middle through the left tackle's spot, going fifty-five yards for a touchdown. Alabama was up 14–7.

Then, just as it seemed as if Alabama had taken control, Joey Jones, normally a sure-handed punt returner, fumbled the ball, and Auburn recovered it at the Alabama two. On the second play, future San Diego Chargers star Lionel James, Auburn's 170-pound dynamo, scored to tie the game again.

Almost unbelievably, a few minutes later Joey Jones fumbled again and Auburn recovered at the Tide thirty-three-yard line. Tiger fans, whose chants of "War Eagle!" were rolling over the stadium in waves, were in a state of near-delirium. But at the two-yard line, the Tide defense once again rose up and stopped the Tigers. Al Del Greco (who would go on to a fourteen-year NFL career) kicked the field goal to put Auburn ahead, 17–14. On the sidelines, Pat Dye, pumping his fist in the air, led the cheers for his team as it came off the field of play. On the Alabama sideline, Bryant remained calm, his substitution charts still rolled up in his hand. It was impossible to tell from his demeanor whether his team was winning or losing.

Finding themselves in the unexpected position of trailing in the fourth quarter, the Tide players finally exhibited the class that Bryant knew was there. Walter Lewis, back in the game as quarterback, drove Alabama to the Auburn thirty-eight, then, faking a handoff and fading back to throw, spotted single coverage on split end Jessie Bendross, who beat his man and broke free to gather in a thirty-eight-yard pass, catching the ball right on the goal line and scoring a touchdown. Alabama was up, 21–17, with eight minutes left to play, but the game seemed far from over. It was almost as if everyone was waiting to see how Auburn would bounce back. Following an Auburn punt, Lewis took the team near midfield, where Linnie Patrick, emerging from Bryant's doghouse in spectacular fashion, took a pitch from Lewis on a sweep and headed to his right. Two Auburn tacklers converged on Patrick almost parallel to the line of scrimmage; it looked as if the play would yield no gain. Patrick, legs churning, spun around and cut back to the inside, taking a glancing hit from a third Auburn tackler, then careening off a fourth before breaking upfield. Two more Auburn men had clean shots at him. Patrick shook one off and pulled his ankle out of the grasp of another. Finally, at the seventeen-yard line, two more Auburn players, the seventh and eighth defenders to hit him on the run, combined to knock him off balance. The play went for thirty-two yards and all but put Bear Bryant's 315th victory away. Bryant would later compare it to the run John David Crow had made for him back at Texas A&M thirty-four years earlier, the one Bryant had previously called "the greatest single run I've ever seen."

More than twenty years later, Walter Lewis watched a replay of the game on video. "Watching Linnie make that run," he says, "I realized it was the same play that Coach Bryant made him run over and over that day in practice when he walked off the field."

Two plays later, Patrick took the same pitch on the same play, headed to his right, cut back upfield, and knocked down only three Auburn tacklers to score the touchdown and make the game 28–17, which stood as the final score.

In anticipation of the national press blitz, a specially designed "media trailer" had been placed behind the south end zone. Bryant arrived, weaving his way through the swarms of former players and associates and friends, just as Pat Dye was ending his press conference. The coaches embraced. Bryant, with his arm around his former assistant, told him, "I want you to know, Pat, that Jimmy Carter called me on the telephone in the dressing room." What about President Reagan, Dye asked. "I'm talking about Governor Carter," Bryant laughed. "You're from Georgia, I figured you'd appreciate that more." "I'm not a politician, Coach," said Dye. "But," he asked, pretending to needle his mentor, "what about President Reagan? Didn't he call you?" "Why, he sure did call me. I don't guess he's ever called you, has he?"

To hear Bryant's patter on *The Bear Bryant Show*, one would have never thought that the greatest record in college football history had been broken. At times it was more like a small-town high school football broadcast interlaced with community news.

"That was plain old vanilla" [an off-tackle run] . . . Mr. Sloan Bashinsky's up here, come to visit . . . We fumbled and now they're on our ten. Merciful heavens! . . . I'm real sorry Carney Laswell and Frank Moseley weren't here yesterday. I want to say hello to my good friends who both have cancer and are recovering. And Ermil Allen had a heart attack in Dallas . . ."

Misidentifying one of the Alabama passers, Bryant explains, "I called that quarterback Babe [Parilli]. Sometimes I get mixed up and call the quarterback Parilli."

When Alabama falls behind, "Now things don't look so good . . . There's lot of people here. I had breakfast this morning with Joe Drach and Harry Bonk, who I had the privilege of being with at Mary [pronounced "Mayree"]–land [hard accent on the "land"]."

"Tommy Wilcox made that tackle, from Hanrahan, Louisiana. Great play by Mike Pitts. He can get right in your mustache and have it off before you know it."

In the final period, with Auburn leading 17–14, "Now we're behind, and that's not a very good feeling in the fourth quarter. This is when our players, I think, begin to show their class . . . Robbie Jones made the tackle. I think Robbie made a lot of tackles yesterday. Woodrow did, too—not Woodrow, I mean Eddie, Woodrow's younger brother."

After Linnie Patrick's great run, "That was maybe as fine a run as I've ever seen." Then, in a moment of rare candor, "What I wouldn't give if I could reach that young man. He would be somethin'. He would be some-thin'." When Patrick scored the touchdown, "Another great run by Patrick. If he'd ever study and do everything he's told to do, he'd be a great one."

On Auburn's last series, following an incomplete pass, "Jeremiah Castille really covered his man on that one. Benny Perrin . . . makes a nice intercep-tion there, put the last nail into the coffin. Benny is from Decatur, Alabama. Benny's mother and father came by the other day. And now Alan [Gray, the quarterback] going to run the clock out."

After game films, there were taped congratulations from celebrities. From Alabama president Joab Thomas, Governor James, Bob Hope—"I hope I see you soon on the golf course, Bear, I need the money"—and President Reagan, who offered, "Congratulations from a man who has fond memories of his own experiences on the gridiron." Whether Reagan was referring to memories of his experiences as a broadcaster during Alabama's Rose Bowl trip or his movie role as George Gipp in *Knute Rockne All American* was not clear.[21]

THE DEMAND for tickets to the 1981 Auburn game was the greatest of Bryant's career. "In the weeks leading up to the game," recalls Bryant's sec-retary, Linda Knowles, "I'd not sooner answer one call requesting tickets than it'd ring again with another request. I never saw anything like it, not even the Sugar Bowl games in 1979 and 1980 for the national champi-onships. One day a couple of weeks before the game, Coach came into the office and said, 'Lynda, what in the world happened to all those tickets I had to give away? There ain't none of them around, and there's no way I could have given all of them away.' He couldn't find them, and I was days on the phone apologizing to people telling them we were all out.

"About two months later, toward the end of January, I was taking dicta-tion from him in his office, and he remembered something he wanted to look at in his top right-hand drawer. He started to pull on it, but it was stuck. It wouldn't open. He gave it a yank, and a whole mess of papers just flew out. And there was a thick stack of those tickets, maybe two inches of them, wrapped in a rubber band. Coach just stared at the tickets for a moment and didn't say anything. Then he just closed the drawer, and we got back to work."

Knowles had no way of knowing that thirty years earlier, Bryant had done exactly the same thing with a stack of tickets to the first big game of his coaching career, the 1951 Sugar Bowl against Bud Wilkinson's Oklahoma Sooners.*

DESPITE THE high drama of Bryant's pursuit of Stagg's record, Alabama was not given its usual nod for the Sugar Bowl. Bryant was disappointed, but knew that co-SEC champion Georgia, with the sensational Herschel Walker, was more deserving. (The Bulldogs had won not only the SEC but the national championship the year before.) Alabama, with just one defeat, was ranked in the top five in both major polls and thus still in line for a shot at the national title. But there had been a listlessness about the Tide's play for most of the season, and few thought the team had earned a crack at number one.

Alabama accepted a bid to the Cotton Bowl against Texas, which in most years would not have been a bad consolation, but at the end of 1981 it had a kind of anticlimactic feel to it. Bryant admitted as much, perhaps unwisely, when he told a local reporter that his players were "not feeling any great pressure. It's not like when we play Auburn or Tennessee. We had a coaches' meeting this morning and nobody puked." Perhaps not, but there were some upset stomachs in the second half of the Cotton Bowl. After breezing to a 12–0 lead, the gas ran out and the Tide sagged to a 14–12 defeat. It was its first bowl loss since falling to Notre Dame in the Orange Bowl at the end of the 1974 season.

In March, Paul and Mary Harmon went to Washington, D.C., for a gala black-tie event, "America's Tribute to Paul (Bear) Bryant." The event, of

---

* Somehow, some of those unused tickets worked their way into sports memorabilia shops in Birmingham and Tuscaloosa. My mother paid thirty-five dollars for one for my birthday a few years ago. It's framed and hanging on my office wall as I write this.

course, was emceed by Bob Hope. More than two hundred of Bryant's former players and rival coaches were there. Babe Parilli, his great quarterback from Kentucky, recalled that his coach "smiled and joked and laughed, and I couldn't help thinking all the while about how old he looked, and I wondered if he still had it in him to go through the recruiting grind."

It was a good question. In point of fact, Bryant was no longer recruiting at all. His staff did that, and he confined himself largely to greeting prospects when they came on campus. Bryant's age and increasingly haggard appearance were used against him in the bitterly competitive SEC recruiting wars. Two days before national signing day, when high school players had to commit to a college, the *Birmingham Post-Herald* ran a photo, a large close-up of Bryant's face, which, according to former *Post-Herald* columnist Paul Finebaum, looked like "crevices in the moon's surface." Finebaum, who had come to Birmingham from the *Shreveport Times*, was something new in Alabama sports; brash and iconoclastic, he presented his opinions without sentiment or fear of public relations fallout. He was among the first to sense the coming story, which was that Bryant was losing his monopoly on the best football players in the state, and that when it happened, the Alabama program would change quickly and drastically. Finebaum insists that Pat Dye revealed having purchased "fifty copies of that *Post-Herald* and mailing them to the top recruits all over the state." Dye denies it: "I didn't have to do that. There wasn't a top high school player in the state who couldn't look at a picture of Coach Bryant and know that he had health problems." What was undeniable was that a boy considering playing at Alabama knew he would not be playing all four years for Bear Bryant.

The point was driven home with painful clarity when Vincent "Bo" Jackson of McAdory High School—some said the best football prospect Alabama had seen in years, and some even said the equal or superior of Herschel Walker over at Georgia—signed with Pat Dye and Auburn. "My mother," Bo told Paul Finebaum, "doesn't feel right about me going to Alabama. They've had so much trouble this past season, she wouldn't rest with me down there." Bryant, whose strategy had always been to court a player's mama, must have winced when he read this. An uncharacteristic note of defeatism began to creep into his interviews. "Coaching is a young man's game," he told a Mississippi reporter just before the start of the season. "You never see old men winning championships. We are surrounded. All these people are recruiting better than we are."[22]

Bryant was not a vain man, but he had been disturbed by the *Post-Herald*'s picture and was determined to present a better, fitter-looking image to the public. After spring practice, he told friends that he would be taking a vacation to North Africa to revisit the places he had been stationed while with the navy during World War II. In truth, Bryant had calmed Mary Harmon's misgivings and agreed to some minor plastic surgery. It's doubtful that he would have done so if the surgeon had been anyone but E. Gaylon McCollough, who had been the center on his 1964 national championship team. McCollough took off some of what Bryant referred to as "turkey wattle" around his neck. When he returned to the office, everyone said he looked a few years younger, though no one said it to Bryant himself because plastic surgery just wasn't the kind of thing one talked about.*

"THE SECOND thing I look at in the paper every morning is the stock-market tables," Bryant once told an interviewer, "the first thing is Ann Landers, usually on page six." For years Bryant had clipped her columns and read them to his freshman teams. The two began corresponding; in August 1982, Bryant phoned Landers. Landers was thrilled at being sought out by "The Bear." Bryant was calling to request a copy of a column she had written several years before that he had misplaced. The column, "Dead at 17," was a fictitious account of a teenage boy who sees himself killed when he drives recklessly. The story made a deep impression on Bryant.

Landers knew little about football, but she was impressed with Bear Bryant.

"He must be a very sensitive, warm person to care so much about the kids who pass through his life," she told the *New York Times*'s Ira Berkow.

"I have a feeling he cares more about them than he does his record of being the coach with all those wins."

* In 1986 McCullough published a book, *Shoulders of Giants*, subtitled *A Facial Surgeon's Prescriptions for Life's Dilemmas*. I have not read the book, but the press material passed on to me indicates that one of its major themes is an application of Bryant's philosophy of the "price of victory" applied to "the chances, choices, and challenges that have to be faced every day." The brochure's centerpiece is a photo of Bryant alongside his credo: "If you believe in yourself and have dedication and pride—and never quit—you'll be a winner. The price of victory is high—but so are the rewards."

What was Ann Landers's advice to Coach Bryant? "I'd say, hang in there, Bear. They need you. Don't let a bum season discourage you, you've still got plenty to give."[23]

Privately, Bryant was beginning to wonder how much he did have left to give. In a trip back home to Fordyce, he confided to Jimmy "Red" Parker, football coach for his old Fordyce Redbugs, that he was thinking of retiring. "He told me 'I just feel like takin' Mary Harmon and goin' on a long cruise, give us both some time away from football. She'd sure appreciate that.'" But Bryant knew that as long as he was coaching for Alabama, there could be no such thing as a life away from football, and that left only one alternative. "Privately he had asked a lot of people in the family if they thought he should retire," says Marc Tyson. "Nobody wanted to say yes, nobody wanted to admit the time might have come. He said to me, 'But Marc, you don't know how tired I am.'"

In an interview with Al Browning that appeared in the *Huntsville Times* just prior to the 1982 football season, Bryant sounded almost elegiac.

> I've had a full life in one respect, but I've had a one-track deal in another respect. Whether it's been good, I'll never know. That'll be decided by wiser men later. My life has been so tied up in football that it has flown by. I wish it wasn't that way, but it had gone by mighty fast. Practice, recruiting and games. Football, football and more football. There hasn't been much else. It has become a void, as it has to when your next minute, next hour and next day all revolve around one thing.
>
> Frankly, I don't know if that's good. I know I've made the journey, but I'm not sure I've enjoyed all of it. You miss a lot of things you shouldn't miss. . . .
>
> When I look back, there are good things I wouldn't take anything for. But still, you never know if it has been worth it. . . .
>
> . . . I haven't even gotten to know my neighbors well. I've reached a point where thirty minutes after the last game, I start thinking about the next game. That's ridiculous.[24]

Bryant told Browning that his life had been changed by a simple devotional, the author of which he did not know. "I found this last year, read it and liked what it had to say. It says that God has given us this life, has traded days with us, and that we should make a point of putting something back into it. It asks what we're going to trade for today. I wish I had read this 30 years ago. If I had, I wouldn't have wasted so much valuable time."[25] Who would have imagined that Bear Bryant felt that he had wasted so much valuable time?

THE CRIMSON Tide began the 1982 season, Bryant's twenty-fifth at Alabama, with a roar. The 45–7 victory over Georgia Tech was the most impressive opening-day game Alabama had played in years. Bryant had modified his wishbone offense, working in more I-formation plays to take advantage of Walter Lewis's passing ability, though some suspected it had as much to do with the team's lack of depth at running back. With the wishbone, one needed a fleet of good backs to shuffle in and out of the lineup, and some felt Alabama hadn't been able to recruit enough talent to stock a strong wishbone team. But no one was thinking that through the first victory.

Then came the big one at Legion Field: Joe Paterno's Nittany Lions looked as if they were on the fast track to the national championship, winning their first four games with quarterback Todd Blackledge and future All-Pro running back Curt Warner putting up points even faster than the Tide had. Penn State fans were sure this was the year the Lions would have their revenge. The game, televised nationally, proved to be a stunner, not so much because Alabama won by such a large margin, 42–21, but because of how poorly Penn State played. Walter Lewis and wide receiver Joey Jones humiliated the much-touted Penn State defense on long passes, and on consecutive possessions Penn State's punter kicked the ball right into the back side of his own blocker. After the game, a benevolent Bryant put his hand on the shoulder of a disconsolate Joe Paterno and told him not to despair, that there was a lot of football left in the season.

Bryant had no idea how right he was. No team that ever went on to win a national championship (as Penn State would when it defeated Herschel Walker and Georgia in the Sugar Bowl on January 1) ever suffered a worse drubbing during the regular season. For Alabama, despite its 5–0 record and its number-one rank in the polls, the season was about to collapse.

Alabama lost to Tennessee, 35–28, the first time Bryant failed to break out the cigars since 1970. The Tide won the next two games before losing to LSU in Birmingham. The defeat was ominous, coming as it did to the second of Alabama's big three rivals. After the game, Don Klauser Jr. of the *Birmingham News* dropped a bombshell.[26] He openly called for Bryant's retirement. The *News* offices were flooded with angry phone calls, letters, and death threats. Bryant made no comment about the story.

The next week was even more depressing because it was so unexpected. Southern Miss and its scrambling quarterback, Reggie Collier, embarassed Alabama 38–29. Another streak had come to an end: it was the first time in fifty-eight games that Alabama had lost at Bryant-Denny Stadium. Afterward, Bryant walked across the field and singled out Collier for praise. The next day, on *The Bear Bryant Show*, he seemed almost in a state of despair. "I don't know why I didn't put eight or nine players up on the line of scrimmage to try and stop that boy," he told co-host Steadman Shealy, his quarterback on the 1979 national championship team. "I just don't know why I didn't do that."[27] On Monday Bryant gave an interview to the *Atlanta Constitution*'s Ed Hinton. In the middle of the interview, Bryant surprised Hinton by stating flatly, "I can't coach them any more."

In the season finale, the Crimson Tide faced an Auburn team with the same 7–3 record Alabama had. In the third quarter, Auburn led 14–13 before Alabama came back with a field goal and an eight-yard burst by the Tide's fine running back, Paul Carruth. Alabama led 22–14, and Tide fans raised their right hands with all four fingers extended: "The fourth quarter belongs to us."

But the fourth quarter belonged to the man Bryant failed to recruit. Bo Jackson broke free for a fifty-three-yard run to set up a field goal and then, to cap a sixty-six-yard drive, went over the top of the Alabama line from the one-yard line to make it 23–22 with about two minutes left to play. That's how it ended. The Tide had riddled the Tigers' defense for 507 yards and twenty-seven first downs and held Auburn to 257 yards and eleven first downs. But Tide mistakes, penalties, and turnovers, the kind of thing that never happened to Bryant's teams in big games, had kept Auburn in the game and finally given it a chance to win. Auburn fans were jubilant; nine years of humiliation had finally come to an end. The coach was not quite so ebullient. In the postgame press conference at Legion Field, Pat Dye, speaking into the microphone, in so low a voice that some reporters could not hear him, said, "To tell you the truth, I'd rather beat anybody in the world but Coach Bryant. He's done so much for me, there's no way I could repay him. It's kind of sad for me."

The unthinkable had happened: Alabama had lost three consecutive games, all of them at home, to end the season. Recognizing that the Coach would need some extra support on this bleak day, several of Bryant's friends accompanied him to the taping of his show. "Despite a brave front," Tide broadcaster John Forney would recall, "it was obvious he was totally exhausted and despondent."[28]

HERSCHEL NISSENSON was a veteran sportswriter whose beat for many years had been college football in the Southeast. Nissenson loved Alabama—the sports bars, the barbecue stands, the country and blues joints—more than his home. He stayed close to Alabama football year-round. Football coaches, he had learned over the years, "gossip worse than a bunch of old ladies in a sewing circle." Football writers, too. Two weeks after the Auburn game, Nissenson got a phone call from David Housel, Auburn's sports information director, who was in Orlando, where the Tigers were to play Boston College in the Tangerine Bowl. Housel told Nissenson that some of the Auburn coaches were in touch with some former Alabama coaches who were now on Ray Perkins's staff in New York; they had heard that Bryant was ready to step down and Perkins would be named his successor. Perkins, an All-America wide receiver on the great 1965 and 1966 Alabama teams, had become head coach of the New York Giants in 1979 and restored them to football respectability by taking them to the playoffs in 1981, only to watch in disgust as his team unraveled in the strike-shortened 1982 season. He had always been one of Bryant's favorites.

That's it, thought Nissenson, Bear is going to retire and Perkins will leave New York and go to Alabama. But should he run with the story? Nissenson called Sam Bailey, Bryant's close friend and assistant athletic director, and asked him, "Sam, if I run this story, am I going to look stupid?" After a pause, Bailey told him, "Naw, go ahead."

Nissenson had only a couple of hours to put together the biggest football story of the year. He got on the phone from his home in Long Island and dialed the Bryants' home in Tuscaloosa. The line was busy. Then he called Logan Young, a close friend of Bryant's in Memphis. Young confirmed that that's what he had heard—Bryant would be stepping down and Perkins would be the new head coach.

He decided to try the Bryant home one more time. Mary Harmon picked up the phone. The Coach was out, she told him, recruiting a player in Mississippi, she thought, or something like that. "But Herschel," she said, "you bein' such a good friend with Paul, can't you just wait for the press conference?" Nissenson, of course, could not allow himself to be scooped. Half-apologizing, he told her, "I have to put this out for the morning editions." The story went out on the AP wire. On New York's Channel 2 eleven-o'clock newscast, sports anchor Warner Wolf read the as-yet-unsubstantiated report that Bear Bryant would be retiring and Ray Perkins would be replacing him. Wolf tossed the report over his shoulder, saying, "That's what I think of that!" The following night, Wolf apologized.

Alf Van Hoose of the *Birmingham News* was scheduled to break the story. But the *Birmingham News* was the afternoon paper, and the AP report ran in nearly every morning paper in the country. "Every time I'd see Alf after that," says Nissenson, "he'd say, 'Damn you!'"

Rumors of Bryant's retirement had been swirling for a week, but nobody in Alabama believed them, or, maybe, as Paul Finebaum says, "It wasn't so much that people didn't believe he'd retire as that they couldn't comprehend what that meant. How could you wake up one day and not have this towering figure to look up to? For years people had been seeing him as a monument. Well, how can a monument retire?"

The press conference on December 15, 1982, proved anticlimactic. "There comes a time in every profession when you need to hang it up, and that time has come for me as head football coach at the University of Alabama." The team had been a disappointment that year, and, as always, he took full responsibility. "We lost two big football games this season that we should have won, and we played only four or five like a Bryant-coached team should play"—the newspapers, which used a written handout of his speech for their stories the next day, did not include Bryant's ad-lib, muttered under his breath after those words—"whatever that is."

"I love the players, but in my opinion they deserve better coaching than they've been getting from me, and that's why I'm stepping down, in an effort to see they get better coaching from someone else." He accounted that he would stay on as athletic director.

Then came the formality of naming Ray Perkins as his successor. Alabama president Joab Thomas said that a special committee formed to screen the leading candidates—Bryant was not on it—had decided "the obvious choice was Perkins." The choice may not have been obvious to

Bryant. He would not speak publicly on the issue because he was in an unwinnable position; he had produced so many qualified coaches—all of them, by now, close friends—that it would have been agonizing to narrow the choice down to one. Some thought Gene Stallings, who was then working for the Dallas Cowboys as an assistant to Tom Landry, was Bryant's first choice; others thought Bryant was leaning toward his own assistant, Mal Moore.* Still others thought another assistant, Ken Donahue, would be the best choice. Bryant, probably for fear of offending his protégés, never made his preference public.

"Before the announcement was made," says Jack Rutledge, a trusted Bryant assistant, "Coach called me and asked me to meet him in his office on a Sunday. He wanted to set up a meeting with the players to discuss what was going to happen, but when I met him on that Sunday, he said, 'Never mind, it's all changed. They took it away from me, and I can't do anything about it.'" Bryant, he recalls, was in tears.

Why wasn't Bryant included in the selection process? Probably for several reasons, beginning with the obvious one that a decision by the university that didn't involve Bryant would shield him from any acrimony resulting from that decision. Even though Bryant was hurt by being kept out of the review process, he must have realized that, in the final analysis, it was none of his business. He had always been a university man and had taken pains to identify himself in interviews as a university employee. Surely part of him had to understand that the power to select another football coach—another faculty member, he had always insisted—could not rest with him.

Anyway, there was something else to think about right now. There was one game left to play, against the University of Illinois in the Liberty Bowl, and, as Walter Lewis says, "Nobody, and I mean nobody, wanted to be on the team that lost Bear Bryant's last game."

THE LIBERTY Bowl had been the first one Bryant had taken Alabama to back in 1959. It was now played in Memphis, Tennessee, a locale that was supposed to guarantee warmer conditions in late December than Philadelphia. It seldom worked out that way; UCLA players complained about the

---

* Moore is currently Alabama's athletic director.

bitter cold when Alabama whipped them there in 1976, and the 1982 game was one of the coldest Tide fans could remember sitting through. Bowl teams are generally selected to provide not only the most attractive but also the fairest matches. The Fighting Illini were a good team, well matched against Alabama with the same 7–4 record. They had one genuine weapon: quarterback Tony Eason, who would become a standout in the NFL and guide the New England Patriots to the 1986 Super Bowl. In public, Bryant played down the game. "I don't have any emotion whatsoever," he said at a pregame press conference. "I'll probably have a lot of emotion this time next week when it's all over. But now it's just another game."

In private, though, it was a different matter. The day before the game, nearly one hundred players and coaches gathered in a room to watch Illinois game films. Bryant stopped the films, started talking to the assemblage, and then began crying. The players and coaches were silent. One of the players, Russ Wood, recalled,

> He went over the game plan format like he always did, but all of a sudden, he got off on football, told us how much he loved it, and how much he cared about us. He told us he wanted us to do well in the game for ourselves and Alabama and not for him. He got choked up, and his mouth was moving, but no words were coming out and the tears were flowing.
>
> It seemed like eternity, but it was probably just eight or nine seconds. Finally, somebody turned off all the lights and started the projectors.[29]

An entire room full of football players and coaches looked toward the screen but couldn't see the films through their tears.

SHORTLY BEFORE the game, Bryant was shaking hands with a swarm of friends and former players when he spotted Joe Drach from the Maryland team of thirty-seven years ago. Drach remembers Bryant calling him over. "'Joe,' he told me, 'I wanna talk to you about something. Right now this is all a madhouse, but when it's over I'm gonna get settled down and do some things that I've been wantin' to do for years, and I want you to help me.' What he wanted was to get all the vets from the Navy Pre-Flight team that played at Maryland and some of the other guys who had played on the team, too. He said, 'Joe, I want for all of us to get together and talk about life. I want to know if any of them are still bitter because I left and to apologize to them in the right way. Would you help me do that?' I said of course I would. But I was surprised. I mean, I was mad at him for leaving, but I had forgiven him years ago. To be honest, I don't think I had thought about it much in thirty years. But here he was, just a few hours before the end of his career, and it was still on his mind."

ON DECEMBER 29, the day of the game, emotions were running rampant in the Alabama locker room. First Jeremiah Castille, Alabama's best defensive back, and then Eddie Lowe, whose brother Woodrow had starred on the 1973 national championship team, got up to make heartfelt speeches. If it was possible to be too emotional before a football game, then the Crimson Tide may have passed that point.

If the Alabama players had been expecting Illinois to cooperate in making Bear Bryant's final game a happy occasion for him, they were badly mistaken. The weather didn't cooperate either. The stadium was frigid; Bryant exchanged the familiar houndstooth hat for an Alabama baseball cap tucked inside a parka hood. The chill factor was eight degrees; just before kickoff, someone reminded Bryant of what he had told the team back in Tuscaloosa: "Coldness is in the mind."

"Well," Bryant replied, "I can tell you now that was a bunch of bull. I'm freezing to death."

The Tide defense seemed to have no answer to Tony Eason's passing, and the Fighting Illini riddled the Alabama defense on that night for 444 yards. Alabama players, overwhelmed by the significance of the game, could not focus. The Illini made an early drive deep into Alabama territory, but then, inside the ten-yard line, the Tide defense stiffened. Defensive tackle Randy Edwards broke unexpectedly through the middle of the line and blocked Illinois's field goal attempt. The Tide settled down. Walter Lewis hit end Joey Jones for a fifty-yard completion, and Ricky Moore scored the first touchdown, to make it 7–0.

But Illinois drove back into Tide territory again and again; five times in the first half they drove inside the Alabama twenty-five. No one could remember the last time that had happened; John Forney thought it was the 1970 game with Southern Cal, where Sam Cunningham and Clarence Davis had run wild. Finally, just before the half, Illinois scored a touchdown but missed the extra point. Alabama clung to a precarious 7–6 lead. In the halftime locker room, Bryant refused to appeal to his team's emotions. "You got class," he told them, "it's going to show." The players were not so sure. They felt better in the third quarter when Lewis spearheaded another scoring drive, which ended with another of Bryant's favorite trick plays, a reverse with Jessie Bendross coming around to take a handoff and going eight yards, untouched, into the Illinois end zone. The reliable Peter Kim made it 14–6. Once again, though, Illinois came back. Eason, looking as if he couldn't be stopped, led the Illini on a thirteen-play drive that culminated in a touchdown pass. Illinois then went for the two-point conversion to tie the game; it failed. The score was 14–12 Alabama with minutes to play.

Unnoticed by the television press, the intensity on the Alabama sideline nearly boiled over. Walter Lewis had not realized it before taking the field, but Bryant's plan had essentially allowed him to call his own game with little interference from the sideline. In his final game, Bryant was restoring to his last quarterback some of the freedom his earlier quarterbacks such as Blanda, Parilli, Namath, and Stabler had enjoyed before college football became as sophisticated as the pros. On this night, Lewis would not always make the right decisions; after he threw an interception early in the game, Bryant confronted him as he came off the field. "What in hell were you doing on that play?" "I thought I had made the right decision," says Lewis, "so next time we got the ball back I called the same play again. Well, I was wrong again—the pass was intercepted. This time I came off the field *way down* at the end of the line so I didn't have to face Coach."

On the whole, though, Lewis's play calling and his execution had been good—he would be selected as Alabama's Offensive Player of the Game— and he had kept the Tide in front all afternoon. Now, late in the game and leading by just two points, there was no margin for error. Bryant wanted a particular running back in the game but Lewis did not think he was reliable; Lewis wanted someone else. On the sideline, Lewis openly questioned his coach's decision. "I got in his face," says Lewis, "and he jumped on me. I had forgotten for a moment who made the final decisions, and I paid the price." Luckily, no one in the media spotted what could have been an embarrassing flare-up between Bryant and his black star quarterback in the Coach's last game—or if they did, everyone chose to ignore it.

Lewis shook off the reprimand and led the most impressive scoring drive of the day for Alabama. Fullback Craig Turner bulldozed to the end zone from the two-yard line in the fourth period. The Tide now led by nine points, 21–12, and it seemed safe to relax. It was not safe. Tony Eason completed a flurry of passes to bring the ball down to the Alabama six; once again the bloodied Tide defense held on and forced a field goal. That made the score 21–15, and everyone knew what that meant: if the Illini could get one more touchdown, they could win the game merely by kicking the extra point that had eluded them in their previous two tries. Alabama got the ball, was forced to punt, and Eason drove his team downfield, completing desperation pass after desperation pass. With less than a minute to go and the crowd at frenzied pitch, Eason took the Illini to the six-yard line. He dropped back to throw and from his left side, defensive end Russ Wood beat his blocker and crashed into Eason from behind, for a ten-yard loss. In a state of euphoria, Wood jumped to his feet and began leaping up and down. In the center of the jubilation on the Alabama sideline was a slightly annoyed head coach. Bryant turned to assistant coach Steve Hale and asked him, "Haven't you coached him to lay on the quarterback when we're trying to run the clock out?" Just because there were only seconds left in his career wasn't a reason to get sloppy.

Eason was injured on Wood's sack, and on the next play his replacement's pass was intercepted by Eddie Lowe, who had made one of the fiery pregame speeches in the locker room. Alabama ran the clock out, and the game, and Bryant's career, was over. The journey that had begun one day in Fordyce when he walked by the Redbugs practice field had come to an end. His players carried him on their shoulders for the last time. For one of the few times in his career, Bryant allowed himself a smile at the postgame press conference. "We won in spite of me," he said, shaking his head. "I actually had little to do with what they were doing. I don't recall making a decision all night." He singled out for praise his fine defensive back, Jeremiah Castile, who had intercepted three passes, and his quarterback, Walter Lewis, with whom he had clashed on the sideline. Castille was named the MVP in Bryant's last game.

After nearly forty-five minutes of politely answering questions from reporters and commentators from all over the country, Bryant, looking terribly drained, left the stadium in a car waiting to take him to the celebration. A woman, an Alabama fan, was waiting outside the stadium to bid him farewell. "We're going to miss you, Coach Bryant," she sobbed. "Thank you," Bryant replied, "but you remember to keep rooting for Alabama."

A few days later, Walter Lewis, feeling as if he had to get something off his chest, walked from the dorm to Bryant's office. He found Bryant in a jovial mood. "Coach," he said, "I just wanted to tell you that I was wrong to challenge you like that, and I know it. I apologize." Bryant laughed. "Walt," he said, "that's part of the game. You're learning how to be a quarterback." Twenty-two years later, Lewis was scheduled to deliver a speech before a Boy Scout group in Anniston, Alabama. He bumped into his old teammate, Major Ogilvie, and recounted the story to him. Paul Bryant Jr. overheard it. "Paul told me, 'I don't think my father ever got a chance to tell you how much he felt about you.' I got goose bumps," Lewis recalls. "I said, 'Paul, I'd appreciate it if you'd tell me.' He said that Coach Bryant had said I reminded him of his grandson, Marc. I knew Marc, and I knew how much he meant to his grandfather. I think it's the greatest compliment anyone ever paid me, even if I had to wait more than twenty years to hear it." (After graduating, Lewis would return to Alabama as an assistant coach.)

WHAT WOULD Bear Bryant's life after football be like? John Underwood phoned him shortly after the announcement and asked him why he had stepped down. "Because four damn losses is too damn many. I'm up to my ass in alligators, John. These new young coaches just have too much energy for me. We need someone younger." "So you really are tired?" Underwood asked. "Naw. To tell you the truth, I feel great. I got so many things I've been wantin' to do for so long, and now I'm gonna get to 'em." "Like what?" Underwood wanted to know. After a pause, Bryant replied, "I'm not sure just yet."

On January 25, just twenty-seven days after his final game, Bryant complained of severe chest pains and was rushed to Druid City Regional Medical Center in Tuscaloosa. His doctors did not seem overly disturbed, but decided to keep him overnight for observation. The feeling was that he would be released the following day. Shortly after he was admitted, a nurse, Tammy Kilgore, came to check his vital signs. Kilgore was more than seven months' pregnant. Bryant, in a cheerful mood, asked if he could pat her tummy while she went about her duties. She said she'd be delighted. "He's going to be an Alabama football player," he told her. Kilgore replied that she was expecting a girl and said, "No, she's going to be a cheerleader."

Bryant laughed and said, "That's O.K., so long as she cheers for Alabama."[30] Even after his retirement, Bryant was still recruiting talent for Alabama, and in this case he landed another one. Almost twenty years later, the baby, Emily Kilgore, would be enrolled at Alabama and work as a student assistant in the athletic department's media relations office.

In the morning, Ray Perkins dropped by to visit; Bryant chided him for wasting time when he should be out recruiting. It was the same jest Pat Trammell had made when Bryant visited him in the hospital shortly before Trammell's death. Bryant had been taking notes the whole time he was in the hospital, listing bits of business that needed to be dealt with. There was a player, the son of one of Bryant's Kentucky boys who had also been an assistant coach for him at Alabama—did Perkins think the boy was good enough to merit a football scholarship? Perkins was honest: he did not think the boy was good enough, but he would see to it that the boy got his education through the Bryant scholarship program. That would be fine, Bryant replied.

"He didn't skip a single beat," says Jack Rutledge. "Even while he was in a hospital bed, he was keeping in communication with everybody and knew everything that was going on."

Shortly afterward, Billy Varner brought Mae Martin by to see her father; they found the Coach in a good mood. When Varner got home, he called Linda Knowles, Bryant's secretary, to check in. She told him there had been a turn for the worse, and Varner hurried back to the hospital. At 12:24 p.m., Bryant had been sitting up in bed trying to eat lunch when he suffered cardiopulmonary arrest. Attempts to revive him failed. He was pronounced dead at 1:30 p.m., January 26, 1983. "He was a very courageous man," Dr. William Hill told the *New York Times*, "I seriously doubt there were many people who could overcome what he did the last three years to accomplish so much."[31]

"If I ever quit coaching," he had often told friends, "I'd croak in a week." He was off by twenty-one days.

Chapter 12

Like Having John Wayne for Your Grandfather

. . . to have been in the city of Tuscaloosa in October when you were young and full of Early Times and had a shining Alabama girl by your side—to have had all that and then to have seen those red shirts pour onto the field, and, then, coming behind them, with that inexorable big cat walk of his, the man himself, The Bear—that was very good indeed.

—Howell Raines[1]

I MADE IT BACK to my apartment in Brooklyn in time to switch on the TV and hear Tom Brokaw say, "The Bear is dead. The most successful coach in college football history, Paul 'Bear' Bryant, today died of a heart attack in Alabama." I tried to return the calls on my answering machine, but all I got when I called was a fast beep—I later learned that first the hospital switchboard, then all Tuscaloosa exchanges, and finally the area code for the entire state of Alabama had gone down from overload.

Great pains were taken to see that the funeral service did not turn into a media circus. The Reverend Duncan Hunter of the First United Methodist Church in Tuscaloosa recalled, "Mary Harmon was very composed. Her interest was that the funeral would be dignified and worshipful." There were far too many close friends for the Bryants' church to accommodate, so closed-circuit television cameras were installed in order that mourners at two other churches could view the brief service. The eulogy was delivered by Steadman Shealy, who had gone into the ministry after spending a year on Bryant's coaching staff. The pallbearers were eight members of the team chosen by the Bryant family: Walter Lewis, Jeremiah Castile, Eddie Lowe, Tommy Wilcox, Gerill Sprinkle, Mike McQueen, Paul Fields, and Darryl White. After the service, as the casket, draped in red and white roses, was carried down the church steps to the hearse, Reverend Hunter "heard a noise. I'll always remember what it sounded like, almost like thunder. There must have been two hundred photographers, and the sound of those shutters clicking at the same time is something I'll never forget."

The procession ran three miles long and included six buses loaded with current and former players and staff members. When the white hearse left the church, it drove by Bryant-Denny Stadium and paused. The motorcade drove down Tenth Street—since renamed Bryant Drive—turned on McFarland Boulevard, and onto Interstate 20/59, carrying Bear Bryant west to Birmingham's Elmwood Cemetery. Viewers across the nation turned on their nightly news to an astonishing sight: all along the fifty-five-mile route an estimated quarter of a million people*—perhaps one out of twelve people in the state of Alabama—lined the highways and crowded the overpasses to view the procession. Old men holding their fedoras over their hearts, truck drivers with baseball caps removed, black and white, young and old, mothers with young children, all tearfully watched as the hearse passed. The overwhelming majority had never attended any college, let alone the University of Alabama.

Some journalists later compared it to the slow train cortege that carried Franklin Roosevelt's body from Warm Springs, Georgia, to Washington in

---

* This estimate appeared in the *Birmingham News* and *Birmingham Post-Herald*. Tommy Ford, in his 1983 book, *Bama Under Bear: Alabama's Family Tides*, estimated the number at 500,000 to 700,000. This seems excessive, though it probably didn't to those in the motorcade.

1945. My Brooklyn neighbors said, "My God, I've never seen anything like that." No, I replied, and you never will again.

Marc Tyson would remember, "That was the first time I realized how many people loved Papa besides me."

Paul Finebaum, then of the *Birmingham Post-Herald*, had always been a bit skeptical of the Bryant legend; while viewing the procession, he says, "I suddenly got it. I realized for the first time what he had meant to everyone. Without realizing exactly why, I found myself overcome."

"It was the most amazing sight I've ever seen," said Bryant's old friend, former Southern Cal coach John McKay. "It was like a presidential funeral procession. No coach in America could have gotten that. No coach but him. But then, he wasn't just a coach. He was *the* coach."

"When I heard on the radio that he had died, and I started to cry," wrote Ian Frazier in the "Talk of the Town" column in the February 14 *New Yorker*, "I knew I was just part of a big chorus."

Woody Hayes had probably been the football coach closest to Bryant in terms of the country's esteem—that is, until he was fired by Ohio State for punching a player in the 1978 Gator Bowl. After the service, he recalled for the *Tuscaloosa News* the feeling of being on the practice field the day Knute Rockne died. "I have the same feeling today," he said. "Rockne was the greatest coach of his era. Bryant was the greatest coach of his era. There'll never be another like him."[2]

At the cemetery, there were flowers from all living former American presidents, Nixon, Carter, and Ford, as well as from President Reagan—but no floral arrangement outshone the one from the Alabama Booster Club of Bridgeport, Pennsylvania. The mourners included Joe Namath, Lee Roy Jordan, and Darrell Royal, as well as a crowd of newsmen from the *New York Times*, *Washington Post*, *Houston Chronicle*, and *Los Angeles Times*. The first football coach to arrive was Grambling's Eddie Robinson, who had coached the all-black school to numerous championships and had become fast friends with Bryant at coaching clinics. At the time, the sports media was only dimly aware of how close Robinson was to breaking Bryant's record for victories. George Allen, head coach of the Washington Redskins, represented President Reagan, who could not get away from official business.

Mickey Herskowitz arrived late because his flight from Houston had been delayed. At Birmingham International Airport, he got flustered and forgot the name of the cemetery. His cab driver knew exactly where to take him. Arriving at Elmwood, Herskowitz spotted Richard Gay, one of Bryant's Aggies from the 1957 team, with his son. Weaving their way through the crowd, they moved toward Mary Harmon and the Bryant family. Without realizing it, Herskowitz stepped directly in front of a man in a wheelchair; he stopped to apologize to George Wallace for nearly running into him. Wallace acknowledged his apology with a sad smile.

The graveside service lasted for perhaps five minutes. As the mourners made their way back to their cars, Paul Jr. motioned to Herskowitz and Gay to come over. Gay had been Paul Jr.'s favorite player back at A&M; Herskowitz overheard Paul Jr. say, "When Papa died we took this off his finger. It was the only jewelry he was wearing." He handed Gay the Junction Boys ring that had been presented to Bryant at the twenty-fifth-anniversary reunion back in 1979.

On the way back to Texas, Herskowitz was flipping through the *Birmingham News* and came across a story about a black man who had run a barbecue stand a block from the campus. Occasionally, when there were no team meetings at lunchtime, Bryant would walk across the road alone, sit at a bar stool under the tin roof over the stand, and have a barbecue sandwich on white bread. "Apparently they were about the same age," recalls Herskowitz. "The story said they would talk about things like hunting and fishing and dogs. One of their big topics was how things had changed since they were young men. The thing I remember best, though, was that the man said, 'One thing Coach Bryant and I never talked about was football.'"

Four months before Bryant's death, I had written in the *Village Voice*, "In another season, two maybe, Bear Bryant will step down. . . . And, for better or worse, kids in Alabama will grow up not knowing what's it like to have John Wayne for a grandfather."[3] I just hadn't realized it was going to happen so soon.

MARY HARMON BRYANT survived Paul by only two and half years. She suffered a stroke and died on August 26, 1984, at age sixty-eight. The Alabama beauty queen who had married the football hero was buried next to her husband of forty-eight years. She left behind two children, five grandchildren, and thousands of surrogate children and grandchildren— former players and assistants and their families with whom she kept in regular contact long after they left the University of Maryland, Kentucky, Texas A&M, and Alabama.

Ray Perkins lasted four years as Alabama's head coach. He wasn't a bad coach, though a 32–15–1 record was not what Alabama fans were used to. (Perkins had one losing season, his second, in 1984, with a record of 5–6; he was 2–2 against Auburn; and his teams won all three of their bowl games.) But Perkins was devoid of the media-handling skills that Bryant had possessed in such abundance, and he angered many fans at the start by removing Bryant's famous tower from the practice field. Early in 1983, I went to Tuscaloosa to profile Perkins for *Us* magazine and found him amazingly sullen and uncommunicative; he would repeatedly make what he believed to be big, defining statements, such as "I'm right where I want to be," and then stare out the window as if there was nothing more to discuss. I made a note to myself that this man is "temperamentally unsuited for any of the duties of a football coach off the football field." It did not help that Perkins repeatedly clashed with Paul Finebaum, who had become the most talked-about sportswriter in the state. "I know he felt I had it in for him," says Finebaum, "but that's just not true. Ray did himself in. I mean, he was the only coach I've ever seen who alienated more fans than he made on his own radio call-in show. He told one man that his question was 'stupid.' He scolded another caller by saying, 'I'm the coach of this team, and I make the decisions I think are best for the team.' Alabama fans weren't expecting the second coming of Bear Bryant, but they needed somebody who had more personality than a drill sergeant." By 1987, Perkins had departed Tuscaloosa for the NFL's Tampa Bay Buccaneers with a five-year, $3.7 million contract.

The next head coach of the Crimson Tide, Bill Curry, never really had a chance. Not only had he coached at Georgia Tech, a school many Alabama fans still recalled with animosity, he had no direct coaching or playing ties to Bear Bryant. "If folks had known how fond Coach Bryant was of Coach Curry, it might have made a big difference," says Walter Lewis, but they had no way of knowing. If Curry did not know what he was getting into when he took the job, he found out when he arrived at the Montgomery airport and was picked up by Mae Martin Tyson, who told him, "It broke my heart when they didn't hire one of Papa's boys as head coach. But you're the coach now, and I'm going to support you." Curry, whose courtly public demeanor contrasted vividly with Perkins's churlishness, was head coach for three years. His contract was not renewed at the end of the 1989 season. Curry had the best winning percentage of any of Bryant's successors, but he could not beat Auburn in three tries. If he had won those games, he probably would have been accorded the status of Honorary Bryant Boy. Curry made some lasting friends, though, by restoring Bryant's tower.

Gene "Bebes" Stallings finally got his chance as head coach at Alabama in 1990 and did well, winning the national championship in 1992 when the Crimson Tide went undefeated and scored a major upset, beating the University of Miami and its Heisman-winning quarterback Gino Torretta, 34–13, in the Sugar Bowl. (It should be noted that several of the star players on that 1992 national championship team had been recruited by Bill Curry.)

In 1997 Stallings retired, and the job went to Mike DuBose, a defensive end on the 1973 national championship team who had served as defensive coordinator under Stallings. Under DuBose, things began to get messy. DuBose's record was 4–7 in his first year, improved to 7–5 in his second, and then to 10–3 in his third year, 1999. Several preseason polls for the 2000 season predicted Alabama would be in contention for the national title. The team flopped miserably, finishing 3–8. Far worse, DuBose was accused of sexual harassment by a former university employee. Alabama settled with the woman, but inexplicably gave DuBose a two-year contract extension and announced that the $360,000 cost of the settlement would be deducted from his salary.

In 2001, after having had bad luck twice with "Bear's boys," Alabama once again decided to go outside its tradition and hired Dennis Franchione of Texas Christian University. Franchione survived two stormy seasons in which the program was crippled because of NCAA infractions that occurred under DuBose. Franchione publicly implored his boys to "grab the rope and hold on!"—even using the phrase on his Web site—to convince the players, who were entitled to change schools after the sanctions were levied, to stay on with him. Then, when he could no longer stand the pressure, he bolted for Texas A&M.

The sad tale of Mike Price, who was supposed to be Franchione's successor, left Tide fans wondering if Bear Bryant had left a curse behind. Price, a successful coach at Washington State, accepted the job at Alabama and was fired before the season, for, as reported by *Sports Illustrated*, having sex with two women in his hotel room while on university business. The two women charged over a thousand dollars in food and drink to Price's room.[4] Price denied, and continues to deny, all allegations. When I wrote about the Price situation for the *New York Times* on May 11, 2003, I talked to Ted Miller, who had known Price while working for the *Seattle Post-Intelligencer*, and who knew Alabama football from a stint at the *Mobile Press Register*. "Pullman, where the Washington State campus is located, is tranquil compared to Tuscaloosa," he told me. "I think Price went dizzy with the sudden rush of money, power and attention. It's very easy for a man who comes in from the outside world to forget that in exchange for those things, accepting the head coaching job at Alabama means you no longer have a private life." Paul Finebaum, who by this time had the most popular radio talk show in the Southeast, was harsher in his assessment: "Mike Price came across as a small-time football coach. He was a mope who thought he had turned into a stud." (Price made a comeback in 2004 at the University of Texas at El Paso, taking the team to an 8–4 record after a 2–11 season under its previous coach.)

The controversy was not yet over. In 2003, Mike Shula, age thirty-eight, became the youngest Alabama head coach since Frank Thomas, age thirty-three, back in 1931. Shula, son of the longtime Miami Dolphins coach Don Shula—the man who got the job that Bear Bryant turned down—did not have a Bear connection, but he had played quarterback brilliantly for three years under Ray Perkins and had worked as an offensive coordinator at Tampa Bay and as quarterback coach for the Dolphins.

But in hiring Shula, Alabama bypassed an older, even more experienced candidate who *did* have a connection with the Bear. Sylvester Croom had been chosen by Bryant as a student assistant in 1976 and had spent twenty-eight years coaching, seventeen at the professional level, including three years as running back coach for the Green Bay Packers. Amid a blizzard of editorials suggesting or even accusing the University of Alabama of racism, Croom himself kept silent and took the head coaching job with the Mississippi State Bulldogs, the first black head coach in SEC history.

"I think it's a biblical thing," says Finebaum. "Twenty-five years of glory followed by twenty-five years of plagues." If the plague era began with Bryant's death, then a new golden age should be dawning for the Crimson Tide around 2007.

SOMETIME IN the summer of 1982 I attended a press conference in Birmingham where the Coach himself announced that a deal had been made for a movie based on his life. I snapped several pictures of him at that press conference; he looks rather glum in all of them. Our brief interview later was polite and cheerless. I got the impression that since John Wayne's death, the desire to see himself depicted on the screen had faded and that he was only agreeing to the film in order to leave something more behind for his family.

Bryant died long before the film was released, and Mary Harmon passed away only a few days before its premiere in Birmingham. Perhaps it was a blessing. *The Bear*, directed by Richard C. Sarafian, who had made the 1971 cult film *Vanishing Point*, was compromised and probably doomed from the start. The family would not allow reference to any of the Coach's rough edges or unsavory habits, and thus, in just one scene in the film, at a Christmas party where the Bear is seen dressed as Santa Claus gulping down a cup of spiked punch, is there a reference to alcohol. Gary Busey, a former high school football player back in Oklahoma, was woefully miscast as Bryant, though he struggled heroically with the voice and eventually managed an approximation of Bryant's growl. Harry Dean Stanton, a fine actor, was cast as Frank Thomas, and the young rising TV star Jon-Erik Hexum played the ill-starred Pat Trammell (in a bitter twist of fate, Hexum would die in an on-set accident while filming a movie shortly after *The Bear* was released). Bill Conte, who won the Academy Award for the soundtrack of *Rocky*, did the music, and the football sequences, choreographed with aid from Tommy Brooker, Billy Neighbors, and Gene Stallings, were surprisingly realistic. But the story was such a whitewash of Bryant's life that it made *Knute Rockne All American* seem like Greek drama.

I had an assignment to write a piece for *Sports Illustrated* on the film for what used to be called "Regionals," short, page-long features that appeared before the main articles in the magazine. The task was impossible. The internecine feuding among the Bryant family members and friends regarding who should control the content dogged the production from start to finish. The Alabama State Film Commission stopped cooperating with the production, and most of the film was shot in Georgia. Busey, off camera, was dangerously erratic. It was no secret among local journalists that the man playing Bear Bryant was using cocaine on a regular basis; Busey later admitted to having a drug problem as early as 1979 and nearly overdosed from coke in 1995. We were supposed to collaborate on a piece for *Inside Sports* on how he approached the role of Bear Bryant, but during the interview Busey was virtually incoherent. The story that appeared in "the Fan" column in the February 1985 *Inside Sports* under Busey's name was written by me, almost entirely from whole cloth. The only part that came from Busey was the end: "I want my Bear to go into the Smithsonian so that 100 years from now people can go and see something of his contributions to their time, their fears, their braveries."

I don't think *The Bear* was released anywhere but in Alabama, and even there it was quickly forgotten. To my knowledge it has never been released on video or DVD. I thought I was the only one in the world with a poster for the film until I saw one on the wall of a back hallway at the Paul W. Bryant Museum.

WHAT, ULTIMATELY, are Bryant's legacies? I think of that question every time I pass the sports section of a bookstore and see the latest tome from a star-of-the-moment college coach extolling the principles of leadership or some such nonsense. The coach has usually released his book just as he bolted to the professional ranks for more money; that's the principle he neglected to tell you about in his book. This isn't to deny that college football has been a business from the time of Walter Camp and Pudge Heffelfinger, but the most dedicated and most principled of college coaches have always stood for something greater than the business side of the game—or at least regarded the business of the football team as being to support the university rather than professional football.

Bear Bryant represented the last generation of college coaches who came of age when college football *was* football to America. By the time he retired, college football had already become to many, if not most, American sports fans a semiprofessional minor league whose primary purpose is to prepare young men for the professional ranks. No one has ever adequately explained how or why this process came about or, for that matter, why it can't be reversed. If, as college football analyst Murray Sperber claims, the overwhelming number of college football programs lose money, it may sooner or later dawn on America's colleges that they have everything to gain and nothing to lose by throwing off their subservience to the NFL and going back to the old-time college game. If they do, the university officials who bring about the counterrevolution might consider calling themselves "The Bear Bryant Society." Bryant never stopped wishing for the return of "eleven man and sic 'em" football. In one of his last interviews broadcast on WVUE-TV in Louisiana six months before his death, he told the host, Ron Gaspar, "If I could change one thing about college football, I'd go back to having the players play both sides of the ball. That was pure football."

As the great college football writer Dan Jenkins once reminded me, "Pro football could not survive without the colleges, but college football wouldn't notice if pro football disappeared tomorrow." Bear Bryant is a monument to the time when college football was the dog and pro football the tail; that is still true, though the colleges don't know it.

That speaks of Bryant the symbol. What of the man? Could a man personify so much that is virtuous to so many without necessarily possessing all those virtues himself? After nearly two years of listening to me expound on the subject of Bear Bryant during long phone conversations, my friend Kevin Baker, the novelist, posed this question to me: "If you had a son, would you want him to be like Bear Bryant? Is he the role model you'd choose for him?" And after nearly two years of what feels like having lived with Bryant night and day, I can finally answer—no, I wouldn't.

Twenty-two years after his death, Bear Bryant still intimidates me, not so much the memory of his overpowering demeanor when I saw him up close, as his intensity and will to win and his unshakable belief that these qualities, when applied to a higher purpose, can make you a better person. Not that I don't believe that. I just don't know whether or not, if I had to, I could commit to those principles as strongly as might be demanded of me by someone like Bear Bryant. In Bryant's case, faith and determination were products born of a desperation that I have never known and that I hope my child will never know. The America I grew up in was, I'm aware, a much easier place to live, largely because of men and women with the strength and tenacity of Bear Bryant. I understand and accept that fact but I don't know that I can ever fully appreciate it. But I never have and probably never will need anything as badly as Paul Bryant needed that football scholarship when he was trying to get out of Fordyce, Arkansas, and I pray to God my daughter will never need anything that badly either. But if I do, and if she does, Bear Bryant is there to inspire us. There is an important difference between being a role model and being the kind of man who can mold and shape role models. I am sure, now, after talking to scores of men and women who knew him well, that Bear Bryant was one of the latter.

Regarding his private life, I am reasonably certain that there are many more unpleasant stories about him than what I heard from his friends, and even now, after all these years, that people are not willing to be entirely honest about him. There are also far more extraordinary stories about his loyalty and generosity than I could fit into this book. As Pat Dye told me, "There's a lot of people walking around out there—friends, former players, students who attended college on the scholarship fund he helped set up—people who hit on hard times that don't even know they were helped by him and who he never wanted to know because he thought it might embarrass them."

But, finally, his character defects and good qualities are not even the point; in time, the memory of them will fade as those who knew him will pass on. What will matter, what will endure about Bryant, will be the legacy he left behind of the power of simple adherence to good principles, such as the ones on a devotional he carried in his wallet:

This is the beginning of a new day.
God has given me this day to use as I will.
I can waste it or use it for good.
What I do today is very important
because I am exchanging a day of my life for it.
When tomorrow comes, this day will be gone forever,
Leaving something in its place I have traded for it.
I want it to be a gain, not loss—good, not evil.
Success, not failure in order that
I shall not forget the price I paid for it.*

The sophisticated are ill advised to sneer at these words.

Though I never really knew Paul "Bear" Bryant, I think, like Richard Price when he went to Tuscaloosa in 1979 to profile him for *Playboy*, I finally understand what it is like to want Bear Bryant's respect. If I have probed more deeply into some areas of his life than he would have been comfortable with, it's because I could not imagine looking him in the eye and presenting him with anything less than the truth as I found it.

I suppose, in the end, like just about everyone else who knew him, in my own way I want Bear Bryant's approval.

---

* I carry a copy of these words in my wallet, courtesy of Bryant's grandson, Marc Tyson.

Appendix 1

Bud and Bear

PAUL WILLIAM "BEAR" BRYANT and Charles Burnham "Bud" Wilkinson were good friends from two very different backgrounds who were brought together by football. Wilkinson was born in Minnesota in 1916 and was raised mostly by his father after his mother died when he was seven. Bryant was born in Arkansas in 1913; by the time he was seven, his father was a semi-invalid, and he was raised almost entirely by his mother. Wilkinson was sent to a military academy before college, where he excelled in several sports, was a fine student, and even studied dramatics. Bryant had virtually no discipline save that enforced by his mother and, later, his high school football coach. Although he loved baseball his entire life, the only sport Paul ever really learned to play was football. He was so poorly prepared for college that he had to study at Tuscaloosa High a full year before he was admitted to the University of Alabama. Bryant never entirely overcame his inferiority complex and looked to Wilkinson as the ideal of how a college coach should look and act. He often sought Wilkinson's advice on everything from offensive formations to neckties.

In 1934, both men were stars on powerhouse teams that claimed the national championship. Bryant and the Alabama Crimson Tide under Frank Thomas, unbeaten, went to the Rose Bowl at the end of the 1934 season; Wilkinson and the equally unbeaten Minnesota Golden Gophers, under Bernie ("The Silver Fox of the Northland") Bierman, felt their team should have gone.

Both Wilkinson and Bryant served in the U.S. Navy during World War II and began their head coaching careers with Navy Pre-Flight School teams. (Bryant was with the North Carolina team, Wilkinson with Iowa's.) Wilkinson was hired by Jim Tatum in 1946 to be an assistant coach at the University of Oklahoma. Tatum, who later became a good friend of Bryant's, left the Sooners the next year for Maryland, which Bryant had left in 1945. Bryant was thirty-two when he got his first head coaching job with the Terps; Wilkinson was thirty-one when he became Oklahoma's head coach. They were the young Turks of college coaching, the men who learned football under the old masters and were now ready to carry it into the high-powered postwar era.

Both Bryant and Wilkinson were immediately successful; Bryant was 6-2-1 in 1945 with Maryland, and Wilkinson was 7-2-1 in his first year, 1947, at Oklahoma. The difference is that Wilkinson inherited a good team: the Sooners were 8-3 under Jim Tatum the year before Wilkinson took over. Bryant took on a team that had previously gone 1-7-1.

Wilkinson was just about everyone's choice as college football coach of the 1950s. In fact, he would probably top most sportswriters' polls as the greatest coach of his era, from his first year as head coach at Oklahoma to his final season, 1963. But over that same period, Bear Bryant was the greater coach. Let's look at their records for those seventeen seasons:

Years 1947–1963

	Wins	Losses	Ties	Won-Loss %	Bowl Game Record	National Titles
Bud Wilkinson	145	29	4	.826	6-2	3
Paul Bryant	128	44	12	.728	6-3-1	1

Bryant's numbers are excellent; Wilkinson's are amazing. He won seventeen more games than Bryant, lost fifteen fewer, and tied eight fewer. He won three national championships to Bryant's one and posted a won-lost percentage 98 points higher than Bear's.

At least up until 1963, clearly the argument that Bryant was the better

coach is not a simple one. First of all, Wilkinson's edge in national championships is not what it seems. His Sooners were awarded the 1950 national
title by the major wire-service polls only because the vote was held before
the Sugar Bowl, in which Bryant's Kentucky Wildcats beat Oklahoma 13-
7. Had the vote been held after the bowl game, then both their teams
would have won two titles between 1947 and 1963. It would have been
interesting to see what would have happened if Bryant's unbeaten 1956
Texas A&M Aggies had been allowed to play Wilkinson's unbeaten 1956
Sooners in a bowl game, but the Aggies were on probation that year and
not allowed to go to a bowl game. (The national champion Sooners did
not play in a bowl that year either because the Big Eight champion was
locked into the Orange Bowl and the conference would not allow the
same team to represent the conference two consecutive years. The Big Ten
had a similar irritating rule about the Rose Bowl.)

Wilkinson and Bryant coached against each other one more time,
in the 1963 Orange Bowl. Bryant and Alabama won easily, 17-0. So,
for their only two games against each other, Bryant's teams outscored
Wilkinson's 30-7.

The problem with simply comparing won-lost records is that it doesn't
take into account one very important fact: Wilkinson coached his entire
college career at Oklahoma. From 1947 to 1963, the period that covers
Wilkinson's career, Bryant coached for three different schools; from 1945
through 1963, he coached at four schools. Wilkinson was never faced with
the responsibility of building a program. Each time Bryant was faced with
the task of turning the football program around, he succeeded. In the three
seasons before Bryant came to Kentucky, the Wildcats' record was 8-20-1; in
their first three years under Bryant, it was 20-9-2 and the team was a serious
contender for the national championship, the only time in the school's history. The Texas A&M Aggies' record was 12-14-4 in the three years before
Bear arrived; over the next three seasons, it was 17-11-2, and that includes
the 1954 season when they went 1-9. After Bear's radical rebuilding program, from 1955 through 1957, the Aggies' record was 24-5-2.

Bryant's greatest reclamation project, though, was the University of
Alabama. In the three seasons before Bryant started coaching there, 1955
through 1957, the Crimson Tide's record was 4-24-1. Alabama had won
just three conference games, and those by a combined total of eight points;
it had lost eighteen SEC games by a combined total of 355 points. Vander-

bilt was traditionally the weakest team in the conference, but over those three seasons the Commodores won all three games against the Tide. Perhaps most unbearable of all, Alabama had gone *three years without scoring a point against Tennessee*. In Bryant's first three years, 1958 through 1960, Alabama's record was 20-7-5.

There is one more important factor that mitigates the difference between Wilkinson's and Bryant's won-lost percentages: Bryant was coaching against much tougher competition. Wilkinson dominated in the Big Eight, a conference many observers, including Pudge Heffelfinger in his 1954 book, *This Was Football*, regarded as one of the weakest. Pudge quoted an unnamed Texan as saying the Sooners "should win. Their schedule is on the soft side year in and year out. Wilkinson doesn't have to keep his squad up week after week, so has time to rest his players and sharpen them up for the toughies."[1] Of course, a Texan might be expected to say such a thing about Oklahoma, but many other coaches of the time had similar feelings, including Bryant. As he wrote in his autobiography *Bear*, recalling his game plan for the upset in the 1951 Sugar Bowl, "Bud was used to playing against those children in the Big Eight (it's a tougher conference now), and I wanted him to see some men."

Whether Pudge's and Bear's assessments are entirely fair, there's no question that the SEC was the tougher conference. In his first seven seasons at Kentucky, Bryant had to contend with one of the game's all-time great coaches, General Neyland of Tennessee, and he had to do it with far less recruiting clout. He never did succeed in beating Neyland, losing five games and tying two (though six of the games were decided by a total of just seventeen points). When Bryant returned to Alabama in 1958, he was caught between two powerhouses: the Auburn Tigers had won the national championship in 1957, and the LSU Tigers, coached by Bryant's former Kentucky assistant Paul Dietzel, would win in 1959.

Bryant is generally regarded as the greatest college coach of the 1960s and 1970s, but his claim for greatest coach of the 1950s should not be overlooked.

Appendix 2

Was Bear the
Greatest Coach Ever?

WAS PAUL BRYANT THE greatest college football coach of all time? The question became more or less rhetorical after Bryant won his 315th game in 1981, passing up what was then believed to be Amos Alonzo Stagg's career record.

Incredibly, as it turns out, Bryant may not have broken Stagg's record in 1981 with the 315th win against Auburn. Some overly diligent researchers have now uncovered four more early victories by Coach Stagg, though against schools so obscure that whether or not they qualify as major college opponents is a matter of opinion.* No matter. If that's the case, Bryant would have passed Stagg's mark the following season with the victory over Arkansas State in Birmingham. (Though how less satisfying it would have been for Bryant to break the record against Arkansas State rather than Auburn!) Legitimate record or no, the hoopla surrounding the Stagg hunt simply served to put Bryant's greatness in perspective; the record, as such,

---

* There is no clear consensus on exactly how many games Stagg did win. The College Football Data Warehouse lists him with 340 wins, while the American Football Coaches Association still shows him with 314. Some researchers dispute whether Stagg was actually head coach for some of the victories he is given credit for, contending that his status in some seasons was not head coach but closer to what we call an assistant coach today.

had nothing to do with it. Stagg never knew he had set a "record"; Bryant coached for more than twenty-five years without knowing he was approaching one.

How does one compare the greatest coaches from the first half of the twentieth century with those of the second half? For instance, how would one compare Bryant to Stagg (who coached from 1890 to 1946)? Or even Knute Rockne (1918–1930)? Bryant was probably correct when he said that the game that Stagg had coached and the one that he knew were too different to make for a fair comparison. This is also probably true of the football Knute Rockne coached in the 1920s. The only fair way to rank them is to say that each was generally regarded by his peers as the greatest coach in his time. Let's call Stagg the great innovator, Rockne the great modernizer, and Bryant the perfecter.

The tougher question to answer is how Bryant compares to the great coaches who came just before him and who were still coaching when he began his career: his predecessors at Alabama, Wallace Wade (who coached from 1923 to 1941 and 1946 to 1950) and Frank Thomas (1925–1946); Army's Earl "Red" Blaik (1934–1958); Frank Leahy (1939–1953, his first two years at Boston College, the rest at Notre Dame); and Bryant's great nemesis, Tennessee's General Neyland (1926–1940, 1946–1952). These men, at least in the later stage of their careers, all coached a style of football that would be more or less recognizable to the modern fan. All of them have one thing in common: except for a brief interval in the early 1950s when substitution limits were removed, they all coached in the era of what is now referred to as "one-platoon football." Simply defined, this means the players were expected to play on offense and defense. The end of one-platoon football is not clearly delineated; the rules were gradually liberalized nearly every year until 1964, when they were abolished altogether.

It cannot be argued with any real certainty that Bryant was the greatest coach of the one-platoon era. Let's compare his record in the era of limited substitution with the records of the other great coaches whose careers began before World War II and ended shortly after. They are listed in chronological order of their first year. (I am excluding Bud Wilkinson and Woody Hayes from this discussion as I have already compared Bryant's career and theirs elsewhere in this book.)

Era of Limited Substitution

	Seasons Coached	Wins	Losses	Ties	Won-Loss %
Wallace Wade	24	171	49	10	.765
Frank Thomas	19	141	33	9	.795
Robert Neyland	21	173	31	12	.829
Red Blaik	25	166	48	14	.759
Paul Bryant	19	141	49	13	.727

One can argue, with much validity, that Bryant's record has mitigating factors, such as his having to revive *four* moribund football programs. If we exclude Bryant's first season at Texas A&M, 1954, in which he gutted the program and finished 1-9, his only losing season, his won-lost percentage jumps from .727 to .751, just eight points behind Red Blaik. But such arguments are not really needed here. In his first nineteen seasons, Bryant's teams won one national championship (1961), should have won another (1950), and was unbeaten in yet another (1956), proving that he ranked with the greatest coaches of the limited-substitution era. And there is every reason to believe that if Bryant had had the same player talent the other coaches in this comparison had, his record would have been at least their equal.

But what of the coaches in the modern, two-platoon era? Since the early 1960s, only two men stand in genuine comparison with Bryant, Joe Paterno and Bobby Bowden, both of whom have surpassed him in career victories.

There are, of course, two other coaches who have passed Bryant's record. John Gagliardi, who coached football at St. John's Minnesota, is so far ahead on the all-time list with 421 victories that it's unlikely anyone will ever come close to his mark (but then, that was said about both Stagg and Bryant). Bryant's old friend Eddie Robinson of Grambling—who had coached at the school since 1941 and produced such NFL greats as Willie Davis, Doug Williams, Charlie Joiner, Ernie Ladd, and Buck Buchanan, to name just a few—was the first to beat Bryant's mark in 1984. When I interviewed Coach Robinson for the November 1984 issue of *Inside Sports*,* he told me,

---

* Reprinted in *Big Play: Barra On Football*.

When I attended Coach Bryant's funeral, I heard someone say "There's the guy who will break his record." I didn't like that. I don't want to be remembered that way, any more than Coach Bryant wanted to be remembered as the man who broke Amos Alonzo Stagg's record. No one really "replaces" anyone else, regardless of what records you make or break. Bear Bryant, Stagg, Pop Warner, they all have to be considered in the context of their own time and circumstances. I'm sure as far as the people of Alabama are concerned, nobody will ever replace Bear Bryant no matter how many games he wins. I'm sure that whites *and* blacks in Alabama feel that way. I would, however, like to be remembered as a guy who made the same contributions that Bryant did, who influenced people's lives and made an impact on the game.

Coach Robinson was one of the finest gentlemen I have ever met. He lives in Louisiana, suffering from Alzheimer's; his story is the story of black college football in this country and deserves to be told with the same detail with which I have tried to chronicle Paul Bryant's life.

However, without intending to diminish the accomplishments of Coach Gagliardi and Coach Robinson, I should note that they coached at the small-college level.

Bowden and Paterno are another matter. At the end of the 2004 season Bowden's career record was 351-102-4 for a won-lost percentage of .772, while Paterno's was 343-116-3 for a mark of .746. Bryant's career won-lost percentage was .780. Let's compare Bryant's record after the era of unlimited substitution with Paterno and Bowden (and I'm excluding the first four years of Bowden's career at Samford, a small college where he was 34-6):

Era of Unlimited Substitution

	Seasons Coached	Wins	Losses	Ties	Won-Loss %
Paul Bryant	19	182	36	4	.829
Joe Paterno	39	343	116	3	.746
Bobby Bowden	35	317	96	4	.765

Looked at from this perspective, Bryant leaves his modern challengers in the dust. Not only is his won-lost percentage 64 points higher than Bowden's and 83 points higher than Paterno's, he won more national championships in this period than Bowden and Paterno combined. Over the entire course of his career, Bryant won *six* national titles to their combined four. For what it's worth, Bryant was 4-0 in head-to-head meetings with Paterno. (Bryant never coached against Bowden.)

In fact, Bryant, from 1964 to 1982, the era of unlimited substitution, is tied in percentage points with the great General Neyland. Neyland coached his entire career at Tennessee; Bryant coached from 1964 to the end of his career at Alabama. In the second half of Bryant's career, his won-lost percentage was *102 points higher than in the first half.* In other words, freed from the burden of having to revive dead football programs, Bryant proved that he could compile a record as great as any coach's in college football history. (Both Knute Rockne and Frank Leahy had higher won-lost percentages than either Neyland or Bryant, but their careers were much shorter, just thirteen years.)

General Neyland coached at Tennessee for twenty-one seasons; just for fun, let's take Bryant back two seasons at Alabama to include 1963 and 1962, so we can make a twenty-one-season comparison of both men.

Twenty-one-Season Comparison

	Seasons Coached	Wins	Losses	Ties	Won-Loss %
Robert Neyland	1926–1940, 1946–1952	173	31	12	.829
Paul Bryant	1962–1982	201	39	4	.832

The difference in the total number of victories isn't quite fair to Neyland, since fewer games were scheduled in his day and there were fewer bowl possibilities at the end of each season. But one thing is clear: Bryant at his peak established a record slightly better than the legendary Neyland, and he did it in a period when college football was far more sophisticated and competitive in terms of recruiting and NCAA scholarship limitations than in Neyland's day.

There is, however, one major point about Bryant's career that, to my knowledge, has never been made. We can speculate as to how well Stagg and Warner and Rockne and Neyland and other great coaches might have done in the era of two-platoon football and unlimited substitution. And we can also speculate as to how all the great coaches of the last forty-odd years might have done back in the era of limited substitution and one-platoon football. *But Bryant is the only great coach whose career spans both periods. His career is split exactly between the two eras, and he is the only coach in the history of college football who was great in both of them.*

A Point After: Bear Bryant vs. the Hall of Famers

One yardstick for measuring greatness is how a coach performed against the best of his contemporaries. During his career, Bryant faced twenty-four men who would eventually be inducted into the College Football Hall of Fame. In order of the number of times he faced them, here are the results.

Bear's Record against Hall of Fame Coaches

	Wins	Losses	Ties
Ralph "Shug" Jordan	18	5	0
Charlie McClendon	14	2	0
John Vaught	7	6	1
Bobby Dodd	7	2	0
Wally Butts	5	3	0
Robert Neyland	0	5	2
Bowden Wyatt	2	4	1
Vince Dooley	4	2	0
Frank Howard	5	0	0
Joe Paterno	4	0	0
Darrell Royal	0	3	1
Red Sanders	2	2	0
Jerry Claiborne	4	0	0
Bob Devaney	2	1	1
Bud Wilkinson	2	0	0
Ara Parseghian	0	2	0

Dan Devine	0	2	0
Frank Broyles	2	0	0
Pat Dye	1	1	0
John McKay	1	1	0
Tom Osborne	1	1	0
Terry Donahue	1	0	0
Don James	1	0	0
Woody Hayes	1	0	0
Clarence "Biggie" Munn	1	0	0
Totals	**85**	**42**	**6**

Bryant coached 129 games—roughly the equivalent of eleven full seasons—against these coaches. His won-lost percentage against them, .661, is higher than the career won-lost percentage of many coaches in the College Football Hall of Fame.

Appendix 3

Bear by the Numbers

Record as Head Coach

Year	Team	Wins	Losses	Ties	Won-Loss %	Points Scored	Points Gave Up	Differ-ence
1945	Maryland	6	2	1	.722	219	105	114
1946	Kentucky	7	3	0	.700	233	90	143
1947	Kentucky	8	3	0	.727	175	73	102
1948	Kentucky	5	3	2	.600	199	128	71
1949	Kentucky	9	3	0	.750	317	74	243
1950	Kentucky	11	1	0	.917	393	69	324
1951	Kentucky	8	4	0	.667	314	121	193
1952	Kentucky	5	4	2	.545	161	173	−12
1953	Kentucky	7	2	1	.750	201	116	85
1954	Texas A&M	1	9	0	.100	97	177	−80
1955	Texas A&M	7	2	1	.750	160	89	71
1956	Texas A&M	9	0	1	.950	223	81	142
1957	Texas A&M	8	3	0	.727	158	50	108
1958	Alabama	5	4	1	.550	106	75	31

1959	Alabama	7	2	2	.727	95	59	36
1960	Alabama	8	1	2	.818	183	56	127
1961	Alabama	11	0	0	1.000	297	25	272
1962	Alabama	10	1	0	.909	289	39	250
1963	Alabama	9	2	0	.818	227	95	132
1964	Alabama	10	1	0	.909	250	88	162
1965	Alabama	9	1	1	.864	256	107	149
1966	Alabama	11	0	0	1.00	301	44	257
1967	Alabama	8	2	1	.773	204	131	73
1968	Alabama	8	3	0	.727	184	139	45
1969	Alabama	6	5	0	.545	314	268	46
1970	Alabama	6	5	1	.542	334	264	70
1971	Alabama	11	1	0	.917	368	122	246
1972	Alabama	10	2	0	.833	406	150	256
1973	Alabama	11	1	0	.917	477	113	364
1974	Alabama	11	1	0	.917	329	96	233
1975	Alabama	11	1	0	.917	374	72	302
1976	Alabama	9	3	0	.750	327	140	187
1977	Alabama	11	1	0	.917	380	139	241
1978	Alabama	11	1	0	.917	345	168	177
1979	Alabama	12	0	0	1.000	383	67	316
1980	Alabama	10	2	0	.833	352	98	254
1981	Alabama	9	2	1	.792	296	151	145
1982	Alabama	8	4	0	.667	338	216	122
Totals		323	85	17	.780	10,265	4,268	5,997

National Championships
1961, 1964, 1965, 1973, 1978, 1979

Conference Titles (15)
1950 (SEC), 1956 (SWC), 1961, 1964, 1965, 1966, 1971, 1972, 1973, 1974, 1975, 1977, 1978, 1979, 1981 (SEC)

Coach of the Year
1961, 1971, 1973

Complete Records

Player		Wins	Losses	Ties	Won-Loss %
1933	Alabama	7	1	1	.833
1934	Alabama	10	0	0	1.000
1935	Alabama	6	2	1	.722
Totals		23	3	2	.857

Assistant Coach

1936	Alabama	8	0	1	.938
1937	Alabama	9	1	0	.900
1938	Alabama	7	1	1	.833
1939	Alabama	5	3	1	.611
1940	Vanderbilt	3	6	1	.350
1941	Vanderbilt	6	1	2	.778
Totals		38	12	6	.732

Head Coach

Maryland	1 year	6	2	1	.722
Kentucky	8 years	60	23	5	.710
Texas A&M	4 years	25	14	2	.634
Alabama	25 years	232	46	9	.824
Totals	38 years	323	85	17	.780

Bear against His Own

Bryant was 43-6 over his career against his former players and assistant coaches. As Charley McClendon was reputed to have said, "He taught us everything we know, but not everything *he knew*."

	Wins-Losses
Charley McClendon	14-2
Bob Tyler	6-0
Bill Battle	6-1
Steve Sloan	5-0
Jerry Claiborne	4-0
Paul Dietzel	4-1
Charley Pell	1-0
Howard Schnellenberger	1-0
Larry Lacewell	1-0
Pat Dye	1-1
Gene Stallings	0-1

Bowl Records

Kentucky

1947	Great Lakes Bowl (Cleveland, Ohio)	12-6-1947	Villanova	W	24-14
1949	Orange Bowl (Miami)	01-01-1950	Santa Clara	L	13-21
1950	Sugar Bowl (New Orleans)	01-01-1951	Oklahoma	W	13-7
1951	Cotton Bowl (Dallas)	01-01-1952	TCU	W	20-7

Texas A&M

1957	Gator Bowl (Jacksonville)	12-28-1957	Tennessee	L	0-3

Alabama

1959	Liberty Bowl (Philadelphia)	12-19-1959	Penn State	L	0-7
1960	Bluebonnet Bowl (Houston)	12-17-1960	Houston	T	3-3
1962	Sugar Bowl (New Orleans)	01-01-1962	Arkansas	W	10-3
1963	Orange Bowl (Miami)	01-01-1963	Oklahoma	W	17-0
1964	Sugar Bowl (New Orleans)	01-01-1964	Ole Miss	W	12-7
1965	Orange Bowl (Miami)	01-01-1965	Texas	L	17-21
1966	Orange Bowl (Miami)	01-01-1966	Nebraska	W	39-28
1967	Sugar Bowl (New Orleans)	01-02-1967	Nebraska	W	34-7
1968	Cotton Bowl (Dallas)	01-01-1968	Texas A&M	L	16-20
1968	Gator Bowl (Jacksonville)	12-29-1968	Missouri	L	10-35
1969	Liberty Bowl (Memphis)	12-13-1969	Colorado	L	33-47
1970	Astro-Bluebonnet Bowl (Houston)	12-31-1970	Oklahoma	T	24-24
1972	Orange Bowl (Miami)	01-01-1972	Nebraska	L	6-38
1973	Cotton Bowl (Dallas)	01-01-1973	Texas	L	13-17
1973	Sugar Bowl (New Orleans)	12-31-1973	Notre Dame	L	23-24

1975	Orange Bowl (Miami)	01-01-1975	Note Dame	L	11-13
1975	Sugar Bowl (New Orleans)	12-31-1975	Penn State	W	13-6
1976	Liberty Bowl (Memphis)	12-20-1976	UCLA	W	36-6
1978	Sugar Bowl (New Orleans)	01-02-1978	Ohio State	W	35-6
1979	Sugar Bowl (New Orleans)	01-01-1979	Penn State	W	14-7
1980	Sugar Bowl (New Orleans)	01-01-1980	Arkansas	W	24-9
1981	Cotton Bowl (Dallas)	01-01-1981	Baylor	W	30-2
1982	Cotton Bowl (Dallas)	01-01-1982	Texas	L	12-14
1982	Liberty Bowl	12-29-1982	Illinois	W	21-15
	Totals		15	12	2

Bear by the Decade

		Record	Won-loss %	
1940s	(1945–1950)	46-15-3	.742	
1950s	(1951–1960)	64-31-10	.657	
1960s	(1961–1970)	98-20-3	.822	(Best in Country)
1970s	(1971–1980)	107-13	.892	(Best in Country)
1980s	(1981–1982)	17-6-1	.724	

Appendix 4

Chronology

September 11, 1913

Paul William Bryant is born in Moro Bottom in south central Arkansas. Moro Bottom isn't a town but merely a plot named for nearby Moro Creek. Paul is the eleventh of twelve children born to William Monroe and Ida Mae Kilgore Bryant (three other Bryant children died in infancy).

1924

The Bryant family moves a few miles south to Fordyce, Arkansas, a railroad junction town of perhaps 3,700 people. Ida Mae's family owns substantial property in Fordyce, and there is a school for Paul to attend.

1926

Paul is walking by the practice field for the Redbugs football team of Fordyce High School when he sees his first scrimmage. The coach, or so the legend goes, recruits him on the spot.

1927

The most likely year for the first legendary event in Paul's life. At the Fordyce Theatre, Paul wrestles a muzzled bear from a local traveling carnival. He does it to impress a local girl and also for the money—the extraordinary sum of one dollar a minute. The owner of the bear skips town without paying, and all Paul got out of it was some bruises and a nickname.

1930

Paul—now called "Bear" by his teammates—helps lead the Redbugs to a perfect season and the state championship of Arkansas.

1931

University of Alabama assistant coach Hank Crisp—Coach Hank, as he will come to be known—comes to Fordyce to tap the school's pipeline of football talent. He doesn't get the players he came for, but he does return to Tuscaloosa with Paul Bryant.

1934

Paul, a junior, is a standout on Frank Thomas's 10-0 Crimson Tide led by quarterback Dixie Howell and end Don Hutson. (Bryant, playing in Hutson's shadow, is referred to as "the other end.") Alabama, a substantial underdog, goes to the Rose Bowl and defeats mighty Stanford, 29-13, to win several polls as the national champions of college football.

1935

Paul and his college sweetheart, Mary Harmon Black, are married in Ozark, Alabama. They keep the marriage a secret; Coach Thomas doesn't want his players to be married, and Paul fears the loss of his football scholarship.

In October, Paul plays against Alabama's biggest rival, Tennessee, with a broken bone in his leg, making newspaper headlines across the South. (Alabama beats Tennessee, 25-0.)

1936

Frank Thomas offers Paul a job as an Alabama assistant coach at $1,250 a year. Paul needs the job; Mae Martin, his first child, is born that year.

1937

Paul goes to California as an assistant coach with the Alabama football team. In Hollywood, he renews an acquaintance with former-Alabama-player-turned-cowboy-star Johnny Mack Brown and gets a screen test. He is offered a contract, but an indignant Mary Harmon isn't moving. Paul abandons his dreams of Hollywood glory and returns to football.

1940

Bryant takes a job at Vanderbilt under head coach Red Sanders and helps coach the Commodores to a much-publicized 7-0 upset over Alabama.

1941

His Vanderbilt job is cut short after a falling-out with Sanders that is never explained. With the help of New York Yankees catching great Bill Dickey, Arkansas's most famous athlete, Bryant has the inside track for the head coaching job at the University of Arkansas. Then, on December 7, Pearl Harbor is bombed and Bryant enlists in the U.S. Navy.

1943

The troop ship USS *Uruguay* is rammed by another ship in the convoy while sailing to North Africa. Bryant disobeys the order to abandon ship and survives; at least two hundred soldiers and sailors died.

1944

Lieutenant Commander Paul Bryant is sent to North Carolina to train new enlistees. He assembles the North Carolina Navy Pre-Flight football team, the nucleus of his first winning team at Maryland. Paul Bryant Jr. is born on December 19.

1945

Accepting the head coaching job at Maryland, he turns the Terrapins football program around in one season, with a 6-2-1 record. His stars are the players he took with him from North Carolina Navy Pre-Flight.

1946

Following a dispute with Maryland president Curley Byrd over the suspension of a player, Bryant leaves Maryland and accepts the head coaching job at Kentucky. The Wildcats go from 2-8 to 7-3 in their first season under Bryant.

1947

Achieving an 8-3 record, Bryant takes the Wildcats to a Great Lakes Bowl victory over Villanova, the first ever postseason appearance ever by Kentucky.

1950

After an 11-1 season marred only by a 7-0 loss to General Neyland's Tennessee Volunteers, the Wildcats, with Babe Parilli at quarterback, win their first (and so far only) Southeastern Conference title. On New Year's Day, they win the biggest victory in Kentucky football history, a 13-7 victory in the Sugar Bowl over Bud Wilkinson's Oklahoma Sooners. The loss ends Oklahoma's thirty-one-game winning streak. Many regard Kentucky as the number-one team in the country.

1953

After posting a 7-2-1 record, Bryant asks to be released from his contract at Kentucky for the head coaching job at Texas A&M. His decision to leave Kentucky was precipitated by Adolph Rupp's decision not to resign—or by Kentucky President Donovan's failure to force Rupp to retire—in the wake of a basketball scandal that rocked Kentucky athletics.

1954

Bryant inherits yet another dismal football team at Texas A&M and decides to torch the program and start nearly from scratch. Fewer than thirty players returned with him from a brutal practice session at Junction, Texas. The Aggies finish 1-9, the only losing season in Bryant's career. To Bryant's and the school's astonishment, the Aggies are put on probation by the NCAA for recruiting violations.

1955

In the ninth game of the season, at Rice, the Aggies trail 12-0 with about two minutes left to play. They stage a miracle rally that turns their season around. Texas A&M finishes 7-2-1.

1956

Bryant guides Texas A&M to a 9-0-1 record and the Southwest Conference title, defeating Texas. It is the first time the Aggies have ever defeated the hated Longhorns on their home field.

1957

John David Crow becomes Bryant's only Heisman Trophy winner, but at the end of the season it is revealed that Bryant has accepted an offer to return to his alma mater, the University of Alabama. The dispirited Aggies lose to Tennessee 3-0 in the Gator Bowl.

1958

Bryant begins the turnaround of a fourth football program, at Alabama. The team goes from 2-7-1 in 1957 to 5-4-1 under Bryant.

1959

Alabama beats cross-state rival Auburn for the first time since 1953, to finish the regular season 7-1-2. Bryant accepts a bid to the Liberty Bowl in Philadelphia, where Alabama faces its first racially integrated team, the Penn State Nittany Lions. On a frozen field, they lose 7-0.

1960

ABC's new head of sports programming, Roone Arledge, selects the Alabama-Georgia game to showcase his revolutionary techniques for broadcasting college football. The country gets its first substantial look at Bear Bryant and the Crimson Tide. Arledge and Bryant will give the country many memorable TV games in the years to come.

1961

Bryant delivers on his promise to his 1958 freshmen that if they believed in themselves and in him, they would win the national championship. They finished the season 10-0 and then swept the polls by defeating Arkansas in the Sugar Bowl.

In the ninth game of the season, Alabama's Darwin Holt smashes into Georgia Tech's Chick Graning on a punt return play and sends him to the hospital. The play will get national publicity and trigger the most publicized controversy of Bryant's career.

1962

An article by the *Atlanta Constitution*'s Furman Bisher in the *Saturday Evening Post* accuses Bryant of coaching brutal football. Bryant sues Curtis Publishing,

1963

On New Year's Day, Alabama, led by future NFL stars Joe Namath and Lee Roy Jordan, defeats Oklahoma and Bryant's old friend Bud Wilkinson, 17-0, in the Orange Bowl. President Kennedy snubs Alabama to pay a visit to the Sooners' locker room.

In March, the *Saturday Evening Post* published a second story accusing Bryant and Georgia athletic director Wally Butts of having fixed the 1962 Georgia-Alabama game. Both Butts and Bryant initiate lawsuits. On August 20, Butts wins his case. Five months later, Curtis decides to settle out of court with Bryant for $360,000. One *Saturday Evening Post* editor later says Butts's and Bryant's victories helped to put the magazine out of business.

In the fall of 1963, Bryant makes more national headlines by suspending his quarterback, Joe Namath, for breaking team rules.

1964

The Crimson Tide wins its second national championship under Bryant, finishing the regular season 10-0.

1966

The Crimson Tide, which began New Year's Day ranked number four, beats Nebraska 39-28 in the Orange Bowl on New Year's Day to win its second-straight national title.

1968

On December 10, Dr. Pat Trammell, quarterback of Bryant's first national championship team, dies of cancer at age twenty-eight. In his autobiography, Bryant calls it "the saddest day of my life."

1970

On September 12, the University of Southern California, led by fullback Sam "The Bam" Cunningham, beats Alabama 42-21 at Birmingham's Legion Field. It is the first time an integrated college football team comes to play in the state of Alabama.

Wilbur Jackson becomes the first black player to accept a grant-in-aid from Alabama.

1971

Alabama stuns Southern Cal at the Los Angeles Coliseum on September 10 when Bryant unveils Alabama's new "wishbone" attack. John Mitchell becomes the first black player to start for the Crimson Tide.

1973

On New Year's Eve, Alabama and Notre Dame, both unbeaten, face each other for the first time, playing for the national championship in the Sugar Bowl. The lead changes hands six times, with Notre Dame winning 24-23, the margin of a missed extra point. Many call it the greatest college football game ever played.

Before the start of the football season John Mitchell becomes Alabama's first black assistant coach.

1978

On January 2 in the Sugar Bowl, Bryant and the Crimson Tide square off against the Ohio State Buckeyes and Woody Hayes, the active coach who is closest to Bryant in number of victories. Alabama wins easily, 35-6.

1979

On New Year's Day, Alabama defeats number one–ranked Penn State 14-7 to win the national title. The game is decided when Alabama stops Penn State at the one-yard line late in the fourth quarter in what is probably the most famous defensive stand in college football history.

1980

January 1, Alabama defeats Arkansas 24-9 in the Sugar Bowl, finishing 12-0 and winning Bryant's sixth and final national championship.

1981

Alabama defeats Auburn 28-17 in Birmingham for Bryant's 315th career victory. At the time, Amos Alonzo Stagg was known to have only 314 wins, making Bryant the winningest coach ever in college football.

1982

Bryant officially announces his retirement as head coach of the University of Alabama football team on December 15.

On December 29, in the Bear's last game, Jeremiah Castille intercepts three passes in the Liberty Bowl as Alabama wins 21-15. It is Bryant's 323rd and final victory.

1983

After being admitted to Druid City Hospital in Tuscaloosa with chest pains, Bryant suffers a heart attack on January 26 and is pronounced dead at 1:30 p.m. CST. He is sixty-nine years old.

Paul Bryant is interred at Elmwood Cemetery in Birmingham on January 28 after a funeral procession that began in Tuscaloosa and was witnessed by perhaps a quarter of a million people.

Acknowledgments

I SUPPOSE I HAVE been planning to write a book on Bear Bryant for more than thirty years and did not realize it. When I finally decided to embark on this project and began looking through my own collection, I found I had saved nearly three boxes of newspaper clippings, magazine articles, programs, and books, some dating back to the mid-1960s. I had lugged them to Houston, to Chicago, to Brooklyn, and, finally, to South Orange, New Jersey, where they formed the core of the research for this book. If I hadn't been planning to write this all along, why had I saved all these things?

Still, I truly did not understand what a massive undertaking I had begun, and how much about Bryant's life and career I did not know, until I was well into it. Many times over the years, I've seen the phrase in acknowledgments "this book could not have been written without the assistance of . . ." and I don't think I really appreciated what those words meant until I finished *The Last Coach*.

The Paul W. Bryant Museum in Tuscaloosa is a biographer's dream, a place that never fails to give me goose bumps every time I return. Ken Gaddy, Brad Green, and Taylor Watson never let me leave without bags of materials and, when I returned home, answered questions for me by email on an almost daily basis for a year and a half. Coach Clem Gryska was my closest and most direct link to Alabama history and Coach Bryant. He sat for two long interview sessions and several extended telephone conversations, and, perhaps most important of all, he vouched for me with scores of former players, coaches, and friends of Coach Bryant. Thanks to Matt Pulsifer, an Alabama student from Massachusetts who overcame the neurological disorder of being a Red Sox fan and did yeoman work locating and researching photographs.

Mrs. Agnes Phillips and her husband, Colonel Jimmy, opened up to me the history and lore of the wonderful little town of Fordyce, Arkansas. Not only did Mrs. Phillips supply me with names and telephone numbers of numerous friends and relations of Coach Bryant, she gave me letters, newspaper clippings, and, perhaps most invaluable of all, videotaped interviews of the Coach's family and friends, all of whom have since passed on. It was a thrill to see them and hear their voices; their recollections conveyed the post–World War I life that Paul grew up in in a way that no print material could have. I feel honored to have known these people, if only secondhand. There were times when I felt as if I had been in the theater with young Paul Bryant the night he wrestled the bear.

I attended the University of Alabama in Birmingham with George McAdams in the 1970s, lost track of him over the years, and was surprised and delighted when he contacted me two decades later when he saw my column in the *Wall Street Journal.* George sent me tapes and DVDs with rarely seen interviews with Coach Bryant, old Alabama game films such as the 1979 Sugar Bowl against Penn State and the 315th win against Auburn, and media accounts of Bryant's 315th win, retirement, and death as well as his funeral. Best of all, he sent me several episodes of *The Bear Bryant Show.*

David Briley, assistant professor of political science at East Tennessee State University, has been working on his own book on the integration of the Alabama football team and generously shared his time, material, contacts, and, above all, his own insight. The time he saved me is incalculable.

Jake Reiss of the Alabama Booksmith honed the manuscript for errors and supplied me with scrapbooks and pictures from his years with the Birmingham Touchdown Club. His tape from Coach Bryant's sixty-fifth surprise birthday party was priceless. The late Sid Studin, father of my friend Robert, took me to my first Alabama-Auburn game.

Mickey Herskowitz allowed me to quote generously from his memoir, *The Legend of Bear Bryant,* spent hours re-creating Coach Bryant's years at Texas A&M in detail, and shared personal photos. Mickey's assistance on this book was essential because he had a longer unbroken relationship with Bryant than did any other journalist, and remained close friends with him after Bryant left Texas A&M in 1957. It's possible that no other living person has a better perspective on Bryant's life and work than Mickey.

In addition to Coach Gryska, former Alabama assistant coaches Larry "Dude" Hennessey, Mal Moore, and Jack Rutledge all took time to explain Coach Bryant's strategy, tactics, and training methods in great detail.

For background on Bryant's years in Moro Bottom and Fordyce, I would like to thank, again, Colonel and Mrs. Phillips, Coach Bryant's late sister Louise Goolsby, the Coach's grandnephew Ray Bryant, Larry Lacewell, Coach Jimmy "Red" Parker, Ruth Jordan, Buster Garlington, and Dr. Garth Russell. The late Mel Allen was a wealth of information on the University of Alabama in the 1930s when I interviewed him in 1982 for an intended *Inside Sports* profile on Bryant that I never got to write. Vic Turyn, Joe Drach, Harry Bonk, Sammy Behr, and Frank Sadler shared their Maryland experiences with me. George Blanda, Babe Parilli, Bob Gain, Walt Yowarksy, Dude Hennessey, Howard Schnellenberger, Frank Sadler, Paul Dietzel, Steve Meilinger, Darrell Royal, and Russell Rice were all enormously helpful on Coach Bryant's years at Kentucky. For the Texas A&M years, Jim Dent shared stories with me that he did not use in his own book. I also relied heavily on the late Jones Ramsey (who was introduced to me by Mickey Herskowitz) and his son, Paul Ramsey, Gene Stallings, Ken Hall, Jack Pardee, Bobby Drake Keith, Henry Clark, John David Crow, and, most of all, Dennis Goehring, who is one of the most amazing talkers I have ever had the privilege of listening to. Bart Starr was helpful in describing Alabama football in the 1950s before Coach Bryant.

On Coach Bryant's return and his first few seasons at Alabama, Tom Stoddard contributed much, as did Tommy Brooker, Billy Richardson, Billy Neighbors, Steve Wright, Darwin Holt, Bill Battle, Mal Moore, Coach Gryska, and Lee Roy Jordan. On Alabama's first big nationally televised game and Coach Bryant's special relationship with Roone Arledge, I thank Andy Sidaris and Curt Gowdy. I also derived much information on Arledge and his grand design for college football from Bert Randolph Sugar.

Jay Wilkinson, son of the late great coach Bud Wilkinson, shared his memories of his father's relationship with Coach Bryant. Chick Graning and Darwin Holt were gracious in recalling the calamitous 1961 Georgia Tech game. On the similarities between Coach Bryant and Coach Vince

Lombardi, as well as the friendship between Coach Bryant and Coach Bobby Dodd, I thank Bill Curry. On the investigation of Coach Bryant by Curtis Publishing, I am indebted to Bard Lindeman. On the settlement of Coach Bryant's lawsuit against Curtis Publishing, I thank Francis Hare Jr. Steve Sloan gave me background on the 1965 championship team, and Jerry Duncan helped me with the 1965 and 1966 teams. On Coach Bryant's uneasy relationship with George Wallace and the struggle to integrate the Alabama football team, I wish to thank my good friend Diane McWhorter, the late Marshall Frady, David Briley, Jimmy Bryan, Clyde Bolton, and Dr. Wayne Flint. On the first integrated football game in Birmingham against Southern Cal and the following year's game against the Trojans in Los Angeles, I thank Doug Layton, Craig Fertig, Jimmy Bryan, and Bill Lumpkin. On Coach Bryant's conversion to the wishbone formation, I thank Darrell Royal. On the first two seasons of integration of the Alabama football team, I thank Coach Gryska, John David Crow, Wilbur Jackson, and John Mitchell.

On the 1970s, I am indebted to the late Al Browning, Bill Lumpkin, Coach Bryant's secretary Linda Knowles, the late Charley Thornton, Johnny Musso, Scott Hunter, Sylvester Croom, Ozzie Newsome, Gary Rutledge, Buddy Aydelette, Marty Lyons, and Barry Krauss. For an inside look on the classic 1973 Sugar Bowl, I thank former Notre Dame quarterback and current Buffalo Bills offensive coordinator Tom Clements. A special thanks to Kent Waldrep for sharing his personal experiences with Coach Bryant and Mary Harmon after his accident in the 1974 game against Texas Christian University, and for opening up his personal photo album. Joan Perry and Julie Strauss gave me an inside look at *The Bear Bryant Show*. Coach Bill Battle detailed the marketing of Bear Bryant for me. I thank John Nicola Jr. for his recollections of Coach Bryant's visit to the Alabama Booster Club of Bridgeport, Pennsylvania.

On Coach Bryant's final seasons, I especially thank the late Al Browning, the late Charley Thornton, Pat Dye, Walter Lewis, Kirk McNair, and Paul Carruth. For the story on the announcing of Coach Bryant's retirement, I thank Herschel Nissenson. Thanks to the late Pat James for sharing anecdotes about Bryant at Kentucky and especially the story of Coach Bryant's relationship with Shug Jordan. On Coach Bryant's astute handling of the national media, I thank Hoyt Harwell. Gene Schoor offered insight into Coach Bryant's shrewd handling of the eastern press. Special thanks to

George Steinbrenner for several anecdotes on his long friendship with Coach Bryant. Special thanks, too, to the Coach's grandson, Marc Tyson, who offered me a rare inside look at Coach Bryant's family life and passed on to me the inspirational poem that Bryant carried in his wallet for years.

Thanks to Bob Blalock, Bob Carlton, Alec Harvey, and Linda Stafford of the *Birmingham News* for their time, patience, and research. Jimmy Smothers, sports editor of the *Gadsden Times*, was generous in recounting moments from his long friendship with Coach Bryant and Mary Harmon. Thanks to Lynda Cardwell for her inside account of Coach Bryant's last press conference.

And thanks, too, to Paul Finebaum for recollecting Bryant's last seasons in Birmingham and the transition to Ray Perkins. Also, thanks to Pat Smith for digging out so many phone numbers and addresses.

I single out for thanks John Underwood, who generously allowed me to quote extensively from Coach Bryant's memoir, *Bear: The Hard Times and Good Life of Alabama's Coach Bryant*. There are so many places in this book where the sound of Bryant's own voice has an authority and richness that simply could not be conveyed by paraphrasing. In allowing me to quote from *Bear* frequently, Underwood has given me a direct connection to Coach Bryant that would have otherwise been impossible.

Sadly, a number of people who spoke to me on this book passed away before it was finished. I'd like to mention their names again—Marshall Frady, Louise Goolsby, Pat James, Charlie McClendon, Jones Ramsey, Charley Thornton. Mel Allen, John Forney, and Al Browning were all sources of great Alabama stories over the years, and I wish they had lived long enough to see this book in print.

I want to thank my agent, Jay Mandel of William Morris Agency, for being skeptical about this project when I first approached him, forcing me to think it through clearly. My editor, Robert Weil, was enthusiastic about the book from the get-go. Special thanks to Tom Mayer of W. W. Norton, who proved to know a great deal about Alabama football for an infidel, for carrying this project into overtime. The enthusiasm of Norton's director of sales, Bill Rusin, sustained me at times when this project seemed overwhelming, and my publicist, Winfrida Mbewe, made the last phase of this book a genuine pleasure.

Three more people who urged me to write a book on Bryant years ago should also be mentioned: the late Willie Morris, with whom I helped contribute a Bryant anecdote to the script of *Mississippi Burning* when we visited the set; Kent Carroll, who edited my 1998 book, *Inventing Wyatt Earp*, and who loves to gas about Bear Bryant and Alabama; and Michael Anderson of the *New York Times Book Review*, who nagged me to "stop wasting your [meaning me] time and write a book about Bear Bryant."

Also at the *New York Times*, thanks to the many editors from different departments over the years who have edited my stories on football: Jon Landman, Tom Kuntz, Scott Veale, Katy Roberts, Toby Harshaw, Susan B. Adams, Sam Tanenhaus, and Kyle Chrichton. Marty Gottlieb is now at the *Times*, but at the *Village Voice* many years ago he edited the first story I ever wrote on Bear Bryant, for which I am eternally grateful.

From the *Wall Street Journal*, I am indebted to the late Lee Lescaze, who first encouraged me to write about the football there; Paul Steiger, who gave me such free reign; and my several fine editors, including Erin Friar, Steve McKee, Eric Gibson, Barbara Phillips, and Michael Philips.

Thanks to Geoff Norman, Roy Blount Jr., and Richard Price for sharing their Bear Bryant stories. Thanks, also, to Ian Frazier for allowing me to identify him as the author of the *New Yorker* "Talk of the Town" piece written after Bryant's death. Special thanks to Mark Mayfield, former editor of the *Crimson White* and current editor in chief of *House Beautiful* for sending me his copies of the *Saturday Evening Post* with the controversial stories on Bryant.

Thanks to the *New York Times*'s Bill Pennington, the go-to guy for Heisman Trophy information, who pointed out to me that Joe Namath never finished in the top ten in Heisman voting. I will always be grateful to Steve Wasserman, former editor of the *Los Angeles Times Book Review*, for telling me a couple of years ago, "I don't know much about football, but that's a great idea for a book." Keith Jackson made the 1979 Sugar Bowl come alive for me a second time in our conversations.

As always, I want to thank my mother, Lorraine Arnwine, who proves that good biographers, like good football players, come from good mamas, and my stepfather, Grover Arnwine, who has held together a family of Alabama and Auburn fans without bloodshed for over twenty-five years. Finally, thanks to my wife, Jonelle, with whom I lived most of the memories of this book and then relived them in the course of writing and editing, and my daughter, Maggie, who can't wait to go to her first Alabama-Auburn game and shake hands with Alabama's mascot, Big Al.

Notes

Introduction

1. Norman, *Alabama Showdown*, p. 219.
2. *Newark Star-Ledger*, Nov. 12, 2003.
3. Interview on *ESPN Classic Sports Century*: "Bear Bryant", Dec. 13, 2002.

Prologue

1. Videotapes of Bryant's retirement speech, Dec. 15, 1982.

Chapter 1: Up from the Bottom

1. Forney, *Above the Noise of the Crowd*, p. 32.
2. *Birmingham News*, quoted in Bolton, *Crimson Tide—A Story*, p. 38.
3. *Los Angeles Evening Herald*, Jan. 2, 1926.
4. Heffelfinger, *This Was Football*, p. 131.
5. Williams, *Paul Bryant*, p. 20.
6. Cash, *Mind of the South*, p. 24.
7. Ibid., p. 46.
8. Interview with Dean Kilgore, on videotape, courtesy of the Dallas County Museum, Fordyce, Arkansas.
9. Interview (cousin not specified), on videotape, courtesy of the Dallas County Museum.
10. Interviews with Kelsey Kaplinger, on videotape, courtesy of the Dallas County Museum.
11. Interview with Dean Kilgore, on videotape, courtesy of the Dallas County Museum.
12. Dunnavant, *Coach*, p. 23.

13. John Underwood, *Sports Illustrated*, Aug. 15, 1966.

14. Ibid.

15. Interview with Jack Benham, on videotape, courtesy of the Dallas County Museum.

16. Interview with Dean Kilgore, on videotape, courtesy of the Dallas County Museum.

17. Story related by Mickey Herskowitz, *The Legend of Bear Bryant*, p. 41.

18. Interview with Dean Kilgore, on videotape, courtesy of the Dallas County Museum.

19. Videotape, courtesy of the Paul W. Bryant Museum, Tuscaloosa, Alabama.

20. Arkansas Gazette, Sunday Magazine, Nov. 18, 1956.

21. Ibid.

22. Ibid.

23. Interview made available courtesy of the Dallas County Museum.

24. Interview with Dean Kilgore, on videotape, courtesy of the Dallas County Museum.

25. Interview with Click Jordan, on videotape, courtesy of the Dallas County Museum.

Chapter 2: You Gotta Be a Football Hero

1. Heffelfinger, *This Was Football*, p. 20.

2. McCallum and Pearson, *College Football, U.S.A., 1869–1971*.

3. Heffelfinger, *This Was Football*, p. 28.

4. Bolton, *Crimson Tide—A Story*, p. 23.

5. *Birmingham Daily News*, Dec. 26, 1925.

6. Bolton, *Crimson Tide—A Story*, p. 13.

7. Ibid., p. 73.

8. *Birmingham Daily News*, Dec. 26, 1925.

9. *Los Angeles Times*, Dec. 19, 1925.

10. Bolton, *Crimson Tide—A Story*, p. 33.

11. Furman Bisher, *Sport* magazine, May 1958.

12. Noble, Introduction, in Huie, *Mud on the Stars*, p. x.

13. John Underwood, *Sports Illustrated*, Aug. 15, 1966.

14. Bolton, *Crimson Tide—A Story*, p. 32.

15. Stone, *Coach Tommy of the Crimson Tide*, p. 27.

16. *New York Herald-Tribune*, Oct. 19, 1924.

17. Stone, *Coach Tommy of The Crimson Tide*, p. 20.

18. Ibid., p. 68.

19. Ibid., p. 81.

20. Browning, *I Remember Bear Bryant*, p. 17.

21. Bolton, *Crimson Tide—A Story*, p. 48.

22. *Tuscaloosa News*, Sept. 2, 1971.

23. Groom, *Crimson Tide—An Illustrated History*, p. 124.

24. *San Diego Union*, Jan. 2, 1935.

25. *Los Angeles Times,* Jan. 2, 1935.
26. Browning, *I Remember Bear Bryant,* p. 16.
27. Ibid.
28. Ralph McGill, *Atlanta Constitution,* Oct. 20, 1935.

Chapter 3: Coach in Progress
1. McCallum and Pearson, *College Football, U.S.A., 1869–1971,* p. 422.
2. Interview with Collins Kilgore, on videotape, courtesy of the Dallas County Museum.
3. John Underwood, *Sports Illustrated,* Aug. 22, 1966.
4. Heffelfinger, *This Was Football,* p. 144.
5. John Underwood, *Sports Illustrated,* Aug. 22, 1966.
6. CBS, *The Bear: The Legend of Coach Paul Bryant,* Jan. 12, 2002.
7. Interview on *ESPN Classic Sports Century,* "Bear Bryant," Dec. 13, 2002.
8. Letter, courtesy of the Paul W. Bryant Museum.

Chapter 4: New Kentucky Home
1. Twombly, *Blanda,* p. 114.
2. Ibid., p. 108.
3. Letter, courtesy of George Blanda and the Paul W. Bryant Museum.
4. Heffelfinger, *This Was Football,* p. 114.
5. Ibid., p. 103.
6. Sugar, *SEC,* p. 105.
7. John Underwood, *Sports Illustrated,* Aug. 22, 1966.
8. *The Adolph Rupp Show,* on videotape, winter 1970.
9. *Time,* Sept. 29, 1980.
10. Quoted by Carter, *Politics of Rage,* p. 355.

Chapter 5: Gone to Texas
1. Dent, *Junction Boys,* p. 3.
2. Browning, *I Remember Bear Bryant,* p. 43.
3. Popularly attributed to Sheridan, when he was assigned as military governor of Texas after the Civil War.
4. Charles Hall to an interviewer in CBS, *The Bear: the Legend of Coach Paul Bryant,* Jan. 12, 2002.
5. Bum Phillips to Adam Schefter, *Denver Post,* Jan. 27, 2004.
6. John Underwood, *Sports Illustrated,* Aug. 22, 1966.
7. *Fort Worth Star Telegram,* May 26, 1955.
8. John Underwood, *Sports Illustrated,* Oct. 22, 1966.
9. *Houston Post,* Nov. 20, 1956.
10. Heffelfinger, *This Was Football,* p. 123.
11. Furman Bisher, *Sport* magazine, May 1958.
12. Bryant, *Building a Championship Football Team,* p. 12.
13. Bolton, *Crimson Tide—A Story,* p. 190.

14. Herskowitz, *Legend of Bear Bryant*, p. 117.

Chapter 6: The Second Coming

1. *Birmingham Daily News*, Feb. 23, 1893.
2. Norman, *Alabama Showdown*, p. 27.
3. Stoddard, *Turnaround*, p. 19.
4. Ibid., p. 39.
5. John Underwood, *Sports Illustrated*, Aug. 29, 1966.
6. Forney and Townsend, *Talk of the Tide*, p. 79.
7. Stoddard, *Turnaround*, p. 92.
8. Ibid., p. 59.
9. Ibid., p. 60–61.
10. Gunther and Carter, *Monday Night Mayhem*, p. 6.
11. Ibid., p. 7.
12. Arledge, *Roone*, p. 114.
13. Gunther and Carter, *Monday Night Mayhem*, p. 8.
14. Bryant, *Building a Championship Football Team*, p. 1.
15. Ibid., p. 4.
16. Ibid., p. 186.
17. Ibid., p. 24.

Chapter 7: Bear Accused

The Southeastern Conference no longer has a file on the suits involving Wally Butts, Paul Bryant, and Curtis Publishing. All quotes relating to the lawsuits are taken from *Fumble—Bear Bryant, Wally Butts, and the Great College Football Scandal* by Professor James Kirby, who was the SEC's official observer. I am also grateful to the inside account of the workings of Curtis Publishing provided to me by Mr. Bard Lindeman and to Francis Hare Jr., Bryant's Birmingham attorney, for an inside look at his father's work on the suit.

1. John Underwood, *Sports Illustrated*, Aug. 29, 1966.
2. *Time*, Oct. 27, 1961.
3. *Atlanta Journal*, Nov. 19, 1961.
4. *Atlanta Constitution*, Nov. 19, 1961.
5. John Underwood, *Sports Illustrated*, Aug. 29, 1966.
6. *Atlanta Constitution*, Nov. 20, 1961.
7. Wright, *I'd Rather Be Wright*, p. 6.
8. Ibid., p. 12.
9. Herskowitz, *Legend of Bear Bryant*, p. 147.
10. Kriegel, *Namath*, p. 20.
11. Ibid., p. 67.
12. Ibid.
13. *Saturday Evening Post*, Oct. 20, 1962.
14. Ibid.
15. Ibid.

16. Ibid.
17. Kriegel, *Namath*, p. 85.
18. Wilkinson and Hirsch, *Bud Wilkinson*, p. 97.
19. Identified by Professor James Kirby in his book on the trial, *Fumble*, as "a Chicago beer dealer who gambled on college football games," p. 31.
20. Otto Friedrich, quoted in Kirby, *Fumble*, p. 57.
21. Graham, *Farewell to Heroes*, p. 290.
22. Ibid., p. 289.
23. Ibid., p. 295.
24. John Underwood, *Sports Illustrated*, Aug. 29, 1966.
25. Herskowitz, *Legend of Bear Bryant*, p. 133.
26. Ibid.
27. *Saturday Evening Post*, Mar. 23, 1963.
28. Ibid.
29. *New York Herald-Tribune*, Mar. 20, 1963.
30. *Sports Illustrated*, Apr. 8, 1963.
31. John Underwood, *Sports Illustrated*, Sept. 5, 1966.
32. Graham, *Farewell to Heroes*, p. 297.
33. Friedrich, *Decline and Fall*, p. 274.
34. Graham, *Farewell to Heroes*, p. 290.

Chapter 8: High Tide

1. Frady, *Wallace*, p. 82.
2. Carter, *Politics of Rage*, p. 104.
3. Ibid., p. 71.
4. Ibid., p. 112.
5. Bob Philips, *Birmingham Post-Herald*, Dec. 11, 1963.
6. Al Browning, *Bowl, 'Bama, Bowl*, p. 149.
7. *New Orleans Times-Picayune*, Dec. 29, 1963.
8. *New Republic*, Jan. 24, 1983.
9. *Look*, Nov. 16, 1965.
10. *Sports Illustrated*, Nov. 28, 1966.

Chapter 9: Ebb Tide

1. Stabler and Stainback, *Snake*, p. 46.
2. Ibid.
3. Ibid., p. 40.
4. Interview on *ESPN Classic Sports Century*, "Bear Bryant," Dec. 13, 2002.
5. Stabler and Stainback, *Snake*, p. 54.
6. Ibid., p. 55.
7. Ibid., p. 56.
8. *Birmingham News*, Dec. 3, 1967.
9. Groom, *Crimson Tide: An Illustrated History*, p. 132.
10. *Los Angeles Times*, Sept. 13, 1970.

11. *USC Report*, Sept. 5, 2000.
12. *Mobile Register*, Aug. 24, 2003.
13. McKay, *McKay*, pp. 14–15.
14. Briley, "*Second Reconstruction*."
15. Ibid.
16. Interview with U. W. Clemon by David Briley.

Chapter 10: Bear Redux

1. Forney, *Above the Noise of the Crowd*, p. 133.
2. *Los Angeles Herald-Examiner*, Sept. 11, 1971.
3. *Sports Illustrated*, Oct. 4, 1971.
4. Reprinted in Jenkins's *Saturday's America*, "The Cream Gravy Game," p. 175.
5. Ford, *Bama under Bear*, p. 223.
6. *Sports Illustrated*, Jan. 7, 1974.
7. *Birmingham Post-Herald*, Jan. 1, 1974.
8. Recorded in Browning, *Bowl, 'Bama, Bowl*, p. 223.
9. Herskowitz, *Legend of Bear Bryant*, p. 211–212.
10. *Esquire*, Sept. 1975.
11. Browning, *I Remember Bear Bryant*, p. 268.
12. Michener, *Sports in America*, p. 276.
13. Ibid., p. 278.

Chapter 11: The Bear in Winter

1. Townsend, *Tales from 1978–79 Alabama Football*, p. 28.
2. Browning, *I Remember Bear Bryant*, p. 141.
3. Ibid., p. 142.
4. *ABC Sports Pregame Show*, Jan. 1, 1979.
5. Bryant, *Building a Championship Football Team*, p. 43.
6. Townsend, *Tales from 1978–79 Alabama Football*, p. 85.
7. Bryant, *Building a Championship Football Team*, p. 204.
8. Ibid., p. 25.
9. Ibid., p. 49.
10. Ibid.
11. Paterno, *Paterno*, p. 215.
12. Dent, *Junction Boys*, p. 281.
13. NBC, *The Bob Hope Show*, Sept. 1979.
14. ABC, *The Dick Cavett Show*, 1980.
15. Browning, *I Remember Bear Bryant*, p. 127.
16. Ibid., pp. 197–198.
17. *Sports Illustrated*, Oct. 20, 1980.
18. Herskowitz, *Legend of Bear Bryant*, p. 220.
19. *Birmingham News*, Nov. 24, 1981.
20. *Sports Illustrated*, Nov. 23, 1981.
21. *The Bear Bryant Show*, Nov. 29, 1981.

22. *Jackson Daily News*, Aug. 26, 1982.

23. *New York Times*, Dec. 10, 1982.

24. *Hunstville Times*, Sept. 7, 1982.

25. Ibid.

26. *Birmingham News*, Nov. 8, 1982.

27. *The Bear Bryant Show*, Nov. 14, 1982.

28. Forney, *Above the Noise of the Crowd*, p. 201.

29. Forney and Townsend, *Talk of the Tide,* p. 153.

30. Mark Edwards, "Two Decades Later, Bear Not Forgotten," *Decatur Daily*, Jan. 24, 2003.

31. *New York Times*, Jan. 27, 1983.

Chapter 12: Like Having John Wayne for Your Grandfather

1. *New Republic*, Jan. 24, 1983.

2. *Tuscaloosa News*, Jan. 29, 1983.

3. *Village Voice*, Sept. 28, 1982.

4. *Sports Illustrated*, May 7, 2003.

Appendix 1: Bud and Bear

1. Heffelfinger, *This Was Football*, p. 103.

Bibliography

THE LITERATURE ON THE career of Paul Bryant was so extensive that I had at least one good book to guide me through every phase of *The Last Coach*. The most helpful, of course, was Bryant's own *Bear*, cowritten with John Underwood. Unfortunately, *Bear* only brought Bryant's story up to 1973. After that, Keith Dunnavant's *Coach: The Life of Paul "Bear" Bryant* offered a reliable narrative. Mickey Herskowitz's *The Legend of Bear Bryant* is part biography and part memoir from the sportswriter who knew him longer, and probably better, than any other. Jim Dent's best-seller, *The Junction Boys*, is the definitive work on Bryant's years at Texas A&M, and Tom Stoddard's *Turnaround* is a revealing look at Bryant's return to Alabama in 1958.

For understanding the Coach's own football strategy and tactics, *Building a Championship Football Team* is a positive revelation, and for the history and lore of the Southeastern Conference, Bert Randolph Sugar's *The SEC* was essential. A compact history of Alabama football, Clyde Bolton's *The Crimson Tide* was indispensable.

College Football, U.S.A., 1869–1971 is the best one-volume history of college football I've ever come across.

Arledge, Roone. *Roone: Memoir*. HarperCollins, New York, 2003.

Birmingham News staff. *Remembering Bear*. News & Features Press, Indianapolis, 1983.

Birmingham Post-Herald. Bloodfeud—The Storied Rivalry of Alabama-Auburn Football. Epic Sports, Birmingham, Ala., 2000.

Bolton, Clyde. *The Crimson Tide; a Story of Alabama Football*. Strode Publishers, Huntsville, Ala., 1979.

Briley, J. David. "Second Reconstruction," unpublished paper.

Browning, Al. *Bowl, 'Bama, Bowl: Sixty-One Years of Crimson Tide Glory*. Rutledge Hill Press, Nashville, 1987.

Browning, Al. *I Remember Bear Bryant*. Cumberland House, Nashville, 2001.

Bryant, Paul W. *Building a Championship Football Team*. Prentice-Hall, Englewood Cliffs, N.J., 1960.

Bryant, Paul W., and John Underwood. *Bear; The Hard Life and Good Times of Alabama's Coach Bryant*. Little, Brown, Boston, 1975.

Carter, Dan T. *The Politics of Rage: George Wallace, the Origins of the New Conservatism, and the Transformation of American Politics*. Simon & Schuster, New York, 1995.

Cash, W. J. *The Mind of the South*. Random House, New York, 1969.

Dent, Jim. *The Junction Boys: How Ten Days in Hell with Bear Bryant Forged a Championship Team*. St. Martin's Press, New York, 1999.

Dent, Jim. *Monster of the Midway: Bronko Nagurski, the 1943 Chicago Bears, and the Greatest Comeback Ever*. Thomas Dunne Books, New York, 2003.

Dunnavant, Keith. *Coach: The Life of Paul "Bear" Bryant*. Simon & Schuster, New York, 1996.

Flint, Wayne. *Alabama in the Twentieth Century (The Modern South)*. University of Alabama Press, Tuscaloosa, 2004.

Ford, Tommy. *Bama under Bear: Alabama's Family Tides*. Strode Publishers, Hunstville, Ala., 1983.

Forney, John. *Above the Noise of the Crowd—Thirty Years behind the Alabama Microphone*. Albright & Company, Huntsville, Ala., 1986.

Forney, John, and Steve Townsend. *Talk of the Tide: An Oral History of Alabama Football since 1920*. Crane Hill Publishers, Birmingham, Ala., 1993.

Frady, Marshall. *Wallace*. Signet, New York, 1976.

Friedrich, Otto. *Decline and Fall: The Death Struggle of the* Saturday Evening Post. Ballantine Books, New York, 1971.

Graham, Frank Jr. *A Farewell to Heroes*. University of Southern Illinois Press, Carbondale, 2003.

Groom, Winston. *The Crimson Tide: An Illustrated History of Football at the University of Alabama*. University of Alabama Press, Tuscaloosa, 2000.

Gunther, Marc, and Bill Carter. *Monday Night Mayhem: The Inside Story of ABC's Monday Night Football*. Beech Tree Books (William Morrow), New York, 1988.

Heffelfinger, W. W. *This Was Football*. Barnes, New York, 1954.

Herskowitz, Mickey. *The Legend of Bear Bryant*. McGraw-Hill, New York, 1987.

Huie, William Bradford. *Mud on the Stars*. University of Alabama Press, Tuscaloosa, 1996.

Jenkins, Dan. *Saturday's America*. Berkley Medallion Books, New York, 1970.

Kirby, James. *Fumble: Bear Bryant, Wally Butts, and the Great College Football Scandal*. Harcourt Brace Jovanovich, San Diego, 1986.

Kriegel, Mark. *Namath: A Biography*. Viking, New York, 2004.

Maraniss, David. *When Pride Still Mattered: A Life of Vince Lombardi*. Simon & Schuster, New York, 1999.

Marshall, Benny. *Winning Isn't Everything, But It Beats Anything That Comes in Second*. Parthenon Press, Nashville, 1965.

McCallum, John, and Charles H. Pearson. *College Football, U.S.A., 1869–1971*. Hall of Fame Publishing, Greenwich, Conn., 1971.

McKay, John. *McKay: A Coach's Story*. Atheneum, New York, 1974.

McWhorter, Diane. *Carry Me Home: Birmingham, Alabama: The Climactic Battle of the Civil Rights Revolution*. Simon & Schuster, New York, 2002.

Michener, James. *Sports in America*. Random House, New York, 1976.

Norman, Geoffrey. *Alabama Showdown: The Football Rivalry between Auburn and Alabama*. H. Holt, New York, 1986.

Paterno, Joe. *Paterno: By the Book*. Random House, New York, 1989.

Pont, Sally. *Fields of Honor: The Golden Age of College Football and the Men Who Created It*. Harcourt, New York, 2001.

Schoor, Gene. *100 Years of Alabama Football*. Longstreet Press, Atlanta, 1991.

Stabler, Ken, and Berry Stainback. *Snake*. Doubleday, Garden City, N.Y., 1986.

Stoddard, Tom. *Turnaround: The Untold Story of Bear Bryant's First Year as Head Coach at Alabama*. Black Belt Press, Montgomery, Ala., 1996.

Stone, Naylor. *Coach Tommy of the Crimson Tide*. Vulcan Press, Birmingham, Ala., 1954.

Sugar, Bert Randolph, ed. *The SEC: A Pictorial History of the Southeastern Conference Football*. Bobbs-Merrill, Indianapolis, 1979.

Sugar, Bert Randolph. *"The Thrill of Victory": The Inside Story of ABC Sports*. Hawthorn Books, New York, 1978.

Townsend, Steve. *Tales from 1978–79 Alabama Football: A Time of Champions*. Sports Publishing, Champaign, Ill., 2003.

Twombly, Wells. *Blanda, Alive and Kicking*. Nash Publishing, Los Angeles, 1972.

Williams, Sylvia B. *Paul Bryant: Football Legend*. Seacoast, Birmingham, Ala., 2002.

Wilkinson, Jay, and Gretchen Hirsch. *Bud Wilkinson: An Intimate Portrait of an American Legend*. Sagamore, Champaign, Ill., 1994.

Wright, Steve. *I'd Rather Be Wright; Memoirs of an Itinerant Tackle*. Grosset & Dunlap, New York, 1975.

Television Broadcasts

CBS, *The Bear: The Legend of Coach Paul Bryant*, Jan. 12, 2002.

ESPN Classic Sports Century, "Bear Bryant," Dec. 13, 2002.

More praise for *The Last Coach*

"*The Last Coach* is a remarkable piece of digging into, and reporting of, a magnificent life story written at a length more commonly reserved for a Founding Father.... Barra's book devotes a lot more time to inspecting the nature of the man than to the secret of his success, but after a while it becomes obvious that the nature of the man *was* the secret of his success."
—Michael Lewis, *The New Republic*

"A thorough and well-written biography of Paul 'Bear' Bryant along with a compelling discussion of Coach Bryant's standing among the most successful college football coaches ever. Sport fans and historians will devour this outstanding book."　　—Bart Starr, former quarterback, Green Bay Packers

"If you were a college football junkie like me, you will welcome this book about Bear Bryant. Happily, after all these pages, he still winds up as the greatest college coach who ever thanked the good mamas and papas."
—Dan Jenkins, author of *Semi-Tough* and *Saturday's America*

"In *The Last Coach*, Allen Barra paints a rich portrait of the man in the houndstooth hat."　　—*Sports Illustrated*

"Barra gets it right ... he was born to write this story."
—Don Keith, *Birmingham Weekly*

"A wonderful read. Barra has written a thoughtful, inquiring and evocative look at the life and times of the legendary coach."
—Paul Finebaum, *Mobile Register*

"Admirably ambitious.... Barra is one of the country's most thoughtful writers on the subject.... [Barra] does all the things you would expect from a biography of a sports figure."
—Buzz Bissinger, *New York Times Book Review*

"Barra captures ... the man and the legend, in what, by all odds, should be the last word on the life and times of Paul 'Bear' Bryant."
—Victor Gold, *Weekly Standard*

"A biography with a bite . . . a work of solid fact, airtight and accurate."
—Bill Briggs, *Denver Post*

"An epic . . . the story of the most American of lives: ignorant, up-from-nothing country boy becomes national icon. . . . When Barra calls him 'The Last Coach,' he means, in one sense, that Bryant was the last great coach to span two markedly different eras. . . . Barra tells the stories of the great games well. A fan could love this book solely for that."
—Lee Cearnal, *Houston Chronicle*

"A worthy work that does much to separate myth from fact and restore the sense of Bryant himself." —Michael MacCambridge, *Wall Street Journal*

"Separates the contradictory man from the celebrity myth . . . [gives] the reader the private Bear, the one with faults, with contradictions, with nuance. . . . The reporting is prodigious and caring, worthy of one of the major figures in American sports." —*Milwaukee Journal Sentinel*

"Bear has been gone nearly three decades, but he still towers like a colossus over the game of football. This is the best-researched and best chronicle of his life." —Keith Jackson, ABC Sports

"Barra gives a meticulous history of college football and how Alabama became one of the early powers. He is equally meticulous in describing Bryant's life from his first days as a high school athlete." —*USA Today*

"Barra conducts an in-depth investigation into Bryant's carefully constructed mythic persona to show the man behind the curtain, but often the author's analysis raises rather than diminishes Bryant in our estimation."
—Brad Vice, *San Francisco Chronicle*

"Finally a biography worthy of the man. Allen Barra has sifted the truth from the myth. *The Last Coach* . . . tells why Bryant mattered so much to so many." —Mark Kreigel, author of *Namath: A Biography*

"Barra's prose is poignant. . . . *The Last Coach* is riveting in its portrayal of Bryant . . . football at its very best, a must for every football aficionado's reading list." —Elizabeth A. Doehring, *St. Petersburg Times*

"[Barra] has simply penned as definitive an account of Bryant's life as is possible . . . 500-plus pages of intensely researched details, insights and imagination-stirring game accounts. Along the way, Barra manages to make a persuasive argument as to why Bear Bryant was the greatest coach who ever stood on a gridiron sideline." —Gilbert Cruze, *Tuscaloosa News*

"Barra writes winningly." —*Atlanta Journal-Constitution*

"Allen Barra attempts to separate the man and the icon in *The Last Coach*. [This] moving biography is a comprehensive account emboldened by nuance and extensive research."

—Erik Spamberg, *Christian Science Monitor*

"Allen Barra researches a book the way Coach Bryant prepared for a game; this is a perfect fit."

—Mickey Herskowitz, author of *The Legend of Bear Bryant*

"The most complete look at Bryant yet." —Al Burleson, *Huntsville Times*

"Skillfully details the Coach's personality traits and the circumstances of his professional life that converged to elevate the man from Moro Bottom, Ark., into a football legend." —Greg Connors, *Buffalo News*

"Allen Barra, one of our two or three best sportswriters, surpasses Jim Dent's efforts in *The Junction Boys* and those of just about anybody else who's written about Bryant by several touchdowns with this sweeping biography. . . . It is a work that paints Bryant as a man who overcame his hardscrabble, redneck rearing in Arkansas and helped backward Alabamians accept African-American football players and integration. . . . He is revealed as he ever will be in Barra's excellent account." —*Blue Ridge Business Journal*

"Barra has done his research thoroughly and somehow managed to catch both the legendary and the human dimensions of this complex American hero. . . . Finding fault with Barra's book is hard to do."

—Larry Mcgehee, *Southern Scene*

Recent Books of Interest, Editor's Choice, *New York Times Book Review*

A *Washington Post* Best Sports Book